Modelling Single-name and Multi-name Credit Derivatives

To Penny, Rory and Fergal.

Modelling Single-name and Multi-name Credit Derivatives

Dominic O'Kane

John Wiley & Sons, Ltd

Published by   John Wiley & Sons Ltd, The Atrium, Southern Gate, Chichester,
                      West Sussex PO19 8SQ, England

                      Telephone   (+44) 1243 779777

Email (for orders and customer service enquiries): cs-books@wiley.co.uk
Visit our Home Page on www.wiley.com

Other Wiley Editorial Offices

John Wiley & Sons Inc., 111 River Street, Hoboken, NJ 07030, USA

Jossey-Bass, 989 Market Street, San Francisco, CA 94103-1741, USA

Wiley-VCH Verlag GmbH, Boschstr. 12, D-69469 Weinheim, Germany

John Wiley & Sons Australia Ltd, 42 McDougall Street, Milton, Queensland 4064, Australia

John Wiley & Sons (Asia) Pte Ltd, 2 Clementi Loop #02-01, Jin Xing Distripark, Singapore 129809

John Wiley & Sons Canada Ltd, 6045 Freemont Blvd, Mississauga, ONT, L5R 4J3, Canada

Wiley also publishes its books in a variety of electronic formats. Some content that appears in print may not be
available in electronic books.

Library of Congress Cataloging in Publication Data

O'Kane, Dominic.
   Modelling single-name and multi-name credit derivatives / Dominic O'Kane.
      p.   cm. — (Wiley finance)
   Includes bibliographical references and index.
   ISBN 978-0-470-51928-8 (cloth : alk. paper)
   1. Credit derivatives.   I. Title.
   HG6024.A3039 2008
   332.64′57—dc22

                                                    2008019031

British Library Cataloguing in Publication Data

A catalogue record for this book is available from the British Library

ISBN 978-0-470-51928-8 (HB)

Typeset in 10/12pt Times by Integra Software Services Pvt. Ltd, Pondicherry, India
Printed and bound in Great Britain by Antony Rowe Ltd, Chippenham, Wiltshire

Contents

Acknowledgements

Many thanks go to all the quants I have worked with on credit derivative modelling. First and foremost is Lutz Schloegl, a superb quant and a good friend with whom I have collaborated for many years. Other quants with whom I have collaborated and whose help I gratefully acknowledge are Ren-Raw Chen, Andrei Greenberg, Sebastian Hitier, Matthew Livesey, Sam Morgan, Claus Pedersen, Lee Phillips, Wenjun Ruan and Saurav Sen. I would especially like to acknowledge collaborations with Professor Stuart Turnbull.

On the trading side, I would like to acknowledge many fruitful conversations with Georges Assi. A large debt of gratitude is also owed to Mark Ames, Ugo Calcagnini, Assan Din and Ken Umezaki who all helped me get my head around the basics of credit derivatives way back in the late 1990s when there was nothing to read and the asset swap looked exotic.

Extra special thanks go to all those others who read earlier versions of this book, especially Lutz Schloegl whose extensive comments were a great help. I also thank Robert Campbell and Matthew Leeming who both read the entire manuscript and provided valuable feedback. Thanks also go to Matthew Livesey, Michal Oulik, Claus Pedersen and Jeroen Kerkhof for reading and commenting on selected chapters. In all of these cases, it was a significant request and they all responded generously. It must also be stated that any errors which remain in this book are mine.

I am grateful to Dev Joneja at Lehman Brothers for providing access to the LehmanLive® website, to the British Bankers' Association and Moody's Investor Services for permission to quote from their reports, and to the valuation experts at Markit Group Limited for answering some technical questions. Conversations with Robert McAdie are also gratefully acknowledged.

Finally I would like to reserve my biggest thanks for my wife who provided both support and encouragement. I dedicate this book to her and to my two wonderful boys.

Dominic O'Kane
April 2008.

About the Author

Dominic O'Kane is an affiliated Professor of Finance at the French business school EDHEC which is based in Nice, France. Until May 2006, Dominic O'Kane was a managing director and ran the European Fixed Income Quantitative Research group at Lehman Brothers, the US investment bank. Dominic spent seven of his nine years at Lehman Brothers working as a quant for the credit derivatives trading desk. Dominic has a doctorate in theoretical physics from Oxford University.

Introduction

The aim of this book is to present an up-to-date, comprehensive, accessible and practical guide to the models used to price and risk-manage credit derivatives. It is both a detailed introduction to credit derivative modelling and a reference for those who are already practitioners.

This book is up-to-date as it covers many of the important developments which have occurred in the credit derivatives market in the past 4–5 years. These include the arrival of the CDS portfolio indices and all of the products based on these indices. In terms of models, this book covers the challenge of modelling single-tranche CDOs in the presence of the correlation skew, as well as the pricing and risk of more recent products such as constant maturity CDS, portfolio swaptions, CDO squareds, credit CPPI and credit CPDOs.

For each model, the reader is taken through the underlying assumptions and then the mathematical derivation. The application of the model to pricing and risk-management is explained with the goal of trying to build intuition. There is also a focus on the efficient implementation of each model.

Product coverage is extensive and is split into two parts. Part I covers single-name credit derivatives and Part II covers multi-name credit derivatives. We begin the first part with the traditional credit products including the credit risky bond, the floating rate note and the asset swap. Although they are not credit derivatives, these are included for the sake of completeness and because they are a pricing reference for the credit default swap. We then move on to the credit default swap (CDS) which, reflecting its importance, is covered in considerable detail. We also include a discussion of digital CDS, forward CDS and loan CDS. We then cover other single-name products including the constant maturity default swap and the default swaption.

Part II covers products whose risk is linked to the credit performance of more than one credit. These are known as 'multi-name' products. We begin with the biggest growth product of the credit derivatives market, the CDS index. This then leads us to the many product innovations which have resulted from the arrival of these CDS indices. These include the tranched CDS indices and CDS index swaptions. We also cover advanced correlation products such as the CDO-squared and the leveraged super senior. Dynamically managed structures such as the credit CPPI and CPDO are also examined. Towards the end of the book we consider a number of the newer products which are beginning to be traded. These include forward starting tranches and tranche options.

In this book we set out in detail the models which have been developed to address the challenges posed by these products. Of these challenges, the most important has been the modelling of default correlation. We therefore cover in detail the Gaussian copula and the modelling of default dependency in general, especially within a copula framework. After establishing the arbitrage-free conditions for a correlation model, we devote an entire chapter to *base correlation*, which has become a widely used pricing and risk-management approach. We discuss its implementation and in doing so highlight the advantages and disadvantages of base correlation as a pricing and risk-management framework. We then discuss a range of specific copula models, highlighting the pros and cons of each. This takes us to the subject of much current research – the development of usable dynamic correlation models. In the final two chapters of this book we discuss the two main categories of dynamic models known as bottom-up and top-down. We also set out in detail some specific models which fall into these two categories.

The credit derivatives market has changed significantly in the past four to five years and most of these developments are contained within this book. However, the market continues to evolve. As a result, I would suggest that readers keen to keep abreast of the latest modelling and market developments periodically visit www.defaultrisk.com and the technical forums of www.wilmott.com.

Notation

Symbol	Description
t	today (valuation date).
$t = 0$	Contract initiation date.
t_s	Contract settlement date.
t_E	Option expiry date.
T	Contract maturity date.
t_n	nth cash flow date on the premium leg. Usually $t_0 = t$ and $t_N = T$.
$\Delta(t_{n-1}, t_n, b)$	The year fraction from date t_{n-1} to t_n in a basis b. We typically drop the b.
$Z(t, T)$	Libor zero coupon bond price from time t to T. We sometimes use $Z(t) = Z(0, t)$.
$\hat{Z}(t, T)$	Zero recovery credit risky zero coupon bond price from today time t to time T.
$L(T_1, T_2)$	The observed value of the Libor rate which sets at time T_1 for a period $[T_1, T_2]$.
$L(t, T_1, T_2)$	The value at time t of a forward Libor rate which sets at time T_1 for a period $[T_1, T_2]$.
$D(t, T)$	Present value of \$1 paid at the time of default as seen at time t.
$Q_i(t, T)$	Survival probability from today time t to time T for issuer i. We sometimes use $Q_i(t) = Q_i(0, t)$.
$S(t, T)$	CDS contractual spread at time t for a contract which matures at time T.
$S(t, t_F, T)$	Forward CDS contractual spread at time t for a contract with forward start t_F which matures at time T. Note that $S(t, t, T) = S(t, T)$.
$PV01(t, T)$	The time t present value of a \$1 Libor quality annuity which matures at time T.
$RPV01(t, T)$	The time t present value of a credit risky \$1 annuity which matures at time T.
$r(t)$	The risk-free short interest rate at time t.
$\beta(t)$	Value of the rolled-up money-market account $\beta(t) = \exp(\int_0^t r(s)ds)$.
$\beta(t, T)$	Value of $\beta(T)\beta(t)^{-1}$.
$\lambda(t)$	The hazard rate or intensity process at time t.
$\Pr(x)$	The probability that x is true.
$C(u_1, \ldots, u_n)$	The n-dimensional default copula.
$\hat{C}(u_1, \ldots, u_n)$	The n-dimensional survival copula.

Symbol	Description
$\phi(a)$	The Gaussian density.
$\Phi(a)$	The uni-variate Gaussian cumulative distribution function.
$\Phi_2(a, b, \rho)$	The bi-variate Gaussian cumulative distribution function.
$\Phi_n(\mathbf{a}, \Sigma)$	The n-variate Gaussian cumulative distribution function with correlation matrix Σ.
$t_v(x)$	The uni-variate Student-t cumulative distribution function with v degrees of freedom.
$L(T)$	The fractional portfolio loss at horizon time T.
$L(T, K_1, K_2)$	The fractional tranche loss at horizon time T.
$F(x)$	The cumulative portfolio loss distribution, i.e. $F(x) = \Pr(L \le x)$.
$f(x)$	The density of the portfolio loss distribution $f(x) = \partial F(x)/\partial x$.
$O(x)$	'Order of' x. If $f(x)$ is $O(x^n)$ then n is the exponent of the dominant polynomial term in $f(x)$.
$\text{int}(x)$	Function which returns the integer part of a number without rounding, e.g. int $(5.7322) = 5$.
$\text{ceil}(x)$	Function which returns the smallest integer value greater than or equal to x, e.g. ceil $(5.7322) = 6$.

1
The Credit Derivatives Market

1.1 INTRODUCTION

Without a doubt, credit derivatives have revolutionised the trading and management of credit risk. They have made it easier for banks, who have historically been the warehouses of credit risk, to hedge and diversify their credit risk. Credit derivatives have also enabled the creation of products which can be customised to the risk–return profile of specific investors. As a result, credit derivatives have provided something new to both hedgers and investors and this has been a major factor in the growth of the credit derivatives market.

From its beginning in the mid-1990s, the size of the credit derivatives market has grown at an astonishing rate and it now exceeds the size of the credit bond market. According to a recent ISDA survey,[1] the notional amount outstanding of credit derivatives as of mid-year 2007 was estimated to be $45.46 trillion. This significantly exceeds the size of the US corporate bond market which is currently $5.7 trillion and the US Treasury market which is currently $4.3 trillion.[2] It also exceeds the size of the equity derivatives market which ISDA also estimated in mid-2007 to have a total notional amount outstanding of $10.01 trillion.

In addition to its size, what is also astonishing about the credit derivatives market is the breadth and liquidity it has attained. This has been due largely to the efforts of the dealer community which has sought to structure products in a way that maximises tradabililty and standardisation and hence liquidity. The CDS indices, introduced in 2002 and discussed extensively in this book, are a prime example of this. They cover over 600 of the most important corporate and sovereign credits. They typically trade with a bid–offer spread of less than 1 basis point and frequently as low as a quarter of a basis point.[3]

To understand the success of the credit derivatives market, we need to understand what it can do. In its early days, the credit derivatives market was dominated by banks who found credit derivatives to be a very useful way to hedge the credit risk of a bond or loan that was held on their balance sheet. Credit derivatives could also be used by banks to manage their regulatory capital more efficiently. More recently, the credit derivatives market has become much more of an investor driven market, with a focus on developing products which present an attractive risk–return profile. However, to really understand the appeal of the credit derivatives market, it is worth listing the many uses which credit derivatives present:

- Credit derivatives make it easier to go short credit risk either as a way to hedge an existing credit exposure or as a way to express a negative view on the credit market.

---

[1] These numbers are based on the ISDA Mid-Year 2007 Market Survey report.
[2] *Securities Industry and Financial Markets Association Research Quarterly*, August 2007.
[3] This has certainly been the case for the CDX Investment Grade North America index. In price terms, this is roughly equivalent to a bid–offer of 1 cent on a five-year bond with a price of $100.

- Most credit derivatives are unfunded. This means that unlike a bond, a credit derivative contract requires no initial payment. As a consequence, the investor in a credit derivative does not have to fund any initial payment. This means that credit derivatives may present a cheaper alternative to buying cash bonds for investors who fund above Libor. It also makes it easier to leverage a credit exposure.
- Credit derivatives increase liquidity by taking illiquid assets and repackaging them into a form which better matches the risk–reward profiles of investors.
- Credit derivatives enable better diversification of credit risk as the breadth and liquidity of the credit derivatives market is greater than that of the corporate bond market.
- Credit derivatives add transparency to the pricing of credit risk by broadening the range of traded credits and their liquidity. We estimate that there are over 600 corporate and sovereign names which have good liquidity across the credit derivatives market.[4] The scope of the credits is global as it includes European, North American and Asian corporate credits plus Emerging Market sovereigns.
- Credit derivatives shift the credit risk which has historically resided on bank loan books into the capital markets and in doing so it has reduced the concentrations of credit risk in the banking sector. However, this does raise the concern of whether this credit risk is better managed in less regulated entities which sit outside the banking sector.
- Credit derivatives allow for the creation of new asset classes which are exposed to new risks such as credit volatility and credit correlation. These can be used to diversify investment portfolios.

The relatively short history of the credit derivatives market has not been uneventful. Even before the current credit crisis of 2007–2008, the credit derivative market has weathered the 1997 Asian Crisis, the 1998 Russian default, the events of 11 September 2001, the defaults of Conseco, Railtrack, Enron, WorldCom and others, and the downgrades of Ford and General Motors. What has been striking about all of these events is the ability of the credit derivatives market to work through these events and to emerge stronger. This has been largely due to the willingness of the market participants to resolve any problems which these events may have exposed in either the mechanics of the products or their legal documentation. Each of these events has also strengthened the market by demonstrating that it is often the only practical way to go short and therefore hedge these credit risks.

In this chapter, we discuss the growth in the credit derivatives market size. We present an overview of the different credit derivatives and discuss a market survey which shows how the importance of these products has evolved over time. We then discuss the structure of the credit derivatives market in terms of its participants.

1.2   MARKET GROWTH

The growth of the credit derivatives market has been phenomenal. Although there are different ways to measure this growth, each with its own particular approach, when plotted as a function

---

[4] We calculated this by summing the number of distinct credits across the main CDS indices listed in Table 10.1. These credits have been selected for their liquidity.

of time, they all show the same exponential growth shown in Figure 1.1. Let us consider the three sources of market size data:

1. The British Bankers' Association (BBA) surveys the credit derivatives market via a question-naire every two or so years. Their questionnaire is sent to about 30 of the largest investment banks who act as dealers in the credit derivatives market. Their latest report was published in 2006 and estimated the total market notional at the end of 2006 to be $20.207 trillion.
2. The International Swaps and Derivatives Association (ISDA) conducts a twice-yearly survey of the market. In the most recent, they surveyed 88 of their member firms including the main credit derivatives dealers about the size of their credit derivatives positions. The collected numbers were adjusted to correct for double-counting.[5] The mid-2007 survey estimated the size of the credit derivatives market to be $45.25 trillion, an increase of 32% in the first six months of 2007.
3. The US Office for the Comptroller of the Currency conducts a quarterly survey of the credit derivatives market size. The survey covers just the US commercial bank sector. The June 2007 survey found that the total notional amount of credit derivatives held by US commercial banks was $10.2 trillion, an increase of 86% on the first quarter of 2006. This number is lower than the others partly because it excludes trades done by many non-US commercial banks and investment banks.

Although these numbers all differ because of the differing methodologies and timings, what is beyond doubt is the rapid growth that has been experienced by the credit derivatives market.

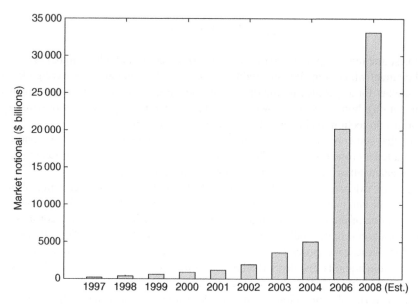

Figure 1.1   Evolution of the credit derivatives market size using estimates calculated in the BBA Credit Derivatives Report 2006. Source: British Banker's Association

[5] A lot of credit derivatives trades occur between dealers. If two dealers have taken the opposite side of a contract, then that contract is only counted once.

Although the size of the credit derivatives market is significant, it is important to realise that credit derivatives do not increase the overall amount of credit risk in the financial system. This is because every credit derivative contract has a buyer and a seller of the credit risk and so the net increase of credit risk is zero. However, credit derivatives can in certain cases be used to increase the amount of credit risk in the *capital markets*. For example, suppose a bank has made a $10 million loan to a large corporate and this loan is sitting on their loan book portfolio. As we will see later, to hedge this risk, the bank can use a credit default swap (CDS) contract. The credit risk of the corporate is therefore transferred from the bank to the CDS counterparty who may then transfer this risk on to another counterparty using another CDS contract. At the end of this chain of transactions will be someone, typically an investor, who is happy to hold on to the risk of the corporate and views that the premium from the CDS is more than sufficient to compensate them for assuming this risk. The loan that was sitting on the bank's loan book is still there. However, the risk has been transferred via the CDS contracts to this investor in the capital markets. Because the credit risk has been transferred without any actual sale of the loan, the credit risk produced by a CDS is 'synthetic'. If a default of the corporate does occur, the loss compensation is paid from the investor to the counterparty and on down the chain of contracts to the bank which was the initial buyer of protection. The bank has successfully hedged its credit exposure to this loan.

The only way in which credit risk has increased is through the counterparty credit risk associated with each contract. This is the risk that the protection seller does not make good a payment of the default loss compensation to the protection buyer. In practice, this risk is usually mitigated through the use of collateral posting as explained in Section 8.8.

1.3   PRODUCTS

The simplest and most important credit derivative is the credit default swap (CDS). This is a bilateral contract which transfers the credit risk of a specific company or sovereign from one party to another for a specified period of time. It is designed to protect an investor against the loss from par on a bond or loan following the default of the issuing company or sovereign. In return for this protection the buyer of the CDS pays a premium.

We note that someone who is assuming the credit risk in a credit derivatives contract like a CDS is called a *protection seller*. The person taking the other side of this trade is insuring themselves against this credit risk and is called a *protection buyer*.

An important extension of the CDS is the CDS index. This is a product which allows the investor to enter into a portfolio consisting of 100 or more different CDS in one transaction. For example, one of the most liquid indices is the CDX NA IG index which consists of 125 investment grade corporate credits which are domiciled in North America. We call this a *multi-name* product because it exposes the issuer to the default risk of more than one credit or 'name'. The considerable liquidity and diversified nature of the CDS index have meant that it has also become a building block for a range of other credit derivatives products.

There are also a number of option-based credit derivatives. These include single-name default swaptions in which the option buyer has the option to enter into a CDS contract on a future date. More recently we have seen growth in the market for portfolio swaptions. As the name suggests, these grant the option holder the option to enter into a CDS index.

Then there are the multi-name contracts such as default baskets and synthetic CDOs which are built on top of a portfolio of CDS. These contracts work by 'tranching' up the credit risk of the underlying portfolio. Tranching is a mechanism by which different securities or 'tranches' are structured so that any default losses in the portfolio are incurred in a specific order. The first default losses are incurred by the riskiest equity tranche. If the size of these losses exceeds the face value of the equity tranche then the remaining losses are incurred by the mezzanine tranche. If there are still remaining losses after this, then these are incurred by the senior tranches. The risk of this credit derivatives contract is sensitive to the tendency of the credits in the portfolio to default together. This is known as default correlation and, for this reason, these derivatives are known as correlation products.

Finally, we have the credit CPPI structure and the more recent CPDO structure. These structures exploit a rule-based dynamic trading strategy typically involving a CDS index. This trading strategy is designed to produce an attractive risk–return profile for the investor. In the case of CPPI, it is designed to provided a leveraged credit exposure while protecting the investor's principal. In the case of CPDO, the strategy is designed to produce a high coupon with low default risk.

Table 1.1   Market share of different credit derivatives products measured by market outstanding notional. We compare the results of the BBA survey for 2002, 2004 and 2006. Source: BBA Credit Derivatives Report 2006

Product type	Market share(%)		
	2002	2004	2006
Single-name credit default swaps	45.0	51.0	32.9
Credit-linked notes	8.0	6.0	3.1
Credit spread options	5.0	2.0	1.3
Full index trades	–	9.0	30.1
Synthetic CDOs	–	16.0	16.3
Tranched index trades	–	2.0	7.6
Basket products	6.0	4.0	1.8
Swaptions	–	1.0	0.8
Others	36.0	8.0	5.7
Market size ($bn)	1 952	5 021	20 207

Table 1.1 shows a breakdown of the various credit derivatives by their market outstanding notional. The data is sourced from the BBA survey of 2006 mentioned earlier. Note that this survey does not consider the CPPI and CPDO products since these have only become important in the time since this survey was carried out. This table already enables us to make the following observations about the current state and also the trends of the credit derivatives market:

- Many of the products which appeared in the 2004 and 2006 surveys did not exist in 2002. The most notable examples of this are the full index trades, which refer to trades on the CDX and iTraxx indices which were launched after 2002. We also see the establishment of a number of synthetic CDO categories and a tranched index trade category.
- We see a relative decline in the importance of more traditional credit derivatives products such as credit-linked notes and spread options. However, this decline in market percentage share is actually an increase in absolute size given the fourfold growth of the credit derivatives market over the 2004–2006 period.

- The market share of CDS fell from 51% to 32.9% over the 2004–2006 period. Over the same period, the portfolio indices rose from 9.1% to 30.1% of a much larger market. This suggests a trend away from single-name credit towards portfolio products. In absolute terms, the CDS market size actually grew significantly over this period.

There is a clear trend towards portfolio index products, i.e. multi-name products.

1.4   MARKET PARTICIPANTS

There are several different types of participants in the credit derivatives market. Each has its own specific rationale for using credit derivatives. Table 1.2 presents a breakdown of the market

Table 1.2   Market share of different market participants. Source: BBA Credit Derivatives Report 2006

Year of survey	2004		2006	
Type of market participant	Protection buyer (%)	Protection seller (%)	Protection buyer (%)	Protection seller (%)
Banks (including securities firms)	67	54	59	44
Trading activities	–	–	39	35
Loan portfolio	–	–	20	9
Insurers	7	20	6	17
Hedge funds	16	15	28	32
Pension funds	3	4	2	4
Mutual funds	3	3	2	2
Corporates	3	2	2	1
Other	1	1	1	1

share of the credit derivatives market by participant. This data is taken from the 2006 BBA Credit Derivatives Report. From this, we make the following observations:

- Banks are the largest participant in the credit derivatives market, both as buyers and sellers of protection. Table 1.2 splits the category of banks into trading activities and loan portfolio which we now consider separately.
- Many banks, in particular the securities houses, have significant trading activities as they act as dealers in the credit derivatives market. Dealers provide liquidity to the credit derivatives market by being willing to take risk onto their trading books which they then attempt to hedge. As a result, they buy roughly as much protection as they sell. They also act as issuers of structured products such as synthetic CDOs which they also hedge dynamically.
- Commercial banks possess loan portfolios. They use credit derivatives to buy protection in order to synthetically remove credit risk concentrations from their loan portfolio. They sell protection on other credits in order to earn income which can be used to fund these hedges, and to diversify their credit risk. One of the main drivers of bank behaviour is their regulatory framework. Until recently, this was based on the 1988 Basel Accord in which the capital a bank had to reserve against a loan or credit exposure was linked to whether the issuer of the

loan was an OECD[6] member government, bank or other. However, the regulatory regime has recently changed to the Basel II capital accord in which the regulatory capital is linked to the credit rating of the asset.

- Insurance companies mainly use credit derivatives as a form of investment which sits on the asset side of their business. They are principally sellers of credit protection and tend to prefer highly rated credits such as the senior tranches of CDOs.
- Hedge funds have grown their credit derivatives activity and have become significant players in the credit derivatives market. They are attracted by the unfunded[7] nature of most credit derivatives products which makes leverage possible. The fact that the credit derivatives market makes it easy to go short credit is another big attraction. Furthermore, credit derivatives also facilitate a number of additional trading strategies including cash versus CDS basis trading, correlation trading and credit volatility trading which hedge funds are free to exploit.
- Mutual and pension funds are not particularly large participants in the credit derivatives market. As investors, they would be primarily sellers of protection. They buy protection to hedge existing exposures. Often, they have restrictions on what sort of assets they can hold which preclude credit derivatives. However, the exact permissions depend on both their investment mandate and the investment regulations governing the jurisdiction in which they operate. Typically, one of their main restrictions is that the credits owned should be investment grade quality.
- Although credit derivatives could be used to try to hedge the credit risk of receivables, corporates have not become significant players in the credit derivatives market. There are a number of reasons why. First, standard credit default swaps do not trigger on the non-payment of receivables since receivables are not classified as *borrowed money* – the term used to encompass the range of obligations which are covered. Typically a contract will only trigger if there is a default of bonds and loans. Second, the payout from a standard credit default swap may not be consistent with the actual loss since it is linked to the delivery of a senior unsecured bond or loan. Finally, the range of traded credits may not overlap with the companies to which the corporate has a credit exposure.

Understanding the motivations of these different participants assists us in understanding why different products are favoured by different participants.

1.5 SUMMARY

In this chapter we have explained the features of credit derivatives which have led to their success and then discussed the market in terms of its size, the types of credit derivatives which are traded and who uses them.

---

[6] Organisation for Economic Co-operation and Development.
[7] Unfunded means that the credit derivatives transaction can be entered into at zero initial cost. Unlike a bond, which is a funded transaction, there is no need to pay an initial bond price of around $100 in order to have a credit exposure of $100.

2
Building the Libor Discount Curve

2.1 INTRODUCTION

This chapter does not focus on credit modelling or credit derivatives. It simply discusses one of the prerequisites for any credit derivative model – a Libor discount curve. Building the Libor discount curve is an important and often overlooked part of credit derivatives pricing and for this reason, we include a description of how it is typically done. In the process, we also introduce some of the instruments which will later be used to hedge the interest rate sensitivities of credit derivatives.

We need a discount curve because the valuation of all credit derivatives securities with future cash flows requires us to take into account the time value of money. This is captured by the term structure of interest rates. The interest rate used to discount these future cash flows can then have a significant effect on the derivative price. The next question is – which interest rate should I use? Since the sellers of credit derivatives, typically commercial and investment banks, need to hedge their risks, the interest rate used to discount cash flows is the one at which they have to fund the purchase of the hedging instruments. This interest rate is known as Libor. It is a measure of the rate at which commercial banks can borrow in the inter-bank market. As a result, derivative pricing requires a discount curve which is linked to the level of the current and expected future level of the Libor index.

2.2 THE LIBOR INDEX

Within the derivatives market Libor is the benchmark interest rate reference index for a number of major currencies including the US dollar and the British pound. Libor stands for the London Inter Bank Offered Rate and is the interest rate at which large commercial banks with a credit rating of AA and above offer to lend in the inter-bank market. It is set daily in London by the British Bankers' Association (BBA) using deposit rates offered by a panel of typically 16 banks. This is done for a range of terms out to one year.[1] The process for determining Libor is as follows:

1. For a given currency and term, the 16 rates are sorted into increasing order.
2. The top and bottom four quotes are removed.
3. The arithmetic average of the remaining eight quotes is calculated.
4. The result becomes the Libor rate for that currency and term and is published on Reuters at 11.00am London time each day.

---

[1] For more information see http://www.bba.org.uk/public/libor/

For the euro currency the BBA produced rate is called euro Libor. However, the more widely used rate for the euro is known as the Euribor. This is calculated daily by the European Banking Federation, also as a filtered average of inter-bank deposit rates offered by a panel of 50 or more designated contributor banks.

As most large derivatives dealers fund at or close to the Libor rate, it has become the reference interest rate for the entire derivatives market. However, Libor is also very important because of the broad range of interest rate products which are linked to it. These include:

- Money market deposits in which short-term borrowing occurs in the inter-bank market.
- Forward rate agreements which can be used to lock in a future level of Libor.
- Exchange-traded interest rate futures contracts in which the settlement price is linked to the three-month Libor rate.
- Interest rate swaps which exchange fixed rate payments for a stream of Libor payments.

In this chapter we will describe in detail these Libor instruments. In particular, we will focus on the interest rate swap because it is a key component of many credit structures such as the asset swap. The interest rate swap is also the main hedging instrument for the interest rate exposure embedded in credit derivatives.

Since the price of these instruments embeds market expectations about the future levels of Libor, we can use them to generate an implied Libor discount curve. As a result, we will show how these instruments can be used to construct the risk free discount curve which will be used in the pricing of credit derivatives in the rest of this book.

2.3   MONEY MARKET DEPOSITS

Money market deposits are contracts in which banks borrow in the inter-bank market for a fixed term of at most one year. Because this is the inter-bank market, in a standard money-market deposit contract, the amount is borrowed at a rate of return equal to the corresponding Libor index.

The deposit rate is agreed at contract initiation time t. We denote the maturity date of the deposit with T. However, it is on the settlement date t_s of the deposit that the deposit is made and the interest begins to accrue. The period between trade date and settlement date is two days for EUR, JPY and USD currency deposits, but can be different for other currencies. The standard terms of money-market deposits go out to one year, with the quoted rates including one week (1W), two week (2W), one month (1M), three months (3M), six months (6M), nine months (9M), and one year (12M) terms.

2.3.1   Mechanics

The mechanics of a money-market deposit in which \$1 is borrowed are shown in Figure 2.1. The trade is done at time 0 and settles at time t_s with the borrower receiving \$1. At the end of the deposit term, the lender is repaid the borrowed cash amount plus interest. The amount paid at time T is given by

$$V(T) = 1 + \Delta(t_s, T)L(t_s, T)$$

where Δ represents the year fraction, also known as the *accrual factor*, between the settlement date and the deposit maturity date defined according to some day count convention. It should be emphasised that every time we encounter a day count fraction, we must take care to apply the correct day count basis convention. In US dollars, Japanese yen and euros, the standard money-market deposit convention is Actual 360. For UK sterling, Actual 365 is used.

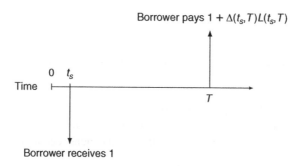

Figure 2.1   Mechanics of a money-market deposit on a face value of $1

Actual 360 means that the value of Δ is given by calculating the number of calendar days between the settlement date and maturity date, and dividing the result by 360. As a result we have

$$\Delta = \frac{\texttt{DayDiff}(t_s, T)}{360}$$

where $\texttt{DayDiff}(t_1, t_2)$ is a function that simply calculates the number of days between two times t_1 and t_2.

We can calculate the current value of the deposit by discounting the expected cash flows using Libor discount factors $Z(t, T)$. We have

$$V(0) = -Z(0, t_s) + (1 + \Delta(t_s, T)L(t_s, T))\, Z(0, T).$$

For a trade done at time 0, the expected present value of the deposit $V(0)$ must be zero. The value of the discount factor from today time 0 until the maturity of the deposit is therefore given by

$$Z(0, T) = \frac{Z(0, t_s)}{1 + \Delta(t_s, T)L(t_s, T)}$$

where $Z(0, t_s)$ is the discount factor from today until the settlement date of the deposit.

However, there is a difficulty in determining the value of $Z(0, t_s)$. Deposits in most currencies and for terms from 1W to 12M settle two days after trade date. This is known as a 'T+2' settlement convention where T represents the trade date and is not to be confused with the deposit maturity date. It means that the associated rates do not provide any information about the discount curve between times 0 and t_s. In order to determine $Z(0, t_s)$, we need to have a deposit or deposits which settle immediately and which can bridge the gap between 0 and t_s. This can usually be done using the overnight (O/N) rate which settles today for maturity tomorrow, and 'tomorrow/next' (T/N) which is the rate that settles tomorrow for payment in two days. By compounding these two rates, we can determine $Z(0, t_s)$.

2.4   FORWARD RATE AGREEMENTS

Forward rate agreements (FRAs) are over-the-counter bilateral agreements to borrow money for a forward starting period at a rate defined today. This rate is known as the FRA rate which we will denote with F_0. FRAs are generally traded over the counter between banks in a broker market and the corresponding FRA rates are shown on electronic broker screens.

2.4.1   Mechanics

To describe the mechanics of an FRA contract we begin by defining the three dates shown in Figure 2.2:

1. The trade date of the FRA contract, time 0.
2. The forward start date T_1 on which the interest period begins.
3. The end date of the FRA, T_2 on which the *effective* payment is equal to

$$\Delta(T_1, T_2) \, (L(T_1, T_2) - F_0)$$

where $L(T_1, T_2)$ is the Libor fixing observed at time T_1 for the period T_1 to T_2, and $\Delta(T_1, T_2)$ is the accrual factor from time T_1 to T_2 quoted according to the FRA basis. F_0 denotes the strike of the FRA and can be thought of as the forward rate of borrowing/lending.

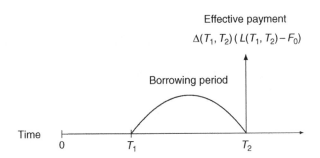

Figure 2.2   Mechanics of a forward rate agreement on a face value of $1

While the final payment is defined as though it occurs at time T_2, in practice the contract is cash settled at time T_1. After all, since we know the value of the Libor rate $L(T_1, T_2)$ at time T_1, then we can use it to calculate the value of the payoff at time T_2 and to discount this payoff to time T_1. As a result, the *actual* payment on the FRA is made at time T_1 and is equal to

$$V(T_1) = \frac{\Delta(T_1, T_2) \, (L(T_1, T_2) - F_0)}{1 + \Delta(T_1, T_2) L(T_1, T_2)}.$$

The breakeven value of the strike of the FRA is the value of F_0 for which the present value of the contract is zero. However, $L(T_1, T_2)$ is the future Libor rate which has not yet been set. Essentially what we need to solve for is the expected value of this future Libor. The good news is that it is also possible to determine the fair-value of F_0 using a replication strategy.

2.4.2   FRA pricing by replication

We begin by noting that the *effective* FRA payoff can be replicated using a combination of T_1 and T_2 maturity zero coupon bonds and a money-market deposit. The steps of the strategy are as follows:

1. Pay $Z(t_s, T_1)$ to purchase \$1 face value of a T_1 maturity zero coupon bond which settles at time t_s.
2. Sell short face value $(1 + \Delta(T_1, T_2)F_0)$ of a T_2 maturity zero coupon bond which settles at time t_s.
3. When the T_1 maturity bonds mature at time T_1, invest the \$1 received in a T_2 maturity money-market deposit. This pays $(1 + \Delta(T_1, T_2)L(T_1, T_2))$ at a later time T_2.

The results of this strategy mean that:

- At time t_s we pay $Z(t_s, T_1) - (1 + \Delta(T_1, T_2) F_0)Z(t_s, T_2)$.
- At time T_2 we receive $\Delta(T_1, T_2)(L(T_1, T_2) - F_0)$.

Since the payoff at time T_2 is the same as an FRA, no-arbitrage requirements mean that the initial payment at time t_s must be equal to zero. Hence we have

$$(1 + \Delta(T_1, T_2)F_0)Z(t_s, T_2) - Z(t_s, T_1) = 0.$$

This implies a fair value for the FRA rate given by

$$F_0 = \frac{1}{\Delta(T_1, T_2)} \left(\frac{Z(t_s, T_1)}{Z(t_s, T_2)} - 1 \right).$$

Hence, given a term structure of Libor discount factors, we can determine the FRA rate. However, once an FRA is transacted the FRA rate becomes fixed. However the value of the forward Libor rate

$$L(0, T_1, T_2) = \frac{1}{\Delta(T_1, T_2)} \left(\frac{Z(t_s, T_1)}{Z(t_s, T_2)} - 1 \right)$$

will continue to change as the Libor curve changes. Although it is beyond the scope of the book, it is possible to demonstrate the same result using a change of numeraire technique. We are then able to interpret F_0 as the expected value of the forward Libor rate under the forward measure. For details see Brigo and Mercurio (2001).

2.5   INTEREST RATE FUTURES

Interest rate futures contracts are exchange-traded contracts where the price at maturity is equal to 100 minus the Libor rate observed on the maturity date. They can therefore be used to express a view on future Libor rates, or to hedge a forward starting interest rate exposure.

The most liquid interest rate futures contracts reference the three-month Libor rate. At any moment in time, several contracts may trade with maturity dates occurring on the IMM date – defined as the third Wednesday of the delivery month. The most liquid delivery months are March, June, September and December. Examples of interest rate futures contract are the Eurodollar contracts which trade on the Chicago Mercantile exchange, plus the euro, UK sterling, Swiss franc and yen contracts traded at the Liffe exchange in London.

2.5.1   Mechanics

Consider a futures contract which matures at time T_1 at a price equal to 100 minus the Libor rate to time T_2. The mechanics of the contract are as follows:

1. At initiation of the contract at time 0, the contract is worth nothing. However, a small percentage of the face value of the contract known as the initial margin will be deposited in the investor's margin account at the exchange. The quoted price of the contract at any time t is given by

$$P(t, T_1, T_2) = 100 - F(t, T_1, T_2)$$

   where $F(t, T_1, T_2)$ is called the futures rate.
2. On each date between time 0 and T_1, *variation margin* is deposited in the investor's margin account at the exchange equal to the daily change in the futures price. The size of the variation margin is calculated by multiplying the price change in *ticks*[2] by the *tick size* of the contract and by the number of contracts. The tick size has been set by the exchange so that the change in the final payment from the contract is consistent with a 3M deposit contract with the same face value. The balance of the margin account is rolled over at Libor.
3. At the contract maturity date T_1, the price of the futures contract is given by

$$P(T_1, T_1, T_2) = 100 - L(T_1, T_2)$$

   where $L(T_1, T_2)$ is the Libor fixing for the period $[T_1, T_2]$ observed and set at time T_1.
4. Time T_2 is the end of the interest rate period referenced by the contract. No payments occur at time T_2.

It is important to realise that the price of a futures contract is not the same as the value of the contract. At the moment it is transacted, the value of the contract is zero to the investor. However, as the market changes its view about what value it expects for Libor at time T_1, the futures price changes, and so does the value of the contract to the buyer. If the futures price falls, the investor will be required to post additional margin with the exchange. If the futures price rises, the exchange deposits the increase into the investor's margin account.

By requiring investors to post daily collateral equal to the change in value of the contract with the exchange, the exchange minimises any counterparty risk it may have to the investor. Equally, if the contract price moves in the investor's favour, the exchange posts daily collateral to the investor's margin account and so the investor minimises counterparty risk to the exchange.

---

[2] Usually a tick is 1 bp but in some cases it can be 0.5 bp.

This margining process is important as it creates what is known as a convexity effect which is best explained using an example.

Example   An investor buys one futures contract which is trading at a price of 95.82, implying a futures rate of 4.18%. The contract face value is $1 million and the tick size is $25. Consider the following two scenarios:

1. If the futures price falls to 95.55, the futures rate has increased to 4.45% and the investor is required to borrow $(95.82-95.55) \times 100 \times \$25 = \$675$ to post as collateral at a higher interest rate.
2. If the futures price increases to 95.90, implying a futures rate of 4.10% then the investor's margin account at the exchange shows a balance of $(95.90-95.82) \times 100 \times \$25 = \$200$ which is then invested by the exchange at the lower spot deposit rate.

We have made the very reasonable assumption here that the futures rate $F(t, T_1, T_2)$ and the spot rate at which the exchange rolls the margin account are very highly correlated.

In both scenarios the margining always works against the futures contract holder. When they receive margin, this will coincide with a drop in the rate at which the balance in the margin account is rolled. When they have to deposit margin, this will coincide with an increase in the borrowing rate. This effect is known as *negative convexity* and the interest rate futures buyer will always lose relative to the investor in the comparable FRA who makes no payments until T_1. If both the quoted futures rate and the FRA rate for the same period and currency are the same, then this will be exploited by arbitrageurs who will lock in a forward borrowing rate using the FRA and sell the futures contract against it in an attempt to profit from the negative convexity. This demand will drive down the futures price and so drive up the futures rate until this convexity bias is cancelled out.

Since the value of the negative convexity depends on the volatility of the interest rate process, we need to have a model of the interest rate process in order to calculate its value. If we model the dynamics of the short interest rate process using the simple one-factor Ho and Lee (1986) model process, i.e. $dr = \theta(t)dt + \sigma dW$, where $\theta(t)$ is used to match the initial term structure, we assume that the short rate at which the margin account is rolled is perfectly correlated with the futures rate. We find that the relationship between the futures rate F and the FRA rate f is given by

$$f(0, T_1, T_2) \simeq F(0, T_1, T_2) - \frac{\sigma^2 T_1 T_2}{2}. \tag{2.1}$$

This equation is only exact if the forward and FRA rates are expressed as continuously compounded rates. However, even if they are not, the small size of the correction and the uncertainty in the value of the parameter σ means that this equation is a perfectly good first approximation which can be used to link futures contracts and FRAs.

Example   Assuming a basis point volatility for the short rate of 100 bp, the convexity correction for the futures contract with $T_1 = 1.0$ and $T_2 = 1.25$ is equal to

$$\frac{\sigma^2 T_1 T_2}{2} = \frac{1}{2}(0.01)^2 \times 1.0 \times 1.25 = 0.625 \, bp.$$

The effect is small but it does grow quadratically with the time to the forward date of the future, and also with the basis point volatility of the short rate process.

The importance of having a convexity adjustment is that by adjusting the futures rate, it allows us to map the prices of highly liquid interest rate futures contracts onto FRAs which we are then able to use in the construction of a discount curve. This will be described later in this chapter.

2.6   INTEREST RATE SWAPS

The global interest rate swap market has been in existence since the early 1980s. Since then it has grown substantially and now has a total market outstanding estimated in mid-2007 to be around \$347 trillion.[3] The interest rate swap plays an extremely important role in the credit derivatives market. It is a building block of many popular credit structures including the asset swap. It is also the main interest rate hedging instrument for credit derivatives.

An interest rate swap (IRS) is a bilateral over-the-counter contract. The standard swap contracts are transacted within the legal framework of the International Swap Master Agreement (ISMA) produced by the swap market's International Swaps and Derivatives Association (ISDA). We now set out the mechanics of the standard interest rate swap contract.

2.6.1   Mechanics

An interest rate swap traded at time 0 settles at time t_s. This typically occurs two days later, i.e the settlement convention is known as 'T + 2'. There is, however, no payment on the settlement date as the coupon on the fixed leg has been set so that the interest rate swap costs nothing to enter into.

Following contract initiation, the two parties exchange fixed rate interest payments for floating rate payments linked to a floating rate index, typically Libor. We call these two streams of payments the fixed leg and the floating leg. Figure 2.3 shows the payments on a five-year interest rate swap in which the fixed flows are assumed to be annual and at a fixed rate which we denote with H. The floating flows are semi-annual and are set at Libor. Each payment leg of the swap can have its own conventions in terms of coupon frequency and accrual basis. Both sets of flows terminate at the swap maturity.

Market terminology is to distinguish between the two parties to an interest rate swap based on whether they pay or receive the fixed rate. The party who pays the fixed rate is known as the

---

[3] ISDA Market Survey for mid-2007. Numbers are adjusted for double-counting and include single currency swaps, cross currency swaps and options.

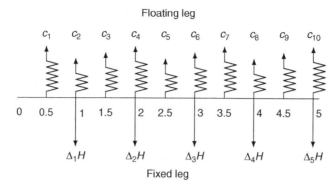

Figure 2.3 Mechanics of a five year interest rate swap which is paying semi-annually on the floating leg and annually on the fixed leg. We define the floating payments $c_m = \Delta(t_{m-1}, t_m) L(t_{m-1}, t_m)$ where $t_m = t_1, \ldots, t_M$ are the floating leg payment times. On the fixed leg we pay $\Delta(t_{n-1}, t_n)H$ where H is the swap rate and $t_n = t_1, \ldots, t_N$ are the fixed leg payment times. Note that $t_M = t_N = T$, the swap maturity

payer and the party who receives the fixed rate is known as the *receiver*. We now consider the valuation of the two legs of an interest rate swap separately.

2.6.2 Valuing the Fixed Leg

We begin by defining the N payment dates of the fixed leg of the swap as $t_1, t_2, \ldots, t_N$. All payments on the fixed leg of a swap are based on the swap rate H which is set at the start of the trade. If we assume that the notional of the swap is \$1, then the cash flow paid on the fixed leg at time t_n is given by

$$H \cdot \Delta(t_{n-1}, t_n),$$

where we remind the reader that the accrual factor is also a function of the basis convention on the fixed leg. The value of the fixed side of the swap at time t is therefore given by discounting the fixed coupons according to a Libor discount factor and then summing over all of the fixed coupons to give

$$V_{Fixed}(0) = H \sum_{n=1}^{N} \Delta(t_{n-1}, t_n) Z(0, t_n).$$

We now consider the floating leg.

2.6.3 Valuing the Floating Leg

The floating leg of a swap consists of a stream of M cash flows linked to the Libor interest rate index. We define the payment times on the floating leg of the swap as $t_1, t_2, \ldots, t_M$. This leg may have a different frequency and basis convention from the fixed leg of the swap. However, the final cash flows of both legs usually coincide so that we have $t_N = t_M = T$, the swap maturity date.

In the standard swap contract, each floating rate coupon is *set in advance, and paid in arrears* meaning that the value of the next coupon payment is determined by observing the appropriate term Libor on the fixing date which typically falls two days before the immediately preceding coupon payment date. This is shown in Figure 2.4. Accrual of the Libor payment then begins on the previous coupon payment date.

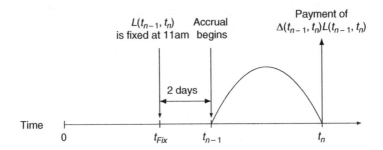

Figure 2.4   Each Libor floating rate payment is set at 11am on the fixing date, which occurs typically two days before the accrual period starts. The accrual period starts on the previous coupon date and is paid in arrears

The present value of the floating side of the swap is then given by discounting the future Libor cash flows and summing over them. We can write this formally as

$$V_{Float}(0) = \sum_{m=1}^{M} \Delta(t_{m-1}, t_m)\, \mathbb{E}\left[\exp\left(-\int_0^{t_m} r(s)ds\right) L(t_{m-1}, t_m)\right]$$

where $r(s)$ is the continuously compounded Libor short rate. In Section 2.9.1 we show that

$$\mathbb{E}\left[\exp\left(-\int_0^{t_m} r(s)ds\right) L(t_{m-1}, t_m)\right] = \frac{1}{\Delta(t_{m-1}, t_m)}\,(Z(0, t_{m-1}) - Z(0, t_m)).$$

This allows us to write

$$V_{Float}(0) = \sum_{m=1}^{M} \Delta(t_{m-1}, t_m) \cdot \frac{1}{\Delta(t_{m-1}, t_m)}\,(Z(0, t_{m-1}) - Z(0, t_m))$$

$$= (Z(0, t_s) - Z(0, t_1)) + \ldots + (Z(0, t_{M-1}) - Z(0, t_M))$$

$$= Z(0, t_s) - Z(0, t_M).$$

The situation becomes more complicated if the floating leg has already begun and we are part way through a coupon payment period. In this case we have a next Libor coupon which is already known and began to accrue at time t_0 to be paid at time t_1. Therefore

$$V_{Float}(0) = \Delta(t_0, t_1)L(t_0, t_1)Z(0, t_1) + (Z(0, t_1) - Z(0, t_M)).$$

2.6.4   The Swap Mark-to-market

The mark-to-market of an interest rate swap is the value of money we would receive if we were to close out the swap contract. Since interest rate swaps usually settle according to a T + 2 convention, i.e. two days after trade date, then the mark-to-market must be based on exchanging the unwind value in two days' time. We call this date the settlement date and it occurs at time t_s.

When an interest rate swap is initially traded, it has zero value. However, as soon as the market swap rates move, the value of the contract moves away from zero.

Example   Consider a scenario in which we have entered into a 5Y receiver swap contract at a swap rate of 7%. A year later, rates have declined so that the 4Y swap contract has a swap rate of 5%. The value of this initial contract will move into positive territory since we are receiving more than the 5% we would receive from a new 4Y swap contract. Indeed, we could enter into the 4Y payer swap and end up with a contract in which we have a net income of 2% on the fixed swap legs while the floating legs cancel out. The question is then – what is this worth?

We consider an interest rate swap contract which was traded in the past at a time 0 and has a fixed rate leg which pays a swap rate $H(0)$. We consider the valuation from the perspective of a receiver, the party to the swap who is receiving the fixed coupon. The mark-to-market from the perspective of a payer is simply the negative of this.

$$W_{Receiver}(t) = -W_{Payer}(t) \tag{2.2}$$

Suppose that we are receiving the fixed leg and paying the floating leg, and suppose that the settlement date is on a coupon payment date for both the fixed and floating legs so that we don't have to consider any floating payment that has already been set. The value of the swap on the settlement date is given by

$$W_{Receiver}(t_s) = H(0) \sum_{n=1}^{N} \Delta(t_{n-1}, t_n) Z(t_s, t_n) - (Z(t_s, t_s) - Z(t_s, T))$$

$$= H(0) \sum_{n=1}^{N} \Delta(t_{n-1}, t_n) Z(t_s, t_n) - (1 - Z(t_s, T)). \tag{2.3}$$

2.6.5   The Breakeven Swap Rate

The breakeven swap rate at time t_s is the value of swap rate $H(t_s)$ which makes the net present value of a swap equal to zero. We therefore have

$$H(t_s) \sum_{n=1}^{N} \Delta(t_{n-1}, t_n) Z(t_s, t_n) = 1 - Z(t_s, t_N).$$

Defining the PV01 as the present value of an annualised coupon of 1 dollar paid on the schedule of the fixed leg of the swap, we have

$$PV01(t_s, T) = \sum_{n=1}^{N} \Delta(t_{n-1}, t_n) Z(t_s, t_n).$$

The breakeven swap rate at time t is therefore given by

$$H(t_s) = \frac{1 - Z(t_s, t_N)}{\text{PV01}(t_s, T)}.$$

We can use this to rewrite Equation 2.3 as

$$W_{Receiver}(t_s) = (H(0) - H(t_s)) \, \text{PV01}(t_s, T).$$

The value of an interest rate swap is roughly linear in the market swap rate $H(t_s)$. It is not exactly linear since the PV01(t_s, T) of the swap also contains an implicit dependence on the term structure of swap rates and therefore on $H(t_s)$.

In the following, we will use the terms 'on-market' and 'off-market'. The term 'on-market' refers to a swap which is quoted in the market for one of the standard fixed terms such as 1Y, 3Y, 5Y, 7Y, 10Y. The breakeven swap rate is the swap rate which makes the net present value of this swap equal to zero. As soon as the swap is traded it goes 'off-market' and its value can move away from zero. This terminology is also used for other sorts of derivatives contracts.

2.6.6 Interest Rate Swap Risk

The value of an interest rate swap is sensitive to changes in the market Libor curve. We can quantify these sensitivities by considering the sensitivity of the swap mark-to-market to changes in market swap rates. We begin by writing the value of a payer interest rate swap as

$$W_{Payer}(t_s) = (H(t_s) - H(0)) \sum_{n=1}^{N} \Delta(t_{n-1}, t_n) Z(t_s, t_n).$$

Differentiating with respect to the market swap rate to the swap maturity $H(t_s)$, we get

$$\frac{\partial W_{Payer}}{\partial H(t_s)} = \text{PV01}(t_s, T) + (H(t_s) - H(0)) \sum_{n=1}^{N} \Delta(t_{n-1}, t_n) \frac{\partial Z(t_s, t_n)}{\partial H(t_s)}.$$

For an *on-market* swap, we know that $H(t_s) = H(0)$ and the value of the swap is zero. As a result we have

$$\frac{\partial W_{Payer}}{\partial H(t_s)} = \text{PV01}(t_s, T).$$

The swap rate sensitivity of the swap value therefore equals its PV01. This result holds for both payer and receiver swaps although the sensitivities have opposite signs. The advantage of this result is that the PV01 is a sensitivity which can be computed analytically without the need to do any bumping of rates and rebuilding of the Libor discount curve.

When the swap is off-market, i.e. $H(t_s) \neq H(0)$, then its interest rate sensitivity must be computed by bumping the swap rates, rebuilding the Libor curve, and then repricing the swap. This requires us to have a methodology for building the Libor discount curve and this is the subject of the next section.

2.7   BOOTSTRAPPING THE LIBOR CURVE

So far, we have introduced and analysed the pricing of money-market deposits, forward rate agreements, interest rate futures and interest rate swaps. We have shown that their pricing is directly linked to the shape of the forward Libor discount curve at today time 0 which is given by $Z(0, T)$. However, we now ask the reverse question. How can we construct a discount curve that is consistent with the prices of deposits, futures, FRAs and swaps? To begin, we write out the set of pricing equations for all of the Libor instruments, except the interest rate futures:

- For deposits $d = 1, \ldots, N_D$ we have

$$Z(t_s, T_d) \left(1 + \Delta(t_s, T_d)L(t_s, T_d)\right) = 1.$$

- For FRAs $f = 1, \ldots, N_F$ we have

$$Z(t_s, t_{1f}) = Z(t_s, t_{2f}) \left(1 + \Delta(t_{1f}, t_{2f})F(t_{1f}, t_{2f})\right).$$

- For swaps $h = 1, \ldots, N_H$ we have

$$H_h \sum_{i=1}^{N_h} \Delta(t_{i-1}, t_i) Z(t_s, t_i) = 1 - Z(t_s, t_{N_h}).$$

These are all linear equations in $Z(t, T)$. This is why we have omitted interest rate futures. Due to their convexity adjustment, interest rate futures do not have a linear pricing equation in $Z(t, T)$. However, we can incorporate futures as a linear product by *mapping them onto equivalent FRAs with the same start and end dates*. To do this, we must convert the futures rate to FRA rates using a convexity adjustment such as the one given in Equation 2.1.

These instruments present a system of $N_D + N_F + N_H$ linear equations. However, the number of discount factors to be solved for will typically be greater than this. Consider the following example.

Example   Suppose we have the following instruments:

- 3M and 6M deposit rates. These have a dependency on discount factors at $T = 0.25$ and $T = 0.5$ years.
- A 5 × 8M FRA with dependency on dates at $T = 0.417$ and $T = 0.75$ years.
- 1Y, 2Y, 3Y, 4Y, 5Y swap rates with semi-annual coupons on the fixed leg. The discount factors needed are at times $T = 0.5, 1.0, 1.5, 2.0, 2.5, 3.0, 3.5, 4.0, 4.5, 5.0$.

We have a total of $2 + 1 + 5 = 9$ linear pricing equations, one for each instrument. However, there are a total of 13 different discount factors to find. The system is underdetermined and can only be solved if we make further assumptions.

It is also possible for the system of equations to be overdetermined. Consider another example:

Example   Suppose we have the following instruments:

- A 6M deposit with payment dates at $T = 0.5$.
- A 6×12M FRA with dates at $T = 0.5$ and $T = 1.0$.
- A one year swap with semi-annual coupon payment dates at $T = 0.5, 1.0$.

We have a total of three pricing equations, but with only two unknowns which are $Z(0, 0.5)$ and $Z(0, 1.0)$. The system is overdetermined.

When the system is overdetermined, we need to reject some instruments, i.e. we should decide which instruments take precedence when building a discount curve. In the example, it may be decided that the 1Y swap is a more liquid and more appropriate measure of the 6M to 1Y discount curve than a 6×12M FRA. We would then remove the 6×12M FRA in order to imply out the 12M discount factor from the 1Y swap rate.

2.7.1   Interpolation

While the case of an overdetermined system is certainly possible, it is much more likely that the system is underdetermined, with more unknowns than equations. We then need additional assumptions. Typically, these assumptions take the form of an interpolation scheme. Using interpolation, we simply reduce the number of unknown discount factors to the number of instruments and then solve for these. Any remaining discount factors are not solved for but simply determined by interpolating the 'skeleton' of solved discount factors.

There are many possible interpolation schemes. Spline methods such as quadratic, tension and b-splines may be used and have been discussed in recent papers by Andersen (2005) and Hagan and West (2004). However, such approaches may be deemed to be overly sophisticated in the context of credit derivatives pricing since credit derivatives have a low interest rate sensitivity and are also fairly insensitive to the shape of the interest rate curve. We therefore choose to use a simple interpolation scheme which assumes that the continuously compounded forward rate is piecewise constant.

2.7.2   The Bootstrap

Given an interpolation scheme, the most common approach to building curves is to use a bootstrap. The idea of a bootstrap is that we start with the shortest maturity product. We then solve for the discount factor at its maturity date, relying upon our interpolation scheme to determine any earlier discount factors which may be required. We then move to the instrument with the next longest maturity and once again solve for its maturity date discount factors. Any cash flows which fall between the previous maturity date and this maturity date are also determined by interpolation. Hence each product requires us to solve for one discount factor and the system is exactly determined. This process is shown in Figure 2.5.

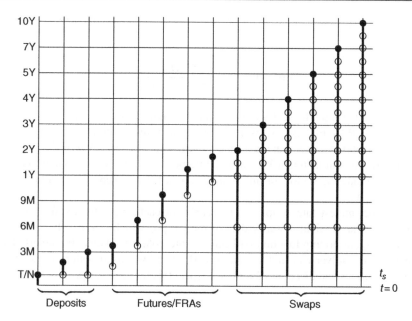

Figure 2.5 The bootstrap methodology works through the instruments from left to right, in order of their increasing final maturity. Discount factors for cash flow dates with the solid circles are solved for, while those discount factors at the cash flow dates with empty circles are interpolated using a chosen interpolation scheme. This means that we have one unknown for each market instrument and the system is exactly solvable. The time grid starts today and then we have T/N, which together with O/N takes us to the settlement date of the deposits and swaps

Different instruments are handled differently. The discount factors implied by the money-market deposits have only one payment date and so can be solved for immediately. However, for the FRA and interest rate swap, although we have one equation and one unknown for each instrument, the equation is not necessarily linear since intermediate dates may have to be interpolated. As a result, we require a one-dimensional root solver. A simple one-dimensional root solver such as Newton–Raphson, or Brent's method can be used. Both can be found in Press *et al.* (1992).

The *internal representation* of the discount curve consists of two vectors of equal length. The first is for times starting with $t = 0$ and then t_s, followed by the maturity dates of all of the instruments. The second vector contains the corresponding discount factors starting with 1.0. We also assume that we have an interpolation function which given both vectors and a future time returns the corresponding interpolated discount factor. The bootstrap algorithm is as follows:

1. Map interest futures onto FRAs by convexity adjusting the futures rate.
2. Sort deposits, FRAs and swaps in order of increasing final maturity date. Check for cases when the system is overdetermined and, if so, remove the appropriate instruments, typically on grounds of liquidity, until the system is solvable.
3. Using the overnight rate L_{ON} and the tomorrow next rate L_{TN} calculate

$$Z(0, t_s) = \frac{1}{(1 + \Delta(0, t + 1 \text{ day})L_{ON}))(1 + \Delta(t + 1 \text{ day}, t_s)L_{TN})}.$$

Insert the time t_s and $Z(0, t_s)$ onto the vector of times and discount factors.

4. Loop over the deposits $d = 1, \ldots, D$. For each, solve for the final maturity discount factor using

$$Z(0, t_d) = \frac{Z(0, t_s)}{(1 + \Delta(t_s, t_d)L(t_s, t_d))}.$$

For each deposit, extend the vector of times and discount factors by inserting t_d and $Z(t, t_d)$.

5. Loop over the FRAs. For each, solve for the final maturity discount factor $Z(0, t_2)$ using a one-dimensional root solver that makes the present value of the FRA zero. The value of the forward start discount factor $Z(0, t_1)$ will be interpolated off the curve. When found, insert t_2 and $Z(0, t_2)$ onto the vectors of times and discount factors. Repeat until all of the FRAs have been fitted.

6. Loop over the interest rate swaps $k = 1, \ldots, K$. For each, we solve for the value of the discount factor at the final maturity date of the swap t_k which reprices the swap to zero. In the process, our pricing function will call the interpolation scheme. Eventually the one-dimensional root solver will find a value of $Z(0, t_k)$ and we insert both t_k and $Z(0, t_k)$ into our vector of times and discount factors. We repeat this for each swap.

Example The market rates for 14 November 2006 are shown in Table 2.1. Although the four deposit rates shown were available, we actually only used the O/N, T/N, 1W and 1M rates. Our reason for not using longer maturity deposits is that the short end of the interest rate futures market is generally considered to be much more liquid than the money-market deposits. For the purpose of converting the futures into FRAs in order to use them to build the curve, we computed the futures–FRA convexity correction using a basis point volatility of 60 bp, implying that a 60 bp movement in interest rates over one year is a one standard deviation move. The sizes of the convexity corrections for the futures contracts were 0.006, 0.037, 0.091, 0.167 and 0.265 bp. The resulting forward curve is shown in Figure 2.6. The piecewise flat continuously compound forward rate interpolation assumption is clearly evident.

Table 2.1 Deposits, futures, FRA and swap rates used to build a Libor curve from 14 November 2006. Source: Lehman Brothers

Instrument	Term	Rate/Price
Deposit	O/N	5.275
Deposit	T/N	5.275
Deposit	1W	5.280
Deposit	1M	5.320
Deposit	2M	5.360
Deposit	3M	5.375
Future	Dec 06	94.6275
Future	Mar 07	94.7450
Future	Jun 07	94.9050
Future	Sep 07	95.0800
Future	Dec 07	95.2000

Swap	2Y	5.0946%
Swap	3Y	5.0241%
Swap	4Y	5.0123%
Swap	5Y	5.0180%
Swap	7Y	5.0481%
Swap	10Y	5.0982%
Swap	12Y	5.1332%
Swap	15Y	5.1747%
Swap	20Y	5.2137%
Swap	25Y	5.2252%
Swap	30Y	5.2217%

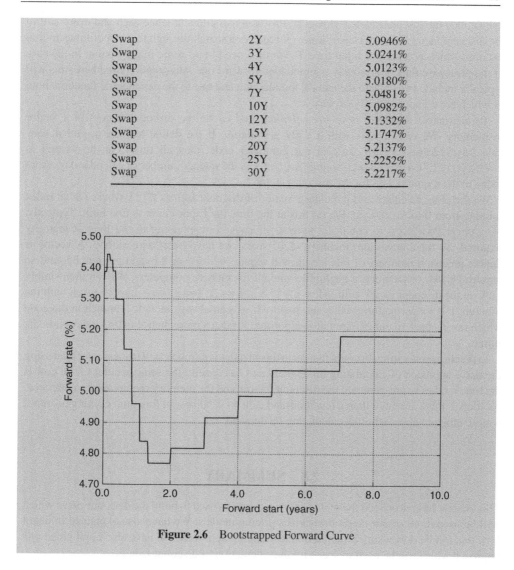

Figure 2.6   Bootstrapped Forward Curve

2.7.3   Caching Discount Factors

We conclude this section with a discussion of how we can improve the numerical performance of generating Libor discount factors. This is a major issue in the pricing of derivatives, especially when Monte Carlo methods are used and large numbers of trials have to be run. It is not uncommon that we have to make several million calls into the discount factor function just to calculate one price. In fact, any profile analysis of Monte Carlo derivative pricing code will invariably find that a large proportion of the time is spent generating Libor discount factors.

Let us first recap what happens when we call for a Libor discount factor $Z(0, T)$. The direct approach which we have described in this chapter is to apply our interpolation scheme to the internal representation of the discount curve consisting of times and discount factors which we have calculated at the maturity times of our bootstrap instruments as and when we need to calculate the discount factor. However, this is not so efficient since each and every call to the discount factor generator takes time – it requires a search through the grid of times to find the ones which bracket our input time T. We then need to do some interpolation. In the case of the piecewise flat continuously compounded forward rate interpolation used here, this will typically include two calls to the natural log function and one to the exponential function, both of which are computationally expensive.

An alternative approach is to *pre-calculate and cache* the discount factors in a vector in memory. We can do this with a daily granularity. If we define and use a global variable `DaysInYear = 365.242` in our computer code, then all times can be written as `t = DayDiff/DaysInYear` where `DayDiff` is the integer number of calendar days from today to the required date for the discount factor.

We therefore calculate and populate a vector of discount factors `Z[i]` where i is an index running from 0 to `MaxDays`. We do this at the time the Libor curve is first built. Typically, we can set `MaxDays` to equal the number of days corresponding to the longest maturity required. So for a maximum maturity of 10 years, we have `MaxDays = 3653`. A vector of double precision numbers of this length will require 64 bits (or 8 bytes) per number and so require 28.5 kb of memory, a negligible amount for modern computers. We can then simply look up the discount factor with index `i = T * DaysInYear` (care must be taken with the rounding). If longer maturity dates are required, we can always include a branch in the code which resorts back to our extrapolation algorithm for dates more than `MaxDays` days into the future.

In practice, generating discount factors in this manner is as much as 10 times faster than using the naïve approach of calculating on demand and has exactly the same accuracy. The cost is the time it takes to pre-generate the discount factors and the memory requirements associated. As soon as there are more than a few thousand calls to the discount function, caching becomes a more efficient approach than calculating on demand.

2.8 SUMMARY

This chapter has introduced the main Libor instruments used to build the discount curve which will be used in all of our credit derivatives pricing models. We have also explained in detail how this can be done using a standard bootstrapping approach. We have also highlighted one approach which can be used to speed up the calculation of discount factors.

2.9 TECHNICAL APPENDIX

2.9.1 Pricing a Floating Rate Payment

We consider a payment of Libor at a future time t_2, based on the rate that was observed at time t_1 for the period $[t_1, t_2]$. This is market standard – the payment is set in advance at time t_1 and paid in arrears at time t_2. The contract is discounted at the Libor quality continuously compounded short rate $r(s)$. The value of the future Libor payment as seen at time t_1 is given by

$$L(t_1, t_2) = \frac{1}{\Delta(t_1, t_2)} \left(\frac{1}{Z(t_1, t_2)} - 1 \right) \quad \text{where} \quad Z(t_1, t_2) = \mathbb{E}_{t_1} \left[\exp \left(- \int_{t_1}^{t_2} r(s) ds \right) \right]$$

where $\mathbb{E}_t[x] = \mathbb{E}[x|\mathcal{F}_t]$ where $\mathcal{F}_t$ is the filtration, i.e. the information until time t. We can therefore write the expected present value of this Libor payment at time 0 as

$$V(0) = \frac{1}{\Delta(t_1, t_2)} \mathbb{E}\left[\exp\left(-\int_0^{t_2} r(s)ds \right) \left(\frac{1}{\mathbb{E}_{t_1}\left[\exp\left(-\int_{t_1}^{t_2} r(s)ds \right) \right]} - 1 \right) \right].$$

Rearranging, we have

$$V(0) = \frac{1}{\Delta(t_1, t_2)} \mathbb{E}\left[\exp\left(-\int_0^{t_1} r(s)ds \right) \left(\frac{\exp\left(-\int_{t_1}^{t_2} r(s)ds \right)}{\mathbb{E}_{t_1}\left[\exp\left(-\int_{t_1}^{t_2} r(s)ds \right) \right]} \right) - \exp\left(-\int_0^{t_2} r(s)ds \right) \right].$$

We can now use the Tower property (see Williams (1991)) which states that

$$\mathbb{E}_{t_1}\left[\mathbb{E}_{t_2}[X] \right] = \mathbb{E}_{t_1}[X] \text{ if } t_1 < t_2$$

to write

$$V(0) = \frac{1}{\Delta(t_1, t_2)} \mathbb{E}\left[\exp\left(-\int_0^{t_1} r(s)ds \right) \left(\frac{\mathbb{E}_{t_1}\left[\exp\left(-\int_{t_1}^{t_2} r(s)ds \right) \right]}{\mathbb{E}_{t_1}\left[\exp\left(-\int_{t_1}^{t_2} r(s)ds \right) \right]} \right) - \exp\left(-\int_0^{t_2} r(s)ds \right) \right]$$

giving finally

$$V(0) = \frac{1}{\Delta(t_1, t_2)} \left(Z(0, t_1) - Z(0, t_2) \right).$$

As a result, the present value of a future Libor payment is simply the difference between the discount factor at the start and end of the Libor period divided by the year fraction in the appropriate basis. This is only true if the Libor is set in advance and paid in arrears.

Part I
Single-name Credit Derivatives

Part 1

Single-name Credit Derivatives

3

Single-name Credit Modelling

3.1 INTRODUCTION

Before we can begin to construct models for pricing credit derivatives, we need to establish a modelling framework which can capture the appropriate risks. These risk are default risk, recovery rate risk, spread risk and interest rate risk. Default risk is the risk that a scheduled payment of interest or principal on a bond or loan is not received. Recovery risk is the risk that following a default, the size of the recovered amount is much less than the amount owed. Spread risk is the risk that the value of a credit security falls as the market's view regarding the credit quality of the borrower changes, causing us to realise a loss if we sell the credit security. Interest rate risk is the risk that changes in the level of the Libor curve will cause the value of the credit security to fall. Since none of credit derivatives we encounter in this book ever condition a payment on a change in credit rating, we do not consider the challenge of modelling credit rating transitions.

The main purpose of this chapter is therefore to set out the modelling framework which is used in the credit derivatives market and which can capture all of these risks. We will provide the theoretical foundation for all of the pricing models used in subsequent chapters for single-name product pricing.

It is important for any credit derivative modeller to also have a feel for the event of default in terms of its historical frequency and severity. For this reason, we begin this chapter by setting out some of the empirical observations that have been made about the default rate of bonds and loans. We also discuss empirical data relating to the recovery rate, explaining the effect of seniority and the difference between bonds and loans.

We then set out the pricing framework in which the credit derivatives market operates. This is known as the *risk-neutral* framework and we discuss the concept of a risk-neutral pricing model. It is important for the reader to understand the idea of risk-neutral pricing as it underpins the pricing and risk management of not just credit derivatives, but all derivatives.

Merton's firm value model is discussed next. Although this is not a model which is typically applied in the risk-neutral framework and is almost never used for pricing credit derivatives, we introduce it for three reasons. First of all, setting out Merton's model and describing how it is used helps to clarify the separation between the structural approach to credit modelling and the reduced form approach to credit modelling. A second reason is that this model was the first attempt to construct a credit model which was both solvable and insightful, and no text on credit modelling is complete without a discussion of it. The third reason is that it is the inspiration behind some of the multi-name models discussed in the second part of this book.

Following Merton's model, we then introduce the standard risk-neutral pricing model used in the market for pricing single-name credit. We describe in detail the mathematical basis for this model and how it can be used to price a number of simple credit risky payoffs. When combined, these payoffs will allow us to price a very broad range of credit risky securities. We also discuss the simplifying assumptions often made when using this model and attempt to quantify and justify them.

Note that by presenting the modelling framework for single-name credits, we are also presenting some of the theoretical foundation for pricing multi-name credit derivatives. After all, these are products which knit together the risks of single-name credits. We have deferred our detailed theoretical discussion of multi-name credit modelling, specifically the modelling of co-dependence, to chapters in Part II of this book.

3.2 OBSERVING DEFAULT

Default is a complex event which can occur for a whole host of reasons. In some cases it is a completely idiosyncratic event which strikes just one company. In other cases it can be a systemic event in which several companies or sovereigns are all affected by the same factor. For an excellent and detailed discussion of the many factors which can lead to default, we refer the reader to Ganguin and Bilardello (2005). In the following, we will try to shed some light on the frequency of default and the size of the recovered amount using empirical data.

3.2.1 Default Rate Statistics

The main source of default statistics are the credit rating agencies. In order to better assess the credit quality of issuers, they have collected a significant amount of data over their lifetimes. For example, Moody's Investor Services has been in existence since 1909 and their default database runs back as far as 1920.

In order to measure default, we need to define what a default is. Moody's Investor Services defines default as 'any missed or delayed payment of interest or principal, bankruptcy, receivership or distressed exchange where (i) the issuer offered bondholders a new security or package of securities that amount to a diminished financial obligation (such as preferred or common stock or debt with a lower coupon or par amount) or (ii) the exchange had the apparent purpose of helping the borrower avoid default'. If a failure to pay principal or coupon occurs as a result of some omission which is quickly rectified, then the event is known as *technical default*. Such an occurrence is not usually included in rating agency default statistics.

The rating agency methodology for calculating default statistics has been to construct data-bases of issuers, and to monitor the rating and default behaviour of the senior unsecured bonds of each issuer through time. This is done by identifying a *cohort* – a group of issuers with the same initial rating. The rating agency then keeps track of the cohort and records if any of the issuers default. As a result, it is possible to calculate the number of defaults in each cohort. Dividing this by the number of issuers in the cohort gives the average default rate of issuers with a specific rating. Each year new cohorts are defined. Averages can then be taken across cohorts with different initial dates but with the same initial rating to give a time-averaged default rate for each rating class.

Table 3.1 shows time-averaged cumulative default rates and so has averaged out any time variability in default rate statistics. In practice, market participants will use these historical default rates as proxies for the default probabilities used within their credit risk models. This assumes that time-averaged historical default rates by rating are a good predictor of future default rates, and that all issuers with the same rating have the same probability of default. It therefore ignores the current state of the credit environment and differences in credit quality which exist within

Table 3.1 Average cumulative default rates of corporate bond issuers by letter rating from 1983 to 2005: Source: Hamilton *et al.* (2005). © Moody's Investors Service, Inc. and/or its affiliates. Reprinted with permission. All rights reserved

Years	Cumulative default rate (%)									
	1	2	3	4	5	6	7	8	9	10
Aaa	0.0	0.0	0.0	0.0	0.1	0.1	0.2	0.2	0.2	0.2
Aa	0.0	0.0	0.1	0.1	0.2	0.3	0.3	0.3	0.4	0.4
A	0.0	0.1	0.3	0.4	0.6	0.7	0.9	1.0	1.1	1.2
Baa	0.2	0.6	1.1	1.6	2.2	2.8	3.3	3.7	4.1	4.5
Ba	1.3	3.6	6.3	9.0	11.1	12.9	14.5	15.8	16.9	17.8
B	5.7	12.1	17.6	21.8	25.1	27.7	29.6	30.8	31.6	32.1
Caa-C	21.0	30.3	36.1	39.5	41.2	42.1	42.6	42.9	43.1	43.3

a rating category. The averages are global, so that differences in the triggering of default and the workout process which may exist across different legal jurisdictions are not captured. The data is also biased towards US corporate credits since this has traditionally been the dominant market for corporate credit bonds. However, this issue is now being addressed by the rating agencies who have recently begun to produce separate statistics for the European credit market.

To get a sense of the large variability in default rates, Figure 3.1 shows the annual default rates of issuers by year and rating.

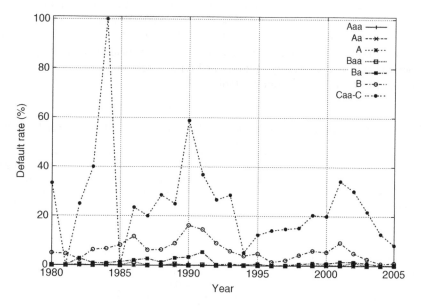

Figure 3.1 One-year default rates by year and rating class, 1980–2005. Source: Hamilton *et al.* (2005). © Moody's Investors Service, Inc. and/or its affiliates. Reprinted with permission. All rights reserved

Historical default data is not used by the market for determining the price of a security. Its use is primarily as a way of calibrating risk models. When we come to pricing credit risky assets such as credit derivatives, we need to be in a world in which we can hedge out the risk that these contracts present. For that, we need to be in a risk-neutral framework.

3.2.2 Recovery Rate Statistics

Credit risk is also about the risk associated with the amount of the claim that can be recovered after default. Care should be taken to distinguish between the recovery price used within the credit derivatives market and the price obtained by bond holders after going through the full workout process in which the assets of the firm are liquidated and distributed to the various debt holders.

In the credit derivatives market, the recovery price is the price of some defined reference obligation determined within 72 days of the default event. Rating agencies typically measure default as the price of a defaulted asset within some period, say 30 days, after a default.

There must clearly be a close link between the recovery price and the amount received after the workout process. However, differences can arise. Significant differences might occur if new information arrives between the setting of the recovery price and the completion of the workout process. The recovery price is also vulnerable to supply and demand effects in the distressed debt market.

3.2.3 Empirical Data on Recovery Rates

The measure of recovery rate used in the credit markets is the defaulted bond price divided by the face value. There are a number of sources for recovery rate data. Once again, the rating agencies are one of the main sources for this data. In addition, there are a number of academics who have access to defaulted bond data provided by dealers. Table 3.2 presents the median and mean recovery rates by seniority and type of debt instrument as determined by Altman *et al.* (2003b). It is clear from this table that:

Table 3.2 Empirical estimates of recovery rates based on prices just after default on bonds and 30 days after default on loans. Source: Altman *et al.* (2003b)

Seniority of debt	Debt type	Number of issues	Median recovery (%)	Mean recovery (%)	Standard deviation (%)
Senior secured	Loans	155	73.00	68.50	24.4
Senior unsecured	Loans	28	50.50	55.00	28.4
Senior secured	Bonds	220	54.49	52.84	23.1
Senior unsecured	Bonds	910	42.27	34.89	26.6
Senior subordinated	Bonds	395	32.35	30.17	25.0
Subordinated	Bonds	248	31.96	29.03	22.5
All bonds and loans		1,909	40.05	34.31	24.9

- The most important driver of the recovery rate is the position of the debt in the capital structure of the firm, i.e. senior debt recovers more on average than subordinated debt.
- The recovery rate of loans exceeds that of bonds. This is because the loans typically contain additional covenants.

- The standard deviation of the recovery rate distributions is rather broad. Indeed, it has been observed by Frank and Torous (1989) that the *absolute priority rule* (APR) is not always obeyed in the US, meaning that in certain circumstances, holders of subordinated debt may recover more than holders of more senior debt.
- The most relevant recovery value for the credit derivatives market is the expected recovery rate for senior unsecured bonds. This is equal to 34.89%. The median value is 42.27%.

Empirical studies have also shown that default data exhibits a strong and long-run correlation between default rates and expected recovery rates. Altman *et al.* (2003a) analysed the default behaviour of a US bond database in the period 1982–2002. The analysis was based on 1300 defaults with reliable post-default prices. The results are plotted in Figure 3.2. They show that the relationship is a negative one – when macroeconomic default rates increase, the average recovery rate falls, and vice versa. The explanation behind this result is mainly one of market supply and demand. The dynamic is that when there is a high default rate, there is an oversupply of defaulted assets in the distressed debt market. As a result, the price of distressed debt falls. The opposite occurs when we are in a period of below average default rates. This risk is systemic and has implications for those who are exposed to broad portfolios of credit bonds either directly or in a derivative format such as a CDO.

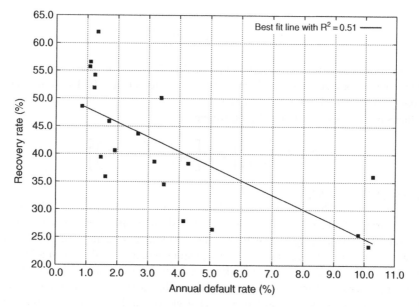

Figure 3.2   Relationship between bond recovery rates and bond default rates for the period 1982–2001 from Altman *et al.* (2003a). We have included a best fit line which has an R^2 of 0.51 and the equation $y = 0.51 - 2.6x$

3.3   RISK-NEUTRAL PRICING FRAMEWORK

The concept of risk-neutral pricing, first introduced by Black, Scholes and Merton, has been the foundation for the massive growth in size, scope and complexity of the derivatives market. The basic idea is that dealers who issue derivatives can hedge them by trading the underlying asset. In some special cases, the hedge may be static. More generally, it is a dynamic hedging strategy. What is important is that at any moment in time, the dealer should have a net portfolio of derivative plus hedging positions which is instantaneously insensitive to market movements – it is *risk free*. The total value of the derivative plus the hedging positions should therefore simply grow at the *risk-free rate*. The cost of the derivative can then be considered to be the cost of hedging it, taking into account the fact that the hedging instruments may have to be funded by borrowing at some interest rate. As a result, the effective risk-free rate becomes the rate at which the hedges are funded, which for most dealers is Libor.

Within a risk-neutral framework, it can be shown that the value of a derivative contract is given by the discounted expectation of the payoff. Discounting is done at the risk-free rate and the expectation is taken in the risk-neutral measure, i.e. a probability distribution in which the price of a forward calculated using this probability measure equals the price of a forward in the market. Mathematically, we can write the expected present value at time 0 of a payoff at time T as

$$V(0) = \mathbb{E}\left[\frac{V(T)}{\beta(T)}\right]$$

where $\mathbb{E}[x]$ represents an expectation of x in the risk-neutral measure, and

$$\beta(T) = \exp\left(\int_0^T r(s)ds\right)$$

discounts the payment at time T to today time 0. It is the value at time T of the rolled-up risk-free money-market account in which \$1 was deposited at time 0. The term $r(t)$ is the continuously compounded risk-free short rate.

Note that since the risk-free rate is Libor, we have

$$Z(0, T) = \mathbb{E}\left[\frac{1}{\beta(T)}\right] = \mathbb{E}\left[\exp\left(-\int_0^T r(s)ds\right)\right]$$

as the Libor quality discount factor.

The assumptions on which this risk-neutral framework is based, which include continuous hedging, zero transaction costs and zero counterparty risk, all break down in practice. However, if the market for the underlying asset is liquid, allowing frequent trading with small bid–offer spreads, and counterparties enter into collateral posting agreements, then such a limit is certainly approachable and the whole idea of risk neutrality works well enough to make it feasible.

Initially, the risk-neutral framework was applied to the large and highly liquid equity, FX and interest rate markets. Now, with the significant growth in the depth and liquidity of the credit default swap market, it has become possible to create a whole family of credit derivatives for which the credit default swap is the underlying asset which is used to dynamically hedge out the credit risk.

The implications of the risk-neutral framework are quite profound. For a start, when the market is *complete* the dealer does not need to take a view on the direction of the market. Market completeness means that it is possible for the dealer to find hedging instruments which allow him to create a portfolio of derivative plus hedges which is instantaneously risk free. For example, an equity option trader is able to hedge the first-order stock price sensitivity of his position by trading a delta amount of the underlying stock. However, he is not able to immunise his portfolio to first-order changes in volatility without using products which embed some volatility sensitivity. This risk can only be hedged using other liquid options.

Since the pricing model needs to use all of the necessary underlying products to hedge out all of the risks, one important requirement is that the pricing model must also be able to reprice all of the hedging instruments. This is essential since a model which does not reprice the market is by definition not arbitrage free.

These pricing models will not tell the user whether the credit derivative is a good investment. They are not predictive. They simply extract information about the market's expectations embedded in the prices of credit risky instruments to which they are calibrated. This information can then be used to price other more complex credit derivative securities. As a result, we have an internally consistent approach – our model is calibrated to fit the observable market prices of instruments which become the hedging instruments for more complex credit derivative structures.

Calibration to the prices of market instruments is a basic requirement of a no-arbitrage model provided the market prices do not exhibit arbitrage. For example, consider *put–call parity*. This is a mathematical relationship between the price of a call option, a put option and the underlying asset which is based on no-arbitrage arguments. If we have a situation in which the market prices of a put option, a call option and the underlying asset violate put–call parity, then we have an arbitrage. In this case, we would *not* want the pricing model to fit to all three market prices simultaneously. Indeed, we would expect the model to refuse to fit and by failing to do so, it would tell us that there is a problem with the market prices. In practice such an arbitrage would be quickly removed by the actions of traders.

We call a model that is able to identify the existence of arbitrage across products which have the same underlying risk but different payoffs a *consistent model*. Even if the market prices are assumed always to be arbitrage free, it is not certain that the prices produced by a model which is *not consistent* would also always be arbitrage free. This is a concern which will arise in our discussion of base correlation in Chapter 20.

Sometimes the market is not *complete*. This means that the product has some risk which we are not able to hedge using the range of available market securities. In this situation, we are forced to move outside a pure risk-neutral framework since the dealer's portfolio can no longer be instantaneously risk free. There are a number of approaches which can then be taken. These include:

1. Quantifying our exposure to the risk using empirical data and allocating some reserve fund against potential losses based on the size and likelihood of this risk.
2. Packaging and selling this risk, although finding a buyer may be difficult.

In both of these cases, hedging this risk will increase the cost of the transaction and this will affect the price of the derivative.

Finally, we make some comments on notation. In all of the pricing formulae, unless otherwise specified, we are using the risk-neutral measure known as the spot Libor measure. This is because our choice of *numeraire* is the rolled-up money-market account which uses the spot Libor rate. The concept of numeraires will be introduced and discussed later in Section 9.3.4. When we calculate this expectation based on information available at time 0, the expectation is unconditional since no events can occur before time 0. However, in many cases, we will price a derivative as of time t, where time t may represent today or it could be a date in the future. In either case, we need to condition this expectation on the information up to time t. As a result, we can rewrite the value of a payoff at time T conditional on information to time t as

$$V(t) = \mathbb{E}\left[\frac{V(T)}{\beta(T)} \mid \mathcal{F}_t\right]$$

where $\mathcal{F}_t$ is the *filtration* or the set of information up to and including time t. We can think of this information set as including price histories and a knowledge of previous defaults. To simplify notation, we prefer to shorten this to

$$V(t) = \mathbb{E}_t\left[\frac{V(T)}{\beta(T)}\right].$$

For a more comprehensive introduction to the concept of the risk-neutral measure, two good references with lots of intuitive discussion are the books by Baxter and Rennie (1996) and Joshi (2003). For a mathematically rigorous discussion of completeness and risk neutrality, the reader is referred to Duffie (1996).

3.4   STRUCTURAL MODELS OF DEFAULT

The history of credit modelling began with the work of Merton (1974), in which he proposed an option-based model for corporate default. Merton's idea was to model default as the event which occurs when the value of the assets of a firm fall below the value of the firm's debt. The model assumed a highly simplified capital structure for a firm consisting of:

- Face value F of T-maturity zero coupon bonds with total value D, and
- Shares with total value E which pay no dividend.

At any moment in time the asset value of the firm $A(t)$ is related to the value of the debt $D(t)$ and equity $E(t)$ via the standard *accounting equation* which states that the value of the firm's assets equals the value of its debt plus equity, i.e.

$$A(t) = D(t) + E(t).$$

Merton further specified that default can only occur at time T which corresponds to the maturity of the debt. On this date, the firm can be in one of two states:

- Solvency: $A(T) \geq F$ and the value of the assets of the firm exceed the face value of the debt. The bond holders are therefore repaid in full leaving $A(T) - F$ for the equity holders.
- Insolvency: $A(T) < F$ and the value of the assets are insufficient to pay off the outstanding debt of the firm in full. In this case, the debt holders have a claim on the remaining assets of the firm taking all of the remaining value $A(T)$. This leaves the equity holders with nothing.

We can write the time T payoffs for the bond holders as

$$D(T) = F - \max[F - A(T), 0] = \min[F, A(T)]$$

and for the equity holders as

$$E(T) = \max[A(T) - F, 0].$$

Figure 3.3 shows that the equity payoff at time T has the same payoff as a call option on the asset value of the firm with a strike price at the face value of the outstanding debt. We also see that the value of the debt is equivalent to being long an amount F in cash and short a put option on the firm struck at F.

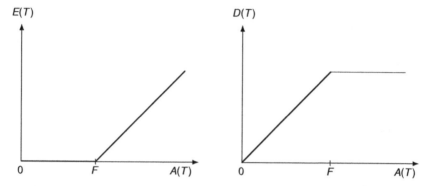

Figure 3.3 Value of debt and equity at maturity as a function of the asset value

To determine the current value of the equity and debt, we need to have a model for the evolution of $A(t)$. Merton assumed that it follows a lognormal process of the form

$$\frac{dA(t)}{A(t)} = \mu dt + \sigma_A dW$$

where σ_A is the percentage volatility of the asset value process. In the risk-neutral measure, we set $\mu = r$ and assuming that the company does not pay dividends, we can write the present value of the debt and the equity using the well-known Black–Scholes equations

$$E(t) = A(t)\Phi(d_1) - F\exp(-r(T-t))\Phi(d_2) \tag{3.1}$$

$$D(t) = F\exp(-r(T-t))\Phi(d_2) + A(t)\Phi(-d_1) \tag{3.2}$$

where $\Phi(x)$ is the Gaussian cumulative distribution function and

$$d_1 = \frac{\ln(A(t)/F) + \left(r + \frac{1}{2}\sigma_A^2\right)(T-t)}{\sigma_A\sqrt{T-t}}$$

$$d_2 = d_1 - \sigma_A\sqrt{T-t}.$$

If we define the credit spread s as the continuously compounded spread over the constant and continuously compounded risk-free rate which reprices the debt we then have

$$D(t) = F\exp(-(r+s)(T-t))$$

so that

$$s = -\frac{1}{(T-t)} \ln\left(\frac{D(t,T)}{F}\right) - r.$$

Substituting Equation 3.2 for $D(t)$ allows us to calculate the term structure of credit spreads for a range of model inputs. Figure 3.4 shows the dependency of the spread implied by

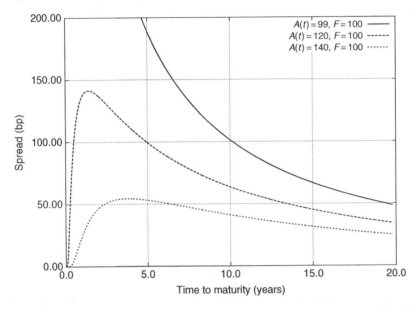

Figure 3.4   Credit spread term structure implied by the Merton model for three values of the initial asset value. We have set $\sigma_A = 20\%$ and use a risk-free rate of $r = 5\%$

the model on the time to maturity of the bond. This is shown for three values of the asset value:

- When $A(t) = \$99$ and $F = \$100$, we have $A(t) < F$. In this scenario, it would not be possible to redeem the bond if it matured immediately. As a result, the credit spread as $T - t \to 0$ tends to infinity. However, for longer maturities, there is a finite probability that the asset value will grow to exceed the face value and the bond becomes more likely to be repaid. As a result, the credit spread falls with increasing time to maturity.
- When $A(t) = \$120$, we have $A(t) > F$ and so a bond maturing immediately can be repaid in full. As a result, the spread tends to zero as $T - t \to 0$. With increasing maturity, the risk of the asset value falling below F increases and so the credit spread rises. However, the growth of the asset value at the risk-free rate means that at longer maturities the default risk of the bond declines.
- When $A(t) = \$140$, the asset value starts even further above the default threshold. The curve shape is the same as the previous case but the higher asset value means that the value of the credit spread is lower.

The probability that the asset value of the firm is above the face value of the debt on its maturity date is its survival probability, which we denote with $Q(t,T)$. This is given by

$$Q(t,T) = \Pr(A(T) \geq F) = \Phi(d_2).$$

We can also determine the expected recovery value of the bond. This is the expected value of the asset value conditional on the final asset value being below the bond face value at maturity. The price of a zero coupon bond which pays in full or pays the recovery fraction R at maturity is given by weighting the two possible payments by their respective probabilities and discounting back to today at the risk-free rate. We therefore have

$$D(t) = F \exp(-r(T-t))(Q(t,T) + (1 - Q(t,T))R)$$
$$= F \exp(-r(T-t))(\Phi(d_2) + \Phi(-d_2)R). \tag{3.3}$$

We define the recovery rate R as the fraction of the recovery value paid at default divided by the face value of the bond. It is determined by setting Equation 3.2 equal to Equation 3.3, and gives

$$R = \frac{A(t)\Phi(-d_1)}{F \exp(-r(T-t))\Phi(-d_2)}.$$

This demonstrates that the Merton model not only allows us to price equity and bonds, it also allows us to determine the recovery rate endogenously. We can also establish a mathematical link between the volatility of the asset value and that of the equity. Since the equity value is a function of $A(t)$, we can use Ito's lemma to write

$$\sigma_E = \frac{\partial E(t)}{\partial A(t)} \frac{A(t)}{E(t)} \sigma_A \tag{3.4}$$

where the partial derivative can be computed analytically to give

$$\sigma_E = \sigma_A \Phi(d_1) \frac{A(t)}{E(t)}.$$

This equation can then be used to calibrate the asset volatility parameter in the Merton model using the volatility of equity prices.

3.4.1   Limitations of the Merton Model

Merton's model is a simple yet very instructive model for analysing corporate default. However its practical applications as a pricing model is very limited. There are a number of reasons why:

- The highly simplified capital structure is unrealistic. Adding other levels of subordination is also difficult since one must consider the *priority of payments* – the rules governing how and in what order debt with different seniorities is repaid.
- The model only allows default at a single time T. It is not possible therefore to consider a capital structure with bonds whose maturities are different.
- Merton's model assumes that the bonds are zero coupon. It is possible to extend Merton's model to handle coupon paying bonds as in Geske (1977). However, the computational complexity of the pricing formulae increases significantly – a coupon paying bond is a compound option, an option on an option in this framework.

- There is limited transparency regarding the value of the assets of a company. Company reports are issued only every three or six months, meaning that it is difficult to obtain an up-to-date snapshot of the capital structure of a firm away from these dates.
- The credit spread for firms for which $A(t) > F$ always tends to zero as $T - t \to 0$. This is not consistent with the credit markets in which even corporates with very high credit ratings have a finite spread at very short maturities.

Structural models perform best as a tool for augmenting the traditional balance sheet analysis methods of credit analysts. Since their default mechanism closely resembles what happens in practice, they can be used to shed light on forward-looking credit risk. A number of proprietary models, most notably that of Moody's KMV,[1] are designed for this exact purpose.

However, for the reasons listed above, structural models are not widely used in credit derivatives pricing. Despite this, the Merton model has been the inspiration behind one of the main correlation pricing models, which will be discussed in Chapter 13.

3.5   REDUCED FORM MODELS

To price single-name credit derivatives we need to establish a risk-neutral modelling approach. Specifically, we would like a model which satisfies the following requirements:

1. The model captures the risk of default as a single event which can occur at some unknown future time.
2. The model captures the risk of an uncertain recovery payment assumed to occur at the default time.
3. The model captures spread risk – the risk that market credit spreads change even though default does not occur.
4. The model is flexible enough to fit exactly the term structure of prices of bonds, CDS and other credit instruments in the market.
5. The model can be extended in a straightforward manner to price a broad range of products – fixed and floating rate bonds, CDS, options and later, multi-name products.
6. The model should be fast to calibrate to market prices, and fast to price.
7. The model should enable us to consider the effect of joint risks such as co-movements in credit risk and interest rate risk.

Such a modelling approach will enable us to price and risk manage products with default, spread, recovery rate and interest rate risks, all within a coherent and consistent framework. Note that we have not included downgrade risk in our model requirements. This is because the credit derivatives market does not use a rating change as a contingent event. Also, any change in the rating of a credit should be priced into the credit spread, either before or after the downgrade event.

In its purest sense, a default model can be seen as a way to model the default time τ for a credit. Clearly, we assume that default is a one-time event – once a credit has defaulted,

---

[1] See www.moodyskmv.com

it can never default again. Also, we assume that if we extend our time horizon to infinity, all credits will eventually default. So every credit has a default time $0 < \tau < \infty$. If our trade has a maturity T, we really only care about the case when $\tau \leq T$. Without actually specifying how we plan to model τ, we can already use this idea to consider how to price a number of simple credit risky structures which will become the building blocks for much of the derivatives pricing that we will encounter in the rest of this book.

3.5.1 Zero Recovery Risky Zero Coupon Bond

Consider a credit risky zero coupon bond with a face value of $1 which is due to mature at time T. Assume also that we know that if there is a default, the recovered amount will be zero. The two possible payments are shown in Figure 3.5. As a result, we can write the present value of this risky zero coupon bond as the discounted expectation of the payoff at time T in the risk-neutral measure. This is given by

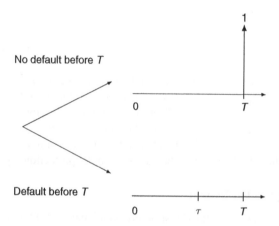

Figure 3.5   A risky zero coupon bond which pays $1 at maturity if there is no default, otherwise zero

$$\hat{Z}(0, T) = \mathbb{E}\left[\exp\left(-\int_0^T r(s)ds \right) \mathbf{1}_{\tau > T} \right]$$

where $r(t)$ is the continuously compounded risk-free short rate, and we use the indicator function to capture the risk of default

$$\mathbf{1}_{\tau > T} = \begin{cases} 1 & \text{if} \quad \tau > T \quad \text{and the bond survives} \\ 0 & \text{if} \quad \tau \leq T \quad \text{and the bond defaults} \end{cases}$$

and the expectation is taken in the risk-neutral measure.

To price this risky zero coupon bond, we do not need to know τ, just the probability that $\tau \leq T$. This is because any cash flows occur at a known time T. This pricing formula is generic – it does not assume any model for τ. We also allow for the possibility that there may be some co-dependence between the risk-free interest rate process and the default time.

3.5.2   Fixed Payment at Default

Consider next a simple credit risky structure which pays $1 *at the time of default τ if $\tau \leq T$*, otherwise nothing. This is shown in Figure 3.6. The price is given by discounting back the payment from the default time as follows

$$D(0, T) = \mathbb{E}\left[\exp\left(-\int_0^\tau r(s)ds\right) \mathbf{1}_{\tau \leq T}\right].$$

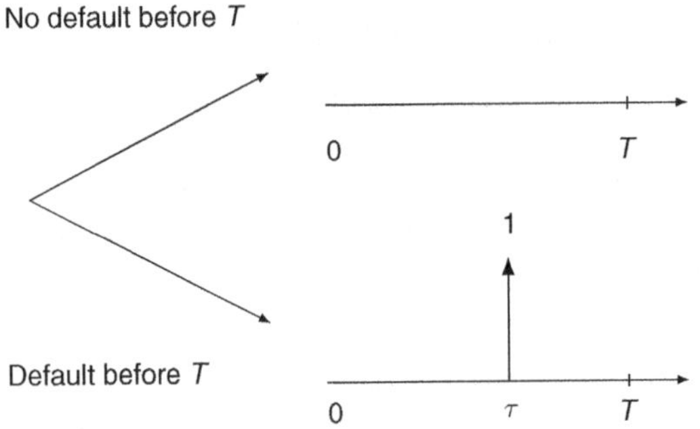

No default before T

Default before T

Figure 3.6   An instrument which pays $1 at the time of default if default occurs before time T

This instrument presents a greater modelling challenge than the risky zero coupon bond since the time of the cash flow is unknown. This would not be a problem if interest rates were zero – we would then only need to know if $\tau \leq T$. However, for non-zero interest rates, we need not just the cumulative distribution $\Pr(\tau \leq T)$, but the full probability density of the default time distribution, i.e. $\Pr(t < \tau \leq t + dt)$. Payments like this occur commonly in bonds as recovery payments and in credit default swaps as the payment on the protection leg.

3.5.3   Random Payment at Default

Finally, we consider a simple credit risky structure which pays a random quantity $\Phi(\tau)$ *at the time of default τ if $\tau \leq T$*, otherwise nothing. The price is given by

$$\hat{D}(0, T) = \mathbb{E}\left[\exp\left(-\int_0^\tau r(s)ds\right) \Phi(\tau)\mathbf{1}_{\tau \leq T}\right].$$

The key question here is whether the size of the payment $\Phi(\tau)$ has any dependency on the default time τ or if it has any link to the interest rate process. Once again, we need to know not just the cumulative distribution $\Pr(\tau \leq T)$ but the full probability density of the default time distribution, i.e. $\Pr(t < \tau \leq t + dt)$. This sort of term can be used to price a random recovery rate, or a contract which makes some payment at default whose value is linked to the default time or the level of interest rates.

3.6   THE HAZARD RATE MODEL

To proceed beyond these generic pricing formulae, we need to specify a model for the default times of the portfolio. The model which most closely satisfies all of the requirements listed above follows the framework initially established in Jarrow and Turnbull (1995) and later in

Lando (1998). This approach is based on the idea of modelling default as the first arrival time τ of a Poisson process. The *intensity* or *hazard rate* for this process is given by $\lambda(t)$. Mathematically, we can define $\lambda(t)$ as follows

$$\lim_{dt \to 0} \frac{1}{dt} \Pr[\tau \le t + dt | \tau > t] = \lambda(t). \tag{3.5}$$

The hazard rate multiplied by dt is the probability of a credit defaulting in the time period from t to $t + dt$ *conditional* on it having survived to time t. An important property of the hazard rate approach is that default is always a surprise – since we are modelling default by modelling the *probability of a default* we do not know whether default will occur in the next period of length dt. We only know that it will default with probability $\lambda(t)dt$.

To see this more clearly, we can build a simple Monte Carlo simulation of default according to this model using Bernoulli trials.[2] The following algorithm shows how we would simulate one path of the default process to determine the time of a default, conditional on it being before time T. The steps are:

1. Set $t = dt$.
2. At time t, draw an independent uniform random number u.
3. Perform a Bernoulli trial and check if $u \le \lambda(t)dt$. If this is the case, default has occurred in the period $[t - dt, t]$ and we terminate this algorithm at the default time $\tau = t$. If $u > \lambda(t)dt$ then we continue to step (4).
4. Set $t = t + dt$.
5. If $t > T$ terminate, else go back to (2).

It is clear from this algorithm[3] that at time t we cannot know until we do the test in step (3) whether a default will occur. Also, although the probability of defaulting in time dt tends to zero as $dt \to 0$, the probability of defaulting per unit of time does not.

It is worth contrasting this with the Merton model default mechanism. If at time $T - dt$, just before maturity of the debt T, we observe that $A(t) < F$ then we know that the probability of defaulting per unit time before T tends to 100% as $dt \to 0$. Likewise, if $A(t) > F$, we know that the probability of defaulting per unit time before T tends to zero. To use the jargon of stochastic calculus, the default time is *predictable*, i.e. in the limit of $dt \to 0$, we can know with certainty whether or not the credit will default in the next interval of time dt. Within a hazard rate approach the default time is not predictable.

Is this a problem? In general the answer to this question is 'no'. Indeed, the fact that default is a surprise helps us to fit the short end of the credit curve – we usually find that the probability of default per unit time of a very short dated credit instrument does not go to zero as the maturity goes to zero. The market does price in some *jump to default* premium which the hazard rate can more easily capture than a Merton-style model. The observation of a non-zero spread at short maturities can be explained by viewing it as a measure of market uncertainty about the state of credit health of the corporate which means that the probability of a sudden default is not zero.

---

[2] A Bernoulli trial is an experiment with two possible outcomes which occur with probabilities p and $1 - p$. This can be simulated by drawing a random uniform u, using the fact that $\Pr(u \le p) = p$. If $u \le p$, then outcome 1 occurs, otherwise outcome 2 occurs.
[3] An algorithm like this is easy to implement provided we have a uniform random number generator. The Excel rand() function will return a random uniform draw.

3.6.1   Calculating the Survival Probability

From the definition of the hazard rate in Equation 3.5, assuming the hazard rate is deterministic, we can calculate the probability of surviving from time $t = 0$ to a time T. We do this by dividing the entire period into N intervals of length $dt = T/N$. In each interval we calculate the probability of surviving. The probability of surviving to time T is then given by

$$\Pr(\tau > T) = (1 - \lambda(dt)dt)\,(1 - \lambda(2dt)dt)\ldots(1 - \lambda(T)dt).$$

In the continuous time limit, we let $dt \to 0$, and this becomes

$$\Pr(\tau > T) = \exp\left(-\int_0^T \lambda(t)dt\right).$$

We can also write the probability density of default times which can be obtained by differentiating the cumulative distribution function

$$\Pr(T < \tau \le T + dT) = -\frac{\partial \Pr(\tau > T)}{\partial T}dT.$$

Substituting from above gives

$$\Pr(T < \tau \le T + dT) = \lambda(T)\exp\left(-\int_0^T \lambda(t)dt\right)dT. \tag{3.6}$$

The density of default times is very useful when we want to price securities which have a payment at the default time.

3.7   MODELLING DEFAULT AS A COX PROCESS

In the previous section, we assumed that $\lambda(t)$ is deterministic. While this is sufficient to allow us to model a random default time, it does not enable us to model the fact that $\lambda(t)$ changes over time as the arrival of new information in the market changes expectations about the default risk of the credit. This manifests itself in the form of changing credit spreads. As a result, there is an incentive to generalise the model to allow for stochastic hazard rates. This means that the model will incorporate two sources of randomness – one from the Poisson jump process and one from the random evolution of $\lambda(t)$. We say that the model is *doubly stochastic*.

We now show how to update the pricing formulae in this doubly stochastic framework. If $\lambda(t)$ is stochastic, the Poisson default process is then known as a *Cox process*, first introduced into credit modelling by Lando (1998). If we assume that $\lambda(t)$ is stochastic, then we also need to consider its correlation with the Libor short rate process $r(t)$.

3.7.1   Zero Recovery Risky Zero Coupon Bond

We want to compute the price of an instrument which pays \$1 at time T as long as the credit has not defaulted, i.e. as long as $\tau > T$. It pays nothing otherwise. Once again, we write the price as

$$\hat{Z}(0, T) = \mathbb{E}\left[\exp\left(-\int_0^T r(t)dt\right)\mathbf{1}_{\tau > T}\right]. \tag{3.7}$$

To price this risky payoff, consider the following Monte Carlo algorithm. We model both the evolution of $\lambda(t)$ and the short risk-free interest rate $r(t)$ using stochastic processes which may be correlated. We simulate over $m = 1, \ldots, M$ paths. The steps in the simulation are as follows:

1. Set the simulation path index $m = 1$.
2. Set $t = dt$.
3. Compute $\lambda_m(t)$ and $r_m(t)$ according to their respective stochastic processes.
4. Draw an independent random uniform u.
5. If $u \leq \lambda_m(t)dt$ then default has occurred and $\tau = t$. Set $\hat{Z}_m = 0$ and go to step (8).
6. Set $t = t + dt$. If $t < T$ go to step (3).
7. The credit has survived to maturity time T. Set $\hat{Z}_m = \exp\left(-\int_0^T r_m(t)dt\right)$.
8. Set $m = m + 1$. If $m \leq M$ return to step (2).
9. Calculate $\hat{Z} = \frac{1}{M} \sum_{m=1}^{M} \hat{Z}_m$.

This algorithm makes it very clear how we need to handle the three sources of randomness due to the stochastic hazard rate, the stochastic interest rate, and the Bernoulli trial. Note that because of all the sources of randomness, this algorithm is slow to converge in terms of statistical accuracy. Part of the problem is that for typical investment grade credits the hazard rate is small, of the order of 1–2% and most bonds have a maturity of around 5 years. As a result, defaults occur in only a few per cent of the M simulation paths. A lot of paths are therefore required to make the standard error of the estimate converge to an acceptable accuracy.

Fortunately, it is possible to analytically average out one source of randomness from Equation 3.7. Using the law of iterated expectations we have

$$\hat{Z}(0, T) = \mathbb{E}\left[\exp\left(-\int_0^T r(t)dt\right) \mathbf{1}_{\tau > T}\right]$$

$$= \mathbb{E}\left[\mathbb{E}\left[\exp\left(-\int_0^T r(t)dt\right) \mathbf{1}_{\tau > T} | \{\lambda(t)\}_{t \in [0,T]}\right]\right]$$

where the inner expectation conditions on the realised path of hazard rates from time 0 to time T. From before, we know that

$$\mathbb{E}\left[\mathbf{1}_{\tau > T} | \{\lambda(t)\}_{t \in [0,T]}\right] = \exp\left(-\int_0^T \lambda(t)dt\right).$$

Substituting back, the price of the risky \$1 paid at time T becomes

$$\hat{Z}(0, T) = \mathbb{E}\left[\exp\left(-\int_0^T (r(t) + \lambda(t))\, dt\right)\right].$$

Let us now revisit the previous simulation using this new result. A more efficient procedure would now be:

1. Set the simulation path index $m = 1$.
2. Set $t = dt$.
3. Compute $\lambda_m(t)$ and $r_m(t)$ according to their respective stochastic processes.

4. Set $t = t + dt$. If $t < T$ return to (3).
5. Calculate the discount factor using $Z_m = \exp(-\int_0^T r_m(t)dt)$.
6. Calculate the survival probability using $Q_m = \exp(-\int_0^T \lambda_m(t)dt)$.
7. Set $m = m + 1$. If $m \leq M$ then return to step (3).
8. Calculate $\hat{Z} = \frac{1}{M}\sum_{m=1}^{M} Q_m Z_m$.

This process avoids the need to generate uniform random deviates and to perform the Bernoulli tests. It does require that all paths run to time T rather than terminate at $\min[\tau, T]$. This has only a small computational cost since for typical hazard rates of say 1%, a five-year horizon would mean that roughly 95% of paths would survive to time T. The great advantage of this approach is that we have already averaged out the randomness from the Bernoulli tests, and so the standard error of the price is significantly lowered for only a small increase in computational cost.

3.7.2   Fixed Payment at Default

Consider again the credit instrument which pays $1 at the time of default τ if $\tau \leq T$. This is shown in Figure 3.6. The price is given by

$$D(0,T) = \mathbb{E}\left[\exp\left(-\int_0^\tau r(t)dt\right) \mathbf{1}_{\tau \leq T}\right].$$

This is a more challenging pricing problem since it requires knowledge of the probability density of τ given in Equation 3.6. As a result, the price of $1 paid at the time of default, provided $\tau \leq T$, requires us to integrate over the density of default times out to T as follows

$$D(0,T) = \mathbb{E}\left[\int_0^T \lambda(t)\exp\left(-\int_0^t (r(s) + \lambda(s))ds\right) dt\right].$$

Although this is not difficult to calculate, numerically, it is more expensive to calculate than the price of a fixed payment made conditional on surviving since we have two integrals to perform inside the expectation.

3.7.3   Uncertain quantity at default

Finally, consider the credit instrument which pays an uncertain quantity $\Phi(\tau)$ at the time of default τ if $\tau \leq T$. The price is given by

$$\hat{D}(0,T) = \mathbb{E}\left[\exp\left(-\int_0^\tau r(t)dt\right) \Phi(\tau)\mathbf{1}_{\tau \leq T}\right].$$

If $\Phi(\tau)$ is random, but is independent of the short rate and the hazard rate processes then

$$\hat{D}(0,T) = \mathbb{E}\left[\Phi\right] \mathbb{E}\left[\int_0^T \lambda(t)\exp\left(-\int_0^t (r(s) + \lambda(s))ds\right) dt\right] = \mathbb{E}\left[\Phi\right]D(0,T).$$

This case is relevant as it shows that if we assume independence, we can value a random independent payment at default using just its expectation.

3.8 A GAUSSIAN SHORT RATE AND HAZARD RATE MODEL

The focus of our discussion so far has been to establish a modelling framework for credit risky securities. We have not specified any dynamic process for the interest rate or the hazard rate. In this section, we choose perhaps the simplest non-trivial model dynamics which has the advantage of being analytically tractable. We model the dynamics of the short interest rate process r according to a Gaussian process of the form

$$dr = \theta(t)dt + \sigma_r dw_r,$$

where $\theta(t)$ is a time-dependent drift and σ_r is the volatility. We use a similar process to model the hazard rate process given by

$$d\lambda = \mu(t)dt + \sigma_\lambda dw_\lambda.$$

Once again, $\mu(t)$ is a time-dependent drift and σ_λ is the process volatility. Both processes are specified in the risk-neutral measure and are correlated via

$$\mathbb{E}\left[dw_\lambda dw_r\right] = \rho dt.$$

The advantage of having a time-dependent drift for the interest rate is that we can use it to fit the current term structure of Libor discount factors. Likewise, the hazard rate drift can be used to fit the current term structure of credit bond prices or CDS contracts.

The attraction of using a Gaussian model to represent the dynamics of the risk-free short rate and the hazard rate is that we can compute a closed-form expression for the risk-free zero coupon bond price as a function of the spread–interest rate correlation. The disadvantage of Gaussian processes is that we allow negative interest rates and negative hazard rates. Despite this caveat, we hope that by fitting the processes to market prices through their drifts, and provided the volatilities are not too high, the probability of negative rates will be low.

We can integrate the short rate and the hazard rate directly to give

$$r(T) = r(0) + \int_0^T \theta(t)dt + \sigma_r W_r(T) \tag{3.8}$$

where $W(T) = \int_0^T dW(s)$ and

$$\lambda(T) = \lambda(0) + \int_0^T \mu(t)dt + \sigma_\lambda W_\lambda(T). \tag{3.9}$$

We now show how to calculate the price of a zero recovery risky zero coupon bond given these dynamics.

3.8.1 Zero Recovery Risky Zero Coupon Bond

We now wish to calculate the price of a risky zero coupon bond which pays zero recovery on default. We therefore need to calculate

$$\hat{Z}(0, T) = \mathbb{E}\left[\exp\left(-\int_0^T (r(s) + \lambda(s))\, ds\right)\right].$$

Setting

$$y(T) = \int_0^T (r(s) + \lambda(s))ds$$

we can then write this as

$$\hat{Z}(0,T) = \mathbb{E}\left[\exp(-y(T))\right].$$

As the term $y(T)$ is a sum of Gaussian random variables, it is also a Gaussian random variable. In order to perform the expectation we will need to calculate the mean and variance of $y(T)$. Using the integrated processes in Equations 3.8 and 3.9 we have

$$y(T) = \int_0^T \left[r(0) + \int_0^t \theta(s)ds + \lambda(0) + \int_0^t \mu(s)ds \right] dt + \int_0^T [\sigma_r W_r(t) + \sigma_\lambda W_\lambda(t)]\, dt.$$

Changing the order of integrations in the drift term,[4] this can be simplified to

$$y(T) = (r(0) + \lambda(0))T + \int_0^T (T-t)\,(\theta(t) + \mu(t))\, dt + \int_0^T [\sigma_r W_r(t) + \sigma_\lambda W_\lambda(t)]\, dt.$$

Taking the expectation of $y(T)$ gives

$$\mathcal{M} = \mathbb{E}\,[y(T)] = (r(0) + \lambda(0))T + \int_0^T (T-t)(\theta(t) + \mu(t))dt.$$

The variance of $y(T)$ is given by

$$\mathcal{V} = \mathbb{E}\,[y(T)^2] - \mathbb{E}\,[y(T)]^2 = \mathbb{E}\left[\left(\int_0^T [\sigma_r W_r(t) + \sigma_\lambda W_\lambda(t)]\, dt\right)^2\right].$$

Expanding and using the Ito isometry property that

$$\mathbb{E}\left[W(t)W(t')\right] = \min(t,t')$$

we have

$$\mathcal{V} = \left(\sigma_r^2 + 2\sigma_r\sigma_\lambda\rho + \sigma_\lambda^2\right) \int_{t=0}^T \int_{t'=0}^T \min(t,t')dt'dt.$$

To handle the $\min(t,t')$, we simply partition the integral over t' into $t' < t$ and $t' > t$. This gives

$$\mathcal{V} = \left(\sigma_r^2 + 2\sigma_r\sigma_\lambda\rho + \sigma_\lambda^2\right) \frac{T^3}{3}.$$

Using the result derived in Section 3.13.1, we can then write the risky zero coupon bond price as

$$\hat{Z}(0,T) = \exp\left(-(r(0) + \lambda(0))T - \int_0^T (T-t)\,(\theta(t) + \mu(t))\, dt + \left(\sigma_r^2 + 2\sigma_r\sigma_\lambda\rho + \sigma_\lambda^2\right) \frac{T^3}{6}\right).$$

---

[4] We use the fact that

$$\int_0^T dt \int_0^t f(s)ds = \int_0^T ds f(s) \int_s^T dt = \int_0^T f(s)(T-s)\, ds.$$

This can be written as $\hat{Z}(0,T) = Z(0,T)Q(0,T)\Theta(0,T,\rho)$ so that the effect of a non-zero correlation on the risky zero coupon bond price is a multiplicative correction of the form

$$\Theta(0,T,\rho) = \exp\left(\frac{\rho\sigma_r\sigma_\lambda T^3}{3}\right).$$

This model implies that the price of a risky zero bond increases with correlation. This is because scenarios in which both the hazard rate is low and the interest rate is low are more likely, as are scenarios in which the hazard rate is high and the short rate is high. The first scenario means that the bond is more likely to survive in situations when the present value is higher. The second scenario means that the bond is more likely to default with zero recovery when the present value is lower. The combined effect is to make the expected present value of the bond increase.

Example It is worth considering a real example in order to assess the magnitude of the correlation multiplier on the pricing of a zero coupon bond. For the basis point volatilities, we set $\sigma_\lambda = 125$ bp and $\sigma_r = 100$ bp. Table 3.3 shows the correlation multiplier term $\Theta(t,T,\rho)$ which must be applied to the zero correlation price to get the correlation adjusted price. This table shows that the sensitivity of a risky zero coupon bond to the correlation between interest rates and hazard rates is small. For example, for $T = 5$ and a correlation of $\rho = 20\%$, the correction multiplier Θ is 1.001, meaning a correction of 0.1%.

Table 3.3 Correlation multiplier Θ for different values of T and correlation ρ

T (years)	Correlation multiplier $\Theta(0,T,\rho)$				
	$\rho = -20\%$	$\rho = -10\%$	$\rho = 0\%$	$\rho = 10\%$	$\rho = 20\%$
1	0.99999	0.99999	1.00000	1.00000	1.00000
3	0.99977	0.99988	1.00000	1.00011	1.00022
5	0.99896	0.99948	1.00000	1.00052	1.00104
7	0.99714	0.99857	1.00000	1.00143	1.00286
10	0.99170	0.99584	1.00000	1.00417	1.00836

The small size of the correction does not mean that we should always ignore the effect of correlation. However, it shows that it is not significant and is one reason why most credit derivatives pricing models choose not to incorporate correlated stochastic hazard and interest rates.

3.9 INDEPENDENCE AND DETERMINISTIC HAZARD RATES

So far, we have considered the general case of stochastic correlated hazard and interest rates. However, in practice, we tend to make simplifying assumptions for the sake of analytical tractability. There are two types of assumptions which are typically made:

1. Assume that the hazard rate and risk-free short rate processes are independent.
2. Assume that the hazard rate process is deterministic.

We now consider the implications of these two assumptions.

3.9.1   Independence

Assuming independence is a less restrictive assumption than assuming that the hazard rate process is deterministic since it enables us to include stochastic hazard rate effects in the model. In the case of pricing a risky zero coupon bond, what it allows us to do is to separate the expectation of a product into a product of expectations

$$\hat{Z}(0,T) = \mathbb{E}\left[\exp\left(-\int_0^T (r(t) + \lambda(t))\, dt\right)\right]$$

$$= \mathbb{E}\left[\exp\left(-\int_0^T r(t))dt\right)\right] \mathbb{E}\left[\exp\left(-\int_0^T \lambda(s)ds\right)\right].$$

As a result we can write the price of the zero recovery zero coupon bond as the product of the risk-free zero coupon bond price and the survival probability

$$\hat{Z}(0,T) = Q(0,T)Z(0,T),$$

where

$$Z(0,T) = \mathbb{E}\left[\exp\left(-\int_0^T r(t)dt\right)\right]$$

and

$$Q(0,T) = \mathbb{E}\left[\exp\left(-\int_0^T \lambda(t)dt\right)\right].$$

Clearly, independence implies zero correlation. With the assumption of independence, we can also simplify the price of $1 paid at the time of default. This is given by

$$D(0,T) = \mathbb{E}\left[\int_0^T \lambda(t)\exp\left(-\int_0^t (r(s) + \lambda(s))ds\right)dt\right]$$

$$= \int_0^T \mathbb{E}\left[\exp\left(-\int_0^t r(s)ds\right)\right] \mathbb{E}\left[\lambda(t)\exp\left(-\int_0^t \lambda(s)ds\right)\right]dt.$$

which can be written as

$$D(0,T) = -\int_0^T Z(0,s)dQ(0,s).$$

What makes the assumption independence attractive is that we can price both of the types of payment discussed if we have knowledge of the term structures of $Z(0,T)$ and $Q(0,T)$.

3.9.2   Deterministic Hazard Rates

When the hazard rate is deterministic many of the pricing formulae simplify. This assumption is only usually appropriate for products which have a very low dependency on the volatility of hazard rates and when the credit spread curve is relatively flat. The price of the credit risky zero recovery zero coupon bond is given by

$$\hat{Z}(0, T) = Z(0, T) \exp\left(-\int_0^T \lambda(s)ds\right).$$

The price of $1 paid at the time of default becomes

$$D(0, T) = \int_0^T Z(0, t)\lambda(t) \exp\left(-\int_0^t \lambda(s)ds\right) dt.$$

3.9.3 Constant Hazard Rates

We can further simplify if we assume constant hazard rates, i.e. $\lambda(t) = \lambda$. The price of the credit risky zero recovery zero coupon bond is given by

$$\hat{Z}(0, T) = Z(0, T) \exp(-\lambda T).$$

The price of $1 paid at the time of default becomes

$$D(0, T) = \lambda \int_0^T Z(0, t) \exp(-\lambda t) dt.$$

Since the default time density is given by

$$\Pr(t < \tau \le t + dt) = \lambda \exp(-\lambda t) dt$$

we can then calculate the expected default time using integration by parts

$$\mathbb{E}[\tau] = \lambda \int_0^\infty s \exp(-\lambda s) ds = \left[se^{-\lambda s}\right]_0^\infty + \int_0^\infty e^{-\lambda s} ds = \frac{1}{\lambda}.$$

We can also calculate the variance of the default time. This is given by

$$\mathbb{E}[\tau^2] - \mathbb{E}[\tau]^2 = \int_0^\infty s^2 \lambda \exp(-\lambda s) ds - \frac{1}{\lambda^2} = \left(\frac{2}{\lambda^2} - \frac{1}{\lambda^2}\right) = \frac{1}{\lambda^2}.$$

Example A credit with a hazard rate of 1% therefore has a default time distribution with a mean of 100 years and a variance equal to 10 000 years.

This example makes it clear that any simulation of default times for a credit with a very small λ requires a large number of paths to ensure an acceptably low standard error.

In practice, this assumption only works if the spread curves are flat. However, even when they are not flat, an assumption of a constant hazard rate can serve as a good approximation. At the very least, assuming a constant hazard rate allows us to simplify the pricing equations and so helps us to better understand the dependence on the model parameters.

If we also assume a constant risk-free short rate, i.e. $r(t) = r$, the price of a risky zero recovery zero coupon bond is given by

$$\hat{Z}(0, T) = \exp(-(r + \lambda)T).$$

We can also calculate the price of $1 paid at the time of default.

$$D(0, T) = \int_0^T \lambda \exp(-(r + \lambda)t)\, dt = \frac{\lambda}{r + \lambda}(1 - \exp(-(r + \lambda)T)).$$

These are useful results which are often used to help us build intuition when used in the pricing of different securities.

3.10   THE CREDIT TRIANGLE

Let us use what we have derived so far to calculate a very useful result. Let us suppose that we have a contract linked to an issuer with a deterministic hazard rate $\lambda(t)$. The contract pays $(1 - R)$ at the time of default if default occurs before contract maturity time T. Let us also suppose that in order to pay for this 'protection', a premium or spread S is paid continuously until maturity or default, whichever occurs first. The value of the spread is set so that the net present value of the contract equals zero at inception.

Let us consider the value of the 'premium leg' of this contract. Between time t and time $t + dt$ we have a payment of $S.dt$ provided the credit has not defaulted. Discounting this payment and integrating over the lifetime of the contract gives

$$\text{Premium leg PV}(0, T) = S \int_0^T Z(0, t)Q(0, t)dt.$$

Now let us consider the payment on the protection leg. The value of this is given by

$$\text{Protection leg PV}(0, T) = (1 - R) \int_0^T Z(0, t)(-dQ(0, t)).$$

Since $dQ(0, t) = -\lambda(t)Q(0, t)dt$, this can be written as

$$\text{Protection leg PV}(0, T) = (1 - R) \int_0^T Z(0, t)\lambda(t)Q(0, t)dt.$$

If we then make the final assumption that the hazard rate is constant, we have

$$\text{Protection leg PV}(0, T) = \lambda(1 - R) \int_0^T Z(0, t)Q(0, t)dt.$$

The value of the spread S which makes the protection and premium leg values equal is given by

$$S = \lambda(1 - R).$$

We call this relationship the *credit triangle* because it is a function of three variables and knowledge of any two is sufficient to calculate the third. What it states is that the required continuously paid spread compensation for taking on a credit loss of $(1 - R)$ equals the hazard rate times $(1 - R)$.

The contract we have described here is a very close approximation to the credit default swap which will be discussed later in this book, and this credit triangle is a very useful equation which is commonly used as a quick way to relate spreads, risk-neutral default probabilities and recovery rates.

3.11   THE CREDIT RISK PREMIUM

If we compare the risk-neutral default probability implied by credit spreads against the default probabilities implied by historical data, we find that the risk-neutral probability is almost always much larger. Finance theory explains this phenomenon through the concept of risk premia. To make this clear, we break the market spread of a credit into the following components:

- Actuarial spread: This is what an investor in a credit security has to be paid to compensate them for the expected loss of the security as implied by historical default probabilities and historical recovery rates.
- Default risk premium: This is the additional spread paid to compensate the investor for the risk that the historical default rate and recovery rate statistics do not reliably predict the default risk of the credit to which the investor is exposed. The uncertainty in the prediction, and the fear that the true default risk is higher than that implied by the actuarial spread, commands a premium.
- Volatility risk premium: This is the additional spread paid to compensate the investor for the risk that the credit quality of the issuer changes, as evidenced by a change in the market spread of the issuer. This may cause the value of the position to fall, even if there is no default. If the investor then wishes to sell the credit position, this will result in a realised loss.
- Liquidity risk premium: This premium compensates the investor for the risk that a reduction of the liquidity of the instrument prevents the investor from being able to sell the bond when they wish due to a lack of demand for the credit.

The difference between the market spread and the actuarial spread of an issuer is known as the *risk premium* and is shown in Figure 3.7.

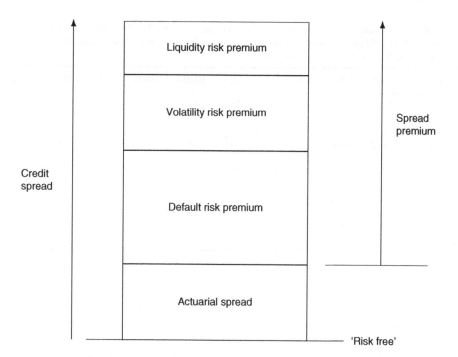

Figure 3.7   Decomposition of the credit spread into the actuarial spread, the default risk premium, the volatility risk premium and the liquidity risk premium

If the credit spread is quoted versus Libor, then the credit risk of the bond is being measured relative to the credit risk of AA-rated commercial banks which Libor represents. If the credit spread is quoted versus Treasury bonds, then it will be larger since the default risk of Treasury bonds is typically lower than that of the AA-rated commercial banking sector. While we should strictly choose the government curve as the 'risk-free' curve, it is not clear that the swap spread – the difference between the yield on AA-rated commercial bank bonds and government bonds – is driven by just credit considerations. Other technical effects, especially the demand and supply for government debt, can play a role in driving the value of the swap spread. By referencing against Libor, we remove such effects.

It is difficult to decompose spreads into these different components. However, it is possible to estimate the actuarial spread, and from this the spread premium which we define as

$$\text{Spread premium} = \text{Credit spread} - \text{Actuarial spread}$$

where we choose to use the credit spread relative to the Libor curve. It is also possible to calculate the coverage ratio. This is the number of times a spread 'covers' the actuarial default risk of a credit

$$\text{Coverage ratio} = \frac{\text{Credit spread}}{\text{Actuarial spread}}.$$

In O'Kane and Schloegl (2002b), we calculated these numbers using the credit default swap spread levels in the market in January 2002. We did this by taking a large pool of credits for which we had liquid CDS quotes. We grouped the pool by rating and then calculated the average spread by rating category. We also used Moody's historical default and recovery rates to determine the actuarial spreads. The results are shown in Table 3.4.

Table 3.4 Calculation of coverage ratio and risk premium by rating. For the spreads, we took a typical universe of CDS credits and grouped them by rating. In each group, we calculated the average spread. See O'Kane and Schloegl (2002b) for details

Rating	AA	AA−	A+	A	A−	BBB+	BBB	BBB−	BB+	BB
5Y avg. spread (bp)	28	37	47	61	75	116	164	265	349	463
Probability (%)	0.76	0.88	0.98	1.11	1.33	1.84	2.50	4.39	7.87	11.25
Expected loss (%)	0.45	0.53	0.59	0.67	0.80	1.10	1.50	2.63	4.72	6.75
Actuarial spread (bp)	9	11	12	13	16	22	30	53	98	145
Coverage ratio	3.12	3.52	4.05	4.67	4.77	5.33	5.54	5.02	3.56	3.19
Spread premium	19	26	36	48	59	94	134	212	251	318

1. We see that the spread premium increases as we descend the rating spectrum. This makes sense since we would probably expect the volatility risk premium, the default risk premium and liquidity risk premium to increase as we move out of investment grade and into the high yield CDS universe.
2. We see that the coverage ratio tends to remain fairly constant as a function of rating.

Note that if we measured the credit spread relative to Treasury bonds, the numbers presented would change; however, both of the effects described would still be present. Finally, we note that in Section 12.3, we will discuss how certain products can be structured to increase the coverage ratio or spread premium and so change the credit risk profile faced by an investor.

3.12 SUMMARY

This chapter has covered the theoretical basics for many of the credit pricing models which will be used throughout the rest of this book. We have discussed both the structural and reduced form modelling paradigms and explained why the reduced form approach is the one used for credit derivatives pricing. We have also presented a broad range of empirical default data including default rates and recovery rates. We have demonstrated how to price a number of simple credit risky instruments which will be used later as the building blocks for our pricing of credit derivatives payoffs. Finally, we have described the concept of the spread premium, which motivates many of the credit derivatives products discussed later.

3.13 TECHNICAL APPENDIX

3.13.1 Computing the Expectation of exp(−y)

In this section, we show how the method of 'completing the squares' can be used to take an expectation of exp(−y) where y is a Gaussian distributed random variable with mean $\mathcal{M}$ and variance $\mathcal{V}$.

$$\mathbb{E}\left[e^{-y}\right] = \frac{1}{\sqrt{2\pi\mathcal{V}}} \int_{-\infty}^{\infty} e^{-(y-\mathcal{M})^2/2\mathcal{V}} \cdot e^{-y} dy.$$

Changing variables to $x = (y - \mathcal{M})/\sqrt{\mathcal{V}}$ so that $y = x\sqrt{\mathcal{V}} + \mathcal{M}$ gives us

$$\mathbb{E}\left[e^{-y}\right] = e^{-\mathcal{M}} \frac{1}{\sqrt{2\pi}} \int_{-\infty}^{\infty} e^{-x^2/2 - x\sqrt{\mathcal{V}}} dx.$$

Completing the square, i.e. $(x^2/2 + x\sqrt{\mathcal{V}}) = (x + \sqrt{\mathcal{V}})^2/2 - \mathcal{V}/2$, we then have

$$\mathbb{E}\left[e^{-y}\right] = e^{-\mathcal{M}+\mathcal{V}/2} \frac{1}{\sqrt{2\pi}} \int_{-\infty}^{\infty} e^{-(x+\sqrt{\mathcal{V}})^2/2} dx.$$

Finally, changing variables to $z = (x + \sqrt{\mathcal{V}})$ and integrating gives

$$\mathbb{E}\left[e^{-y}\right] = e^{-\mathcal{M}+\mathcal{V}/2}.$$

4

Bonds and Asset Swaps

4.1 INTRODUCTION

Although bonds are not credit derivatives, credit derivatives and bonds are fundamentally related since they both embed the same risks. For example, the pricing of credit default swaps and cash bonds are linked by no-arbitrage relationships as we will discuss in Chapter 5. For this reason, we begin this chapter with an introduction to the mechanics, pricing and risk of bonds. We begin with fixed rate bonds and then cover floating rate bonds. We then discuss the asset swap. The asset swap is a way to repackage a fixed rate bond which removes most of its interest rate risk, making it an almost pure credit play. We conclude the chapter with a discussion of the pricing and risk of the asset swap.

We can generally divide credit risky bonds into two categories – corporate bonds and sovereign bonds. Corporate bonds are those bonds which are issued by corporations and typically are issued with a maturity greater than one year. According to the Bond Market Association, the size of the US corporate debt market in 2007 was $5.7 trillion.[1] Sovereign bonds are those issued by national governments and may be denominated in a currency other than that of the issuing country.

Each bond is governed by a contract known as an indenture, whose provisions are verified over the bond's life by a trustee who acts on behalf of the bond holders. This indenture will state the explicit seniority of the debt within the capital structure of the firm.

Since bonds are traded in the capital markets and can be purchased by private individuals, regulators usually expect a large degree of transparency regarding the financial status of the borrower/issuer. In addition, it is customary for a bond to be rated by two or more credit rating agencies. These rating agencies which include Moody's Investor Services, Standard and Poor's and Fitch IBCA, assign a credit rating to the bond based on its assessed credit risk.

The rating categorisations are shown in Table 4.1 for the three main credit rating agencies. There is an important rating boundary between *investment grade* and *sub-investment grade* due to the stipulation that many investment funds are only allowed to hold bonds designated investment grade. If a bond is downgraded to a sub-investment grade category, these funds will be required to sell it.

Bonds which are issued with ratings below investment grade are known as *high yield*, reflecting the high coupons that they pay to compensate investors for assuming the higher credit risk. These are usually bought by specialist credit funds, hedge funds and banks. A bond may also achieve high yield status by being downgraded from investment grade as a result of a perceived deterioration in the credit quality of the issuer. These bonds are known as *crossover* credits or *fallen angels*.

---

[1] *Securities Industry and Financial Markets Association Research Quarterly*, August 2007.

Table 4.1 Rating categories for the main credit rating agencies.

Credit quality description	Rating agency		
	Moody's Investor Service	Standard and Poor's	Fitch IBCA, Duff & Phelps
Investment grade			
Highest quality	Aaa	AAA	AAA
High	Aa1	AA+	AA+
quality	Aa2	AA	AA
(very strong)	Aa3	AA−	AA−
Upper	A1	A+	A+
medium grade	A2	A	A
(strong)	A3	A−	A−
Medium grade	Baa1	BBB+	BBB+
	Baa2	BBB	BBB
	Baa3	BBB−	BBB−
Sub-investment grade			
Lower	Ba1	BB+	BB+
medium grade	Ba2	BB	BB
(somewhat speculative)	Ba2	BB−	BB−
Low	B1	B	B+
grade	B2	B	B
(speculative)	B3	B	B−
Poor quality	Caa	CCC	CCC
(may default)			
Most speculative	Ca	CC	CC
No interest being paid or bankruptcy petition filed	C	C	C
In default	C	D	D

4.2 FIXED RATE BONDS

In this section we discuss a category of bonds called fixed rate bonds. The term *fixed rate* reflects the fact that we are discussing bonds which pay a fixed coupon. These are therefore distinct from floating rate notes which pay a variable coupon and which are discussed in the next section. As we shall see, fixed rate and floating rate bonds have very different interest rate risk profiles.

Fixed rate bonds are one of the main mechanisms which corporates and sovereigns use to raise funds. They are initially issued into the primary market, a process in which a syndicate of dealers price, structure and sell the bond on behalf of the borrower. Determining the structure means determining the bond's characteristics in terms of coupon and maturity in a way that strikes a compromise between the borrowers' need to minimise their funding costs and the desire of investors to be compensated for assuming the credit risk of the issuer. The issue price is typically par. Those who buy the bond in the primary market may then sell the bonds which are subsequently traded in what is called the *secondary market*.

4.2.1 Mechanics

To buy a fixed rate bond which has previously been issued, an investor executes a trade in the secondary bond market which is then settled on a date which can vary depending upon the type of bond. Some bonds settle $T + 1$, i.e. on the business day following the trade date. Others, such as Eurobonds, settle on $T + 3$.

On the settlement date, the purchaser of the bond pays the *full* bond price to the seller. The full bond price is determined by adding the *clean* price of the bond, which is how the bond price is quoted in the market, and the accrued interest calculated according to some accrual convention. The determination of the accrued interest will be discussed in the next section. The investor then receives a fixed periodic coupon until maturity when the investor also receives back the principal.

Corporate bonds are generally issued with terms of about 10 years. Typically, the coupon is paid semi-annually. For example, if the quoted coupon is c and is paid semi-annually, then each coupon payment will be $c/2$ per dollar of face value. The coupon on the bond is set at a level which enables the bond to be issued at a price of par. After issue, the price of the bond will evolve, reflecting changes in the level of interest rates and changes in the perceived credit quality of the issuer.

Both the coupon and principal payments are vulnerable to the credit risk of the issuer. If there is a default, this will result in the termination of the coupon payments. There is then typically some workout process at the end of which the creditors of the firm, who include the bond holders, are paid some fraction of the residual value of the company. The amount received is a function of the position of the bond in the capital structure of the firm, the size of the bond holders' claim, which is the face value of the bond, and the residual value of the company. The amount received is known as the recovery price, and when divided by the face value of the bond, is known as the *recovery rate*.

4.2.2   Accrued Interest

The bond price quoted in the market is known as the clean price. It is different from the amount which is actually paid to buy a bond which is known as the full or dirty price. The difference between the clean price and the full price is known as the accrued interest.

The purpose of accrued interest is to avoid a sudden drop in the *quoted* price of bonds as we pass through a coupon payment which is what must happen with the bond full price. These effects are not helpful to investors as they do not represent a change in credit quality or interest rates.

The market therefore prefers to quote bonds using a *clean price*. This is calculated by subtracting the *accrued interest* from the full price of the bond. The accrued interest is defined as the portion of the next coupon payment which has accrued since the previous coupon date. Suppose that a bond pays a coupon c/f at time t_2 and the previous coupon was paid at time t_1. Suppose that the bond settles at time t_s. The accrued coupon is therefore defined as

$$\Delta\left(\frac{c}{f}\right)$$

where $\Delta = d_1/d_2$ is the fraction of the coupon period between t_s and t_1. The exact calculation of d_1 and d_2 depends upon the day count convention associated with the bond. For example, if the day count convention is Actual 365, then d_1 is the actual number of days between the last coupon date and the settlement date of the bond, and $d_2 = 365$. Other conventions include 30/360, Actual/360 and Actual/Actual. The full price is then computed from the clean price as follows

$$P = P_C + \Delta\left(\frac{c}{f}\right).$$

Figure 4.1 shows the cash flows of a five-year fixed rate bond which pays a 6% coupon with a semi-annual frequency. The bond has been sold part way through its second coupon period and so the full bond price takes into account the 28 days of accrued interest which have accrued. Economically the full price is the important one as it measures what is actually paid. It represents the expected present value of future cash flows.

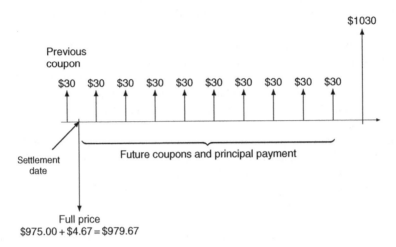

Figure 4.1   Cash flow schedule of $1000 face value of a five-year fixed rate bond paying a semi-annual coupon of 6%. The bond clean price is 97.50 and the accrued interest is based on 28 days since the first and previous coupon was paid and so using the Actual 360 day count convention equals $28/180 \times \$30 = \$4.67$

4.2.3   Yield Measures

The credit risk of the issuer is factored into the price of the corporate bond. For example, it will generally be found that a corporate bond will trade at a discount to the same maturity Treasury bond *paying the same coupon*. This lower price is to attract the investor to prefer the credit risky corporate bond over the almost certain coupon payments of the government issued bond. In order to compare bonds with different coupons and maturities, it is more meaningful to compare their yields rather than their prices.

Market practice is that traders tend to price the bond off the issuer's yield curve where the market uses the concept of *yield to maturity*. Consider a corporate bond with coupon c, paid with a frequency of f. We define the corporate bond yield y as the solution to the equation

$$P = \sum_{n=1}^{N} \frac{c/f}{(1+y/f)^n} + \frac{1}{(1+y/f)^N} \tag{4.1}$$

where P is the full price of the bond and we assume that today is a coupon payment date so that there is a full coupon period to the next coupon. As with all such yield measures, this measure of yield assumes that all coupons are reinvested at the same yield y.

Figure 4.2 shows a snapshot of the term structure of yields for bonds issued by Ford Motor Company taken in early 2006. We see clearly that the term structure of Ford yields is upward sloping. This is explained by the fact that investors demand a higher yield in order to buy longer

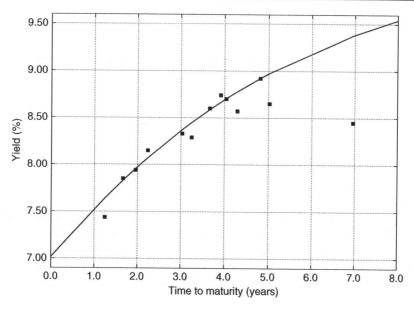

Figure 4.2 This graph shows the yield curve for USD denominated Ford Motor Company bonds. We also show a best-fit line fitted using a cubic polynomial. Source data: Lehman Brothers

maturity Ford bonds. We see that there is a reasonable amount of dispersion in the yields around the fitted curve. This reflects a number of factors not captured by the yield calculation. These include differences in liquidity caused by different bonds being issued in different sizes and at different times in the past.

4.2.4   Risk Management

We can decompose the yield of a defaultable fixed rate bond into an interest rate component and a credit component by writing $y = y_T + s$ where y_T is the yield of the most liquid Treasury bond with a maturity equal to or close to the maturity of the credit risky bond. The quantity s is known as the *yield spread*. The corporate bond full price is given by

$$P = \frac{c}{f} \sum_{n=1}^{N} \frac{1}{(1 + (y_T + s)/f)^n} + \frac{1}{(1 + (y_T + s)/f)^N}.$$

The price sensitivity of a corporate bond to changes in y_T and s is given by the Taylor expansion

$$dP = \frac{\partial P}{\partial y_T}(dy_T) + \frac{1}{2}\frac{\partial^2 P}{\partial y_T^2}(dy_T)^2 + \frac{\partial P}{\partial s}(ds) + \frac{1}{2}\frac{\partial^2 P}{\partial s^2}(ds)^2 + \frac{\partial^2 P}{\partial s \partial y_T}(ds)(dy_T) + \dots.$$

The first-order sensitivity to changes in y_T and s is known as the *modified duration*, D. The second-order sensitivity is known as the *convexity*, C. As a result, we can write

$$\frac{dP}{P} = -D_{y_T}.dy_T + \frac{1}{2}C_{y_T}dy_T^2 - D_S.ds + \frac{1}{2}C_S ds^2 + \dots.$$

We ignore the second-order cross term since we assume that on average, y_T and s are weakly correlated. Note that the modified duration is defined with a negative sign in front so that the modified duration term D of a fixed rate bond will be positive.

4.2.5   The Modified Duration

The modified duration of a bond is the proportional change in the price movement in yield. Given a bond with a full price P and yield to maturity y the modified duration is defined by

$$D_y = -\frac{1}{P}\frac{\partial P}{\partial y}. \tag{4.2}$$

This can be computed numerically by calculating finite differences

$$D_y = -\frac{P(y + \Delta y) - P(y - \Delta y)}{2P\Delta y}$$

where Δy is typically 1 bp. Duration is defined with a negative sign so that it will typically have a positive value.

In the case of a defaultable bond, we wish to manage the interest rate risk and credit risk separately. We therefore wish to calculate the duration with respect to changes in the Treasury yield, and also with respect to changes in the yield spread. We can calculate the sensitivity of the corporate bond price P to changes in the Treasury yield analytically. The analytical form of the interest rate duration D_{y_T} is given by the partial derivative with respect to y_T

$$D_{y_T} = \frac{1}{Pf}\left(\frac{c}{f}\sum_{n=1}^{N}\frac{n}{(1 + (y_T + s)/f)^{n+1}} + \frac{N}{(1 + (y_T + s)/f)^{N+1}}\right).$$

Similarly, we can calculate the yield spread duration D_S by taking the partial derivative with respect to s. By symmetry, we also have

$$D_S = D_{y_T}.$$

We see that for the defaultable bond the interest rate duration and spread duration *are exactly the same*. A fixed rate corporate bond is therefore as much an interest rate play, as it is a credit play, i.e. a change of 1 bp in the yield spread has the same effect on the price as a change of 1 bp in the Treasury yield.

4.2.6   Duration Hedging

The prices of both a fixed rate credit risky bond and a Treasury bond are sensitive to changes in the Treasury yield y_T. This means that we can use a Treasury bond to hedge out the interest rate risk of the credit risky bond, rendering it an almost pure credit play. To hedge out the interest rate risk of the corporate bond, market practice is to short a notional F_T the benchmark Treasury against the purchase of face value F of the corporate bond. The benchmark Treasury is a liquid Treasury bond which has a similar maturity to the corporate. This will be done by calculating a value of F_T which allows the credit investor to cancel out the duration of the position. If we define V as the value of the hedged position, then

$$V = FP - F_T P_T$$

where P_T is the full price of the Treasury bond and P is the full price of the credit risky bond. A first-order hedged position to the Treasury yield means that

$$\frac{\partial V}{\partial y_T} = 0.$$

As a result we can solve for the face value of Treasury bonds which hedge the first-order Treasury yield sensitivity of a credit risky bond to give

$$F_T = \left(\frac{\partial P_T}{\partial y_T}\right)^{-1} \left(\frac{\partial P}{\partial y_T}\right) F.$$

4.2.7 The Bond DV01

This is a good moment to introduce the concept of the DV01. This is the *absolute change* in the full price of a bond per 1 bp increase in the yield. It is defined by

$$\mathrm{DV01} = -\left(P(y + 1\,\mathrm{bp}) - P(y)\right) \simeq -\frac{\partial P}{\partial y}\Delta y$$

where $\Delta y = 1\,\mathrm{bp}$. The minus signs ensures that the DV01 of a fixed rate bond is a positive quantity. When risk managing a portfolio of bonds, the DV01 becomes a useful tool because it is additive across bonds, i.e. if we have a portfolio of $k = 1, \ldots, K$ bonds, each with a face value F_k, a price P_k and with total value V, we can write

$$V = \sum_{k=1}^{K} P_k$$

so that

$$\mathrm{DV01}_{\mathrm{Portfolio}} = \sum_{k=1}^{K} F_k \mathrm{DV01}_k.$$

This is not the case for the modified duration.

4.2.8 Convexity

Once a position has been duration hedged, the next order of risk is the second-order sensitivity of the corporate bond price to changes in the level of interest rates or spreads. This is known as the convexity, and it is defined as

$$C_y = \frac{1}{P}\frac{\partial^2 P}{\partial y^2}. \tag{4.3}$$

In practice, we can compute it by taking the numerical derivative of the bond price via second differences, i.e.

$$C_y = \frac{P(y + \Delta y) - 2P(y) + P(y - \Delta y)}{P(y)(\Delta y)^2}$$

where we usually set $\Delta y = 1\,\mathrm{bp}$. We can write the convexity contribution to changes in the Treasury yield and yield spread as

$$C_{y_T} = \frac{1}{P}\frac{\partial^2 P}{\partial y_T^2} \quad \text{and} \quad C_S = \frac{1}{P}\frac{\partial^2 P}{\partial s^2}.$$

We can calculate these convexity terms analytically so we have a Treasury yield convexity

$$C_{y_T} = \frac{1}{Pf^2} \left(\frac{c}{f} \sum_{i=1}^{N} \frac{n(n+1)}{(1 + (y_T + s)/f)^{n+2}} + \frac{N(N+1)}{(1 + (y_T + s)/f)^{N+2}} \right).$$

Once again, by symmetry it is clear that the yield spread convexity is given by

$$C_S = C_{y_T}.$$

Simple hedging based on using the yield to maturity and the yield spread works best only if the assumption of parallel movements in the yield curve comes true. Although parallel movements are the principal component of yield curve dynamics, they are not the only component. We find in practice that both the slope and curvature of the yield curve can change. As a result, a better interest rate hedging approach would involve some combination of Treasury bonds at different points of the yield curve. For more on this see Tuckman (2002).

Example To demonstrate the interest risk hedging of a fixed corporate bond, we consider how to hedge a five-year to maturity corporate bond using a Treasury bond. The bond details are given in Table 4.2. The value date is 1 May 2007, with the maturity date of both bonds set five-years later on 1 May 2012. Figure 4.3 shows the dependency of the prices of the corporate bond and the Treasury bond on the Treasury yield. We have assumed a yield spread of 2%. The face value of the short position hedge in the Treasury bond for each $100 of the corporate bond is given by taking the ratio of the DV01s

$$F_T = \frac{4.3668}{4.4879} \times \$100 = \$97.30.$$

The face value of the Treasury position is less than $100, reflecting the higher interest rate sensitivity of the Treasury bond.

To measure the quality of the hedge, we can calculate the sensitivity of the value of the combined position to changes in the Treasury yield. This is shown in Figure 4.4. We also see that the value of the net position is a concave function of the field. This is known as being *short yield convexity*.

We note that the Treasury yield sensitivity of the hedged position is tiny. For example, a reasonably large 1% movement in the Treasury yield from 5% to 6% causes the hedged position to lose 0.32 cents on a $100 face value corporate bond position. This is small compared to the $4.26 the bond holder would lose on the unhedged position.

Table 4.2 Bond indicatives and risk measures for the example hedged portfolio

	Treasury bond	Corporate bond
Maturity date	1 May 2012	1 May 2012
Coupon	6%	9%
Frequency	2	2
Yield	5.00%	7.00%
Price	104.38	108.32
Duration	4.2998	4.0315
DV01	4.4879	4.3668

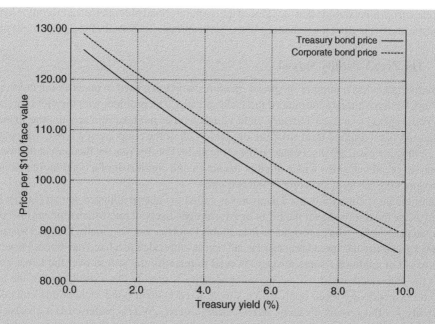

Figure 4.3   Price–yield relationship for a five-year Treasury bond with a semi-annual coupon of 6% and for a corporate bond with a 9% coupon

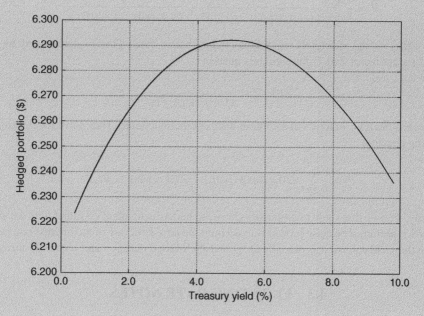

Figure 4.4   Combined value of the corporate bond plus Treasury bond hedge

It is clear from this example that the value of the corporate bond plus interest rate duration hedge is almost exclusively driven by changes in the yield spread, i.e. it is almost a pure credit play.

4.2.9   The Zero Volatility Spread

The credit market has a number of spread measures which are used to quantify the credit risk of a bond. We have already introduced the yield spread s. The problem with the yield spread is that it is the spread to a fixed Treasury yield y_T and so does not take into account the shape of the Treasury bond implied term structure of yields – all of the coupons of a bond, irrespective of when they are paid, are discounted at the same yield. For this reason, there are a number of alternative spread measures which attempt to capture the credit risk of a bond more precisely by incorporating the term structure of interest rates.

One of the most commonly used measures is called the option adjusted spread (OAS). It is defined as the fixed spread over the Libor or government discount rate which reprices the bond. The concept of the OAS has its origins in the callable bond market. Originally, the OAS was used as a way to quantify the spread impact of a call option embedded in a fixed rate bond. However, in the world of credit, the same measure is used to quantify the spread over the Libor curve due to the embedded credit risk where no optionality is present. As a result, use of the term OAS can be confusing when applied to a simple fixed coupon bond without any embedded optionality. For this reason, the name *zero volatility spread* (ZVS) is preferred as it makes clear that it is not a volatility measure, even though it is calculated in exactly the same way.

The ZVS for a specific bond is defined as the fixed spread adjustment to the Libor discount rate which reprices the bond. If we use the symbol θ to represent the ZVS, we can write this as

$$P = \frac{c}{f} \sum_{n=1}^{N} \frac{1}{(1 + (r(0, t_n) + \theta)/f)^n} + \frac{1}{(1 + (r(0, t_N) + \theta)/f)^N}$$

where $r(0, t)$ is the discretely compounded Libor zero rate. This is determined by the Libor discount factor $Z(0, t)$ through the equation

$$Z(0, t_n) = \frac{1}{(1 + r(0, t_n)/f)^n}.$$

Some define the ZVS in terms of a continuously compounded rate. They solve for θ using the following equation

$$P = \frac{c}{f} \sum_{n=1}^{N} Z(0, t_n) \exp(-\theta t_n) + Z(0, t_N) \exp(-\theta t_N).$$

Finally, we note that some practitioners choose to hedge using the ZVS rather than the yield. The ZVS is preferred because it takes into account the term structure of the interest rate curve. As with the yield spread, it is possible to write a ZVS-based duration and convexity measure.

4.3   FLOATING RATE NOTES

A floating rate note (FRN) is a bond which pays a coupon linked to some variable interest rate index. For almost all FRNs, the index used for determination of the bond coupon is Libor, which was described in detail in Chapter 2. Although initially a small market, the issuance of floating rate notes has grown steadily over the past 20 years and is now comparable in size to that for fixed rate bonds. In 2006, the total of fixed rate corporate bond issuance was \$542 billion versus \$518 billion for floating rate debt.[2]

4.3.1   Mechanics

An investor can buy an FRN either at origination or in the secondary market. If bought at origination, the price of the FRN is usually equal to or close to par. If bought after origination, the price paid for the bond may no longer be close to par – as we will see the price will reflect changes in the credit quality of the issuer since the FRN was issued. This full price is given by the clean price, quoted in the market plus any accrued interest. This price is paid on the settlement date of the bond.

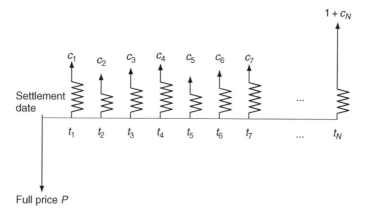

Figure 4.5   Cash flow schedule of a floating rate note paying a regular coupon of $c_n = \Delta(t_{n-1}, t_n)(L(t_{n-1}, t_n) + F(0))$ at time t_n where the size of the coupon is determined according to a specified frequency and day count convention

Figure 4.5 shows the mechanics of an FRN. Following purchase of the bond, the investor receives a floating coupon of Libor plus an annualised fixed spread $F(0)$ which is paid according to a specified frequency and day count convention. The coupon frequency is typically quarterly. We represent the times to the coupon payment dates as $t_1, \ldots, t_N$ and set $t_0 = t_s$, the settlement date of the bond.

This fixed spread was set on the issue date of the bond so that the bond price was close to par. It is known as the *quoted margin*. We will show later that the value of this spread can be shown to be a measure of the credit quality of the issuer when the bond was issued.

Determination of the Libor rate to be used in a coupon payment occurs just before the preceding coupon date following the same mechanism as the floating leg of an interest rate swap. As a result, the investor always knows the next coupon with certainty. This convention is known as *set in advance, paid in arrears* and is market standard.

To have a model-based valuation of a floating rate note would require us to determine the expected present value of the floating and fixed component of the coupons. To do this correctly,

---

[2] Source: Thomson Financial.

we would need a pricing model which can correctly account for the payment of the unknown future Libor and take into account any correlation with interest rates and the default time. This would require us to specify a dynamics for the interest rate process and the hazard rate process and the correlation between them. However, such an approach is not necessary since the price of a floating rate note can be obtained in the market.

4.3.2   The Par Floater Spread

What we really want is a simple way to assess the credit risk of a floating rate note. One approach is to discount the cash flows at a fixed spread to Libor as follows

$$P(t) = \sum_{n=1}^{N} \frac{\Delta_n \left(L(t_{n-1}, t_n) + F(0) \right)}{\prod_{m=1}^{n} \left(1 + \Delta_m (L(t_{m-1}, t_m) + F(t)) \right)} + \frac{1}{\prod_{m=1}^{N} \left(1 + \Delta_m (L(t_{m-1}, t_m) + F(t)) \right)}$$

where we have set $\Delta_n = \Delta(t_{n-1}, t_n)$ in order to simplify the notation. We call $F(t)$ the time t *par floater spread*. It is simply the flat spread to Libor at which we have to discount the coupon and principal payments of the FRN in order to reprice the bond at time t. Note that this is not a proper model-based pricing equation. The par floater spread is simply a convention for discounting the cash flows which takes into account the term structure of Libor rates. Rearranging, and assuming that the current settlement date is a coupon payment date so that the full price and clean price are the same, we can rewrite the pricing equation as

$$P(t) = 1 + (F(0) - F(t)) \sum_{n=1}^{N} \frac{\Delta_n}{\prod_{m=1}^{n} \left(1 + \Delta_m (L(t_{m-1}, t_m) + F(t)) \right)}. \tag{4.4}$$

Examining this equation, we see that there are three distinct cases to consider:

1. If $F(t) = F(0)$ the price of the FRN equals par. This reflects the fact that the market perceived credit quality of the bond is the same as when the bond was issued at par.
2. If $F(t) > F(0)$ the price of the FRN will be less than par, reflecting the fact that the market perceived credit quality of the bond has declined since it was issued.
3. If $F(t) < F(0)$ the price of the FRN will be above par. The bond trades at a premium, reflecting the fact that the market perceived credit quality of the bond has improved since it was issued.

It is clear that the par floater spread is a measure of the credit risk embedded within the par floater as seen at time t. This also shows that we can tell how the credit quality of the bond, as viewed by the market, has changed since the bond was issued by looking to see whether the bond price is above or below par.

4.3.3   Risk Management

The two types of market risk for floating rate notes in which we are interested are interest rate risk and credit risk. The former is the risk to changes in the forward Libor curve. The second can be captured by understanding the effect of changes in $F(t)$. We start with the interest rate risk. We define the interest rate DV01 as the negative of the dollar value change in the FRN price for a 1 bp increase in all forward Libor rates

$$\text{Libor DV01} = - \left(P(\text{Libor} + 1\,\text{bp}) - P(\text{Libor}) \right).$$

The credit DV01 is defined as the dollar change in the value of the position for a 1 bp increase in the par floater spread $F(t)$. In both cases we have put a negative sign in front so that the quantity will be consistent with the definition used for fixed rate bonds

$$\text{Credit DV01} = -(P(F(t) + 1\,\text{bp}) - P(F(t)))\,.$$

We now consider an example FRN.

Example Consider a $1 million face value FRN with a maturity of five years. The quoted margin is 75 bp and the current par floater spread is 100 bp. Table 4.3 shows the cash flow schedule complete with the Libor and spread payments. We discount them using the discount factors which have been computed using the par floater spread and the Libor schedule. We then sum over all discounted cash flows to give the present value.

Table 4.3   Cash flow schedule and payments for the floating rate note discussed in the text

Payment date	Year fraction	Forward Libor (%)	FRN payment	Discount factor
25 October 2006				1.000000
25 January 2007	0.2556	5.375	15 653.66	0.983968
25 April 2007	0.2500	5.369	15 296.42	0.968547
25 July 2007	0.2528	5.272	15 221.79	0.953432
25 October 2007	0.2556	5.155	15 090.03	0.938668
25 January 2008	0.2556	5.105	14 963.28	0.924248
25 April 2008	0.2528	5.034	14 620.21	0.910363
25 July 2008	0.2528	4.965	14 446.37	0.896840
25 October 2008	0.2556	4.898	14 433.82	0.883523
25 January 2009	0.2556	5.077	14 890.38	0.870012
25 April 2009	0.2500	5.066	14 539.24	0.857016
25 July 2009	0.2528	5.051	14 662.97	0.844105
25 October 2009	0.2556	5.035	14 784.85	0.831284
25 January 2010	0.2556	5.090	14 924.57	0.818544
25 April 2010	0.2500	5.083	14 582.57	0.806283
25 July 2010	0.2528	5.076	14 726.44	0.794087
25 October 2010	0.2556	5.068	14 868.33	0.781961
25 January 2011	0.2556	5.197	15 196.69	0.769771
25 April 2011	0.2500	5.199	14 872.59	0.758024
25 July 2011	0.2528	5.202	15 044.46	0.746324
25 October 2011	0.2556	5.203	1 015 214.05	0.734677
		Present value	989 175.90	

The price of the FRN is $98.92 (to 2 decimal places). We can calculate the interest rate and credit DV01s. We find that the interest rate DV01 is −$2.70 – there is a small *increase* in the value of the position for a 1 bp increase in the forward Libor curve. The reason why the change in the value of the position is positive is because we can see from Equation 4.4 that we are long both a par amount paid at maturity and a five-year annuity with an annualised coupon of $(F(0) - F(t))$. Since this coupon equals $75 - 100 = -25$ bp, the value of this liability to us increases (or becomes less negative) when Libor increases. We also note that the magnitude of the interest rate risk is much smaller than that of the equivalent maturity fixed rate bond.

We find that the credit DV01 is much larger at $430. The credit modified duration is 4.348. This *is similar to a fixed rate corporate bond of the same maturity.*

These results make it very clear that a floating rate note is predominately a credit play. The interest rate sensitivity is small. However, the credit risk remains and is comparable to that of a fixed rate bond of a similar maturity.

4.3.4   The Discount Margin

In addition to the par floater spread, the market has another spread measure for floating rate notes known as the *discount margin*. We denote this as d where the price–discount margin relationship is given by

$$P = \frac{\left(\Delta_1 \, (L^* + F(0)) + \sum_{n=2}^{N} \frac{\Delta_n \, (L + F(0))}{\prod_{m=2}^{n} (1 + \Delta_m (L + d))} + \frac{1}{\prod_{m=2}^{N} (1 + \Delta_m (L + d))}\right)}{(1 + \Delta_s (L_s + d))}$$

and

- d is the discount margin.
- L^* is the next Libor payment which has already fixed and is known.
- L_s is the current Libor rate from today to the first cash flow. This is not fixed and can be determined from the term structure of Libor rates which are quoted in the market.
- Δ_s is the year fraction from today to the first coupon date.
- Δ_n is the year fraction from t_{n-1} to t_n in the appropriate basis, typically Actual 360.
- L is the current Libor rate to a date which has the same term as the Libor coupons on the bond, i.e. if the FRN coupons are semi-annual, then this will be the 6M Libor rate.

This measure has the advantage that it does not require any special analytics to build a Libor curve and to calculate the implied forward Libor rates. All of the Libor rates used can be read from a screen of Libor quotes. A simple one-dimensional root searching algorithm can then be used to determine d. As a result, this measure is used widely in the market to the extent that floating rate notes are often quoted and traded using the discount margin as the basis for negotiation. The disadvantage of the discount margin relative to the par floater spread is that it ignores the term structure of Libor rates.

4.4   THE ASSET SWAP

The asset swap is a structure in which a credit investor effectively synthesises a floating rate bond by combining a fixed rate bond with an interest rate swap. Since the inception of the asset swap in the early 1980s, it has become an extremely important product for credit investors. It is also a preferred tool of banks who use the floating rate coupons which it pays to match their floating rate liabilities on depositor accounts. Since it combines a credit risky bond and an interest rate swap, the asset swap is considered by some to be the first credit derivative.

4.4.1   Mechanics

An asset swap is a package consisting of a bond and an interest rate swap which together cost par. The full mechanics of the asset swap structure are shown in Figure 4.6. On the settlement date of the trade the mechanics are as follows:

1. The asset swap seller delivers to the asset swap buyer a fixed rate bond which has a full price P and pays a coupon c at a frequency f in return for a payment of par.
2. The asset swap buyer enters into a payer interest rate swap. The payment schedule of the fixed leg is set so that it is identical to that of the fixed rate bond. On the floating leg, the asset swap buyer receives payments of Libor plus A, where A is known as the *asset swap spread*. These are paid at a frequency and with a day count convention which may be different from those of the fixed leg.

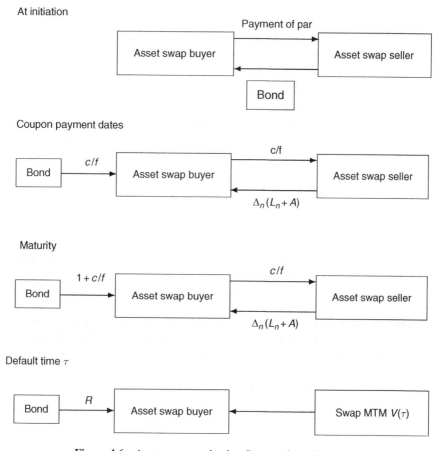

Figure 4.6   Asset swap mechanics. See text for a discussion

We now consider what happens after the asset swap has settled.

- On the floating leg payment dates, the asset swap buyer receives payments of

$$\Delta(t_{m-1}, t_m)(L(t_{m-1}, t_m) + A)$$

where $m = 1, \ldots, M$ and $t_1, \ldots, t_M$ are the floating rate payment dates. These are calculated according to the floating leg day count convention.
- On bond coupon payment dates, assuming the bond has not defaulted, the asset swap buyer receives the scheduled coupon of c/f from the bond. On the same date, the asset swap buyer

pays a coupon of c/f to the asset swap seller on the swap fixed leg. It is essential to realise that these swap fixed leg payments are *non-contingent*, meaning that they are scheduled to be paid even if the bond defaults.

- At maturity, assuming that the fixed rate bond has not defaulted before the maturity date of the asset swap, the asset swap buyer receives par from the bond.
- If there is a default before the maturity of the asset swap, the asset swap buyer can sell the bond for its recovery value R. However, the interest rate swap payments *do not cancel*. The asset swap buyer can continue the swap or may decide to unwind it at its current mark-to-market value.

We can value the asset swap by thinking of it as two separate transactions in which the investor buys a bond with full price P and enters into an interest rate swap with value V. The combined cost is par. Hence, we have

$$V + P = 1 \tag{4.5}$$

Note that if $P > 1$ then the initial value of the swap must be negative, and vice versa. When structuring an asset swap, the degree of freedom which allows us to ensure that Equation 4.5 holds is the asset swap spread A. In the next section, we show how this is determined.

4.4.2 Determining the asset swap spread

To calculate the asset swap spread for a particular bond, we need to consider the risk of the cash flows. We do this from the perspective of the asset swap buyer.

At the settlement of the asset swap, which we call time 0, the bond is delivered, par is paid and the interest rate swap begins. The upfront payment from the perspective of the asset swap buyer is therefore simply

$$+P - 1$$

where P is the full price of the bond. At the same time, the asset swap buyer has entered into an interest rate swap in which they pay a fixed coupon c/f and receive Libor plus a fixed asset swap spread which we denote with $A(0)$. The swap payments are not *contingent* – they do not cancel if the bond defaults. As a result, we discount them on the risk-free Libor curve. The present value of the floating leg of the interest rate swap is therefore

$$\sum_{m=1}^{M} Z(0, t_m) \Delta(t_{m-1}, t_m) \left(L(t_{m-1}, t_m) + A(0) \right).$$

At initiation, the present value of the fixed leg of the swap is also non-contingent and so we discount these coupons on the risk-free Libor curve to give a present value of

$$-\frac{c}{f} \sum_{n=1}^{N} Z(0, \hat{t}_n).$$

Note that the fixed leg schedule payments are at times $\hat{t}_1, \ldots, \hat{t}_n$ and so can be different from those on the floating leg. As a result, the total value of the asset swap at initiation equals

$$-1 + P + \sum_{m=1}^{M} Z(0, t_m) \Delta(t_{m-1}, t_m) \left(L(t_{m-1}, t_m) + A(0) \right) - \frac{c}{f} \sum_{n=1}^{N} Z(0, \hat{t}_n).$$

It is important to understand that the value of the risky coupon and principal payments of the bond is captured within the bond full price P. The net present value of the initial exchange plus future flows must be zero at initiation. This allows us to write

$$A(0) = \frac{c/f \sum_{n=1}^{N} Z(0, \hat{t}_n) + 1 - P - \sum_{m=1}^{M} Z(0, t_m) \Delta(t_{m-1}, t_m) L(t_{m-1}, t_m)}{\sum_{m=1}^{M} Z(0, t_m) \Delta(t_{m-1}, t_m)}.$$

Since the value of the forward Libor rate is given by

$$L(t_{m-1}, t_m) = \frac{1}{\Delta(t_{m-1}, t_m)} \left(\frac{Z(0, t_{m-1})}{Z(0, t_m)} - 1 \right)$$

and since both legs mature at the same time, we have $t_N = t_M = T$, and we can write

$$A(0) = \frac{c/f \sum_{n=1}^{N} Z(0, \hat{t}_n) + Z(0, T) - P}{\text{PV01}(0, T)}$$

where

$$\text{PV01}(0, T) = \sum_{m=1}^{M} Z(0, t_m) \Delta(t_{m-1}, t_m)$$

is the present value of 1 bp paid on the floating leg of the swap. If we write

$$P_{Libor} = \frac{c}{f} \sum_{n=1}^{N} Z(0, \hat{t}_n) + Z(0, T) \tag{4.6}$$

then the asset swap spread can be written as

$$A(0) = \frac{P_{Libor} - P}{\text{PV01}(0, T)}.$$

What this tells us is that an asset swap is equivalent to going long a defaultable bond and short a risk-free bond with the same coupon schedule. The asset swap spread is then the amortised payment of the price difference over the life of the asset swap. The amortisation continues to the maturity of the asset swap-it is risk free.

The asset swap spread is therefore a measure of the credit quality of the fixed rate bond. If the bond issuer has the credit quality of the AA commercial banking sector, then it will probably have a price close to P_{Libor} and the asset swap spread will be close to zero. If the credit quality of the issuer falls, the price of the fixed coupon bond will fall below P_{Libor} and the asset swap spread will increase.

Example Consider a fixed rate five-year bond with a coupon of 7.25%, paid semi-annually. It is currently trading at a price of $94.38. We wish to asset swap $1million face value of this bond. The asset swap spread is computed by calculating the present value of the fixed flows discounted via the Libor curve. The flows are shown in Table 4.4.

(*Continued*)

The PV01 is calculated to be 4.4396, and the value of P_{Libor} is found to equal 1.0876 per $1 of facevalue. As a result, the asset swap spread is given by

$$A(0) = \frac{1.0876 - 0.9438}{4.4396} = 323.9 \, bp.$$

Table 4.4 Cash flow schedule of an asset swap showing the fixed and floating payments. We also show the implied forward Libors and the Libor discount factors

Payment dates	Fixed flows	Floating flows	Accrual factor	Forward LIBOR	Discount factor
25 Oct 2006					1.000000
25 Jan 2007		22 014	0.25556	5.375%	0.986449
25 Apr 2007	36 250	21 519	0.25000	5.369%	0.973385
25 Jul 2007		21 513	0.25278	5.272%	0.960584
25 Oct 2007	36 250	21 451	0.25556	5.155%	0.948095
25 Jan 2008		21 324	0.25556	5.105%	0.935885
25 Apr 2008	36 250	20 912	0.25278	5.034%	0.924126
25 Jul 2008		20 738	0.25278	4.965%	0.912671
25 Oct 2008	36 250	20 795	0.25556	4.898%	0.901388
25 Jan 2009		21 251	0.25556	5.077%	0.889844
25 Apr 2009	36 250	20 762	0.25000	5.066%	0.878715
25 Jul 2009		20 955	0.25278	5.051%	0.867638
25 Oct 2009	36 250	21 146	0.25556	5.035%	0.856615
25 Jan 2010		21 285	0.25556	5.090%	0.845615
25 Apr 2010	36 250	20 805	0.25000	5.083%	0.835005
25 Jul 2010		21 018	0.25278	5.076%	0.824427
25 Oct 2010	36 250	21 229	0.25556	5.068%	0.813885
25 Jan 2011		21 557	0.25556	5.197%	0.803219
25 Apr 2011	36 250	21 095	0.25000	5.199%	0.792913
25 Jul 2011		21 336	0.25278	5.202%	0.782622
25 Oct 2011	36 250	21 575	0.25556	5.203%	0.772352

4.4.3 Valuation of an asset swap

The mark-to-market today of a derivative is what we receive if we unwind the position in the market. To unwind an asset swap we can enter into an offsetting asset swap position which converts the risky asset swap into a stream of risk-free payments. The mark-to-market of the position is then the present value of these risk-free payments.

To begin with, consider the asset swap from the perspective of an asset swap buyer who we shall call 'party A'. The asset swap seller is 'party B'.

1. Party A pays $100 at initiation to party B.
2. Party A receives the fixed rate bond which pays a coupon of c/f from party B.
3. Party A pays a coupon of c/f on the swap to party B.
4. Party A receives Libor plus $A(0)$ on the swap from party B.

To unwind this trade at time t, party A sells an asset swap package on the same bond to another asset swap buyer, party C, at a new asset swap spread $A(t)$. The cash flows are as follows:

1. Party A receives \$100 from C. This repays the \$100 used to enter into the asset swap package at initiation.
2. Party A delivers the fixed rate bond to party C.
3. Party A receives a coupon of c/f on the swap from C which is paid to B on the initial swap fixed leg.
4. Party A receives a coupon of Libor plus $A(0)$ from party B on the initial swap and pays a coupon of Libor plus $A(t)$ on the new swap to C.

Party A no longer owns the bond and its credit risk. All that is owned is a pair of offsetting interest rate swaps in which both the fixed legs and Libor payments cancel. The only payments that do not cancel are the spread payments of $(A(0)-A(t))$. These payments are non-contingent, i.e. they are risk free and are made for the remaining life of the asset swap. The mark-to-market value of the asset swap is therefore

$$\text{MTM}(t) = (A(0) - A(t)) \sum_{m=1}^{M} Z(t, t_m) \Delta(t_{m-1}, t_m)$$

which can be written more succinctly as

$$\text{MTM}(t) = (A(0) - A(t)) \cdot \text{PV01}(t, T).$$

Clearly, the mark-to-market value of an asset swap is zero at initiation when $A(t) = A(0)$. The mark-to-market can then move away from zero depending on how the asset swap spread changes.

Example   Consider a fixed rate corporate bond with five years to maturity which pays an annualised coupon of 7.25%. The bond is currently trading at a price of \$94.38 and we enter into an asset swap on a face value of \$10 million at a spread of 323.9 bp. A year later, the bond is trading at a price of \$96.00, a price increase of \$1.62. Over the year, we also suppose that Libor swap rates have risen by 25 bp across the curve. Due to the shortening of the time to maturity by one year and the increase in Libor rates, the PV01 has fallen to 3.622. The new asset swap spread equals 284 bp. As a result, the mark-to-market of the asset swap position is

$$\text{MTM} = (323.9 - 284.0)\,\text{bp} \times 3.622 \times \$10\,\text{million} = \$144\,518.$$

What we have is a position in which the asset swap buyer is long the credit risk of the issuer, the credit quality of the issuer has improved, as shown by the increase in the bond price, and the position has made money.

4.4.4 Risks of an Asset Swap

If the bond in the asset swap does not default, the asset swap package continues until maturity with the buyer simply passing through the bond coupons to the asset swap seller. In return the asset swap buyer receives the floating rate payments of Libor plus the asset swap spread. As they have paid par for this, provided the issuer does not default, this is equivalent to buying a floating rate note at par where the quoted margin equals the asset swap spread.

However, this is no longer true if the bond defaults. In this case, the value of the asset swap to the asset swap buyer is:

- R from the sale of the defaulted bond.
- $V(\tau)$ from the unwind of the interest rate swap.

If default occurs soon after the asset swap begins, then we can assume that $V(\tau) \simeq V(0)$, the initial value of the interest rate swap. As the investor paid par, the loss is $1 - (R + V(0))$. However, we also know that on the settlement date of the asset swap $V(0) + P = 1$. Hence $V(0) = 1 - P$ and the loss to the investor is

$$1 - (R + V(0)) = 1 - (R + (1 - P)) = (P - R).$$

Since $P > R$, the asset swap buyer makes a loss. Note that *the size of the default loss is exactly the same as if the asset swap buyer had simply purchased the bond without any asset swap package*. This asset swap can be compared to buying a par floater if the price of the fixed rate bond is also par, i.e. $P = 1$. In this case the value of the interest rate swap is zero at the start of the asset swap and should remain close to zero over the life of the asset swap provided there are no large interest rate movements.

This simple analysis assumes that default happens soon after the start of the asset swap. This allowed us to assume that the value of the interest rate swap had not changed. However, in practice, when a default occurs, the value of the interest rate swap will have changed. As a result, the asset swap buyer can make a gain or loss due to interest rate movements if there is a default, i.e. *we have a default contingent interest rate risk*. This is different from the risk of a floating rate note.

4.5 THE MARKET ASSET SWAP

The standard par asset swap can present a counterparty risk to either party on initiation. Since the asset swap buyer pays par in exchange for a bond worth P, they are exposed to a default by the asset swap counterparty if the bond is trading at a discount, i.e. $P < 1$. If the bond is trading at a premium $P > 1$, then the asset swap seller is taking the counterparty risk of the asset swap buyer. Over time this counterparty risk will be reduced by the payments on the asset swap, the pull to par of the bond, and the pull to zero of the swap.

However, for those who wish to avoid this counterparty risk, it is possible to adapt the par asset swap structure to what is known as *the market asset swap*. In this, the cost of entering into the asset swap is the full bond price P. Furthermore, the face value of the floating swap leg is set equal to the full bond price P. The mechanics of the market asset swap are as follows:

1. On the settlement date, the bond is delivered and the bond price P is paid.
2. On the settlement date, the asset swap buyer enters into an interest rate swap in which they pay a fixed coupon c/f on a face value of 1, and receive Libor plus the *market asset swap spread $A^*(0)$* on a face value of P.
3. At maturity, the floating rate leg of the swap pays P while the fixed leg of the swap pays 1. The net payment received by the asset swap buyer is $P - 1$.

We can now try to determine the value of $A^*(0)$.

At the settlement date of the asset swap, time 0, the net upfront transfer from the asset swap buyer has a value of

$$-P + P = 0.$$

There is no counterparty risk. At the same time, the asset swap buyer has entered into an interest rate swap. The present value of the floating leg of the interest rate swap is therefore

$$P \sum_{m=1}^{M} Z(0, t_m) \Delta(t_{m-1}, t_m) \left(L(t_{m-1}, t_m) + A^*(0) \right)$$

and the present value of the fixed leg of the swap is

$$-\frac{c}{f} \sum_{n=1}^{N} Z(0, \hat{t}_n).$$

The present value of the payment at maturity time $T = t_M = t_N$ is

$$Z(0, T)(P - 1).$$

As a result, the total value of the asset swap at initiation, which must equal zero, is given by

$$P \sum_{m=1}^{M} Z(0, t_m) \Delta_m \left(L(t_{m-1}, t_m) + A^*(0) \right) - \frac{c}{f} \sum_{n=1}^{N} Z(0, \hat{t}_n) + Z(0, T)(P - 1) = 0.$$

This simplifies to

$$P + P \cdot A^*(0) \cdot \text{PV01}(t, T) - P_{Libor} = 0$$

where P_{Libor} was defined in Equation 4.6. We can solve for $A^*(0)$ and find that

$$A^*(0) = \frac{A(0)}{P}$$

where $A(0)$ is the *equivalent par asset swap spread* derived previously. The market asset swap spread is higher for a discount bond than the par asset swap spread and is lower than the par asset swap spread for a premium bond.

Since the asset swap buyer simply pays the bond price, the value of the interest rate swap must be zero at initiation. If there is a default soon after initiation, the loss to the asset swap buyer is therefore $(P - R)$, which is exactly the same as the par asset swap and the same as buying the fixed rate bond. If the bond defaults later, interest rate effects come into play as discussed earlier in this section.

The ingenious feature of the market asset swap is that it has reversed both the timing and direction of the counterparty exposure.

1. The counterparty risk has been shifted from the front to the back end of the trade, i.e. it grows as we reach maturity since the two final payments on the swap do not cancel. A residual payment of $1 - P$ from the asset swap buyer to the asset swap seller remains to be paid.
2. The market asset swap reverses the counterparty risk. An asset swap buyer who does a par asset swap has an initial exposure of $1 - P$ to the asset swap seller. In the market asset swap, the initial exposure is zero. An asset swap buyer who does a par asset swap has no counterparty risk at maturity. However, at the end of the life of the market asset swap, the asset swap buyer has an exposure of $P - 1$ to the asset swap seller. The direction of the exposure has been reversed.

This is an example of a how a structure may be amended in order to change its counterparty risk profile. Finding ways to structure a transaction in order to mitigate counterparty risk is a frequent concern in the credit derivatives markets.

4.6   SUMMARY

This chapter has taken us through the simplest credit instruments starting with the fixed rate bond and the floating rate note. Not only are these important instruments in themselves, they are also key to understanding the pricing of credit derivatives. As we shall see, the price of a credit default swap is linked via arbitrage arguments to the prices of bonds and floating rate notes.

This chapter has also provided a detailed analysis of the asset swap. This is a hybrid product, being part bond, part derivative. It is also an important product as it is the simplest way to turn a standard fixed coupon bond into an almost pure credit play. As we shall see, it is also an important reference in the pricing of credit default swaps.

5

The Credit Default Swap

5.1 INTRODUCTION

The credit default swap (CDS) contract is the most liquid single-name credit derivatives contract, comprising 32.9% of the notional of all outstanding credit derivatives contracts according to the 2006 BBA Credit Derivatives report. It is also the building block for most of the other credit derivatives products. An understanding of credit derivatives therefore must be underpinned by a full understanding of the CDS contract.

To fully understand how the CDS contract works, there are a number of legal terms with which we must become familiar. This is because even simple concepts like default need to be defined with a wording that is legally watertight. Otherwise, there is scope for error or ambiguity and hence legal risk. In order to minimise legal risk, the credit derivatives market has adopted the definitions proposed by the International Swaps and Derivatives Association (ISDA). Since 1999, ISDA has been instrumental in creating a level of standardisation of these terms which has been one of the main contributors to the significant liquidity of the market that we see today.

Our aim in discussing these concepts is to make the credit modeller aware of the precise rules which govern a CDS contract. Since these rules are based on the ISDA definitions, an appreciation of these definitions is essential in order to understand these contracts. As the CDS market evolves, ISDA continues to monitor and evolve these definitions over time. As a result, we cannot claim that the definitions presented here will remain correct, and market participants should always seek up-to-date professional legal advice.

The credit default swap is an over-the-counter[1] product and the ISDA definitions allow for a lot of flexibility in terms of which features a specific CDS contract may possess. However, one of the advantages of the ISDA definitions is that it has enabled the market to develop the concept of a *standard CDS contract*. The standard contract is one which has a specific set of features generally viewed as being the most commonly used at a particular moment in time. By definition, the market standard contract is the one with the highest liquidity. In the following, we will try to highlight which features of a CDS are standard and which are not.

This chapter begins with a description of the mechanics of the CDS. We focus on how the contract is structured with a *protection leg* and *premium leg*. We discuss how the premium payment schedule is generated, what triggers the credit default swap protection payment, and how this payment process works. We then discuss a simple arbitrage argument for determining

---

[1] Over the counter means that the contract is not exchange traded. It is usually executed via the telephone or via some other tool such as a web page or Bloomberg screen. It is also usually a private transaction conducted between two parties.

the CDS premium via the bond market. We conclude with a discussion of the *CDS basis* – the spread difference between cash bonds and CDS – and the factors that drive it.

5.2 THE MECHANICS OF THE CDS CONTRACT

A credit default swap is a bilateral over-the-counter contract whose purpose is to protect one party, the *protection buyer*, from the loss from par on a specified face value of bonds or loans following the default of their issuer. This protection lasts from the *effective date*[2] which falls on the calendar date after the trade date, until a specified maturity date also known as the *scheduled termination date*. The specified bonds and loans which are protected are known as the *deliverable obligations* and the issuer is known as the *reference entity*.

There is no initial cost in entering into a credit default swap. Instead, we have two 'legs' as shown in Figure 5.1. These are:

- The protection leg: If a default, or as it is more formally called, a *credit event*, occurs before the contract maturity date, the *protection seller* has to compensate the *protection buyer* for the loss from par on the face value on the *deliverable obligations*. How this is done is discussed later in this section.
- The premium leg: In return for assuming the credit risk associated with the deliverable obligations, the protection seller receives a regular, typically quarterly, payment from the protection buyer. These payments terminate following a *credit event*, the credit derivative term for a default, or at contract maturity, whichever occurs sooner. Any payment which has accrued since the previous coupon date is also paid to the protection seller. The payment size is quoted in the market as an annualised spread called the *default swap spread*.

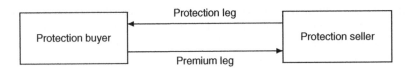

Figure 5.1   The mechanics of a credit default swap

Since a protection buyer receives a payment following a credit event, they have effectively gone short the credit risk of the reference entity. As a result, a long protection CDS contract represents a way to take an outright short position on a credit. Similarly, a protection seller has effectively gone long the credit risk of the reference entity. We shall see later that this risk is very similar to buying a floating rate note on the same issuer to the same maturity date. To summarise:

$$\text{Long protection} = \text{Short credit risk}$$

$$\text{Short protection} = \text{Long credit risk.}$$

---

[2] The effective date is the calendar day after the trade date. This convention is called 'T + 1 calendar'. It means that the effective date can fall on a Saturday or on a holiday. It does not need to be a business day. Since corporates can file for default or bankruptcy on a weekend or holiday, there is certainly some value in being able to have the protection start on a non-business day.

Note that in CDS market terminology, 'buying' a CDS contract means buying protection, i.e. going short the credit. This is opposite to the convention in the cash credit market where 'buying' means going long the credit. This difference in terminology can cause confusion and care needs to be taken to check whenever there is any doubt.

5.2.1 The Quarterly Roll

Since 2003, the market has changed its convention for determining the maturity date of a standard CDS contract. Until 2003, the most liquid CDS contract was the contract with an exact term of three, five, seven or 10 years *from the effective date*. However, this convention presented problems for dealers wishing to hedge recently transacted CDS contracts – unless a hedge was executed on the exact same day as the original trade, a *forward credit exposure* would result due to the difference between the maturity of the initial contract and that of its CDS hedge. Trading a CDS contract to the same maturity date as the recently transacted contract is non standard and so has a higher cost, i.e. a higher spread for a protection buyer than the standard five year contract.

To overcome these issues the market decided to begin trading contracts to rolling quarterly maturity dates. Inspired by the IMM[3] dates used in the interest rate futures markets, they set these standard maturity dates to be 20 March, 20 June, 20 September and 20 December of each year.[4] This new convention was widely adopted and these 'IMM' maturity contracts are now market standard. At any moment in time, the most liquid T-year contract is the one which matures on the first 'IMM' date T years after the trade date. This is shown in Figure 5.2 where we show how the maturity for the most liquid five-year CDS contract changes as we move the trade date through 2007.

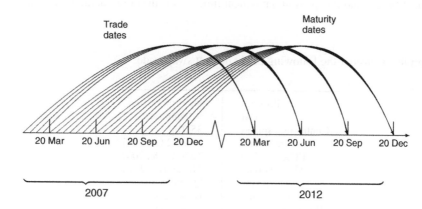

Figure 5.2   The evolving maturity date of a five-year fixed maturity CDS. The arrows link the trade date with the maturity date of the standard 'IMM' contract. As we move through 20 March, June, September or December, we see that the standard contract maturity switches to the following 'IMM' date five years ahead

---

[3] IMM stands for the International Money Market, a division of the Chicago Mercantile Exchange where the Eurodollar interest rate futures contract trades.

[4] Note that although we use the term IMM date, the date is not always the same as the corresponding IMM date. The CDS market always chooses the 20th date of the month while the official IMM date is the 3rd Wednesday of the month.

5.3   MECHANICS OF THE PREMIUM LEG

The premium leg is the series of payments made by the protection buyer to the protection seller to pay for the protection being provided. These payments are typically made quarterly according to an Actual 360 basis. The payments terminate at the contract maturity or immediately following a *credit event*. The sizes of the premium payments are specified in terms of a credit default swap spread. The process for calculating the payments for a T maturity credit default swap is as follows:

1. The maturity date is calculated as the first 'IMM' date T years after the effective date.
2. Starting at the maturity date, we step back in time in three-month steps, landing on earlier 'IMM' dates until we arrive at the last date which falls after the effective date.
3. All of these dates are then adjusted so as not to fall on weekends or holidays. This is typically done by rolling them forward to the next business day. Since holidays are country specific, a holiday *calendar* will need to be specified. For example, a contract traded on a US credit in NY will generally use a US holiday calendar. A CDS contract traded in Paris on a European credit may use the European holiday calendar known as TARGET.
4. Once we have the dates, the payments are calculated using the Actual 360 day count convention. According to this convention the size of the premium payment at time t_2 per \$1 of contract face value is given by

$$S \times \frac{\texttt{DayDiff}(t_1, t_2)}{360}$$

where $\texttt{DayDiff}(t_1, t_2)$ is the number of calendar days between the previous premium payment time t_1 and this premium payment time t_2. S is the credit default swap spread.

Example   Consider the following credit default swap trade:

Position	Short protection
Notional	\$10 million
Contractual spread	35.0 bp
Trade date	Mon 22 Oct 2007
Effective date	Tues 23 Oct 2007
Maturity date	Thu 20 Dec 2012
Frequency	Quarterly
Schedule rule	Backward
Business day rule	Following
Basis	Actual 360
Calendar	TARGET

The premium leg cash flow schedule is shown in Figure 5.3. We see that the cash flows are not all equal amounts, reflecting the small but real differences in the time between payments caused by adjustments to avoid weekends and public holidays. There is also a *short stub* at the beginning reflecting the shorter period to the first premium payment.

Flow date	Day count fraction	Actual flow
Thu 20 Dec 2007	0.161111	5,638.89
Thu 20 Mar 2008	0.252778	8,847.22
Fri 20 Jun 2008	0.255556	8,944.44
Mon 22 Sep 2008	0.261111	9,138.89
Mon 22 Dec 2008	0.252778	8,847.22
Fri 20 Mar 2009	0.244444	8,555.56
Mon 22 Jun 2009	0.261111	9,138.89
Mon 21 Sep 2009	0.252778	8,847.22
Mon 21 Dec 2009	0.252778	8,847.22
Mon 22 Mar 2010	0.252778	8,847.22
Mon 21 Jun 2010	0.252778	8,847.22
Mon 20 Sep 2010	0.252778	8,847.22
Mon 20 Dec 2010	0.252778	8,847.22
Mon 21 Mar 2011	0.252778	8,847.22
Mon 20 Jun 2011	0.252778	8,847.22
Tue 20 Sep 2011	0.255556	8,944.44
Tue 20 Dec 2011	0.252778	8,847.22
Tue 20 Mar 2012	0.252778	8,847.22
Wed 20 Jun 2012	0.255556	8,944.44
Thu 20 Sep 2012	0.255556	8,944.44
Thu 20 Dec 2012	0.252778	8,847.22

Figure 5.3 Premium leg payments for a CDS contract with a face value of $10 million and a credit default swap spread of 35 bp.

An important feature of the premium leg is the *payment of the coupon accrued at default*. In the standard contract, following a credit event, the protection buyer must pay the fraction of the premium which has accrued since the previous premium payment date. This is a contingent cash flow which must be captured by any valuation model for CDS since a CDS contract which does not pay the coupon accrued at default must have a different present value to one that does. This standard feature of a CDS contract has nothing to do with the convention of quoting the accrued interest on CDS discussed later in Section 6.6.3.

5.4 MECHANICS OF THE PROTECTION LEG

The protection leg is the contingent payment made by the protection seller to the protection buyer to make up to par the value of a deliverable obligation following a credit event. There are two ways to effect the payment of the protection leg which are both shown in Figure 5.4. They are:

1. Physical settlement: The protection buyer delivers face value of *deliverable obligations* to the protection seller. In return, the protection seller makes a simultaneous payment of the face value in cash to the protection buyer.
2. Cash settlement: The protection seller pays the protection buyer the face value of the protection minus the recovery price of the *reference obligation* in cash. The reference obligation is a single specified bond or loan of the reference entity. All deliverable obligations must be *pari passu* or senior to the reference obligation. The recovery price is determined by a dealer poll or auction process.

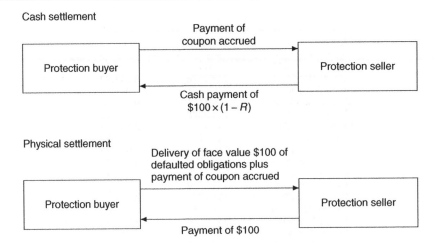

Figure 5.4 After a credit event, the protection leg can be paid either by cash settlement or physical settlement. We assume a contract face value of $100

In both cases there will also be a payment of the coupon accrued at default from the protection buyer to the protection seller. This is, however, handled separately as it is part of the premium leg.

The current market standard for default swaps is to prefer physical settlement over cash settlement. However a recent survey[5] suggests there is a trend towards cash settlement for CDS, especially in the CDS index and STCDO markets discussed later in this book. The allowance for cash settlement is intended to overcome the problem of sourcing physical assets to deliver, especially when the amount of credit default protection sold is similar to or greater than the outstanding notional of deliverable obligations.

Typically, there can be many bonds and loans which qualify as deliverable obligations and so can be delivered into the default swap. The advantage of defining a basket of deliverables is that we can use one standard contract to hedge any of the bonds or loans which satisfy the criteria for a deliverable obligation. This removes the need to have different contracts for individual securities and so enhances liquidity. A side-effect of this is the protection buyer's right to choose the deliverable asset which means that the protection buyer is effectively long a *delivery option*. This is discussed in Section 5.4.3.

5.4.1 The Credit Event

The *credit event* is the legal term for the event which triggers the payment of the protection leg. It is an event which is similar to default but, as we will see, it is not exactly the same as the event of default as defined by the rating agencies. In the credit derivatives market and in this book, the term 'default' is often used when the precise term 'credit event' is meant.

A description of the most commonly used credit events is provided in Table 5.1. The market generally divides these into *hard* and *soft* credit events. Hard credit events are those which

---

[5] BBA Credit Derivatives Report 2006.

Table 5.1 Description of the most commonly used credit events

Credit event	Hard or soft	Description
Bankruptcy	Hard	Corporate becomes insolvent or is unable to pay its debts. The bankruptcy event is not relevant for sovereign issuers.
Failure to pay	Hard	Failure of the reference entity to make due payments, taking into account some grace period.
Obligation acceleration	Hard	Obligations have become due and payable earlier than they would have been due to default or other and have been accelerated. This event is used mostly in certain emerging market contracts.
Obligation default	Hard	Obligations have become due and payable prior to maturity. This event is hardly ever used.
Repudiation/moratorium	Hard	A reference entity or government authority rejects or challenges the validity of the obligations. Used in emerging market sovereign CDS.
Restructuring	Soft	Changes in the debt obligations of the reference creditor but excluding those that are not associated with credit deterioration such as a renegotiation of more favourable terms.

would cause all the debt of the reference entity to become immediately due and payable and hence trade at the same price. It is what the rating agencies would traditionally call default.

Restructuring is the only soft credit event. Following a restructuring event, debt can continue trading with a term structure of prices. Short dated assets will tend to trade at higher prices than long dated assets, and assets with higher coupons will trade with a higher price than those with lower coupons.

5.4.2 Triggering the Protection Leg

Under almost all circumstances the protection buyer will trigger the payment of the protection leg as soon as they become aware that a credit event has occurred on any of the obligations of the issuer. In certain cases the protection buyer may delay triggering. For example, they may expect that by waiting, a restructuring may turn into a full default possibly producing a larger payoff. Once a decision to trigger has been made, the timeline around the physical settlement of a credit default swap following a credit event then consists of three steps:

1. The protection buyer must give the protection seller a Credit Event Notice which informs the protection seller that a credit event has occurred. The event must be evidenced by at least two sources of Publicly Available Information, e.g. a news article on Reuters, the *Wall Street Journal*, the *Financial Times* or some other recognised publication or electronic information service. The date that the Credit Event Notice is delivered to the protection seller is referred to as the Event Determination Date.
2. Within 30 calendar days of the Event Determination Date, the protection buyer must give Notice of Physical Settlement. The date on which the notice of Intended Physical Settlement is delivered is called the Conditions of Payment date. This must give information

about what the deliverable obligations will be. According to ISDA 2003, this notice may be updated at any time between the Conditions of Payment date and the Physical Settlement date, with the last one being binding.

3. Within 30 business days of the Conditions of Payment date, the protection buyer must effect the physical delivery in return for par. This is the Physical Settlement date.

In the case of physical settlement, the whole process is shown in Figure 5.5. It is worth noting that there are up to 72 calendar days after initial notification until a payment on the protection leg must be made.

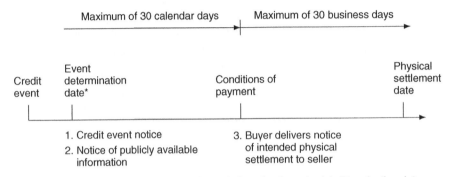

Figure 5.5   The default swap physical settlement timeline

In some circumstances, the amount of outstanding protection that has been written which specifies physical settlement can be as large or even larger than the face value of deliverable obligations. This can also lead to a 'short squeeze' as protection buyers who do not hold a deliverable cash bond attempt to buy deliverable obligations to deliver into the contract. In this case, this demand can increase the price of the defaulted assets, thereby reducing the value of the loss payment. Recently, market participants have introduced a number of mechanisms to alleviate these situations. For example, if for some reason beyond the control of the protection buyer and seller it is not possible or legal to effect the physical settlement, then there is a mechanism to allow a fallback to cash settlement.

5.4.3   The Delivery Option

Once the credit event has been triggered, the protection buyer can choose one or more bonds or loans from a range of deliverable obligations in order to physically settle a default swap. We call this the delivery option. This option only has value if different deliverables trade at different prices following a credit event. We would therefore expect price differences to occur only for a *soft* credit event like restructuring since after a soft credit event, the assets of the reference entity can continue to trade with a term structure.

For a protection buyer who is using the CDS to hedge a specific security, the value of the delivery option following a credit event is simply the difference between the value of the security they hold and the value of the cheapest deliverable.

> **Example**   Consider a protection buyer holding $100 face value of an asset which trades at a price of $43 and $100 of protection. Suppose that a restructuring credit event occurs and that another deliverable asset is trading at a price of $37. To maximise his profit, the protection buyer can sell the original asset for $43, buy the cheaper asset for $37, and deliver that for par, making an additional profit of $6 from the delivery option.

However, this delivery option, while positive for the protection buyer, is negative for the protection seller as it exposes them to a greater payout. These concerns of protection sellers were shown to be real following the restructuring of loans of the US insurer Conseco, Inc. in September 2000. Holders of default swap protection on Conseco triggered the protection and using the ISDA 1999 definitions on deliverable obligations, they were allowed to deliver long maturity and hence deep discount bonds trading in the 65–80 range in return for par. At the same time, shorter dated loans which were held by banks were trading at higher prices. It was claimed that banks were able to exploit the delivery option by selling their short dated loan assets, and buying the longer dated assets to deliver into the protection. In doing so they were able to receive more than the loss on the loans they were using the CDS to hedge. As a consequence, the inclusion of restructuring as a credit event was discouraged by protection sellers.

5.4.4   The Restructuring Clause

In order to minimise the value of the delivery option while retaining the clear advantages of having a basket of deliverables, the US and then the European market decided to change the delivery mechanism *if the credit event is a restructuring*.

Unfortunately, this has resulted in regional differences in the standard CDS contract. In the US the issue of the delivery option was addressed by the introduction of the Modified-Restructuring (Mod-Re) clause in May 2001. This restricted the maturity of deliverable obligations following a restructuring credit event.

In 2003, Europe introduced another mechanism for dealing with restructuring known as Modified-Modified-Restructuring (Mod-Mod-Re). This allows a slightly broader range of deliverables following a restructuring than the US Mod-Re standard. The reason for these regional differences is due to the banking sectors and their regulators in the different regions having a different emphasis regarding the importance of being able to hedge a debt restructuring using a CDS.

To complicate matters even further, some contracts in the US now trade without including a restructuring credit event. These contracts are known as No-Restructuring (No-Re). The treatment of restructuring which applied before 2003 is now known as Old-Restructuring (Old-Re). Table 5.2 outlines the four main restructuring choices used in the market. It also shows the abbreviations used in the market for these specifications.

The choice of restructuring clause should affect the CDS spread for that contract. After all, the protection buyer who is long the delivery option should expect to have to pay for this optionality by paying a slightly higher spread than if the contract had no delivery option. The value of the delivery option is linked to the breadth of the range of deliverables. The broadest range of deliverables occurs when the old restructuring clause is used. The delivery option has

Table 5.2 The different restructuring clauses and a short description of their constraints on deliverable obligations. For a full description, readers should refer to the ISDA 2003 definitions

Clause	Short name	Description
Old-Restructuring	Old-Re (OR)	This is the original standard for deliverables in default swaps in which the maximum maturity deliverable is 30 years.
Modified-Restructuring	Mod-Re (MR)	This is the current standard in the US market. It limits the maturity of deliverable obligations to the maximum of the remaining maturity of the swap contract and the minimum of 30 months and the longest remaining maturity of a restructured obligation. It only applies when the credit event has been triggered by the protection buyer.
Modified-Modified-Restructuring	Mod-Mod-Re (MMR)	This is the standard for the European market. It limits the maturity of deliverable obligations to the maximum of the remaining maturity of the CDS contract and 60 months for restructured obligations and 30 months for non-restructured obligations. It also allows the delivery of conditionally transferable obligations rather than only fully transferable obligations. This should widen the range of bonds/loans that can be delivered. It only applies when the credit event has been triggered by the protection buyer.
No-Restructuring	No-Re (NR)	This contract removes restructuring as a credit event.

the least value when restructuring is not included as a credit event. We therefore find that

$$S_{\text{Old-Re}} > S_{\text{Mod-Mod-Re}} > S_{\text{Mod-Re}} > S_{\text{No-Re}}.$$

The exact spread difference due to this option is hard to determine since we would need to estimate the probability that any credit event is a restructuring and then estimate the dispersion in the prices of the deliverable obligations. This value would then need to be present valued and amortised over the life of the CDS. This problem has been studied in O'Kane et al. (2003). It is possible to observe the CDS quotes on a reference entity with different restructuring clauses. Indeed, care must be taken when comparing different CDS quotes to ensure that the same restructuring clause is being used.

5.5   BONDS AND THE CDS SPREAD

The premium payments in a default swap contract are defined in terms of a default swap spread. It is possible to show that the default swap spread can, subject to some assumptions, be proxied by the quoted margin of a newly issued par floating rate note with the same maturity and seniority which has been issued by the same reference entity. Consider the following strategy shown in Figure 5.6. It begins as follows:

1. An investor buys face value $100 of a floating rate note with a full price of par. The FRN has maturity time T. The purchase of the asset for par can be funded on balance sheet or on repo – in which case we make the assumption that the repo rate can be locked into the bond's maturity. The funding cost of the $100 is set at Libor plus B.
2. The investor hedges the default risk of the floating rate note by purchasing face value $100 of CDS protection to maturity date T. The CDS spread is S. The floating rate note pays a coupon of Libor plus F.

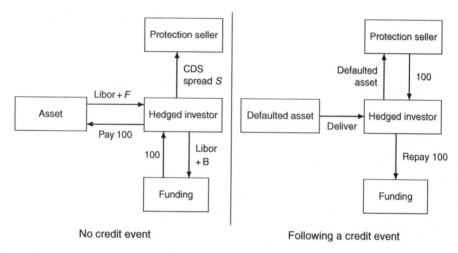

Figure 5.6   Theoretical default-risk-free hedge for an investor who buys protection. We have shown initial payments and coupon payments on the left. On the right we show payments following a credit event

We assume that all coupon payments have the same payment schedule. Consider what happens in the scenarios of credit event and no credit event:

- No credit event: The CDS hedge terminates at time T. At the same time the hedged investor receives the par redemption from the asset and uses it to repay the borrowed par amount. All cash flows at maturity net out to zero.
- Credit event: The hedged investor delivers the floating rate asset to the protection seller in return for par of $100. They then use the $100 to repay the funding.

Both scenarios make it clear that, subject to some assumptions which are listed below, the hedged investor has no credit risk. As the strategy is risk free and has no initial cost, the hedged investor should not earn (or lose) anything on the payment dates. This implies that

$$\text{CDS spread } (S) = \text{Par floater quoted margin}(F) - \text{Funding spread } (B).$$

Example Suppose the par floater pays Libor plus 25 bp and the protection buyer funds the asset on balance sheet at Libor plus 10 bp. For the protection buyer the breakeven default swap spread equals $F - B = 25 - 10 = 15$ bp. However, suppose the protection buyer has a very high credit rating and funds at Libor minus 10 bp. In this case, the breakeven cost of protection is $F - B = 25 - (-10) = 35$ bp. If the market CDS spread is 25 bp, the protection buyer who funds at $+10$ bp has a negative carry of $25 - 10 - 25 = -10$ bp while the protection buyer who funds at -10 bp has a positive carry of $25 + 10 - 25 = +10$ bp.

This analysis has shown that there should be a close relationship between cash and default swap spreads. However, it is not exact as it relies on several assumptions which could result in small but observable differences. Some of these assumptions are listed below.

1. We assumed existence of a newly issued par floater with the same maturity date as the CDS contract.
2. We assumed a funding level of Libor plus B until the maturity time T.
3. If the credit event occurs between premium payment dates, the payment of par from the protection does not exactly cover cost of unwinding the funding leg.
4. We have also ignored the effect of the accrued coupon at default which is paid on the CDS following a credit event.
5. We have ignored counterparty risk on the CDS.
6. We ignore tax effects which may treat coupon and principal differently.
7. We ignore transaction costs.

Despite these assumptions, cash market spreads usually provide the starting point for where the default swap spreads should trade. Although this analysis was done using a par floating rate note, it is also possible to repeat it for asset swaps. However, the initial full price of the fixed rate bond in the asset swap must be par for the comparison to work. This is because the initial loss on an asset swap of a bond trading with a full price P is $P - R$, while the credit loss on a CDS is $100 - R$. The credit risk is then only comparable to a default swap when $P = 100$. However, even when this is true, the difference between a CDS and asset swap also depends on the expected value of the interest rate swap in the asset swap following a credit event.

5.6   THE CDS–CASH BASIS

In our demonstration of the relationship between cash and CDS spreads, we made a number of assumptions. However, there are other reasons why this relationship may not hold, thereby creating and maintaining a *default swap basis*. We define the CDS basis as:

$$\text{CDS basis} = \text{CDS spread} - \text{Bond Libor spread}.$$

This definition is not explicit in that it does not define which bond Libor spread should be used. For a fixed rate bond, the natural choice is the asset swap spread of a bond trading close to par. For floating rate bonds, the natural choice is the par floater spread.

There are now a significant number of market participants who actively trade the default swap basis, viewing it as a new relative value opportunity. To do this, it is important to understand what factors drive the dynamics of the CDS basis and what their effect is. Following O'Kane and McAdie (2001), we divide these factors into fundamental and market factors.

5.6.1 Fundamental Factors

Fundamental factors are those which relate to the contractual differences between the cash bond and the default swap contract. They are:

1. Funding: Default swaps are unfunded transactions and bonds are funded. For the same spread, CDS are favoured by investors who have funding costs above Libor while bonds are favoured by those who fund below. As a result, the basis is affected by the differing funding levels of the market participants.
2. The delivery option: In a CDS contract, the protection buyer is able to choose which physical asset out of a basket of obligations to deliver following a credit event. In certain circumstances, this option can be valuable. However, there is no such option in a bond. This therefore makes a long protection CDS position more valuable than a short cash position. As a result the CDS spread should be wider and hence the basis should increase. As discussed earlier, the value of this option depends on the choice of restructuring clause.
3. Technical default: The standard credit events may be viewed as being broader than those which constitute default on a bond. As a result, protection sellers in a CDS may demand a higher spread as compensation for the increased risk of the protection being triggered. This widens the basis.
4. Loss on default: The protection payment on a CDS following a credit event is a fraction $(1 - R)$ of the face value of the contract. The default risk on a bond (or asset swap) purchased at a full price of P is to a loss of $P - R$. As a result, the loss on a bond is different if the bond is not initially trading at par. We would therefore expect the CDS basis to reflect this difference.
5. Premium accrued at default: Following a credit event, a CDS pays the protection seller the premium which has accrued since the previous payment date. However, when a bond defaults, the owner's claim is on the face value, and so any accrued coupons are lost. The effect on the inclusion of coupon accrued on default is to lower the CDS spread and so reduce the basis.
6. Default swap spreads cannot be negative: In the case of an asset swap or par floater, it is possible to show that if the credit quality of the issuer is better than AA-rated commercial banks, the spread over Libor paid by the bond may be negative. For example, it is possible to asset swap a US Treasury bond and find that the asset swap spread is negative. However, CDS spreads can never go negative as the protection seller is taking on the default risk of the reference entity and, though small, the probability of triggering can never be negative. The CDS spread must at the very least cover the administration costs of the CDS trade.

5.6.2   Market Factors

The other factors which drive the basis are *market factors*. These refer to the nature of the market in which the cash and CDS contracts are traded and so include effects such as liquidity, and supply and demand. We list the main market factors below:

1. Relative liquidity: The liquidity of the cash and CDS markets is different across the term structure and can result in differences in the basis as a function of maturity. For example, the cash market consists of points of liquidity at the maturity dates of the issued bonds. However, the CDS market has its liquidity points at fixed term points with most liquidity concentrated at the three-, five-, seven- and 10-year maturity 'IMM' dates.
2. Synthetic CDO technical short: When dealers issue synthetic CDOs, they then hedge their spread risk by selling CDS credit protection on each of the 100 or more credits in the reference portfolio. CDO issuance is therefore usually accompanied by a tightening (reduction) in CDS spreads. This reduces the CDS basis.
3. New issuance/loans: When bonds are newly issued by a corporate, CDS spreads often widen in order to make them more attractive relative to the bonds. There is also a dynamic in which banks who have assumed large credit exposures to corporates by granting them loans, hedge this risk in the CDS market, thereby driving out CDS spreads and temporarily increasing the basis.
4. Convertible issuance: The issuance of convertible bonds often results in a demand to buy protection on the issuer. This is because convertible hedge funds seek to hedge out the credit risk in order to isolate the equity volatility risk in the convertible bond. This drives out the CDS spread resulting in a temporary increase of the basis.
5. Demand for protection: It is much easier to go short a credit by buying protection in the CDS market than by shorting a cash bond. As a result, if there is negative news on a credit, it will tend to result in a flurry of protection buying in the CDS market thus increasing the CDS basis.
6. Funding risk: Since the CDS is unfunded, it effectively locks in a funding rate of Libor flat until maturity or a credit event, whichever occurs first. There is therefore no funding risk. This is not true if the exposure is taken in the cash market. This should reduce the CDS spread and so reduce the basis.

All of these fundamental and market factors are reasons why the CDS and cash market spreads should diverge. It is difficult to assign degrees of importance to the individual factors as it is hard to tease them apart empirically.

5.7   LOAN CDS

One of the most recent developments in the CDS market has been the advent of loan CDS, known as LCDS for short. As the name suggests, these are CDS in which the only allowed deliverable obligations are syndicated secured loans. For US loan-only CDS, the credit events are just bankruptcy and failure to pay. In Europe, restructuring is included as a credit event. Physical settlement following a credit event involves the delivery of a senior secured loan to the protection seller in return for par. Cash settlement using a dealer poll is also possible.

The mechanics of a loan CDS are very similar to a standard CDS with one main exception. The LCDS may terminate early if the underlying loan is refinanced. Although the treatment of this event was initially handled differently between Europe and the US, in September 2007 market participants led by the ISDA agreed a new standard which applies in both regions. According to the new standard, the contract will only cancel if the reference obligation is fully repaid and no substitute reference obligation can be identified. In Section 6.9, we discuss how to amend our standard CDS pricing model to handle this cancellation feature.

There is another important difference between US and European LCDS. The European LCDS can only be triggered by the default of the reference obligation, which is a loan. The US LCDS can be triggered by all borrowings of the reference entity.

In general, loan CDS trade at a tighter (lower) credit default spread than standard CDS on the same name. This effect can be ascribed to the generally superior recovery rates of secured loans as opposed to the recovery rates of the *bond and loan* deliverable obligations of traditional CDS.

5.8   SUMMARY

Before we can start to model a credit default swap, we need to understand how it works. This chapter has explained the mechanics of the contract. In particular, we have focused on the triggering of the protection leg and how this process works. Subject to several assumptions, we have also demonstrated the link between the default swap spread and the spread of a floating rate note. We are now ready for the next chapter in which we build a model for pricing CDS contracts.

6

A Valuation Model for Credit Default Swaps

6.1 INTRODUCTION

Since a new default swap contract costs nothing to enter into, it has no initial value. However, soon after inception this will no longer be true as the CDS market spreads of the reference entity move. In this chapter we set out in detail how the value of a CDS contract is defined. We describe why we need a pricing model, and we discuss in detail what has become the market standard model for valuing a CDS position. Armed with a model we are then in a position to understand the pricing and risk characteristics of CDS. We postpone calibration of the model until Chapter 7 and will discuss the risk of CDS in Chapter 8.

6.2 UNWINDING A CDS CONTRACT

Having the ability to calculate the daily value of a CDS contract is essential for those who are required to mark their derivatives positions to market. By definition, the mark-to-market represents the unwind cost of the contract, i.e. how much we would have to pay or receive to remove the contract from the trading book. Therefore, while we may not wish to close out our contract, it is only by considering the close-out cost that we can mark it to market.

For example, consider a protection buyer, who we will call party A, who buys $10 million of protection in a five-year default swap contract at a default swap spread of 75 bp. The protection seller is party B. One year later, spreads have moved and the cost of 4Y protection in the CDS market is 320 bp. The protection buyer will see that the contract now has a positive value since they are only paying 75 bp for protection for which the market is now charging 320 bp. To put it another way, party A went short the reference credit by buying protection, spreads have widened due to a deterioration in the market perceived credit quality of the reference entity, and this has resulted in a positive gain.

Although we know that the value of the contract is now positive to party A, we want to be able to determine exactly how much it is worth. The value of contract is the value at which the contract can be unwound. This is also known as the *unwind value, tear-up value*, or *mark-to-market value*. There are three ways that this gain can be realised:

1. Party A to the CDS requests party B to agree a cash payment at which the contract can be closed out. In this example, the cash amount will be positive. If party B is a dealer, then this unwind value will be provided by unwinding CDS hedges executed by party B when the CDS was first traded with party A.
2. Party A to the CDS agrees with a third party, C, an unwind value and then requests to party B that the default swap be reassigned to party C. The mark-to-market amount is paid from

party C to party A. This has the effect of removing party A from the CDS which is now between parties B and C. If party C is a dealer, they will almost certainly go into the market and hedge the contract using a combination of on-market CDS swaps.

3. Party A enters into an offsetting transaction in which they sell 4Y protection at 320 bp. The protection leg is therefore perfectly hedged. What remains is a series of net premium leg payments which continue until default or maturity, whichever occurs earlier. In this case, the net premium payments will be $320 - 75 = 245$ bp. These payments are not risk free.

In theory, the unwind value of (1) and (2) should be identical since from A's perspective, they accomplish exactly the same objective. These values should also be equal to the present value of (3) since this is how counterparties B and C will hedge the risk of the initial CDS contract. However, choice (3) is fundamentally different from the first two *since there is no immediate realisation of the value of the CDS contract*. Consider choice (3) and the following two scenarios:

- If the reference entity were to survive for another four years, the realised income would be (ignoring time value) 4×245 bp $\times$ \$10 million $= \$980\,000$.
- If the reference entity experiences a credit event immediately, the realised income would be \$0 (ignoring accrued interest paid at default).

The difference between (3) and choices (1) and (2) is that in (1) and (2) a fixed amount of cash is received and there is no further credit exposure. In choice (3), we receive an uncertain payment. The present value of this uncertain payment equals the unwind value of the contract and depends on the market's expectation of the default risk of the reference entity. Once discounted, the two values just calculated provide the upper and lower bounds for the value of the contract. The unwind value of the contract must lie between these bounds.

To determine the value of the CDS contract, we require a model. Another way to look at the mark-to-market is to write the value of the contract in terms of the present values of the protection and premium legs. In the example above, from the perspective of counterparty A, the value of the long protection contract is given by

$$V(t) = \text{PV of 4Y of protection} - \text{PV of 4Y of risky premium payments at 75 bp.}$$

The definition of the CDS spread in the market is that it is the spread which makes the initial value of the CDS contract equal to zero. Since the current 4Y market spread is 320 bp, we can write

$$\text{PV of 4Y of protection} - \text{PV of 4Y of risky premium payments at 320 bp} = 0.$$

Substituting the value of the protection leg into the previous equation we have

$$V(t) = \text{PV of 4Y of risky premium payments at 320 bp}$$
$$- \text{PV of 4Y of risky premium payments at 75 bp}$$
$$= \text{PV of 4Y of risky premium payments at 245 bp}$$

i.e. the value of the contract is the expected present value of the net credit risky payments. We can generalise this example to write the general CDS pricing formula. Consider a *long protection* position initially traded at time 0 with a maturity time T. We wish to value this contract today, time t. The value of the contract per \$1 of face value is

$$V(t) = (S(t, T) - S(0, T)) \times \text{RPV01}(t, T)$$

where

- $S(0, T)$ is the contractual CDS spread at which protection was bought at time 0.
- $S(t, T)$ is the current time t CDS spread to maturity date T.
- $\text{RPV01}(t, T)$ is the time t present value of a risky 1 bp paid on the premium leg of the CDS until the maturity time T or default, whichever is sooner.

For a short protection position, the contract value is the negative of the value of a long protection position.

The modelling challenge for pricing a CDS is to incorporate into the calculation of the RPV01 the risk that the reference entity may experience a credit event resulting in the loss of the subsequent premium payments. This requires a model.

6.3   REQUIREMENTS OF A CDS PRICING MODEL

Before we launch into the model specification, it is worth spending a moment to determine the criteria for a successful CDS pricing model. They are:

1. The model should be able to capture the timing of any default. This is important since the timing of any payments can have an important effect on present values.
2. The model should take into account the recovery rate following a default. This will allow us to distinguish between the different levels of the capital structure.
3. The model should have the flexibility to exactly refit the term structure of CDS spreads.
4. The model should allow for quick, stable and accurate pricing of CDS. A model which is overly complex for simple CDS will present significant challenges when used for pricing more complex instruments.
5. The model should be as simple as possible, while satisfying all of these requirements.

One of the main modelling assumptions made in the following valuation model is *to assume the independence of interest rates and the default time*. The benefits of this assumption are that it simplifies the pricing equation as it enables us to express all of our pricing formulae in terms of a risk-free discount curve and a credit risky survival curve. The assumption of independence is justified on the following reasons:

- For reasonable model parameters, the correlation between interest rates and the default intensity process has only a small effect on the pricing of a risky zero coupon bond. This was demonstrated in Section 3.8.
- The interest rate sensitivity of a CDS contract is much smaller than that of a zero coupon bond of a similar maturity. As a result, the correlation dependence of the value of a CDS must also be much smaller than that of a zero coupon bond, which is already small.

For these reasons, the assumption of independence is market standard.

6.4   MODELLING A CDS CONTRACT

In the following we will model the value of a CDS contract using the reduced form modelling approach introduced in Chapter 3. We assume that the hazard rate process, interest rates and recovery rate are all independent. This is the standard model for pricing CDS in the markets which we discuss and follows the work of Duffie (1998), Hull and White (2000a) and O'Kane and Turnbull (2003).

Within a valuation model we need to use times. We define our unit of time to be years and the time between two dates d_1 and d_2 is given by

$$t = \frac{\mathtt{DayDiff}(d_1, d_2)}{\text{Days in year}}$$

where $\mathtt{DayDiff}(d_1, d_2)$ is a function which returns the number of calendar days between d_1 and d_2. The value of the denominator is a measure of the number of days per year. We typically fix it equal to 365.242.

When building models, we must keep in mind that it has to be numerically stable. For example, we would not like a model which caused the value of a derivative to change simply because of some numerical inaccuracy in the implementation. For this reason, we will attempt to enforce a relative accuracy of 10^{-7} on our CDS pricing model. This is consistent with an error of $1 per $10 million of face value. For notational simplicity, we will also assume that the face value of the CDS contract is $1.

We value all CDS cash flows to the valuation date t. Our convention is to calculate the mark-to-market of the CDS as of '$T + 0$ close of business'. This means that we take a snapshot of the Libor and CDS quotes at or close to 5pm on the valuation date and use those quotes to value the contract. Time zero on our Libor discount factor curve and our CDS survival probability curve corresponds to one minute past midnight on '$T + 1$' calendar. This is the time at which the effective date begins. At this time both the discount factor and survival probability equal 1.0. They both immediately begin to decrease since the contract becomes exposed to the risk of the reference credit at this time.

Although the risk of a CDS contract begins on the effective date which is '$T + 1$ calendar', the settlement of the unwind value of an existing CDS typically occurs at '$T + 3$ business', i.e. three business days after the contract was traded. If we need to determine the unwind value we simply roll the '$T + 0$' mark-to-market three days forward at the risk-free Libor rate.

We now establish the following notation:

t is the effective date of the CDS contract.

$Z(t, T)$ is the Libor discount curve which is anchored to the CDS effective date.

$Q(t, T)$ is the time t survival probability of the reference entity to time T.

t_n for $n = 1, \ldots, N$ are the premium payment dates. We set $t_0 = t$.

T corresponds to when the protection ends. Typically $t_N = T$.

S_0 represents $S(0, T)$, the fixed contractual spread of a contract traded at time 0 which matures at time T.

$\Delta(t_{n-1}, t_n)$ is the day count fraction between dates t_{n-1} and t_n in the appropriate day count convention, typically Actual 360.

R is the expected recovery rate as a percentage of par.

We now develop a pricing model for the CDS contract. To start with, we split the pricing of a CDS contract into its two legs – the premium leg and the protection leg.

6.5   VALUING THE PREMIUM LEG

To begin our valuation of the premium leg, we assume that we are on a coupon payment date. There are therefore two types of contribution to the premium leg value. First, there are the scheduled premium payments which are paid as long as the reference credit survives to the payment date. Second, if there is a credit event, there is a payment of the premium which has accrued from the previous premium payment date.

We start with the expected present value of the risky premium payments made conditional on surviving to their payment dates. Payments with this risk profile were introduced in Section 3.5.1 and discussed in Chapter 3 where we showed that the present value of \$1 which is to be paid at time t_n, but which cancels with zero recovery on a default before t_n, is given by

$$\hat{Z}(t, t_n) = \mathbb{E}_t \left[\exp\left(-\int_t^{t_n} r(s)ds \right) \mathbf{1}_{\tau > t_n} \right]$$

where $r(t)$ is the continuously compounded risk-free rate. Assuming independence between the short interest rate process and the default time, the expectation separates into a product of expectations to give

$$\hat{Z}(t, t_n) = Z(t, t_n)Q(t, t_n).$$

Following our independence assumption, the present value of the premium leg then becomes

$$S_0 \sum_{n=1}^{N} \Delta(t_{n-1}, t_n)Q(t, t_n)Z(t, t_n).$$

We have summed over each of the premium payments, weighting each by the probability of surviving to the payment date and then discounted the payment back to today at the risk-free rate.

We then need to consider the effect of premium accrued at default. This is the payment made from the protection buyer to the protection seller immediately following a credit event. It equals the amount of premium which has accrued from the previous premium payment date to the default time. The amount of premium accrued at default is therefore determined by the timing of the credit event, if indeed there is a credit event. This is a contingent payment with the risk profile discussed in Section 3.5.2 where it was shown that the price today of \$1 paid at default which occurs in the interval $[s, s + ds]$ is given by

$$Z(t, s)(-dQ(t, s)). \tag{6.1}$$

If the credit event happens at the start of a premium period, then no premium will have accrued. If the credit event happens at the end of the period then a full premium payment will have to be paid. If the credit event happens at time s between two premium payment dates $t_{n-1} < s < t_n$ then protection buyer needs to pay an extra amount of accrued premium given by

$$S_0 \Delta(t_{n-1}, s)$$

to the protection seller. This is calculated according to the same basis convention as used for the other premium payments. The expected present value of the premium accrued due to a default in the interval s to $s + ds$ in the nth premium period is therefore given by

$$S_0 \Delta(t_{n-1}, s) Z(t, s)(-dQ(t, s)).$$

However, default can happen any time during this coupon period. The value of the premium accrued due to this is therefore

$$S_0 \int_{t_{n-1}}^{t_n} \Delta(t_{n-1}, s) Z(t, s)(-dQ(t, s)).$$

We then also need to sum over all of the premium payments to calculate the expected present value of the premium accrued. As a result, the value of the premium accrued is given by

$$S_0 \sum_{n=1}^{N} \int_{t_{n-1}}^{t_n} \Delta(t_{n-1}, s) Z(t, s)(-dQ(t, s)).$$

Consequently, the present value of the premium leg is given by

$$\text{Premium Leg PV} = S_0 \cdot \text{RPV01}(t, T) \tag{6.2}$$

where the risky PV01 is given by

$$\text{RPV01}(t, T) = \sum_{n=1}^{N} \Delta(t_{n-1}, t_n) Z(t, t_n) Q(t, t_n)$$

$$+ \sum_{n=1}^{N} \int_{t_{n-1}}^{t_n} \Delta(t_{n-1}, s) Z(t, s)(-dQ(t, s)). \tag{6.3}$$

Performing the integration in the second term in the risky PV01 in Equation 6.3 can be slow. Fortunately, we can approximate this integral as follows

$$\int_{t_{n-1}}^{t_n} \Delta(t_{n-1}, s) Z(t, s)(-dQ(t, s)) \simeq \frac{1}{2} \Delta(t_{n-1}, t_n) Z(t, t_n)(Q(t, t_{n-1}) - Q(t, t_n)).$$

This approximation is based on the observation that if there is a default during a coupon period, on average it will occur close to halfway through the period and so the accrued premium at default will be $S_0 \Delta(t_{n-1}, t_n)/2$. The probability of a default during the nth premium payment period is $Q(t, t_{n-1}) - Q(t, t_n)$, and we then discount this payment back to today using the discount factor to the end of the period. To be consistent with the approximation we should use a discount factor to time $(t_{n-1} + t_n)/2$. Our reason for discounting to the end of the period is that it means we have one less discount factor to calculate and it also simplifies the form of the final PV01 equation below.

This approximation is reasonably accurate, with an error in the premium leg risky PV01 of $O(10^{-5})$. Given that the spread which will multiply this term is of the order of $O(10^{-2})$, the final PV error on a CDS contract with a face value of $1 will be about $O(10^{-7})$, which is at the required tolerance. We can therefore write the premium leg risky PV01 which combines the risky premium payments plus the payment of coupon accrued at default as

$$\text{RPV01}(t, T) = \sum_{n=1}^{N} \Delta(t_{n-1}, t_n) Z(t, t_n) Q(t, t_n)$$

$$+ \frac{1}{2} \sum_{n=1}^{N} \Delta(t_{n-1}, t_n) Z(t, t_n) \left(Q(t, t_{n-1}) - Q(t, t_n) \right)$$

which simplifies to become

$$\text{RPV01}(t, T) = \frac{1}{2} \sum_{n=1}^{N} \Delta(t_{n-1}, t_n) Z(t, t_n) \left(Q(t, t_{n-1}) + Q(t, t_n) \right). \tag{6.4}$$

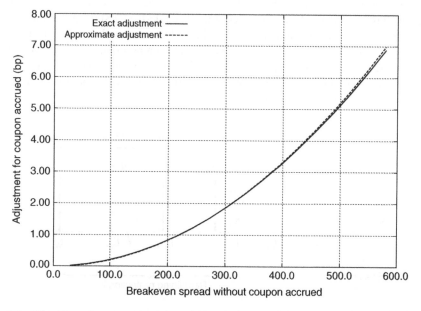

Figure 6.1 The effect of coupon accrued on the breakeven spread of a CDS as a function of the CDS spread without accrued coupon. We show the effect calculated using a full integration and one using the approximation derived in the text. The quadratic dependency is very clear. Note that the effect of incorporating the accrued premium at default is to lower the breakeven spread

There is a simple approximation for the spread adjustment implied by the specification of coupon accrued. The argument is as follows. Define f as the annual frequency of the premium payments. The probability of the issuer defaulting in the ith premium payment period of length $1/f$ years conditional on surviving to the start of the period is given by λ_i/f. If it does default in a coupon period, on average it will default midway, resulting in a payment of approximately $S/2f$. We multiply each potential payment by the probability of surviving to the start of each coupon period and then discounting back to today. The effect of coupon accrued is therefore $(S/2f) \cdot (1/f) \sum_{i=1}^{N} Q_i Z_i \lambda_i$. To get this into spread terms we need to divide by the risky PV01 given by $1/f \sum_{i=1}^{N} Q_i Z_i$. If we assume that the CDS curve is flat so that $\lambda_i = \lambda$, then the spread impact is $S\lambda/(2f)$. Using the credit triangle relationship, we can write $\lambda \simeq S/(1 - R)$ so we have finally

$$S(\text{Without accrued at default}) - S(\text{With accrued at default}) \simeq \frac{S^2}{2(1-R)f}.$$

We see that the effect of including coupon accrued at default is to reduce the fair CDS spread below the fair CDS spread of a contract which does not include coupon accrued at default. This is no surprise since the same protection value must be paid by both contracts. By having an extra premium payment at default, the contract with coupon accrued at default should have a slightly lower spread to offset this additional payment. Figure 6.1 shows that this approximation for the spread difference works very well. This approximation works best when the spread curve is flat.

6.5.1 Valuation Between Premium Payment Dates

Equation 6.2 for the value of the premium leg takes into account the effect of the payment of the accrued premium at default. However, it has been derived assuming that the valuation date falls on a premium payment date. As a result, we have assumed that there is no accrued premium today. This is no longer true when we are between premium payment dates. This is shown in Figure 6.2. Let us define t_{n*} as the first cash flow time after today. We need to ensure the correct treatment of the next payment. We must therefore update the formula for the present value of the premium leg. The exact formula is given by

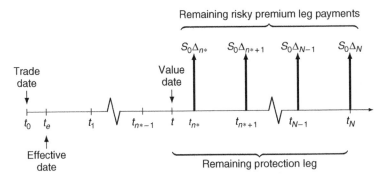

Figure 6.2   Seasoned CDS contract in which the valuation date is between two premium payment dates. We assume a face value of $1

$$\text{Premium PV} = S_0 \int_t^{t_{n*}} \Delta\,(t_{n*-1}, s)\, Z\,(t, s)\, (-dQ(t, s))$$

$$+ S_0 \sum_{n=n*+1}^{N} \int_{t_{n-1}}^{t_n} \Delta(t_{n-1}, s) Z(t, s)(-dQ(t, s))$$

$$+ S_0 \sum_{n=n*}^{N} \Delta(t_{n-1}, t_n) Z(t, t_n) Q(t, t_n).$$

The first term is the new one which takes into account the fact that even if the reference credit defaults today, we are paid the fraction of the next coupon which has accrued since the previous coupon date. Note how the accrual factor in the integral starts at the previous payment date while the integral starts from today. This payment of what has already accrued is effectively risk free since we will receive it either as the coupon accrued at default or as part of the next coupon payment. The only difference is a small amount of time value. Using the same approximation as above, we can write

$$\text{Premium PV} = S_0 \Delta(t_{n^*-1}, t) Z(t, t_{n^*}) (1 - Q(t, t_{n^*}))$$

$$+ \frac{S_0}{2} \Delta(t, t_{n^*}) Z(t, t_{n^*})(1 - Q(t, t_{n^*}))$$

$$+ S_0 \Delta(t_{n^*-1}, t_{n^*}) Z(t, t_{n^*}) Q(t, t_{n^*})$$

$$+ \frac{S_0}{2} \sum_{n=n^*+1}^{N} \Delta(t_{n-1}, t_n) Z(t, t_n) (Q(t, t_{n-1}) + Q(t, t_n)).$$

The first term is the payment of the part of the coupon which has accrued in the time period between the previous coupon payment date and the valuation date. This is paid in full if there is a credit event between now and the next coupon date. The second term expected present value of the part of the premium which accrues from the value date to the next coupon date. As before, this assumes that if we default during the period, on average it will occur halfway and so half the accrued coupon will be paid. The third term is the full coupon which is paid as long as there is no credit event before the next coupon date. The fourth and final term represents the remaining coupons which are handled as described earlier in this section.

6.6   VALUING THE PROTECTION LEG

The protection leg is the contingent payment of par minus recovery on the face value of the credit following a credit event (Figure 6.3). It is an uncertain quantity paid at default. The modelling of such payments has already been discussed in Section 3.7.3, where it was shown that the price of a security which pays an uncertain quantity $\Phi(\tau)$ at the time of default τ if $\tau \leq T$ is given by

$$\hat{D}(t, T) = \mathbb{E}_t \left[\exp\left(-\int_t^\tau r(s)ds \right) \Phi(\tau) \mathbf{1}_{\tau \leq T} \right].$$

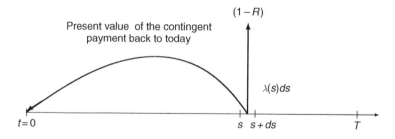

Figure 6.3   Pricing the protection leg

Here we assume that the expected value of the protection payment $\mathbb{E}[\Phi(\tau)] = (1 - R)$ is independent of interest rates and the default time. We have already assumed that the default time is independent of interest rates. We can therefore write

$$\text{Protection PV}(t, T) = (1 - R) \int_t^T Z(t, s)(-dQ(t, s)).$$

This integral over s can be performed by discretising the time between t and T into $K = \text{int}(M \times (T - t) + 0.5)$ equal intervals, where M is the number of integration steps per year. Increasing M improves the accuracy of the integration. Defining $\epsilon = (T - t)/K$ we have

$$\text{Protection PV} = (1 - R) \sum_{k=1}^K Z(t, k\epsilon)\, (Q(t, (k - 1)\epsilon) - Q(t, k\epsilon)).$$

The percentage error of this approximation is $O(r\epsilon)$. So if $r = 5\%$ and $M = 10$, we have a percentage error of the order of $5\% \times 1/10 = 0.5\% = 0.005$. Given that a typical protection PV on a contract with a face value of \$1 would be between 0.10 and 0.50, the size of the error is $O(10^{-4})$, which is outside our desired tolerance of $O(10^{-7})$. To get this level of accuracy would require so many time steps in the integration that our analytics would become extremely slow.

Fortunately, there is a way to significantly improve the accuracy for a very small additional cost. Since the discount function $Z(t, T)$ is a monotonically decreasing function of T, we can write upper and lower bounds for the value of the protection leg. The lower bound is

$$L = (1 - R) \sum_{k=1}^K Z(t, t_k)\, (Q(t, t_{k-1}) - Q(t, t_k))$$

and the upper bound is

$$U = (1 - R) \sum_{k=1}^K Z(t, t_{k-1})\, (Q(t, t_{k-1}) - Q(t, t_k)).$$

The distance between the bounds scales as $U - L \sim O(\epsilon)$. One way we can significantly improve our approximation of the integral is by setting the value of the protection leg equal to the average of these two bounds. The present value of the protection leg becomes

$$\text{Protection PV} = \frac{1}{2}(L + U) = \frac{(1 - R)}{2} \sum_{k=1}^K (Z(t, t_k) + Z(t, t_{k-1}))\, (Q(t, t_{k-1}) - Q(t, t_k)).$$

If we write $Z(t, T) = \exp(-r(T - t))$ and $Q(t, T) = \exp(-\lambda(T - t))$ and do a first-order expansion in ϵ, it is possible to show that the percentage error is now $O(r(r-\lambda)\epsilon^2/12)$. The good news is that the error is now quadratic in ϵ. We find that with monthly time steps, the accuracy is typically $O(10^{-7})$ and so it is in line with our required tolerance. With weekly time steps, it falls to $O(10^{-8})$. Although these scaling arguments are calculated using a flat interest rate curve and a flat hazard rate curve, we find that they work well even if the CDS curves are sloped.

6.6.1 The Full Mark-to-market

The full mark-to-market value of a long protection position with a face value of \$1, a contractual spread S_0, a maturity time T, at time t is given by

$$V(t) = \frac{(1 - R)}{2} \sum_{k=1}^K (Z(t, t_{k-1}) + Z(t, t_k))\, (Q(t, t_{k-1}) - Q(t, t_k)) - S_0 \cdot \text{RPV01}(t, T)$$

where

$$\text{RPV01}(t, T) = \Delta(t_{n^*-1}, t)Z(t, t_{n^*})(1 - Q(t, t_{n^*}))$$
$$+ \frac{1}{2}\Delta(t, t_{n^*})Z(t, t_{n^*})(1 - Q(t, t_{n^*}))$$
$$+ \Delta(t_{n^*-1}, t_{n^*})Z(t, t_{n^*})Q(t, t_{n^*})$$
$$+ \frac{1}{2}\sum_{n=n^*+1}^{N} \Delta(t_{n-1}, t_n)Z(t, t_n)(Q(t, t_{n-1}) + Q(t, t_n)).$$

The full mark-to-market of the same short protection position is just the negative value of this.

6.6.2   Determining the Breakeven Spread

The breakeven spread is the credit default swap spread paid on a new contract. Since a new CDS contract costs nothing to enter, on the contract initiation date at time $t = 0$, we must have

$$V(0) = 0.$$

This can only be achieved by setting the spread S_0 equal to the value which solves this equation. We therefore have

$$S_0 = \frac{(1 - R)\sum_{k=1}^{K}(Z(0, t_{k-1}) + Z(0, t_k))(Q(0, t_{k-1}) - Q(0, t_k))}{2 \cdot \text{RPV01}(0, T)}. \tag{6.5}$$

Note that the RPV01 at the initiation of a CDS is simpler than the general case shown above since there is no accrued premium to worry about. It is given by

$$\text{RPV01}(0, T) = \frac{1}{2}\sum_{n=1}^{N}\Delta(t_{n-1}, t_n)Z(0, t_n)(Q(0, t_{n-1}) + Q(0, t_n)).$$

6.6.3   Quoting CDS with Accrued Interest

Just as with bonds, the mark-to-market value of CDS can expressed in terms of a full price or a clean price. A full price is the present value of the full economic value of the credit default swap and is the value which is exchanged when a default swap is unwound. It is the expected present value of all future cash flows which have been contractually agreed. It is therefore what we have been considering so far in all of our pricing formulae.

The clean market value is simply a market convention in which the quoted market value excludes the component of the premium which has been accrued since the last premium payment date. The advantage of the clean market value is that, unlike the full market value, it does not experience a sudden jump as we move through a coupon payment date. Of course, in a trading book, this sudden jump in the CDS mark-to-market will be offset exactly by a payment (positive or negative depending on whether we are short or long protection) into the cash account.

The clean price is therefore only something we need to consider when we are quoting prices with other counterparties on valuation dates which are not premium payment dates. The sign of the accrued interest depends on whether we are long or short protection. The accrued interest of a short protection CDS position has a positive accrued interest since the investor receives the coupon. However, for a long protection position, the accrued interest is negative since the coupon is being paid. In either case, we define a clean mark-to-market (MTM) value as

$$\text{Clean MTM} = \text{Full MTM} - \text{Accrued}$$

where

$$\text{Accrued} = \begin{cases} +\Delta(t_{n^*-1}, t)S_0 & \text{for a short protection position} \\ -\Delta(t_{n^*-1}, t)S_0 & \text{for a long protection position.} \end{cases}$$

Example   To make this clear, consider a trade in which we buy $10 million of protection for five years at a spread of 200 bp and wish to value it after 1.5 months, i.e. halfway between quarterly premium dates. To close out this position, we would need to pay the accrued premium to the counterparty who is buying back the position, for the protection received since the previous premium date. The payment would be $25 000. This payment is opposite to what happens in a simple bond where it is the buyer of the bond who pays the bond holder for the accrued premium. As a result the accrued interest is a negative quantity, − $25 000 in this example.

A final comment. Do not confuse the quotation of accrued interest with the CDS paying or not paying coupon accrued following a credit event. The quotation of accrued interest is simply a quotation convention, and has no effect on the cash flows of the CDS contract. The payment of coupon accrued at default is a contingent payment on the CDS which changes the actual cash flows of a CDS and so has a value which must be captured by the pricing model.

6.7   UPFRONT CREDIT DEFAULT SWAPS

An upfront CDS is a simple variation on the standard CDS contract in which the investor receives the premium leg not as a *running* stream of credit risky payments, but as a single upfront amount at the start of the contract (Figure 6.4). The protection leg remains identical to that of a standard CDS.

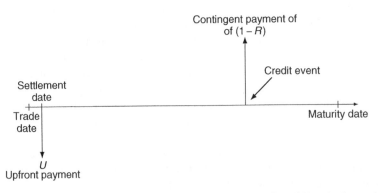

Figure 6.4   Mechanics of an upfront CDS with an initial upfront price of U and a face value of $1

Upfront contracts are non-standard for most issuers. However, when an issuer is in distress – typically the market CDS spread is of the order of 1000 bp – the market switches from trading using the standard *running* spread to trading in an upfront format. This is because protection sellers prefer to receive a sure but heavily discounted premium now rather than wait for a very risky stream of premium cash flows.

Example   Consider an example in which an investor has a choice of selling protection for two years on a distressed credit for which the market is shown in Table 6.1. Both upfront payments and the equivalent maturity running spreads are shown. These have been calculated using the market standard model. The investor can choose between selling protection in upfront format or in a running spread format. The deal notional is $10 million.

Table 6.1   The term structure of upfront payments and the corresponding running spreads for a distressed credit for different contract maturities

CDS term	Running spread (bp)	Upfront payment (%)
6M	2300	10.17
1Y	1500	12.77
2Y	1025	16.35
3Y	800	18.19

Table 6.2   The profit and loss of two trades, one with a running spread format and one with an upfront format for different default times of the reference credit. The trade maturity is two years. The upfront payment is $1 635 359 while the running spread is 1025 bp. We assume a 25% recovery rate

Default time	Upfront P&L ($)	Running P&L ($)
Immediate	− 5 864 641	− 7 500 000
1 year	− 5 864 641	− 6 475 000
2 years	− 5 864 641	− 5 450 000
No default	1 635 359	2 050 000

Table 6.2 compares the profitability of two trades in each format from the perspective of a protection seller. The trade maturity is two years so that the upfront payment is $1 635 359 while the equivalent running spread is 1025 bp. On default, the recovery rate is assumed to be 25%. We consider four scenarios:

1. First, we consider the case of an immediate default. The upfront trade loses $7 500 000 − $1 635 359 = $5 864 641. However, the running trade, which had no upfront payment and in which the investor has received no spread, immediately loses $7 500 000.
2. If there is a default at one year, the trade loses money in both formats. We see that the running spread format loses more than the upfront.

(Continued)

3. If there is a default at two years, the running loses less than the upfront. Therefore, we observe that the timing of the default event determines which of the two formats is the better investment.
4. The trade makes money in both formats as long as default does not occur within the life of the trade, i.e. no default before two years. The running format makes more money than the upfront.

6.7.1   Valuation of Upfront CDS

The upfront CDS replaces the premium leg of a CDS with a single payment of $U(0)$ at the initiation of the contract. The two legs of the contract are therefore the payment of the upfront value and the protection leg. We can therefore determine $U(0)$ by setting the net value of the CDS contract equal to zero at initiation. Consider a long protection buyer who has paid the upfront $U(0)$ to buy protection to time T. The value of the contract at initiation time $t = 0$ is

$$V(0) = (1 - R) \int_0^T Z(0, s)(-dQ(0, s)) - U(0) = 0$$

so that

$$U(0) = (1 - R) \int_0^T Z(0, s)(-dQ(0, s)).$$

Once the upfront payment has been made, it goes into the cash account of the protection seller. The mark-to-market value of the contract for the protection buyer at a later time t is given by

$$V(t) = (1 - R) \int_t^T Z(t, s)(-dQ(t, s))$$

i.e. it is simply the value of the protection leg of the standard CDS. This increase in the value of the position from zero to the price of the protection leg is offset in the protection buyer's cash account by the payment out of $U(0)$. This is probably funded by borrowing at some rate close to Libor. For the protection seller, the value of the contract will be negative since they are short protection with no incoming flows to offset the protection leg. However, this negative value is offset by the initial payment of $U(0)$ and may be invested at some rate close to Libor. The absence of a risky premium leg means that the market risk of an upfront CDS position is quite different from that of running CDS.

6.8   DIGITAL DEFAULT SWAPS

The contingent payment on a standard default swap is determined by the price of the deliverable obligations following the credit event. As a consequence, if one is using a credit default swap to hedge a *fixed* loss, the protection buyer is exposed to a recovery rate risk, meaning that the loss payment on the CDS is not guaranteed to equal the fixed loss we are hedging. For this reason, the market has introduced a variation on the standard default swap contract known as the *digital default swap*. This is a cash settled contract which pays the fixed notional contract amount following a credit event. It is also known as a zero recovery default swap or a binary default swap.

The value of the premium leg of a digital default swap paying a spread S_D is analogous to a standard CDS paying the same spread. However, the value of the protection leg is different. It is given by

$$\text{Digital protection PV}(t, T) = \int_t^T Z(t, s)(-dQ(t, s))$$

and so is analogous to a standard CDS in which the recovery rate is set to zero. As a result, given the same survival curve $Q(t, T)$, the relationship between the standard *floating* breakeven CDS spread, which we denote with S, and the digital spread S_D is given by

$$\frac{S}{S_D} = (1 - R). \tag{6.6}$$

Assuming an expected recovery rate of 50%, the digital default swap spread will be *twice* the standard CDS spread. This makes sense because the loss amount on the digital CDS for each $1 of notional will be $1 which is twice the expected loss conditional on default of $0.50 in the standard CDS case.

The fact that the payoff is known means that market quotes for the digital CDS spread can be used to imply out the risk-neutral default probability. Given this, we can then use standard CDS spreads to extract information about market-implied (or risk-neutral) recovery rates using Equation 6.6. However, although possible in theory, this is not possible in practice. Digital CDS have only a tiny fraction of the liquidity of standard CDS and are restricted to a fairly small number of names. This is mainly because users of CDS are buying protection to hedge the default risk of cash assets whose loss on default is not known in advance. The demand for digital CDS is therefore small.

6.9 VALUING LOAN CDS

Loan CDS, which were introduced in Section 5.7, are a type of CDS which only accept loans as deliverable obligations. This distinguishes LCDS from the standard CDS contract which typically allows both bonds and loans to be used as deliverables obligations. The LCDS also differs from the standard CDS in another important respect – an LCDS cancels if the reference obligation loan is refinanced and no replacement reference obligation can be found. In this event, the protection buyer pays the accrued premium to the cancellation date, and the protection seller pays nothing. As a result, it can be treated like a credit event in which the recovery rate is 100%. To model the LCDS contract we define:

- $\lambda_D(t)dt$ is the probability that the issuer defaults in the period $[t, t + dt]$ conditional on surviving to time t.
- $\lambda_C(t)dt$ is the probability that the loan cancels in the period $[t, t + dt]$ conditional on not cancelling before time t. If the loan cancels, the protection leg cancels with no cost and the premium leg cancels with the payment of the coupon accrued.

If we assume that the cancellation time and default time are independent and that the two hazard rates are deterministic, the price of the protection leg is given by

$$\text{Protection leg } PV(t, T) = (1 - R_L) \int_t^T Z(t, s) \lambda_D(s) \exp\left(-\int_t^s (\lambda_C(u) + \lambda_D(u)) du\right) ds$$

$$= (1 - R_L) \int_t^T Z(t, s) Q_C(t, s)(-dQ_D(t, s))$$

where R_L is the loan recovery rate. This is often higher than the recovery rate of standard CDS as loans often contain additional covenants. There is no need to consider the cancellation event as it has a zero payoff. The premium leg also has to be handled differently. It is the same as the ordinary premium leg where we set

$$Q(t, T) = Q_D(t, T) Q_C(t, T)$$

and the corresponding breakeven spread for the loan CDS, which we denote with S_L, becomes

$$S_L(t, T) = \frac{(1 - R_L) \int_t^T Z(t, s) Q_C(t, s)(-dQ_D(t, s))}{\frac{1}{2} \sum_{n=1}^N \Delta(t_{n-1}, t_n) Z(t, t_n) \left(Q(t, t_{n-1}) + Q(t, t_n)\right)}.$$

If the CDS is not cancellable, we have $Q_C(t, T) = 1$ and the standard CDS pricing formula is returned, albeit with a loan-specific recovery rate. Calibrating to LCDS then becomes a two-stage process:

1. First, we use standard CDS to build the $Q_D(t, T)$ survival curve using a standard CDS recovery rate assumption.
2. We then bootstrap the $Q_C(t, T)$ cancellation curve from the term structure of LCDS spreads using a loan recovery rate R_L.

Because the seniority of loan CDS and by extension its recovery rate is typically higher than that of the equivalent CDS, the typical LCDS spread should be lower than the CDS equivalent spread. The spread difference between cancellable and non-cancellable LCDS contracts on the same issuer is typically very small. In fact, it is possible to show that both callable and non-callable CDS obey the same credit triangle, i.e. $S_L \simeq \lambda_D(1 - R_L)$. Their differences in value are therefore only a result of accrued interest and the discrete payment times of the premium leg.

Finally, recall that we have assumed independence between default and refinancing times. In practice, we might expect there to be some negative correlation between the probability of refinancing and that of default since firms are more likely to refinance when their credit improves and they are able to obtain lower refinancing costs. This effect would tend to raise the LCDS spread since it would make the contract more (less) likely not to be cancelled early when the risk of a default increases (decreases), requiring a higher compensation for the protection seller.

6.10 SUMMARY

Using a simple hazard rate model in which we have assumed that the interest rate dynamics and the hazard rate dynamics are independent, we have been able to write simple pricing formulae for the value of a CDS position. However, in order to mark a CDS position to market, we need to calibrate the model to the market. We have already shown in Chapter 2 how to calibrate the Libor term structure. Building the market implied survival curve from the market prices of CDS is the subject of the next chapter.

7

Calibrating the CDS Survival Curve

7.1 INTRODUCTION

We saw in the previous chapter that a CDS contract can be priced given the issuer survival curve $Q(t, T)$, a Libor curve $Z(t, T)$, and an assumption for the expected recovery rate, R. However, if the survival curve has not been calibrated to the CDS market spreads of the reference entity, any CDS mark-to-market computed with it is meaningless. The objective of this chapter is to show how to build a survival curve that is able to reprice the full term structure of quoted CDS spreads. This will complete all of the steps needed to allow us to finally value a CDS contract.

We begin this chapter by setting out the requirements which we would like our curve building methodology to satisfy. We then discuss curve building approaches and explain why we focus on linear approaches. We discuss a number of possible quantities for our interpolation scheme, and choose the one which best satisfies our requirements. We then explain how given a linear interpolation scheme and an appropriate interpolation quantity we can construct the market survival curve. Finally, we present an example in which we calibrate to the CDS curve and use the resulting curve to value an existing contract.

7.2 DESIRABLE CURVE PROPERTIES

Building the survival curve is essentially a process of constructing a full term structure of survival probabilities from a finite number of CDS market quotes. There are in theory an infinite number of ways of doing this. The method we choose must be selected according to what we believe are the desired properties. We list below what we consider these to be in a rough order of importance:

1. We want the methodology to provide an *exact* fit to the CDS market quotes provided. Since we require a minimum PV accuracy of $O(10^{-7})$, we define *exact* to mean an error of $O(10^{-4})$ basis points or less in the spread.
2. The method should interpolate between the market quotes in a sensible manner. Given a CDS curve with CDS quotes at 1Y, 3Y, 5Y, 7Y and 10Y, we can have gaps of up to 3Y to interpolate.
3. We would like the construction method to be *local*. For example, if we bump the 5Y CDS spread and rebuild the CDS curve, we would prefer a method which only changes the spread of CDS with a maturity close to 5Y. We want to avoid methods which cause the bump to 'leak' into more distant curve points. Satisfying this requirement makes it easier to understand the model-implied hedges and to explain P&L movements.

4. The curve building algorithm should be fast. For example, a typical CDS book may have $O(10^4)$ CDS positions linked to $O(10^3)$ different issuer curves. This need for speed is even greater when we encounter the pricing and risk management of multi-name credit derivatives.
5. We would like the curve to be smooth. However, there is usually a conflict between localness and smoothness since smoothness necessarily links together different parts of the curve via their derivatives. We prefer localness to smoothness.

For these reasons, we choose a curve construction approach based on the bootstrap approach.

7.3 THE BOOTSTRAP

The bootstrap is one of the fastest and most stable curve construction approaches and is the standard approach for constructing CDS survival curves. It was already encountered in Chapter 2 in the context of constructing the Libor discount curve.

A bootstrap works by starting with the shortest dated instrument and works out to the longest dated instrument, at each step using the price of the next instrument to solve for one parameter which determines how to extend the survival curve to the next maturity point. The result is a survival curve which can reprice the market exactly and which can be constructed very quickly.

However, we cannot just bootstrap from one instrument to the next without having to think about what happens between these maturity points. This is because a CDS contract requires knowledge of the survival probabilities at all times between today and CDS maturity in order to calculate the time integral on the protection leg. A bootstrap algorithm therefore requires an interpolation scheme. However, this interpolation scheme can only have one free variable since given one additional CDS quote, we can only solve for one unknown.

There has been a lot of work done on the fitting of interest rate curves which can be applied directly to the building of credit curves. In fact, there is a strong analogy between both problems as shown in Table 7.1. The methods which have been used range from simple linear splines to polynomial methods. For a comprehensive review of spline methods see Hagan and West (2004).

The advantage of polynomial splines is that they provide a smoother curve shape than linear splines. This has become important in the Libor interest rate market, especially at the short end

Table 7.1　Analogy between curve building in interest rates and credit

Interest rates		Credit
Discount curve	$\Longleftrightarrow$	Survival curve
Short rate $r(s)$	$\Longleftrightarrow$	Hazard rate $\lambda(s)$
No-arbitrage $r(s) > 0$	$\Longleftrightarrow$	No-arbitrage $\lambda(s) > 0$
Discount factor $Z(t)$	$\Longleftrightarrow$	Survival probability $Q(t)$
$Z(t) = E[\exp(-\int_0^t r(s)ds)]$	$\Longleftrightarrow$	$Q(t) = E[\exp(-\int_0^t \lambda(s)ds)]$
Zero rate $z(t)$	$\Longleftrightarrow$	Zero default rate $z(t)$
$z(t) = -(1/t)\ln Z(t)$	$\Longleftrightarrow$	$z(t) = -(1/t)\ln Q(t)$
Forward rate $f(t)$	$\Longleftrightarrow$	Forward default rate $h(t)$
$f(t) = -Z(t)^{-1}\partial Z(t)/\partial t$	$\Longleftrightarrow$	$h(t) = -Q(t)^{-1}\partial Q(t)/\partial t$

where the large number of short-term instruments[1] and their high liquidity provide a great deal of accurate information about the shape of the curve. By comparison, the CDS curve is fairly sparse. Therefore the cost of these more sophisticated splines, which is usually less localness and slower curve construction, is hard to justify in a CDS context. The speed issue is also more important in the credit derivative world. Consider that in a typical global interest rate swap trading book 90% or more of contracts will be denominated in USD, EUR, GBP and JPY. As a result there will be just four Libor curves to build to cover all of these trades. However, in a global CDS trading book we may need to build over 1000 different issuer curves. For this reason, we focus solely on linear splines.

Although we are proposing linear interpolation, we have not yet specified what quantity we are linearly interpolating. We discuss various interpolation quantities in the next section. In Section 7.5 we describe how to implement the bootstrap algorithm.

7.4   INTERPOLATION QUANTITIES

Having chosen linear interpolation, we also need to choose what quantity we are interpolating. This choice is crucial to the success of our pricing model in its pricing and risk management of our trading book. We therefore need to ensure that the interpolation quantity satisfies as many of the criteria specified in Section 7.2 as possible. In this section, we set out and discuss several alternative interpolation quantities.

All interpolation quantities will be expressed in terms of the survival curve. Regarding notation, we set today to be time 0. We can then write the survival curve as

$$Q(t) = Q(0, t).$$

All of the interpolation schemes we discuss are posed as linear interpolations of some function $f(t)$ as shown in Figure 7.1 where we have been supplied with a *skeleton* of survival probabilities $Q(t_n)$ at time points t_n. The standard linear interpolation formula to some time $t^* \in [t_{n-1}, t_n]$ is given by

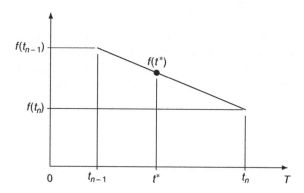

Figure 7.1   A linear interpolation scheme for $f(t)$

---

[1] These include deposits, interest rate futures, overnight index swaps and FRAs.

$$f(t^*) = \frac{(t_n - t^*)f(t_{n-1}) + (t^* - t_{n-1})f(t_n)}{(t_n - t_{n-1})}. \tag{7.1}$$

To assist the interpolation, we introduce the continuously compounded forward default rate, $h(t)$ given by

$$Q(t) = \exp\left(-\int_0^t h(s)ds\right). \tag{7.2}$$

This equals the hazard rate when the hazard rate process is deterministic. We now consider a number of candidates for the choice of $f(t)$.

7.4.1   Linear Interpolation of $f(t) = -\ln Q(t)$

We begin with an interpolation method which linearly interpolates the log of the survival probability. This can also be described as exponentially interpolating the survival probability. We define

$$f(t) = -\ln Q(t).$$

Since $0 < Q(t) \leq 1$, the minus sign ensures that $f(t)$ is a positive number. From Equation 7.2 we can write

$$f(t) = \int_0^t h(s)ds.$$

We therefore have

$$h(t) = \frac{\partial f(t)}{\partial t}.$$

We can therefore write this interpolation scheme to some time t^* in terms of $f(t)$ by differentiating Equation 7.1 to give

$$h(t^*) = \frac{\partial f(t^*)}{\partial t^*} = \frac{f(t_n) - f(t_{n-1})}{(t_n - t_{n-1})}.$$

Since $h(t^*)$ does not depend on t^*, this interpolation shows that $h(t)$ is constant between the interpolation limits. We conclude that *linear interpolation of the log of the survival probability is equivalent to assuming a piecewise constant forward default rate $h(t)$*. We therefore define the constant continuously compounded forward default probability at time t^* where $t_{n-1} < t^* < t_n$ as

$$h(t^*) = h(t_{n-1}) = \frac{1}{(t_n - t_{n-1})} \ln\left(\frac{Q(t_{n-1})}{Q(t_n)}\right).$$

The formula for a survival probability to some time t^* is therefore

$$Q(t^*) = Q(t_{n-1}) \exp(-(t^* - t_{n-1})h(t_{n-1})).$$

No-arbitrage requires that $h(t) \geq 0$. Provided this is the case at each of the skeleton points, which is the case if $Q(t_n) \leq Q(t_{n-1})$, this piecewise constant interpolation of $h(t)$ will also ensure no-arbitrage between these points.

7.4.2   Linear Interpolation of the Zero Default Rate

The zero default rate is the credit equivalent of what is known as the zero rate for bonds. It is the flat default rate $z(t)$ to some maturity time t, i.e.

$$Q(t) = \exp(-z(t)\,t)\,.$$

We therefore define our choice of interpolation function

$$f(t) = z(t) = -\frac{1}{t}\ln Q(t).$$

There is a simple mathematical relationship between the continuous forward default rate $h(t)$ and the zero default rate given by

$$h(t) = \frac{\partial}{\partial t}\,(z(t)t) = z(t) + t\left(\frac{\partial z(t)}{\partial t}\right). \tag{7.3}$$

This equation suggests that a linear interpolation scheme for $z(t)$ can cause sudden jumps in the shape of $h(t)$ since it will involve joining together different linear sections of $z(t)$ which will have different gradients. Sudden jumps in the forward default rate for simple slope changes in $z(t)$ are not desirable. In addition, if $Q(t_n) \leq Q(t_{n-1})$, it is not guaranteed that all points which have been interpolated using this algorithm will also be arbitrage free.

7.4.3   Linear Interpolation of the Instantaneous Forward Default Rate

This interpolation methodology assumes that the forward default probability $h(t)$ is linearly interpolated between the skeleton points, i.e. $f(t) = h(t)$. In terms of the survival probability we have

$$f(t) = -\frac{1}{Q(t)}\frac{\partial Q(t)}{\partial t}.$$

However, it is well known that there are stability problems with this interpolation method in the sense that the resulting forward default rate curve tends to oscillate with a 'saw-tooth' pattern, i.e. oscillations of the forward default rate with alternately positive and negative slopes. This algorithm is also not able to guarantee that the interpolation will be arbitrage free between skeleton points even if the skeleton is arbitrage free.

7.4.4   Conclusion

We have proposed three choices for the quantity which is to be linearly interpolated. Out of these three, we now reject linear interpolation of the zero default rate and linear interpolation of the instantaneous forward default rate. This is done because of their instabilities and their inability to guarantee an arbitrage-free interpolation. However, to emphasise that the problems with these schemes are not just theoretical but are real and do appear in practice, we will present them later in our analysis.

7.5   BOOTSTRAPPING ALGORITHM

What we now wish to do is to build the survival curve using the curve building approach known as bootstrapping. We begin by defining the set of CDS market quotes $S_1, S_2, \ldots, S_M$

which are for contracts with times to maturity $T_1, T_2, T_3, \ldots, T_M$. These are sorted in order of increasing maturity. We also have an expected recovery rate assumption R which we assume is the same for all maturities. Let us consider in detail the steps of the bootstrap algorithm. Its basic aim is to produce a vector of discount factors $Q(T_m)$ at the $M + 1$ times (where we include time 0) which reprice the CDS market quotes given the chosen interpolation scheme.

Before we present the bootstrap algorithm, we note that we also have to extrapolate the survival curve below the shortest maturity CDS and beyond the longest maturity CDS. Therefore, between $t = 0$ and $t = T_1$, we assume that the forward default rate is flat at a level of $h(0)$. Beyond the last time point T_M we assume that the forward default rate is flat at its last interpolated value.

The bootstrap algorithm is as follows:

1. Initialise the survival curve starting with $Q(T_0 = 0) = 1.0$.
2. Set $m = 1$.
3. Solve for the value of $Q(T_m)$ for which the mark-to-market value of the T_m maturity CDS with market spread S_m is zero. The equation to be used is 6.5. All of the discount factors required to determine the CDS mark-to-market will be interpolated from the values of $Q(T_1), \ldots, Q(T_{m-1})$ which have already been determined, and $Q(T_m)$ which is the value we are solving for. The no-arbitrage bound on $Q(T_m)$ is $0 < Q(T_m) \leq Q(T_{m-1})$. Since the PV is linear in $Q(t)$, the required PV tolerance can be controlled via a tolerance in the value of $Q(t)$.
4. Once we have found a value of $Q(T_m)$ which reprices the CDS with maturity T_m, we add this time and value to our survival curve.
5. Set $m = m + 1$. If $m \leq M$ return to step (3).
6. We end up with a survival curve consisting curve of $M + 1$ points with times at $0, T_1, T_2, \ldots, T_M$ and values $1.0, Q(T_1), Q(T_2), \ldots, Q(T_M)$.

Solving for the next maturity survival probability in step (3) requires the use of a one-dimensional root search algorithm. There are a number to choose from including bisection, Newton–Raphson, and Brent's method. These are all described in Press *et al.* (1992).

We may sometimes find that the root search fails to converge. This typically occurs when the CDS spread curve is steeply inverted and implies that there is an arbitrage in the input spread curve. The code should therefore handle this case, and it is up to the user to decide whether to allow this case to proceed or not by changing the bounds on the root solver. If a curve which does not have a monotonically decreasing survival curve is allowed, the fact should be reported to the user so that the problem can be addressed either by remarking the input spreads or by adjusting the expected recovery rate assumption. We will discuss the issue of arbitrage detection in more detail in Section 7.7.

7.6 BEHAVIOUR OF THE INTERPOLATION SCHEME

Once we have the bootstrap algorithm working we can then study the behaviour of our interpolation scheme. To do so, we consider some realistic market curves. The CDS quotes are shown in Table 7.2. We have taken three CDS curve shapes: (i) a flat curve with a single

Table 7.2   Example CDS term structures

CDS term	Flat with step at 4Y (bp)	Upward sloping (bp)	Steeply inverted (bp)
6M	50	100	800
1Y	50	120	700
2Y	50	140	600
3Y	50	160	500
4Y	60	180	450
5Y	60	200	400
7Y	60	220	350
10Y	60	220	350

step which rises from 50 bp to 60 bp at the four-year maturity, (ii) an upward sloping curve going from 100 bp at the six-month term to 220 bp at 10 years, and (iii) a steeply inverted curve implying a distressed credit. For all three curves, we have assumed a 40% recovery rate.

For each of these curves, we have constructed the credit curve using the piecewise constant interpolation of the forward default rate which was the interpolation scheme we chose earlier. For comparison, we have also examined the two other interpolation methods rejected earlier. We have plotted the forward default probability curves in Figure 7.2 and we now consider what they show:

- The top graph shows the forward default rate curve for the flat CDS curve with a step at 4Y. It is clear that the different interpolation schemes produce very different results. All of the curves have in common the fact that they are flat out to 3Y, reflecting the constant nature of the CDS spread. All of the interesting behaviour takes place between 3Y and 5Y. The curve which is linear in $\ln Q(t)$ is piecewise flat and behaves in a stable manner as expected. The same is true for the piecewise linear interpolation in $z(t)$. However, the interpolation scheme which is linear in $h(t)$ is extremely unstable, exhibiting a violent saw-tooth shape. It even manages to find negative values for the forward default rate and so has generated an arbitrage. We therefore reject this scheme and do not include it in the remaining graphs.
- The middle graph compares just the linear in $z(t)$ and the linear in $\ln Q(t)$ schemes using the upward sloping CDS term structure. Both curves follow the same general shape with one being piecewise constant and the other piecewise linear as expected.
- The bottom graph compares the linear $z(t)$ and the linear in $\ln Q(t)$ schemes using the steeply inverted CDS term structure. Once again we see that both curves seem similar although one is flat and the other linear. The jagged pattern of the forward default curve given by the $z(t)$ interpolation scheme could have implications for the pricing of forward starting products.

These results confirm that the interpolation scheme which is piecewise constant in $h(t)$ is clearly the most stable and is the preferred of the three schemes considered.

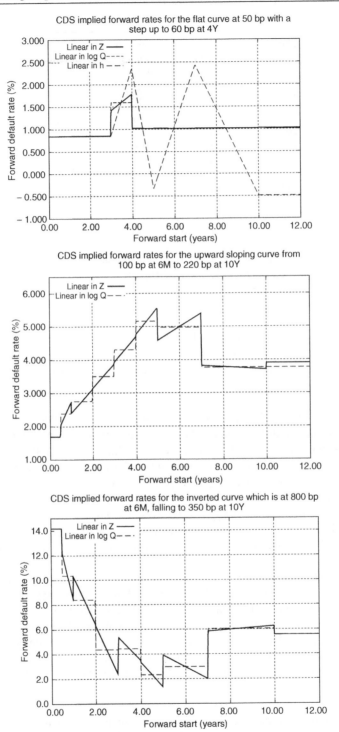

Figure 7.2 The interpolated forward default rate curves for the three CDS curve term structures in Table 7.2. For the stepped CDS curve we show all three different interpolation methods. For the upward sloping curve and inverted curves we only show the $z(t)$ and $\ln Q(t)$ interpolations

7.7   DETECTING ARBITRAGE IN THE CURVE

When constructing spread curves, we need to take care to identify the presence of arbitrages. The no-arbitrage constraint is that the forward default rate[2] $h(t)$ has to be positive. In other words, we require that the survival probabilities have to be flat or monotonically decreasing with horizon time. We can write this as a condition on the derivative of the survival probability to time t

$$\frac{\partial Q(0, t)}{\partial t} \le 0 \text{ for all } 0 < t < \infty. \tag{7.4}$$

Arbitrage occurs in a CDS term structure as soon the value of protection leg for T_m years is the same as the value of the protection leg for T_{m-1} years where $T_m > T_{m-1}$. This is because we are getting the extra protection in the period $[T_{m-1}, T_m]$ for free. If we hold S_{m-1} fixed, what we wish to determine is the value of S_m at which this arbitrage first occurs. We denote this value with S_m^*. For $S_m > S_m^*$, the cost of the longer protection is greater than the cost of the shorter protection and there is no arbitrage. For $S_m < S_m^*$, the cost of the longer protection is less than the cost of the shorter protection and we have an arbitrage. The value of S_m^* is therefore given by solving for the value of S_m at which the two protection legs have the same value. This is given by the following equation

$$S_{m-1} \text{RPV01}(0, T_{m-1}) = S_m^* \text{RPV01}(0, T_m).$$

Note that since there is a dependency on S_m^* in RPV01$(0, T_m)$ this equation has to be solved by a root search in which the CDS curve has to be bootstrapped for each value of S_m^*.

We note that at the arbitrage limit when $S_m = S_m^*$, the value of the forward protection in the period $[T_{m-1}, t_m]$ must equal zero so $Q(0, T_{m-1}) = Q(0, T_m)$ and $\partial Q(0, t)/\partial t = 0$ for $t \in [T_{m-1}, t_m]$. This shows that this arbitrage condition is equivalent to the arbitrage condition expressed in Equation 7.4.

We can calculate an approximation for S_m^* if we replace the ratio of the risky PV01s with the ratio of their maturities. The no-arbitrage condition $S_m > S_m^*$ therefore becomes

$$S_m \gtrsim S_{m-1} \left(\frac{T_{m-1}}{T_m} \right). \tag{7.5}$$

We can use this approximation to calculate the arbitrage lower bound for an entire CDS term structure starting with a 6M CDS spread of 800 bp. The approximate lower bound for subsequent spreads is shown in the second column of Table 7.3 and the exact result is shown in the third column of Table 7.3. Assuming bid–offer spreads of zero, any inverted spread curve that starts with a 6M spread of 800 bp which drops below this curve is arbitrageable.

7.7.1   Calibrating the Recovery Rate

To calibrate to the CDS spread curve, we need to input an expected recovery rate R. However, there is no liquid and transparent market in recovery rates. While a comparison of digital and standard default swap spreads should in theory provide information to imply out risk-neutral expected recovery rates, the digital default swap market has not achieved the necessary breadth and liquidity that this would require. Perhaps this will change over time. However, what this

---

[2] This is equivalent to the hazard rate for deterministic hazard rates.

Table 7.3   Example CDS term structure arbitrage limits for
an inverted curve which starts with a fixed spread of 800 bp
at 6M. This includes a simple arbitrage limit and the model-
based limit for the $\ln Q(t)$ interpolation scheme

CDS term	Approximate lower bound (bp)	Exact $\ln Q(t)$ lower bound (bp)
6M	800	800
1Y	400	419
2Y	200	219
3Y	133	150
4Y	100	116
5Y	80	96
7Y	57	72
10Y	40	54

means in practice is that the calculated unwind value of a CDS contract can differ between counterparties who, despite using the same CDS spreads and the same model for extracting survival probabilities, disagree on their views around expected recovery rates.

The starting point for recovery rate estimates is the data collected by the rating agencies. However, what then happens is that a consensus value arises in the market which then becomes widely used. Currently the consensus value for the expected recovery rate is 40% for investment grade senior unsecured debt. However, if the credit market were to enter a period with higher default rates and lower observed recovery rates, the consensus would probably change and this estimate would be reduced.

What mitigates the problem of agreeing a common recovery rate when unwinding CDS is that the recovery rate sensitivity of the mark-to-market of a CDS with investment grade quality spread levels is very low. This is discussed in detail in the next chapter. The sensitivity to the value of the recovery rate only becomes significant when the issuer spreads become very large and the credit is distressed. However, in this scenario we would expect that the prices of the bonds issued by the reference entity would have fallen in value and so their price may give a more precise indication about where the market anticipates the final recovery rate to be.

One thing the market certainly does is to distinguish between the recovery rates of CDS linked to reference assets at different levels of the capital structure. It is therefore worth noting that there is a simple relationship between the spreads and expected recovery rates of CDS at different levels of the capital structure of the same reference entity. Suppose we have CDS linked to the senior and subordinated debt of the same issuer which trades at a spread of S_{Sen} and S_{Sub}. We assume that they have *expected* recovery rates of R_{Sen} and R_{Sub} where, assuming that the absolute priority rule is obeyed, we have $R_{Sub} \leq R_{Sen}$. Cross-default provisions, which are written into most debt, mean that the senior and subordinated debt of a reference entity must default together, and so both a senior and subordinated linked CDS will trigger on the same credit event. We can therefore use the same hazard rate $\lambda(t)$ for both senior and subordinated debt. Assuming $\lambda(t) = \lambda$, from the credit triangle we have

$$S_{Sub} = \lambda(1 - R_{Sub}) \quad \text{and} \quad S_{Sen} = \lambda(1 - R_{Sen}).$$

Dividing, we can write

$$\frac{S_{Sub}}{S_{Sen}} = \frac{(1 - R_{Sub})}{(1 - R_{Sen})}.$$

We therefore have a simple relationship between senior and subordinated CDS spreads. In practice, this relationship is only a rough guide. Market technicals will often mean that it is not obeyed exactly. However, it does reminds us that we should take care to price different levels of the capital structure consistent with their expected recovery rates.

7.8   EXAMPLE CDS VALUATION

We conclude this section with an example of a CDS pricing which finally puts all of the components together. These components are:

- Construction of a Libor curve.
- Calibration of the survival curve to a term structure of CDS spreads.
- Use of both of these curves to price a CDS contract.

Recall that we choose to value the trade according to 'T + 0 close of business'. This means that both the CDS survival curve and Libor discount factor curve should be anchored with a value of 1.0 at 1 minute past midnight on 'T + 1'. Thereafter the contract is exposed to the risk of the credit defaulting and so the survival probability should decline.

Example   We value an existing CDS position with the following trade details:

Face value	$10 million short protection
Valuation date	18 January 2008
Effective date	15 November 2006
Maturity date	15 November 2012
Contractual spread	180 bp
Business day convention	Modified following

Note that the deal is a non-standard CDS in the sense that it does not mature on one of the 'IMM' dates. At initiation, the trade had 6 years to maturity. Now on the valuation date, the deal has approximately 4.8 years remaining to maturity and we are part way through a premium accrual period. Both the CDS swap curve and the Libor rates are shown below. Although the CDS contract does not mature on an 'IMM' date, the contracts underlying the CDS quotes do and this must be taken into account in the calibration of the survival curve.

Libor curve		CDS curve	
6M deposit	4.650%	6M	145 bp
1Y swap	5.020%	1Y	145 bp
2Y swap	5.019%	2Y	160 bp
3Y swap	5.008%	3Y	175 bp
4Y swap	5.002%	4Y	190 bp
5Y swap	5.030%	5Y	220 bp
7Y swap	5.041%	7Y	245 bp
10Y swap	5.080%	10Y	270 bp

(Continued)

We assume a 40% recovery rate and use these market rates to imply out the CDS survival curve. We also calculate the premium payment dates of the CDS contract and in the table below we show the Libor discount factors and implied survival probability. The calibrated terms structure of forward default rates is shown in Figure 7.3.

Schedule dates	Accrual factor	Actual cash flow	Libor discount factors	Survival probability
Fri 18 Jan 2008			1.000000	1.000000
Fri 15 Feb 2008	0.25556	46 000.00	0.996449	0.997409
Thu 15 May 2008	0.25000	45 000.00	0.985213	0.990054
Fri 15 Aug 2008	0.25556	46 000.00	0.973973	0.983247
Mon 17 Nov 2008	0.26111	47 000.00	0.961504	0.976340
Mon 16 Feb 2009	0.25278	45 500.00	0.947857	0.969701
Fri 15 May 2009	0.24444	44 000.00	0.936601	0.963323
Mon 17 Aug 2009	0.26111	47 000.00	0.924726	0.956556
Mon 16 Nov 2009	0.25278	45 500.00	0.913373	0.950051
Mon 15 Feb 2010	0.25278	45 500.00	0.902181	0.943590
Mon 17 May 2010	0.25278	45 500.00	0.891177	0.935912
Mon 16 Aug 2010	0.25278	45 500.00	0.880308	0.927585
Mon 15 Nov 2010	0.25278	45 500.00	0.869570	0.919332
Tue 15 Feb 2011	0.25556	46 000.00	0.858799	0.911063
Mon 16 May 2011	0.25000	45 000.00	0.848282	0.902223
Mon 15 Aug 2011	0.25278	45 500.00	0.837779	0.892895
Tue 15 Nov 2011	0.25556	46 000.00	0.827293	0.883562
Wed 15 Feb 2012	0.25556	46 000.00	0.816938	0.874327
Tue 15 May 2012	0.25000	45 000.00	0.806934	0.862391
Wed 15 Aug 2012	0.25556	46 000.00	0.796834	0.848531
Thu 15 Nov 2012	0.25556	46 000.00	0.786860	0.834893

Using these we are then able to calculate the risky PV01 for the contract and its mark-to-market. These are:

Full mark-to-market	−110 785
Accrued interest	+32 000
Clean mark-to-market	−142 785
Risky PV01	4.2082
Replication spread	206.3 bp

The risky PV01 is 4.2082 and takes into account the full accrued coupon which will be received at the end of the current premium payment period. The mark-to-market is negative as the position is short protection at 180 bp and the market spread to 5Y is now 40 bp wider at 220 bp. The accrued interest equals $32 000, corresponding to 64 days of accrued interest since the previous coupon payment date which falls on 15 November 2007. The replication spread is the breakeven spread for a new contract starting today and maturing on the same date as this contract. However, as it is a new contract, it has a smaller 'short-stub' payment for the first premium payment than the existing CDS contract being valued.

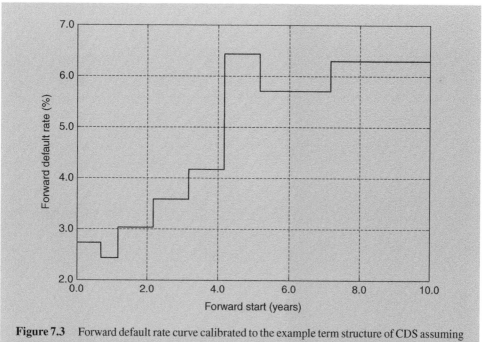

Figure 7.3   Forward default rate curve calibrated to the example term structure of CDS assuming a 40% recovery rate

One subtle aspect of this valuation example is that the standard CDS which were used to build the CDS curve are quoted on the basis of IMM dates, meaning that the 5Y quote is for a contract which matures not on 18 January 2013 but on the next IMM date which is 20 March 2013. This explains why the steps in the instantaneous forward default rate curve occur at times which are not exactly 0.5, 1.0, 2.0, ... years in the future but are closer to 0.67, 1.17, 2.17, ... years in the future, with the extra 0.17 being the year fraction from 18 January to 20 March.

7.9   SUMMARY

In this chapter we have completed the process of defining, building and calibrating a model for pricing CDS. Specifically, we have investigated a number of alternative linear interpolation schemes and demonstrated that the piecewise constant forward default rate interpolation is more stable, and less prone to create arbitrages than the alternatives presented.

8

CDS Risk Management

8.1 INTRODUCTION

The aim of this chapter is to establish a risk-management framework for hedging credit default swaps (CDS). The risks that we want to consider are sensitivities to:

- Changes in the credit spread curve.
- Changes in the Libor rate curve.
- Changes in the expected recovery rate assumption.
- A sudden default and the resulting recovery rate risk.
- The shortening life of a contract.

The first four of these are sensitivities to random changes in market prices or a default event which are not known in advance. The final sensitivity is the sensitivity to the shortening life of the contract which changes in a predictable way and which we may wish to hedge.

Since there are so many variables that affect the value of a CDS contract, we begin this chapter by introducing a simple model for valuation which we can use to gain some insight and intuition. This is based on a simple analytical approximation for the CDS mark-to-market in which the dependency on all of these market risks is explicit. Although simplified, this model is rich enough to allow us to understand the behaviour of a CDS mark-to-market, and the interplay between the different model inputs.

Following this, we move on to use our full valuation model set out in the previous chapters. We begin by defining a general risk-management framework for a credit default swap position. We show mathematically how to hedge the credit and interest rate risks. Then, with a realistic example, we calculate both spread and interest rate hedges. This allows us to see what the residual risks are. We then discuss how to extend this to the pricing of an entire CDS book.

8.2 MARKET RISKS OF A CDS POSITION

The mark-to-market value of a CDS position at time t, which we denote with $V(t)$, is sensitive to movements in the term structure of credit spreads S, the term structure of swap rates $\mathbf{H}$, and the passage of time t. It is also sensitive to the assumed *expected* recovery rate R. The sensitivity of the value of a CDS position to these market inputs can therefore be expressed in a Taylor expansion as a sum of partial first- and second-order derivatives as follows

$$dV(t) = \frac{\partial V}{\partial \mathbf{S}}(d\mathbf{S}) + \frac{\partial V}{\partial \mathbf{H}}(d\mathbf{H}) + \frac{\partial V}{\partial t}(dt) + \frac{\partial V}{\partial R}(dR)$$

$$+ \frac{1}{2}\frac{\partial^2 V}{\partial \mathbf{S}^2}(d\mathbf{S})^2 + \frac{1}{2}\frac{\partial^2 V}{\partial \mathbf{H}^2}(d\mathbf{H})^2 + \frac{1}{2}\frac{\partial^2 V}{\partial R^2}(dR)^2 + \dots . \qquad (8.1)$$

We ignore the second order cross terms such as

$$\frac{\partial^2 V}{\partial \mathbf{S}\partial \mathbf{H}}(d\mathbf{S})(d\mathbf{H})$$

since their magnitude depends on the correlation between the different market observables we assume to be small. Note that when we take the partial derivative

$$\frac{\partial V}{\partial H_m}$$

we are calculating the change in the price of the CDS contract for a small change in the mth swap rate, *holding all the other market rates, i.e. the other swap rates and all the CDS spreads, fixed*. Also, we use the bold text to denote a vector so that $\mathbf{S} = \{S_1, S_2, \dots, S_M\}$. The first- and second-order partial derivatives are

$$\frac{\partial V}{\partial \mathbf{S}} = \sum_{m=1}^{M}\frac{\partial V}{\partial S_m} \quad \text{and} \quad \frac{\partial^2 V}{\partial \mathbf{S}^2} = \sum_{m=1}^{M}\frac{\partial^2 V}{\partial S_m^2}.$$

The first row of Equation 8.1 consists of the first-order sensitivities. These are the main risks of the position as they are the largest and they are also direction sensitive. On the second line of Equation 8.1 we have the second-order sensitivities. Since these are quadratic in the market move, these are changes which depend only on the magnitude of the market move, and not the direction. For a small change in spreads or interest rates, the second-order risks are smaller than the first-order risks. These are the residual risks once the first-order risks have been hedged. Higher-order risks are ignored since they are considered to be even smaller.

The Taylor expansion deals with risks which change smoothly and have a first- and higher-order derivatives. It therefore does not include the 'jump to default' risk in which a credit suddenly defaults. This risk will also be covered later when we will use the Value on Default (VOD) to describe the change in value of a CDS contract from before to after a default. VOD is something of a misnomer since we might expect value on default to be the *value* of the position after default. However, we define it as the *change* in value due to default.

To help us understand the behaviour of these different risks, we now propose a simple model which allows us to calculate the sensitivities analytically.

8.3 ANALYTICAL CDS SENSITIVITIES

It is often useful to have a simple approximate model for the purpose of better understanding the general characteristics of a more exact model. In the world of credit default swap pricing, we can formulate a simple analytical equation for the pricing of CDS by assuming that:

- The hazard rate term structure observed at time t is flat at a value equal to λ_t.
- The continuously compounded interest rate observed at time t is also flat and equal to r_t.

We can therefore write the present value of the protection leg as

$$\text{Protection Leg PV}(t, T) = (1 - R) \int_t^T \lambda_t \exp(-(r_t + \lambda_t)s)\, ds$$

$$= \frac{\lambda_t(1 - R)\,(1 - \exp(-(r_t + \lambda_t)(T - t)))}{(r_t + \lambda_t)}.$$

The contractual spread, S_0, on the premium leg is typically paid with a quarterly frequency. For simplicity, we assume that all premium payment periods have an equal accrual period of Δ years. In accordance with the standard Actual 360 convention, we approximate the accrual period with

$$\Delta = \frac{365.25}{360 \times 4} \simeq 0.254.$$

The present value of the premium leg is given by

$$\text{Premium Leg PV}(t, T) = S_0 \Delta \sum_{n=1}^{N} \exp(-(r_t + \lambda_t)(t_n - t))$$

where $n = 1, \ldots, N$ indexes the N premium payments between time t and time T. The last premium payment date falls on the maturity date of the contract so we have $t_N = T$.

We assume that the current effective date falls on a premium payment date so that we do not have to consider the credit risk of partly accrued coupons. In order to keep the analytical approximation simple, we have also ignored the payment of premium accrued on default since its effect on the value of a CDS is small. The aim of this exercise is not to build an exact pricing model, but rather to have a nice approximate analytical form for the value and risk of a CDS contract which we can use to understand its behaviour.

8.3.1   The Approximate CDS Mark-to-market

The value of a short protection CDS contract that we observe in the market today at time t with a time T maturity and with contractual spread S_0 is given by

$$V(t) = S_0 \Delta \sum_{n=1}^{N} \exp(-(r_t + \lambda_t)\tau_n) - \frac{\lambda_t(1 - R)\,(1 - \exp(-(r_t + \lambda_t)(T - t)))}{(r_t + \lambda_t)}. \quad (8.2)$$

For notational simplicity, we set $\tau_n = t_n - t$. The value of a new CDS contract to the same maturity date and with contractual spread S_t is zero by definition. Hence we can write

$$S_t \Delta \sum_{n=1}^{N} \exp(-(r_t + \lambda_t)\tau_n) = \frac{\lambda_t(1 - R)\,(1 - \exp(-(r_t + \lambda_t)(T - t)))}{(r_t + \lambda_t)}.$$

Therefore, the mark-to-market value of an existing short protection CDS position with a face value of $1 is given by

$$V(t) = (S_0 - S_t)\Delta \sum_{n=1}^{N} \exp(-(r_t + \lambda_t)\tau_n) .\tag{8.3}$$

Substituting for λ_t using the credit triangle equation[1]

$$\lambda_t \simeq \frac{S_t}{(1 - R)}$$

the net mark-to-market value of a short protection CDS position is given by

$$V(t) = (S_0 - S_t)\Delta \sum_{n=1}^{N} \exp\left(-(r_t + S_t(1 - R)^{-1})\tau_n\right) .\tag{8.4}$$

This equation is very useful as it makes the spread dependence, the interest rate dependence, and the recovery rate dependence of a CDS contract explicit. We can also calculate the analytical derivatives with respect to S_t, r_t and R to understand the market risk sensitivities of a CDS position. While this is only approximate, and assumes a flat interest rate and credit curve, this simplistic model allows us to develop our intuition before we encounter the full CDS model risk management described later in this chapter.

Despite its simplicity, this approximation is good. To show this, we have computed the mark-to-market of a $10 million short protection CDS contract traded at a contractual spread of 100 bp. We have done this using both an exact model as described in the previous chapter, and using the approximation in Equation 8.4. This has been done for CDS with a maturity of 5 Y where we have priced the CDS position with a *flat* CDS curve at 60, 80, 100, 120 and 140 bp. The results are shown in Table 8.1. In general, the percentage error in the mark-to-market is small and is typically less than 0.50%. While not accurate enough for a production pricing model, this is certainly sufficient for intuition building or for a quick estimate.

Table 8.1 Comparison of the exact and approximate value of a 5Y CDS $10 million short protection position with a contractual spread of 100 bp as a function of the CDS spread curve level

	5Y CDS MTM		
Spread (bp)	Exact	Approx.	Error %
60	174 357	173 996	0.25
80	86 486	85 103	0.29
100	0	0	0
120	−85 125	−84 858	0.36
140	−168 909	−168 322	0.39

---

[1] Strictly speaking, we should also adjust the credit triangle to handle the accrual convention as follows

$$\lambda_t \simeq \frac{4\Delta S_t}{(1 - R)}.$$

However, doing so only has a second-order effect on the accuracy of the approximation and we therefore choose not to in order to keep the equation as simple as possible.

Finally, the valuation in Equation 8.4 has been defined for a short protection position. For a long protection position, we simply need to multiply the mark-to-market by minus one. The symmetry of a credit default swap means that the same applies to all of the sensitivities defined in the forthcoming pages.

8.3.2   The Credit DV01

The most important market risk of a CDS position is to changes in the level of the CDS spread curve. This is typically quantified using the Credit DV01. This is the change in the value of the CDS position for a one-basis point parallel increase in the CDS curve. We define it as

$$\text{Credit DV01} = -V(S + 1\,\text{bp}) - V(S)$$

where the negative sign is used to ensure that the Credit DV01 of a short protection position will be positive. We can calculate an analytical approximation to the Credit DV01 by taking the partial derivative with respect to S_t,

$$\text{Credit DV01} \simeq -\frac{\partial V}{\partial S} \times 1\text{bp}.$$

The partial derivative of Equation 8.4 with respect to the current market spread S_t is given by

$$\frac{\partial V(t)}{\partial S_t} = -\Delta \sum_{n=1}^{N} \exp\left(-(r_t + S_t(1-R)^{-1})\tau_n\right)$$

$$-\frac{(S_0 - S_t)\Delta}{(1-R)} \sum_{n=1}^{N} \tau_n \exp\left(-(r_t + S_t(1-R)^{-1})\tau_n\right).$$

Identifying the risky PV01 term

$$\text{RPV01}(t, T) = \Delta \sum_{n=1}^{N} \exp\left(-(r_t + S_t(1-R)^{-1})\tau_n\right)$$

we can rewrite this as

$$\frac{\text{Credit DV01}}{1\text{bp}} = \text{RPV01}(t, T) + \frac{\Delta(S_0 - S_t)}{(1-R)} \sum_{n=1}^{N} \tau_n \exp\left(-(r_t + S_t(1-R)^{-1})\tau_n\right).$$

From this equation, we observe that:

- When $S_t = S_0$, the Credit DV01 equals the RPV01 of the contract times 1bp.
- When S_t deviates from S_0, this is no longer true. The Credit DV01 increases or decreases depending on the value of $(S_0 - S_t)$.

Let us consider a simple example.

Example Consider a short protection position on a $10 million notional contract with a contractual spread of 100 bp. The remaining maturity of the contract is five years. Suppose that the market spread for 5Y protection is now 120 bp and that the continuously compounded short Libor rate is 5%. The risky PV01 is given by 4.240. Setting $r_t = 0.05$, $S_0 = 0.01$ and $S_t = 0.012$, we calculate the Credit DV01 to be $4.240 - 0.035 = 4.205$. A one-basis point increase in credit spreads results in a mark-to-market change

$$\Delta V(t) = -\text{Credit DV01} = -4.205 \times \frac{1}{10\,000} \times \$10m = -\$4,205.$$

8.3.3   The Spread Convexity

The spread convexity, or gamma, is the second-order sensitivity to changes in the market CDS spread. For a short protection position, we write this as

$$\frac{\partial^2 V(t)}{\partial S_t^2} = \frac{2\Delta}{(1-R)} \sum_{n-1}^{N} \tau_n \exp\left(-(r_t + S_t(1-R)^{-1})\tau_n\right)$$

$$+ \frac{\Delta(S_0 - S_t)}{(1-R)^2} \sum_{n=1}^{N} \tau_n^2 \exp\left(-(r_t + S_t(1-R)^{-1})\tau_n\right).$$

For a new short protection CDS position, $S_t = S_0$, and the second term is zero and the spread convexity is just the first term which is positive. As soon as $S_t \neq S_0$ the second term starts to have an effect. However, because this second term is multiplied by $S_0 - S_t$, its contribution is typically much smaller than the first term.

Example Consider a $10 million short protection position with a contractual spread of 100 bp. The remaining maturity of the contract is five years. We suppose that the market spread for 5Y protection is now 120 bp. We can calculate

$$\frac{\partial^2 V(t)}{\partial S_t^2} = 34.837.$$

As a result, we can write (to second order in dS)

$$\Delta V(t) = \frac{\partial V(t)}{\partial S_t} dS + \frac{1}{2} \frac{\partial^2 V(t)}{\partial S_t^2} (dS)^2$$

$$= \left(4.205(dS) + \frac{1}{2}(34.837)(dS)^2\right) \times \$10m$$

$$= \$126\,150 + \$1568 = \$127\,718.$$

We see that 98.8% of the change in the value of the position can be explained by the first-order spread sensitivity.

This example demonstrates that, in general, the effect of spread convexity is small. In addition, when a short protection position is duration hedged by buying protection, the effect of convexity will be reduced as the convexity of the short protection position which is positive will be reduced by the convexity of the long protection position which is negative.

8.3.4   The Interest Rate DV01

We define the Interest Rate DV01 as the change in the value of the CDS position caused by a one-basis point increase in the level of swap rates. We define it as

$$\text{Interest Rate DV01}(t, T) = -(V(H + 1\,\text{bp}) - V(H)).$$

If the risk-free short rate curve is flat, it is possible to show that the breakeven swap rate and the risk-free short rate are close in value. We compare a set of values in Table 8.2.

Table 8.2   Comparison of the risk-free short rate and the corresponding 5Y swap rate

Risk-free short rate (%)	5Y swap rate (%)
2.00	2.011
4.00	4.043
6.00	6.095

This suggests that to a first approximation we can proxy the sensitivity of the CDS mark-to-market by calculating the partial derivative of $V(t)$ with respect to r_t; we have

$$\text{Interest Rate DV01}(t, T) \simeq -\frac{\partial V(t)}{\partial r_t} \times 1\,\text{bp}$$

where

$$\frac{\partial V(t)}{\partial r_t} = -(S_0 - S_t)\Delta \sum_{n=1}^{N} \tau_n \exp\left(-(r_t + S_t(1 - R)^{-1})\tau_n\right).$$

Once again, we can make a few observations:

- The interest rate DV01 of a CDS position is zero when $S_t = S_0$.
- When $S_t \neq S_0$, the interest rate DV01 can be positive or negative.
- The sign of the DV01 is the negative of the sign of the mark-to-market.

Example   Consider again a situation in which we are short protection on $10 million of a contract with a contractual spread of 100 bp. The remaining maturity of the contract is five years. We suppose that the market spread for 5Y protection is now 120 bp. We can calculate the interest rate derivative given above to be 0.02074. A one-basis point increase in interest rates results in a mark-to-market change

(Continued)

$$\Delta V = -\text{Interest Rate DV01} = 0.02074 \times \frac{1}{10\,000} \times \$10\text{m} = \$20.74.$$

The position, which has a negative mark-to-market, actually increases in value if interest rates increase since the expected future cash flows which are negative become less negative as they are discounted at a higher rate.

What is striking is that the interest rate sensitivity is much smaller than the credit spread risk for a similar absolute size movement in their respective underlying rates. *This makes it very clear that the CDS is almost a pure credit product.*

8.3.5 The CDS Theta

The theta (Θ) of a CDS is a measure of the sensitivity of the mark-to-market to the passage of time. As time passes, t increases and the remaining time to maturity, $\tau = (T - t)$, falls. We therefore define Θ as the change in the mark-to-market if we move one day forward in time with everything else remaining fixed. We assume that we do not cross a premium payment date. We can approximate the Θ as

$$\Theta \simeq \frac{\partial V}{\partial t} \cdot dt = -\frac{\partial V}{\partial \tau} \cdot dt$$

where $dt \simeq 1/365$ is one day. We cannot use Equation 8.4 to study the effect of time moving forward for the simple reason that S_t changes with time t even if λ_t is constant.[2] It reflects the fact that between premium payment dates the value of the premium leg does not increase at the same rate as the decrease in the value of the protection leg. We therefore use Equation 8.2 which we differentiate with respect to t to give

$$\frac{\partial V(t)}{\partial t} = S_0(r_t + S_t(1 - R)^{-1}) \cdot \text{RPV01}(t, T)$$

$$+ S_t \exp\left(-(r_t + S_t(1 - R)^{-1})(T - t)\right).$$

Our initial observation is that the value of the premium increases with t while the value of the protection leg falls with t between premium payment dates. This is because:

- The shortening maturity of the contract means that the premium payments are moving closer in time and so have a greater present value. They are also safer in the sense that there is less time in which they can default. Since we are assuming that the credit survives the one day, the value of the premium leg grows at the 'risk-adjusted' rate of $(r_t + \lambda_t)$.
- The shortening maturity of the contract means that the reference credit has less time in which to default. This causes the value of the protection leg to fall with time.

---

[2] The only way to ensure that S_t is constant through time when λ_t is constant through time is to assume that the premium leg is paid continuously, in which case there is no accrued coupon and no sudden change in the mark-to-market as we pass through a premium payment date.

As a result, the value of a short protection position will always increase with time between premium payment dates provided nothing else changes. The reverse is true for a long protection contract.

> **Example** Consider a $10 million short protection position with a contractual spread of 100 bp. The remaining maturity of the contract is five years. We suppose that the market spread for 5Y protection is now 120 bp. Over a one-day period we calculate that the value of the premium leg increases by $82 and the value of the protection leg (which the protection seller is short) decreases by $231, resulting in an overall daily Θ of $313.

Theta does not take into account what happens across a premium payment date. As we move through a premium payment, the value of a short protection CDS falls by the size of the premium payment. The protection leg value changes smoothly as the length of the protection shortens by only one day. As a result, the overall mark-to-market drops from the perspective of a protection seller. As we approach the maturity of the CDS contract, the full value of the CDS tends to the value of the last premium payment.[3]

This is confirmed by the evolution of the full value of a CDS shown in Figure 8.1. We show the value of the premium leg, the protection leg, and the overall mark-to-market of a

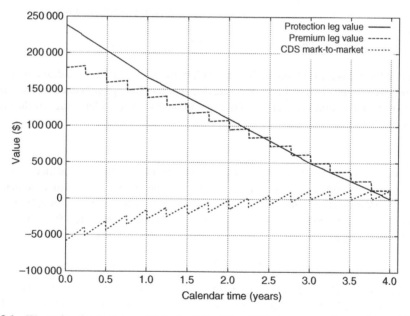

Figure 8.1 We evolve the mark-to-market of a $10 million CDS short protection position with a contractual spread of 50 bp and a market CDS curve fixed at 66 bp. We start with a remaining life of four years. We show the evolution of the protection leg value, the premium leg value and the full mark-to-market. Note how the full mark-to-market drops as we pass through a premium payment date and how it increases between premium payment dates

---

[3] The clean value of the CDS contract calculated by subtracting away the accrued coupon will pull to zero.

$10 million position in a four-year CDS with a contractual spread of 50 bp. The 4Y market spread is currently 66 bp and so the contract currently has a negative mark-to-market. Note how the premium leg value drops after each premium payment date. However, the value of the protection leg evolves smoothly to zero.

There is another factor that affects the value of Θ which we have not included in this simple model. This is the effect of the slope of the CDS curve. A sloped curve will cause the breakeven CDS market spread to the maturity of the CDS to change as we roll through time. If the CDS curve is upward sloping, then the fair market spread of the contract will fall as we move through time. This will cause a short protection position to increase in value.

8.3.6   Recovery Rate Sensitivity

The mark-to-market value of a CDS has an explicit dependency on the expected recovery rate R. In fact, we can calculate the recovery rate sensitivity of a short protection position analytically by differentiating Equation 8.4 to give

$$\frac{\partial V(t)}{\partial R} = \frac{S_t(S_0 - S_t)\Delta}{(1-R)^2} \sum_{n=1}^{N} \tau_n \exp\left(-(r + S_t(1-R)^{-1})\tau_n\right).$$

A number of observations can immediately be made:

- The recovery rate sensitivity is zero if $S_t = S_0$.
- When $S_t \neq S_0$, the sign of the recovery rate sensitivity can be positive or negative depending on the sign of $S_0 - S_t$.
- For typical values of S_t, the recovery rate sensitivity is quadratic in S_t.

The fact that the recovery rate sensitivity of the CDS mark-to-market is quadratic in S_t means that at low spreads, the choice of recovery rate does not have a huge influence on the mark-to-market. However, this quickly changes if the spread blows out to wider values of the order of 500 bp or more.

Example   Consider a $10 million short protection position with a contractual spread of 100 bp. The remaining maturity of the contract is five years. We suppose that the market spread for 5Y protection is now 120 bp. We have assumed a 40% recovery rate. However, we decide to revise our recovery rate estimates by marking this down to 35%. The recovery rate sensitivity at 40% is 0.000704. The change in the value of the position is given by

$$\Delta V = 0.000704 \times 5\% \times \$10m = -\$352.$$

This decrease in value can be explained by noting that a decrease in the recovery rate while holding the CDS spread fixed results in a decrease in the hazard rate. This is clear from the credit triangle. Since the position has a negative mark-to-market, the future cash flows are negative and discounting them at a lower risky rate makes them more negative. The value of the position therefore falls.

If we widen the market spread curve to 500 bp, the sensitivity changes. The recovery rate sensitivity is now 0.0473 and the change in the value of the position for the same recovery rate reduction is −$23 670, a much larger fall than when the curve was at 120 bp.

To compare different positions, practitioners often calculate the change in the mark to market value for an absolute change of 1% in the recovery rate. This is known as the recovery rate DV01.

8.3.7 Value on Default

The value on default (VOD) risk is the change in the value of the CDS contract on an immediate default. We can break this change into the following components.

1. The CDS position cancels and has a mark-to-market value of zero. If $V(t)$ is the value of the position immediately before default, we lose $V(t)$. If $V(t) < 0$ then this is a gain. The change is therefore $0 - V(t) = -V(t)$.
2. If we are a protection buyer, we receive par in return for delivery of a defaulted asset which is a gain of $(1 - R)$. For a protection seller, it is a loss of $(1 - R)$.
3. The protection buyer pays coupon accrued to the protection seller for the fraction of the CDS premium which has accrued since the previous payment date.

The VOD is therefore

$$\text{VOD} = \begin{cases} -V(t) - (1 - R) + \Delta_0 S_0 & \text{for a protection seller} \\ -V(t) + (1 - R) - \Delta_0 S_0 & \text{for a protection buyer} \end{cases}$$

where $\Delta_0 S_0$ is the premium accrued at default.

If default follows a gradual but significant widening in credit spreads, then we should find that the VOD is small. This is because just before default, the value of a long protection contract should converge to $V(t) = (1 - R) - \Delta S_0$. Likewise, for a protection seller we should find that $V(t) = -(1 - R) + \Delta S_0$. Substituting these into the VOD equations, we see that the VOD is zero. As a result, the VOD is in some ways a measure of the 'unexpected shock' of the default.

The biggest uncertainty in the VOD is the value of the recovery payment on default. While the mark-to-market of our position has a fairly small recovery rate sensitivity, *the default contingent recovery rate sensitivity is significant.*

Table 8.3 summarises all of the CDS risk measures discussed and their main characteristics.

Table 8.3 Summary of risks of a CDS position

	Short protection	Long protection
Credit risk	Long the reference entity	Short the reference entity
Mark-to-market	Zero at inception Positive if spreads tighten $S_t < S_0$ Pulls to zero at maturity	Zero at inception Positive if spreads widen $S_t > S_0$ Pulls to zero at maturity
Credit DV01	An increase in credit spreads causes the mark-to-market to fall	An increase in credit spreads causes the mark-to-market to increase
Interest Rate DV01	Zero at contract initiation Opposite sign to mark-to-market Much smaller than the Credit DV01	Zero at contract initiation Opposite sign to mark-to-market Much smaller than the Credit DV01
Recovery Rate DV01	1% increase in R Same sign as mark-to-market Increases quickly for large S_t	1% increase in R Same sign as mark-to-market Increases quickly for large S_t
Spread convexity	Positive	Negative

Table 8.3   (Continued)

	Short protection	Long protection
Theta	Positive	Negative
Premium payment	$V(t)$ jumps down	$V(t)$ jumps up
Value on default	Negative	Positive
	Size depends on the degree of surprise of the default	Size depends on the degree of surprise of the default

8.4   FULL HEDGING OF A CDS CONTRACT

We have used a simplified model of the CDS with some simplified assumptions about the swap curve and CDS curve to build some intuition about how different inputs affect the valuation of a CDS. Specifically, we have used this to demonstrate that the main market risk of a CDS position is to changes in the CDS spreads. As a result, it is clear that the CDS is almost a pure credit play. However, the approximation ignored the term structure of spreads and interest rates. It therefore is too simplistic and imprecise to be used for the pricing and risk management of a CDS book in an industrial environment. We therefore continue this chapter with a description of a full hedging framework for CDS.

We denote the value of a CDS position at time t with maturity T with V. To manage the credit spread risk of this contract will involve buying or selling protection in the liquid on-market CDS contracts. To manage the interest rate risk will involve entering into interest rate swaps in the liquid standard maturity contracts. We assume that our CDS position is hedged with:

- A combination of up to M on-market[4] CDS contracts with times-to-maturity and spreads given by $T_1, T_2, \ldots, T_M$ and $S_1, S_2, \ldots, S_M$. These will present both a CDS spread risk and an interest rate risk. The notional of each is $N_1, N_2, \ldots, N_M$.
- A combination of up to M on-market interest rate swap contracts with times-to-maturity and swap rates given by $\hat{T}_1, \hat{T}_2, \ldots, \hat{T}_M$ and $H_1, H_2, \ldots, H_M$. We have chosen these to correspond to the same tenors as the CDS. However, they do not share the exact same maturity dates since CDS contracts mature on CDS IMM dates while swaps do not. The hedge notional of each swap maturity position is $L_1, L_2, \ldots, L_M$.

We denote the value of the T_m maturity on-market CDS with V_m and the value of the T_m maturity on-market interest rate swap with W_m. The value of our portfolio consisting of our initial position plus hedges in all on-market contracts is

$$\Pi = V + \sum_{m=1}^{M} N_m V_m + \sum_{m=1}^{M} L_m W_m$$

---

[4] An on-market contract is the standard contract of a certain maturity which is quoted in the market today and whose contractual spread is determined so that the contract has no initial value.

where we have dropped the calendar time from $V(t)$ and the CDS and swap values for notational simplicity. At initiation of the CDS hedges, $V_m = 0$ and at initiation of the interest rate swap hedges $W_m = 0$ so that

$$\Pi = V.$$

The first-order change in value of our portfolio consisting of the initial position plus hedges is given by

$$d\Pi = dV + \sum_{m=1}^{M} N_m dV_m + \sum_{m=1}^{M} L_m dW_m.$$

In terms of the first-order sensitivities to the CDS market rates of the hedging instruments we can write

$$d\Pi_S = \sum_{m=1}^{M} \frac{\partial V}{\partial S_m} dS_m + \sum_{m=1}^{M} N_m \sum_{n=1}^{M} \frac{\partial V_m}{\partial S_n} dS_n.$$

This is true because the interest rate swaps have no sensitivity to the CDS curve. The first-order sensitivities to changes in the Libor swap curve are given by

$$d\Pi_H = \sum_{m=1}^{M} \frac{\partial V}{\partial H_m} dH_m + \sum_{m=1}^{M} N_m \sum_{n=1}^{M} \frac{\partial V_m}{\partial H_n} dH_n + \sum_{m=1}^{M} L_m \sum_{n=1}^{M} \frac{\partial W_m}{\partial H_n} dH_n$$

where

$$d\Pi = d\Pi_S + d\Pi_H.$$

Our objective is to determine the spread and interest rate hedges. Since the CDS hedges have an interest rate sensitivity, and the interest rate hedges have no CDS sensitivity, the process is as follows:

1. Calculate the CDS hedges first. We do this ignoring the interest rate hedges which have no spread sensitivity. We only need to consider the spread sensitivity of the position being hedged.
2. Calculate the IRS (interest rate swap) hedges second. This involves calculating the combined interest rate sensitivity of the initial position to be hedged plus the CDS hedges. Once the initial set of IRS hedges start to have a non-zero value, they will present an interest rate sensitivity which will need to be taken into account as the hedge is adjusted.

We now consider these two steps in detail beginning with the CDS spread hedges.

8.5 HEDGING THE CDS SPREAD CURVE RISK

What we want to do is to determine the values of the N_m so that the portfolio is hedged against small first-order movements of the CDS spread curve as represented by the vector of CDS rates. We choose the five most liquid curve points, so that $\{S_1, S_2, S_3, S_4, S_5\} = \{S_{1Y}, S_{3Y}, S_{5Y}, S_{7Y}, S_{10Y}\}$.

The following analysis can easily be generalised to include more curve points. Let us assume that these are also our hedging instruments. In order to be insensitive to first-order movements in these spreads, we require that

$$d\Pi_S = 0.$$

Substituting in from above and setting the coefficients for terms in dS_m equal to zero, we have a set of linear equations, one for each CDS rate

$$-\frac{\partial V}{\partial S_{1Y}} = N_{1Y}\frac{\partial V_{1Y}}{\partial S_{1Y}} + N_{3Y}\frac{\partial V_{3Y}}{\partial S_{1Y}} + \ldots + N_{7Y}\frac{\partial V_{7Y}}{\partial S_{1Y}} + N_{10Y}\frac{\partial V_{10Y}}{\partial S_{1Y}}$$

$$-\frac{\partial V}{\partial S_{3Y}} = N_{1Y}\frac{\partial V_{1Y}}{\partial S_{3Y}} + N_{3Y}\frac{\partial V_{3Y}}{\partial S_{3Y}} + \ldots + N_{7Y}\frac{\partial V_{7Y}}{\partial S_{3Y}} + N_{10Y}\frac{\partial V_{10Y}}{\partial S_{3Y}}$$

$$\vdots \qquad \vdots$$

$$-\frac{\partial V}{\partial S_{7Y}} = N_{1Y}\frac{\partial V_{1Y}}{\partial S_{7Y}} + N_{3Y}\frac{\partial V_{3Y}}{\partial S_{7Y}} + \ldots + N_{7Y}\frac{\partial V_{7Y}}{\partial S_{7Y}} + N_{10Y}\frac{\partial V_{10Y}}{\partial S_{7Y}}$$

$$-\frac{\partial V}{\partial S_{10Y}} = N_{1Y}\frac{\partial V_{1Y}}{\partial S_{10Y}} + N_{3Y}\frac{\partial V_{3Y}}{\partial S_{10Y}} + \ldots + N_{7Y}\frac{\partial V_{7Y}}{\partial S_{10Y}} + N_{10Y}\frac{\partial V_{10Y}}{\partial S_{10Y}}. \qquad (8.5)$$

These equations are linear in the hedging notionals and can be written as

$$-\frac{\partial V}{\partial S_i} = \sum_{j=1}^{M} N_j \frac{\partial V_j}{\partial S_i} \quad \text{for } i = 1, \ldots, M.$$

Clearly, we would expect the largest values of N_j to belong to the CDS contracts which have a T_j close to the contract maturity T, i.e. we would expect a four-year CDS to be hedged with a combination of three-year and five-year maturity contracts.

If we compute sensitivities of a position by bumping one CDS swap spread while holding all the other CDS spreads constant, we find that the value of an on-market CDS is only sensitive to changes in its own maturity CDS spread. To see this, consider a sensitivity of the form

$$\frac{\partial V_{1Y}}{\partial S_{10Y}}.$$

This is the change in value of a 1Y on-market CDS position caused by a change in the 10Y CDS spread, *holding all of the other spreads fixed*. Since the spread of the 1Y on-market contract is held constant as we bump the 10Y spread, its mark-to-market must remain equal to zero and so this sensitivity must also be zero.

Using a bootstrap, we will find that this off-diagonal sensitivity will be exactly zero since the value of the 10Y CDS spread cannot affect the forward default rate between today and the seven-year maturity point. However, if we consider a sensitivity of the form

$$\frac{\partial V_{3Y}}{\partial S_{1Y}}$$

the small increase in the 1Y CDS spread will have an effect on the shape of the forward default curve out to 1Y. There should be no change the 3Y CDS spread as long as the tolerance used in the bootstrap fitting of the survival curve is small enough. We therefore have

$$\frac{\partial V_j}{\partial S_i} = 0 \text{ for } i \neq j. \tag{8.6}$$

Note also that for an on-market CDS

$$\frac{\partial V_i}{\partial S_i} = -\text{RPV01}(t, T_i).$$

We therefore do not need to do any bumping, we can just calculate the risky PV01.

Using the CDS market rates in Table 8.4, we show an example of the on-market CDS sensitivities in Table 8.5.

Table 8.4   Credit default swap curve

CDS maturity	1Y	3Y	5Y	7Y	10Y
CDS market spread	50 bp	60 bp	70 bp	80 bp	100 bp

Table 8.5   Sensitivity of the mark-to-market of a CDS contract with the shown maturities to changes in the 1Y, 3Y, 5Y, 7Y and 10Y rates. See text for a discussion

	Bumped CDS spread maturity				
Hedge	1Y	3Y	5Y	7Y	10Y
CDS 1Y	−0.9791	0	0	0	0
CDS 3Y	0	−2.7745	0	0	0
CDS 5Y	0	0	−4.3530	0	0
CDS 7Y	0	0	0	−5.7382	0
CDS 10Y	0	0	0	0	−7.4629

Using Equation 8.6, we can write Equation 8.5 as

$$-\frac{\partial V}{\partial S_{1Y}} = N_{1Y} \frac{\partial V_{1Y}}{\partial S_{1Y}}$$

$$-\frac{\partial V}{\partial S_{3Y}} = N_{3Y} \frac{\partial V_{3Y}}{\partial S_{3Y}}$$

$$-\frac{\partial V}{\partial S_{5Y}} = N_{5Y} \frac{\partial V_{5Y}}{\partial S_{5Y}}$$

$$-\frac{\partial V}{\partial S_{7Y}} = N_{7Y} \frac{\partial V_{7Y}}{\partial S_{7Y}}$$

$$-\frac{\partial V}{\partial S_{10Y}} = N_{10Y} \frac{\partial V_{10Y}}{\partial S_{10Y}}.$$

Now the inversion to calculate the hedge notionals is trivial. In the general case we now have

$$N_i = \left(-\frac{\partial V}{\partial S_i} \right) \left(\frac{\partial V_i}{\partial S_i} \right)^{-1}. \tag{8.7}$$

These hedges are known as the *CDS equivalent notionals*. They tell us how much of the on-market CDS we have to do in order to immunise our CDS position against small movements in the CDS spread curve.

Within a bootstrap framework, different interpolation schemes will have the same degree of locality, but can have slightly different results. This is because a perturbation in a CDS spread, holding all of the other CDS spreads fixed, will cause a change in the shape of the forward default rate curve. This can affect the value of the premium leg and the protection leg for longer dated contracts which do not fall on the exact maturity dates of the CDS being used to calibrate the survival curve – these are refitted exactly by construction. The effect is usually small, but not negligible.

Table 8.6 The table shows the equivalent notional of hedges to the different maturity points required to hedge a $10 million face value CDS contract. This contractual spread is 50 bp. The contract length is shown in months. In the last row, we show the unbumped CDS curve. We assumed a 40% recovery rate

Contract length (months)	CDS Hedge Notionals at maturity point				
	1Y	3Y	5Y	7Y	10Y
6	−5 031 430	–	–	–	–
12	−10 000 000	–	–	–	–
18	−7 402 730	−2 587 860	–	–	–
24	−4 844 540	−5 136 420	–	–	–
30	−2 392 810	−7 578 420	–	–	–
36	22 614	−9 983 490	–	–	–
42	27 246	−7 341 970	−2 623 110	–	–
48	31 742	−4 791 710	−5 154 570	–	–
54	35 784	−2 329 760	−7 597 340	–	–
60	40 070	59 515	−9 967 090	–	–
66	43 446	64 626	−7 328 610	−2 613 500	–
72	46 780	69 578	−4 749 130	−5 166 790	–
78	49 894	74 270	−2 295 570	−7 593 700	–
84	53 055	78 858	88 771	−9 950 460	–
90	56 769	84 530	94 999	−8 068 620	−1 840 740
96	60 580	90 082	101 337	−6 226 240	−3 641 190
102	63 821	95 021	106 758	−4 536 350	−5 290 520
108	67 144	99 856	112 284	−2 871 860	−6 913 450
114	70 111	104 275	117 231	−1 311 920	−8 432 550
120	72 820	108 370	121 715	173 165	−9 876 980

Table 8.6 shows how the equivalent notionals for a CDS contract depends on the contract maturity in months. The contract is assumed to pay a contractual spread of 50 bp and have a face value of $10 million. The hedging instruments are the 1Y, 3Y, 5Y, 7Y and 10Y on-market CDS. We make the following observations:

- The equivalent notional hedge for a 12-month contract is exactly −$10 million. This is simply because the CDS spread of the 1Y contract is 50 bp, which is exactly the same as the contractual spread of the contract being hedged. This is reassuring as it demonstrates that the model returns the risky position as the hedge if it is one of the available hedging instruments.
- For a CDS contract with the same maturity as one of the hedging instruments but with a different contractual spread, most of the hedge will be in the same maturity CDS. However,

because of the spread difference, the contract value will be exposed to changes in shorter maturity CDS since these affect the value of the risky PV01 of the contract being hedged. As a result, we need to put on smaller hedges in these to offset this sensitivity.

- For a CDS contract with a maturity which does not coincide with the hedge maturities, the hedges are mostly confined to the maturity points adjacent to the maturity of the CDS contract, i.e. they are *local*. For example, the 96-month (eight-year) contract has hedges of −$6.23 million in the 7Y CDS and −$3.64 million in the 10Y CDS. Once again there are smaller hedges in shorter maturity contracts due to the spread difference between the contract and the market.
- There is a difference in sign between the hedge on the maturity buckets close to the CDS position maturity, and the hedges on the earlier maturity buckets. Consider, for example, the 60-month (five-year) contract. The main hedge is a notional of −$9.967 million in the 5Y contract which has a spread of 70 bp. However, there is also a hedge of +$59 515 in the 3Y point and a slightly smaller positive hedge of +$40 070 at the 1Y point. These smaller hedges can be explained by realising that if we bump the 3Y CDS spread while holding the 1Y and 5Y spread fixed, we must push up the forward default rate curve between years 1 and 3. However, the foward default rate between years 3 and 5 will have to fall by about the same amount in order to refit the 5Y CDS spread. While the 5Y spread is unchanged, the 5Y risky PV01 drops because, due to discounting, the effect of the increase in the default rate from year 1 to 3 has a bigger impact than the fall in the default rate from year 3 to 5. This means that the value of a 5Y short protection position with a negative mark-to-market will *increase* by a small amount. However, bumping the 5Y spread causes the mark-to-market of the short protection position to *decrease*. This explains the sign difference.

Despite being hedged with respect to first-order spread movements, we are not hedged with respect to larger spread movements which would be captured by higher-order derivatives. To examine the importance of second-order effects, we write the value of our CDS position plus the M hedges at the different CDS maturity points as

$$\Pi = V + \sum_{m=1}^{M} N_m V_m$$

and consider a specific example.

Example An investor has a CDS position on their book which is a short protection position with four years remaining to maturity. It has a contractual spread of 50 bp and the face value of the position is $10 million. The current CDS spread curve is given in Table 8.4.

The initial mark-to-market of the position is −$58 326. This is because the investor has sold protection at 50 bp, yet the four-year breakeven spread implied by our interpolation scheme is 66.25 bp. As a result, the investor is being paid less now than they could receive in the market and so the contract has a negative value. Or to put it another way, the investor went long the credit at 50 bp and the credit has widened to 66.25 bp, resulting in a loss. To hedge this position, the investor wants to use the main liquid hedging instruments. These are the 1Y, 3Y and 5Y CDS market contracts. We calculate the following equivalent hedge notionals:

(Continued)

CDS maturity	1Y	3Y	5Y	7Y	10Y
RPV01	0.9791	2.7745	4.3530	5.7382	7.4629
$\partial V/\partial S_i$	3.11	−1329.42	−2243.69	0	0
CDS hedge notional ($ thousand)	+31 742	−4 791 710	−5 154 570	0	0

A negative hedge notional means that we buy protection. Figure 8.2 shows the sensitivity of the mark-to-market of the hedged CDS position to parallel movements in the CDS spread curve. We see that the quality of the hedge is excellent with a change in value of only $50 for a 25 bp change in the CDS curve. The gamma of the hedged position is negative.

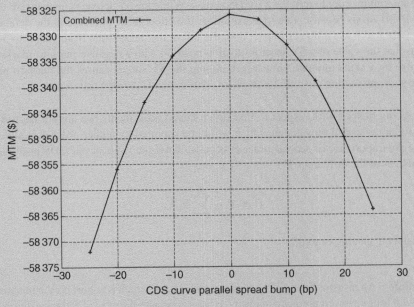

Figure 8.2   MTM of the hedged CDS position as we shift the CDS curve in a parallel fashion

This example shows that the CDS position is very well hedged against parallel movements in the CDS spread curve. This is only a small part of the power of this hedging approach – by computing hedges at different maturity points we are also immunised against first-order changes in the value of the CDS position due to small independent movements in the 1Y, 3Y, 5Y, 7Y and 10Y CDS spreads. Collectively, these movements may cause the shape of the CDS curve to steepen, flatten or twist.

8.6   HEDGING THE LIBOR CURVE RISK

Once we have hedged out the spread risk as described in the previous section, the next risk to hedge is the sensitivity to movements in the Libor curve. We assume that the interest rate hedging instruments are the set of on-market interest rate swaps with maturities of 1Y, 3Y, 5Y, 7Y and 10Y. As these have no credit exposure to the reference entity, they have no spread risk and so do not affect our spread hedge.

We denote the interest rate swap rates as $H_{1Y}, H_{3Y}, H_{5Y}, H_{7Y}$ and H_{10Y}. As with an on-market CDS, the value of an on-market interest rate swap is zero. We define the hedge notionals of interest rate swaps as $L_{1Y}, L_{3Y}, L_{5Y}, L_{7Y}$ and L_{10Y}. We also define their respective mark-to-market values as $W_{1Y}, W_{3Y}, W_{5Y}, W_{7Y}$ and W_{10Y}. Recall that these are all initially equal to zero, though their sensitivities are not. From Equation 8.5 we have

$$\sum_{m=1}^{M} \frac{\partial V}{\partial H_m} dH_m + \sum_{m=1}^{M} N_m \sum_{n=1}^{M} \frac{\partial V_m}{\partial H_n} dH_n + \sum_{m=1}^{M} L_m \sum_{n=1}^{M} \frac{\partial W_m}{\partial H_n} dH_n = 0.$$

Since the hedging interest rate swap instruments are on-market swaps, whose value is zero, they have no sensitivity to changes in other swap rates, i.e.

$$\frac{\partial W_j}{\partial H_i} = 0 \quad \text{if } i \neq j.$$

Also, since the on-market credit default swaps hedges have zero initial value, we set $V_m = 0$. We also showed in Section 8.3.4 that on-market CDS have an Interest Rate 01 of zero. We can therefore write that

$$\frac{\partial V_m}{\partial H_n} = 0.$$

We therefore have

$$\sum_{m=1}^{M} \frac{\partial V}{\partial H_m} dH_m + \sum_{m=1}^{M} L_m \frac{\partial W_m}{\partial H_m} dH_m = 0.$$

This is a systems of M equations which can be solved directly for each L_m.

$$L_m = - \left(\frac{\partial V}{\partial H_m} \right) \left(\frac{\partial W_m}{\partial H_m} \right)^{-1}.$$

This analysis is exact, but only applies to a new position which we are hedging with on-market interest rate swaps and credit default swaps. We also recall that the Interest Rate 01 of an *on-market* interest rate swap position is simply the PV01 of the swap as discussed in Section 2.6.6 multiplied by 1bp so there is no need to do any bumping of swap curves. For a receiver swap, we simply set

$$\frac{\partial W_m}{\partial H_m} = -\text{PV01}(t, T_m).$$

Example Consider the example used in the previous section in which an investor has a $10 million short protection position with four years remaining to maturity with a contractual spread of 50 bp. Recall that this position currently has a negative mark-to-market value of −$58 326. We calculate the equivalent interest rate swap hedge notionals which are shown in Table 8.7. These interest rate hedges take into account the interest rate risk of the initial position plus that of the CDS spread hedges. The sensitivity of the CDS position to increases in the swap rate is positive – as the position has a negative mark-to-market, an increase in rates will make the present value less negative and hence the change in mark-to-market will be positive.

Table 8.7 Calculation of interest rate swap equivalent notionals. These are receiver swaps

IRS maturity	1Y	3Y	5Y	7Y	10Y
PV01	0.96359	2.75609	4.37429	5.84033	7.78047
$\partial V/\partial H_i$	1.0585	9.9134	2.6461	0	0
Receiver swap notional ($)	10 985	35 969	6049	0	0

Table 8.8 shows the value of the unhedged CDS position for various parallel bumps in both the CDS curve and the Libor swap curve. Contrast this with Table 8.9 which shows the value of the hedged position also shown for various bumps in the CDS curve and the Libor swap curve. In the worst shown case of a 25 bp spread widening and an increase in Libor rates of 40 bp the position drops only $166. The value of the portfolio is very insensitive to market spread and interest rate movements and the first-order hedges perform well.

Table 8.8 Change in dollar value of an unhedged $10 million CDS position as we bump the CDS spread curve and the interest rate swap curve in a parallel fashion

Swap rate bump (bp)	CDS spread bump (bp)						
	−15	−10	−5	0	5	10	15
−40	53 775	35 638	17 560	−459	−18 420	−36 323	−54 168
−30	53 783	35 682	17 640	−344	−18 270	−36 138	−53 948
−20	53 792	35 726	17 720	−229	−18 120	−35 953	−53 728
−10	53 800	35 770	17 799	−115	−17 970	−35 768	−53 508
0	53 808	35 814	17 878	0	−17 821	−35 584	−53 290
10	53 817	35 858	17 957	114	−17 672	−35 401	−53 072
20	53 825	35 901	18 035	227	−17 524	−35 218	−52 854
30	53 833	35 945	18 114	340	−17 376	−35 035	−52 638
40	53 841	35 988	18 192	453	−17 229	−34 854	−52 422

Table 8.9 Change in dollar value of a $10 million spread hedged and interest rate hedged CDS position as we bump the CDS spread curve and interest rate swap curve in a parallel fashion

Swap rate bump (bp)	CDS spread bump (bp)										
	−25	−20	−15	−10	−5	0	5	10	15	20	25
−40	0	25	46	64	78	89	97	100	101	98	92
−30	−11	11	30	46	58	67	72	74	72	67	59
−20	−23	−2	14	28	38	44	47	47	43	37	26
−10	−34	−16	−1	10	17	22	23	21	15	6	−6
0	−46	−30	−17	−8	−3	0	−1	−6	−13	−24	−38
10	−57	−43	−33	−26	−23	−22	−26	−32	−42	−54	−70
20	−69	−57	−49	−44	−43	−44	−50	−58	−70	−84	−102
30	−80	−70	−64	−62	−62	−66	−73	−84	−97	−114	−134
40	−91	−84	−80	−79	−82	−88	−97	−110	−125	−144	−166

8.7   PORTFOLIO LEVEL HEDGING

The previous section has shown how we can immunise a CDS position against small spread and interest rate movements using on-market CDS and interest rate swaps. In practice, the situation is never so simple. A trader's book will consist of many legacy CDS and interest rate swap positions. Some of these positions are trades done with investors in the market. Others are trades done to hedge these investor-facing trades. These are usually executed in the broker market. While the situation is then more complicated, the approach to risk managing a CDS book is simply a generalisation of the framework which has already been described. It is as follows:

1. We group the CDS positions by reference entity.
2. For each reference entity, we bump the CDS spreads at the standard hedge maturity points.
3. For each bump, we calculate the change in the value of the CDS positions associated with each reference entity.
4. We use these value changes to generate the equivalent CDS notionals.
5. We repeat until all of the reference entities have been hedged.

As all of the positions in the portfolio present an interest rate sensitivity, the hedging of the interest rate risk is as follows:

1. We bump the interest rate swap rates at the standard hedge maturity points.
2. For each bump, we calculate the change in the value of all the existing positions. This includes legacy CDS positions, new CDS hedges, and legacy interest rate swap positions.
3. We use these value changes to calculate the equivalent interest rate swap notionals.

Although the process is quite simple, it can be computationally intensive. It only needs to be done for each reference credit curve at a time. Since the interest rate and spread risks are typically managed via their first-order sensitivities, they are linear and it is possible to sum them across positions.

One of the advantages of trading a large book is that some of the higher-order risks such as the spread gamma may be largely offset when aggregated over a large number of positions. However, this is far from certain and care should certainly be taken to monitor the higher-order risks to ensure that these risks are not compounding.

A weakness of this hedging approach is that it is only appropriate for fairly small market moves where first-order sensitivities are sufficient to explain the changes in value of the portfolio. What is also important is to complement this analysis by determining the effect on the book of large movements or shocks in market prices and default. This is best captured by generating scenarios in which we stress the market inputs and reprice the book in each scenario. In particular, the VOD of the book should be calculated per trade and per reference credit.

8.8   COUNTERPARTY RISK

Counterparty risk in the context of credit default swaps is the risk that the counterparty in the CDS contract fails to make the contractually obliged payments. For example, a protection buyer may fail to make payments on the premium leg, or a protection seller may fail to make the payment of par following a credit event.

In practice, when two parties enter into a CDS and there is a concern about the counterparty risk of one party, this can generally be mitigated via a process of *collateral posting*. This requires the counterparties to agree to periodically deposit securities equal in value to the CDS mark-to-market with the other counterparty. This means that at worst, a failure of one counterparty will only cause the other to lose the change in value of the contract since the last collateral posting.

If there is a counterparty default then provided the CDS is transacted within the standard framework of the ISDA master agreements, the ISDA claimant is considered to be *pari passu* with senior unsecured bond holders.

There is clearly a fundamental asymmetry in the counterparty exposure of the parties to a CDS contract. We therefore consider counterparty risk from the two perspectives of a protection seller and a protection buyer.

8.8.1   Protection Seller

The scenario in which the protection seller loses due to counterparty risk is one in which the protection buyer stops making the promised payments of premium. If this happens, the contract will terminate and no more protection will be provided. The protection seller could immediately go into the market and reinstate this short protection position at the current market spread. If CDS spreads have tightened, this could result in a mark-to-market loss although the size of the loss is capped by the fact that a CDS spread can never become negative. The size of such a loss is typically less than 10% of the contract face value. Consider the following example.

Example   A short protection position with a notional of $10 million and with a contractual spread of 200 bp with a risky PV01 of 4.0 (roughly five years to maturity) will lose a maximum of approximately $10m × 200 bp × 4.0 = $800 000 if the spread tightens to zero and the protection buyer defaults.

Two factors mitigate this risk:

1. A tightening of spreads is usually a gradual process and so the changes in contract value could be captured through a collateral posting process.
2. Default correlation is generally positive, i.e. it is generally unlikely that one credit is tightening while at the same time the counterparty defaults. The opposite case is much more likely.

8.8.2   Protection Buyer

The worst case scenario for the protection buyer is one in which we have the following sequence of events:

1. The reference credit experiences a credit event.
2. The protection buyer triggers the protection on the CDS.
3. The protection seller fails to deliver the par amount.

On a $10 million face value trade, assuming a recovery rate of 40%, the loss would be $6 million. We call this the worst case since we have no opportunity here to reinstate the protection before the credit event. For example, if we know that the counterparty has failed *before* the reference credit defaults, we can immediately purchase protection on the reference entity and so we are protected in the event of a default of the reference asset. The cost of replacing the protection may be higher than the initial cost and so a loss will be incurred. However, this will typically be smaller than the loss incurred if we only discover that we have no protection after the credit event.

8.8.3   Summary

The protection buyer is therefore the counterparty who has the most counterparty risk. While it is possible to build a pricing model to price in counterparty risk as in Hull and White (2000b) and O'Kane and Schloegl (2002a), hedging this risk assumes the existence of a CDS market in the name of the counterparty, which is not always true. Instead, the market prefers to use the collateral posting approach. In cases when the counterparty risk is assumed to be too great, or the counterparty is not willing to accept the collateral posting arrangements, the trade simply does not get approved and does not happen.

8.9   SUMMARY

This chapter has covered in detail all of the market risks of a CDS contract. We have described a hedging framework for removing almost all of both spread risk and interest rate risk, and we have presented a number of realistic examples to demonstrate this.

9
Forwards, Swaptions and CMDS

9.1 INTRODUCTION

In this chapter we will analyse the following single-name credit derivatives for which the CDS contract is the underlying:

- The forward credit default swap: This is a contract in which a forward starting CDS can be entered into today at a contractual forward spread which is also agreed today. This is a simple product to define and price, and is an important and fairly liquid product in the market.
- The option on a credit default swap: Also known as the *default swaption*, this is the first volatility product we have encountered. We discuss the mechanics of the default swaption and explain the standard pricing model used and discuss its risk management.
- The constant maturity default swap: This is also known as the CMDS or CMCDS for short. A CMDS is a CDS contract in which one of the legs has been replaced with a floating leg. The payments on the *floating* leg are variable and are linked to future observations of a fixed tenor CDS spread in the market. We describe the mechanics of the CMDS and set out a pricing model.

We begin with the forward starting CDS.

9.2 FORWARD STARTING CDS

In the standard CDS, protection comes into effect on the *effective date*, usually the calendar day following trade date. However, it is possible to buy or sell protection at a spread agreed today in which the protection starts weeks or months after the trade date. These are called forward starting CDS or, more simply, forward CDS.

In the standard forward CDS contract, a protection buyer agrees to enter into a contract to buy protection at a forward date t_F and at a contractual spread $S(t, t_F, T)$ which is agreed today. This protection matures on some maturity date T where clearly $T > t_F$. Between today and the forward date there are no payments. Note that:

- If a credit event occurs before the forward date the standard contract cancels at no cost to either party.
- If no credit event occurs before the forward date, the protection buyer pays the premium leg with the first coupon payment date starting after the forward date.

- If a credit event occurs at time after the forward date and before the contract maturity time T then there is a payment of $(1 - R)$ on the protection leg of the CDS at the time of the credit event.

These mechanics are shown in Figure 9.1.

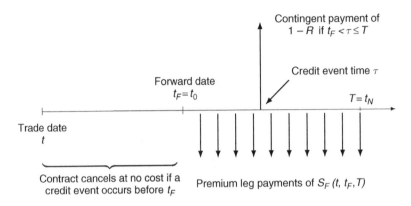

Figure 9.1   Forward starting CDS

Forward starting CDS enable hedgers to lock-in today a cost of protection for a future period. As we will show later, the shape of the forward curve is sensitive to the slope of the CDS term structure. In particular, we find that the forward curve for an upward sloping CDS curve will be higher than the CDS curve. As a result, CDS can be used by a protection seller to lock in a higher spread forward for the same term, e.g. if the CDS curve is upward sloping, a 2Y CDS contract starting six months forward will pay a higher spread than a 2Y contract starting tomorrow. The investor in the forward CDS expects that the forward spread is higher than the 2Y spread will be in six months' time.

9.2.1   Valuation of Forward Starting CDS

We need to establish a clear notation for distinguishing between CDS spreads, forward CDS spreads and future CDS spreads. We therefore define:

- $S(t, T)$: This is the spot starting CDS spread for a contract which starts today at time t and matures at time T.
- $S(t, t_F, T)$: This is the forward CDS spread known at time t for a contract starting at time $t_F > t$ and maturing at time T. By definition $S(t, t, T) = S(t, T)$.
- $S(t_F, T)$: This is the CDS spread observed at time $t_F > t$ in the future for a contract which matures at time T. At time t this quantity is unknown.

To price a product which depends on $S(t_F, T)$, we need to model the uncertainty by assuming some probability distribution for the future spread. This will be discussed in much greater detail later in the chapter when we encounter default swaptions and CMDS.

9.2.2   Determining the Forward CDS Spread

We define the survival probability from today time t, valuation date, to forward time t_F as $Q(t, t_F)$. Each payment on the premium leg which occurs at time t_n needs to condition on the probability that there is no credit event before time t_n. We also take into account the effect of coupon accrued paid at default. The premium leg present value is therefore

$$\text{Premium Leg PV}(t) = S(t, t_F, T) \cdot \text{RPV01}(t, t_F, T)$$

where

$$\text{RPV01}(t, t_F, T) = \frac{1}{2} \sum_{n=1}^{N} \Delta(t_{n-1}, t_n) Z(t, t_n)(Q(t, t_{n-1}) + Q(t, t_n))$$

is the forward starting risky PV01 including the effect of the accrued coupon paid at default. Note that premium payments begin following the forward date so that $t_0 = t_F$ and $t_N = T$. A forward CDS is similar to a standard spot starting CDS since all premium flows have to be conditioned on surviving from the valuation date to the premium payment date.

For the protection leg, the change in the pricing formula is that we only start the time integral from the forward start time t_F

$$\text{Protection Leg PV}(t, t_F, T) = (1 - R) \int_{t_F}^{T} Z(t, s)(-dQ(t, s)).$$

The mark-to-market for a long protection forward position is therefore given by

$$V(t, t_F, T) = (1 - R) \int_{t_F}^{T} Z(t, s)(-dQ(t, s)) - S(t, t_F, T)\text{RPV01}(t, t_F, T).$$

The forward starting CDS spread is therefore given by setting $V(t, t_F, T) = 0$ to give

$$S(t, t_F, T) = \frac{(1 - R) \int_{t_F}^{T} Z(t, s)(-dQ(t, s))}{\text{RPV01}(t, t_F, T)}. \tag{9.1}$$

We can write the forward spread in terms of CDS spreads and spot starting RPV01s. To do this, we note that the forward RPV01 in the denominator can be expressed as the difference between the two spot starting RPV01s

$$\text{RPV01}(t, t_F, T) = \text{RPV01}(t, T) - \text{RPV01}(t, t_F).$$

In addition, the value of the forward starting protection in the numerator of Equation 9.1 can be written as the difference of the value of two spot starting protection legs as follows

$$(1 - R) \int_{t_F}^{T} Z(t, s)(-dQ(t, s)) = (1 - R) \left(\int_{t}^{T} Z(t, s)(-dQ(t, s)) - \int_{t}^{t_F} Z(t, s)(-dQ(t, s)) \right).$$

Given that the value of a spot starting protection leg must equal the value of the premium leg at the market spread, the forward starting spread is given by

$$S(t, t_F, T) = \frac{S(t, T)\text{RPV01}(t, T) - S(t, t_F)\text{RPV01}(t, t_F)}{\text{RPV01}(t, T) - \text{RPV01}(t, t_F)}.$$

This equation makes it possible to calculate the forward spread from a knowledge of the spot starting CDS spreads and their respective risky PV01s. We note that if the spot starting CDS spread curve is flat so that $S(t, T) = S(t, t_F)$, the forward spread becomes

$$S(t, t_F, T) = S(t, T) = S(t, t_F).$$

The forward CDS curve will also be exactly flat.

9.2.3 Valuation of a Forward Starting CDS

As with a standard CDS, the spread of a forward starting CDS is set so that the contract has a value which is initially zero. However, as time passes and the spread curve changes, its value will tend to move away from zero. We suppose that a contract has been transacted at time $t = 0$ with a contractual forward spread $S(0, t_F, T)$ and we want to value it at a time t where $0 < t < t_F$. Since the value of the forward starting protection today at time t is the same as the value of the forward starting premium leg paying the forward spread $S(t, t_F, T)$, the value of a long protection forward starting position is therefore

$$V(t) = (S(t, t_F, T) - S(0, t_F, T)) \cdot \text{RPV01}(t, t_F, T).$$

This formula is very similar to the pricing formula for a spot starting CDS. Indeed, if we set $t_F = t$ then we recover the standard CDS pricing equation as required.

9.2.4 The Shape of the Forward CDS Curve

In general, the CDS curve is not flat and consequently the forward curve is also not flat. To aid intuition about the link between the forward curve shape and the spot CDS curve shape, we write the forward CDS spread to maturity T as

$$S(t, t+\alpha, T+\alpha) \simeq \frac{(1-R)}{(T-t)} \int_{t+\alpha}^{T+\alpha} h(s)ds$$

where $h(t)$ is the forward continuous default rate. This equation is a good first-order approximation[1] and means that we can write the forward starting CDS spread in terms of the spot starting spread as

$$S(t, t+\alpha, T+\alpha) \simeq S(t, T) + \frac{(1-R)}{(T-t)} \left(\int_T^{T+\alpha} h(s)ds - \int_t^{t+\alpha} h(s)ds \right).$$

---

[1] From the credit triangle which assumes a continuously paid spread premium, we have

$$S(t, t+\alpha, T+\alpha) = \frac{(1-R) \int_{t+\alpha}^{T+\alpha} h(s) \exp\left(-\int_{t+\alpha}^s (r(u)+h(u))\right) ds}{\int_{t+\alpha}^{T+\alpha} \exp\left(-\int_{t+\alpha}^s (r(u)+h(u))\right) ds}.$$

If we assume that $\int_{t+\alpha}^{T+\alpha}(r(s)+h(s))ds \ll 1$ then to first order we have

$$S(t, t+\alpha, T+\alpha) \simeq \frac{(1-R) \int_{t+\alpha}^{T+\alpha} h(s)ds}{\int_{t+\alpha}^{T+\alpha} ds} = \frac{(1-R)}{(T-t)} \int_{t+\alpha}^{T+\alpha} h(s)ds.$$

If the CDS curve is upward sloping, then we expect that

$$\int_T^{T+\alpha} h(s)ds - \int_t^{t+\alpha} h(s)ds > 0$$

and that this difference will increase with the length of the forward period α. As a result, the forward curve will be higher than the spot curve, with the difference increasing with the forward time α. If the CDS curve is inverted, then we expect that

$$\int_T^{T+\alpha} h(s)ds - \int_t^{t+\alpha} h(s)ds < 0$$

and the forward curve will be lower than the spot CDS curve. In this case, the forward curve will be lower for increasing α. Table 9.1 shows two examples, one of an upward sloping and one of an inverted spread curve along with their respective forward spread curves. These curves were calculated using a full CDS valuation model and demonstrate the same qualitative results as this simplified analysis.

Table 9.1 Forward spread curves for an upward sloping and an inverted CDS curve. We show the spot CDS curve and forward curves which are 1, 2, 3 and 4 years forward. Units are basis points

Upward sloped						Inverted					
Term (yrs)	Spot (bp)	Forward start (years)				Term (yrs)	Spot (bp)	Forward start (years)			
		1	2	3	4			1	2	3	4
1	105	115	143	167	194	1	180	138	127	103	77
2	110	129	155	180	192	2	160	133	115	91	80
3	120	140	166	183	191	3	150	124	104	88	80
4	130	152	171	184	189	4	140	114	99	87	64
5	140	157	174	184	188	5	130	109	96	74	55
7	150	163	175	183	186	7	120	96	77	59	44
10	155	166	176	183	185	10	100	80	64	50	37

9.2.5 Hedging Forward Starting CDS

If the CDS curve is exactly flat, then there is a static hedge for the forward CDS using spot starting CDS. To see this, consider a CDS curve which is flat at 100 bp. We consider a 1 × 5 forward short protection CDS. This is a forward CDS which starts in one year and matures five years later which is six years from today. Because of the flat CDS curve, the contract will also have a forward spread of 100 bp. The hedge for this position is:

• Sell $10 million of protection at a CDS spread of 100 bp with a maturity of six years.
• Buy $10 million of protection at a CDS spread of 100 bp with a maturity of one year.

Any default before one-year will cause the one-year and six-year CDS contracts to trigger and cancel with no net cost. This is the same as the forward CDS contract which simply cancels. After one year, the one-year contract has matured and our six-year contract is now a five-year short protection contract at a spread of 100 bp. This is exactly the same as the forward contract.

When the CDS curve is no longer flat, the situation is a little bit more complex. Hedging forward starting CDS contracts is then done by calculating the sensitivity of the contract value to changes in the different points along the CDS curve and then calculating the corresponding equivalent notionals of CDS to buy and sell. We can calculate the hedges by perturbing the individual hedge maturity points on the CDS curve and determining the equivalent notional of the CDS hedge. Let us consider an example.

Example   Consider a $10 million long protection 2 × 5 forward CDS position initially traded exactly a year ago at a forward spread of 300 bp. The contract is now a 1 × 5 forward. Given the current CDS term structure in Table 9.2, we calculate the current 1 × 5 forward rate to be 267 bp.

Table 9.2   CDS term structure and equivalent notional hedges calculated for a $10 million face value 1 × 5 forward starting CDS

CDS term	Spread (bp)	Mark-to-market change ($)	Risky PV01	Hedge notional ($m)
1Y	100	−991	0.979	−10.126
2Y	120	−3	1.895	−0.016
3Y	145	−9	2.765	−0.032
5Y	220	2027	4.306	4.707
7Y	245	2930	5.604	5.229
10Y	270	0	7.166	0.000

We wish to calculate the CDS equivalent notional hedges. We do this by bumping each of the spreads, holding the other spreads fixed, and determining the change in the value of the forward. We then divide the value change by the risky PV01 of the CDS hedge. The resulting hedge notionals are shown in Table 9.2. We see that a long protection 1 × 5 CDS can be hedged to spread movements by going long $10.126 million of protection to one year and short a total of $9.936 million of protection split across the 5Y and 7Y CDS spread buckets. We did not include a 6Y point on our curve since we consider the 5Y and 7Y CDS contracts to be more liquid and so prefer to express our hedges in those instruments.

9.3   THE DEFAULT SWAPTION

The default swaption is an over-the-counter product which grants the holder the right, but not the obligation, to enter into a credit default swap on some future date at a spread fixed today. In this section we will start by discussing the mechanics of the standard credit swaption product. We then introduce the standard pricing model.

9.3.1   The Mechanics

The default swaption is simply an option on a forward starting credit default swap. Almost all default swaptions are European style, meaning that the option holder can only exercise the option on one specific date known as the option expiry date t_E. Borrowing from the world of interest rate swaptions, we name an option to buy protection a *payer* swaption, since on exercise of this option, the option owner pays the premium leg at the strike CDS spread. An option to sell protection and receive the premium leg is a *receiver* swaption.

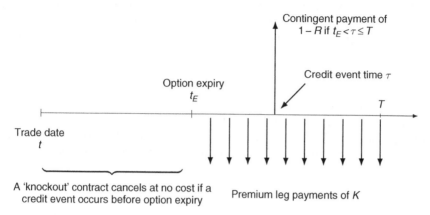

Figure 9.2   CDS knockout payer swaption – an option to buy protection – showing the payments if the option holder decides to exercise the option

There are two variations on the mechanics of a default swaption. They are:

- A knockout swaption cancels with no payments if there is a credit event before the option expiry date. This version of the contract seems to be standard practice outside the US, although this is not a hard rule.
- A non-knockout swaption does not cancel if there is a credit event before the option expiry date. In this case the holder of a non-knockout payer swaption is able to take delivery of the underlying long protection CDS on the expiry date and exercise the protection, delivering a defaulted obligation in return for par. This is the standard version of the contract within the US.

Note that the holder of a receiver non-knockout swaption will never exercise the swaption if the reference credit has defaulted since it would result in delivery of a short protection position on a defaulted credit and a loss of $(1 - R)$.

Figure 9.2 shows the cash flows associated with a standard knockout CDS swaption. We denote the strike CDS spread with K. This is the contractual spread of the CDS into which the option holder can exercise the option at time t_E. A payer and a receiver swaption only differ through the direction of the arrows on the payment and protection legs.

In the following we will focus on the knockout swaption. We do this because the non-knockout payer swaption can be decomposed into a knockout swaption plus the front end protection provided by the non-knockout feature. We can simply write

Value of non-knockout payer = Value of knockout payer + Value of front end protection.

Calculation of the front end protection value will be discussed later. Because of this simple decomposition, we now focus on pricing just knockout swaptions.

9.3.2 The exercise decision

Consider a knockout default swaption with option expiry at time t_E. If exercised, the option holder enters into a CDS contract with final maturity at time T. We now consider the decision to exercise. We assume that the option is European style – the option can only be exercised on its expiry date. An option holder will only exercise if the value of CDS protection which they are buying or selling is less than the cost of the same contract in the market. To see this, consider a payer swaption. The value at time t_E of the long protection CDS with contractual spread K received on exercise is given by

$$(S(t_E, T) - K) \times \text{RPV01}(t_E, T)$$

where $S(t_E, T)$ is the T-maturity CDS market spread as seen at time t_E. $\text{RPV01}(t_E, T)$ is the associated risky PV01 also seen at time t_E. In this formula, we are on the option exercise date so both $S(t_E, T)$ and the $\text{RPV01}(t_E, T)$ are known with certainty. The cost of entering into the current market CDS from time t_E to T at the market spread $S(t_E, T)$ is zero. Hence we should exercise the payer option if

$$S(t_E, T) > K.$$

We have an option to buy protection at K which we only exercise if the market spread has widened beyond K. The opposite is the case for a contract to sell protection. We only exercise a receiver swaption if

$$S(t_E, T) < K.$$

The fact that a knockout swaption cancels if there is a credit event before option expiry is clearly not good for the holder of a payer swaption. Consider the scenario in which the CDS spread is trading at 2000 bp, the option strike is 100 bp, and there is just one day left to option expiry. The option owner is long protection forward and wants the spread to continue to widen and is even hoping for a credit event but *does not want this to occur before the option expiry.* If there is a credit event on the day before expiry, the option knocks out with no payments. However, if there is a credit event on the following day, the option expires and the option holder can trigger the protection life, receiving $(1 - R)$ on the option face value.

   Because of this large variation in potential payouts, dealers are often unwilling to quote payer knockout swaptions on credits with high spreads. If the two outcomes have significant probabilities, the position becomes very difficult to hedge. This is why dealers tend to prefer to sell non-knockout swaptions.

   Whether the contract does or does not knock out does not matter to the holder of a receiver option as they would never choose to exercise an option to sell protection on a defaulted credit or one with a spread higher than K.

9.3.3 Valuing a Knockout Default Swaption

A valuation model for knockout default swaptions has been derived by a number of researchers including Schönbucher (1999), Jamshidian (2002) and Hull and White (2003a). What they all have in common is that they rely on the use of the *change of numeraire* technique to translate the pricing problem into what is called the *forward risky PV01 survival measure*. In this section we step through the derivation of the general result. In doing so we attempt to explain the change of numeraire technique and show how it is applied to the pricing of default swaptions.

To begin, we note that the value of a payer swaption at option expiry time t_E is given by

$$V_{Pay}(t_E) = 1_{\tau > t_E} \max\left[S(t_E, T) - K, 0\right] \cdot \text{RPV01}(t_E, T)$$

where the indicator function $1_{\tau > t_E}$ is given by

$$1_{\tau > t_E} = \begin{cases} 1 & \text{if } \tau > t_E \\ 0 & \text{if } \tau \leq t_E \end{cases}$$

and ensures that the payoff is zero if the credit event has occurred before the option exercise date. It enforces the knockout feature. Similarly, the value at option expiry of a receiver swaption is given by

$$V_{Rec}(t_E) = 1_{\tau > t_E} \max\left[K - S(t_E, T), 0\right] \cdot \text{RPV01}(t_E, T).$$

We can calculate the present value of the payer option at time t by taking the expectation in the risk-neutral $\mathbb{Q}$-measure which describes the distribution of forward starting CDS spreads. The price of the option at time 0 is given by

$$V_{Pay}(0) = \mathbb{E}^{\mathbb{Q}}\left[\frac{1}{\beta(t_E)} 1_{\tau > t_E} \max\left[S(t_E, T) - K, 0\right] \cdot \text{RPV01}(t_E, T)\right] \qquad (9.2)$$

and similarly for the receiver swaption

$$V_{Rec}(0) = \mathbb{E}^{\mathbb{Q}}\left[\frac{1}{\beta(t_E)} 1_{\tau > t_E} \max\left[K - S(t_E, T), 0\right] \cdot \text{RPV01}(t_E, T)\right] \qquad (9.3)$$

where $\beta(t)$ is the value at time t of \$1 deposited in a Libor money-market account at time 0. It is given by

$$\beta(t) = \exp\left(\int_0^t r(s)ds\right).$$

9.3.4 Changing Numeraires

We now explain the change of numeraire technique. The concept of a numeraire, combined with the concept of a martingale measure, is a foundation of arbitrage-free pricing as pioneered in the seminal papers of Harrison and Kreps (1979) and Harrison and Pliska (1981).

A numeraire is a unit in which we choose to express the price of assets. This numeraire has to be any *strictly positive* price process, e.g. a stock price, the price of a bond, or a unit of a foreign currency. Note that we cannot use the price of a CDS as this can equal zero or can go negative. Using a numeraire $A(t)$ we can take a price process $X(t)$ and create a relative price process $\hat{X}(t)$ where

$$\hat{X}(t) = \frac{X(t)}{A(t)}.$$

If we have a dynamic process for $X(t)$, dividing $X(t)$ by $A(t)$ will produce a new dynamic process for $\hat{X}(t)$. The process for $\hat{X}(t)$ could have very different dynamics to $X(t)$. This all depends on the process for $A(t)$ and its correlation with $X(t)$.

What Harrison and co-workers showed is that in an arbitrage-free pricing framework, there is a probability measure for every choice of numeraire in which the relative price process of every asset is a *martingale*. What this means is that for any choice of $A(t)$ we have a measure $\mathbb{P}$ such that

$$\hat{X}(t) = \mathbb{E}_t^{\mathbb{P}}\left[\hat{X}(T)\right] \tag{9.4}$$

i.e. the price today is the expectation of the future price at all future times. A measure is some probability density function. This expectation is conditional on all market information until t. Martingales in finance reflect the fact that one asset should not, on average, make more or less money than any other (its numeraire). Clearly, the value of a security must be independent of the choice of numeraire. Hence, if we take a price process and change the numeraire we must then change the probability measure in order to ensure that the price remains the same and no arbitrage is permitted. The mathematics for making this change is determined by the Radon–Nikodym process which we now describe.

In all of the pricing so far in this book we have been using the spot martingale measure $\mathbb{Q}$ in which the numeraire is the value of the rolled-up money-market account $\beta(t)$. If we use a numeraire $A(t)$, then using the Radon–Nikodym density process we have a new probability measure $\mathbb{P}$ in which the relative price process is also a martingale. The resulting Radon–Nikodyn derivative is given by

$$\frac{d\mathbb{P}}{d\mathbb{Q}}|_t = \frac{A(t)\beta(0)}{A(0)\beta(t)}.$$

This discussion also applies to derivative securities which are simply examples of other price processes. For example, we can then write the time 0 value of a derivative security with payoff $H(T)$ at time T in the spot measure $\mathbb{Q}$ and then in the new measure $\mathbb{P}$

$$V(0) = \mathbb{E}^{\mathbb{Q}}\left[\frac{H(T)}{\beta(T)}\right] = \mathbb{E}^{\mathbb{Q}}\left[H(T)\frac{A(0)}{A(T)}\frac{d\mathbb{P}}{d\mathbb{Q}}\right] = A(0)\mathbb{E}^{\mathbb{P}}\left[\frac{H(T)}{A(T)}\right]. \tag{9.5}$$

This shows that the price of the derivative security in the spot measure $\mathbb{Q}$ in which we use the rolled-up money market as numeraire can be written in terms of an expectation in the $\mathbb{P}$ measure with a numeraire $A(t)$, in which the value of the relative price in this measure is then multiplied by the time 0 value of $A(0)$. The trick here is noting that a suitable choice of $A(t)$ can be used to simplify the form of a payoff and hence the variable being modelled. This is a trick which has been used in the pricing of options on forwards, and options on interest rate swaps, known as swaptions. We now show how to apply it to the case of default swaptions.

9.3.5   Choosing the Numeraire

In the context of default swaption pricing, we need to define a suitable numeraire. If we inspect the payoff function of the payer default swaption

$$V_{Pay}(t_E) = 1_{\tau > t_E} \max\left[S(t_E, T) - K, 0\right] \cdot \text{RPV01}(t_E, T),$$

we note that this payoff is not easy to model since there is a non-linear dependency on the time t_E term structure of credit spreads embedded in the value of the risky PV01. However, we can use the change of numeraire to remove this dependency. A suitable choice of numeraire would be

$$A(t) = 1_{\tau > t}\text{RPV01}(t, t_E, T),$$

However, this process, which is the expected present value of the future stream of risky premium payments, *is not strictly positive* – if the credit defaults before time t, the premium leg will cancel and we will have $A(t) = 0$. In general, this means that $A(t)$ cannot be used as numeraire. However, we can make an exception to this rule in this situation. Since the CDS option has a knockout feature, we know that when $A(t) = 0$, the value of the option payoff will *also equal zero*. It is this feature of the product payoff which allows us to use $A(t)$ as numeraire. In the spot martingale measure we have

$$V_{Pay}(0) = \mathbb{E}^Q \left[1_{\tau > t_E} \frac{1}{\beta(t, t_E)} \max\left[(S(t_E, T) - K), 0 \right] \cdot \text{RPV01}(t_E, T) \right].$$

We can then change measure to the risky PV01 measure $\mathbb{P}$. Using Equation 9.5, we have

$$V_{Pay}(0) = \text{RPV01}(0, t_E, T) \, \mathbb{E}^{\mathbb{P}} \left[\max\left[S(t_E, T) - K, 0 \right] \right].$$

Hence, the value of a payer swaption is the risky PV01 for the forward starting CDS multiplied by the price of a call option on the forward starting spread as seen at time t_E struck at K. Using the same arguments we can write the analogous equation for a receiver swaption

$$V_{Rec}(0) = \text{RPV01}(0, t_E, T) \, \mathbb{E}^{\mathbb{P}} \left[\max\left[K - S(t_E, T), 0 \right] \right].$$

It is now clear that the change of numeraire has simplified the form of the payoff. The random forward risky PV01 has been removed from within the expectation. All of the uncertainty in the payoff is contained within the distribution of the time t_E CDS spread in the $\mathbb{P}$ measure. Since this measure uses a forward starting numeraire which is only non-zero if $\tau > t$, it is known as a *forward survival measure* or *forward risky annuity measure*.

9.3.6 Put–call Parity

We can use the change of measure technique to demonstrate put–call parity in the context of CDS swaptions. Simple replication arguments show that being long a payer CDS swaption and short a receiver CDS swaption both struck at K and both with the same option expiry date t_E and CDS maturity date T is equivalent to being long a forward starting payer CDS with a forward date t_E, CDS maturity T and forward spread K.

However, it is also possible to show this using the change of numeraire technique. At time 0, the value of a payer swaption minus the value of a receiver swaption is given by

$$\text{Put–call} = \mathbb{E}^Q \left[1_{\tau > t_E} \frac{1}{\beta(t_E)} \max\left[S(t_E, T) - K, 0 \right] \cdot \text{RPV01}(t_E, T) \right]$$

$$- \mathbb{E}^Q \left[1_{\tau > t_E} \frac{1}{\beta(t_E)} \max\left[K - S(t_E, T), 0 \right] \cdot \text{RPV01}(t_E, T) \right]$$

$$= \mathbb{E}^Q \left[1_{\tau > t_E} \frac{1}{\beta(t_E)} \left(S(t_E, T) - K \right) \cdot \text{RPV01}(t_E, T) \right].$$

Changing numeraire to

$$A(t) = 1_{\tau > t} \text{RPV01}(t, t_E, T),$$

we have

$$\text{Put--call} = \mathbb{E}^{\mathbb{P}}\left[S(t_E, T) - K\right] \cdot \text{RPV01}(0, t_E, T)$$

$$= \left(\mathbb{E}^{\mathbb{P}}\left[S(t_E, T)\right] - K\right) \cdot \text{RPV01}(0, t_E, T).$$

To compute the expectation of the future spread $S(t_E, T)$, we note that

$$S(t, T) = \frac{\text{Protection leg PV}(t, T)}{\text{RPV01}(t, T)}$$

which is undefined for $t > \tau$. Since the spread is a relative price in the forward risky annuity or $\mathbb{P}$ measure it must be a martingale, i.e. we have

$$\mathbb{E}^{\mathbb{P}}[S(t_E, T)] = S(0, t_E, T). \tag{9.6}$$

As a result

$$\text{Put--call} = (S(0, t_E, T) - K) \cdot \text{RPV01}(0, t_E, T).$$

This is the time 0 value of a forward starting CDS with forward spread K and is the required result.

9.3.7 Lognormal Forward CDS Spread

Until now everything has been derived without specifying a process for the $\mathbb{P}$ measure dynamics of the CDS spread. The market standard approach is to assume that the $\mathbb{P}$ measure dynamics is a simple lognormal process with volatility σ, i.e. we have

$$dS(t) = \sigma S(t) dW^{\mathbb{P}}(t). \tag{9.7}$$

The choice of a lognormal process for the evolution of the spread is an appealing one. For a start, the lognormal distribution ensures that the spread can never be negative. It is also a skewed distribution, assigning higher probabilities to large realisations of the future spread than to low realisations of the future spread. This seems to concur with our experience of credit spreads.

Figure 9.3 shows the shape of the lognormal distribution after the spread process has evolved for one year. We show the distribution for different values of the volatility σ. The skewed nature of the distribution becomes very apparent as we increase σ. We can write the analytical density of the future spread distribution which we denote with $f(S)dS$ as

$$f(S)dS = \frac{1}{\sqrt{2\pi\sigma^2 t_E}} \exp\left(-\frac{\left(\ln(S/F) + \sigma^2 t_E/2\right)^2}{2\sigma^2 t_E}\right) \frac{dS}{S}$$

where $F = S(0, t_E, T)$ is the forward CDS spread calculated today at time 0. This enforces the martingale condition in Equation 9.6 which in this context is given by

$$\int_0^\infty f(S) S dS = F = S(0, t_E, T).$$

It is important to realise that a distribution which is lognormal in the $\mathbb{P}$ measure is not necessarily going to be a lognormal distribution in the $\mathbb{Q}$ measure. The distribution is only lognormal in

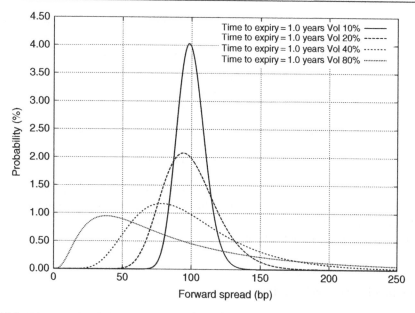

Figure 9.3 Lognormal distribution for the forward CDS spread assuming a time to option expiry of one year and for σ equal to 10%, 20%, 40% and 80%. The mean is set at the forward spread $S(t, t_E, T)$ which equals 100 bp

this forward risky PV01 survival numeraire measure. In this measure, the price of a payer option can be solved using the formula derived in Black (1976)

$$V_{Pay}(0) = \text{RPV01}(0, t_E, T) \, (S(0, t_E, T)\Phi(d_1) - K\Phi(d_2))$$

where

$$d_1 = \frac{\ln(S(0, t_E, T)/K) + \frac{1}{2}\sigma^2 t_E}{\sigma\sqrt{t_E}}$$

$$d_2 = \frac{\ln(S(0, t_E, T)/K) - \frac{1}{2}\sigma^2 t_E}{\sigma\sqrt{t_E}}.$$

We can simply use put–call parity to write the price of a receiver option

$$V_{Rec}(0) = \text{RPV01}(0, t_E, T) \cdot (S(0, t_E, T)\Phi(d_1) - K\Phi(d_2))$$
$$- \text{RPV01}(0, t_E, T) \cdot (S(0, t_E, T) - K)$$
$$= \text{RPV01}(0, t_E, T) \cdot (K\Phi(-d_2) - S(0, t_E, T)\Phi(-d_1)).$$

9.3.8 Valuing the Front End Protection

For a payer default swaption which does not knock out if default occurs before option expiry, we need to take into account the value of the default protection provided from option initiation to option expiry. This is known as the *front end protection*. We assume that the payment of the protection occurs at option expiry, although we note that the pricing formula can easily be adapted to handle a payment which is made immediately following a credit event. To value the front end protection at time $t > 0$, we can write the present value of the front end protection as

$$FEP(t) = (1 - R)\mathbb{E}_t \left[\frac{1_{t < \tau \le t_E}}{\beta(t, t_E)} \right].$$

Making the standard assumption of independence of interest rates and hazard rates we get

$$FEP(t, t_E) = (1 - R)Z(t, t_E) \left(1 - Q(t, t_E) \right).$$

The calculation of the front end protection is therefore simple. All we need to know is the survival probability to the option expiry date which we can get by interpolating the survival curve. We also need the expected recovery rate. We are now therefore in a position to price both knockout and non-knockout default swaptions.

9.3.9 Estimating Spread Volatility

It is not always possible to obtain the market implied volatility quotes we need to calibrate our default swaption model. The broad range of credits and the limited liquidity of this market mean that we generally have to rely upon empirical estimates of the volatility of spreads. However, we should note that the quantity we are modelling in the default swaption model is the forward spread. Historical estimates should therefore be based on forward CDS spreads, not spot CDS spreads. To perform the calibration correctly, we should take a time series of full CDS term structures for the reference entity for a long series of dates. For each date in the time series, we should calculate the forward spread to the remaining option expiry date. This time series of forward spreads should then be used to calculate the volatility using the method described below.

In practice, most practitioners do not do this since typically most CDS curves are fairly flat and sustain mainly parallel movements. As a result the forward volatility will be similar to the spot volatility. Furthermore, if we were to model the term structure of CDS with some more realistic mean-reverting process, we would tend to find that long-dated forwards are not necessarily more volatile than short-dated forwards. For this reason, practitioners generally use the simpler approach of estimating the forward spread volatility from spot starting CDS spreads.

We therefore suppose that we have a series of CDS spreads which we denote with S_i, where $i = 1, \ldots, N_D$. N_D is the number of daily observations. Since we have assumed a lognormal process for S, the volatility is based on the continuously compounded daily return

$$u_i = \ln \left(\frac{S_i}{S_{i-1}} \right) \simeq \frac{(S_i - S_{i-1})}{S_{i-1}}.$$

The unbiased estimate of the daily volatility is then given by

$$\sigma_{Daily} = \sqrt{\frac{1}{N_D - 1} \sum_{i=1}^{N_D} \left(u_i - \hat{u} \right)^2}$$

where the average is

$$\hat{u} = \frac{1}{N_D} \sum_{i=1}^{N_D} u_i.$$

Since we have used daily observations, the resultant volatility is the daily volatility, i.e. the daily change consistent with a 1 standard deviation move in the forward spread. However, since all the times used within our models are in units of years, we need to convert this daily volatility to an annual volatility. This is done by noting that there are typically 252 trading days in a year and that in a Brownian motion the distance moved in time T scales as $\sqrt{T}$. Hence, we have

$$\sigma_{Annualised} = \sqrt{252}\sigma_{Daily}.$$

Since spreads may remain static over a period of days, we may alternatively choose to calculate the volatility using weekly observations. In this case we would simply perform the above calculation of the volatility using weekly data and then annualise the result using

$$\sigma_{Annualised} = \sqrt{\frac{252}{5}}\, \sigma_{Weekly}$$

where we note that each week is made up of five trading days. More sophisticated estimation techniques using exponential or other weighting schemes can be used to change the relative importance of recent versus older spread changes.

9.3.10   Pricing Examples

Before we present the examples, we define our convention for quoting prices. The price of the option is often quoted in 'basis points'. However, here we prefer to use 'cents' since as a rule of thumb we prefer to use basis points for rate-like quantities and cents for price-like quantities. The price of an option can be expressed as a percentage of face value. Here we quote it in terms of 'dollars' and 'cents'. This assumes that the face value of the trade is $100, and so $1 = 1\% $ and 1 cent = 0.01%.

> **Example**   Using the CDS spread curve with the upward sloping structure shown in Table 9.3, we price both payer and receiver default swaptions with the underlying being a forward starting CDS starting in one year with a final maturity five years later. This is known as a 1×5 contract. Assuming a 40% recovery rate, we calculate the forward starting CDS spread to be 266 bp.
>
> - Figure 9.4 shows the price of a knockout payer swaption as a function of strike for different levels of spread volatility. When the strike equals zero, we are long an option

(Continued)

- to buy protection at 0 bp. Given that protection costs 266 bp, the option is deep in-the-money and its value equals the value of the forward protection leg which equals 10.231% or 1023.1 cents. As we increase the strike the option moves out-of-the-money and the price falls.
- Figure 9.5 shows the price of a knockout receiver swaption as a function of strike for different values of spread volatility. This time we see that the option price increases with strike. When $K = 0$, we own an option to sell protection at zero basis points. This is clearly not an option we would wish to exercise and the price is zero. As the strike spread increases, the option becomes increasingly in-the-money. As the strike spread becomes large, the option is so far in the money that we would almost surely choose to exercise it and the price tends to the value of the forward starting protection leg.

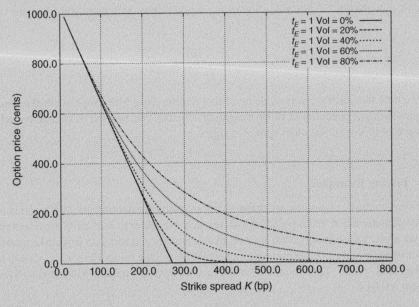

Figure 9.4   Price of payer swaptions on a 1 × 5 CDS with a forward CDS spread of 266 bp as a function of the strike spread and lognormal volatility

We also see that in both the case of the payer and receiver swaptions, increasing the volatility increases the value of the option. This is because a higher volatility increases the probability of the option being deep in-the-money at expiry and having a larger payoff. While it also increases the probability of the option being far out-of-the-money, the option is then not exercised and so the value is floored at zero.

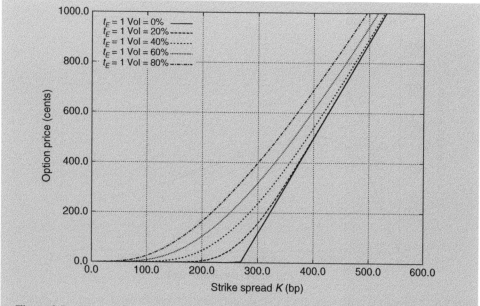

Figure 9.5 Price of receiver swaptions on a 1 × 5 CDS with a forward CDS spread of 266 bp as a function of the strike spread and lognormal volatility

These default swaptions are all knockout. For those payer swaptions that do not cancel in the event of a default before option expiry, the option price also contains the value of the front end protection as discussed in Section 9.3.8. Figure 9.6 compares the price of two 1 × 5 payer swaptions, one which is a knockout swaption and the other a non-knockout swaption as a function of the level of the CDS curve which is assumed to be flat. The difference in the option values is the value of the front end protection which therefore makes the non-knockout option more valuable. We see that as spreads increase, the price of the knockout swaption increases since the option becomes more and more in the money. However, beyond a certain spread, the option value begins to fall. This happens because the spread is now so high that it is implying that the *default is more likely to occur before* the option expires, in which case the knockout option would be worthless. However, the value of the non-knockout swaption increases monotonically with spread and in the limit of the CDS spreads tending to infinity – i.e. when immediate default is certain – the difference in option values tends to the value of the front end protection which in this limit tends to the present value of $(1 - R)$ paid at option expiry.

9.3.11 Hedging a Knockout Default Swaption

The underlying asset for a default swaption is the forward starting CDS. Therefore, hedging a default swaption should require us to buy or sell a delta amount of the forward CDS. However, forward starting CDS are much less liquid than spot starting CDS and so we prefer to express our hedges in terms of CDS equivalent notionals. As before, we calculate these equivalent notionals by perturbing different parts of the CDS curve and then calculating the equivalent notional of spot starting CDS required to hedge the change in value of the option position.

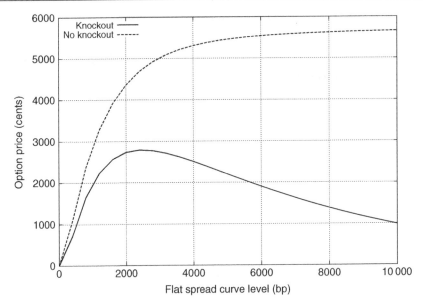

Figure 9.6 Comparison of the value of a 1×5 knockout and non-knockout payer swaption as a function of the spread of the CDS curve which is assumed to be flat. We set the volatility to 60% and the option strike to 200 bp

Example Consider a 1 × 5 payer swaption struck at 200 bp on $10 million face value. We use the CDS term structure shown in the previous example and set the recovery equal to 40% and the volatility to 60%. The forward spread is 266 bp. The option is therefore in-the-money and has a price of 368 cents. We perturb the CDS curve by bumping individual spreads on the CDS curve and determine the equivalent notional of CDS required to hedge this price change where the equivalent hedge notional is given by

$$N(S_T) = \frac{V(S_T + 1\,\text{bp}) - V(S_T)}{1\,\text{bp} \times \text{RPV01}(t, T)}$$

where S_T is the CDS spread to maturity T, and all other CDS spreads and swap rates are held fixed. The results are shown in Table 9.3.

Table 9.3 CDS equivalent notional hedges for a 1 × 5 payer swaption. In this example, a negative hedge notional means we buy protection

CDS Term (yrs)	CDS spread (bp)	Bumped option price (%)	Risky PV01	Equivalent hedge notional ($m)
1	100	3.668	0.979	−7.91
2	120	3.676	1.895	−0.11
3	145	3.675	2.765	−0.14
5	220	3.688	4.306	3.50
7	245	3.698	5.604	4.04
10	270	3.676	7.166	0.00

We see that the spot CDS hedge consists of a 1Y long protection position of almost $8 million plus two short protection positions of $3 million at five and $4.13 million at seven years. This splitting of the hedges between the five- and seven-year points is because we did not assume the existence of a liquid 6Y market in our risk analysis. There is a small residual exposure to the 2Y and 3Y points.

Option hedges are dynamic and so have to be frequently rebalanced. This has cost implications since the hedger needs to cross the bid–offer spread in order to do this and on illiquid credits, this cost can be large.

9.4   CONSTANT MATURITY DEFAULT SWAPS

The constant maturity default swap, also known as a CMDS or a CMCDS, is a variation on the default swap in which the one leg pays a floating spread. On this floating leg, the coupon paid on each payment date is linked to an observation of some M-year tenor CDS spread made on the previous coupon date. This is similar to the way the Libor payment on a floating rate note is set in advance and paid in arrears. Typically, the CDS spread used is the five-year CDS spread of the reference credit as observed on the previous coupon payment date. As the time to maturity of the reference CDS is held fixed, this contract is known as a *constant maturity* default swap. This CMDS floating leg can be combined with other types of CDS legs in a number of ways:

- Floating CMDS leg vs CDS protection leg: One leg is a standard protection leg and the other is a floating leg linked to some CDS constant maturity index.
- Floating CMDS leg vs CDS premium leg: One leg is a standard premium leg and the other is a floating leg linked to some CDS constant maturity index.
- Floating CMDS leg vs floating CMDS leg: Both legs are floating but are referenced to different maturity CDS quotes. For example, one leg may be linked to the 5Y CDS spread while the other may be linked to the 10Y CDS spread.

These different combinations present different risk profiles and so present the investor with a number of ways to tailor a trade to their specific view. The risks of the different legs are discussed later in Section 9.4.10 and we mention some of the conclusions here.

1. When a CMDS floating leg is combined with a standard CDS protection leg, the position has a lower spread sensitivity and hence lower mark-to-market volatility than a standard CDS.
2. By combining the CMDS floating leg with a standard CDS premium leg, we remove the protection leg and hence the investor has no exposure to the recovery rate risk associated with the delivery of a defaulted asset. The only default risk is the risk that the payment legs terminate before contract maturity.
3. By combining the CMDS floating leg with another CMDS floating leg linked to a different maturity, the investor can express a view on the evolution of the slope of the CDS curve without taking any recovery rate risk leaving just the risk of early termination of the payment legs.

We now describe how the floating leg works.

9.4.1 CMDS Contract Mechanics

The floating leg of a CMDS pays coupons that are based on an M-year tenor CDS spread. This spread is fixed on the coupon payment date before the one on which it is paid, i.e. it sets in advance and pays in arrears. Per $1 of face value, the size of the coupon paid at time t_n is given by

$$\alpha S(t_{n-1}, T_n) \Delta(t_{n-1}, t_n)$$

where

- $S(t_{n-1}, T_n)$ is the *floating* M-year tenor CDS maturity spread observed at time t_{n-1} for a contract with an effective date t_{n-1}. For simplicity of notation, we introduce $T_n = t_{n-1} + M$.
- α is the *participation rate* and is a multiplier applied to all coupon payments. It is by varying α that we set the value of the contract equal to zero at initiation.
- $\Delta(t_{n-1}, t_n)$ is the day count fraction in the appropriate basis convention.

The process for setting the CDS rate is one of the complications of this product. There is (as yet) no standard and commonly agreed mechanism for setting the value of the reference spread although there are alternatives. One approach simply involves a dealer poll.

In certain contracts, a cap is imposed on the floating spread. The purpose of this is to ensure certainty about the coupon in cases when a reference credit becomes distressed. When this happens the market begins to trade CDS in an upfront format and the CDS spread curve is no longer quoted. We denote this cap on the spread with K. It is usually set at some high value, typically 500–1000 bp. Taking the cap into account, the coupon paid at time t_n is given by

$$\alpha \Delta(t_{n-1}, t_n) \min \left[S(t_{n-1}, T_n), K \right].$$

The overall mechanics of the floating leg are shown in Figure 9.7

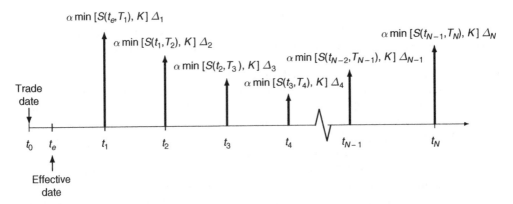

Figure 9.7   The floating leg of a CMDS assuming no credit event during the life of the contract. We assume a face value of $1. The coupon paid at time t_n is the M-year tenor CDS spread observed at time t_{n-1}. We denote this with $S(t_{n-1}, T_n)$ where $T_n = t_{n-1} + M$. We also set $\Delta_n = \Delta(t_{n-1}, t_n)$

We assume that the CMDS makes no payment if default occurs in the period between the coupon reset and payment. There is therefore no need to worry about the payment of premium accrued at default.

9.4.2 Valuation of a CMDS

The challenge of pricing CMDS is the valuation of the floating leg in an arbitrage-free framework. As we shall see, it is not correct to assume that these payments are simply the forward CDS spreads implied by the current CDS curve. This would only be true if CDS spreads evolved so that the today time 0 forward spreads are realised, i.e.

$$S(t_n, T) = S(0, t_n, T).$$

However, since the CDS spread process is a martingale in the forward annuity measure, this is only true *on average*. Mathematically,

$$\mathbb{E}^{\mathbb{P}}[S(t_n, T)] = S(0, t_n, T).$$

Since there is uncertainty in the evolution of spreads, we have to use a pricing model to take this uncertainty into account.

9.4.3 Valuation without a Cap

To start with, we assume there is no cap on the floating spread. The value of the floating leg is therefore given by a sum over the expected present value of the individual payments which occur at times $t_1, \ldots, t_N$. The expected present value today of the payment at time t_n, before it is multiplied by its accrual factor and participation rate is given by

$$X_n = \mathbb{E}^{\mathbb{Q}} \left[\frac{1}{\beta(t_{n-1})} 1_{\tau > t_{n-1}} Z(t_{n-1}, t_n) Q(t_{n-1}, t_n) S(t_{n-1}, T_n) \right]. \tag{9.8}$$

This requires an explanation. First of all $S(t_{n-1}, t_n)$ is the M maturity CDS spread observed at future time t_{n-1}. Conditional on no default before time t_{n-1}, it is only paid at time t_n provided the reference credit survives from time t_{n-1} to t_n. This probability is known at time t_{n-1} and is given by $Q(t_{n-1}, t_n)$. We discount the payment back at the risk-free rate using $Z(t_{n-1}, t_n)$ which is also known at time t_{n-1}. Finally, we condition on no default before t_{n-1} using $1_{\tau > t_{n-1}}$ and discount from time t_{n-1} back to today using the money market numeraire. As a result, the time 0 value of the floating leg in the $\mathbb{Q}$-measure is given by

$$\text{Floating Leg PV}(0, T) = \alpha \sum_{n=1}^{N} \Delta(t_{n-1}, t_n) X_n$$

Once again we can use the change of numeraire to move the payoff into the $\mathbb{P}$ measure corresponding to the forward risky PV01 as numeraire. We have

$$X_n = \text{RPV01}(0, t_{n-1}, T_n) \cdot \mathbb{E}^{\mathbb{P}} \left[\frac{Z(t_{n-1}, t_n) Q(t_{n-1}, t_n) S(t_{n-1}, T_n)}{\text{RPV01}(t_{n-1}, T_n)} \right]. \tag{9.9}$$

Previously when we priced a default swaption, we had a simple payoff function in the unknown future CDS spread. Now the payoff function is more complicated. A dependence on the future

CDS spread $S(t_{n-1}, T_n)$ is contained within the RPV01(t_{n-1}, T_n) term and also within the future survival probability $Q(t_{n-1}, t_n)$.

The question is how to capture the dependency of the payoff on the value of the unknown future spread in a way which is analytically tractable and arbitrage free. Note that the payoff is also a function of the term structure of Libor interest rates. However, the sensitivity of the payoff to interest rates is second order when compared to the spread dependence and can be ignored. We therefore choose to write Equation 9.8 as

$$X_n = \text{RPV01}(0, t_{n-1}, T_n) \int_0^\infty f(S)g(S)S \, dS$$

where $f(S)$ is the probability density function for S and

$$g(S) = \frac{Z(t_{n-1}, t_n)Q(t_{n-1}, t_n)}{\text{RPV01}(t_{n-1}, T_n)}.$$

This reduced form dependency of the payoff on a single spread variable S also implies that the term structure of spreads at future time t_{n-1} can be captured by one number. The exact dependency of $g(S)$ on S has not yet been specified, nor has the probability distribution of S. We only assume that S is positive.

9.4.4   An Analytical Approximation

A number of approximate approaches have been proposed to enable the fast and closed-form pricing of CMDS. For example, Pedersen and Sen (2004) propose an expansion of the value of the floating CMDS payment in terms of the forward hazard rate about the expected value of the hazard rate on the reset date. Another approach, which we will follow here, is that of Andersen (2006a). In this approach we approximate the function $g(S)$ with a linear function in S. We will show below that this approximation works well. We start by introducing the linearised approximation for $g(S)$. This is

$$\hat{g}(S) = c_0 + c_1 S$$

where $\hat{g}(S) \simeq g(S)$. We now solve for the two coefficients:

1. To solve for c_0, we set $S = 0$. In this limit the reference entity is default free after time t_{n-1}. The future survival probabilities are therefore equal to 1.0 and the time t_{n-1} risky PV01 equals the time t_{n-1} risk-free PV01. Hence, we have

$$c_0 = g(0) = \hat{g}(0) = \frac{Z(t_{n-1}, t_n)}{\text{PV01}(t_{n-1}, T_n)} = \frac{Z(t, t_n)}{\text{PV01}(0, t_{n-1}, T_n)}.$$

2. We can then determine the coefficient c_1 by noting that in the forward RPV01 survival measure

$$g(S) = \frac{Z(t_{n-1}, t_n)Q(t_{n-1}, t_n)}{\text{RPV01}(t_{n-1}, T_n)}$$

is a martingale and

$$\mathbb{E}^{\mathbb{P}}[g(S)] = \mathbb{E}^{\mathbb{P}}\left[\frac{Z(t_{n-1}, t_n)Q(t_{n-1}, t_{n-1}, t_n)}{\text{RPV01}(t_{n-1}, T)}\right] = \frac{Z(0, t_n)Q(0, t_n)}{\text{RPV01}(0, t_{n-1}, T_n)}.$$

We impose the same martingale constraint on our approximation

$$\mathbb{E}^{\mathbb{P}}[\hat{g}(S)] = \mathbb{E}^{\mathbb{P}}[c_0 + c_1 S] = c_0 + c_1 S(0, t_{n-1}, T) = \frac{Z(0, t_n)Q(0, t_n)}{\text{RPV01}(0, t_{n-1}, T_n)}.$$

We can solve for c_1 as follows

$$c_1 = \frac{1}{S(0, t_{n-1}, T_n)} \left(\frac{Z(0, t_n)Q(0, t_n)}{\text{RPV01}(0, t_{n-1}, T_n)} - c_0 \right).$$

The coefficients c_0 and c_1 are computed for the CDS term structure and each payment date t_n.

To assess the accuracy of this approximation, we take the CDS term structure in Table 9.3. We then calculate the values of c_0 and c_1 for each of five reset times at 1, 2, 3, 4 and 5 years. The range of forward curves is generated by multiplying the initial CDS spreads by a single common multiplier, thus preserving the general shape of the CDS curve. We have plotted in Figure 9.8 the relative error in the approximation $\epsilon(S) = (g'(S) - g(S))/g(S)$ as a function of S. As expected, we see that the error is zero when $S = 0$ since this was imposed when we solved for c_0. It is also zero when S equals the forward spread, as this is the condition imposed by solving for c_1. Overall, we see that the quality of the approximation is very good, with less than a 1% error across a broad range of spreads.

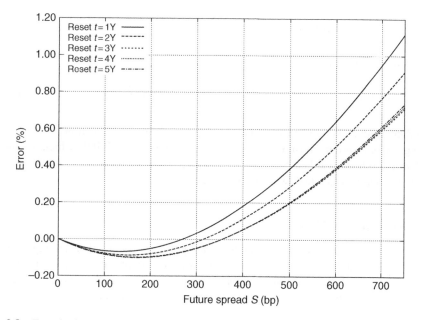

Figure 9.8 Error in the approximation of the function $g(S)$ with its linear expansion $\hat{g}(S) = c_0 + c_1 S$. We plot the percentage error $\epsilon(S) = (\hat{g}(S) - g(S))/g(S)$ for five different reset times from one year to five years

We conclude this section by stating that the expected present value of a CMDS coupon can now be written as

$$\alpha \Delta(t_{n-1}, t_n)\text{RPV01}(0, t_{n-1}, T_n) \int_0^{\infty} f(S)(c_0 S + c_1 S^2)dS$$

where c_0 and c_1 have been defined above. The next step is to assume a model for S which allows us to calculate the density $f(S)$. However, before we do that we consider the added complication of a cap on the CMDS spread.

9.4.5   Valuation with a Cap

It is standard to impose a cap on the forward spread that is paid. Denoting the level of the cap with K, we can once again write the expected present value of the payment at time t_n (before being multiplied by the day count fraction and participation rate) in the forward RPV01 survival measure $\mathbb{P}$ as

$$X_n = \text{RPV01}(0, t_{n-1}, T_n)\mathbb{E}^{\mathbb{P}}\left[\frac{Z(t_{n-1}, t_n)Q(t_{n-1}, t_n)\min\left[S(t_{n-1}, T_n), K\right]}{\text{RPV01}(t_{n-1}, T_n)}\right].$$

Once again we introduce the function $g(S)$ and write the payoff as

$$X_n = \text{RPV01}(0, t_{n-1}, T_n)\int_0^\infty f(S)g(S)\min\left[S, K\right]dS.$$

Approximating $g(S)$ as a linear function

$$X_n = \text{RPV01}(0, t_{n-1}, T_n)\int_0^\infty f(S)(c_0 + c_1 S)\min\left[S, K\right]dS$$

we can then write this as

$$X_n = \text{RPV01}(0, t_{n-1}, T_n)\left(\int_0^K f(S)(c_0 S + c_1 S^2)dS + K\int_K^\infty f(S)(c_0 + c_1 S)dS\right).$$

The coefficients c_0 and c_1 are calculated as described in the previous section.

Having derived a pricing formula for the floating payments of a CMDS, which is a function of the density of the forward CDS spread, the next step is to assume a model for the dynamics of the future CDS spread which will give us the density.

9.4.6   The Lognormal Model

We are now ready to apply a specific model to the pricing of the CMDS floating payments. Ideally, we want a dynamics for the spread which is consistent with our model for default swaptions. This would allow us to share calibrations and to combine risk measures. We therefore assume a lognormal dynamics for the forward spread in the $\mathbb{P}$ measure

$$dS(t) = \sigma S(t)dW^{\mathbb{P}}(t).$$

The density of the distribution of S at some future time t_{n-1} is given by

$$f(S)dS = \frac{1}{\sqrt{2\pi\sigma^2 t_{n-1}}}\exp\left(-\frac{\left(\ln(S/F) + \sigma^2 t_{n-1}/2\right)^2}{2\sigma^2 t_{n-1}}\right)\frac{dS}{S}$$

where $F = S(0, t_{n-1}, T_n)$.

9.4.7 Lognormal Spread without a Cap

We start by pricing the CMDS payment without a cap. We have

$$X_n = \frac{RPV01(0, t_{n-1}, T_n)}{\sqrt{2\pi \sigma^2 t_{n-1}}} \int_0^\infty \exp\left(-\frac{\left(\ln(S/F) + \sigma^2 t_{n-1}/2\right)^2}{2\sigma^2 t_{n-1}}\right)(c_0 + c_1 S)dS.$$

We change variables by defining $u = \ln S$ so that $S = e^u$ and $dS = e^u du$. This then becomes a simple Gaussian integration in u

$$X_n = \frac{RPV01(0, t_{n-1}, T_n)}{\sqrt{2\pi \sigma^2 t_{n-1}}} \int_{-\infty}^\infty \exp\left(-\frac{\left(u - \ln F + \sigma^2 t_{n-1}/2\right)^2}{2\sigma^2 t_{n-1}}\right)(c_0 + c_1 e^u)e^u du.$$

We then integrate to give

$$X_n = RPV01(0, t_{n-1}, T_n)S(0, t_{n-1}, T)\left(c_0 + c_1 \exp\left(\sigma^2 t_{n-1}\right)S(0, t_{n-1}, T_n)\right).$$

9.4.8 The Convexity Adjustment

Using this formula, we can then start to calculate the convexity adjustment on the forward spread. Specifically, we define this as

$$\Gamma_n = \frac{X_n}{Z(0, t_{n-1})Q(0, t_{n-1})} - S(0, t_{n-1}, T_n).$$

where X_n was defined in Equation 9.8. As an example, we take a five-year maturity CMDS leg where the payments are made at quarterly intervals and are linked to the five-year maturity CDS spread observed on the previous coupon date. We assume three different levels of volatility at 20%, 40% and 60% and plot the convexity for the different reset dates in the contract in Figure 9.9.

We see that the size of the forward rate convexity adjustment is primarily a function of the time to the reset. This is because the longer the time to the reset, the more time there is for the realised future CDS spread to deviate from its mean value which is the forward CDS spread. The minor fluctuations in the shape of the convexity reflect the shape of the forward curve. At a volatility of 60%, we see that the convexity correction becomes quite significant. For example, the correction at four years raises the expected value of the five-year CDS forward from 345 bp to 464 bp.

9.4.9 Lognormal Spreads with a Cap

Assuming a lognormal distribution for the future CDS spread, the formula for the present value of the capped future CDS spread is given by

$$X_n = \frac{RPV01(0, t_{n-1}, T_n)}{\sqrt{2\pi \sigma^2 t_{n-1}}} \int_0^K \exp\left(-\frac{\left(\ln(S/F) + \sigma^2 t_{n-1}/2\right)^2}{2\sigma^2 t_n}\right)(c_0 + c_1 S)dS$$

$$+ \frac{RPV01(0, t_{n-1}, T_n)}{\sqrt{2\pi \sigma^2 t_n}} K \int_K^\infty \exp\left(-\frac{\left(\ln(S/F) + \sigma^2 t_{n-1}/2\right)^2}{2\sigma^2 t_{n-1}}\right)(c_0 + c_1 S)\frac{dS}{S}.$$

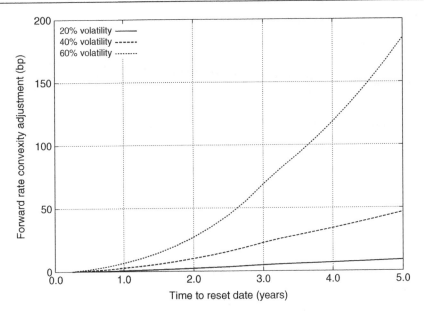

Figure 9.9 CMDS forward rate convexity adjustment as a function of the forward reset date and for three values of the forward CDS rate volatility

Once again we can make a change of variable to $u = \ln S$. This gives

$$X_n = \frac{\text{RPV01}(0, t_{n-1}, T_n)}{\sqrt{2\pi\sigma^2 t_n}} \int_{-\infty}^{\ln K} \exp\left(-\frac{\left(u - \ln F + \sigma^2 t_{n-1}/2\right)^2}{2\sigma^2 t_{n-1}}\right) (c_0 + c_1 e^u) e^u \, du$$

$$+ \frac{\text{RPV01}(0, t_{n-1}, T_n)}{\sqrt{2\pi\sigma^2 t_{n-1}}} K \int_{\ln K}^{\infty} \exp\left(-\frac{\left(u - \ln F + \sigma^2 t_{n-1}/2\right)^2}{2\sigma^2 t_n}\right) (c_0 + c_1 e^u) \, du.$$

Once again we have to perform some Gaussian integrals. This time there are limits on the integrals that require the use of the cumulative normal density function $\Phi(x)$. The final result is

$$X_n = \text{RPV01}(0, t_{n-1}, T_n)$$

$$\times \left(c_0 F \Phi\left(\frac{\ln(K/F) - \sigma^2 t_{n-1}/2)}{\sigma\sqrt{t_{n-1}}}\right) + c_1 F^2 \exp\left(\sigma^2 t_n\right) \Phi\left(\frac{\ln(K/F) - 3\sigma^2 t_{n-1}/2)}{\sigma\sqrt{t_{n-1}}}\right)\right.$$

$$\left. + c_0 K \Phi\left(\frac{\ln(F/K) - \sigma^2 t_{n-1}/2)}{\sigma\sqrt{t_{n-1}}}\right) + c_1 K F \Phi\left(\frac{\ln(F/K) + \sigma^2 t_{n-1}/2)}{\sigma\sqrt{t_{n-1}}}\right)\right)$$

where $F = S(0, t_{n-1}, T_n)$ is the forward CDS spread. Now that we have a pricing formula for the present value of the forward CDS spread observed at time t_{n-1} and paid at time t_n, we are ready to price a CMDS contract with a cap.

9.4.10   Calculating the Participation Rate

The price of a CMDS is often quoted in terms of a participation rate. This is the factor which we use to multiply all of the coupons on the CMDS so that their present value equals the present value of the protection leg. This in turn equals the present value of the premium leg of a CDS at initiation paying the breakeven CDS spread $S(0, T)$. We denote the participation rate with α

$$\alpha \sum_{n=1}^{N} \Delta_n X_n = (1 - R) \int_0^T Z(0, s)(-dQ(0, s)) = S(0, T)\text{RPV01}(0, T)$$

In practice, the participation rate is typically less than one. To see why, consider the zero volatility case in which the forwards are realised. If $\alpha = 1$ and the CDS curve is upward sloping, the future cash flows will be greater than the cash flows from a standard CDS premium leg. As a result we will have to scale down the cash flows on the CMDS leg by reducing α until their expected present value equals the expected present value of the CDS premium leg. In the more unusual case of an inverted spread curve, we would find that the expected future cash flows are lower than the CDS premium leg and that the participation rate has to be greater than one.

Once we have a non-zero volatility, the situation changes. Since the forward curve volatility means that the expected present value of each CMDS payment will be higher than its zero volatility case, the effect of volatility will be to reduce the participation rate even more. This is certainly true if there is no cap on the CMDS rate.

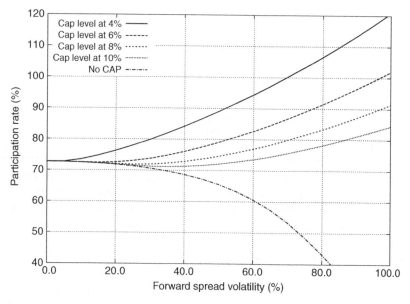

Figure 9.10 CMDS participation rate for a five-year deal on a five-year CDS index. We plot the participation rate versus forward CDS spread volatility and with different levels of cap

Figure 9.10 shows the participation rate for the curve in Table 9.3 as a function of the forward spread volatility and for different values of the cap. We make the following observations:

- For the lowest cap of $K = 4.0\%$ we see that the participation rate actually increases with increasing volatility. This is because the expectation of the CDS spread is the forward rate. By capping the future CDS spread at 4.0%, its expectation will be lower than the forward

rate and so the CMDS payments will on average be lower than the forward and so the participation rate will increase to compensate.
- For the highest cap, which is when there is no cap,[2] we see that increasing volatility increases the expected value of the CMDS payments and so pushes down the participation rate.

9.4.11   CMDS Risk and Hedging

To study the risk of a CMDS trade, we compare the hedges for the three types of legs. These are:

1. Long a five-year standard CDS premium leg with a contractual spread of 220 bp.
2. Long a five-year protection leg. We assume a 40% recovery rate.
3. Long a five-year CMDS leg with the spread referenced to the five-year CDS spread. We impose a spread volatility of 60% and a cap on the spread set at 1000 bp. We set the participation rate to 73.55% so that its value equals that of the premium and protection leg.

All are assumed to have a face value of $10 million. We assume that the market CDS spreads are the ones in Table 9.4.

Table 9.4   Hedge notionals for a $10 million long position in each of a five-year premium leg, a protection leg and a five-year CMDS leg with a five-year reference CDS spread. A positive hedge means short protection

CDS term	Spread (bp)	Hedge RPV01	5Y premium leg hedge ($m)	5Y protection leg hedge ($m)	5Y CMDS leg hedge ($m)
1Y	100	0.979	−0.30	−0.30	−2.13
2Y	120	1.895	−0.31	−0.31	−2.07
3Y	145	2.765	−0.48	−0.48	−2.68
5Y	220	4.306	−0.41	9.59	0.47
7Y	245	5.604	0.00	0.00	4.16
10Y	270	7.166	0.00	0.00	1.85

What we then do is to apply a multiplier to the spreads in the curve shown in Table 9.4 and examine how the value of each of these legs changes with changing spreads. The results are shown in Figure 9.11. All of the lines cross at a spread multiplier of 100% since the participation ratio was set so that the CMDS leg value equals the protection leg value. The fixed spread on the premium leg was also set so that the value of the premium leg equals the value of the protection leg. We consider the different legs:

- The value of the premium leg falls because, given that the contractual spread is fixed, raising the CDS spread curve will mean that the survival probabilities are decreased and so the risky PV01 falls.
- We see that the value of the protection leg increases with spreads. This is as expected – the higher the spread the greater the risk of default and the more valuable is the protection.
- We see that the CMDS leg has a dependency on parallel spread movements which is similar to the protection leg. This is because an increase in spreads causes all of the expected future CMDS flows to be increased.

---

[2] When there is no cap, the *effective cap* is at infinity.

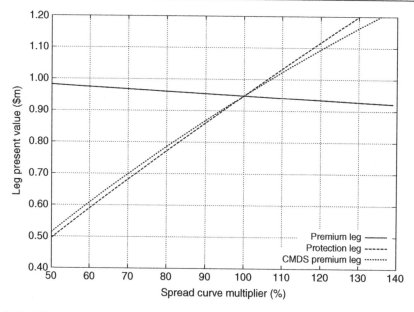

Figure 9.11   The dependence of the premium leg value, the protection leg value and the CMDS leg value to changes in the level of the CDS computed by taking the CDS curve and scaling by a multiplier

We therefore conclude that:

- A CDS premium leg versus a CMDS leg will have almost exactly the same spread curve sensitivity as a standard CDS contract. However, there will be no default-contingent recovery rate risk.
- A CDS protection leg versus a CMDS leg will have a low net spread sensitivity. However, it will present a default-contingent recovery rate risk.

We should be careful about these observations as there is actually a fundamental difference between the sensitivity of a CDS protection leg and a floating CMDS leg. To see this, we need to calculate the CDS hedges.

Once again, we calculate the CDS hedge notionals by bumping the different CDS maturity points. The results are shown in Table 9.4. As expected, the premium leg hedges are small. Combining the premium and protection leg produces a combined hedge of $10 million at the five-year point, which is as expected, i.e. you hedge a five-year CDS with a five-year CDS.

What is interesting is the hedges on the CMDS leg. We see that the hedge of a long CMDS leg is to go long protection out to the 5Y point and to then go short protection beyond. The value of the CMDS is therefore affected differently by spread changes at the short and long end of the CDS curve. There is an exposure out to the 10Y point since the final reset on the 5Y CMDS floating leg is in 4.75 years and it references the 5Y CDS spread. Clearly, the comparison of a protection leg and a CMDS floating leg only works when the CDS spread curve moves in a parallel fashion.

9.5 SUMMARY

This chapter has introduced a number of important extensions of the standard CDS including the forward starting CDS, the default swaption and the constant maturity CDS. We have also presented simple pricing models for all of these which are all sufficient for real pricing and hedging. More sophisticated term structure models could be used but are beyond the scope of our current treatment.

Part II
Multi-name Credit Derivatives

10

CDS Portfolio Indices

10.1 INTRODUCTION

CDS portfolio indices have transformed the credit derivatives markets by providing a highly liquid product which investors can use to assume or hedge the risk of a broad portfolio of credit exposures. The arrival of the first CDS portfolio indices in 2002 heralded the start of a new era for the credit derivatives market. After an uncertain first year, in which the market had a number of competing index products, by mid-2004, these had merged, resulting in a single index product in each region. In Europe and Asia, the indices fell under the banner of iTraxx. In North America, the indices fell under the name CDX. In addition, there are a number of tradable subindices. The general structure of the European, North American and Asian families of indices and subindices is shown in Table 10.1. Growth of these products was so rapid that by 2006, these portfolio indices comprised just over 30% of the credit derivatives market.[1]

Table 10.1 The main CDS indices. All indices are equally weighted. The number of credits in any one index may be lower than the number shown here due to their removal following credit events. Source: Markit

Name	Type of credit	Number of credits
CDX.NA.IG	North American investment grade	125
CDX.NA.HY	North American high yield	100
CDX.NA.XO	North American crossover[a] credits	35
CDX.EM	Emerging market sovereign credits	15
CDX.EM.Diversified	Emerging market sovereign and corporate credits	40
iTraxx Europe	European investment grade	125
iTraxx Europe Crossover	European crossover credits	40
iTraxx Japan	Japanese investment grade	50
iTraxx Asia ex-Japan	Asian non-Japan investment grade	50
iTraxx Australia	Australian investment grade	25

[a] A Crossover credit is one which was previously investment grade but has since been downgraded.

The most liquid CDS portfolio indices are the investment grade indices of iTraxx and CDX. Each contains 125 investment grade reference credits chosen to represent the *most liquid* credits satisfying the index criteria. For iTraxx, these require that all the issuers in the index are domiciled in Europe and are investment grade quality. For CDX, these require that the 125 credits are all domiciled in North America and are also rated investment grade quality.

---

[1] BBA Credit Derivatives Report 2006.

Since there are no published estimates for the trading volume of different issuers in the CDS market, determining which issuers are the most liquid is not easy. To ensure that decisions about which issuers should be admitted to or removed from the index are unbiased, the decision-making process is managed by independent index administrators in consultation with a consortium of investment banks, based on defined and published rules. The details of the rules can vary between the indices. The owner and administrator of the CDX and iTraxx indices is Markit Group Limited, hereafter referred to as Markit.

The format of these indices was driven primarily by the need to make them as easy to trade as possible and by doing so, to encourage liquidity. This has succeeded. Liquidity of this market is now exceptional, with bid–offer spreads of one quarter of a basis point on the most liquid investment grade indices rising to just 4 bp on the high yield index. In the early days of the CDS index, the only tenor was five years. However, there is now a liquid index with a tenor of 10 years and indices with lower liquidity at three and seven years.

The success of the portfolio CDS indices has been a result of the many advantages that a portfolio CDS index presents. We list some of them below:

- Since the indices contain as many as 125 credits, the portfolio CDS index allows investors to take a broad exposure to the credit markets in a single transaction.
- The portfolio CDS index allows hedgers to go short the credit markets in a single transaction. This is useful for credit funds, hedge funds or banks who wish to hedge a broad exposure to the credit markets.
- Since the portfolio CDS indices have a small initial cost, they can be used to take a leveraged credit exposure. In addition, it makes them efficient for those who fund above Libor.
- Portfolio CDS indices can be used as the underlying for other derivative products such as synthetic loss tranches and spread options. These are described later.
- By allowing the trading of constituent subindices, it becomes possible to take relative value views on sectors.

It is important to distinguish the purpose of these CDS indices from the CDS benchmark indices published by a number of investment banks. While the CDS indices are designed with the primary aim of tradability, benchmark indices are more concerned with providing an accurate reflection of the performance of the 'market'.

The CDX and the iTraxx families of indices follow almost exactly the same rules in terms of how they work. We will therefore describe the mechanics of the generic portfolio index. Where they exist, any differences between different contracts will be highlighted.

10.2   MECHANICS OF THE STANDARD INDICES

A CDS portfolio index is an over-the-counter bilateral contract. Each party to the contract is either a buyer or a seller of the CDS portfolio index. It is important to note that the terminology of the CDS index is different from the CDS market. A *buyer* of the CDS index means a buyer of credit risk – the party which receives the spread. This is different from the CDS market in which the buyer is often assumed to be a buyer of protection who is effectively going short credit risk.

Most CDS indices are issued or *rolled* semi-annually with a coupon which is fixed for the lifetime of the issue. From the time a new index is issued to the time that the next series of the index is issued, this index is known as the *on-the-run* index. Issue dates typically fall on one of the CDS 'IMM' dates, i.e. 20 March, 20 June, 20 September or 20 December. Those issued on 20 March will mature on 20 June of the appropriate year depending on the index maturity and likewise those issued on 20 September will mature on 20 December of the appropriate year depending on their index maturity. For example, the five-year index issued on 20 September 2007 matures on 20 December 2012. This is shown in Figure 10.1.

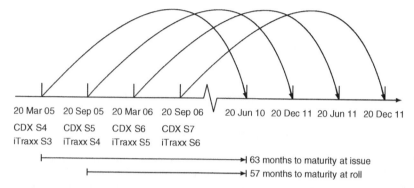

Figure 10.1 Five-year maturity CDS index swaps are issued in March and September for maturity in June and December, respectively, in five years. We also show the corresponding index series numbers for the CDX and iTraxx investment grade series

Indices are issued with a range of maturities. Initially, only a 5Y index was issued. However, it is now possible to trade indices with 3Y, 5Y, 7Y and 10Y maturities, noting that the most liquid points are the 5Y and 10Y maturities. Each of these will share the same underlying list of reference entities. Care must be taken to note that the so-called 3Y, 5Y, 7Y or 10Y *on-the-run* indices do not have exactly 3, 5, 7 or 10 years to maturity on their issue date. At issuance the time to maturity of a T-year index is typically $T + 3$ months, declining to $T - 3$ months when the next index is issued and it is no longer *on-the-run*. For example, a March 2006 issued five-year index will mature on 20 June 2011 and so have 63 months to maturity. On the September roll, it will have a remaining tenor of 57 months.

The constituents of a specific issue of an index remain fixed for the lifetime of the index, except when they default in which case they are removed without replacement. The constituents of new issues of the same index can change from index roll to index roll. Changes are typically due to the removal of credits which no longer satisfy the inclusion criteria. Possible reasons include downgrade out of investment grade, a credit event and a material reduction in liquidity of the credit. Once removed, these credits are replaced with new reference credits which do satisfy the inclusion criteria.

10.2.1 Payment Legs on a CDS Portfolio Index

Figure 10.2 shows the mechanics of a typical CDS portfolio index. The contract is entered into on-trade date t and is cash settled three days later. On this date, the buyer of the contract makes an upfront payment to the seller equal to the value of the contract. On the inception date of an index, this value is typically close to zero. This is because at inception, the index coupon is set close to the fair-value spread of the index. It is not set exactly equal to the fair-value spread as the index coupon is usually chosen to be a multiple of 5 bp.

Following settlement, the index buyer then has a contract which pays the index coupon. This is usually paid quarterly according to an Actual 360 basis. This is the same as the standard

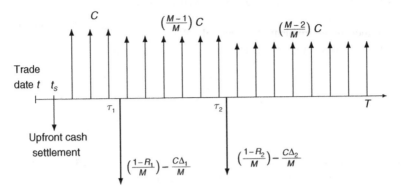

Figure 10.2   CDS index mechanics. An example of a CDS index with a face value of $1. The index coupon is C. We show two defaults on the index at times τ_1 and τ_2. After each default, the size of the coupon is reduced as the face value is reduced by $1/M$. We also have a loss payment. We use Δ_1 and Δ_2 to denote the year fraction which has passed between the previous coupon payment and the default times τ_1 and τ_2, respectively

CDS premium leg convention. If there are no credit events on the underlying portfolio, then the same coupon (ignoring variations in the day count fraction) is paid until the contract matures at time T. However, if there is a default, and assuming that the portfolio consists of M credits, what happens is that:

1. The buyer pays $1/M$ of the face value of the contract to the seller in return for delivery of a defaulted asset also on $1/M$ of the contract notional. In situations where the outstanding notional of derivative contracts exceeds the supply of deliverable obligations, a new protocol was introduced by ISDA in 2005 which allows a fallback to cash settlement in which case an auction method is used to determine a cash settlement price.
2. The buyer receives the fraction of premium which has accrued from the previous coupon date on the defaulted credit.
3. The notional of the contract is reduced by $1/M$. As a result, the absolute amount of spread received on the premium leg is reduced.

Figure 10.2 shows what happens if there are two credit events over the life of a portfolio index. In both cases, we show the default loss and the payment of the accrued coupon at default. We also show how a default reduces the size of the subsequent coupon payments.

While the European iTraxx indices include a restructuring credit event, the North American CDX index protection leg is only triggered by a bankruptcy or failure to pay on a reference credit. Restructuring is not included as a credit event. The CDX is therefore consistent with the No-Re category of CDS which trades at a spread which is lower than the spread of the standard Mod-Re restructuring clause CDS.

Table 10.2 shows the maturity date, coupon and price of the on-the-run indices in November 2006. Note that the price quoted is a 'bond price'. This is the price that should be paid if the

Table 10.2 The on-the-run index quotes as of 21 November 2006. We show the series number, maturity date, the fixed coupon and the current market spread and price if purchased in a funded format. Source: Markit

Index name	Series number	Maturity date	Coupon (bp)	Index spread (bp)	Bond price
CDX.NA.IG	7	20 Dec 2011	40	34	100.27%
CDX.NA.HY	7	20 Dec 2011	325	271	102.18%
CDX.NA.XO	7	20 Dec 2011	165	147	100.79%
CDX.EM	6	20 Dec 2011	140	122	100.72%
CDX.EM.DIVERS.	4	20 Dec 2011	95	86	100.38%
iTraxx Europe	6	20 Dec 2011	30	24	100.28%
iTraxx Europe HiVol	6	20 Dec 2011	55	46	100.39%
iTraxx Europe Crossover	6	20 Dec 2011	280	236	101.88%
iTraxx Japan	6	20 Dec 2011	25	21	100.19%
iTraxx Asia ex-Japan	6	20 Dec 2011	55	47	100.35%
iTraxx Australia	6	20 Dec 2011	35	24	100.52%

index is purchased in a bond format, i.e. the index is effectively packaged with a Libor quality par floater creating an effective credit risky floating rate note. For example, we see that the CDX.IG.NA index spread is 34 bp while the coupon is 40 bp – the credit quality of the index has improved since issue and the floating rate note trades above par. For the standard unfunded CDS index, the value is the 'bond price' minus 100%. A bond price of 102.18% therefore equates to payment of 2.18% of face value to enter into the index. A bond price of 99.5% would equate to a payment *to the investor* of 0.50% of face value to enter into the index.

Most investors prefer to trade the indices in unfunded format. For investment grade contracts such as the CDX IG and the iTraxx Europe, the market quotes an index spread which represents the flat spread at which the index should be priced if it were a simple CDS contract. If that spread is greater than the coupon on the index, then the index has a negative value from the perspective of an index buyer as the spread of the index has widened. As a result, an investor who wishes to enter into this index today would receive an upfront payment. Other lower credit quality indices such as the EM and HY indices are *quoted* using the bond price convention described above in which the upfront value is computed simply by subtracting 100. This convention has the advantage that it avoids any disagreement about the value of the index PV01 which is required to convert a spread-based quotation into an upfront value.

10.2.2   The Index Roll

The indices roll every six months and investors who hold the existing on-the-run index will generally try to roll into the new on-the-run index by selling the old index contract and buying the new one. This will almost certainly result in a P&L impact caused by:

- Any changes in the composition of the index which change its perceived credit quality. For example, the new index will not contain any names which have been downgraded below investment grade or whose liquidity has declined. This does not mean that the new index will be issued at a tighter spread than the current market spread of the old index since liquidity requirements may result in some names being replaced with wider spread names.

- The new index has a longer maturity, by six months, than the previous index. As credit curves tend to be upward sloping, this would tend to cause the new index spread to be wider, all other things being the same.

Calculating the value of a CDS index requires a model. It is also important to establish the relationship between the index spread and the spreads of all the CDS within the index. This is the subject of the next section.

10.3   CDS PORTFOLIO INDEX VALUATION

At time t, an investor enters into a long credit position in a CDS index with maturity time T. The contract pays a *fixed coupon* which we call the contractual index spread, and which we denote with $C(T)$. This spread is paid according to the frequency and accrual convention of the CDS index specification. It is paid on the outstanding notional of the CDS index. To enter into this contract, the investor has to make an initial upfront payment of $U_I(t)$ (note that $U_I(t)$ can be negative so that the investor receives a payment).

In the following, we want to calculate what the value of the upfront payment should be based on the underlying constituent CDS spread curves. We call this the *intrinsic value* and distinguish it from the actual upfront paid by calling it $V_I(t)$. Clearly, if $V_I(t) = U_I(t)$ then the intrinsic price calculated from the underlying CDS equals the upfront price quoted in the market. However, as we will discuss later, this is not always the case. To determine the intrinsic value of the CDS index, we must first determine the intrinsic values of the protection and premium legs separately.

10.3.1   Intrinsic Value of the Protection Leg

We begin by indexing the credits in the CDS index with $m = 1, \dots, M$. The default of a reference entity m in the index portfolio results in an immediate loss of $(1 - R_m)/M$ to the index buyer. We can therefore write the expected present value of the protection leg of the index as the sum over all M reference entities with each paying out the loss $(1 - R_m)$ at time τ_m conditional on τ_m being before the maturity time T of the index. The expected present value of the index protection leg in the risk-neutral pricing measure is given by

$$\text{Index protection Leg } PV(t) = \mathbb{E}_t \left[\frac{1}{M} \sum_{m=1}^{M} (1 - R_m) Z(t, \tau_m) 1_{t < \tau_m \leq T} \right].$$

Once again, we assume independence between default times, interest rates and recovery rates. As this is a linear function in the indicator function, we can move the expectation inside the sum and write the value of the protection leg in terms of the M reference entity survival curves $Q_m(t, T)$ as follows

$$\text{Index protection } PV(t) = \frac{1}{M} \sum_{m=1}^{M} (1 - R_m) \int_t^T Z(t, s)(-dQ_m(t, s)) \qquad (10.1)$$

where

$$Q_m(t, T) = \mathbb{E}_t \left[1_{\tau_m > T} \right].$$

For each reference entity, we can write the protection leg in terms of the breakeven spread and risky PV01 for the individual CDS contracts as follows

$$(1 - R_m) \int_t^T Z(t, s)(-dQ_m(t, s)) = S_m(t, T) \cdot \text{RPV01}_m(t, T)$$

where $S_m(t, T)$ is the breakeven CDS spread for issuer m at time t to the index maturity time T. Therefore we can write the present value of the index protection in terms of the individual name CDS spreads and risky PV01s

$$\text{Index protection leg PV}(t) = \frac{1}{M} \sum_{m=1}^M S_m(t, T) \cdot \text{RPV01}_m(t, T) \tag{10.2}$$

Given the CDS spread curve for each reference entity, we can use our CDS analytics to calculate the present value of the protection leg of the CDS index.

10.3.2 Intrinsic Value of the Premium Leg

Now we consider the premium leg of the CDS index. Contractually, a credit event in the CDS index portfolio results in a reduction in the contractual spread payments by a factor $1/M$. The value of the CDS index premium leg is therefore a sum over the reference entities and cash flows, with the payment only being made if the default is after the payment date

$$\text{Index premium leg PV}(t) = C(T) \cdot \mathbb{E}_t \left[\frac{1}{M} \sum_{m=1}^M \sum_{n=1}^N Z(t, t_n) 1_{\tau_m > t_n} \right] \tag{10.3}$$

For notational simplicity we have not included the contribution of the premium accrued at default in Equation 10.3. However, we do include it implicitly in the RPV01 term in the following equation. This writes the index premium leg value as a sum of all M premium legs of the individual CDS with all of them paying the same contractual spread $C(T)$

$$\text{Index premium leg PV}(t) = \frac{C(T)}{M} \sum_{m=1}^M \text{RPV01}_m(t, T). \tag{10.4}$$

The $\text{RPV01}_m(t, T)$ includes the coupon accrued at default and given in Equation 6.4.

10.3.3 The Intrinsic Value

The value at time t of a short protection position in the index swap is the present value of the premium leg minus the present value of the protection leg. This is given by

$$V_I(t) = \frac{1}{M} \sum_{m=1}^M (C(T) - S_m(t, T)) \cdot \text{RPV01}_m(t, T). \tag{10.5}$$

As a result, arbitrage pricing arguments allow us to value a CDS index in terms of the survival curves of the reference entities. We call this the intrinsic value since we have calculated the value of the index swap as the sum of the values of its constituent parts.

10.4   THE INDEX CURVE

Performing an intrinsic valuation is a slightly cumbersome way of valuing the index since it requires a knowledge of all of the individual constituent CDS spread curves. To simplify things, the market creates an *index curve* as though the index was a single name CDS with a spread curve $S_I(t, T)$. This new curve can then be used for quoting and pricing CDS index swaps. Table 10.3 shows a set of index spread quotes for different maturity investment grade indices. These were the on-the-run indices on 20 November 2006.

Table 10.3 3Y, 5Y, 7Y and 10Y market quotes for the on-the-run series of the CDX NA Investment Grade and High Yield indices, and the iTraxx Europe Investment Grade index on 20 November 2006. Source: Markit

Index term	Index maturity date	CDX NA HY Series 7	CDX NA IG Series 7	iTraxx Europe IG Series 6
3Y	Monday 21 Dec 2009	189 bp	18 bp	12 bp
5Y	Tuesday 20 Dec 2011	276 bp	34 bp	24 bp
7Y	Friday 20 Dec 2013	315 bp	44 bp	32 bp
10Y	Tuesday 20 Dec 2016	315 bp	55 bp	42 bp

Market convention dictates that the index curve used to value an index has a *flat term structure*. So if we wish to value the 7Y CDX NA Investment Grade index, we would simply use a flat CDS curve at a level of 44 bp. As a result, there is an implicit contradiction in our pricing of the different maturity indices. The contradiction is that we use different survival probabilities to weight the same time cash flows on the different maturity indices. As the portfolios are the same, their survival probabilities should also be the same to the same date. As a result, we should not think of a T-maturity index quote as though it were analogous to a T-maturity CDS quote. We should think of it as the spread level of a flat CDS curve which when combined with a 40% recovery rate assumption gives the correct upfront value for the CDS index.

Example Consider an investor who has sold the CDX Investment Grade Series 4 trade, i.e. who is long protection, and wishes to calculate its mark-to-market value on 7 February 2006. A trade executed on this date would become effective on the 8 February and be cash settled two days later on 10 February. The index has a maturity date of 20 June 2010. The index spread curve is assumed to be flat at 48.375 bp. The coupon of the index CDX.NA.IG.4 is 40 bp. We assume an index recovery rate of 40%. The deal characteristics are summarised in the table below.

Deal characteristics	
Position	Short index
Face value	$10 million
Maturity	20 June 2010
Index coupon	40 bp
Previous coupon date	20 December 2005
Effective date	8 February 2006

Cash settlement	10 February 2006
Index curve	Flat at 48.375 bp
Assumed recovery rate	40%

Libor swap curve	
1Y	5.02%
2Y	5.02%
3Y	5.01%
4Y	5.02%
5Y	5.03%
Fixed frequency	Semi-annual
Fixed basis	30/360

We need to generate all of the scheduled cash flows. These are shown below:

Scheduled payment date	Accrual factor $\Delta(t_{n-1}, t_n)$	Risky flow amount	Libor discount factor $Z(t, T_n)$	Survival prob. $Q(t, t_n)$
Mon 20 Mar 2006	0.250000	10 000.00	0.994906	0.999110
Tue 20 Jun 2006	0.255556	10 222.22	0.983289	0.997065
Wed 20 Sep 2006	0.255556	10 222.22	0.971133	0.995025
Wed 20 Dec 2006	0.252778	10 111.11	0.958473	0.993013
Tue 20 Mar 2007	0.250000	10 000.00	0.946447	0.991026
Wed 20 Jun 2007	0.255556	10 222.22	0.934729	0.989000
Thu 20 Sep 2007	0.255556	10 222.22	0.923156	0.986977
Thu 20 Dec 2007	0.252778	10 111.11	0.911850	0.984980
Thu 20 Mar 2008	0.252778	10 111.11	0.900700	0.982987
Fri 20 Jun 2008	0.255556	10 222.22	0.889590	0.980976
Mon 22 Sep 2008	0.261111	10 444.44	0.878381	0.978926
Mon 22 Dec 2008	0.252778	10 111.11	0.867664	0.976945
Fri 20 Mar 2009	0.244444	9 777.78	0.857367	0.975034
Mon 22 Jun 2009	0.261111	10 444.44	0.846432	0.972996
Mon 21 Sep 2009	0.252778	10 111.11	0.835980	0.971027
Mon 21 Dec 2009	0.252778	10 111.11	0.825656	0.969062
Mon 22 Mar 2010	0.252778	10 111.11	0.815421	0.967102
Mon 21 Jun 2010	0.250000	10 000.00	0.805377	0.965167

Valuation output	
Full swap value ($)	27 020
Accrued interest ($)	−5556
Clean swap value ($)	32 575
Risky PV01	4.027
Credit DV01	$3 876

The full price is the expected present value of the protection leg minus all future index coupon payments out (we are long protection). Consistent with market practice, we also compute the accrued interest based on 50 days of accrual using an Actual 360 basis. Since we are long protection, this has a negative sign. The risky PV01 of the index is also calculated as is its credit spread sensitivity, the credit DV01.

In the previous section, we showed how to calculate the intrinsic value of a CDS index seeing it as a sum of its underlying CDS. In the next section, we describe how to imply out the CDS index curve from the spreads of the underlying CDS curves of all M issuers. We call this implied spread the intrinsic spread.

10.5   CALCULATING THE INTRINSIC SPREAD OF AN INDEX

There is a theoretical relationship between this index spread curve and the spread curves of all of the constituent CDS. To begin, let us recall that in Section 10.3.3 we demonstrated that the intrinsic value of the CDS index is given by

$$V_I(t) = \frac{1}{M} \sum_{m=1}^{M} (S_m(t, T) - C(T)) \cdot \text{RPV01}_m(t, T). \tag{10.6}$$

However, we wish to calculate the market index spread $S_I(t, T)$ at time t. This is not the same as the index coupon $C(T)$ which is announced and fixed at the issuance of the index series. Market convention is that the index curve $S_I(t, T)$ is flat. It is found by solving for the value of $S_I(t, T)$ at which a CDS contract with a coupon $C(T)$ has the same upfront value as the index. Mathematically, we calculate the *upfront value* of the index using a flat index curve as

$$U_I(t) = (S_I(t, T) - C(T)) \cdot \text{RPV01}_I(t, T) \tag{10.7}$$

where the subscript I on the index RPV01 should be a reminder that it uses a flat credit curve. Equating the intrinsic upfront and the index curve upfront, we get

$$\frac{1}{M} \sum_{m=1}^{M} (S_m(t, T) - C(T)) \cdot \text{RPV01}_m(t, T) = (S_I(t, T) - C(T)) \cdot \text{RPV01}_I(t, T). \tag{10.8}$$

Since there is an implicit dependency on the index spread $S_I(t, T)$ in the index RPV01$_I$, it is not possible to solve for $S_I(t, T)$ without using a one-dimensional root-searching algorithm. However, if the individual spread curves are flat and reasonably homogeneous, we can make the approximation

$$\text{RPV01}_I(t, T) \simeq \frac{1}{M} \sum_{m=1}^{M} \text{RPV01}_m(t, T).$$

This allows us to cancel out the dependency on the index coupon $C(T)$ and write an approximation for $S_I(t, T)$ explicitly in terms of the individual issuer curve spreads and risky PV01s

$$S_I(t, T) \simeq \frac{\sum_{m=1}^{M} S_m(t, T) \cdot \text{RPV01}_m(t, T)}{\sum_{m=1}^{M} \text{RPV01}_m(t, T)}. \tag{10.9}$$

This approximation is exact if all of the CDS spread curves are flat and identical.[2] However, this condition is not true in practice and we would therefore like to know how approximate it

---

[2] It is also exact if the upfront value of the index and the intrinsic value equal zero, i.e. $U_I(t) = V_I(t) = 0$. However, we want to consider the general case when the upfront value is non-zero.

is. We have therefore tested it by calculating $S_I(t, T)$ using Equation 10.9, and compared it to the value computed using a one-dimensional root search to solve Equation 10.8.

We have performed this exercise on the iTraxx and CDX indices and the results are presented in Table 10.4. They show that the approximation is very accurate for both families of investment grade indices with a maximum spread difference of 0.065 bp on the 10Y iTraxx index. For the 5Y CDX High Yield index, the error is 1.5 bp. The larger size of this error is due to the higher spreads and higher spread dispersion in the high yield portfolio. It is also due to the large upfront value of the HY index – the index coupon is approximately 100 bp wider than the intrinsic index spread.

Table 10.4 Comparison of the index spread calculated using the approximation in Equation 10.9 and the exact using Equation 10.8 for a range of CDS indices

Index name, series and maturity	Index coupon $C(T)$ (bp)	Approximate spread $S_I(t, T)$ (bp)	Exact spread $S_I(t, T)$ (bp)	Difference (bp)
iTraxx Europe Series 6 3Y	20	13.928	13.928	0.000
iTraxx Europe Series 6 5Y	30	23.856	23.842	0.014
iTraxx Europe Series 6 7Y	40	32.372	32.337	0.035
iTraxx Europe Series 6 10Y	50	41.920	41.855	0.065
CDX NA IG Series 7 3Y	25	19.698	19.697	0.001
CDX NA IG Series 7 5Y	40	35.556	35.540	0.016
CDX NA IG Series 7 7Y	50	49.013	49.005	0.008
CDX NA IG Series 7 10Y	65	61.403	61.363	0.040
CDX NA HY Series 7 5Y	325	226.166	224.666	1.500

10.5.1   Intrinsic Index Spread versus the Average Index Spread

The approximation in Equation 10.9 makes it very clear that the index spread is not a simple average of the individual CDS spreads but is close to the *RPV01 weighted average* of the individual CDS spreads. This tells us that if the reference entities in the index have a similar credit quality then the intrinsic index spread will be close to the average spread. However, if there is any dispersion in the spreads of the credits in the index then the intrinsic index spread will be lower than the average.[3] We demonstrate this in Table 10.5 where we show the intrinsic spread calculated using Equation 10.9 and the average spread

$$\overline{S}_I(t, T) = \frac{1}{M} \sum_{m=1}^{M} S_m(t, T)$$

for a range of indices using real CDS market spreads. For the investment grade portfolios we see that the difference between the intrinsic spread and the average spread is small, of the order of 1–2 bp for the DJ CDX NA, rising to about 3 bp for the iTraxx Europe index. The difference between the intrinsic and average spread is greater for the North American investment grade portfolio than for the European investment grade portfolio because on this

---

[3] This can be explained by noting that the RPV01-weighted average spread, which is a good approximation for the intrinsic spread, is a convex function and so its average is less than the simple average.

Table 10.5 Comparison of the intrinsic index spread and average CDS spread for a range of CDS indices. Also shown is the standard deviation of spreads in the index

Index name and series number	Index term	Intrinsic spread (bp)	Average spread (bp)	Standard deviation (bp)
CDX NA IG Series 7	3Y	18.2	18.3	18
CDX NA IG Series 7	5Y	33.1	33.5	36
CDX NA IG Series 7	7Y	44.8	45.6	46
CDX NA IG Series 7	10Y	55.3	56.9	53
iTraxx Europe Series 6	3Y	16.2	16.2	12
iTraxx Europe Series 6	5Y	26.9	27.1	20
iTraxx Europe Series 6	7Y	36.2	36.5	25
iTraxx Europe Series 6	10Y	45.8	46.4	30
CDX NA HY Series 7	3Y	197	213	233
CDX NA HY Series 7	5Y	275	305	340
CDX NA HY Series 7	7Y	307	345	383
CDX NA HY Series 7	10Y	324	371	412

date, the standard deviation of the spreads of the North American index is higher, 36 bp versus 20 bp at five years. The difference is very large for the high yield index. This can be explained by the large standard deviation of the spreads in the high yield index which is 340 bp. The very high standard deviation of the high-yield index spreads can be explained by a number of distressed credits with spreads greater than 1000 bp which were in this index on the date these spreads were quoted.

10.5.2 The Index Basis

In the previous section, we have shown how to derive an accurate approximation for the intrinsic index spread in terms of the CDS spread curves of the index constituents. However, when we look at the index spread quoted in the market, we often find that it is not the same as the intrinsic index spread. A *basis* can arise for reasons which we list below:

- In the case of the North American CDX index, the payment of protection on the index protection leg is only triggered when the credit event is a *bankruptcy or failure to pay*. Restructuring is not included as a credit event. These are called No-Re CDS. However, the market standard for CDS in the US is based on the use of the Mod-Re restructuring clause. Since No-Re spreads are typically about 5% lower than Mod-Re spreads, we have an immediate basis. These restructuring clauses were discussed in Section 5.4.4.
- The considerable size and liquidity of the CDS index market means that the CDS index spread embeds a lower liquidity risk premium than the less liquid CDS spreads.
- As the CDS index is more liquid, it tends to be the preferred instrument used by market participants to express a changing view about the credit market as a whole, or even one specific name in the index. As a result, the CDS index may be considered to lead the CDS market. This is especially true in a widening market where investors use long protection positions in the index to hedge illiquid long credit positions.

An example of the basis is shown in Table 10.6 where we show the quoted index spread and the CDS-implied intrinsic index spread for a range of indices.

Table 10.6 Comparison of the market quoted index spread and the CDS-implied intrinsic index CDS spread for a range of CDS indices

Index name and series number	Index term	Quoted index spread (bp)	Intrinsic index spread (bp)	Index basis (bp)
CDX NA IG Series 7	5Y	34	33.1	0.9
CDX NA IG Series 7	10Y	55	55.3	−0.3
CDX NA HY Series 7	5Y	276	275	1.0
CDX NA HY Series 7	10Y	315	324	−9.0
iTraxx Europe Series 6	5Y	24	26.9	−2.9
iTraxx Europe Series 6	10Y	42	45.8	−3.8

10.5.3 CDS Index Risk

In the simple case when we are managing a book of index swap trades, we can use the index swap spread to map a CDS index onto a single name CDS. We can then manage the spread and interest rate risk using the standard CDS risk measures outlined in Chapter 8. Special care should be taken to ensure that the VOD risk is managed. In this case, a default on the CDS index should be offset by another index swap position of the same face value. One other problem is that if we hedge an *off-the-run* index swap position with an *on-the-run* index swap position, there may be a mismatch in terms of some credits being in one index but not in the other.

However, if we wish to risk manage a CDS index with respect to its individual constituents, the index basis will present problems as we will need to account for it somewhere in our model. One approach to this problem is to simply adjust the individual CDS spreads in a way that ensures that the adjusted index intrinsic spread equals the market quoted spread of the index. The exact nature of the adjustment is somewhat arbitrary, although we will want an approach that is stable, fast and reasonable. We call this the *portfolio swap adjustment*.

10.6 THE PORTFOLIO SWAP ADJUSTMENT

One way to ensure that the index swap spread equals the intrinsic swap spread is to see if there is an adjustment that can be made to the individual issuer curves which can enforce Equation 10.8. We choose to adjust the individual issuer curves rather than the index swap since the index swap is substantially more liquid and so their prices are more certain than the CDS quotes.

The exact nature of the adjustment is somewhat arbitrary. We prefer a proportional adjustment of the spread rather than an absolute spread adjustment, i.e. we would rather increase all spreads by 1% than add say 5 bp to all spreads which would have a large effect on the credit risk of a name trading at 10 bp and a much smaller effect on another trading at 200 bp. We also require an adjustment which does not induce any arbitrage effects, one that preserves the CDS term structure shape of each of the issuer curves, and one which does not change the relative risk ranking of the issuers in the portfolio. Speed is also a major consideration. Adjusting the term structure of 125 issuers in order to refit an index curve is no small task. Furthermore, since it will become a preprocessing layer to much of the correlation product analytics which we will encounter later, it is important that the implementation is as fast as possible. Figure 10.3 depicts the relationship between the index swap, the unadjusted CDS curves and the portfolio swap adjusted CDS curves.

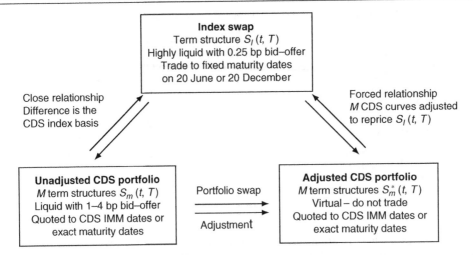

Figure 10.3   The portfolio swap adjustment is a way to adjust the individual CDS issuer curves so that the intrinsic of the adjusted CDS curves exactly matches the CDS index quotes. We use the term CDS IMM dates to mean the rolling maturity CDS contracts which mature on 20 March, June, September and December

10.6.1   Mathematics of the Adjustment

We wish to fit the index spread quotes $S_I(t, T_n)$ at the $n = 1, \ldots, N$ quoted index maturity points $T_1, T_2, \ldots, T_N$. We assume that we have CDS quotes to the same index maturities as we have for the issuer CDS curves. We denote the adjusted issuer $m = 1, \ldots, M$ spreads as $S_m^*(t, T_n)$ and recall that while the individual CDS have a full term structure, the index swaps assume a flat CDS index curve. The swap adjusted CDS spreads to the N index maturities must obey the following equations

$$\frac{1}{M} \sum_{m=1}^{M} \left(S_m^*(t, T_1) - C(T_1) \right) \cdot \text{RPV01}_m(t, T_1, S_m^*(t, T_1)) = U_I(t, T_1)$$

$$\frac{1}{M} \sum_{m=1}^{M} \left(S_m^*(t, T_2) - C(T_2) \right) \cdot \text{RPV01}_m(t, T_2, S_m^*(t, T_2)) = U_I(t, T_2)$$

$$\vdots \quad \vdots$$

$$\frac{1}{M} \sum_{m=1}^{M} \left(S_m^*(t, T_N) - C(T_N) \right) \cdot \text{RPV01}_m(t, T_N, S_m^*(t, T_N)) = U_I(t, T_N)$$

$$(10.10)$$

The index upfront is given by

$$U_I(t, T_n) = (S_I(t, T_n) - C(T_n)) \cdot \text{RPV01}_I(t, T_n)$$

where $S_I(t, T_n)$ is the index spread to maturity T_n.

There are two ways to adjust the issuer spread curves. Either we adjust the issuer spreads directly, or we adjust survival probabilities which in turn adjust the spreads. The adjusted spreads are a function of the adjusted survival probabilities which we denote with $Q^*(t, T)$. In the following, we set out two algorithms, the first based on spread adjustments and the second based on survival probability adjustments.

10.6.2   Using a Spread Multiplier

One very direct approach is to put a simple multiplier on the spreads so that

$$S_m^*(t, T) = \alpha(T) S_m(t, T).$$

We then wish to find the value of $\alpha(T)$ which solves the following equation for each index swap maturity. For each maturity T_n we have to solve

$$\frac{1}{M} \sum_{m=1}^{M} (\alpha(T_n) S_m(t, T_n) - C(T_n)) \cdot \text{RPV01}(t, T_n, \alpha(T_n) S_m) = U_I(t, T_n). \qquad (10.11)$$

For different index maturities, the equations are coupled, i.e. an adjustment to the 3Y CDS spread will change the 5Y, 7Y and 10Y CDS spreads. However, we can solve them using a bootstrap. The idea is that we solve first for $\alpha(T_1)$, then for $\alpha(T_2)$ and so on up to $\alpha(T_N)$. In order to do this, we need to ensure that changing $\alpha(T_{n+1})$ will not break the T_n maturity adjustment which was achieved using $\alpha(T_n)$.

CDS index maturity dates do not always coincide with the standard CDS maturity dates. For example, if the 3Y CDS matures before the 3Y index, then adjusting the 5Y CDS spread will change both the 3Y index spread *and* the 5Y index spread. This will prevent the bootstrap from working. To overcome this problem, we need to move the CDS maturity dates to the index maturity dates. We must therefore determine the *interpolated* CDS spreads to the index maturity dates. We then use these 'virtual' CDS contracts to build our CDS curve. These are then the CDS spreads which should be adjusted in order to fit the index swap quoted spreads. Once the portfolio adjustment has been completed, we can then map the adjusted spreads back onto the standard CDS maturity points since these are the points which we will want to perturb for performing CDS risk management.

Unfortunately, there is no simple linear solution for $\alpha(T_n)$ since there is a dependence within the risky PV01 term. We therefore have to resort to some one-dimensional root solver. However, it is possible to solve the set of equations for $T_n = T_1, \ldots, T_N$, each of the form of Equation 10.11 by fixed point iteration. We assume that we know the upfront values of the different maturity CDS indices given by $U_I(t, T_n)$. The algorithm is as follows:

1. Build all $m = 1, \ldots, M$, survival curves $Q_m(t, T)$ using the standard market CDS maturities.
2. Calculate the interpolated CDS spreads to the index curve maturities $S_m(t, T_n)$. Then rebuild all of the CDS curves using just these spreads.
3. Set $n = 1$.
4. Set $k = 0$, $S_m^{(k)}(t, T_n) = S_m(t, T_n)$ and $\alpha_n(k) = 1.0$.
5. For all the issuers $m = 1, \ldots, M$ adjust the spread $S_m^{(k+1)}(t, T_n) = \alpha_n(k) S_m^k(t, T_n)$.
6. Build all M survival curves using the adjusted spread curves $S_m^{(k+1)}(t, T_n)$.
7. Calculate $\alpha_n(k + 1)$ using the equation

$$\alpha_n(k + 1) = \alpha_n(k) \times \frac{U_I(t, T_n) + C(T_n) \frac{1}{M} \sum_{m=1}^{M} \text{RPV01}_m(t, T_n, S_m^{(k+1)})}{\frac{1}{M} \sum_{m=1}^{M} S_m^{(k+1)}(t, T_n) \cdot \text{RPV01}_m(t, T_n, S_m^{(k+1)})}.$$

8. If $|\alpha_n(k+1) - 1| \le \epsilon$ where ϵ is the required tolerance then continue to step (9). Otherwise set $k = k + 1$ and return to step (5).
9. Set $\alpha(T_n) = \alpha_n(k+1)$.
10. Set $n = n + 1$. If $n > N$ then stop. Otherwise return to step (4).

The output is a vector of N spread multipliers $\alpha(T_n)$. Most of the work of this iteration scheme is done in the first iteration since the dependence of the issuer PV01s on the spread is second order. In most cases we find that the algorithm converges with a tolerance in present value terms of the order of $O(10^{-8})$ within five iteration steps.

The main problem with a spread multiplier approach is that it can be quite slow. This is because in step (6), we have to recalibrate all M issuer curves, and this is done for each iteration of the solver. For this reason, it is more efficient to cut out the curve building step by adjusting the survival probabilities directly.

10.6.3   Using a Forward Default Probability Multiplier

We now adjust the survival probabilities. We write the adjustment as

$$Q_m^*(t, T_n) = Q_m^*(t, T_{n-1}) Q(T_{n-1}, T_n)^{\alpha(n)}$$

i.e. we raise the forward survival probability to the power of $\alpha(n)$. As we manipulate the survival probabilities, this approach avoids the need to bootstrap the survival curves during the search for the adjusted survival curves $Q_m^*(t, T_n)$ which satisfy Equations 10.10.

To better understand this choice of adjustment, let us first write the survival probability curve for issuer m as a function of its forward default rate $h_m(t)$

$$Q_m(t, T_n) = Q_m(t, T_{n-1}) \exp\left(-\int_{T_{n-1}}^{T_n} h_m(s)ds\right)$$

As a result, if we have an adjustment of this type, we can write this as

$$Q_m^*(t, T_n) = Q_m(t, T_{n-1}) \exp\left(-\alpha(n)\int_{T_{n-1}}^{T_n} h_m(s)ds\right).$$

We see that $\alpha(n)$ is a simple multiplier on the forward default rate. As the forward spread is roughly linearly proportional to the forward default rate, we would expect this adjustment to be similar in nature to the spread multiplier described in the previous section. Also, provided we keep α positive, we ensure that the adjusted survival curves remain arbitrage free.

As in the previous section, in order to use a bootstrap approach to solve for the adjustment, we need to take into account the fact that the CDS and CDS index may have different maturity dates. We therefore address this by building our CDS survival curves using the standard CDS market quotes. We then use our curve interpolation scheme to calculate what the issuer survival probabilites should be at the index maturity points. These index maturity time points become the 'skeleton' of points on our new survival curve. Only once we have done this can we then begin our fitting algorithm. This is as follows:

1. Build all $m = 1, \ldots, M$, survival curves $Q_m(t, T)$ using the standard market CDS maturities.
2. Calculate the CDS index maturity survival probabilities $Q_m(t, T_n)$ to the index swap maturities and use these points as the new curve 'skeleton'.
3. Set $n = 1$.
4. Set $k = 0$, $Q_m^{(k)}(t, T_n) = Q_m(t, T_n)$ and $\alpha_n(k) = 1.0$.

5. For all the issuers $m = 1, \ldots, M$ adjust the survival probabilities

$$Q_m^{(k+1)}(t, T_n) = Q_m^*(t, T_{n-1}) \times \left(Q_m^k(T_{n-1}, T_n)\right)^{\alpha(k)}$$

where $Q^*(t, T_0) = 1.0$.

6. Calculate $\alpha_n(k+1)$ using the equation

$$\alpha(k+1) = \alpha(k) \times \frac{U_I(t, T_n) + C(T_n)\frac{1}{M}\sum_{m=1}^{M} \text{RPV01}_m(t, T_n, Q_m^{(k+1)})}{\frac{1}{M}\sum_{m=1}^{M} S_m^{(k+1)}(t, T_n, Q^{(k+1)}) \cdot \text{RPV01}(t, T_n, Q_m^{(k+1)})}.$$

7. If $|\alpha_n(k+1) - 1| \leq \epsilon$ where ϵ is the required tolerance, continue to step (8). Otherwise set $k = k + 1$ and return to step (5).

8. Set $Q_m^*(t, T_n) = Q_m^{(k+1)}(t, T_n)$ for each of the M issuers.

9. Set $n = n + 1$. If $n > N$ then stop. Otherwise return to step (4).

Because we avoid the time-consuming bootstrap of all M curves in each iteration step that we had when we used a spread multiplier for the portfolio swap adjustment, we find that this method is about 50 times faster than the first method and typically takes less than a second for a 125-name portfolio using four maturity points.

Table 10.7 compares the unadjusted and adjusted spread levels of a subset of the reference entities in the iTraxx Europe Investment Grade Series 6 index. This uses our survival probability

Table 10.7 This table shows a selection of credits from the iTraxx Europe Series 6 index. We show the 3Y and 5Y spreads before and after the portfolio swap adjustment. We also show the ratio of the spreads. At the top we show the market quoted spread and the unadjusted intrinsic portfolio spread for 3Y and 5Y. Spread data is courtesy of Lehman Brothers

	3Y Index maturity			5Y Index maturity		
Index spread (bp)	12			24		
Intrinsic spread (bp)	16.2			26.9		
Ratio	0.741			0.892		
Reference entity name	3Y spread unadjusted (bp)	3Y spread adjusted (bp)	Spread ratio	5Y spread unadjusted (bp)	5Y spread adjusted (bp)	Spread ratio
Adecco S A	23.2	17.1	0.737	38.8	34.4	0.89
Bertelsmann AG	16.9	12.5	0.737	28.8	25.7	0.89
DaimlerChrysler AG	34.4	25.4	0.737	52.9	44.6	0.84
Deutsche Telekom AG	21.2	15.6	0.737	37.0	33.5	0.91
Endesa S A	10.4	7.7	0.737	16.4	13.9	0.85
AB Electrolux	22.9	16.9	0.737	34.8	29.1	0.84
Bco Espirito Santo S A	6.2	4.6	0.737	9.1	7.4	0.82
France Telecom	17.9	13.2	0.737	29.8	26.4	0.88
ITV PLC	103.1	76.0	0.737	166.4	145.5	0.87
Kingfisher PLC	29.6	21.9	0.737	50.9	45.7	0.90
Lafarge	25.0	18.5	0.737	38.8	32.9	0.85
Deutsche Lufthansa AG	22.3	16.5	0.737	39.9	36.5	0.92
Safeway Limited	17.8	13.1	0.737	28.7	24.8	0.87
Renault	18.0	13.3	0.737	31.7	28.8	0.91
Telefonica S A	25.1	18.5	0.737	39.8	34.2	0.86
Olivetti Intnl. BV	37.7	27.8	0.737	59.1	50.5	0.86
ThyssenKrupp AG	21.5	15.8	0.737	41.0	38.8	0.95

adjustment. We show the adjustment to the three-year and the five-year issuer curves. We see that the 3Y intrinsic is 16.2 bp versus 12 bp for the market index swap. We therefore need to scale down the hazard rate by some factor until the portfolio intrinsic equals that of the index. We see this requires all spreads to be scaled down by a factor of 0.737, very close to the spread ratio of the intrinsic and the index which is 0.741. At the 5Y maturity, we see that the intrinsic spread of the portfolio is also above the market index spread. To fit the 5Y index, it is necessary to reduce all of the 5Y spreads by an average factor of about 0.878, close to the ratio of the index spread and the intrinsic spread which is 0.89. It is not the same for all credits since the adjustment to the 3Y spreads has already been done and these proportional changes do not affect all issuer survival probabilities by the same amount.

10.7   ASSET-BACKED AND LOAN CDS INDICES

The CDS index family has recently seen the addition of a number of new indices, some of which extend the CDS indices into new parts of the credit markets. We now describe these briefly.

10.7.1   The ABX.HE Index

The ABX.HE indices reference the US subprime home equity mortgage market. Launched in early 2006, the ABX.HE indices consist of a family of five subindices each with a portfolio of 20 US subprime home equity deals. The different subindices contain the different rated tranches of the deals, i.e. the subindices consist of RMBS tranches with initial ratings of AAA, AA, A, BBB and BBB−. The ABX.HE index is owned and administered by Markit. The main rules governing the inclusion of home equity deals are as follows:

- The size of the deal must be at least $500 million and it should have been issued in the previous six months.
- Each security must be floating rate and have a weighted average life between four and six years, except for the AAA index which must have an average life of more than five years.
- No more than four of the deals may have collateral originated by the same lender, and no more than six deals may be selected from the same master servicer.
- More than 90% of the collateral must be first lien, with an FICO[4] less than or equal to 660.

A difference between the ABX and traditional CDS indices is that the index references specify reference obligations, rather than a reference entity. Another difference is that the exposure to the different reference obligations changes through time as the underlying ABS bonds amortise.

Each series pays a fixed coupon. The first series of the ABX.HE index, known as ABX.HE 06-1, was issued on 19 January 2006 and as with other indices, is rolled every six months, with the next roll on 19 July. Table 10.8 shows the coupon and prices of the ABX indices associated with the second series issued in 2007. These are the prices of the index purchased in a funded format. The actual upfront price paid is this price minus par. As a result, an investor in the BBB index would *receive* an upfront payment of $100 − 22.14 = 77.86$ per $100 of face value

---

[4] The FICO is a credit score based on the methodology developed by Fair, Isaac and Company.

Table 10.8   Details of the 2007 series 2 issue of the ABX.HE index showing the index coupon and price in December 2007. Source: Markit

Index	Series	Version	Coupon (bp)	Price
ABX-HE-AAA 07-2	7	2	76	71.00
ABX-HE-AA 07-2	7	2	192	39.83
ABX-HE-A 07-2	7	2	369	31.06
ABX-HE-BBB 07-2	7	2	500	22.14
ABX-HE-BBB- 07-2	7	2	500	21.39

followed by an annualised coupon of 500 bp. The low prices reflect the distressed nature of the subprime market at the end of 2007.

10.7.2   The LCDX.NA Index

Launched in May 2007, LCDX.NA is an index with 100 equally weighted single-name loan-only CDS (LCDS) linked to syndicated first-lien North American loans. These are selected for their liquidity. Although it is very similar to a standard CDS index, there are a number of differences. One difference is that an LCDS may be removed without any payment of protection from the index if the borrower repays the loan without issuing senior syndicated secured debt. This follows the convention used in the LCDS market discussed in Section 5.7. The initial index maturity is set at five years. It is expected that further maturities will be added.

10.7.3   The LevX Index

The LevX index is linked to the European loan CDS market. It was first issued in October 2006, and is administered by Markit. It is broken into two subindices, the senior and subordinated. The LevX senior subindex references the 35 most liquid first-lien credit agreements traded in the European leveraged loan CDS market. The subordinated subindex references the 35 most liquid second- and third-lien credit agreements traded in the European LCDS market.

10.8   SUMMARY

In this chapter we have introduced the CDS portfolio index and focused on its mechanics and risks. We have demonstrated how it can be priced in terms of the underlying CDS, producing an intrinsic value and an intrinsic spread. We have also described how the market quotes the CDS indices in terms of an index spread and explained why the intrinsic spread and index spread do not always agree.

We then showed how to adjust the CDS spread curves in order that the intrinsic and index spread agree. This is a prerequisite for those who wish to build models for products including options on CDS indices and especially the standard tranches which are based on these indices in a way which ensures that there is no built-in basis between the market value and intrinsic value.

Options on CDS Portfolio Indices

11.1 INTRODUCTION

The main growth in credit derivative volatility products has been in options on the CDS portfolio indices. These are also known as portfolio swaptions or index options and we use both terms interchangeably. As the name suggests, the underlying is not one credit but is one of the portfolio indices described in the previous chapter. There is currently active trading in options on all of the traded indices, with most liquidity in the cross-over indices of CDX and iTraxx and the CDX high yield index. These are more popular than the investment grade indices due to the higher volatility of the underlying index. The significant liquidity of the underlying indices has made index options an easier product for dealers to price and hedge, thereby enhancing the liquidity of this product. Investors are attracted to portfolio swaptions for a number of reasons which include:

1. Index options provide a cheap way to take a long or short position on a broad credit index.
2. The non-linear option payoff can be used to produce a risk profile which is more attractive to an investor's view than simply buying or selling the index.
3. They provide a mechanism for expressing a view on the volatility of the macro credit market.

Since index options follow the same mechanics for different underlying indices, we can price options on all of these indices using the exact same model. In the following we will therefore refer generically to index options rather than name a specific index.

11.2 MECHANICS

An index option is a bilateral over-the-counter contract to buy or sell protection on a specified index with a specified maturity time T at an index spread agreed today. The index chosen is usually the 5Y *on-the-run* index at the time of option origination. The option expires at time t_E with typical times to option expiry ranging from one to three months and some going out to six months. Because of the six monthly index roll, option expiries beyond six months are rare since the liquidity of the index drops immediately after the next roll and this can significantly increase hedging costs. The spread of the underlying index is struck at a value K. The index option is a price-based option in which the exercise price is given by

$$G(K) = (K - C(T)) \cdot \text{RPV01}_I(t_E, T, K) \tag{11.1}$$

where $C(T)$ is the fixed coupon on the underlying T-maturity index and $\text{RPV01}_I(t_E, T, K)$ is the risky index PV01 from option expiry to index maturity priced using a flat CDS credit curve at a spread level equal to K. We must also specify whether the option is a payer or a receiver:

- A payer index option is one in which the option holder has the option to enter into a long protection position in the index swap at the strike spread. The option is typically exercised if the index spread widens. It can be used as a way to take a short credit position on the macro credit market.
- A receiver option is an option to enter into a short protection position in the index swap at the strike spread. It is typically exercised when spreads have tightened. As such, it can be a way to take a long credit position on the macro credit market.

There are three important dates in the index option contract:

1. First is the contract initiation date $t=0$ when the option strike is set and the option premium is paid. Any defaults in the index portfolio which occur after this date will affect the valuation of the index option.
2. Second is the option expiry date t_E on which the decision to exercise is taken – almost all default swaptions are European style, meaning that the exercise decision can only be made on option expiry.
3. Last is the maturity time T of the underlying index. Most index options are traded on the 5Y index.

We now consider the calculation of the payoff on the option expiry date and how this determines whether the option is exercised.

11.2.1 The Exercise Decision

At option expiry, the option owner needs to decide whether or not to exercise the option. To determine this, the option holder must be able to determine the value of what is received and what is paid. Figure 11.1 shows the cash flows of a payer index swaption which is exercised.

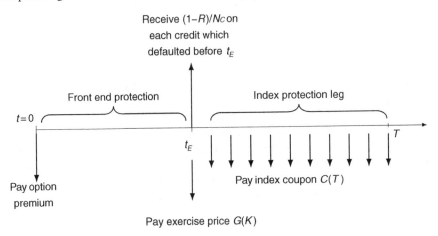

Figure 11.1 Index option payer swaption (option to buy protection) showing the receipt of loss payments on any default credits before t_E and the payment of the exercise price $G(K)$ if the option holder decides to exercise the option. Following option exercise, the option buyer has a long protection position in the index

We consider the case of a payer option in which the investor has the option to enter into a long protection position in the index swap at a fixed spread K. If exercised, the payoff for a payer swaption at expiry is composed of three parts which we now describe:

1. The holder of a payer swaption can immediately settle the protection payment on any credits in the index which have defaulted between option initiation at time 0 and option expiry at time t_E. To do this, the option buyer purchases the defaulted credits in the market and delivers them to the option seller in return for par. Each defaulted credit is therefore worth $(1 - R)$ times its notional exposure in the index where R is its recovery rate.
2. The option buyer pays the exercise price $G(K)$ to the option seller. This is the value of the CDX index (on the full original notional before any defaults) priced using an index spread equal to the strike K. It is calculated according to Equation 11.1. This value is cash settled.
3. The option buyer receives the CDX index (from which the defaulted credits have been removed) from the option seller at the current market index spread $S_I(t_E, T)$. If the option is a payer then the option buyer has a long protection position in the index. The value of this long protection position per dollar of option face value is given by

$$(S_I(t_E, T) - C(T)) \, \text{RPV01}_I(t_E, T, S_I(t_E, T))$$

where the risky PV01 at time t_E is calculated using a flat credit curve at the index spread $S_I(t_E, T)$ on the option expiration date.

The holder of a payer swaption will only exercise if the payoff is greater than zero. As a result we have

$$V^{Payer}(t_E) = \max\left[\frac{1}{M}\sum_{m=1}^{M} 1_{\tau_m \leq t_E}(1 - R_m)\right.$$
$$+ (S_I(t_E, T) - C(T)) \, \text{RPV01}_I(t_E, T, S_I(t_E, T))$$
$$\left. - (K - C(T)) \, \text{RPV01}_I(t_E, T, K), 0\right]. \tag{11.2}$$

Provided there have been no defaults before option expiry, a payoff of zero occurs when $S_I(t_E, T) = K$. However, if there have been defaults, the situation changes as we show in the following example.

Example   Consider an index option deal with the following characteristics:

Option type	European payer
Notional	$10 million
Underlying index	CDX series 7
Index coupon	40 bp
Valuation date	1 August 2007
Option expiry date	1 February 2008
Option strike	55 bp
Maturity date	20 December 2011

(Continued)

Suppose there have been two defaults on the index between option initiation on 1 August 2007 and option expiry on 1 February 2008. We also assume that at option expiry, the index spread curve is at 44 bp and that the Libor curve is flat at 5.00%. The option payoff is made up of three components:

1. We first consider the defaulted assets. Assume that they recover 45% of their face value. At option expiry we are long protection so we can buy $10\,m \times (2/125) = \$160\,000$ face value of the defaulted assets for $72\,000 and deliver them to the option seller for the face value. Overall, we receive $88\,000.
2. We calculate the value of the CDX index at the index spread at expiry of 44 bp. We do this using the method described in the previous chapter in which we build a flat curve at the CDS index curve spread of 44 bp. The risky PV01 of the index is 3.74. Noting that the remaining notional on the index after the two defaults is $123/125 \times \$10m = \$9.84m$, the value of the index equals $\$9.84m \times 3.74 \times (44 - 40)\,bp = \$14\,717$.
3. This is offset by the value of the exercise price $G(K)$ where K is the index strike spread of 55 bp. Assuming a flat curve at 55 bp, the risky PV01 is given by 3.726. As a result, the value of the *full notional* of the exercise price at this spread equals $\$10m \times 3.726 \times (55 - 40)\,bp = \$55\,890$.

Summing these components we get the value of the option payoff at expiry to be

$$\$88\,000 + \$14\,717 - \$55\,890 = \$46\,827.$$

What is important about this example is that although the index spread is below the strike spread of 55 bp, if we take into account the protection payments from the two defaults on the index portfolio, we see that the option value at expiry is actually positive and so should be exercised.

Figure 11.2 extends this example and shows the option payoff value for a payer and receiver option as a function of the index spread for zero, one and two defaults on the index before option expiry. When there is no default, the payer swaption is exercised as soon as the index level exceeds the 55 bp strike spread. However, we see from Figure 11.2 that if there is one default, the holder of a payer option will exercise the option as soon as $S(t_E, T) > 42.7$ bp which is about 12 bp below the option strike. We also see that if there has been one default before expiry, the holder of a receiver option will only exercise if $S(t_E, T) < 42.7$ bp. With two defaults before option expiry, the exercise strike is 30.4 bp, about 24 bp below the option strike. Each default is worth about 12 bp of spread widening.

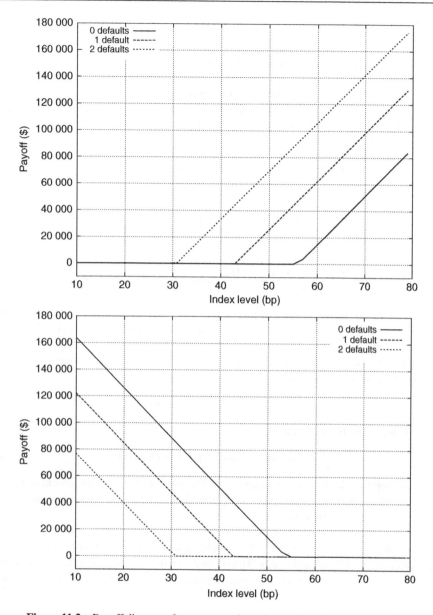

Figure 11.2 Payoff diagrams for a payer and receiver option. See text for details

11.3   VALUATION OF AN INDEX OPTION

In this section we derive a pricing equation for the value of an index option. Before doing so, we discuss the application of Black's model to the pricing of index options.

11.3.1 Black's Model

As shown in Section 9.3.7, Black's model is the standard model for pricing single-name default swaptions which knock out in the event of a default before option expiry. This result is achieved by a change of numeraire following Schönbucher (2003a) so that the expectation over the option payoff is carried out in the risk-neutral forward survival measure.

Let us first recap this model. Denoting the forward spread from option expiry time t_E to the maturity of the underlying CDS as $F = S(t, t_E, T)$, the value of a payer and receiver knockout swaption is given by

$$V^{Pay}(t) = \text{RPV01}(t, t_E, T)\,(F\Phi(d_1) - K\Phi(d_2)) \tag{11.3}$$

and

$$V^{Rec}(t) = \text{RPV01}(t, t_E, T)\,(K\Phi(-d_2) - F\Phi(-d_1)) \tag{11.4}$$

where

$$d_1 = \frac{\ln(F/K) + \sigma^2(t_E - t)/2}{\sigma\sqrt{t_E - t}} \quad \text{and} \quad d_2 = d_1 - \sigma\sqrt{t_E - t}.$$

The modelling assumption is that the future spread $S(t_E, T)$ evolves to time t_E according to a lognormal process with volatility σ. The mean of the distribution is the forward CDS spread $S(t, t_E, T)$.

Non-knockout swaptions are handled by simply adding the value of the front end protection (FEP) to the price of payer swaptions

$$V^{\text{Non-KO pay}}(t) = V^{\text{KO pay}} + \text{FEP}(t) \tag{11.5}$$

where the value of the front end protection is simply given by

$$\text{FEP}(t, t_E) = (1 - R)Z(t, t_E)(1 - Q(t, t_E)). \tag{11.6}$$

The value of non-knockout receiver swaptions is the same as the price of knockout receiver swaptions since a single-name receiver swaption should never be exercised into a short protection CDS on a defaulted credit.

The question we wish to address is *whether this model can be used to price index options*, i.e. can we simply replace all of the single-name spreads and risky PV01s with the index spread, option strike spread and index RPV01 and use the pricing formula for the corresponding non-knockout payer or receiver index options. The answer is 'no' for the following reasons:

1. As described in Pedersen (2003), the single-name swaption model does not correctly capture the exercise decison in an index option. This is most easily seen if we consider a payer swaption in the limit of $K \to \infty$. In this limit, the option to buy protection on the index at a very high strike should tend to zero – we would never exercise an option to pay an infinite spread.[1] However, using Equation 11.5 the value of the option will tend to the value of the

---

[1] There may be an advantage to exercising into an option with a high strike provided this is offset by the income received from a sufficient number of defaults on the portfolio before option expiry.

front end protection. To understand why there is this difference, consider the value of a non-knockout single-name payer swaption when the strike is very high. Its value should tend to the value of the front end protection since there is value in exercising the option if the credit has already defaulted. Also, if the credit has defaulted, the option now cancels and there are no further payments. However, in an index option, the option remains alive even if some of the credits in the portfolio have defaulted. As a result, the owner of a payer swaption will still have to pay the contractual exercise price and if that is very large, they should not exercise. This is the essential difference between the single-name non-knockout swaption and the index option.

2. Second, Black's formula does not reprice the underlying correctly. Specifically, Black's model does not capture the put–call parity relationship correctly. For example, it implies that being long a payer swaption and short a receiver swaption has a value equivalent to that of a long protection position in a forward starting CDS at a forward spread K plus front end protection

$$V^{\text{Non-KO pay}}(t) - V^{Rec}(t) = (S_I(t, t_E, T) - K) \cdot \text{RPV01}_I(t, t_E, T)$$

$$+ \text{FEP}(t, t_E).$$

Instead it should be

$$V^{\text{Non-KO pay}}(t) - V^{Rec}(t) = (S_I(t, t_E, T) - C(T)) \cdot \text{RPV01}_I(t, t_E, T)$$

$$- (K - C(T)) \cdot \text{RPV01}_I(t, t_E, T, K)/Q(t, t_E)$$

$$+ \text{FEP}(t, t_E)$$

where $\text{RPV01}_I(t, t_E, T, K)$ is the forward starting risky PV01 using a flat index curve at a spread K. Note that we divide this by the index survival probability to option expiry to capture the fact that the exercise price is risk-free until the option expiry date since it is based on the initial notional. Recall that $\text{RPV01}_I(t, t_E, T)$ is the forward starting risky PV01 using a flat index curve at a forward index spread $S_I(t, t_E, T)$. As a result, Black's model only ensures put–call parity is observed when $K = C(T)$.

3. Black's model typically assumes a flat term structure of index spreads for the purpose of calculating the term structure of survival probabilities. This is not necessarily consistent with the spreads of the underlying CDS or the price of shorter maturity CDS indices.

Black's model is therefore not appropriate for pricing index options in the form described here. However, later in this chapter we will revisit this model to show how it may be adapted to overcome these limitations.

11.4   AN ARBITRAGE-FREE PRICING MODEL

Most index option modelling approaches used in the markets follow the approaches discussed in Pedersen (2003) and Andersen (2006a). Here we will follow the latter approach. We start by considering the value of a payer index option. We denote the expiry date of the option as

t_E, the maturity of the index with T, the option strike as K, the coupon on the index as $C(T)$, and the index spread at expiry as $S_I(t_E, T)$. We begin by recalling Equation 10.8 which links the index swap spread to that of the M underlying CDS in the index

$$\frac{1}{M} \sum_{m=1}^{M} (S_m(t, T) - C(T)) \cdot \mathrm{RPV01}_m(t, T) = (S_I(t, T) - C(T)) \cdot \mathrm{RPV01}_I(t, T)$$

where the 'I' subscript on the risky PV01 reminds us that it is calculated using a flat index curve. The pricing analysis presented here is based on the assumption that this relationship holds true. For a variety of reasons discussed in the previous chapter, this assumption often breaks down in practice. As a result, we recommend an approach in which a portfolio swap adjustment is first applied to all of the individual CDS as discussed in Section 10.6.

In this pricing analysis, we consider the valuation of an index option at time t. We assume that the index option was initially traded at time 0. We begin our analysis by considering the value of the option at expiry.

11.4.1   Option Value at Expiry

The value of the payer index option at expiry time t_E is given by

$$V^{Pay}(t_E) = \max\left[H(t_E, \{S_m(t_E, T)\}) - G(K), 0\right]$$

where assuming a face value of $1

$$H(t_E, \{S_m(t_E, T)\}) = \frac{1}{M} \sum_{m=1}^{M} (1 - R_m) 1_{0 < \tau_m \leq t}$$

$$+ \frac{1}{M} \sum_{m=1}^{M} (1 - R_m) 1_{t < \tau_m \leq t_E}$$

$$+ \frac{1}{M} \sum_{m=1}^{M} 1_{\tau_m > t_E} (S_m(t_E, T) - C(T)) \mathrm{RPV01}_m(t_E, T). \qquad (11.7)$$

The first term captures the default payments made at time t_E on credits which have already defaulted, i.e. credits which defaulted in the period from when the option was first initiated at time 0 and the valuation time t. This term is known with certainty[2] at valuation time t. The second term captures the default payments made on any credits which have defaulted in the period from valuation date to option expiry date. The value of this term is unknown as of valuation time t. The third term captures the value of all of the CDS on the surviving credits in the index at time t_E. The CDS index is represented as a collection of CDS contracts in which the contractual spread equals the index coupon $C(T)$. This term is also unknown as of valuation time t.

---

[2] To price an ongoing index option we need to maintain a list of which, if any, credits in the reference portfolio have defaulted since the option was initially traded.

11.4.2   Option Value at Time t

To price the option as of time t, we wish to calculate the discounted expectation of the final payoff in the risk-neutral measure

$$V(t) = \mathbb{E}_t \left[\frac{1}{\beta(t, t_E)} \max \left(H(t_E, \{S_m(t_E, T)\}) - G(K), 0 \right) \right]$$

where $\beta(t, T) = \exp \left(\int_t^T r(s)ds \right)$ is the value of the rolled-up money-market account.

There is an interest rate dependency in this payoff since the value of the CDS index depends on the level of interest rates, both through the value of the rolled-up money-market account and the dependence on the interest rate curve seen at time t_E which is contained within the risky PV01 terms. However, because the interest rate sensitivity of the value of the CDS index and the exercise price $G(K)$ is small, we assume deterministic interest rates and just focus on the uncertainty due to credit. This allows us to write

$$V(t) = Z(t, t_E) \, \mathbb{E}_t[\max \left(H(t_E, \{S_m(t_E, T)\}) - G(K), 0 \right)].$$

Pricing the option is then an exercise in determining the probability distribution for $H(t_E, \{S_m(t_E, T)\})$.

Let us examine the properties of $H(t_E, \{S_m(t_E, T)\})$ starting with its expectation. Breaking it into its different terms, the expectation of the first random component at time t_E is given by

$$\frac{1}{M} \sum_{m=1}^{M} (1 - R_m) \mathbb{E}_t \left[1_{t < \tau_m \le t_E} \right] = \frac{1}{M} \sum_{m=1}^{M} (1 - R_m)(1 - Q_m(t, t_E)).$$

The time t expectation of the second random component is given by

$$\frac{1}{M} \sum_{m=1}^{M} \mathbb{E}_t \left[1_{\tau_m > t_E} \left(S_m(t_E, T) - C(T) \right) \cdot \text{RPV01}_m(t_E, S_m(t_E, T)) \right].$$

Following Section 9.3.5, we can calculate this expectation by changing measures. We do this by choosing the following as numeraire for each credit

$$A_m(t) = 1_{\tau_m > t} \text{RPV01}_m(t, t_E, T).$$

Using Equation 9.5, this allows us to write

$$\mathbb{E}_t \left[1_{\tau_m > t_E} \left(S_m(t_E, T) - C(T) \right) \text{RPV01}_m(t_E, T) \right]$$
$$= \frac{\left(S_m(t, t_E, T) - C(T) \right) \text{RPV01}_m(t, t_E, T)}{Z(t, t_E)}.$$

As a result we have

$$\mathbb{E}_t \left[H(t_E, \{S_m(t_E, T)\}) \right] = H_0 + \frac{1}{M} \sum_{m=1}^{M} (1 - R_m)(1 - Q_m(t, t_E))$$

$$+ \frac{1}{MZ(t, t_E)} \sum_{m=1}^{M} \left(S_m(t, t_E, T) - C(T) \right) \text{RPV01}_m(t, t_E, T) \qquad (11.8)$$

where the term

$$H_0 = \frac{1}{M} \sum_{m=1}^{M} (1 - R_m) 1_{0 < \tau_m \le t}$$

is known today with certainty.

11.4.3   The Terminal Payoff Distribution

Pricing the option requires a knowledge of not just the expectation but the entire distribution of $H(t_E, \{S_m(t_E, T)\})$. We could choose to model the distribution of H as a function of the joint distribution of all M individual forward issuer spreads. However, this is not practical. There would be too many parameters to calibrate given that we can only typically observe a single implied option volatility. It would also make the pricing computationally slow. Instead, we choose to assume a homogeneous index portfolio with a single 'composite' flat spread S and recovery R. We approximate the spread dependence of H by writing

$$H(t_E, \{S_m(t_E, T)\}) = \hat{H}(S)$$

where

$$\hat{H}(S) = H_0 + (S - C(T))\, \text{RPV01}_I(t_E, T, S).$$

Market convention requires that the risky index PV01 is calculated using a flat curve at the index spread S. We can therefore justify the use the credit triangle[3] to approximate the individual survival probabilities and so approximate the explicit spread dependence of the risky PV01

$$\text{RPV01}_I(t_E, T, S) = \sum_{n=1}^{N_T} \Delta(t_{n-1}, t_n) Z(t_E, t_n) \exp\left(-\frac{S(t_n - t_E)}{(1 - R)}\right).$$

The summation in this equation is over the payment dates of the index swap from the option expiry date to the index swap maturity. The present value of the payoff at expiry as a function of S is therefore

$$Z(t, t_E) \max\left(\hat{H}(S) - G(K), 0\right).$$

We therefore have a functional form for the value of the terminal payoff in terms of the distribution of the future index spread S. The value of the option can then be calculated as

$$V(t) = Z(t, t_E) \int_0^\infty \max\left(\hat{H}(S) - G(K), 0\right) f(S) ds$$

where $f(S)$ is the distribution of S. A natural choice is to choose a lognormal distribution

$$S = X \exp\left(-\frac{1}{2}\sigma^2(t_E - t) + \sigma Z \sqrt{t_E - t}\right)$$

---

[3] The credit triangle relationship assumes that the spread is paid continuously and that the spread curve is flat. In this case, the latter condition is true. In this context the relationship is approximate because the spread on the underlying index is paid quarterly.

where X is used to enforce a no-arbitrage constraint as described below, and $Z \sim N(0, 1)$. The pricing equation then becomes

$$V(t) = Z(t, t_E) \int_{-\infty}^{\infty} \max \left[\hat{H}(S(X, Z)) - G(K), 0 \right] \phi(Z) dZ$$

where $\phi(x)$ is the Gaussian probability density function. The value of X is chosen in order to ensure no-arbitrage by enforcing Equation 11.8. We perform a one-dimensional root search to solve for the value of X which satisfies

$$\int_{-\infty}^{\infty} \hat{H}(S(X, Z)) \phi(Z) dZ = \mathbb{E}_t [H(t_E, \{S_m(t_E)\})].$$

Here and in the pricing equation, the integration over the Gaussian density function must be performed numerically.

11.4.4   Put–Call Parity

The value of a receiver swaption is related to the value of a payer swaption through put–call parity. This is based on observing that being long a payer and short a receiver swaption has a value given by

$$V^{Payer}(t) - V^{Receiver}(t) = \mathbb{E}_t \left[\frac{1}{\beta(t, t_E)} \max(H(t_E, S_I(t_E, T) - G(K), 0) \right]$$

$$- \mathbb{E}_t \left[\frac{1}{\beta(t, t_E)} \max(G(K) - H(t_E, S_I(t_E, T), 0) \right]$$

$$= \mathbb{E}_t \left[\frac{1}{\beta(t, t_E)} (H(t_E, S_I(t_E, T) - G(K)) \right]$$

$$= Z(t, t_E) \mathbb{E}_t [H(t_E, S_I(t_E, T))] - Z(t, t_E) G(K).$$

The expected value of $H(t_E, S_I(t_E, T))$ is given in Equation 11.8. The advantage of a put–call parity relationship is that we can use it to calculate both payer and receiver option values for the numerical cost of calculating just one option value.

The model described here overcomes the problems of Black's model which were described in Section 11.3.1. For a start, the model captures the exercise decision correctly, taking into account the value of the front end protection. It will also reprice the underlying index exactly through the enforcement of the expected value of $\hat{H}(S)$.

11.5   EXAMPLES OF PRICING

We now present a set of example pricings to make clear the behaviour of the value of index swaptions. We use the example presented at the beginning of this chapter in which the underlying index is CDX Series 7. We calculate the value of payer and receiver options on 1 August 2007 with expiry date 1 February 2008 for a range of option strikes, using a volatility of 50%

in all cases. In all cases we assume that there have been no defaults on the index portfolio between option initiation and valuation time t. We therefore set $H_0 = 0$.

Table 11.1 shows the price of payer and receiver options as a function of the option strike and the level of the index. These prices are based on the example trade introduced at the beginning of this chapter.

Table 11.1 Table showing prices of payer and receiver index swaptions as a function of the option strike and the level of the index using a volatility of 50%. Also shown is the forward index risky PV01, the exercise price $G(K)$, the parameter X and the expected value of $H(S)$

Strike (bp)	Index (bp)	Index PV01	Payer price (cents)	Receiver price (cents)	$G(K)$ (cents)	X (bp)	$\mathbb{E}[H]$ (cents)
20	20	3.563	16.6	6.4	−71.2	23.1	−60.8
20	30	3.548	50.9	1.0	−71.2	34.4	−20.1
20	40	3.534	88.3	0.1	−71.2	45.4	19.1
20	50	3.520	124.9	0.0	−71.2	56.1	56.7
20	60	3.506	169.1	0.0	−71.2	69.0	102.1
30	20	3.563	4.3	29.0	−35.4	23.1	−60.8
30	30	3.548	24.5	9.5	−35.4	34.4	−20.1
30	40	3.534	56.0	2.8	−35.4	45.4	19.1
30	50	3.520	90.8	0.8	−35.4	56.1	56.7
30	60	3.506	134.4	0.2	−35.4	69.0	102.1
40	20	3.563	1.0	60.3	0.0	23.1	−60.8
40	30	3.548	10.1	29.7	0.0	34.4	−20.1
40	40	3.534	31.5	12.9	0.0	45.4	19.1
40	50	3.520	60.7	5.3	0.0	56.1	56.7
40	60	3.506	101.4	1.7	0.0	69.0	102.1
50	20	3.563	0.2	93.9	35.2	23.1	−60.8
50	30	3.548	3.9	57.8	35.2	34.4	−20.1
50	40	3.534	16.2	31.9	35.2	45.4	19.1
50	50	3.520	37.6	16.6	35.2	56.1	56.7
50	60	3.506	72.3	7.0	35.2	69.0	102.1
60	20	3.563	0.1	127.8	70.1	23.1	−60.8
60	30	3.548	1.4	89.4	70.1	34.4	−20.1
60	40	3.534	7.9	57.7	70.1	45.4	19.1
60	50	3.520	22.0	35.1	70.1	56.1	56.7
60	60	3.506	49.1	17.9	70.1	69.0	102.1

For each value of the strike, we see that the value of the payer option increases with the index spread as the option to buy protection at the strike spread becomes more valuable. We also see the value of the receiver option fall as the index spread increases. Keeping the index swap level fixed and increasing the option strike moves the payer swaptions out-of-the-money. As the strike grows much larger than the index level, the value of the payer option falls to zero.

Also shown in Table 11.1 is the value of parameter X, which is determined by solving Equation 11.8. Because of how it is defined, we can think of X as an effective adjusted forward spread which takes into account the value of any defaults which have already occurred plus the value of the front end protection.

11.6   RISK MANAGEMENT

Computing index option hedges can be done using the standard bump and price approach. Using the model it is possible to compute the sensitivity of the option value to spread changes in the underlying index and to use this to work out the corresponding hedge ratio in the underlying forward starting index. The main practical complication in this process is that a bump at any point in the index spread curve will require a readjustment of the portfolio CDS spreads to ensure that the CDS index curve is exactly refitted. This can be time consuming as discussed in Section 10.6. The other complication is that the underlying, which is a forward starting CDS index with front end protection, is not at all liquid.

An alternative and more practical approach is to build a proper index curve – an index curve with a non-flat[4] term structure at 3Y, 5Y, 7Y and 10Y which reprices the term structure of index upfront prices. The CDS spreads also need to be adjusted to ensure that they also fit the quoted index prices using the process described in section 10.6. We can then apply the same bump and price approach to these curves in order to determine the equivalent notional hedges in the spot starting CDS indices of different maturity.

11.7   BLACK'S MODEL REVISITED

Although this full pricing model is not difficult to implement, it may be considered too complicated to be used as the standard model for quoting volatilities for index options. In fact, this may be one reason why the market tends to simply quote in terms of option premium. However, it would be useful to have some commonly agreed and fairly simple convention for quoting volatilities.

We do not want to use the non-knockout payer swaption version of Black's formula since this has a number of problems pricing index options as described in Section 11.3.1. We need to amend Black's model to overcome these problems. One way to do this is to drop the front end protection from the pricing equation and to incorporate it into an adjustment to the forward spread used in the knockout swaption formulae presented earlier in Equations 11.3 and 11.4. This can therefore be expressed through an increase in the forward spread used. We therefore adjust the forward spread as follows

$$F^{Adjusted} = S_I(t, t_E, T) + \frac{FEP(t, t_E)}{RPV01_I(t, t_E, T)}$$

where $FEP(t, t_E)$ is the present value of the front end protection given by Equation 11.6 and $RPV01_I(t, t_E, T)$ is the forward starting risky PV01 for the index using the forward index spread $S_I(t, t_E, T)$. Table 11.2 shows how the size of the adjustment depends on the level of the index curve where we have used the example trade discussed at the start of this chapter.

A second problem with Black's model was that it mispriced the underlying. However, this can be overcome if we replace the strike in Black's model with K' where

$$K' = C(T) + (K - C(T)) \frac{RPV01_I(t, t_E, T, K)}{RPV01_I(t, t_E, T)Q(t, t_E)}. \tag{11.9}$$

---

[4] Unless the CDS index quotes really are all the same.

Table 11.2   Dependence of the forward spread adjustment used to account for the value of the front end protection in the index option on the level of the index curve

Index spread (bp)	Fwd. index spread (bp)	Front end protection (cents)	Fwd. index RPV01	Spread increase	Fwd. adjusted spread (bp)
20	19.9	10.3	3.563	2.9	22.8
30	29.8	15.4	3.548	4.4	34.2
40	39.8	20.6	3.534	5.8	45.6
50	49.7	25.7	3.520	7.3	57.0
60	59.7	30.8	3.506	8.8	68.5
70	69.6	36.0	3.492	10.3	79.9

Note that the risky PV01 in the denominator uses a flat index curve at the index spread $S_I(t, t_E, T)$. The risky PV01 in the numerator is calculated using a flat index curve at the strike spread. To capture the fact that the exercise price is based on the initial notional, we discount it at the risk-free rate from option expiry back to today. In practice this requires us to divide the risky PV01 by the index survival probability from today to option expiry. This ensures that the model correctly reprices the underlying in the zero volatility case and observes put–call parity in all cases.

It is also worth noting that all of the discounting within Black's model assumes flat index curves. This is therefore not consistent with the underlying CDS curves of the index which may have a non-flat term structure. It may also not be consistent with the spreads of other

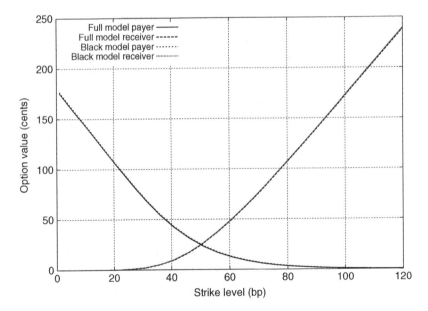

Figure 11.3   Comparison of the value of payer and receiver options calculated using the full model and the adjusted forward and adjusted strike implementation of Black's model as a function of the option strike. The same option volatility of 50% is used in both models and for all strikes. There is almost no visible difference between the two models since the largest difference is about 0.3 cents

maturity indices. However, it is done because it is simple and because the size of the pricing difference between flat and non-flat index curves is typically small.

To test this 'adjusted Black's model', we have priced the payer and receiver options using the example trade discussed throughout this chapter, first using the full model, and then using Black's formulae with the adjusted forward spreads and the adjusted strike.

Figure 11.3 compares the prices of payer and receiver options using both models as a function of the option strike. We use the same lognormal volatility of 50% in both models and for all strikes. What is obvious is that there is almost no visible difference between both models. For both the payer and receiver swaptions, the difference in option premia between the two models is at most 0.3 cents for the range of values shown. This suggests that the Black model with the spread and strike adjustment is a very reasonable alternative to the full model and can also be used for the purpose of quoting implied option volatility.

11.8 SUMMARY

The index option market has been the most liquid of the credit option markets given the extremely high liquidity of its underlying and the macro credit views it enables investors to assume. In this chapter we have discussed the mechanics of index options and how they are priced. We have explained why using Black's model to price index options is not strictly appropriate and have described in detail a method for how it may be adapted to overcome this problem and in doing so become a fast and accurate alternative.

An Introduction to Correlation Products

12.1 INTRODUCTION

Following the credit default swap and the CDS portfolio index, the third significant achievement of the credit derivatives market has been to create a liquid market in credit default correlation. When we speak of credit default correlation, we generally mean the risk of two or more credits defaulting jointly with a probability that is greater than if they were independent. This may be a result of some common feature which these credits may share such as being in a common industry sector or a common region. In some cases, we could have a negative default correlation meaning that the probability of both credits defaulting is less than if they were independent. This could arise if the future prospects of one company could be improved by the default of a competitor. However, since the default correlation represents an average over future scenarios, we generally find that positive correlation effects outweigh negative correlation effects.

The range of products now available which embed this risk has grown substantially since the advent of this market in the very late 1990s. The focus of this chapter is first to describe the mechanics of the two main products, default baskets and synthetic CDO tranches, and to explain why they are exposed to default correlation. We also establish no-arbitrage pricing bounds for these products, and do so without reference to any specific valuation models. We also discuss a pricing framework for these products based on the notion of a basket or tranche survival curve. We now begin with the default basket.

12.2 DEFAULT BASKETS

Default baskets first started to trade in the late 1990s and currently comprise about 1.8% of the credit derivative outstanding notional according to the 2006 BBA Credit Derivatives Report, having declined from 6% of the market share in 2002. However, the significant increase in the size of the credit derivatives market means that this is still an increase in absolute terms. Default baskets were initially the dominant credit derivative correlation product that was sold to investors. This position has since been taken by the synthetic CDO product. Despite this, default baskets continue to exist thanks to their unique characteristics which make them appealing to certain types of credit investor. The advantage of default baskets are discussed at the end of this section.

12.2.1 Mechanics

A default basket is a contract which is almost identical to a credit default swap. The difference is that the event which causes the payment leg to trigger and the premium leg to terminate is the nth default in a basket of N credits, where typically N is between 5 and 10. If $n = 1$ then the contract is called a *first-to-default* (FTD) basket. If $n=2$ then we have a *second-to-default* (STD) basket and so on. The basket of reference credits is chosen at trade initiation and remains fixed over the life of the contract.[1]

As with a standard CDS, the basket consists of a premium leg and a protection leg. The premium leg is typically a stream of quarterly payments calculated using an Actual 360 day convention. This continues until contract maturity time T, or to the time of the nth credit event on the basket, whichever occurs sooner. We denote the fixed nth-to-default basket spread with S_n.

On the protection leg, a payment is only made following the nth credit event, provided this occurs before the contract maturity T. We index the credits in the basket with $i = 1,\ldots,N$ and denote the index of the nth credit to default with $i(n)$. Assuming a contract face value of $1, the size of the payment following the nth default is given by

$$(1 - R_{i(n)})$$

where $R_{i(n)}$ is the expected value of the recovery rate associated with credit $i(n)$. It is important to note that the face value of the loss is the same as the face value of the contract. It is the same as the loss on a CDS on credit $i(n)$ with the same face value as the basket. This is shown clearly in Figure 12.1 where we see that the protection leg payment on the first default in the basket is $6 million, assuming all credits have a 40% recovery. Note that the first-to-default basket has a five-year term and pays a spread of 320 bp. Also shown are the individual five-year CDS spreads for the credits in the basket. What is clear is that the first-to-default spread is over three times the average spread of the credits in the basket.

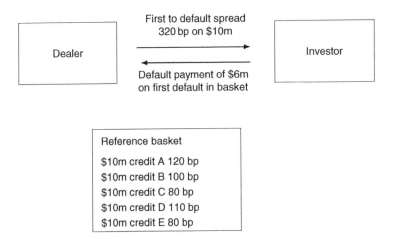

Figure 12.1   Example n-to-default basket on five credits. The payment of the spread terminates after the first default in the basket. We have assumed a recovery rate of 40% on the first default resulting in a default payment of $6 million

Table 12.1 shows spread quotes for second-to-default and higher order contracts on the same 5-name basket. Specifically, we see n-to-default 5Y market quotes for $n=2$ to $n=5$. These

---

[1] The exception to this is *merger substitution*, i.e if two credits in the basket merge then a new credit can be added to the basket subject to criteria.

Table 12.1   Example n-to-default basket spread quotes for 5Y nth-to-default contracts on a basket of five credits with flat spread curves at 120, 100, 80, 110 and 80 bp

nth-to-default	1	2	3	4	5
Basket spread (bp)	320	120	51	20	6

have been generated using a model which will be described in Chapter 15. Our reason for showing them now is to give a sense of the values of basket spreads and how they depend on the order of the basket n. We see that the first-to-default basket spread is more than three times the average spread of the basket which is 98 bp. This is not because the basket has increased the size of the loss to which the investor is exposed. The FTD spread is high because the probability of one out of the five credits in the basket defaulting is over three times the average default probability of the credits in the basket. We also see that the spread falls with n. This is because the probability of $n + 1$ defaults on the basket has to be equal to or lower than the probability of n defaults. Clearly, the probability of n defaults within the basket maturity must depend on the tendency of credits to default together. We therefore consider the effect of default dependency on the basket triggering probability.

12.2.2   Default Baskets and Default Dependency

To understand the relationship between the triggering probability of default baskets and default dependency, we start by taking a very simple basket consisting of two assets, which we label A and B. We denote the default times of A and B with τ_A and τ_B and define their horizon time T risk-neutral default probabilities as seen at time zero as

$$P_A(T) = \mathbb{E}\,[1_{\tau_A \leq T}] = 1 - Q_A(T)$$

and

$$P_B(T) = \mathbb{E}\,[1_{\tau_B \leq T}] = 1 - Q_B(T)$$

where $Q(T) = Q(0, T)$. Both of these probabilities can be extracted from the CDS market spreads of issuers A and B as described in Chapter 7. We then define the joint default probability

$$P_{AB}(T) = \mathbb{E}\,[1_{\tau_A \leq T} 1_{\tau_B \leq T}].$$

This is the probability that *both* A and B default on or before time T. If we define $Q_{AB}(T)$ to be the probability that *both* A and B survive, then we have the relationship

$$Q_{AB}(T) = 1 - P_A(T) - P_B(T) + P_{AB}(T).$$

A first-to-default basket is triggered if one or more defaults occur in the basket before time T. This probability of this is given by

$$P_{FTD}(T) = 1 - \mathbb{E}\,[1_{\tau_A > T} 1_{\tau_B > T}] = P_A(T) + P_B(T) - P_{AB}(T).$$

Likewise, the probability of a second-to-default triggering event is the probability of both credits defaulting before time T and this is given by

$$P_{STD}(T) = P_{AB}(T).$$

Both $P_A(T)$ and $P_B(T)$ are determined by calibrating them to their individual spread curves. However, the FTD and STD spreads are also exposed to the joint probability of default $P_{AB}(T)$. It is therefore clear that the triggering probability of a basket is a function of the degree of

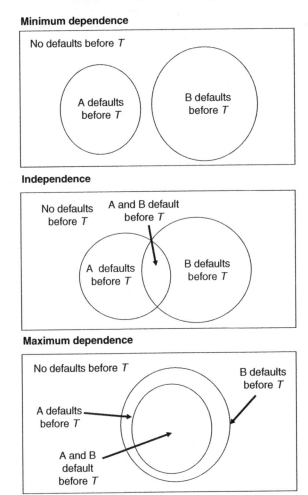

Figure 12.2 The three limiting cases of correlation discussed in the text. At the top is minimum dependence, then independence and at the bottom is maximum dependence

default dependency between the credits in the basket. We therefore consider three important limits shown in Venn diagram form in Figure 12.2:

1. Minimum dependence: $P_{AB}(T) = \max[P_A(T) + P_B(T) - 1, 0]$. In this case the default of credit A and credit B are mutually exclusive events if $P_A(T) + P_B(T) < 1$, which is typically the case for investment grade credits within the typical trade maturity T. In this case, the probability of the FTD or STD being triggered is

$$P_{FTD}(T) = P_A(T) + P_B(T)$$

$$P_{STD}(T) = 0.$$

If $P_A(T) + P_B(T) \geq 1$ then the defaults are no longer mutually exclusive and

$$P_{FTD}(T) = 1$$

$$P_{STD}(T) = P_A(T) + P_B(T) - 1.$$

2. Independence: $P_{AB}(T) = P_A(T)P_B(T)$. In this case the probability of the FTD or STD being triggered is

$$P_{FTD}(T) = P_A(T) + P_B(T) - P_A(T)P_B(T)$$

$$P_{STD}(T) = P_A(T)P_B(T).$$

3. Maximum dependence: $P_{AB}(T) = \min[P_A(T), P_B(T)]$. Whenever the better quality asset defaults, the lower credit quality asset also defaults. The lower quality asset can also default by itself. In this limit we have

$$P_{FTD}(T) = \max(P_A(T), P_B(T))$$

$$P_{STD}(T) = \min(P_A(T), P_B(T)).$$

To calculate the expected loss in each of these cases, we simply multiply the triggering probability by the corresponding expected loss. This is $(1 - R_A)$ or $(1 - R_B)$, depending on which is the nth credit to default. Two effects are clear:

1. The triggering probability of the FTD basket decreases with increasing dependency from $P_A(T) + P_B(T)$ to $\max(P_A(T), P_B(T))$.
2. The triggering probability of the STD basket increases with increasing dependency from 0 to $\min(P_A(T), P_B(T))$.

To translate these probabilities into spread levels, we need to take into account the timing of cash flows on the premium and protection legs. This requires the introduction of the basket survival curve. However before we do so, we briefly consider a measure of default correlation which considers the linear correlation of the random default indicators.

12.2.3 Default Indicator Correlation

We can define a measure of default correlation in terms of the default indicators

$$\rho_{AB}(T) = \frac{\mathbb{E}\left[1_{\tau_A \leq T} 1_{\tau_B \leq T}\right] - \mathbb{E}\left[1_{\tau_A \leq T}\right]\mathbb{E}\left[1_{\tau_B \leq T}\right]}{\sqrt{\left(\mathbb{E}\left[(1_{\tau_A \leq T})^2\right] - E[1_{\tau_A \leq T}]^2\right)\left(\mathbb{E}\left[(1_{\tau_B \leq T})^2\right] - E[1_{\tau_B \leq T}]^2\right)}}.$$

Since $\mathbb{E}\left[1_{\tau_A \leq T}\right] = P_A(T)$ and $\mathbb{E}\left[1_{\tau_A \leq T}^2\right] = P_A(T)$ and $\mathbb{E}\left[1_{\tau_A \leq T} 1_{\tau_B \leq T}\right] = P_{AB}(T)$, we have

$$\rho_{AB} = \frac{P_{AB}(T) - P_A(T)P_B(T)}{\sqrt{P_A(T)(1 - P_A(T))P_B(T)(1 - P_B(T))}}.$$

Note that in the minimum correlation limit when $P_{AB}(T) = 0$, we have

$$\rho_{AB} = -\frac{\sqrt{P_A(T)P_B(T)}}{\sqrt{(1 - P_A(T))(1 - P_B(T))}}.$$

This only equals -100% if $P_A(T) = (1 - P_B(T))$. In the independence limit when $P_{AB}(T) = P_A(T)P_B(T)$, we have

$$\rho_{AB} = 0.$$

In the maximum dependence limit when $P_{AB}(T) = \min[P_A(T), P_B(T)]$ we have, assuming $P_B(T) \leq P_A(T)$,

$$\rho_{AB} = \frac{\sqrt{P_B(T)(1 - P_A(T))}}{\sqrt{P_A(T)(1 - P_B(T))}}.$$

This is only equal to 100% if $P_A(T) = P_B(T)$. It is worth noting that this measure of default correlation does not interpolate between the values of -100% and $+100\%$ as we go from minimum to maximum dependency. Instead, the limiting values of correlation are a function of the default probabilities $P_A(T)$ and $P_B(T)$. For this reason, this measure of default correlation is not widely favoured.

12.2.4   The Basket Survival Curve

We wish to price an nth-to-default basket on a basket of homogeneous loss credits – a basket in which we assume the same expected recovery rate R for all credits. We start by defining a process $n(t)$ which counts the number of defaults in a basket of N credits which have occurred between time zero and time t. This is shown in Figure 12.3. In the case of an nth-to-default basket, the triggering probability to time T is the probability that n or more credits in the portfolio default. This is given by

$$\Pr(n(T) \geq n) = 1 - Q(n(T) < n).$$

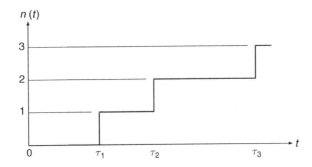

Figure 12.3   Counting function $n(t)$

This will allow us to write the expected present value of the premium leg at time 0 using the *basket survival curve* $Q(n(T) < n)$ as follows

$$\text{Premium leg PV}(0, T) = S_n \sum_{i=1}^{N_T} \Delta(t_{i-1}, t_i)Z(t_i)Q(n(t_i) < n)$$

where S_n is the contractual nth-to-default spread and the summation is over the N_T premium payment dates. We have ignored the payment of the accrued premium following the triggering of the basket. However this can easily be incorporated as described previously in Section 6.5. Similarly, the protection leg present value is triggered as soon as $n(t) > n$ so that

$$\text{Protection leg PV}(0, T) = (1 - R) \int_0^T Z(t)(-dQ(n(t) < n)).$$

We can therefore conclude that a default basket with homogeneous losses can be priced using standard CDS analytics once we have the corresponding basket survival curve $Q(n(t) < n)$.

12.2.5   Basket Spreads and Dependency

Consider again a two-name basket on credits A and B with the same recovery rate. The breakeven spread for the two T maturity CDS contracts for A and B is given by

$$(1 - R) \int_0^T Z(s)dQ_A(s) + S_A(T) \sum_{i=1}^{N_T} \Delta(t_{i-1}, t_i)Q_A(t_i)Z(t_i) = 0$$

$$(1 - R) \int_0^T Z(s)dQ_B(s) + S_B(T) \sum_{i=1}^{N_T} \Delta(t_{i-1}, t_i)Q_B(t_i)Z(t_i) = 0$$

where we have omitted the payment of premium accrued at default for simplicity (this does not change any of the results discussed in this section). Similarly, the breakeven spreads for the FTD and STD baskets are given by

$$(1 - R) \int_0^T Z(s)dQ_1(s) + S_1(T) \sum_{i=1}^{N_T} \Delta(t_{i-1}, t_i)Q_1(t_i)Z(t_i) = 0$$

$$(1 - R) \int_0^T Z(s)dQ_2(s) + S_2(T) \sum_{i=1}^{N_T} \Delta(t_{i-1}, t_i)Q_2(t_i)Z(t_i) = 0$$

where $Q_n(t) = Q(n(t) < n)$. Let us now revisit the dependency limits discussed earlier.

- Minimum dependence: In this limit we assume that $Q_A(T) + Q_B(T) \geq 1$ so that the default events are mutually exclusive to time T and we can write

$$Q_1(t) = Q_A(t) + Q_B(t) - 1$$
$$Q_2(t) = 1.$$

In this case the FTD spread is given by

$$S_1(T) = \frac{S_A(T) \cdot \text{RPV01}_A(T) + S_B(T) \cdot \text{RPV01}_B(T)}{\text{RPV01}_A(T) + \text{RPV01}_B(T) - \text{PV01}(T)}$$

where $\text{PV01}(T)$ is the risk-free Libor PV01. Since the same maturity Libor PV01 is always greater than either of the risky PV01s, it is possible to show that

$$S_1(T) > S_A(T) + S_B(T).$$

Since $Q_2(t) = 1$, we have $dQ_2(t) = 0$ and therefore

$$S_2(T) = 0.$$

This reflects the fact that in the case of minimum dependence, there can never be two defaults before time T and hence the STD basket never triggers.

- Independence: In the case of independence, we have

$$Q_1(t) = Q_A(t)Q_B(t)$$
$$Q_2(t) = Q_A(t) + Q_B(t) - Q_A(t)Q_B(t).$$

However, there is no exact relationship between spreads. All we can say is that

$$S_1(T) \simeq S_A(T) + S_B(T).$$

In the independence case the STD spread is reasonably well approximated by

$$S_2(T) \simeq \frac{P_A(T)P_B(T)(1-R)}{T}.$$

- Maximum dependence: In the case of maximum dependence, we have

$$Q_1(t) = \min[Q_A(t), Q_B(t)]$$
$$Q_2(t) = \max[Q_A(t), Q_B(t)].$$

If $Q_A(t) \geq Q_B(t)$ or $Q_A(t) \leq Q_B(t)$ for all $t \in [0, T]$ then

$$S_1(T) = \max [S_A(T), S_B(T)]$$
$$S_2(T) = \min [S_A(T), S_B(T)].$$

From this analysis we can make the following observations:

1. The FTD spread decreases with increasing correlation and a short protection position will be long correlation, i.e. an investor who has sold FTD protection will see the value of their position increase as the default correlation increases.
2. Since the fair-value STD spread increases with increasing correlation, a short protection position will be short correlation, i.e. an investor who has sold STD protection will see the value of their position fall as the default correlation increases.

Finally, consider the value V of a long protection FTD position plus a long protection STD position. This is given by

$$V = (1-R) \int_0^T Z(s)dQ_1(s) - S_1(T) \sum_{i=1}^{N_T} \Delta(t_{i-1}, t_i)Q_1(t_i)Z(t_i)$$

$$+ (1-R) \int_0^T Z(s)dQ_2(s) - S_2(T) \sum_{i=1}^{N_T} \Delta(t_{i-1}, t_i)Q_2(t_i)Z(t_i).$$

In a two-name basket $Q_1(T) + Q_2(T) = Q_A(T) + Q_B(T)$ so that

$$V = (1 - R) \int_0^T Z(s)(dQ_A(s) + dQ_B(s))$$

$$- S_1(T) \sum_{i=1}^{N_T} \Delta(t_{i-1}, t_i) Q_1(t_i) Z(t_i) - S_2(T) \sum_{i=1}^{N_T} \Delta(t_{i-1}, t_i) Q_2(t_i) Z(t_i).$$

We see that the combined protection legs are equivalent to being long the protection leg of A and B and so have no net correlation sensitivity. However, the correlation dependence of the combined premium legs does not cancel out. This result extends to baskets of an arbitrary number of credits and also applies to baskets with inhomogeneous recovery rates.

12.2.6 Advantages of default baskets

At the start of this section we stated that baskets have a number of attractive feaures which make them useful to investors. These are as follows:

- The basket spread paid can be a multiple of the average spread of the credits in the basket while the notional exposure is equal to that of selling protection on just one of the credits.
- Since the credits in a default basket are typically well-known investment grade quality credits, an investor who knows the credits well may be more comfortable with the credit risk of the basket than with the credit risk of a lesser known credit paying the same spread.
- The first-to-default mechanism enables the investor to leverage the spread premium and so improve the relative risk-return profile when compared to other similar yielding credit investments.
- A hedger may decide that buying protection on the first default in a set of credits using a default basket may be a more efficient hedge than buying protection on each credit individually.

The third of these discusses the ability of baskets to leverage the spread premium. We now analyse this in detail.

12.3 LEVERAGING THE SPREAD PREMIA

One of the key attractions of correlation products is that they allow the investor to leverage the spread premium embedded in credit spreads. The spread premium was introduced in Section 3.11. To explain this, we continue to use the example of a simple two-name default basket containing credits A and B. At time zero, we can approximate the first and second to default spreads to maturity time T in terms of the risk-neutral default probabilities as follows

$$S_1(T) \simeq \frac{(1 - R)\,(P_A(T) + P_B(T) - P_{AB}(T))}{T}$$

and

$$S_2 \simeq \frac{(1 - R)P_{AB}(T)}{T}.$$

This approximation assumes zero interest rates. We also assume that we have the analagous *real-world* measure probabilities. This allows us to approximate the *actuarial* spreads introduced previously in Section 3.11 in terms of their real-world probabilities

$$\tilde{S}_1(T) \simeq \frac{(1-R)\left(\tilde{P}_A(T) + \tilde{P}_B(T) - \tilde{P}_{AB}(T)\right)}{T}$$

and

$$\tilde{S}_2(T) \simeq \frac{(1-R)\tilde{P}_{AB}(T)}{T}.$$

We assume that the expected recovery rates are the same in both measures.

Let us also suppose that the ratio of risk-neutral to real-world probabilities, known as the single-name coverage ratio, is given by k so that $P_A = k\tilde{P}_A$ and $P_B = k\tilde{P}_B$. We expect that the risk premium is positive so that $k > 1$. Typical values for k as a function of credit rating are the single-name coverage ratios shown in Table 3.4. We then define two quantities.

1. The first is the *spread premium*. This is the spread difference between the market spread and the actuarial spread. We drop the T argument from the probabilities for notational simplicity

$$\text{FTD spread premium} = S_1 - \tilde{S}_1 = \frac{(1-R)}{T}\left(P_A + P_B - P_{AB} - \tilde{P}_A - \tilde{P}_B + \tilde{P}_{AB}\right)$$

and

$$\text{STD spread premium} = S_2 - \tilde{S}_2 = \frac{(1-R)}{T}\left(P_{AB} - \tilde{P}_{AB}\right).$$

2. The second is the *coverage ratio* for each basket. This is defined as the number of times the risk-neutral spread covers the actuarial spread. Hence we have

$$\text{FTD coverage ratio} = \frac{S_1}{\tilde{S}_1} = \frac{P_A + P_B - P_{AB}}{\tilde{P}_A + \tilde{P}_B - \tilde{P}_{AB}}$$

and

$$\text{STD coverage ratio} = \frac{S_2}{\tilde{S}_2} = \frac{P_{AB}}{\tilde{P}_{AB}}.$$

We know that P_{AB} ranges from 0 through independence $P_A P_B$ to maximum dependence $\min[P_A, P_B]$. The equivalent is true of $\tilde{P}_{AB}$. To model dependency of two credits we prefer to think about the joint default probability through a correlation measure. We therefore define

$$P_{AB} = \Phi_2(\Phi^{-1}(P_A), \Phi^{-1}(P_B), \rho)$$

and

$$\tilde{P}_{AB} = \Phi_2(\Phi^{-1}(\tilde{P}_A), \Phi^{-1}(\tilde{P}_B), \tilde{\rho})$$

where $\Phi(x)$ is the cumulative distribution function of the Gaussian distribution, and $\Phi_2(x, y, \rho)$ is the bi-variate cumulative distribution function with correlation parameter ρ. This is our first encounter with what is known as a Gaussian copula model of default. This will be discussed in detail in Chapter 13. Here we just note that $\rho = -100\%$ gives the minimum dependency case, $\rho = 0$ gives independence and $\rho = 100\%$ gives maximum dependence. Let us consider a realistic example.

Example   We set $R=40\%$ and suppose that $S_A=60$ bp and $S_B=120$ bp. Using a horizon of five years, this implies that $P_A=5\%$ and $P_B=10\%$. We set $k=5$, implying that single-name risk-neutral spreads are five times single-name actuarial spreads. We also assume that the real-world and risk-neutral correlations agree, i.e. $\rho=\tilde{\rho}$. The spread premium of the two credits in the basket is given by

$$\left(120-\frac{120}{5}\right)=96\,\text{bp} \quad \text{and} \quad \left(60-\frac{60}{5}\right)=48\,\text{bp}.$$

We then calculate the spread premium and coverage ratio of a FTD and STD basket as a function of correlation. The results are shown in Table 12.2. We can make a number of observations:

- The spread premium of the FTD basket is always greater than the maximum of any of its constituent CDS. For minimum correlation, it equals the sum of the spread premia of the constituent CDS, tending to the maximum of the CDS at maximum correlation.
- The spread premium of an STD basket is small for most values of correlation and is lower than that of either of the two credits in the basket.
- The coverage ratio of the FTD basket is fairly constant and is close to that of the constituent credits.
- The coverage ratio of the STD basket is much higher than that of the constituent CDS for low values of correlation tending to the portfolio coverage ratio at maximum correlation. At 25% correlation it is close to 14, implying that the investor in an STD basket at this correlation is being paid 14 times the actuarial spread.

Table 12.2   Spread premium and coverage ratio for an FTD and STD basket on two credits with spreads 60 bp and 120 bp. We highlight the results for a correlation of 25%. See text for discussion

Correlation (%)	FTD spread premium (bp)	STD spread premium (bp)	FTD coverage ratio	STD coverage ratio
−100	144.0	0.0	5.00	–
−75	143.9	0.0	5.00	–
−50	143.7	0.3	4.99	392.20
−25	142.1	1.9	4.95	63.39
0	138.2	5.8	4.87	25.00
25	131.9	12.0	4.77	14.06
50	123.2	20.8	4.67	9.42
75	111.1	32.9	4.65	6.89
100	96.0	48.0	5.00	5.00

These numbers change when we consider baskets with more credits and different spread levels. However, the general result holds which is that FTD baskets leverage the spread premium of the credits in the basket while STD baskets increase the coverage ratio. For investors who wish to receive a high spread, FTD baskets may therefore present an attractive alternative to descending the rating spectrum. For investors who wish to buy low risk investments, STD baskets may also be attractive as they increase the spread paid per unit of actuarial risk.

12.4   COLLATERALISED DEBT OBLIGATIONS

Collateralised debt obligations (CDOs) are securities whose payments are linked to the incidence of default on an underlying portfolio of credit risky assets. This is done in a way which transforms the credit risk of the underlying portfolio into a set of securities with different credit profiles.

In a traditional cash flow CDO, the CDO securities are sold to investors in a funded form at a price of par. The sale proceeds are used to purchase the collateral portfolio of credit risky assets, typically bonds and loans, which is then sold into a structure known as a special purpose vehicle or SPV. The SPV then issues the CDO securities. Note that the term CDO is used in two ways – it can be used to refer to the entire structure consisting of SPV and issued securities. It is also used to refer to a specific security issued by the CDO, i.e. a CDO issues a set of CDOs.

These issued CDO securities are typically divided into three classes known as senior, mezzanine and equity.[2] Using a mechanism called *structural subordination*, the scheduled coupon and principal payments on the different securities are paid according to a set of rules known as the *waterfall*. The interest and principal payments on the senior securities are paid first. It is then the turn of the mezzanine security holders to receive their coupon and principal. The equity security holders receive their coupon and principal last. A simplified version of a CDO is shown in Figure 12.4. The waterfall, described in the *priority of payments* section of the issuing documents of the CDO is often quite complex. For example, it may contain triggers which cause the more senior tranches to amortise early if there have been a large number of defaults on the underlying portfolio.

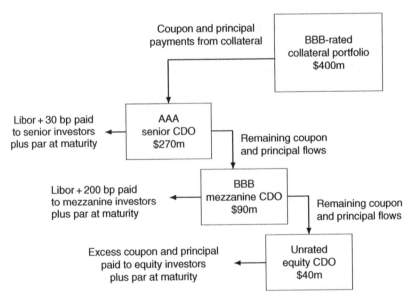

Figure 12.4   Simplified waterfall of a cash flow CDO

---

[2] By analogy to the capital structure of a company, the term 'equity' simply means the first loss or most subordinate part of the CDO structure. It should not be confused with equity in the sense of stocks.

The effect of structural subordination is that if there are defaults in the collateral, they will first impact the coupon and principal payments to the equity holders. If the number of defaults is so great that the equity holders cannot be paid, the mezzanine holders start to see a reduced coupon and principal. In the extreme case of a very high number of defaults the mezzanine holders receive no further payments and the senior holders may also see a reduced coupon and may not receive their promised principal payment. Clearly, the equity securities are the most vulnerable to defaults on the underlying portfolio while the senior securities are the least vulnerable.

To encourage investors to purchase these CDO securities, the coupon on the security is set at a level which takes into account the market's view on the risk of the security. The main indicator of the risk of a CDO security is its rating. This is determined by one or more of the credit rating agencies who assess the risk of the tranche on the basis of the credit quality of the collateral, the mechanics of the waterfall and a proprietary rating model which essentially runs the CDO through a range of default scenarios. Given the credit rating, the coupon of each CDO security is determined by observing the credit spread of other CDO securities with the same rating and then choosing a coupon which allows the security to be issued and sold at par. This coupon may be a fixed coupon or a spread over Libor. We find that the initial coupon on the equity tranche is greater than the initial coupon on the mezzanine tranche which in turn is greater than the initial coupon on the senior tranche.

What makes the concept of structural subordination so appealing is that it can be used to transform the risk–return profile of a set of credit assets into a set of securities whose risk–return characteristics can be tuned to the requirements of different classes of investor. For example, it may be possible to take a portfolio of subinvestment grade credits for which there may only be a limited demand, and to use these in the portfolio of a CDO to issue a set of securities ranging from AAA grade down to unrated equity. The AAA securities may appeal to an insurance company, the investment grade securities may appeal to an investment fund, and the unrated securities may appeal to a high yield credit fund. Structural subordination can be seen as a way to enhance liquidity.

There are several variations on the CDO structure including arbitrage CDOs, balance sheet CLOs and market value CDOs. What these variations all have in common is the fact that the entire credit risk of the credit portfolio is held within an SPV and then sold to the investors via the issued securities. We call these types of CDO *full capital structure deals* since the entire capital structure – meaning all of the CDO tranche securities – are sold, leaving the issuer with no risk. In some cases the equity tranche might be retained by the issuer for moral hazard reasons, i.e. by requiring the issuer to buy and hold the riskiest part of the deal, the interests of the issuer are closely aligned with those of the investors and this incentivises the issuer to ensure that the credits in the collateral portfolio have been carefully selected.

Since the different securities of a full capital structure CDO are sold to a range of investors, the details of the structure usually reflect some compromise between the differing investment requirements and market views of the investors. As a result, traditional CDOs provide little single-investor control over the precise format of the deal in terms of the credit selection, the waterfall, the rating, and the maturity of the CDO security. These deals also typically take months to arrange and sell. They may also incur significant legal and administrative costs to set up. For this reason, many CDO investors prefer the single-tranche synthetic CDO.

12.5   THE SINGLE-TRANCHE SYNTHETIC CDO

The single-tranche synthetic CDO (STCDO) is an over-the-counter derivative version of the CDO security. There are a number of important differences between the traditional CDO and the STCDO which we list below:

1. There is no SPV in an STCDO. Instead, there is a bilateral contract between a dealer and an investor.
2. The reference portfolio is linked to 50–150 reference entities with each reference entity equating to a position in a CDS on that reference entity. The credit risk is in a *synthetic* format.
3. The structure is unfunded. This means that the contract typically costs nothing to enter into. In some cases there may be an upfront payment as in an upfront CDS.
4. Only one CDO security, or tranche, is issued. There is no need to issue the other tranches.
5. The STCDO can typically be issued within a few days of the initial enquiry. This is assisted by the use of standard ISDA documentation.
6. The STCDO waterfall is trivial when compared to the waterfall of a typical cash flow CDO. This is discussed in the next section.
7. The tranche is tailored to the exact requirements of the investor.

This last difference is the one which has made the STCDO so attractive to traditional CDO investors. The investor in an STCDO can select:

- The size of the investment.
- The number of credits in the underlying reference portfolio.
- The name of each reference credit in the reference portfolio.
- The exact level of structural subordination of the tranche.
- The desired rating and choice of rating agencies.
- The exact maturity date.
- The currency.

The most important difference between the STCDO and the traditional CDO from the dealer's perspective is that the dealer retains the credit risk of the STCDO. This is exactly analogous to the way they retain a risk if they buy protection on a CDS. However, unlike a CDS, the risk held by the dealer is a CDO tranche and so includes an exposure to all of the credits in the reference portfolio and their *default correlation*. These risks must be hedged dynamically.

This approach to CDO issuance has only been made possible by three important and recent developments:

1. The growth of a broad and highly liquid CDS market which can be used for sourcing the risk and hedging the risk sensitivities.
2. The development of risk-neutral pricing models which are able to calibrate to all of the CDS curves in the reference portfolio and can calculate the resulting value of the CDO position.
3. The massive increase in computing power that has occurred over the past 10 years which allows all of the risk numbers to be produced within the required time.

Before we can discuss pricing models, we need to set out the STCDO 'waterfall'.

12.5.1   The STCDO Waterfall

The mechanism for introducing structural subordination in an STCDO is not a waterfall in the traditional sense. There are no rules which dictate how interest and principal flows from the reference portfolio should be paid to senior then mezzanine and then the equity tranche. Instead, we have a simple payoff function which defines how the fractional loss on the tranche depends on the cumulative percentage default losses $L(T)$ on the reference portfolio. We first need to define two further quantities:

1. K_1: This is the attachment point, also known as the *subordination* or *lower strike* of the tranche. This is the percentage loss on the reference portfolio below which the tranche loss is zero. As soon as $L(T) > K_1$, the tranche loss is non-zero.
2. K_2: This is the detachment point, also known as the *upper strike*. The quantity $K_2 - K_1$ is the *tranche width*. If $L(T) \geq K_2$, the tranche loss is 100%.

Between these two limits of 0% tranche loss at $L(T) = K_1$ and 100% tranche loss at $L(T) = K_2$, the tranche loss is a linear function of $L(T)$. If we define the fractional loss of the tranche at time T as $L(T, K_1, K_2)$ then the payoff takes the form shown in Figure 12.5. Mathematically, this payoff is defined as follows

$$L(T, K_1, K_2) = \frac{\max(L(T) - K_1, 0) - \max(L(T) - K_2, 0)}{K_2 - K_1}. \qquad (12.1)$$

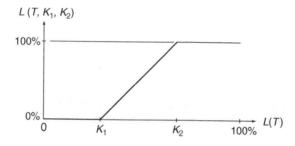

Figure 12.5   Tranche loss $L(T, K_1, K_2)$ as a function of the percentage portfolio loss $L(T)$

We now consider how the evolution of $L(t, K_1, K_2)$ through time determines the payments on the premium and protection legs of the STCDO.

12.5.2   The Premium Leg

The premium leg is the series of cash flows made by the tranche protection buyer to the tranche protection seller. The size of the payments is determined by the contractual tranche spread. For a tranche with attachment and detachment points at K_1 and K_2, this is given by $S(K_1, K_2)$.

The coupons on the premium leg are paid on the *surviving notional* of the tranche according to a schedule which is typically quarterly and uses an Actual 360 day count convention. Per $1 of face value, the size of a single premium payment at time t_i is given by

$$\Delta(t_{i-1}, t_i) S(K_1, K_2)(1 - L(t_i, K_1, K_2)).$$

As a result, the absolute value of the premium payments declines as $L(t, K_1, K_2)$ increases.

Premium payments also take into account the timing of the default of credits in the reference portfolio. As a result, a default loss which occurs immediately before a premium payment has no effect on the premium paid. However, if the default and loss occurred at the start of the accrual period, the entire coupon is based on the reduced surviving notional. If a loss occurs between premium payment periods, the next coupon is calculated on the pro-rated notional exposure over the coupon period. As an approximation, we can assume that losses occur midway through the period so that the tranche notional during this period is the average of the start and end notional. There is a direct analogy between the outstanding tranche notional and the survival probability in a standard CDS which means that we can incorporate the tranche amortisation in the same way as we handle the payment of premium accrued at default on a standard CDS.

12.5.3   The Protection Leg

The protection leg consists of the loss payments made by the investor to the dealer to cover default losses on the tranche. The size of the loss is simply the change in the value of the tranche loss function $L(t, K_1, K_2)$, which will only change if there is a credit event on the reference portfolio such that after the default $K_1 < L(T) \leq K_2$. In practice, losses on the underlying CDS are usually settled using the cash settlement process described in Section 5.4.

If we suppose that the reference portfolio consists of N_C credits which all have the same face value and recovery rate R, then the percentage loss on the portfolio for each default is given by $u = (1 - R)/N_C$. Therefore, the number of defaults in the portfolio before a loss on the tranche occurs is $n_1 = \texttt{ceil}(K_1/u)$, where $\texttt{ceil}(x)$ is the first integer greater than or equal to x. Equally, the number of defaults required to reduce the tranche notional to zero is given by $n_2 = \texttt{ceil}(K_2/u)$.

Example   The best way to make the mechanics of an STCDO clear is to consider a specific STCDO deal. We choose one with the following characteristics:

- A reference portfolio consisting of 100 credits each with a face value exposure of $10 million so that the total notional of the reference portfolio is $1bn.
- A tranche with a face value of $30 million, a contractual spread of 250 bp, an attachment point at 3%, a width of 4% and a maturity of five years.

We now consider the payments if we have a series of semi-annual defaults over the life of the trade. Defaults are assumed to occur immediately before premium payment dates. We assume a 30% recovery rate on default for each credit. We choose such an extreme scenario simply to allow us to see the mechanics of the synthetic CDO. The cash flows in this scenario are set out in Table 12.3.

The first column to note is the portfolio loss. Assuming 100 credits and a recovery rate of 30%, each default results in a $(100\% - 30\%)/100 = 0.70\%$ loss on the reference portfolio. The cumulative loss column therefore increases by 0.70% as each default occurs. Losses do not hit the tranche until the number of defaults equals 5. At this point the cumulative portfolio loss is 3.5% and the tranche loss equals $(3.5\% - 3.0\%)/4\% =$

12.5%. The tranche notional therefore falls from \$30 million to $30 \times (1.0 - 0.125) =$ \$26.25m, and the quarterly coupon payment is calculated on this new notional. The loss payment equals $12.5\% \times \$30m = \$3.75m$.

Table 12.3 Coupon and loss payments on the synthetic CDO example discussed in the text

Payment date	Number of defaults	Portfolio loss (%)	Tranche loss (%)	Notional ($m)	Coupon payment	Protection leg ($m)	Net flow
20 Mar 2007		0.00	0.0	30.00			
20 Jun 2007	1	0.70	0.0	30.00	191 667		191 667
20 Sep 2007		0.70	0.0	30.00	191 667		191 667
20 Dec 2007	2	1.40	0.0	30.00	189 583		189 583
20 Mar 2008		1.40	0.0	30.00	189 583		189 583
20 Jun 2008	3	2.10	0.0	30.00	191 667		191 667
22 Sep 2008		2.10	0.0	30.00	195 833		195 833
22 Dec 2008	4	2.80	0.0	30.00	189 583		189 583
20 Mar 2009		2.80	0.0	30.00	183 333		183 333
22 Jun 2009	5	3.50	12.5	26.25	195 833	−3.75	−3 554 167
21 Sep 2009		3.50	12.5	26.25	165 885		165 885
21 Dec 2009	6	4.20	30.0	21.00	165 885	−5.25	−5 084 115
22 Mar 2010		4.20	30.0	21.00	132 708		132 708
21 Jun 2010	7	4.90	47.5	15.75	132 708	−5.25	−5 117 292
20 Sep 2010		4.90	47.5	15.75	99 531		99 531
20 Dec 2010	8	5.60	65.0	10.50	99 531	−5.25	−5 150 469
21 Mar 2011		5.60	65.0	10.50	66 354		66 354
20 Jun 2011	9	6.30	82.5	5.25	66 354	−5.25	−5 183 646
20 Sep 2011		6.30	82.5	5.25	33 542		33 542
20 Dec 2011	10	7.00	100.0			−5.25	−5 250 000
20 Mar 2012		7.00	100.0				

Finally, it is important to be clear that the reference portfolio does not actually exist as a distinct portfolio of CDS on the dealer's book. It is simply a list of reference entities whose defaults affect the payments of the STCDO via the waterfall. It can be thought of as a *virtual* reference portfolio.

12.5.4 The Senior Tranche

The payoff rules described above only apply to tranches whose upper strike K_2 is *below* the maximum portfolio loss. For tranches with a K_2 above the maximum portfolio loss, the payoff rule needs to be adapted slightly. To see why, consider the case of a portfolio of 100 credits, each \$1 million notional. Suppose also that on this portfolio we have issued a senior tranche with $K_1 = 10\%$ and $K_2 = 100\%$. Let us assume a scenario in which all 100 of the credits in the portfolio default with a 40% recovery resulting in a portfolio loss $L(T) = 60\%$. If we use the previous rules, the tranche loss is

$$\frac{\max[60\% - 10\%, 0] - \max[60\% - 100\%, 0]}{100\% - 10\%} = \frac{50\%}{90\%} = 56\%.$$

It is not a 100% loss as we might expect. According to this rule the senior investor should continue receiving a premium payment on 44% of the original tranche face value. This makes no sense as all of the credits in the portfolio have defaulted.

The solution is to ensure that the notional value of the senior most tranches is reduced by an amount R/N_C following any default in the portfolio. This does not mean that the senior investor pays out a loss. However, it does mean that subsequent premium payments will be reduced. Revisiting the example, this would mean that the senior tranche upper strike K_2 would be reduced from 100% to $100\% - 40\% = 60\%$. The tranche loss is then

$$\frac{\max[60\% - 10\%, 0] - \max[60\% - 60\%, 0]}{60\% - 10\%} = \frac{50\%}{50\%} = 100\%.$$

In practice, the effect of this adjustment need only be considered for the senior tranches which have a detachment point above the maximum portfolio loss. Note that it is fairly unusual to encounter such senior tranches. However, if we do trade such a tranche, this effect should not be ignored.

12.6   CDOs AND CORRELATION

CDOs are credit correlation products. The best way to see this is to introduce the portfolio loss distribution. The portfolio loss distribution tells us the probability of a certain loss on the portfolio at some future time horizon. Here we define a continuous[3] loss distribution $f(L(T))$ as follows

$$f(k) = \frac{\partial}{\partial K} \Pr(L(T) \le K)$$

where

$$L(T) = \frac{1}{N_C} \sum_{i=1}^{N_C} (1 - R_i) \mathbf{1}_{\tau_i \le T}.$$

The loss $L(T)$ is a sum over the N_C credits in the portfolio, each weighted by the loss on default $(1 - R_i)$ and the default indicator function. We assume that the credits all have the same face value. The expected portfolio loss is given by

$$\mathbb{E}[L(T)] = \frac{1}{N_C} \sum_{i=1}^{N_C} (1 - R_i)(1 - Q_i(0, T)) \tag{12.2}$$

where $Q_i(0, T)$ is the survival probability of issuer i from time zero to time T. The expected loss is clearly independent of the correlation between credits. We can also write this in terms of the portfolio loss distribution density

$$\mathbb{E}[L(T)] = \int_0^1 f(k) \cdot k \cdot dk.$$

---

[3] The portfolio loss distribution can also be discrete. However here we just consider the continuous case. The discrete case will be considered later.

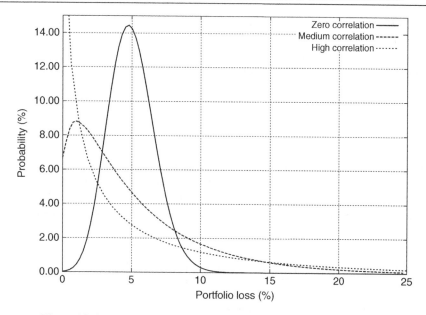

Figure 12.6   The portfolio loss distribution for three levels of correlation

Figure 12.6 shows the portfolio loss distribution $f(k)$ implied by three different values of correlation. This has been generated using the Gaussian copula model discussed in Chapter 13. We present these loss distributions here simply to demonstrate the link between default correlation and the risk of an STCDO tranche. We make the following observations:

- As shown in Equation 12.2, the expected loss of a portfolio is independent of the default correlation. We can see that in this case, the loss distribution has an expected loss of 5%.
- Even though all of the curves have the same expected loss, they have very different shapes. When the correlation is zero, the credits are independent and do not tend to survive or default together. As a result the losses are distributed close to the expected loss in a range between 0% and just over 10% loss. This suggests that the risk of senior tranches with an attachment point above 10% is very low.
- In the high correlation case credits become more likely to default and survive together. We therefore see that there is a reasonable probability of the losses exceeding 10%. This suggests that there is an increased probability of the senior tranche incurring a loss.
- We also see that the probability of very few defaults is high when the correlation is high. There is therefore an increased probability of the equity tranche incurring no loss.

We can therefore conclude that senior investors prefer low correlation and equity investors prefer high correlation portfolios.

12.7   THE TRANCHE SURVIVAL CURVE

The mechanics of the STCDO make it much easier to model than the cash flow CDO. This is because the premium and protection payments at time t are purely a function of the tranche loss $L(t, K_1, K_2)$ which in turn is simply a function of the portfolio loss $L(t)$. We can therefore reduce the pricing problem to modelling the distribution of the reference portfolio loss $L(t)$.

In order to price an STCDO, we consider the valuation of the premium and protection legs. We assume a face value of \$1 and we denote the contractual spread with $S(K_1, K_2)$. The present value of the premium leg at time zero is therefore

$$\text{Premium Leg PV} = S(K_1, K_2) \sum_{i=1}^{N_T} \Delta(t_{i-1}, t_i) Z(t_i) \mathbb{E}[1 - L(t_i, K_1, K_2))].$$

We assume that the premium paid at time t_i is paid on the tranche notional at time t_i. A more accurate pricing formula for the premium leg would take into account the fact that the spread is paid on the pro-rated tranche notional since the previous coupon date. A useful and accurate approximation is to assume that the spread is paid on the *average* tranche notional since the previous coupon payment date. This gives

$$\text{Premium Leg PV} = S(K_1, K_2) \sum_{i=1}^{N_T} \Delta(t_{i-1}, t_i) Z(t_i) \mathbb{E}\left[1 - \frac{(L(t_{i-1}, K_1, K_2) + L(t_i, K_1, K_2))}{2}\right].$$

As discussed earlier, this formula only applies to tranches which have detachment points below the maximum loss.

We now consider the protection leg. The protection leg pays out the tranche loss amount at the time of the loss. The amount lost on the tranche over a small period dt is given by $dL(t, K_1, K_2)$. Hence, the present value of the protection leg is given by

$$\text{Protection Leg PV} = \int_0^T Z(s) \mathbb{E}[dL(s, K_1, K_2)].$$

There is a clear analogy between these pricing equations and those of a CDS. If we write the *tranche survival probability* as

$$Q(t, K_1, K_2) = \mathbb{E}[1 - L(t, K_1, K_2)]$$

then the premium leg value can be rewritten as

$$\text{Premium Leg PV} = \frac{S(K_1, K_2)}{2} \sum_{i=1}^{N_T} \Delta(t_{i-1}, t_i) Z(t_i) \left[Q(t_{i-1}, K_1, K_2) + Q(t_i, K_1, K_2)\right].$$

The protection leg value can be written as

$$\text{Protection Leg PV} = \int_0^T Z(s)(-dQ(s, K_1, K_2)).$$

As a result, the value at time zero of a short protection tranche position is given by

$$V(K_1, K_2) = \frac{S(K_1, K_2)}{2} \sum_{i=1}^{N_T} \Delta(t_{i-1}, t_i) Z(t_i) \left(Q(t_{i-1}, K_1, K_2) + Q(t_i, K_1, K_2)\right)$$

$$- \int_0^T Z(s)(-dQ(s, K_1, K_2)).$$

We see that there is an exact mapping between pricing a CDS and pricing an STCDO tranche. We replace the issuer survival curve with the tranche survival curve $Q(t, K_1, K_2)$ and assume a zero recovery rate in the CDS. This mapping is very useful since it means that once an STCDO model has output a *tranche survival curve*, we can immediately use the curves in our CDS analytics, along with a zero recovery rate assumption, to produce the tranche breakeven spread, the mark-to-market and the interest rate risk sensitivity. Unfortunately, this mapping does not extend to those STCDOs with a detachment point above the maximum portfolio loss. These must be priced directly in terms of $L(t)$.

12.7.1   Conservation of Expected Loss

Suppose we buy protection on $m = 1, \ldots, M$ contiguous tranches with strikes $[K_{m-1}, K_m]$ where $K_0 = 0$ and $K_M = 1$. The face value of each tranche equals $(K_m - K_{m-1})$. The value of the sum of the expected losses to some horizon time T is given by

$$\text{Total expected loss} = \mathbb{E}\left[\sum_{m=1}^{M} (K_m - K_{m-1}) L(T, K_{m-1}, K_m) \right]$$

$$= \mathbb{E}\left[\sum_{m=1}^{M} (\min[L(T), K_m] - \min[L(T), K_{m-1}]) \right]. \qquad (12.3)$$

Expanding the sums and cancelling, this reduces to

$$\mathbb{E}[\min(L(T), K_M) - \min(L(T), K_0)] = \mathbb{E}\,[L(T)]$$

which is the expected loss of the reference portfolio, i.e.

$$\mathbb{E}\left[\frac{1}{N_C} \sum_{i=1}^{N_C} L_i(T) \right] = \mathbb{E}[L(T)].$$

As a result, we conclude that the present value of the protection legs of the STCDOs, which is the discounted expected losses, summed across the capital structure is identical to owning the protection legs of all of the CDS in the reference portfolio. This makes sense since a trade which involved buying all the STCDO protection legs and selling all the CDS protection legs would be perfectly hedged as any default on the reference portfolio would involve an equal and opposite payment from the tranches to the CDS.

However, buying protection with tranches across the capital structure and selling protection on all of the CDS is not an exact hedge since the timing and sizes of the tranche and CDS premium flows do not match exactly. For example, suppose a 0–3% equity tranche on a portfolio of 100 credits pays a spread of 1000 bp and the first credit to default pays a spread of 50 bp and has a 40% recovery. Assuming a $10 million face value for each name in the reference portfolio, the loss on the equity tranche which has a face value of $30 million is $6 million. The notional of the equity tranche is reduced from $30 million to $24 million and the reduction in the annualised coupon payments is $(30 − 24)m × 1000 bp = $600 000. However, the annualised loss of coupon on the defaulted CDS is simply $10m × 50 bp = $50 000. As a result, the premium legs do not offset.

12.8   THE STANDARD INDEX TRANCHES

In mid-2003 an interdealer market appeared for a standardised set of synthetic CDO tranches. These took as their underlying reference portfolio the CDS index portfolios described in Chapter 10. The market for these *standard* index tranches has grown significantly since then. Standard tranches can now be traded on iTraxx, CDX NA IG and the CDX NA HY indices. While the five-year maturity is the most liquid maturity point, it is also now possible to trade tranches at the seven-and 10-year maturity points. The characteristics of the most liquid standard tranches are shown in Table 12.4.

Table 12.4   The attachment and detachment points of the CDX NA, the iTraxx Europe and the CDX NA HY set of tranches

Tranche	CDX IG NA		iTraxx Europe		CDX NA HY	
	K_1 (%)	K_2 (%)	K_1 (%)	K_2 (%)	K_1 (%)	K_2 (%)
Equity	0	3	0	3	0	10
Junior mezzanine	3	7	3	6	10	15
Senior mezzanine	7	10	6	9	15	25
Senior	10	15	9	12	25	35
Super senior	15	30	12	22	35	60

The standard tranches have exactly the same mechanics as the STCDOs already discussed. They differ from bespoke STCDOs in that they are much more liquid and so present much tighter bid–offer spreads. Since they are quoted in the dealer market, their pricing is transparent. As we will see in later chapters, these prices allow us to extract the implied correlations the market is assigning to the reference portfolios.

12.9   SUMMARY

We have introduced the main correlation products and described their mechanics and no-arbitrage properties. This has been done without reference to any specific pricing models. We now begin to discuss models which can be used to price and risk manage these products.

13

The Gaussian Latent Variable Model

13.1 INTRODUCTION

The Gaussian latent variable model has been the standard model for most of the pricing and risk management of the products traded in the credit correlation market since its inception in the late 1990s. It is the 'Black–Scholes' model of the correlation market, and continues to be widely used, although now mostly within a base correlation framework.

The earliest published use of the Gaussian latent variable model can be found in Vasicek (1987). For this reason, it is also known as 'Vasicek's' portfolio model. It is a very simple yet powerful model which already found a number of applications before the advent of the correlation markets. In its multi-state form[1] it was chosen as the underlying model for the CreditMetrics risk management framework by Gupton *et al.* (1997). It has also been adopted by the Basel committee as its base model for assigning capital to bank loan portfolios as discussed in Gordy (2003).

The aim of this chapter is to introduce, describe and analyse the Gaussian latent variable model. We especially wish to highlight the structure of the model and what this implies for the pricing behaviour it produces. We also wish to highlight its flexibility and the fact that it allows us to perform very rapid pricing calculations.

13.2 THE MODEL

We introduce a random variable A_i for a credit which we label with i. We assume that A_i is drawn from a Gaussian distribution with mean zero and unit standard deviation. In the spirit of Merton's structural model discussed in Section 3.4, we specify that default occurs before time T if the value of A_i is less than a time dependent threshold $C_i(T)$. More formally, we write

$$\Pr(\tau_i \leq T) = \Pr(A_i \leq C_i(T)) = 1 - Q_i(T) \tag{13.1}$$

where $Q_i(T)$ is the time T survival probability of credit i implied by the CDS market. Since $A_i \sim N(0, 1)$ the probability that $A_i \leq C_i(T)$ is given by $\Phi(C_i(T))$ where $\Phi(x)$ is the Gaussian cumulative distribution function. As a result, this model can be calibrated to the issuer i survival curve by setting

$$\Phi(C_i(T)) = 1 - Q_i(T).$$

---

[1] The Gaussian latent variable model can model credits which assume one of many credit states, e.g. credit ratings. In the form used in the correlation markets, the Gaussian latent variable model is a two-state model. The two states of any credit are defaulted and non-defaulted.

Calibration involves solving for the value of $C_i(T)$ at each future time for which

$$C_i(T) = \Phi^{-1}(1 - Q_i(T)).$$

Table 13.1 shows the calibrated default thresholds for three term structures of survival probabilities with flat deterministic hazard rates. For very short times when $Q_i(T)$ is close to 1, the threshold becomes large and negative. When $Q_i(T) = 1/2$, we have $C_i(T) = 0$. At very long times when $Q_i(T)$ tends to zero, $C_i(T)$ becomes large and positive.

Table 13.1   Time dependence of the survival probabilities and default thresholds $C(T)$ for issuer curves with the flat deterministic hazard rates shown

	$\lambda = 1.0\%$		$\lambda = 2.0\%$		$\lambda = 3.0\%$	
T	$Q(T)$	$C(T)$	$Q(T)$	$C(T)$	$Q(T)$	$C(T)$
0.1	0.9990	−3.0904	0.9980	−2.8785	0.9970	−2.7483
1	0.9900	−2.3282	0.9802	−2.0579	0.9704	−1.8874
5	0.9512	−1.6569	0.9048	−1.3096	0.8607	−1.0835
10	0.9048	−1.3096	0.8187	−0.9105	0.7408	−0.6459
100	0.3679	0.3375	0.1353	1.1015	0.0498	1.6469

Even though we have introduced a time horizon T, and shown how to calibrate A_i to fit the term structure of survival probabilities, A_i itself has no dynamics. It is a random number drawn from a Gaussian distribution and fixed at time zero. It is also not observable, i.e. it is *latent* or hidden. All we know is the distribution from which it is drawn. As a result, this model is fundamentally different from a Merton style model in which we can observe the evolution of the asset value through time.

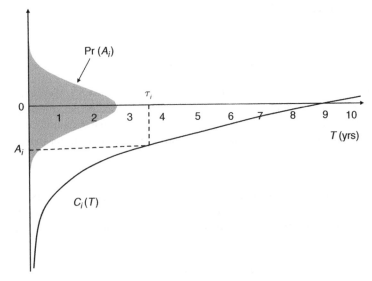

Figure 13.1   The realisation of the latent variable A_i determines the default time τ_i given a default boundary calibrated to the risk-neutral survival probabilities

Knowledge of A_i immediately tells us the default time of credit i. As shown in Figure 13.1, this is simply the value of T for which $C_i(T) = A_i$. We therefore have

$$Q_i(\tau_i) = 1 - \Phi(C_i(\tau_i)) = 1 - \Phi(A_i).$$

This link between the realisation of A_i and τ_i makes it possible to perform a Monte Carlo simulation of the default time of issuer i. Noting that if $x \sim N(0,1)$ then $\Phi(x) \sim U(0,1)$ where $U(0,1)$ is a uniform distribution defined on the interval $[0,1]$, we can calculate the expected default time using the following algorithm:

1. Set $p = 1$.
2. Draw an independent uniform random number u.
3. Solve for $\tau_i^p = Q_i^{-1}(u)$.
4. Set $p = p + 1$. If $p \leq P$ then go to step (2).
5. Calculate $\tau_i = \dfrac{1}{P} \sum_{p=1}^{P} \tau_i^p$.

Since the threshold has been calibrated to the issuer survival curve, there is no need to simulate A_i directly and then to calculate $\Phi(A_i)$. Drawing a random uniform is also faster than drawing a Gaussian since it avoids the numerically more expensive call to the $\Phi(x)$ function. Furthermore, if we have a flat hazard rate, then $Q_i(t) = \exp(-\lambda_i t)$ and we can generate many realisations of τ_i using

$$\tau_i = Q_i^{-1}(u) = -\frac{\ln u}{\lambda_i}.$$

A basic check of any default-time simulation is to show that the expected first jump time of a Poisson process with deterministic hazard rate λ_i is given by $\mathbb{E}[\tau_i] = 1/\lambda_i$.

13.3   THE MULTI-NAME LATENT VARIABLE MODEL

To price correlation products, we need to extend this model into a multi-name setting. We therefore introduce an A_i for each of the $i = 1, \ldots, N_C$ credits in our portfolio. However, we want to do this in a way which allows us to correlate default. This can be achieved by correlating the A_i and A_j. The simplest way to do this is through a single-factor model. We specify a one-factor correlation structure writing

$$A_i = \beta_i Z + \sqrt{1 - \beta_i^2}\, \varepsilon_i$$

where Z is the *market factor* seen by all of the credits in the portfolio, and the ε_i are the idiosyncratic factors specific to each credit. Both are Gaussian distributed with mean zero and unit standard deviation, i.e.

$$Z \sim N(0,1) \quad \text{and} \quad \varepsilon_i \sim N(0,1).$$

They are also independent. The weighting on the idiosyncratic factor ensures that A_i retains its mean of zero and its unit standard deviation.

In a factor model, default can happen when $A_i \leq C_i(T)$. This depends on the market factor and idiosyncratic factor realisations. It can be caused by a large and negative realisation of Z. It could also be caused by a large and negative realisation of ε_i. Or it could occur because both ε_i and Z are large and negative. Whether the default is caused by Z or ε_i also depends on the value of β_i. A higher value of β_i will make it more likely that the default is caused by Z. If credit i defaults because Z is large and negative, then we would expect that other credits in the portfolio which share this factor are more likely to default. If it is the idiosyncratic term which causes default, then we would not expect to see an increased number of other defaults since this default is independent of the other credits.

13.3.1 Asset Correlation and Dependency

The *asset* correlation between A_i and A_j is given by

$$\rho_{ij} = \frac{\mathbb{E}\left[A_i A_j\right] - \mathbb{E}[A_i]\mathbb{E}\left[A_j\right]}{\sqrt{\left(\mathbb{E}\left[A_i^2\right] - \mathbb{E}\left[A_i\right]^2\right)\left(\mathbb{E}\left[A_j^2\right] - \mathbb{E}\left[A_j\right]^2\right)}} = \beta_i \beta_j. \tag{13.2}$$

The value of this credits correlation has a significant effect on the tendency of the credits to default jointly and enables us to interpolate between the limits of minimum and maximum dependence.

To see this, consider two credits i and j. Both will default before time horizon T if $A_i \leq C_i(T)$ and $A_j \leq C_j(T)$. Since both asset values are $N(0, 1)$ distributed, we can write the probability of both credits defaulting before time T in terms of the bi-variate normal cumulative distribution function. We have

$$p_{ij}(T) = \Phi_2\left(C_i(T), C_j(T), \rho_{ij}\right).$$

We can then consider some standard dependence cases:

- Minimum dependence: In the limit of $\beta_i = -\beta_j = 100\%$, we have an asset correlation $\rho = -100\%$. In this limit $A_i = -A_j$ and

$$p_{ij}(T) = \max[1 - Q_i(T) - Q_j(T), 0].$$

  In this limit, the joint default probability of credits i and j is zero as long as $Q_i(T) + Q_j(T) > 1$.
- Independence: In the limit of $\beta_i = \beta_j = 0$, only the idiosyncratic factors are left. In this case $\rho = 0$ and the credits are independent.

$$p_{ij}(T) = \Phi(C_i(T))\Phi(C_j(T)) = (1 - Q_i(T))(1 - Q_j(T)).$$

- Maximum dependence: In the limit of $\beta_i = \beta_j = 1$, we have $\rho = 100\%$ asset correlation. In this case, $A_i = A_j$. If both credits have the same hazard rate then $\tau_i = \tau_j$. However, in general $\lambda_i \neq \lambda_j$ so that not every default of credit i means a similar time default of credit j or vice versa. That depends on the value of their respective thresholds $C_i(T)$ and $C_j(T)$ which are in turn calibrated to their respective survival probability curves. The joint default probability is given by

$$p_{ij}(T) = \min\left[1 - Q_i(T), 1 - Q_j(T)\right].$$

This analysis demonstrates that this model is able to handle the full range of dependency by varying the asset correlation from -100% to $+100\%$. Note that this measure of correlation is therefore more useful than the default indicator correlation presented in Section 12.2.3.

Figure 13.2 shows how the joint default probability of two credits, one with a 3% default probability and the other with default probabilities of 1%, 3%, 5% and 7%, depend on the asset correlation. At -100% correlation, the joint default probability tends to zero. At zero

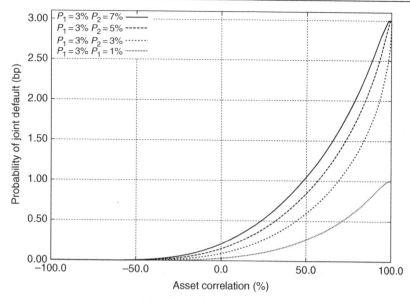

Figure 13.2 The joint default probability as a function of the asset correlation. We consider four examples of different pairs of issuer default probabilites

correlation, the joint default probability equals the product of the individual default probabilities. In the limit of 100% correlation, we see that the joint probability equals the minimum of the two issuer default probabilities.

13.3.2 Conditional Hazard Rates

We can also think about the dependency of the latent variable model in terms of the distribution of *conditional hazard rates*. We recall that credit i defaults before time T if

$$A_i = \beta_i Z + \sqrt{1 - \beta_i^2}\, \varepsilon_i < C_i(T).$$

Rearranging, this condition can be written as

$$\varepsilon_i < \frac{C_i(T) - \beta_i Z}{\sqrt{1 - \beta_i^2}}.$$

Since $\varepsilon_i \sim N(0, 1)$, conditional on the realisation of the random market factor Z, the probability of issuer i defaulting before time T is given by

$$p_i(T|Z) = 1 - Q_i(T|Z) = \Phi\left(\frac{C_i(T) - \beta_i Z}{\sqrt{1 - \beta_i^2}}\right).$$

Assuming for simplicity a flat and deterministic conditional hazard rate, i.e. $Q_i(T|Z) = \exp(-\lambda_i(T|Z)T)$, we have

$$\lambda_i(T|Z) = -\frac{1}{T} \ln \Phi\left(\frac{\beta_i Z - C_i(T)}{\sqrt{1 - \beta_i^2}}\right).$$

For each value of Z there is a corresponding value of $\lambda_i(T|Z)$. This tells us that the Gaussian latent variable model implies a distribution of conditional hazard rates. Figure 13.3 shows the conditional hazard rate distribution for three values of β.

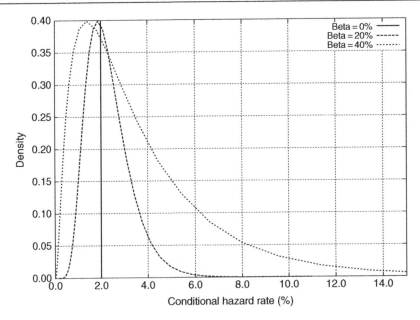

Figure 13.3 Plot showing the conditional hazard rate distribution for $\beta = 0, 0.2, 0.4$. We assume an unconditional hazard rate of 2% and a one-year horizon

It is clear that the variance of the distribution is driven by the value of β. If β is high, we find that the variance of the distribution of $\lambda_i(T|Z)$ is large and scenarios with very high and very low values of $\lambda_i(T|Z)$ become more probable. Low realisations of $\lambda_i(T|Z)$ imply that a lot of credits survive together. High realisations of $\lambda_i(T|Z)$ imply that a lot of credits default together. These two scenarios therefore represent a high correlation environment. As the value of β falls, the variance in the distribution of $\lambda_i(T|Z)$ falls. If $\beta = 0$, the distribution of $\lambda_i(T|Z)$ is a single point mass on the unconditional hazard rate

$$\lambda_i(T|Z) = \lambda_i(T).$$

In this case there is no correlation between the credits, they are independent.

13.4   CONDITIONAL INDEPENDENCE

The major advantage of assuming a one-factor correlation structure is that we can use conditional independence to speed up the calculation of the portfolio loss distribution. The portfolio loss distribution is required in order to price most correlation products. If we condition on the one common factor Z, all of the credits in the portfolio are independent and calculation of the conditional portfolio loss distribution is greatly simplified. Once we have the conditional loss distribution for each value of the market factor, we can calculate the unconditional loss distribution by integrating over the density of the market factor. If we denote the density of the loss distribution with $f(L(T))$ and that of the conditional loss distribution with $f(L(T)|Z)$, we have

$$f(L(T)) = \int_{-\infty}^{+\infty} f(L(T)|Z)\phi(Z)dZ.$$

The conditional loss distribution $f(L(T)|Z)$ is easy to compute as the credits are conditionally independent. Conditional on Z, the default probability of credit i was shown in the previous section to be given by

$$p_i(T|Z) = \Phi\left(\frac{C_i(T) - \beta_i Z}{\sqrt{1 - \beta_i^2}}\right).$$

If the portfolio is homogeneous so that $p_i(T|Z) = p(T|Z)$, and all credits share the same recovery rate R, the conditional loss distribution is simply the binomial distribution, i.e.

$$f(L(T)|Z) = \Pr\left(L(T) = \frac{n(1 - R)}{N}|Z\right) = \frac{N!}{n!(N - n)!}\,p(T|Z)^n\,(1 - p(T|Z))^{N-n}.$$

Example Figure 13.4 shows the conditional loss distribution of a homogeneous independent portfolio of $N_C = 100$ credits. We have assumed an *unconditional* default probability of 4%. We show the conditional loss distribution for different values of Z. When $Z = -1$, the conditional default probability is approximately 7.4% and the expected loss is close to 4.4%. When $Z = +1$, the conditional default probability is small at 0.47% and the conditional loss distribution has almost all of its mass on the zero loss and one loss points.

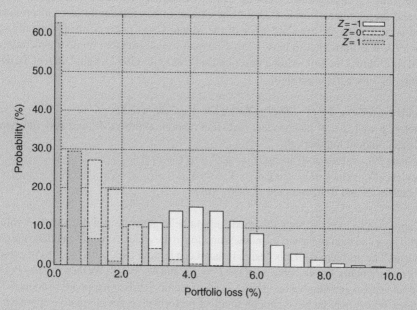

Figure 13.4 Plot showing the conditional loss distribution for $Z = -1, 0, 1$. We assume 100 credits in the portfolio, $\beta = 50\%$, $R = 40\%$ and an unconditional default probability of 4%

It is clear that although the binomial distribution is simple, it can assume a range of shapes. In Chapter 18 we will set out a number of extremely efficient algorithms used to calculate the full loss distribution for a portfolio of independent heterogeneous credits.

13.5 SIMULATING MULTI-NAME DEFAULT

One of the main benefits of the one-factor Gaussian latent variable model is that we can use conditional independence to speed up the numerical calculation of the portfolio loss distribution. Despite this, in some cases, most notably second-to-default and higher inhomogeneous loss baskets, it may be preferable to have a Monte Carlo implementation. This will be discussed in more detail in later chapters. Our aim here is to simply demonstrate how this model can be simulated.

Although the Monte Carlo approach that will be described below does not exploit conditional independence, we will show that it is much easier and faster to draw random numbers from a one-dimensional correlation structure than from a generic correlation structure. The one-factor approach also makes it easier to employ some importance sampling approaches.

We can price a security whose value is a function of the joint distribution of default times via Monte Carlo using the formula

$$V = \lim_{p \to \infty} \frac{1}{P} \sum_{p=1}^{P} V_p(\{\tau^p\})$$

where P is the number of random trials and $V_p(\{\tau^p\})$ is the present value of the security as a function of the vector of default times in trial p of the Monte Carlo simulation. The realisations of default times $\{\tau^p\}$ are drawn from the joint distribution of default times implied by the model, and the number of trials P should be chosen to be sufficiently large to provide the required accuracy. As the standard error of the Monte Carlo price estimate typically scales as $O(1/\sqrt{P})$, it is important to have a fast Gaussian pseudo-random number generator. One standard algorithm is the Box–Muller described in Press *et al.* (1992). Simulation of the default times uses the following algorithm:

1. Calculate $C_i(T) = \Phi^{-1}(1 - Q_i(T))$ for all $i = 1, \ldots, N_C$ credits.
2. Generate $p = 1, \ldots, P$ independent Gaussian random numbers Z^p, and PN_C independent Gaussian random numbers ε_i^p.
3. Calculate PN_C values of A_i^p using $A_i^p = \beta_i Z^p + \sqrt{1 - \beta_i^2} \varepsilon_i^p$.
4. Calculate PN_C values of u_i^p using $u_i^p = 1 - \Phi(A_i^p)$.
5. For each asset and trial, compute $\tau_i^p = Q_i^{-1}(u_i^p)$.

One approach to implementing this model might be to generate and store all $N_C P$ values at the start. These can then be passed to another function in the code in order to calculate the payoff in each trial. The problem with this design is that it can be very expensive in terms of computer memory requirements. For example, suppose $P = 10^6$ and $N_C = 10^2$. We then have $N_C P = 10^8$. With a double precision number requiring 8 bytes of memory, this corresponds to about 0.78GB of memory, which may be large enough to affect performance. An alternative approach is to simply draw the default times one trial at a time and then calculate the corresponding payoff. As all of the random draws are independent, this is easy. It then means that very large numbers of paths can be run for very large portfolios without hitting any computer memory limits.

Another potential source of inefficiency can be found in step (5) of the algorithm in which we map the uniform deviate u to a default time τ by inverting the survival curve according to $\tau = Q^{-1}(u)$. This is shown pictorially in Figure 13.5. One approach is to invert Q by performing a search, using the knowledge that $Q^{-1}(u)$ is a monotonically decreasing function

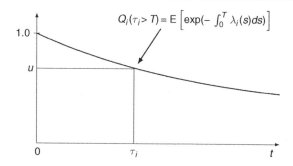

Figure 13.5 The random default time τ_i is linked to the realisation of the random asset value via $u = \Phi(-A_i) = Q(\tau_i)$

of u. However, this can be slow. It can be made faster if we know what algorithm we are using for the interpolation of the survival curve. For example, if we are using the piecewise flat forward default rate approach proposed in Chapter 7, we know that

$$u = \exp\left(-\frac{(t_i - \tau)(-\ln Q(t_{i-1})) + (\tau - t_{i-1})(-\ln Q(t_i))}{(t_i - t_{i-1})}\right)$$

where t_{i-1} and t_i are the two times on the survival curve skeleton which bracket default time τ. $Q(t_{i-1})$ and $Q(t_i)$ are their corresponding skeleton survival probabilities. We can then invert this equation to give

$$\tau = \frac{t_{i-1} \ln\left[Q(t_i)/u\right] + t_i \ln\left[u/Q(t_{i-1})\right]}{\ln\left[Q(t_i)/Q(t_{i-1})\right]}.$$

13.5.1 Using Antithetic Variables

The main problem with a Monte Carlo pricing approach is the statistical error due to the fact that the number of paths P is finite. The simplest way to reduce the statistical error is to increase P. However, while the computation time is linear in P, the standard error in the pricing estimate only falls as $1/\sqrt{P}$. An increase in accuracy therefore necessitates a longer calculation time. There are, however, a range of variance reduction tricks that can be adopted.

One approach is to use antithetic variables. In the case of the algorithm above, this means an extra step in which we note that the symmetry of the Gaussian distribution means that the probability of the asset value equalling A_i is the same as the probability of the asset value equalling $-A_i$. However, we also need to ensure that the dependency structure is preserved. Since A_i is correlated to all of the other credits in the portfolio, we must therefore flip the sign of the value of A_i for every credit. The step is simply:

5. Compute the antithetic default times $\hat{\tau}_i^p$ by solving $\hat{\tau}_i^p = Q_i^{-1}(1 - u_i^p)$ for all $i = 1, \ldots, N_C$.

The advantage here is that we generate two sets of default times for each draw of A_i for $i = 1, \ldots, N$. Also, if one default time is low, its antithetic will tend to be large, so that overall, we increase the likelihood of one of the default times occurring within the lifetime of the deal being priced.

13.5.2 Importance Sampling

Another variance reduction approach is to do importance sampling. Suppose that the product has a payoff function $\Theta(L(T))$ where $L(T)$ is the portfolio loss at time T given by

$$L(T) = \frac{1}{N_C} \sum_{i=1}^{N_C} \mathbf{1}_{\tau_i \leq T} \cdot (1 - R_i).$$

We can write the expected value of the time T payoff as

$$V = \mathbb{E}\left[\Theta\left(L(T)\right)\right].$$

Suppose that

$$\Theta(x) = \begin{cases} (x - K) & \text{if } x \geq K, \\ 0 & \text{otherwise.} \end{cases}$$

If we perform this integration using Monte Carlo techniques by simulating default times, we may find the portfolio loss only exceeds K in a very small fraction of the default time realisations.

Example   Consider an STCDO with 100 independent credits in the portfolio each with a 5% default probability, and suppose that the subordination of the tranche is removed after 10 or more defaults. This is consistent with a 6% subordination level. The probability of this occurring is approximately 1.147%. This means that a naïve Monte Carlo simulation will only find a non-zero payoff in about one out of every 100 paths.

An alternative approach is to exploit the one-factor correlation structure of the model. First, we can write V in terms of the conditional loss distribution $L(T|Z)$

$$V = \frac{1}{\sqrt{2\pi}} \int_{-\infty}^{\infty} \Theta(L(T|Z)) \exp(-Z^2/2) dZ.$$

Known as importance sampling, the idea is that by shifting the mean of the distribution of Z to make it negative, we can change the mean of the conditional loss distribution to make defaults more likely. This will increase the value of $L(T|Z)$ and so give more non-zero realisations of Θ. This will then be offset by a change in the density of the distribution which is analytic and so does not introduce any Monte Carlo error. Overall, we reduce the standard error of our pricing estimate. To show how to do this, we make the following change of variable

$$\hat{Z} = Z + \mu$$

and so we have

$$V = \frac{1}{\sqrt{2\pi}} \int_{-\infty}^{\infty} \exp(-Z^2/2) \Theta(L(T|\hat{Z})) \exp\left(\mu^2/2 - \mu\hat{Z}\right) dZ.$$

The new Monte Carlo algorithm is then as follows:

1. Draw a random Gaussian deviate Z_p from a standard $N(0, 1)$ distribution.
2. Calculate $\hat{Z}_p = Z_p + \mu$.
3. Calculate default times using the algorithm described earlier and using these, calculate $L(T|\hat{Z}_p)$ and the corresponding payoff $\Theta(L(T|\hat{Z}_p))$.
4. Multiply the payoff by the *likelihood ratio* $\exp(\mu^2/2 - \mu\hat{Z}_p)$ to give $\hat{\Theta}(L(T)|\hat{Z}_p)$.
5. Repeat until P trials have been performed and calculate $V = \frac{1}{P}\sum_{p=1}^{P}\hat{\Theta}(L(T|Z_p)$.

We will demonstrate the use of this variance reduction methodology in Section 15.4.1 where we use it to price default baskets.

Making the value of μ negative makes the probability of a large number of defaults more likely. The optimal value μ^* is the value which minimises the standard error of the price. This is a function of the payoff but is not always easy to determine. For a discussion of possible methods for determining μ^*, see Joshi and Kainth (2003) and Joshi (2005). Another important reference on variance reduction methods is Glasserman (2004).

13.5.3   Limitations of the One-factor Correlation Structure

The use of a one-factor model reduces the richness of the allowed correlation structure. One way to quantify this restriction is to count the number of inputs used to describe the correlation structure. In the one-factor model we have N_C correlation parameters β_i, each constrained so that $|\beta_i| \leq 1$. In the case of a full correlation matrix, we have $N_C(N_C - 1)/2$ correlation parameters, also with the requirement that each pairwise correlation $|c_{ij}| \leq 1$. There is also the requirement that the correlation matrix be positive semi-definite. When the number of credits in the portfolio is large, a general correlation matrix has roughly $N_C/2$ times as many parameters as the one-factor structure.

An important question to ask is to what extent a one-factor correlation structure limits the ability of the model to capture the default dependency within a portfolio of credits. For example, does the one-factor structure prevent us from modelling 'sectors', i.e. different groups of credits in the portfolio which have a strong positive correlation within the sector but have a much lower or even negative correlation between sectors.

To examine this, we consider a simple portfolio of four credits grouped into two sectors A and B with $\beta_1 = \beta_2 = \beta_a$ and $\beta_3 = \beta_4 = \beta_b$. The correlation matrix is given by

$$C = \begin{array}{c} \\ \\ \end{array}\begin{pmatrix} \overset{\text{Sector A}}{\begin{array}{cc} 1 & \beta_a^2 \\ \beta_a^2 & 1 \\ \beta_a\beta_b & \beta_a\beta_b \\ \beta_a\beta_b & \beta_a\beta_b \end{array}} & \overset{\text{Sector B}}{\begin{array}{cc} \beta_a\beta_b & \beta_a\beta_b \\ \beta_a\beta_b & \beta_a\beta_b \\ 1 & \beta_b^2 \\ \beta_b^2 & 1 \end{array}} \end{pmatrix}$$

Without loss of generality, suppose that $\beta_a \geq \beta_b > 0$. This implies that $\beta_a^2 \geq \beta_a\beta_b \geq \beta_b^2$. The consequence is that the magnitude of the correlation between the sectors A and B is determined fully by the values of β_a and β_b. The correlation between sectors is constrained to be between the inter-sector correlations of A and B. Consider an example.

Example We show an example correlation matrix below.

$$
C = \begin{array}{c} \\ \end{array}
\begin{array}{cc}
\overbrace{\hspace{4em}}^{\text{Sector A}} & \overbrace{\hspace{4em}}^{\text{Sector B}}
\end{array}
\left(
\begin{array}{cc|cc}
100\% & 64\% & 40\% & 40\% \\
64\% & 100\% & 40\% & 40\% \\
\hline
40\% & 40\% & 100\% & 25\% \\
40\% & 40\% & 25\% & 100\%
\end{array}
\right)
$$

We have set $\beta_a = 0.8$ and $\beta_b = 0.5$. We see that the inter-sector correlation of 40% is higher than the sector B correlation of 25%. As a result, sector B is not really captured. The exact same matrix occurs if $\beta_a = -0.8$ and $\beta_b = -0.5$.

We can only conclude that if β_a and β_b both have the same sign, we cannot have sectors since the intra-sector correlation for sector B, β_b^2, will always be lower than the positive correlation $\beta_a \beta_b$ between sectors A and B.

Let us now consider a two-factor version of this model to see if this changes our ability to model sectors. The asset return equations for credits i and j become

$$
A_i = \beta_{1i} Z_1 + \beta_{2i} Z_2 + \sqrt{1 - \beta_{1i}^2 - \beta_{2i}^2}\, \varepsilon_i
$$
$$
A_j = \beta_{1j} Z_1 + \beta_{2j} Z_2 + \sqrt{1 - \beta_{1j}^2 - \beta_{2j}^2}\, \varepsilon_j
$$

and the correlation matrix is given by

$$
c_{ij} = \beta_{1i}\beta_{1j} + \beta_{2i}\beta_{2j}.
$$

Suppose that we revisit the case of four credits grouped into two in each sector. Now we have two parameters for each sector. In sector A, the credits have a first factor weight β_{1a} and second factor weight β_{2a}. In sector B, the credits have a first factor weight β_{1b} and second factor weight β_{2b}. Now we have a correlation matrix of the form

$$
C = \begin{array}{c}\\ \end{array}
\begin{array}{cc}
\overbrace{\hspace{10em}}^{\text{Sector A}} & \overbrace{\hspace{12em}}^{\text{Sector B}}
\end{array}
\left(
\begin{array}{cc|cc}
1 & \beta_{1a}^2 + \beta_{2a}^2 & \beta_{1a}\beta_{1b} + \beta_{2a}\beta_{2b} & \beta_{1a}\beta_{1b} + \beta_{2a}\beta_{2b} \\
\beta_{1a}^2 + \beta_{2a}^2 & 1 & \beta_{1a}\beta_{1b} + \beta_{2a}\beta_{2b} & \beta_{1a}\beta_{1b} + \beta_{2a}\beta_{2b} \\
\hline
\beta_{1a}\beta_{1b} + \beta_{2a}\beta_{2b} & \beta_{1a}\beta_{1b} + \beta_{2a}\beta_{2b} & 1 & \beta_{1b}^2 + \beta_{2b}^2 \\
\beta_{1a}\beta_{1b} + \beta_{2a}\beta_{2b} & \beta_{1a}\beta_{1b} + \beta_{2a}\beta_{2b} & \beta_{1b}^2 + \beta_{2b}^2 & 1
\end{array}
\right)
$$

Example   Let us now try to create a realistic correlation matrix using a two-factor model. Suppose that all four credits are equally correlated to the first factor Z_1 so that $\beta_{1a} = \beta_{1b} = 0.6$. Then suppose that the credits in sector A are negative correlated to the second factor Z_2 so that $\beta_{2a} = -0.4$ while the credits in sector B are positively correlated to this second factor so that $\beta_{2b} = 0.5$. The correlation matrix is shown below.

$$
\begin{array}{cc}
\quad\text{Sector A} & \quad\text{Sector B}
\end{array}
$$

$$
C = \left(
\begin{array}{cc|cc}
100\% & 52\% & 16\% & 16\% \\[2mm]
52\% & 52\% & 16\% & 16\% \\[2mm]
\hline
16\% & 16\% & 100\% & 61\% \\[2mm]
16\% & 16\% & 61\% & 100\%
\end{array}
\right)
$$

We see that there is a strong positive correlation within each of sectors A and B and that there is a lower positive correlation between sectors.

This is exactly the sort of correlation structure that we require if we are to capture the effect of sectors. However, a two-factor model is not going to be able to model three sectors. For that we need to go to a three-factor model. What we conclude is that we need M factors if we are to model an M-sector portfolio.

We conclude that a one-factor latent variable model is not able to model the correlation structure of a portfolio consisting of credits which exhibit sectors, and that modelling a portfolio consisting of M sectors requires an M-factor model. In mitigation, we note that this may not be as significant a problem as we might expect because:

- The price of most portfolio credit derivatives depends to first order on the average correlation level rather than the correlation factor structure.
- While we would expect that sectors do exist, in practice, much of the positive correlation between credits in different sectors is due to global or national economic factors. The sector level contribution to the correlation may only be a small part of the overall correlation.

Later we will see that the market for implied correlation does not provide enough data for us to be able to imply out correlations at a sector level. In this case market practice is to assume a flat correlation structure, i.e. $c_{ij} = \rho$ for $i \neq j$.

13.6   DEFAULT INDUCED SPREAD DYNAMICS

Within the latent variable framework, there are no explicit spread dynamics. The only events that we can observe are the defaults of credits. This does not mean that there are no spread dynamics at all. A credit does have spread dynamics *but only when we condition on the default and survival behaviour of the other credits to which this credit is correlated.* For example, consider two credits A and B. If credit A defaults at future time t and it has a non-zero asset correlation with credit B, then we would expect this default to have an impact on the conditional default probability of credit B and so B's credit spread should change. This is shown in Figure 13.6.

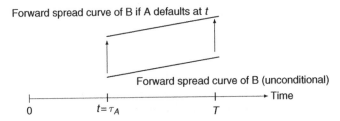

Figure 13.6   If we condition on the default of credit A at time $t = \tau_A$, the forward spread curve of B will be shifted relative to the unconditional forward spread curve of B

We can actually calculate the new spread for credit B if credit A defaults at a future time $t = \tau_A$. We do this for a CDS contract which starts at time t and matures at time T. We denote the default time for credit B as τ_B. If we condition on the fact that credit A defaults at time t then the default time distribution for credit B will change. Specifically, we wish to calculate the forward survival curve for credit B *conditional on default of credit A at time t*. This is defined as

$$\hat{Q}_B(t,T) = 1 - \Pr(\tau_B \leq T | \tau_A = t, \tau_B > t)$$

where $T > t$. This is different from the forward starting survival curve of credit B given by

$$Q_B(t,T) = 1 - \Pr(\tau_B \leq T | \tau_B > t) = 1 - \frac{\Pr(t < \tau_B \leq T)}{\Pr(\tau_B > t)}$$

$$= 1 - \frac{(\Phi(C_B(T)) - \Phi(C_B(t)))}{1 - \Phi(C_B(t))}.$$

We return to the conditional forward default curve $\hat{Q}_B(t,T)$. This can be written as

$$\hat{Q}_B(t,T) = 1 - \frac{\Pr(t < \tau_B \leq T | \tau_A = t)}{\Pr(\tau_B > t | \tau_A = t)}. \tag{13.3}$$

According to the one-factor latent variable model

$$\Pr(\tau_A \leq T_1, \tau_B \leq T_2) = \Phi_2(C_A(T_1), C_B(T_2), \rho)$$

where $\rho = \beta_A \beta_B$ and

$$C_A(T_1) = \Phi^{-1}(1 - Q_A(0, T_1)) \quad \text{and} \quad C_B(T_2) = \Phi^{-1}(1 - Q_B(0, T_2)).$$

We define latent variables $A_A = \beta_A Z + \sqrt{1 - \beta_A^2}\,\varepsilon_A$ and $A_B = \beta_B Z + \sqrt{1 - \beta_B^2}\,\varepsilon_B$. Without loss of generality we can write $\beta_A = 1$ and $\beta_B = \rho$ so that $A_A = Z$ and $A_B = \rho Z + \sqrt{1 - \rho^2}\,\varepsilon_B$. Imposing the condition that $\tau_A = t$ then involves setting $A_A = C_A(t)$. We can therefore determine the probability of τ_B being in a certain range conditional on $\tau_A = t$ by integrating over the density of A_B as follows

$$\frac{\Pr(t < \tau_B \le T|\tau_A = t)}{\Pr(\tau_B > t|\tau_A = t)} = \frac{\int_{C_B(t)}^{C_B(T)} \phi\left(x; \rho C_A(t), \sqrt{1-\rho^2}\right) dx}{\int_{C_B(t)}^{\infty} \phi\left(x; \rho C_A(t), \sqrt{1-\rho^2}\right) dx}$$

where $\phi(x; m, \sigma)$ is the density of a Gaussian distribution with mean m and standard deviation σ. We can write these integrals in terms of the cumulative distribution function of the Gaussian distribution, and substituting into Equation 13.3 gives a conditional survival curve for credit B

$$\hat{Q}_B(t, T) = 1 - \frac{\Phi\left(\frac{C_B(T) - \rho C_A(t)}{\sqrt{1-\rho^2}}\right) - \Phi\left(\frac{C_B(t) - \rho C_A(t)}{\sqrt{1-\rho^2}}\right)}{1 - \Phi\left(\frac{C_B(t) - \rho C_A(t)}{\sqrt{1-\rho^2}}\right)}.$$

If $\rho = 0$, it is straightforward to show that $\hat{Q}_B(t, T) = Q_B(t, T)$, i.e. the forward survival curve for credit B conditioning on the default of credit A at time t is exactly the same as the forward survival curve which does not condition on the default of credit A. This makes sense, if there is no correlation between A and B, the spread curve of credit B should not change after a default of credit A.

We have calculated values of the 5Y spread for credit B after a default of credit A. We assume that the initial credit curve for A is flat at 60 bp and the credit curve for B is flat at 120 bp. The results are shown in Figure 13.7 in which we have plotted the 5Y maturity CDS

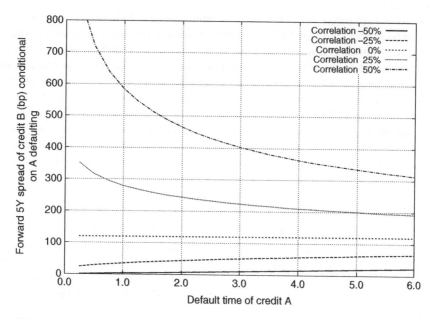

Figure 13.7 Forward 5Y spread curve conditional on a default of credit A at time t as a function of t. We show this for asset correlations $\rho = \beta^2$ of -50%, -25%, 0%, 25% and 50%

spread as a function of the future time at which credit A defaults. We make the following observations:

- When the correlation is zero, the conditional spread curve of credit B after default is flat at 120 bp. It is the same as the unconditional forward spread curve.
- When the correlation is positive, the conditional spread curve jumps up. The size of the jump increases with correlation.
- When the correlation is negative, the conditional spread curve jumps down. The magnitude of the downward jump increases as the correlation becomes more negative.
- The size of the spread jump declines with $t = \tau_A$, i.e. how far in the future credit A defaults. There is no reason why this should be the case. This behaviour occurs as a result of the non-stationary behaviour of the Gaussian latent variable model.

We now consider what time stationarity means in the context of default correlation models.

13.6.1 Time Stationary Models

It is worth spending a moment to consider the issue of *time stationary* correlation models. Time stationarity means that the price of some forward starting fixed tenor product whose payoff depends on the probability of a future joint default and which only exists conditional on surviving to the forward start date, should not depend upon the time to the forward start date if the interest rate and credit curves are flat and the model parameters are constant through time. The problem of a model which is not time-stationary is that it implies a non-flat term structure of default co-dependence which has implications for the pricing and hence the hedging of correlation products.

The non-stationary behaviour of the latent variable model, and Gaussian copula models in general, can be attributed to their lack of any true dynamics. The fact that the default times of all the credits are known at time 0 if the A_i are known means that correlating the A_i together to produce correlated default can lead to some unrealistic effects. It suggests that when we have products to price whose value depends in any important way on the term structure of default correlation, we should be careful when using the Gaussian copula model to ensure that the term structure of default is realistic. However, it is hard to eliminate this time dependence without creating other problems. The approach of incorporating a term structure of correlation into the model by making the correlation maturity-dependent, i.e. $\rho = \rho(T)$ can create problems as it means that the model is no longer guaranteed to be arbitrage free in the time dimension.

13.6.2 The Gaussian Copula and Default Clustering

One empirically observed feature of the credit markets is default clustering. This occurs when groups of credits with different current credit qualities default within some short future time period. When this has happened in the past, it has typically been due to some pre-existing link, e.g. they belong to a common industrial sector. A classic example of default clustering is the 1970 default of Penn Central Railroad which was then followed by the default of 25 of its affiliates.

Our question is whether a Gaussian latent variable model can capture this sort of phenomenon. To answer this question we consider two credits with deterministic flat hazard rates

λ_1 and λ_2. The properties of a Poisson process tell us that the average default time of each credit is given by

$$\mathbb{E}[\tau_1] = \frac{1}{\lambda_1} \quad \text{and} \quad \mathbb{E}[\tau_2] = \frac{1}{\lambda_2}.$$

As we are interested in default clustering, we wish to know the joint distribution of default times. We could determine this by simulation. We can simulate default times for issuers i and j according to

$$\tau_1 = -\frac{\ln \Phi(-A_1)}{\lambda_1} \quad \text{and} \quad \tau_2 = -\frac{\ln \Phi(-A_2)}{\lambda_2}$$

where A_1 and A_2 are correlated random draws from a bivariate Gaussian distribution. In the limit of maximum correlation when we would expect default clustering to be greatest, we have $A_1 = A_2$ and it is possible to write a fixed relationship between the ratio of the default times

$$\frac{\tau_1}{\tau_2} = \frac{\lambda_2}{\lambda_1}.$$

This tells us that in the limit of maximum correlation, the ratio of the default times is the inverse ratio of their hazard rates. For example, if $\lambda_2 = 2\lambda_1$ then $\tau_1 = 2\tau_2$. This is a somewhat strange result since it suggests that if credits 1 and 2 are maximally dependent they do not default together, but at default times which are a fixed ratio to each other. For example, if $\tau_2 = 5$ years then $\tau_2 = 10$ years. This implies that company 2 'remembers' the default of company 1 for five years and only then does it default. This does not seem realistic. Default clustering, meaning that $\tau_1 \simeq \tau_2$, only occurs if both credits have a very high correlation *and* have similar hazard rates, i.e. $\lambda_1 \simeq \lambda_2$.

13.7   CALIBRATING THE CORRELATION

The calibration of correlation models to empirical data is a challenging task for a number of reasons. For a start, default is a rare event so that the quantity of historical data is small. Also, default is a one-time event, so we can only calibrate the default correlation of an asset by referring it to some similar proxy asset, e.g. by looking at the default correlation of defaulted credits within the same sector or with the same rating and country. Calibrating our model directly to historic default correlation is therefore hard.

Despite these problems, we need to start somewhere. Within the latent variable model, we need a way to calibrate the asset correlation by associating the A_i with some observable. Because A_i is a latent variable there is no obvious observable that we can use. However, there is an approach we can use based on the idea of relating the A_i to a structural model of default.

In Hull *et al.* (2005), it was demonstrated that subject to assumptions a Merton-style asset diffusion model and a Gaussian latent variable model both produce very similar pairwise default probabilities if we use the same correlation between the different asset processes as we use for the Gaussian latent variable asset correlation. In terms of pricing, it was shown that the pricing difference between a one-factor latent variable model and the fully dynamic model for a range of STCDOs was close enough to recommend the one-factor latent variable model as a good approximation to the full dynamic model.

The conclusions of this analysis are positive for two reasons. First, we can be reassured that for spot starting CDO products, the pricing of a Gaussian latent variable model is reasonably close to that of a model with true dynamics. Second, we can use the link to the Merton model to argue that the asset correlation of the latent variable model can be linked to the correlation of equities prices. Merton showed that the time t value of the equity of firm i, which we denote with $E_i(t)$ can be expressed as a call option on the firm asset value

$$E_i(t) = C_E(V_i(t), \ldots)$$

where $V_i(t)$ is the asset value of firm i at time t. The change in the equity price for a change in $V_i(t)$ can be calculated in terms of the delta of the call option, $\Delta_i(t)$,

$$dE_i(t) \simeq \frac{\partial C_E(t)}{\partial V_i(t)} dV_i(t) = \Delta_i(t) dV_i(t).$$

If we calculate the correlation of the returns over a small time period, we can assume that the option delta is constant, and so the correlation of the equity returns is given by

$$\mathrm{Corr}\left(\frac{dE_i}{E_i}, \frac{dE_j}{E_j}\right) \simeq \mathrm{Corr}\left(\frac{dV_i}{V_i}, \frac{dV_j}{V_j}\right).$$

Since the latent variable A_i has a Gaussian distribution about a mean zero, we can think of it as an 'asset return' rather than an asset value. This suggests that the correlation of equity returns can be used as a proxy for the correlation of the latent variables A_i and A_j. This is a very useful result since equity data is easy to obtain and is updated regularly. Also, equity coverage is very broad – most companies who issue debt also issue equity. Problems arise with this approach when we need to include sovereigns and there are a number of workarounds, one being to use the main stock index of that country as a proxy for its stock price.

Once we have the equity correlation matrix C_{ij}, we then need to map it onto the one-factor correlation matrix $\beta_i \beta_j$. One approach is to set up a quadratic optimisation problem with an objective function which minimises the distance between the observed correlation matrix and the one-factor matrix as follows

$$\text{Objective function}(\{\beta\}) = \sum_{i=1}^{N} \sum_{j=1}^{i-1} \left(C_{ij} - \beta_i \beta_j\right)^2$$

with the constraint $\beta_i^2 < 1$. This is an N-dimensional optimisation where N is the number of credits in the portfolio and should be reasonably fast to compute. An alternative iterative scheme for performing a factor reduction of a correlation matrix is given in Andersen et al. (2003).

13.8 SUMMARY

The Gaussian latent variable model is a simple model which can be easily calibrated to the term structure of issuer survival probabilities. It allows us to vary the degree of dependence between credits going from minimum to maximum dependence by varying the asset correlation from -100% to $+100\%$. In addition, the one-factor version of the model allows for very fast numerical computation of the portfolio loss distribution through the use of conditional independence. A one-factor model limits the richness of the correlation structure, especially in terms of capturing the effect of sectors. However, it remains to be seen whether this has a significant effect on pricing. The latent variable model does not imply explicit spread dynamics in the absence of default. However, if we condition on the default of a credit, we find that it implies a jump in the implied credit spread of other credits to which the defaulted credit is correlated.

Finally, it has been shown that a latent variable model produces similar prices for STCDO tranches when compared to a dynamic asset diffusion model using the same value for the correlation parameter. This link makes it possible to argue that we can proxy the asset correlation with the correlation of equity price changes.

14
Modelling Default Times using Copulas

14.1 INTRODUCTION

The first application of copula methods to the modelling of credit derivatives was by Li (2000) who applied the Gaussian copula to the pricing of default baskets. In its one-factor version, the Gaussian copula model is equivalent to the one-factor Gaussian latent variable model discussed in the previous chapter. However, what is important about the copula framework is that it provides greater flexibility for modelling default dependency than the latent variable approach and is therefore why we now consider the copula approach in detail.

A copula is a mathematical tool for defining associations between different random variables. Formally, it is a mechanism which links uni-variate marginals to a full multi-variate distribution. Since it does this by separating the choice of uni-variate marginal from the choice of multi-variate marginal, it provides more flexibility than simply specifying one multi-variate distribution.

Because it separates the choice of marginal distribution from the choice of the multi-variate distribution, it is especially suited to the modelling of credit correlation products. This is because the marginal distributions are defined by the single-name survival curve which is determined by calibrating to the CDS market. This leaves us free to choose whichever joint default distribution we desire to capture the joint default behaviour of the credits in the portfolio.

In this chapter, we begin by formally defining a copula and then show how it is used in the context of modelling the default time dependency of a portfolio of credits. We then discuss linear correlation as a measure of dependency and explain why it is not always appropriate. This leads us to introduce the concepts of rank correlation and tail dependency. We then set out the main copulas which have been used within credit modelling, and discuss how these may be implemented and used in practice. We conclude with a discussion of the Monte Carlo pricing of correlation products.

14.2 DEFINITION AND PROPERTIES OF A COPULA

We first define the properties of a copula C. For each property we then describe the meaning of each property within the context of a copula of default times.

1. An N-dimensional copula function C is a multi-variate cumulative distribution function with N uniform marginals with probabilities $u_1, u_2, \ldots, u_N$. We can write the copula as

$$\Pr(\hat{u}_1 \leq u_1, \hat{u}_2 \leq u_2, \ldots, \hat{u}_n \leq u_N) = C(u_1, u_2, \ldots, u_N) \tag{14.1}$$

where the $\hat{u}$ represent random draws from a uniform distribution. *We can model the dependence structure of the default times of N credits using a copula C. Defining $u_i = 1 - Q_i(t_i)$ to be the probability of credit i defaulting before time t_i, we have*

$$C(u_1(t_1), u_2(t_2), \ldots, u_N(t_N)) = \Pr(\tau_1 \le t_1, \tau_2 \le t_2, \ldots, \tau_n \le t_N)$$

where the copula is telling us the joint default probability for the credits to default before times $t_1, t_2, \ldots, t_N$. This copula is known as the default copula.

2. As cumulative distribution functions are increasing, the copula is increasing for an increase in any of $u_1, \ldots, u_N$. *If we increase the default probability of any one credit, we increase the joint default probability.*

3. The copula function can be reduced to the marginal distribution u_k by setting $u_i = 1$ for all $i \ne k$. *If all of the credits have a 100% default probability except credit k, then the probability that they all default is simply the probability that credit k defaults.*

4. The copula function is zero if any element $u_i = 0$. *If any of the credits have a 0% default probability then the probability that they all default is zero.*

5. The dimensionality of the copula can be reduced from N to $N - 1$ simply by setting one of the $u_i = 1$. The result is still a copula as long as the dimensionality $N \ge 2$. As a result, the many properties of copulas can be understood simply by studying the $N = 2$ case.

14.2.1 Dependency Limits

There are a number of limiting dependence cases which we wish to consider:

- Independence: In the case of independence, we have

$$C(u_1, u_2, \ldots, u_N) = u_1 u_2 \ldots u_N = \prod_{i=1}^{N} u_i.$$

In a default copula context, this says the probability that all of the credits default if they are independent is simply the product of all N default probabilities. This is known as the *independence copula*.

- Perfect positive dependence: In the case of perfect positive dependence, the *Fréchet–Hoeffding upper bound* is given by

$$C(u_1, u_2, \ldots, u_N) = \min(u_1, u_2, \ldots, u_N).$$

This is the case of maximum dependence in which default of the all of the N credits is triggered by default of the credit with the lowest default probability.

- Perfect negative dependence: In the case of perfect negative dependency, we have the lower *Fréchet–Hoeffding bound* which is given by

$$C(u_1, u_2, \ldots, u_N) = \max\left[\sum_{i=1}^{N} u_i + 1 - N, 0\right].$$

For $N > 2$, perfect negative dependence is not a meaningful bound. For example, it is not possible to have three credits with perfect negative dependence since this means that default of one always means survival of the other two, and this must be true simultaneously for all three credits. In this limit, the copula function no longer satisfies the requirements of a copula. The *Fréchet–Hoeffding bound* is simply a mathematical limit.

14.2.2   Sklar's Theorem

The definition of a copula in Equation 14.1 shows that the copula is simply a multi-variate distribution function. However, what Sklar (1959) showed is that the opposite is also true. He showed that any multi-variate distribution function can be written as a copula and that this copula representation is unique if the marginal distributions are continuous.

We can write any N-dimensional distribution function H with marginal distributions $F_1, \ldots, F_N$ for random variables $X_1, \ldots, X_N$ as

$$H(x_1, x_2, \ldots, x_N) = \Pr(X_1 < x_1, \ldots, X_N < x_N)$$

$$= \Pr(F_1(X_1) \leq F_1(x_1), \ldots, F_N(X_N) \leq F_1(x_N)).$$

Writing $\hat{u}_i = F_i(X_i)$ and $u_i = F_i(x_i)$, we have

$$H(x_1, x_2, \ldots, x_N) = \Pr(\hat{u}_1 < x_1, \ldots, \hat{u}_N < x_N)$$

This is simply a copula function C and so

$$H(x_1, x_2, \ldots, x_N) = C(F_1(x_1), F_2(x_2), \ldots, F_n(x_N)).$$

Moreover, if the marginal distributions $F_1, \ldots, F_N$ are continuous then C is unique. The converse is also true

$$C(u_1, u_2, \ldots, u_N) = H(F_1^{-1}(u_1), \ldots, F_N^{-1}(u_N)).$$

The advantage of working with the copula function C rather than the multi-variate function H is that it separates the choice of the marginal from the choice of dependence structure. Rather than specify a multi-variate distribution H, we can model the dependence by specifying a marginal function F_i and a copula C. Thanks to Sklar, we know that given H and F_i, the copula C is unique.

14.2.3   Survival Copulas

When modelling the dependence structure of default times using a copula C, we have defined

$$C(u_1(t_1), u_2(t_2), \ldots, u_N(t_N)) = \Pr(\tau_1 \leq t_1, \tau_2 \leq t_2, \ldots, \tau_N \leq t_N)$$

where $u_i(t_i) = 1 - Q_i(t_i)$. However, there is an alternative copula which is called the *survival copula*. This is given by

$$\hat{C}(1 - u_1(t_1), 1 - u_2(t_2), \ldots, 1 - u_N(t_N)) = \Pr(\tau_1 > t_1, \tau_2 > t_2, \ldots, \tau_n > t_N).$$

As the name suggests, the survival copula marginal distributions are specified in terms of the probability of each credit surviving to time t. In the bi-variate case, we can write the simple relationship between the copula $C(u, v)$ and the survival copula $\hat{C}(u, v)$ as

$$\hat{C}(u, v) = u + v - 1 + C(1 - u, 1 - v).$$

In practice, either copula can be chosen. However, once a choice is made, it is worth sticking to it to prevent confusion and to ensure consistency.

14.2.4   The Latent Variable Model

The Gaussian latent variable model introduced in Chapter 13 is a Gaussian copula model. To show this we recall that within this model

$$\Pr(\tau_i \leq t_i, \tau_j \leq t_j) = \Pr\left(A_i \leq D_i(t_i),\ A_j \leq D_j(t_j); \rho\right)$$

$$= \Phi_{2,\rho}\left(\Phi^{-1}(1 - Q_i(t_i)), \Phi^{-1}(1 - Q_j(t_j))\right)$$

$$= C\left(u_i(t_i),\ u_j(t_j)\right)$$

where $u_i(t_i) = 1 - Q_i(t_i) = \Phi(D_i(t_i))$, $u_j(t_j) = 1 - Q_j(t_j) = \Phi(D_j(t_j))$ and $\rho = \beta_i \beta_j$. We can recognise this as a Gaussian copula model in which the marginal distribution $F_i(X_i) = \Phi_i(X_i)$, and the copula is the Gaussian bi-variate cumulative distribution function

$$C_{\rho}^{GC}(u_i, u_j) = \Phi_2\left(\Phi^{-1}(u_i), \Phi^{-1}(u_j), \rho\right).$$

Hence, the survival copula is given by

$$\hat{C}_{\rho_{ij}}^{GC}(u_i, u_j) = \Phi_2\left(\Phi^{-1}(1 - u_i), \Phi^{-1}(1 - u_j), \rho\right)$$

$$= \Phi_2\left(-\Phi^{-1}(u_i), -\Phi^{-1}(u_j), \rho\right)$$

$$= \Phi_2\left(\Phi^{-1}(u_i), \Phi^{-1}(u_j), \rho\right)$$

$$= C_{\rho}^{GC}(u_i, u_j).$$

The symmetry of the Gaussian distribution ensures that the default and survival Gaussian copulae are the same, i.e. $\hat{C}^{GC} = C^{GC}$.

14.3   MEASURING DEPENDENCE

Measuring dependence between different observables is the first step in deciding how to model dependence. Most practitioners in the field of finance are very familiar with the correlation measure, more precisely known as the *linear correlation* or *Pearson correlation coefficient*. However, our familiarity with this measure is mainly due to the widespread use of Gaussian or Gaussian-related distributions such as the lognormal distribution in financial modelling. As the dependencies we measure in the world of credit can be highly non-Gaussian, being skewed or fat-tailed or both, we need to use dependency measures which are able to detect this type of joint behaviour.

In the next section we set out the advantages and limitations of the linear correlation measure. We then introduce two additional measures of correlation based on the ranking of the observations. We then explain why rank correlation measures are unable to distinguish between copulas which allow for extreme joint realisations and in doing so motivate the use of the tail dependence measure.

14.3.1   Pearson Linear Correlation

The most commonly used measure of dependence is known as *the correlation*. To be more precise, we should actually call it the linear correlation or Pearson correlation coefficient. This is a way to capture the strength of the relationship between two (or more) sets of random variables X and Y using their linear product. It is defined as follows

$$\rho_P = \frac{\mathbb{E}[XY] - \mathbb{E}[X]\mathbb{E}[Y]}{\sqrt{(\mathbb{E}[X^2] - \mathbb{E}[X]^2)(\mathbb{E}[Y^2] - \mathbb{E}[Y]^2)}}.$$

The popularity of the linear correlation measure is largely due to the widespread use of Gaussian and other elliptic distributions. We list some advantages of the Pearson linear correlation coefficient:

1. It is easy to understand and easy to calculate.
2. It is invariant under linear transformations, i.e. $X \rightarrow \alpha_X X + \beta_X$ and $Y \rightarrow \alpha_Y Y + \beta_Y$, allowing us to change the mean and variances of the distributions X and Y without affecting the correlation.
3. If the marginals of the distribution are Gaussian, then a linear correlation of 0% implies independence, a linear correlation of 100% implies maximum positive dependence and a linear correlation of -100% correlation implies maximum negative dependence between X and Y.

This last advantage explains why the linear correlation coefficient is so well suited to Gaussian distributed random variables. However, when the marginal distributions are non-Gaussian, linear correlation may not behave in the desired manner. We list some of the problems with linear correlation below:

1. Linear correlation is only invariant under linear transformations. The linear correlation of a lognormal random process is not the same as the correlation of the two normal processes from which the lognormal process is derived.
2. The correlation parameter does not range from -100% to $+100\%$ as we go from minimum to maximum dependency. For example, the linear correlation of Bernoulli default indicators, $X = 1_{\tau_i \leq T}$ and $Y = 1_{\tau_j \leq T}$, does not exhibit the qualities we would expect of a correlation measure. As discussed in Section 12.2.3, this measure of correlation has minimum and maximum dependence values which are both a function of the marginal probabilities. As a result, the linear correlation of the default indicators is not always a useful measure of dependency since we also need to know the marginal probabilities and the correlation to be able to assess the degree of dependency. In other words, linear correlation is not guaranteed to be a pure function of the copula as it can also be a function of the marginals.
3. A linear correlation of zero does not imply independence. This is already true for the Student-t distribution, a member of the family of elliptic distributions, which is discussed in detail later in this chapter.

For these reasons, we need to consider alternative measures of dependence when we move beyond elliptic distributions. One alternative approach is to use *rank correlation*.

14.4   RANK CORRELATION

Rank correlation is an alternative measure of dependency. To understand what we mean by rank correlation, consider two random distributions X and Y from which we draw n pairs (X_i, Y_i) where $i = 1, \ldots, n$. We define R_i as the rank of X_i, i.e. we sort all n realisations of random number X into increasing order and R_i is the rank of X_i in this list. For example, suppose the data series X takes the values

$$X = \{10, 8, 12, 5, 6, 2\}.$$

Sorting it into increasing order, we have

$$\text{Sorted } X = \{2, 5, 6, 8, 10, 12\}.$$

The rank vector R is therefore given by

$$\text{Rank } R = \{5, 4, 6, 2, 3, 1\}.$$

The value of $R_1 = 5$ represents the fact that $X_1 = 10$ is the 5th value in the sorted vector X. The value of $R_6 = 1$ represents the fact that $X_6 = 2$ is the 1st value in the ordered X. We can do the same for another data series vector Y. If we define S_i is the rank of Y_i, we note that

$$1 \le R_i \le n \quad \text{and} \quad 1 \le S_i \le n.$$

The average rankings are given by

$$\hat{R} = \frac{1}{n} \sum_{i=1}^{n} R_i \quad \text{and} \quad \hat{S} = \frac{1}{n} \sum_{i=1}^{n} S_i.$$

Since the sum is over all ranks, i.e. all numbers from 1 to n, we have an arithmetic progression

$$\hat{R} = \hat{S} = \frac{1}{n} \frac{n(n+1)}{2} = \frac{n+1}{2}. \tag{14.2}$$

Another way to represent rank correlation is in terms of the prevalence of concordant versus discordant draws. Given two different random draws (X_1, Y_1) and (X_2, Y_2), they are

$$\text{Concordant if } (X_1 - X_2)(Y_1 - Y_2) > 0.$$
$$\text{Discordant if } (X_1 - X_2)(Y_1 - Y_2) < 0.$$

This is shown in Figure 14.1.

The link between the prevalence of concordance/discordance and rank is that if we find that all pairs of data points (X_i, Y_i) are concordant then we know that the rank vectors R and S are

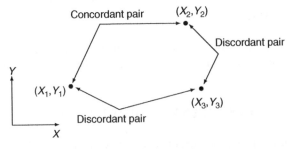

Figure 14.1 Concordant and discordant draws. We show three draws from the joint distribution of X and Y and identify which are the concordant pairs and which are the discordant pairs

identical and the rank correlation will be 100%. As the number of discordant points increases, the vectors R and S begin to differ and the rank correlation falls.

Example: For example, if we have a set of concordant data points (X, Y) of the form $(2.4, 529)$, $(4.2, 737)$, $(1.6, 56)$ and $(10.9, 821)$, then we have

$$X = (2.4, 4.2, 1.6, 10.9) \quad \text{and} \quad Y = (529, 737, 56, 821)$$

which gives the identical rank vectors

$$R = (2, 3, 1, 4) \quad \text{and} \quad S = (2, 3, 1, 4).$$

The rank correlation will be 100%.

In the next sections we will examine two measures of rank correlation. We will see that the advantage of rank correlation is that it can be shown to be a function of the copula alone – *it is independent of the marginal probabilities*. Also, the correlation measure is invariant under monotonic transformations, i.e. any transformation which does not alter the rankings. For example, this means that the rank correlation of a normal distribution will be the same as that of a lognormal distribution since the function $f(x) = \ln(x)$ is a monotonic transformation.

14.4.1   Kendall's Tau

Kendall's tau measures the dependence between two random variables X and Y, each distributed according to some marginal distribution F_X and F_Y, by measuring the probability that two random pairs (X_1, Y_1) and (X_2, Y_2) are concordant versus discordant. Given two series consisting of n pairs, we define the value of Kendall's tau as

$$\tau = \frac{c - d}{c + d}$$

where c is the number of concordant pairs and d is the number of discordant pairs. The total number of distinct pairs $c + d = n(n - 1)/2$. The sample estimator of Kendall's is therefore given by

$$\tau = \frac{2 \sum_{i=1}^{n} \sum_{j=i+1}^{n} \text{sign}[(X_i - X_j)(Y_i - Y_j)]}{n(n - 1)}$$

where

$$\text{sign}[x] = \begin{cases} +1 & \text{if } x \geq 0 \\ -1 & \text{if } x < 0 \end{cases}$$

and n is the number of observations of pairs (X, Y).

Consider the three dependency limits:

- Independence: When X and Y are independent, we have $\tau = 0$.
- Maximum dependence: Setting $Y_1 = X_1$ and $Y_2 = X_2$, we get $\tau = 1$.
- Minimum dependence: Setting $Y_1 = -X_1$ and $Y_2 = -X_2$ we get $\tau = -1$.

As a result, we have a correlation measure which interpolates between -1 and $+1$ and assigns a value of zero to independence. The Kendall's tau of a set of continuous random variables X and Y can be written in terms of their two-dimensional copula $C(u, v)$ as follows

$$\tau_{XY} = 4 \int_0^1 \int_0^1 C(u, v) dC(u, v) - 1.$$

From this, it is clear that *the value of the Kendall's tau is simply a function of the copula and does not depend on the choice of marginals*. It is a pure measure of dependence.

14.4.2   Spearman's Rho

Spearman's rho is a measure of dependence between two random variables X and Y. It is literally the linear Pearson correlation of the ranks R_i and S_i of the random data pairs X and Y, i.e.

$$\rho_S = \frac{\sum_{i=1}^n (R_i - \hat{R})(S_i - \hat{S})}{\sqrt{\sum_{i=1}^n (R_i - \hat{R})^2 \sum_{i=1}^n (S_i - \hat{S})^2}}$$

where $\hat{S}$ and $\hat{R}$ are the mean values of the ranks. It is possible to show that

$$\rho_S = \frac{12 \sum_{i=1}^n (R_i - \hat{R})(S_i - \hat{S})}{n(n^2 - 1)}.$$

Spearman's rho can also be written as an explicit function of the copula

$$\rho_S = 12 \int_0^1 \int_0^1 (C(u, v) - uv) du\, dv$$

$$= 12 \int_0^1 \int_0^1 C(u, v) du\, dv - 3.$$

We see that this measure of rank correlation is also a pure function of the dependency.

14.4.3   Summary

Rank correlation measures have the following useful properties:

1. Rank correlation is only a function of the copula and so is a much purer measure of dependence than linear correlation.
2. Rank correlation captures the range of dependency by assuming a value in the range $[-1, 1]$
3. Rank correlations are invariant under monotonic transformations.

However, rank correlations do not take into account the magnitude of the random variables being measured, and so they cannot distinguish between large and small co-movements. In a financial setting, a measure of the size of the co-movements is essential when calculating risk measures and rank correlations are therefore inadequate. For this reason, it is important to complement rank correlation with a measure of tail dependence.

14.5   TAIL DEPENDENCE

The downside of using rank as a way to measure dependency is that it does not actually take into account the absolute magnitude of the realisations of X and Y. For example, if there is a tendency for the two realisations X and Y to have joint extreme values, this would not be seen by either of these rank correlation measures since it would not change the ranking of the data or equivalently the number of concordant versus discordant data pairs. To capture extremal joint behaviour, we need another measure of dependence known as the *tail dependence*.

Tail dependence is a way to measure dependence which captures the tendency for joint extreme movements in X and Y. In a two-dimensional plot, we are looking at the tendency for X and Y to be both in the extreme lower left quadrant or in the extreme upper right quadrant. This is shown in Figure 14.2.

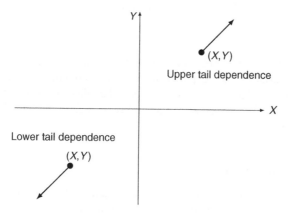

Figure 14.2 Tail dependence is a measure of the tendency for large positive co-movements and large negative co-movements. We distinguish between upper tail dependency and lower tail dependency

At first glance, one measure of tail dependence might be to compute the probability of X and Y both being in their extreme tails. However, this will necessarily be zero in the limit. Instead, what we need is to consider the probability of Y being in the tail of its marginal distribution F_Y *conditional* on X being in the tail of its marginal distribution F_X. We therefore define an upper tail dependence parameter

$$\lambda_U = \lim_{u \to 1} \Pr\left(Y > F_Y^{-1}(u) \mid X > F_X^{-1}(u)\right).$$

This can be thought of as the probability of one extremal positive event conditional on another extremal event. If $\lambda_U > 0$ then X and Y are *upper tail dependent*. If $\lambda_U = 0$ then they are asymptotically independent. This upper tail dependence can be written in terms of the copula

$$\lambda_U = \lim_{u \to 1} \frac{(1 - 2u + C(u, u))}{(1 - u)}.$$

We can also define a lower tail dependence parameter

$$\lambda_L = \lim_{u \to 0} \Pr\left(Y \leq F_Y^{-1}(u) \mid X \leq F_X^{-1}(u)\right)$$

which likewise can be expressed in terms of the copula

$$\lambda_L = \lim_{u \to 0} \frac{C(u, u)}{u}.$$

We will later see that some copulas, most notably the Gaussian copula, are asymptotically independent but that others such as the Student-t copula possess tail dependence.

14.6   SOME IMPORTANT COPULAE

We now apply this framework to the modelling of the dependency of default. We begin by identifying the marginal distribution for the default times as

$$F_i(t) = \Pr(\tau_i \leq t) = 1 - Q_i(t)$$

where $Q_i(t)$ is the issuer survival probability curve. This is calibrated directly to the CDS curve.

Now that we have established a copula framework for modelling dependence, we wish to apply it to the modelling of default times of correlated credits. We therefore examine a range of copulas chosen either for their analytic tractability or because they are believed to closely fit empirical observations.

14.6.1   The Gaussian Copula

The Gaussian copula belongs to the family of elliptic copulas which also includes the Student-t copula. A variable X has a Gaussian distribution with mean zero and unit standard deviation if it has a density which satisfies

$$\phi(x) = \frac{\exp(-x^2/2)}{\sqrt{2\pi}}$$

so that its marginal or cumulative distribution function is given by

$$\Phi(y) = \int_{-\infty}^{y} \phi(x)dx.$$

In the n-dimensional Gaussian survival copula, this is extended to give

$$\hat{C}_{\Sigma}^{GC}(u_1, u_2, \ldots, u_n) = \Phi_{n, \Sigma}\left(\Phi^{-1}(u_1), \Phi^{-1}(u_2), \ldots, \Phi^{-1}(u_n)\right)$$

where $u_n = Q_n(t_n)$ is the survival probability to some time t_n and the $n \times n$ correlation matrix is Σ. In $n = 2$ dimensions we have the bi-variate copula

$$\hat{C}_\rho^{GC}(u_1, u_2) = \frac{1}{2\pi\sqrt{1-\rho^2}} \int_{-\infty}^{\Phi^{-1}(u_1)} \int_{-\infty}^{\Phi^{-1}(u_2)} \exp\left(-\frac{x_1^2 - 2\rho x_1 x_2 + x_2^2}{2(1-\rho^2)}\right) dx_1 dx_2.$$

The rank correlation measures for the Gaussian copula take a simple analytical form. Lindskog *et al.* (2001) showed that the value of Kendall's tau and Spearman's rho is given by

$$\tau = \frac{2}{\pi}\arcsin(\rho_P) \quad \text{and} \quad \rho_S = \frac{6}{\pi}\arcsin\left(\frac{\rho_P}{2}\right)$$

where ρ_P is the Pearson linear correlation coefficient. Figure 14.3 shows that both rank dependency measures as a function of the Pearson linear correlation. All three correlation measures are close across the entire range of linear correlation values.

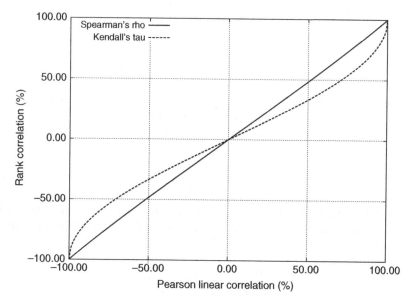

Figure 14.3   Spearman's rho and Kendall's tau plotted as a function of the Pearson linear correlation for the bi-variate Gaussian copula. Note that Spearman's rho is almost identical to the Pearson linear correlation (not shown) which is simply the line $y = x$

Looking at the tail dependency parameters of the Gaussian copula, we find that

$$\lambda_U = \lambda_L = \begin{cases} 0 & \text{if } \rho < 1 \\ 1 & \text{if } \rho = 1. \end{cases}$$

This tells us that the *Gaussian copula does not exhibit either lower or upper tail dependence* for typical values of correlation. So if one Gaussian draw is in the tail of its distribution, the probability that another draw is also in its tail is zero in the limit for all values of $\rho < 1$.

In order to simulate the default times from a Gaussian copula with correlation matrix $\mathbf{C}$, we perform the following steps:

1. Generate P sets of correlated Gaussian random variables $\hat{g}_i^p$ where $i = 1, \ldots, n$ and $p = 1, \ldots, P$ using the Cholesky algorithm in Section 14.10.1.
2. Map each correlated random Gaussian variable $\hat{g}_i^p$ to a uniform random variable using the marginal $u_i^p = \Phi(g_i^p)$.
3. Map each of the uniform random variables to a default time by solving $\tau_i = Q_i^{-1}(u_i^p)$.

This algorithm takes a generic multi-factor correlation matrix Σ and so uses a Cholesky approach to generate the correlation Gaussian random numbers. As a result, it means that we have to generate our random numbers in advance. However, if we are happy to assume a one-factor correlation structure, it is both faster and less memory intensive to use the algorithm in Section 13.5.

Figure 14.4 shows a simulation of default times for two credits. In one figure we assumed a value of $\rho = 20\%$ and in the other $\rho = 90\%$. The increase in co-dependence is clear.

14.6.2 The Student-t Copula

The Student-t copula is one of the most widely used copulas. It is based on the multi-variate version of Student-t distribution. Like the Gaussian copula, the Student-t copula is also a member of the family of elliptic copulas. However, the Student-t distribution can present fatter tails than the Gaussian and so is better able to model tail dependence.

A random variable X is said to have a Student-t distribution if it is generated according to the formula

$$X = \frac{Z}{\sqrt{\xi_\nu/\nu}}, \qquad (14.3)$$

where $Z \sim N(0, 1)$ and ξ_ν is an independent chi-square distributed random variable distributed random variable with ν degrees of freedom. The probability density function of the Student-t distribution is given by

$$f_\nu(t) = \frac{\Gamma((\nu+1)/2)}{\sqrt{\nu\pi}\Gamma(\nu/2)} \left(1 + \frac{t^2}{\nu}\right)^{-(\nu+1)/2} \qquad (14.4)$$

where $\Gamma(x)$ is the gamma function defined in Appendix A. The Student-t distribution has the following properties:

1. It is symmetric about $t = 0$ and so has a mean of zero.
2. It has a variance equal to $\nu/(\nu - 2)$ where parameter ν is known as the *degrees of freedom*. The variance is therefore defined only if $\nu > 2$.
3. In the limit $\nu \to \infty$, the distribution converges to a Gaussian distribution. This is made clear in Figure 14.5 which plots the probability density function for different values of ν.

We define the cumulative distribution function of the Student-t distribution as

$$t_\nu(y) = \int_{-\infty}^{y} f_\nu(t)dt. \qquad (14.5)$$

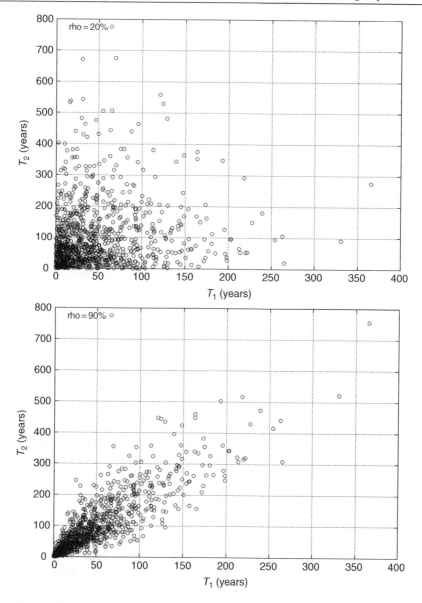

Figure 14.4 Default time simulation using the Gaussian copula for $\rho = 20\%$ and $\rho = 90\%$. We assume that the marginals are set so that $Q_1(t) = \exp(-\lambda_1 t)$ and $Q_2(t) = \exp(-\lambda_2 t)$ where $\lambda_1 = 0.02$ and $\lambda_2 = 0.01$

The n-dimensional Student-t copula with v degrees of freedom is given by

$$C^T_{\Sigma, v}(u_1, u_2, \ldots, u_n) = \frac{1}{\sqrt{|\Sigma|}} \frac{\Gamma(\frac{v+n}{2})}{\Gamma(\frac{v}{2})} \left(\frac{\Gamma(\frac{v}{2})}{\Gamma(\frac{v+1}{2})} \right)^n \frac{(1 + \frac{1}{v}\omega^T \Sigma^{-1}\omega)^{-(v+n)/2}}{\prod_{i=1}^{n}(1 + \omega_i^2/v)^{-(v+1)/2}}$$

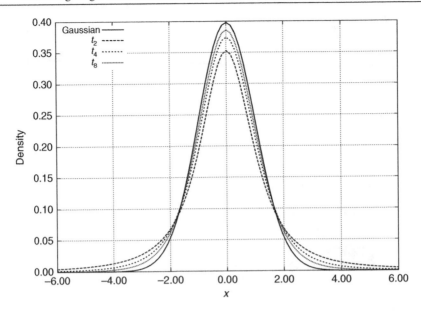

Figure 14.5 Probability density function for the Student-t distribution for $v = 2, 4, 8$. For comparison we also plot the Gaussian density to which the Student-t distribution converges for $v \to \infty$

where $\omega_i = t_v^{-1}(u_i)$. In $n = 2$ dimensions we have the bi-variate Student-t copula

$$C_{\rho,v}^T(u_1, u_2) = \frac{1}{2\pi \sqrt{1 - \rho^2}} \int_{-\infty}^{t_v^{-1}(u_1)} \int_{-\infty}^{t_v^{-1}(u_2)} \left(1 + \frac{x_1^2 - 2\rho x_1 x_2 + x_2^2}{v(1 - \rho^2)}\right)^{-(v+2)/2} dx_1 dx_2.$$

It is important to note that if we set $\rho = 0$, the Student-t copula *does not reduce to the independence copula*. We can understand this by recalling that we can simulate two random Student-t draws X and Y as follows

$$X = \frac{Z_X}{\sqrt{\xi_v/v}} \quad \text{and} \quad Y = \frac{Z_Y}{\sqrt{\xi_v/v}} \tag{14.6}$$

where Z_X and Z_Y are independent Gaussian draws. Both X and Y see the same value of ξ_v. This means that if ξ_v is small, both $|X|$ and $|Y|$ will tend to be large. If ξ_v is large, then both $|X|$ and $|Y|$ will tend to be small. So while the signs of X and Y are determined independently through the independent Gaussian draws, their magnitudes are not independent and they are therefore not independent random variables. This explains why $\rho = 0$ does not imply independence.

The rank correlation measures for the Student-t copula are the same as those for the Gaussian copula. Hence, Kendall's tau and Spearman's rho are given by

$$\tau = \frac{2}{\pi} \arcsin(\rho_P) \quad \text{and} \quad \rho_S = \frac{6}{\pi} \arcsin\left(\frac{\rho_P}{2}\right)$$

where ρ_P is the Pearson linear correlation. Clearly, a zero rank correlation also does not imply independence. However, unlike the Gaussian copula, the Student-t copula possesses tail dependence. Due to the symmetry of the probability density function, it has been shown by Lindskog *et al.* (2001) that the upper and lower tail dependence for the Student-*t* copula is the same and is given by

$$\lambda_L = \lambda_U = 2t_{\nu+1}\left(-\frac{\sqrt{\nu+1}\sqrt{1-\rho}}{\sqrt{1+\rho}}\right).$$

Figure 14.6 shows the tail dependence parameter as a function of ρ for three different values of ν. We first observe that even when $\rho = 0$, the tail dependence parameter is not zero. This is a manifestation of the lack of independence at zero correlation. We see that when $\rho = 0$ and $\nu = 2$, the probability of an extreme tail event in one random variable conditional on an extreme tail event in the other is close to 20%. As the degrees of freedom parameter ν increases, the tail dependence falls. In the limit of $\rho \to 1$, we see that the tail dependence tends to 1 for all values of ν.

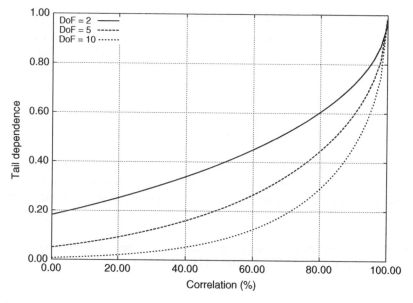

Figure 14.6 Tail dependence of the Student-*t* copula as a function of correlation ρ. We show this for different values of the degrees of freedom (DoF) parameter $\nu = 2, 5, 10$

Once again, our aim is to generate default times τ_i^p consistent with this copula. The steps are as follows:

1. Generate P sets of correlated Gaussian random variables $\hat{g}_i^p$ where $i = 1, \ldots, n$ and $p = 1, \ldots, P$ using the Cholesky algorithm in Section 14.10.1.
2. Draw P random numbers ξ^p from a chi-square distribution with ν degrees of freedom. There are a number of ways to generate a chi-square random number with ν degrees of freedom. One is by generating a uniform random number and then using the inverse chi-squared cumulative distribution function to convert the uniform to a chi-square distributed random number. Another is to use the definition of a chi-square with ν degrees of freedom which is that $\xi_\nu = \sum_{i=1}^{\nu} g_i^2$ where g_i is an independent Gaussian random number.

3. Calculate the Student-t distributed random number for each credit i and realisation p as follows: $\eta_i^p = \hat{g}_i^p / \sqrt{\xi_v^p / v}$.
4. Map each correlated random Student-t distributed variable η_i^p to a uniform random variable using the marginal $u_i^p = t_v(\eta_i^p)$.
5. Map each random uniform to a default time by solving $\tau_i^p = Q_i^{-1}(u_i^p)$.

14.6.3   The Marshall–Olkin Copula

In its simplest form, the Marshall–Olkin copula can be motivated as a model for a pair of credits which are exposed to two types of default-inducing shocks:

1. An idiosyncratic shock which causes a credit to default independently of the other.
2. A common shock that causes both credits to default simultaneously.

The common shock creates a dependency between otherwise independent credits. We can model the arrival of both types of shocks as the first jump of a Poisson process. In the case of two credits, we can model the idiosyncratic shocks using constant hazard rates λ_1 and λ_2. We model the common shock using λ_{12}. We denote the times of the idiosyncratic shocks as τ_1, τ_2 and the time of the common shock as τ_{12}. Credit 1 can then default in a small time interval of length Δt in one of three ways:

1. An idiosyncratic shock to credit 1 but no systemic shock. This occurs with probability $\lambda_1 \Delta t (1 - \lambda_{12} \Delta t)$.
2. A common shock but no idiosyncratic shock. This occurs with probability $\lambda_{12} \Delta t (1 - \lambda_1 \Delta t)$.
3. Both shocks occur with probability $\lambda_1 \lambda_{12} (\Delta t)^2$. Since the probability of both shocks happening in the small time step Δt scales as $(\Delta t)^2$, we can ignore this scenario in the continuous time limit.

Combining these, we find that the composite hazard rate for credit 1 is given by $\lambda_1 + \lambda_{12}$. As a result, we can write the survival probability of credit 1 as

$$\Pr(\tau_1 > t) = \exp\left(-(\lambda_1 + \lambda_{12})t\right).$$

Similarly, the survival probability for credit 2 is

$$\Pr(\tau_2 > t) = \exp\left(-(\lambda_2 + \lambda_{12})t\right).$$

The joint survival distribution is the probability that both credits survive until times t_1 and t_2, i.e. it is the probability that $\tau_1 > t_1$ and $\tau_2 > t_2$. It is given by

$$\Pr(\tau_1 > t_1, \tau_2 > t_2) = \exp\left(-\lambda_1 t_1 - \lambda_2 t_2 - \lambda_{12} \max(t_1, t_2)\right).$$

The Marshall–Olkin survival copula $\hat{C}$ is therefore given by

$$\hat{C}_{\alpha_1, \alpha_2}^{MO}(u, v) = uv \min\left(u^{-\alpha_1}, v^{-\alpha_2}\right)$$

where

$$u = \exp\left(-(\lambda_1 + \lambda_{12})t_1\right) \quad \text{and} \quad v = \exp\left(-(\lambda_2 + \lambda_{12})t_2\right)$$

and we define

$$\alpha_1 = \frac{\lambda_{12}}{\lambda_1 + \lambda_{12}} \quad \text{and} \quad \alpha_2 = \frac{\lambda_{12}}{\lambda_2 + \lambda_{12}}.$$

It is shown in Nelsen (1999) that we can write Spearman's rho and Kendall's tau for the Marshall–Olkin copula as

$$\rho^S = \frac{3\alpha_1\alpha_2}{2\alpha_1 + 2\alpha_2 - \alpha_1\alpha_2} \quad \text{and} \quad \tau = \frac{\alpha_1\alpha_2}{\alpha_1 + \alpha_2 - \alpha_1\alpha_2}.$$

For example, if $\lambda_{12} = 0$ then $\alpha_1 = \alpha_2 = 0$ and both rank correlations are zero. If $\lambda_1 = \lambda_2 = 0$ then $\alpha_1 = \alpha_2 = 1$ and both rank correlations equal 100%. The value of the upper tail dependence measure is given by

$$\lambda_U = \min(\alpha_1, \alpha_2).$$

14.6.4 The Archimedean Copulas

The Archimedean copula is a family of copulas which take the form

$$C(u_1, u_2, \ldots, u_n) = \psi^{-1}\left(\psi(u_1) + \psi(u_2) + \ldots + \psi(u_n)\right).$$

There are a number of conditions on $\psi(x)$ which is known as the *generator* of the copula:

1. The inverse function $\psi^{-1}(x)$ must map to [0, 1] so that it corresponds to a probability.
2. We require the function $\psi(x)$ to be a convex, decreasing function where we confine x to the range $[0, \infty)$.
3. $\psi(1) = 0$ and $\psi(0) = \infty$.

There are a number of functions which satisfy these requirements and so result in a number of *families* of Archimedean copulas. We summarise the properties of the most popular ones below.

14.6.4.1 Independence

The generator is given by $\psi(x) = -\ln x$. As a result we have $\psi^{-1}(x) = e^{-x}$ and we can write the copula as

$$C(u_1, u_2) = \exp\left(-(-\ln(u_1) - \ln(u_2))\right) = u_1 u_2.$$

which is the definition of the independence copula.

14.6.4.2 Gumbel

The generator is given by $\psi(x) = (-\ln(x))^\theta$ where $\theta \geq 1$ is the generator for the Gumbel family of copulas. This has upper tail dependence and a value of Kendall's tau given by $\tau = 1 - 1/\theta$.

14.6.4.3 Frank

This generator is given by $\psi(x) = -\ln(\exp(-\theta x) - 1)/(\exp(-\theta) - 1)$ where $\theta \in \mathbb{R}$ and $\theta \neq 0$. The Frank copula possesses radial symmetry so that the default and survival copula are the same. The value of Kendall's tau is given by $\tau = 1 - 4/\theta + 4D_1(\theta)/\theta$ where D_1 is defined below.[1] The Frank copula has neither upper nor lower tail dependence.

14.6.4.4   Clayton

The generator is given by $\psi(x) = (x^{-\theta} - 1)/\theta$ where $\theta \in [-1, \infty]$, and $\theta \neq 0$ is the Clayton family. This copula has zero upper tail dependence, but has a lower tail dependence equal to $\lambda_L = 2^{-1/\theta}$ for $\theta > 0$ and a value of Kendall's tau given by $\tau = \theta/(\theta + 2)$. A value of $\theta = -1$ corresponds to maximum negative dependence while maximum positive dependence occurs in the limit of large θ.

Of all of these Archimedean copulas, the one which most interests us is the Clayton copula. This is because it is the only one of the Archimedean copulas listed above which possesses lower tail dependence. This occurs when $\theta > 0$. In some sense, a copula with more lower tail dependence than upper tail dependence seems appropriate for modelling in the financial markets since we expect that large negative co-movements are more probable than large positive co-movements.

14.7   PRICING CREDIT DERIVATIVES FROM DEFAULT TIMES

A Monte Carlo simulation of default times enables us to price any credit derivative whose price is a function of the identity and timing of defaults on the reference portfolio. Such products include the main correlation products discussed so far, i.e. default baskets and most variations on the CDO.

The main challenge when pricing credit derivatives using Monte Carlo is minimisation of the standard error of the price estimate. Since the standard error only falls as $O(1/\sqrt{P})$ but the Monte Carlo time scales as $O(P)$, we need to ensure that the code executes as quickly as possible. This requires a combination of careful code design, and the use of variance reduction methods. Methods such as control variates, importance sampling and quasi-random number generators can all be utilised. For further reading, we recommend Glasserman (2004) and Jaeckel (2002). With regard to code design, we can divide the Monte Carlo pricing of credit derivatives into two approaches:

1. We use the default times to *directly* calculate the discounted payoff of each of the premium and protection legs in each path and then average over these to calculate the discounted expectation of each leg.
2. We use the default times to compute the tranche survival curve which we then supply to our CDS analytics for the purpose of calculating the value of the different legs. This is the *indirect* approach. This of course is only possible if the product can be priced using just a survival curve, i.e. it includes STCDOs and homogeneous loss default baskets.

We now consider the advantages and disadvantages of both approaches.

---

[1] $D_1(x)$ is the first Debye function given by

$$D_1(x) = \frac{1}{\theta} \int_0^x \frac{s}{e^s - 1} ds.$$

14.7.1   The Direct Approach

Using the direct approach requires us to write an algorithm which prices the premium and protection legs given a vector of N randomly generated default times for each of the P Monte Carlo trials. We denote this vector with $\{\tau_i^p\}$ and assume that these default times have already been generated. The steps are as follows:

1. We set $p = 1$.
2. We remove the default times $\tau_i^p > T$ where T is the final trade maturity.
3. We order the default times τ_i^p into ascending order using some efficient sorting algorithm such as QuickSort as described in Press *et al.* (1992).
4. We loop through the default times of all of the credits which default before time T and calculate the flows on the protection and payment legs. We know the identity of the credits which default so we can assign the appropriate recovery rate.
5. We present value the flows on the principal and protection leg using the Libor curve to give protection leg PV_p and RPV01_p.
6. We set $p = p + 1$. If $p \leq P$ we return to step (2).
7. We average the premium leg and protection leg present values

$$\text{Tranche risky PV01} = \frac{1}{P} \sum_{p=1}^{P} \text{RPV01}_p$$

and the average protection leg value

$$\text{Tranche protection leg PV} = \frac{1}{P} \sum_{p=1}^{P} \text{Protection leg PV}_p.$$

The advantage of this approach is that it is very generic and can handle any credit derivative whose payments are contingent on default times and on the loss associated with each credit. For example, it can handle nth-to-default default baskets where the losses are inhomogeneous. Although it does make many calls to the Libor discount factor function, this can be speeded up by implementing a caching of the discount factor curve as described in Section 2.7.3.

14.7.2   The Indirect Approach

The alternative indirect approach involves calculating the tranche survival curve. This is the expected tranche surviving percentage notional at each future time. To calculate this, we use the following steps:

1. Discretise the period $[0, T]$ into N_T buckets of width $\Delta T = T/N_T$ and create a vector $Q(k)$ where $k = 0, \ldots, N_T$. We initialise $Q(k) = 1.0$ for all k.
2. Set $p = 1$.
3. Strip out all default times where $\tau_i^p > T$, the trade maturity.
4. Sort all of the default times into ascending order.
5. Determine the loss on the tranche corresponding to the default time τ_i^p of each credit $i = 1, \ldots, N$ which falls before time T. We reduce the value of $Q(k)$ by the loss fraction divided by P where k is the time bucket corresponding to τ_i^p.

6. Set $p = p + 1$. If $p \leq P$ then return to step (3).
7. The survival curve is now stored in vector $Q(k)$.

The advantages of this approach over the direct approach are that:

1. It does not require us to calculate Libor discount factors within the simulation.
2. We can use the tranche survival curve to price tranches with the same attachment and detachment points, but with different maturities without having to rerun the Monte Carlo.
3. We do not have to write code to deal with the calculation of the cash flows on the protection and premium legs. We can just reuse our existing CDS analytics. This approach decouples the model implementation from the product.

While such an approach may be attractive from a design perspective, it is only useful for those products whose pricing can be performed using just a curve. These products are homogeneous loss baskets and STCDO tranches where the upper strike is below the maximum loss. The bucketing also introduces a small discretisation error into the default times.

14.7.3   Conclusion

We conclude that the direct approach is the more flexible one. Indeed, if a flexible payoff language can be put onto the front end of the direct times-to-default simulation, this can be a very powerful tool for pricing and risk managing new types of structures, as well as being a very useful cross-check for analytical approaches. When we are just pricing homogeneous loss baskets or tranches with an upper strike below the maximum loss, the indirect approach may be preferable.

14.8   STANDARD ERROR OF THE BREAKEVEN SPREAD

When pricing a credit derivative using Monte Carlo, we typically wish to calculate a breakeven spread. We would also like to have an estimate of the uncertainty in this estimate of the spread. However, the breakeven spread is the value of the *fixed spread* on the premium leg which makes the present value of the contract equal to zero. From the perspective of a protection buyer, we have

$$\mathbb{E}\left[\text{Protection leg PV}\right] - S \cdot \mathbb{E}\left[\text{RPV01}\right] = 0.$$

To determine the breakeven spread, we need to calculate

$$S = \frac{\mathbb{E}\left[\text{Protection leg PV}\right]}{\mathbb{E}\left[\text{RPV01}\right]}.$$

It is the *ratio of two expectations*. For an analytical model, this calculation can often be performed exactly. However, in a Monte Carlo framework, there is an inherent Monte Carlo pricing error in calculating the expectations of the premium and protection legs. We want to know how these pricing errors on the legs translate into a pricing error on the breakeven spread. We therefore begin by considering the general problem. We define

$$S = \frac{\mathbb{E}\left[X\right]}{\mathbb{E}\left[Y\right]}$$

where X and Y are random variables drawn from unspecified distributions and are not necessarily independent. The ratio of the expectations of two random variables X and Y does not equal the expectation of the ratios,[2] i.e.

$$\frac{\mathbb{E}\,[X]}{\mathbb{E}\,[Y]} \neq \mathbb{E}\left[\frac{X}{Y}\right].$$

This means that if we have a Monte Carlo simulation we must calculate the breakeven spread by taking the expectation of the values of the protection and premium legs across all P trials and then take the ratio. We write

$$\hat{X} = \frac{1}{P}\sum_{p=1}^{P}X_p \quad \text{and} \quad \hat{Y} = \frac{1}{P}\sum_{p=1}^{P}Y_p$$

where X_p and Y_p are the values of the random variables in Monte Carlo trial $p = 1, \dots, P$. We then take the ratio $S = \hat{X}/\hat{Y}$. We can easily calculate the standard deviations of $\hat{X}$ and $\hat{Y}$ as

$$\sigma_{\hat{X}}^2 = \frac{1}{P}\sum_{p=1}^{P}\left(X_p - \hat{X}\right)^2 \quad \text{and} \quad \sigma_{\hat{Y}}^2 = \frac{1}{P}\sum_{p=1}^{P}\left(Y_p - \hat{Y}\right)^2.$$

Calculation of the standard error of S gives

$$\text{Standard error} = \frac{1}{\sqrt{P}}\frac{\hat{X}}{\hat{Y}}\sqrt{\left(\frac{\sigma_{\hat{X}}}{\hat{X}}\right)^2 + \left(\frac{\sigma_{\hat{Y}}}{\hat{Y}}\right)^2 - 2\rho_{XY}\frac{\sigma_{\hat{X}}\sigma_{\hat{Y}}}{\hat{X}\hat{Y}}}$$

where ρ_{XY} is the standard Pearson correlation between X and Y. This equation makes sense. Suppose $X = -Y$. We would find that $\mathbb{E}\,[X] = -\mathbb{E}\,[Y]$ so that $S = -1$. We would also find that $\sigma_X = \sigma_Y$ and that $\rho = -1$ so that $\sigma_S = 0$, i.e. the value of S is the same in every Monte Carlo trial and so there is no uncertainty in the estimate.

We can then use this formula to calculate the standard error of the spread. We set $X_p = $ Protection leg PV_p and $Y_p = $ RPV01$_p$ to calculate the standard deviation of X and Y. In the process we also compute their correlation ρ_{XY}. We then compute the standard error using the above formula.

14.9 SUMMARY

Copulas have become an important tool in the modelling of default dependency thanks largely to the way they separate the choice of marginal and dependency structures. In this chapter we have shown that the Gaussian latent variable model falls into the Gaussian copula model family. We have also discussed dependency and how to measure it using both linear and rank correlation. We have introduced a number of other copula choices and discussed their dependency properties. For a more comprehensive and detailed discussion of copulas, including their estimation, we refer the reader to Cherubini *et al.* (2004).

---

[2] Except in the case where X and Y are linearly dependent, i.e. $X = \alpha Y + \beta$.

14.10   TECHNICAL APPENDIX

14.10.1   Sampling a Multi-variate Gaussian Distribution

This section describes how to sample a multi-variate Gaussian distribution using the method commonly known as Cholesky decomposition. We define an $N \times N$ correlation matrix $\mathbf{C}$. The steps are as follows:

1. First, do a Cholesky decomposition of the correlation matrix. We want to solve for the lower diagonal matrix $\mathbf{A}$ such that $\mathbf{A} \cdot \mathbf{A}^{\mathsf{T}} = \mathbf{C}$. We can solve for the matrix $\mathbf{A}$ in terms of the matrix elements of $\mathbf{C}$ to give

$$A_{ii} = \left(C_{ii} - \sum_{k=1}^{i-1} C_{ik}^2 \right)^{1/2} \quad \text{and} \quad A_{ji} = \frac{1}{A_{ii}} \left(C_{ii} - \sum_{k=1}^{i-1} C_{ik}C_{jk} \right)^{1/2} \quad \text{for } j > i.$$

   This can be done by calling into the Cholesky algorithm in Press *et al.* (1992).
2. We then generate a matrix of independent Gaussians g_i^p where $i = 1, \ldots, N$ and $p = 1, \ldots, P$. This simply requires $N \times P$ repeated calls into our Gaussian random number generator, e.g. Box–Muller.
3. To ensure that the random draws have mean zero and unit variance, we can adjust them *ex post*. If we calculate the sample mean and variance

$$m_i = \frac{1}{P} \sum_{p=1}^{P} g_i^p \quad \text{and} \quad v_i = \frac{1}{P} \sum_{p=1}^{P} (g_i^p - m_i)^2$$

then we can adjust the independent Gaussians' random variables as follows

$$g_i^p = \frac{g_i^p - m_i}{\sqrt{v_i}}.$$

4. To generate correlated Gaussians $\hat{g}_i^p$, we then multiply the independent Gaussians by the Cholesky matrix as follows

$$\hat{g}_i^p = \sum_{j=0}^{i} A_{ij} g_j^p.$$

We can then post-compute the sample correlation as a check using

$$C_{ij} = \frac{1}{P} \sum_{p=1}^{P} \hat{g}_i^p \hat{g}_j^p.$$

Pricing Default Baskets

15.1 INTRODUCTION

In this chapter we discuss the pricing of nth-to-default baskets. Although not as liquid nor as widely traded as synthetic CDOs, default baskets are still preferred by many credit investors. Their advantage is that they permit the investor to focus on a smaller selection of 5–10 credits which can be monitored more easily than say the large portfolio of 100–150 credits found in the typical synthetic CDO. At the same time, the investor can receive a large spread.

Since we have already introduced the concept, mechanics and basic no-arbitrage properties of the default basket in Section 12.2, we begin this chapter by moving straight to their modelling. We begin with the Gaussian copula approach. We focus mainly on the one-factor version of this model. We discuss in detail how the price of an nth-to-default basket depends on the different market variables. Following this, we discuss the effect of going beyond the one-factor correlation structure. We also discuss the impact of pricing baskets using the Student-t copula. The latter part of the chapter is spent discussing the risk management of default baskets.

15.2 MODELLING FIRST-TO-DEFAULT BASKETS

A default basket is a contract similar to a CDS in which the trigger of payment on the protection leg is linked to the incidence of default on a basket of N_C credits. In an nth-to-default basket, it is the default of the nth credit before maturity time T which triggers a payment of $(1 - R_{i(n)})$ per $1 of face value. We use $i(n) \in \{1, \ldots, N_C\}$ to represent the index of the nth credit to default. We denote the default times of the credits in the basket by $\tau_{i(1)}, \tau_{i(2)}, \ldots, \tau_{i(N_C)}$.

When pricing default baskets, we usually treat the case of what we call *homogeneous loss baskets* and *inhomogeneous loss baskets* separately. This is purely a modelling consideration and has nothing to do with the contract itself. When we speak of a homogeneous loss basket, we mean one in which we assume that each of the credits in the basket incurs the same loss amount following a credit event. They may, however, have different correlations and different CDS spread curves. If we define the loss following a credit event for credit i in the basket as $L_i = (1 - R_i)$ then in a homogeneous recovery basket, $L_i = L$ for all $i = 1, \ldots, N_C$.

The reason why we make this distinction is that a homogeneous loss basket is simpler to model than an inhomogeneous loss one. If we have a homogeneous loss basket, then we need to model the probability of having fewer than n defaults through time. We *do not need to know the identity of the nth defaulted credit* since all credits incur the same loss amount.

However, we often have to assume different recovery rates, i.e. inhomogeneous losses. For example, some of the credits in the basket may be linked to subordinated debt while others may be linked to senior secured debt. Another case is when a particular name has been downgraded and is trading at a very wide spread but has not yet experienced a credit event. Looking at the prices of short dated bonds[1] of the issuer may require us to revise our recovery rate assumption. In this case we cannot simply model the number of defaults through time, we also have to know the identity of the defaulting credits so that the correct payoff is applied on the protection leg.

We begin with the simpler case of homogeneous loss first-to-default (FTD) baskets and follow this with a discussion of inhomogeneous loss FTD baskets.

15.2.1 FTD Baskets with Homogeneous Loss

We showed in Section 12.2.4 that to price a first-to-default basket on a basket of homogeneous loss credits, we need to generate the appropriate *basket survival curve*. This will allow us to price a default basket swap using the CDS analytics derived earlier.

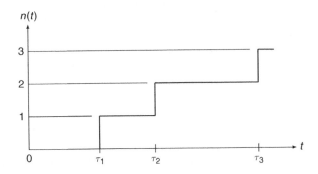

Figure 15.1 Counting function $n(t)$

To do so, we start by defining a function $n(t)$ which counts the number of defaults in a portfolio which have occurred before a time t (Figure 15.1). In the case of a first-to-default basket, the triggering probability to time t is the probability that one or more credits in the portfolio defaults. This is given by

$$Q(n(t) = 0) = 1 - \Pr(n(t) > 0).$$

This allows us to write the value of the premium leg as follows, where we have assumed the payment of coupon accrued following the first default

$$\text{Premium leg PV}(0) = \frac{S_1}{2} \sum_{n=1}^{N_T} \Delta_n Z(0, t_n) \left(Q(n(t_{n-1}) = 0) + Q(n(t_n) = 0) \right)$$

where S_1 is the contractual FTD spread and the sum is over the N_T premium payment dates. Similarly, the protection leg present value is

$$\text{Protection leg PV}(0) = (1 - R) \int_0^T Z(0, s)(-dQ(n(s) = 0)).$$

---

[1] For example, if deliverable bonds are all trading at a price of $27 on a face value of $100, we should not mark the expected recovery rate above 27%.

The survival probability is the probability that the basket has not triggered before time t, i.e. $\Pr(n(t) = 0)$. The basket survival curve is therefore defined as

$$Q(n(t) = 0) = \Pr\left(\tau_1 > t, \tau_2 > t, \ldots, \tau_{N_C} > t\right).$$

Within the one-factor latent variable model we can write this survival probability by first conditioning on the market factor Z. Since the credits are then independent, the conditional probability of none defaulting is simply the product of their conditional survival probabilities, i.e.

$$Q(n(t) = 0\,|Z) = \prod_{i=1}^{N_C} \left(1 - \Pr\left(A_i \leq C_i(t)|Z\right)\right).$$

The unconditional survival probability can be calculated by integrating over the distribution of the market factor

$$Q(n(t) = 0) = \int_{-\infty}^{\infty} \phi(Z) \left[\prod_{i=1}^{N_C} \left(1 - \Pr\left(A_i \leq C_i(t)|Z\right)\right) \right] dZ.$$

The probability of an issuer surviving to time t conditional on the value of the market factor can be written in terms of the cumulative normal distribution function $\Phi(x)$ as follows

$$\Pr\left(A_i > C_i(t)|Z\right) = \Pr\left(\varepsilon_i > \frac{C_i(t) - \beta_i Z}{\sqrt{1 - \beta_i^2}}|Z\right) = \Phi\left(\frac{-C_i(t) + \beta_i Z}{\sqrt{1 - \beta_i^2}}\right).$$

Therefore, the first-to-default basket curve is given by

$$Q(n(t) = 0) = \int_{-\infty}^{\infty} \phi(Z) \left[\prod_{i=1}^{N_C} \Phi\left(\frac{-C_i(t) + \beta_i Z}{\sqrt{1 - \beta_i^2}}\right) \right] dZ. \tag{15.1}$$

The integral in this equation is a simple one-dimensional integral which can be calculated using either a simple trapezium rule or Gaussian quadrature. An implementation of this equation will also need to choose an appropriate time discretisation for the survival curve. Typically, we choose a time discretisation of 0.25 years or less so that the time interpolation of the FTD survival curve is done by the correlation model and not by the CDS survival curve interpolation scheme. When pricing using a basket survival curve, we pass the vector of times and discount factors into our CDS analytics where we set the recovery rate equal to the basket's homogeneous recovery rate.

15.2.2   Factors that Determine the FTD Spread

The FTD spread is the fixed spread which must be paid by the basket in order that the expected present value of the premium leg and protection leg are equal. As a result, it embeds the risk of a first-to-default credit event. The main factors which play a role in determining the FTD spread of a homogeneous loss basket are:

1. The default correlation between the credits in the basket.
2. The number of credits in the basket.
3. The average spread level of the credits in the basket.
4. The time-to-maturity of the basket.

To examine these, we take the example of a homogeneous loss five-name basket. We set all the credit curves identically. The maturity of the basket is set to five years.

15.2.2.1 Correlation Sensitivity

We have calculated the dependency of the FTD breakeven spread on the asset correlation for different levels of the single issuer curves ranging from 30 bp to 150 bp. These are shown in Figure 15.2. We make the following observations:

- The FTD spread falls with increasing asset correlation since higher correlation increases the probability of no defaults. We conclude that a short protection position in an FTD basket is *long correlation*.
- In the limit of zero correlation the FTD spread tends towards a value close to the sum of the spreads.
- In the limit of 100% correlation, the FTD spread tends to the spread of the riskiest credit – the one with the widest spread.
- Between these two limits the FTD spread falls monotonically.

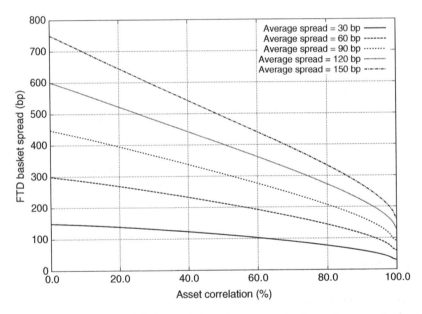

Figure 15.2 Breakeven first-to-default spread for a five-year contract on a five-name basket with all credits having the same spread curves. We show baskets with flat CDS spread curves at 30, 60, 90, 120 and 150 bp, as a function of the asset correlation

15.2.2.2 Number of Credits

The dependence of the FTD spread on the number of credits is shown in Figure 15.3. This shows the FTD spread for a basket of $N_C = 1, \ldots, 10$ credits as a function of correlation. All CDS curves have been set to 90 bp. We make the following observations:

- The FTD spread increases as the number of credits increases. This is because the more credits there are in the basket, the more likely it is that one or more of them will default.
- The slope of the increase in the FTD spread versus the number of credits in the basket depends on the asset correlation. The lower the asset correlation, the greater the slope reflecting the fact that when the credit correlation is low, it is easier for just one or more credits to default idiosyncratically, triggering the basket.
- At zero correlation, the dependence is almost exactly linear as the FTD spread is close to the sum of the spreads in the basket which is simply $90\,bp \times N_C$.
- In the limit of 100% correlation, the FTD spread is the spread of the riskiest credit – the one with the widest spread. As all credits have a 90 bp spread, this is the FTD spread.

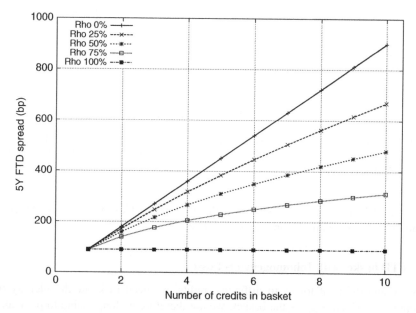

Figure 15.3   Breakeven FTD spread for a five-year contract on a basket with CDS spreads of 90 bp as a function of the number of credits in the basket. We show this for values of the asset correlation equal to 0%, 25%, 50%, 75% and 100%. The lines are drawn as a visual guide

15.2.2.3   Time-to-Maturity

In Figure 15.4 we show the dependence of the FTD spread on the maturity of the basket. The individual spread curves of the five-name basket are set at 90 bp flat. We make the following observations:

- At zero correlation, the term structure of the FTD spread is almost flat and close to 450 bp. This is expected since in this limit, the FTD spread is close to the sum of the issuer spreads and as the CDS curves are flat, so is the FTD spread.
- As the time-to-maturity tends to zero, the FTD spreads approach 450 bps for all values of asset correlation. The credits in the basket become effectively independent. This reflects the fact that at small times and for $\rho < 1$ the probability of two or more defaults falls off quickly, shifting the entire default risk of the basket to an FTD event.

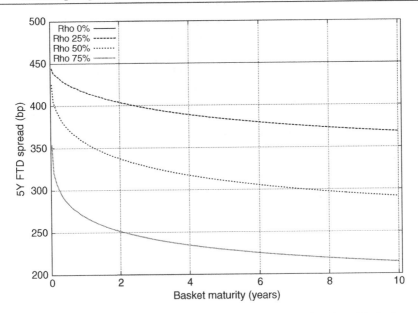

Figure 15.4 Breakeven first-to-default spread on a five-name basket as a function of the basket maturity. The individual name curves are all flat at 90 bp. We show results for four values of the asset correlation of 0%, 25%, 50% and 75%.

Spread and correlation dispersion also change the FTD spread. However, the size of their effect is second order compared to the ones just described.

15.2.3   FTD basket with Inhomogeneous Losses

Once we assign different losses to different credits, we need to know the identity of the defaulting credit which triggers the basket. We are therefore no longer able to price an FTD basket by calculating the survival curve $Q(n(t) = 0)$. We need to calculate the probability of each credit in the portfolio being the first to default before the contract maturity. Conditional on the identity of the first credit to default, we assign the corresponding loss.

Formally, we wish to compute the probability that one credit, which we label as credit number i, defaults in the period $[t, t + dt]$ while all the others survive to time $t + dt$. This recalls the definition of the hazard rate, albeit in a multi-name setting. Mathematically, we write this as

$$h_i(t) = \Pr(\tau_i \in [t, t + dt], \tau_j > t + dt \quad \text{for all } j = 1, \ldots, N_C, j \neq i).$$

We first need to calculate the probability

$$\Pr(\tau_j > t \quad \text{for all } j = 1, \ldots, N_C, \ j \neq i | \tau_i = t).$$

Using conditional independence, and conditioning on the value of Z, this can be written in terms of the asset values

$$\prod_{j \neq i}^{N_C} \Pr(A_j > C_j(t) | A_i = C_i(t))$$

where we have enforced the condition that $\tau_i = t$ by setting

$$A_i = \beta_i Z + \sqrt{1 - \beta_i^2} \varepsilon_i = C_i(t).$$

By requiring that $\tau_i = t$, we have fixed the value of A_i equal to $C_i(t)$. Conditioning on the fact that credit i has defaulted at time t changes the distribution of A_j if credit j is correlated to credit i. Following Laurent and Gregory (2002), we can capture this by rewriting Z as

$$Z = \beta_i C_i(t) + \sqrt{1 - \beta_i^2} \omega$$

where $\omega \sim N(0, 1)$ and is independent. Substituting for Z, we have

$$\prod_{j \neq i}^{N_C} \Pr(A_j > C_j(t) | A_i = C_i(t)) = \prod_{j \neq i}^{N_C} \Phi \left(\frac{\beta_j \sqrt{1 - \beta_i^2} \omega + \beta_j \beta_i C_i(t) - C_j(t)}{\sqrt{1 - \beta_j^2}} \right).$$

To price the protection leg, we then integrate this probability from today to the maturity of the protection leg. At each time interval, we need to consider the probability of each of the credits defaulting first and then paying out the associated recovery rate. Since we have conditioned on the credit i defaulting at time t, we need to weight each term by the probability of that issuer surviving to time t and then defaulting in the next time interval. The present value of the protection leg is therefore given by

$$\text{Protection leg PV}(0, T) = \int_0^T Z(0, s) \int_{-\infty}^{\infty} \phi(\omega) \tag{15.2}$$

$$\times \left[\sum_{i=1}^{N_C} (1 - R_i) \lambda_i(s) Q_i(0, s) \prod_{j \neq i}^{N_C} \Phi \left(\frac{\beta_j \sqrt{1 - \beta_i^2} \omega + \beta_j \beta_i C_i(s) - C_j(s)}{\sqrt{1 - \beta_j^2}} \right) \right] d\omega \, ds.$$

Determining the value of the premium leg is trivial since it does not depend on the identity of the first credit to default. It is handled in exactly the same way as the premium leg of a homogeneous basket for which we simply calculate the survival curve using Equation 15.1.

15.2.4 The FTD Spread for Inhomogeneous Loss Baskets

Roughly speaking, there are three scenarios in which we have inhomogeneous loss baskets:

1. One credit suffers a significant credit deterioration such that its credit curve widens substantially and the market decides, based on observations of the prices of the issuer's bonds, that the recovery rate should be substantially reduced.
2. We have a basket in which the reference credits are linked to different seniorities of debt. A common example of this is when we have baskets with credits linked to subordinated bank debt.
3. We assign different face value exposures to different credits in the basket which may or may not have homogeneous recovery rates. This is very unusual but is easily handled by setting $(1 - R_i)$ in the protection leg value to $F_i(1 - R_i)$ where F_i is the face value exposure to credit i.

To analyse the effect of the first of these we consider a five-name basket in which four credits have a flat spread curve of 90 bp and recovery rate of 40%. The fifth credit has a spread which has widened to 1000 bp and the recovery rate has been marked at 0%. In Figure 15.5 we have plotted the FTD spread of this basket as a function of the asset correlation and compared it to the FTD spread of the homogeneous loss basket.

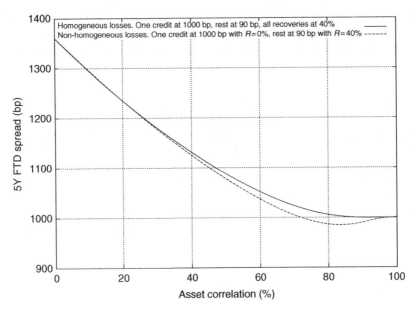

Figure 15.5 Breakeven first-to-default spread for a five-year contract on a five-name basket versus asset correlation. We compare a basket with spreads of { 1000 bp, 90 bp, 90 bp, 90 bp, 90 bp} and recovery rates all at 40% with one for which the spreads are { 1000 bp, 90 bp, 90 bp, 90 bp, 90 bp} but the recovery rates are no longer homogeneous and are given by {0%, 40%, 40%, 40%, 40%}

Below 30% correlation, we see that the effect of the lack of loss homogeneity is almost negligible. At 25% correlation, the difference in the breakeven spread is only 1 bp on an FTD spread of 1206 bp. We can start to understand this by noting that at zero correlation, the FTD spread is close to the sum of the spreads and at maximum correlation, the FTD spread is the widest spread. Both limits are independent of the recovery rates. The inhomogeneous loss has only a second-order effect on the FTD spread which is only evident at high correlations. One curious phenomenon is the initial fall in the FTD spread as the correlation falls below 100%. This can be explained by noting that in the limit of 100% correlation it is the 1000 bp asset with a loss of 100% which always defaults first. However, below 100% correlation there is a growing probability that one of the other four credits defaults first. Since they have lower losses, the FTD spread actually falls slightly. However, as the correlation continues to fall, the probability of an FTD trigger event increases and the FTD spread starts to rise again.

This and other studies we have carried out demonstrate that the price of an inhomogeneous loss FTD basket is highly insensitive to a lack of loss-homogeneity in the basket. This is a positive result to the extent that it means that we can, subject to checks, price all FTD baskets using the simpler homogeneous loss analytics.

15.3   SECOND-TO-DEFAULT AND HIGHER DEFAULT BASKETS

When we move to second-to-default (STD) and higher order default baskets, the pricing problem becomes more difficult. To understand why, recall that an FTD basket can be priced by computing the probability that all of the credits survive. This can only happen in one distinct way. However, if we have a second-to-default basket, we have to consider the N_C ways in which one credit can default before the second default. If the losses are inhomogeneous, we have the added complexity of needing to know the identity of the asset which defaulted in order to know the identity of the surviving credits. As before, we split our analysis into homogeneous loss default baskets and inhomogeneous loss default baskets.

15.3.1   Homogeneous Loss Basket with $n > 1$

Let us start by considering an nth-to-default basket which is homogeneous in terms of the loss. Calculating the nth-to-default survival curve, defined as $Q(n(t) \leq n)$, is more complicated than before since we need to calculate the probability of $n - 1$ credits defaulting first, and this can happen in more than one way.

We can price the basket by building the basket survival curve. To do so, we need to build the default distribution at periodic intervals through time. We define the basket default distribution $f(k(t))$ as the probability of having $k(t)$ defaults in the basket at time t. It does not contain enough information to tell us the identity of the defaulting credits. However, since we are considering the case in which the losses are homogeneous, we do not need this information.

To build the default distribution, we use conditional independence. After conditioning on the value of the common market factor Z, all of the credits in the portfolio are independent, and the conditional default probability for credit i is given by

$$p_i(t|Z) = \Phi \left(\frac{C_i(t) - \beta_i Z}{\sqrt{1 - \beta_i^2}} \right).$$

When the credits in the basket are independent, we can use *recursion* to build the conditional default distribution. The recursion approach is based on the idea of starting with a basket with no credits, and then successively adding credits, updating the previous default distribution with each new addition, until all of the credits have been added. The result is a conditional distribution $f(k(t)|Z)$. We repeat this for different values of the market factor and then integrate the results over the market factor distribution to calculate the unconditional default distribution. The algorithm for calculating the conditional default distribution is as follows where $f^{(j)}(k(t)|Z)$ is the conditional probability of $k(t)$ defaults at time t after j credits have been added to the basket:

1. Initialise the default distribution

$$f^{(0)}(k(t)|Z) = \begin{cases} 1 & \text{if } k = 0 \\ 0 & \text{if } 1 \leq k \leq N_C. \end{cases}$$

2. We begin a loop over credits $j = 1, \ldots, N_C$.
3. For each credit j with a conditional default probability $p_j(t|Z)$, we first adjust the zero loss probability which requires the survival of credit j

$$f^{(j)}(0|Z) = f^{(j-1)}(0|Z)(1 - p_j(t|Z)).$$

4. We then loop over losses starting from $k = 1$ up to $k = j$, and update the default distribution in the case when credit j defaults and survives. We have

$$f^{(j)}(k(t)|Z) = f^{(j-1)}(k(t)|Z)(1 - p_j(t|Z)) + f^{(j-1)}(k(t) - 1|Z)p_j(t|Z).$$

5. We return to step (3) to complete the loop over j, finishing when all N_C credits have been added.

Once we have computed the conditional default distribution to a specific time horizon t, we repeat for different values of Z. To compute the unconditional loss distribution $f(k(t))$ to time t, we then integrate these over the Gaussian density as follows

$$f(k(t)) = \int_{-\infty}^{\infty} \phi(Z)f(k(t)|Z)dZ.$$

The result is a default distribution at time t. We repeat this at regular time steps out to the maximum maturity. We can then represent the nth-to-default basket in terms of its survival curve using

$$Q(n(t) < n) = \sum_{k=0}^{n-1} f(k(t))$$

and then input this survival curve into our CDS analytics in order to compute premium and protection leg present values and the nth-to-default breakeven spread. For our CDS recovery rate assumption, we simply use the recovery rate which is common to all the credits in the basket.

Figure 15.6 shows the dependency of the second-, third-, fourth- and fifth-to-default spreads on the asset correlation in a five-name basket with issuer spreads at 30, 60, 90, 120 and 150 bp. We see that the spreads all increase with asset correlation, reflecting the fact that higher correlation makes multiple defaults more probable. Note that in the limit of maximum correlation, the second-to-default spread tends to the second widest spread of 120 bp, the third-to-default spread tends to the third widest spread of 90 bp and so on until the fifth-to-default tends to the least wide spread which is 30 bp.

In Figure 15.7 we see the second-, third-, fourth- and fifth-to-default spreads as a function of the basket maturity. What is notable is that as the time-to-maturity falls to zero, so do the spreads, reflecting the fact that the probability of two or more defaults falls rapidly to zero at T falls. As a result, the $n > 1$ baskets all become risk free in this limit. This explains why we see the FTD spread tend to the sum of the spreads in the limit of $T \to 0$ as shown in Figure 15.4. In this limit, all of the risk of the basket is in the FTD basket.

15.3.2   Inhomogeneous Loss Basket with $n > 1$

The pricing of an inhomogeneous loss basket requires us to identify which credit was the nth to default. Knowledge of the default distribution is not sufficient. We need to know more and hence the calculation needs to condition on the identity of the nth default in the basket. At this point, it becomes simpler to use a Monte Carlo approach. This is the subject of the next section.

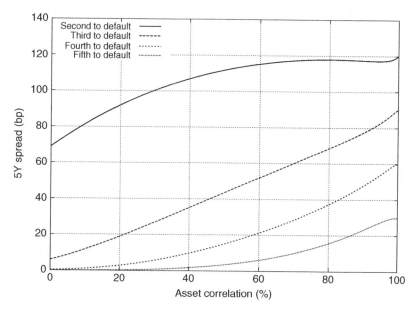

Figure 15.6 Breakeven spread for a five-year contract on a five-name basket with issuer spreads of 30, 60, 90, 120 and 150 bp and recovery rates all at 40% as a function of the asset correlation

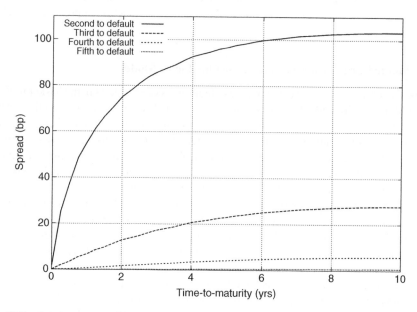

Figure 15.7 Breakeven spread for a five-year contract on a five-name basket with issuer spreads of 30, 60, 90, 120 and 150 bp and recovery rates all at 40% as a function of the time-to-maturity

15.4 PRICING BASKETS USING MONTE CARLO

The advantages of using a Monte Carlo times-to-default simulation of the type discussed in Chapter 14 are:

1. Through the simulation we have direct access to the default time of each asset in the portfolio. This means that we have all the information required in order to price inhomogeneous as well as homogeneous baskets.
2. The approach is generic and so can handle first, second and higher orders of default basket.
3. The Monte Carlo default times simulation can easily handle 1, 2 and generally N-factors.
4. It is fairly easy to switch the choice of copula from say a Gaussian copula to a Student-t copula.

The main disadvantage of Monte Carlo in a rare event setting like credit is that the standard error on the pricing estimate can be significant. This also creates problems when we wish to use the Monte Carlo scheme to compute hedges. However, there are powerful variance reduction techniques which can be used in order to minimise these pricing errors.

In Section 13.5, we showed how to simulate default times using the one-factor latent variable model and in Section 14.6.1 we showed how to generalise this to the full factor Gaussian copula model. In this section, we will first apply the one-factor model to the pricing of generic nth-to-default baskets. We will then do the same using a Gaussian copula approach and then a Student-t copula. This will allow us to answer two questions: (i) what is the pricing impact of the dimensional reduction we impose on our correlation structure by requiring it to be one factor? and (ii) what is the pricing impact of a tail-dependent copula on basket pricing? In the process, we will describe some of the variance reduction approaches which can be used.

15.4.1 Monte Carlo Basket Pricing in the One-factor Model

In the one-factor model, we can calculate the default times of all credits in the basket in P trials using the Monte Carlo method described in Section 13.5. Then, calculating the nth-to-default payoff in each trial requires us to determine which of the credits in the basket is the nth to default. To do this efficiently for a generic nth-to-default basket means that we first remove all default times for which $\tau > T$, the basket maturity. We then sort the remaining default times up to the nth default. Once we have identified the triggering default, we can easily look up the corresponding recovery rate and the discount factor to the default time.

Figure 15.8 shows the prices of an $n = 1, 2, 3, 4, 5$-to-default basket on a five-name basket calculated using a direct Monte Carlo simulation approach. For a comparison, we have also shown the $n = 1$ FTD spread computed using the analytical recursion-based approach described earlier in this chapter and we see close agreement. We use 100 000 trials. As expected, we see that there is Monte Carlo noise in the price.

One variance reduction approach is the importance sampling approach described in Section 13.5.1. In this approach we shift the mean of the market factor distribution by an amount μ in order to make defaults more likely. The important question is how to determine the size of shift μ we should apply. One approach is to try different values of μ and to choose the value μ^* which minimises the standard error of the price estimate. We have done this for different orders of baskets and the results are shown in Figure 15.9. We see that the percentage standard

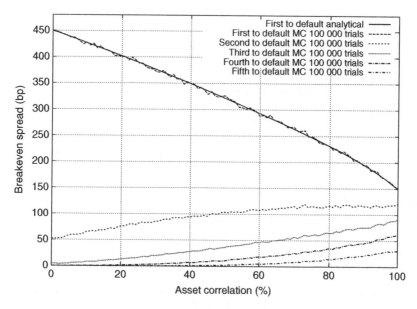

Figure 15.8 Dependence of the breakeven spread of a five-year maturity first-, second-, third-, fourth-and fifth-to-default contract on a five-name basket with issuer curves at 30, 60, 90, 120 and 150 bp. We also plot the analytical first-to-default basket spread as a comparison

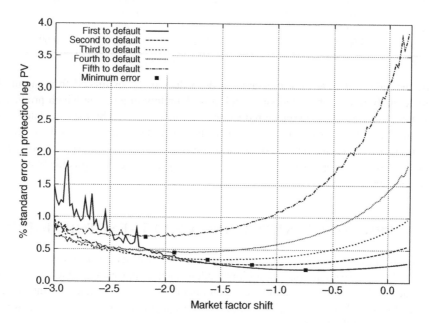

Figure 15.9 The percentage standard error of the PV of the protection leg for a five-year first-, second-, third-, fourth- and fifth-to-default basket as a function of the market factor shift μ using 500 000 Monte Carlo trials. We have marked with black squares the value of μ^* which minimises the standard error

error curve is a roughly parabolic function of μ with a clear value of μ^* at which the standard error is minimised. We also see that the decrease in the standard error from its $\mu = 0$ value is greatest for the higher order baskets such as the fifth-to-default.

Determining μ^* by running through lots of values of μ is computationally expensive. One alternative ad hoc approach suggested in Joshi (2005) is to shift the expected loss of the default distribution so that the expected loss of the basket is equal to loss required to trigger the contract being priced. An nth-to-default basket triggers at an average loss of $(n - 0.5)(1 - R)/N_C$. Mathematically, we solve for $\mu = \hat{\mu}$ where

$$\frac{1}{N_C} \sum_{i=1}^{N_C} (1 - R_i) \int_{-\infty}^{\infty} \phi(Z) \Phi\left(\frac{C_i(T) - \beta_i(Z + \hat{\mu})}{\sqrt{1 - \beta_i^2}}\right) dZ = \frac{1}{N_C}\left(n - \frac{1}{2}\right)(1 - R)$$

where we have used the same value $\hat{\mu}$ for all of the credits in the basket. We can solve this for the basket shown in Figure 15.9 and the results are presented in Table 15.1.

Table 15.1 Estimated value of $\hat{\mu}$ for nth-to-default baskets analysed in Figure 15.9. We also show the decrease in the standard error when we go from $\mu = 0$ to $\mu = \mu^*$. These are taken from the Monte Carlo simulation with 500 000 trials

Basket order n	Theoretical loss trigger	Theoretical adjustment $\hat{\mu}$	Monte-Carlo adjustment μ^*	$\mu = 0$ standard error (%)	$\mu = \mu^*$ standard error (%)
1	0.50	−0.60	−0.74	0.26	0.19
2	1.50	−1.71	−1.22	0.47	0.27
3	2.50	−2.47	−1.62	0.69	0.34
4	3.50	−3.24	−1.92	1.42	0.45
5	4.50	−4.35	−2.18	3.09	0.69

While the values of $\hat{\mu}$ are not the same as the values of μ^* estimated from simulation, they are certainly in the same 'ballpark', and most definitely in a region which produces an improvement in terms of the variance reduction. The main reason why the calculated values of $\hat{\mu}$ are not closer to μ^* is because the adjustment fails to take into account the correlation between the credits which has an important impact on determining whether a basket is triggered. Nonetheless, using this approximation provides an easily implemented and effective variance reduction methodology.

15.5   PRICING BASKETS USING A MULTI-FACTOR MODEL

So far we have priced baskets using a one-factor correlation structure. To move beyond one-factor to N_F factors, we could use a conditional independence approach in which we condition on the value of all N_F factors, compute the conditional loss distribution, and then integrate this conditional loss distribution over all N_F factors. Given a payoff at time T of $\Theta(L(T))$, we have a pricing equation of the form

$$V_T = \int_{-\infty}^{\infty} \left(\prod_{f=1}^{N_F} \phi(Z_f)\right) \Theta\left(L(T)|Z_1, Z_2, \ldots, Z_{N_F}\right) dZ_1 dZ_2 \ldots dZ_{N_F}.$$

This series of nested integrations suffers from the 'curse of dimensionality', meaning that the computation time for computing V_T scales exponentially in N_F and quickly becomes too slow to be practical. This typically occurs for $N_F \gtrsim 3$. The alternative is to use a Monte Carlo approach. The advantage of Monte Carlo is that the computation time is usually fairly linear in the number of factors N_F.

If the *true* correlation matrix used is simple enough to be captured by a one-factor structure, then it is faster to use the one-factor simulation described in Section 13.5, since there is no need to perform a Cholesky factorisation. Also, since we only need to draw independent Gaussian random variables, there is no need to store large numbers of random draws, allowing us to run very large numbers of trials. It is also very easy to implement the importance sampling variance reduction methodology which works well as described in the previous section.

However, most correlation matrices are not one factor and we would like to understand to what extent this may cause us to misprice the basket. Let us therefore suppose that we have a six-name basket with a correlation matrix of the form

$$
\rho = \left(
\begin{array}{cc|cc|cc}
1 & \rho_1 & \rho_2 & \rho_2 & \rho_2 & \rho_2 \\
\rho_1 & 1 & \rho_2 & \rho_2 & \rho_2 & \rho_2 \\
\hline
\rho_2 & \rho_2 & 1 & \rho_1 & \rho_2 & \rho_2 \\
\rho_2 & \rho_2 & \rho_1 & 1 & \rho_2 & \rho_2 \\
\hline
\rho_2 & \rho_2 & \rho_2 & \rho_2 & 1 & \rho_1 \\
\rho_2 & \rho_2 & \rho_2 & \rho_2 & \rho_1 & 1
\end{array}
\right)
$$

where ρ_1 is the intra-sector correlation and ρ_2 is the inter-sector correlation, and where $|\rho_1| > |\rho_2|$. This correlation matrix represents a portfolio of six credits grouped into three sectors. To understand the effect of this multi-factor correlation structure on the price of a basket, we wish to compare it to the price of a basket priced using a flat correlation structure in which we set the flat correlation equal to the average pairwise correlation

$$
\beta^2 = \hat{\rho} = \frac{2}{N_C(N_C - 1)} \sum_{i=1}^{N_C} \sum_{j=1}^{i-1} \rho_{ij}.
$$

To examine this, we use an example of a five-year nth-to-default basket on a portfolio of six credits with 5Y spreads trading at 30, 60, 90, 120, 150 and 180 bp. We assume $\rho_1 = 25\%$ and vary ρ_2 from 20% down to 0%. The results are shown in Table 15.2.

Table 15.2 Comparison of the breakeven basket spread for a full sector correlation and a flat correlation structure for a six-name basket with spreads at 30, 60, 90, 120, 150 and 180 bp

n to default	Breakeven spread (basis points)					
	Full $\rho_1 = 25\%$ $\rho_2 = 20\%$	Flat $\hat{\rho} = 21\%$	Full $\rho_1 = 25\%$ $\rho_2 = 10\%$	Flat $\hat{\rho} = 13\%$	Full $\rho_1 = 25\%$ $\rho_2 = 0\%$	Flat $\hat{\rho} = 5\%$
1	540.9	537.2	572.2	571.4	596.8	606.3
2	128.5	129.1	119.6	118.1	110.8	105.8
3	31.3	30.9	21.5	22.2	15.2	13.4

As expected, the difference in the spreads is largest when the difference between the intra-sector and inter-sector correlation is largest since this is when the one-factor model is least appropriate. However, even in this case, the spread differences are small. This shows that the effect of sectors is very much second order and helps to justify the use of a one-factor correlation structure.

15.6   PRICING BASKETS IN THE STUDENT-*T* COPULA

In Section 13.7, we argued that it is possible to use equity return correlations as a proxy for the asset correlation used in the Gaussian copula model. We also discussed in section 14.6.1 the fact that the Gaussian copula model does not exhibit tail dependence. This raises the question of whether equity returns exhibit tail dependence, and, if so, whether this suggests the use of an alternative copula which also exhibits tail dependence.

This question was investigated by Mashal and Naldi (2002) and Mashal and Zeevi (2002) who demonstrated that the Student-*t* copula is a better fit to the joint distribution of equity price changes than the Gaussian. Since the Student-*t* copula has a non-zero tail dependence parameter, it is better able to capture the tendency for joint extreme events found in the equity data. We would therefore like to understand what impact such a copula has on the pricing of default baskets.

Using a Monte Carlo default times simulation with a Student-*t* copula, we produced the breakeven spreads shown in Table 15.3. This shows how the first- and second-to-default spreads of a five-name basket depend upon the degrees of freedom parameter ν. We recall from Section 14.6.2 that reducing the value of ν increases the tail dependency of the copula, resulting in more extreme joint realisations. It is roughly equivalent to increasing correlation. As a result, we see that reducing ν makes the FTD spread fall as it increases the probability of none of the credits in the basket defaulting. At the same time, it also increases the probability of lots of defaults occurring and so the second-to-default spread increases.

Table 15.3   This table shows the dependency of the 5Y FTD and STD spreads on the degree of freedom parameter ν for a five-name basket with spreads at 30, 60, 90, 120 and 150 bp. We assume a 25% flat correlation. The case $\nu = \infty$ corresponds to the Gaussian copula

Degrees of freedom ν	First-to-default spread (bp)	Second-to-default spread (bp)
3	331.30	101.55
5	351.20	94.70
10	367.85	88.35
20	379.10	84.90
100	386.08	82.30
∞	386.90	79.90

A number of market dealers do price their default baskets using the Student-*t* copula. The implementation does not need to be Monte Carlo based. As with the Gaussian copula, the

Student-t copula can also be cast into a *conditionally independent* framework with a latent variable given by

$$A_i = \left(\beta_i Z + \sqrt{1 - \beta_i^2} \, \varepsilon_i \right) \sqrt{\frac{\nu}{\xi_\nu}}$$

where Z and ε_i are independent Gaussian random draws with mean zero and unit variance, and ξ_ν is a chi-square random variable with ν degrees of freedom. Default occurs before time t if $A_i \leq C_i(t)$ where $C_i(t)$ is given by inverting the cumulative distribution function of the Student-t distribution, i.e. $C_i(t) = t_\nu^{-1}(1 - Q_i(t))$. Therefore, default occurs before time t if

$$\left(\beta_i Z + \sqrt{1 - \beta_i^2} \, \varepsilon_i \right) \sqrt{\frac{\nu}{\xi_\nu}} \leq C_i(t).$$

This can be written as a condition on ε_i

$$\varepsilon_i \leq \frac{C_i(t)\sqrt{\xi_\nu/\nu} - \beta_i Z}{\sqrt{1 - \beta_i^2}}.$$

The conditional default probability is then given by

$$p_i(t|Z, \xi_\nu) = \Phi \left(\frac{C_i(t)\sqrt{\xi_\nu/\nu} - \beta_i Z}{\sqrt{1 - \beta_i^2}} \right).$$

The main disadvantage of the semi-numerical Student-t copula approach when compared to the Gaussian version is that the calculation of the default thresholds requires the inversion of a Student-t cumulative distribution function. Furthermore the integration over the conditional loss distribution requires a joint integral over both a Gaussian and chi-square distribution. As a result, pricing takes several times as long as when using the Gaussian copula. For many this renders the Student-t copula model impractical for pricing and risk managing a large book of default baskets.

In a completely homogeneous basket we have $\beta_i = \beta$ and $C_i(t) = C(t)$, and we can introduce a single *mixing variable*

$$\eta = C(t)\sqrt{\frac{\xi_\nu}{\nu}} - \beta Z$$

conditional on which all the credits are independent. In certain asymptotic limits it is possible to compute the probability density for η analytically as in Schloegl and O'Kane (2005). The implementation of the Student-t copula model is revisited in Section 21.5 in which we discuss its application to the pricing of single tranche CDOs.

15.7   RISK MANAGEMENT OF DEFAULT BASKETS

The value of an nth-to-default basket is sensitive to changes in the level of the credit curves of the basket members, changes in the level of the Libor rates, the assumed recovery rates, the passing of time, and changes in the correlation matrix. Of these, the main risk is the sensitivity to changes in the credit spread and this is the risk we will focus on here.

15.7.1 The Default Basket Delta

Since CDS spreads move around daily, and since a first-to-default basket is a leveraged play on the spreads of the credits in the basket, the most important risk to hedge is the spread risk. We can measure the sensitivity of the price of a first-to-default basket to changes in the spreads of the constituent's credits using the basket spread delta which we define as

$$\Delta_i = \frac{\partial V_{FTD}}{\partial S_i} \left(\frac{\partial V_i}{\partial S_i} \right)^{-1}$$

where V_{FTD} is the mark-to-market value of the first-to-default basket and V_i is the mark-to-market of an on-market CDS with the same maturity as the basket. For a dealer who has purchased FTD protection from an investor, the delta is the amount of credit protection which should be sold in each name to neutralise the combined position against small movements in the CDS spreads.

If the credits in the basket are not identical, each credit in the basket will have a different delta. In addition, rather than hedge each credit with a CDS to the basket maturity, liquidity concerns will mean that we will generally calculate the basket deltas for the standard CDS maturity points. However, we ignore that for the moment since we assume for simplicity that we can trade an on-market CDS to the exact basket maturity.

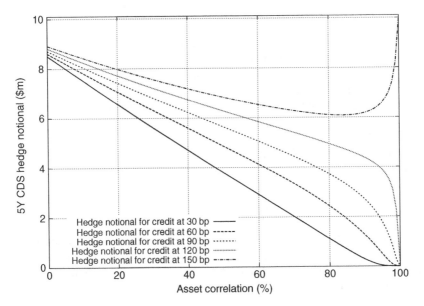

Figure 15.10   The CDS hedge notional for a $10 million face value 5Y first-to-default basket on five credits with flat spread curves at 30, 60, 90, 120 and 150 bp. For each correlation level, the contractual basket spread is set to the breakeven spread

In Figure 15.10 we have plotted the delta for each credit in a $10 million face value first-to-default basket as a function of the flat asset correlation. The credits in the basket have flat CDS spread curves at 30, 60, 90, 120 and 150 bp. For each value of the correlation, we have set the basket spread equal to its breakeven spread so that it is always an on-market basket and so has a mark-to-market value of zero. From this figure we can make a number of observations:

1. In an FTD basket with flat correlations, the delta is highest for the credit most likely to default first and trigger the basket. This is most likely to be the credit with the highest default probability, which, given that all the recovery rates are the same, is the one with the widest spread. Likewise, the next highest delta is for the second most risky credit and so on.
2. The delta of a credit in a first-to-default basket declines with increasing asset correlation. This reflects the decreasing leverage of the basket caused by increasing the default correlation between the credits. This is true for all credits except the riskiest credit.
3. In an FTD basket, the delta of the riskiest credit decreases for low values of correlation. However, it then increases as we approach the maximum correlation limit. In this case, either all the credits survive, or the riskiest credit defaults first. As a result, in this limit, all of the CDS hedge shifts into the riskiest CDS name and the CDS hedge notional for this credit is the basket notional $10 million.

We also wish to be able to delta hedge higher order baskets. Table 15.4 displays the CDS delta hedges for a first-, second-, third-, fourth- and fifth-to-default basket of five credits with spreads of 30, 60, 90, 120, 150 bp at an asset correlation of 20%. As expected, we see that the size of the hedges declines as we go to higher order baskets, reflecting their low spread and lower triggering probability.

Table 15.4   This table shows the notional of the CDS delta hedges required to hedge a $10 million face value five-name 5Y basket with issuer spreads at 30, 60, 90, 120 and 150 bp. We show the hedge for each credit and for the different orders of basket protection using an asset correlation of 20%

Basket order n	CDS delta hedge ($m)				
	30 bp	60 bp	90 bp	120 bp	150 bp
1	6.557	7.057	7.415	7.710	7.971
2	3.152	2.918	2.692	2.461	2.220
3	1.042	0.814	0.653	0.532	0.444
4	0.230	0.145	0.101	0.076	0.060
5	0.027	0.012	0.008	0.006	0.004

15.8   SUMMARY

Baskets are an interesting product which provide a challenge for modellers wishing to price and risk manage them. We have set out how to price them in the context of the one-factor Gaussian copula, and shown that the pricing complexity depends largely on whether the basket has homogeneous or inhomogeneous losses. We have shown the effect of a multi-factor correlation structure, and also the effect of switching to the Student-t copula.

16

Pricing Tranches in the Gaussian Copula Model

16.1 INTRODUCTION

The purpose of this chapter is to explain the pricing of a single tranche CDO (STCDO). We do this using a limiting case of the Gaussian copula model which we call the large homogeneous portfolio (LHP) model. Although we also derive the LHP model within the Student-t copula later in this chapter, the Gaussian copula is the one that we focus on for all our analyses.

The Gaussian LHP model is a limiting case of the Gaussian copula in the sense that it assumes that the reference portfolio contains infinitely many credits, and that the credits have the same default probability, recovery rate and correlation. The first presentation of this analytical limit was provided by Vasicek (1987). It has also found use within the Basel II framework for calculating bank regulatory capital (Gordy 2003).

Our justification for using this model is that it allows us to write a simple closed-form equation for the density of the portfolio loss distribution and for the price of a tranche. The advantage of this is that this implementation is typically 100 times faster[1] than a model which calculates the exact portfolio loss distribution. The percentage error between the exact price and the LHP price is typically within 5%. As a result, we have found that the LHP model, while perhaps not accurate enough for the purposes of full-blown industrial pricing and hedging of synthetic tranches, is extremely useful as an approximation against which we can quickly and easily test our intuition.

Indeed, intuition building is something which is a serious challenge to practitioners working in the correlation market. Not only do we need to understand the behaviour of tranche prices, we also need to understand the spread delta, the spread gamma, the value-on-default and the theta if we are to hedge appropriately. With so many moving parts, it is often hard to find a way to build intuition. Also, playing with scenarios in real time is difficult if the pricing model is slow and if we have to deal with and keep track of large numbers of inputs. The LHP model is the perfect compromise as it is simple and fast to use, yet is close enough to an exact model to present the same behaviour. In the next chapter we will extend the LHP model to what we call the 'LH+' model. This has the added advantage that it enables us to measure idiosyncratic risk.

16.2 THE LHP MODEL

The LHP model is based on the one-factor Gaussian latent variable model. We define

$$A_i = \beta_i Z + \sqrt{1 - \beta_i^2} \varepsilon_i$$

---

[1] This ratio depends on the nature of the reference portfolio in terms of the number of credits and the homogeneity of the losses. For more details see Chapter 18.

where $i = 1, \ldots, N_C$ and Z, ε_i are independent Gaussian random variables with mean zero and unit variance. We recall that default time $\tau_i \leq T$ if $A_i \leq C_i(T)$ where $C_i(T)$ is the default threshold which is calibrated to the term structure of survival probabilities for issuer i, i.e. $C_i(T) = \Phi^{-1}(1 - Q_i(T))$. Conditional on the market factor Z, default occurs before time T with a probability

$$p_i(T|Z) = \Phi\left(\frac{C_i(T) - \beta_i Z}{\sqrt{1 - \beta_i^2}}\right).$$

Furthermore, conditional on Z, all of the N_C credits in the portfolio are independent. If we assume that the portfolio is homogeneous so that $\beta_i = \beta$, $R_i = R$ and $p_i(T|Z) = p(T|Z)$, then the conditional loss distribution for the portfolio is the binomial distribution. We show in Section 16.7.1 that the variance of the portfolio loss distribution for independent credits with default probability $p(T|Z)$ is given by

$$\mathbb{V}[L(T|Z)] = \frac{p(T|Z)(1 - p(T|Z))(1 - R)^2}{N_C}.$$

As N_C increases, the variance of the conditional loss distribution falls as $O(N_C^{-1})$. This is shown clearly in Figure 16.1 in which we have calculated and plotted the portfolio loss distribution for a portfolio of $N_C = 100$, 1000 and $10\,000$ independent credits. In the limit of the number of credits N_C tending to infinity, the conditional loss distribution tends to unit point mass of probability located at the expected portfolio loss

$$\mathbb{E}[L(T)|Z] = (1 - R)p(T|Z).$$

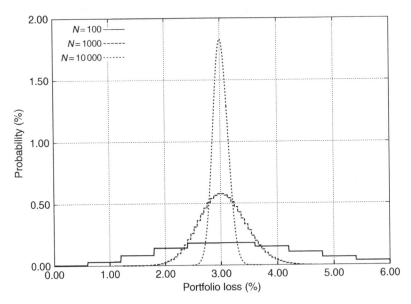

Figure 16.1 Binomial loss distribution for a portfolio of independent and homogeneous credits with $p = 5\%$, $R = 40\%$ as a function of the number of credits in the portfolio, N_C

This result is a manifestation of the *law of large numbers*. We can consider two limits of the market factor Z:

1. In the limit $Z \to -\infty$, the conditional loss of the portfolio tends to $(1 - R)$. This corresponds to a 'bad' state of the world in which all of the credits in the portfolio default.
2. In the limit $Z \to +\infty$, the conditional loss of the portfolio tends to 0. This represents a 'good' state of the world in which nothing defaults.

By integrating the conditional loss distribution over Z, we can calculate the unconditional portfolio loss distribution which can then be used to price tranches.

16.2.1 The Portfolio Loss Distribution

We denote the cumulative distribution function of the time T portfolio loss distribution with $F(K)$ which we define as

$$F(K) = \Pr(L(T) \le K).$$

This is an increasing function of K. Within the LHP model, the portfolio loss conditional on the value of Z is given by

$$L(T) = (1 - R)p(T|Z) = (1 - R)\Phi\left(\frac{C(T) - \beta Z}{\sqrt{1 - \beta^2}}\right).$$

As a result, the horizon T cumulative loss distribution function is given by

$$F(K) = \Pr\left((1 - R)\,\Phi\left(\frac{C(T) - \beta Z}{\sqrt{1 - \beta^2}}\right) \le K\right).$$

This can be recast as a condition on the market factor Z of the form

$$Z \ge A(K)$$

where

$$A(K) = \frac{1}{\beta}\left(C(T) - \sqrt{1 - \beta^2}\,\Phi^{-1}\left(\frac{K}{1 - R}\right)\right).$$

Since $Z \sim N(0, 1)$, we can write the cumulative distribution function as

$$F(K) = 1 - \Phi(A(K)).$$

The probability density function for the loss distribution $f(K)$ can then be calculated analytically by noting that

$$f(K) = \frac{\partial F(K)}{\partial K}$$

to give

$$f(K) = \frac{\phi(A(K))\,\sqrt{1 - \beta^2}}{(1 - R)}\,\frac{\sqrt{1 - \beta^2}}{\beta}\left(\phi\left(\Phi^{-1}\left(\frac{K}{(1 - R)}\right)\right)\right)^{-1}.$$

Example: Figure 16.2 shows the LHP loss distributions for a portfolio with a spread of 50 bp to a five-year horizon for $\beta^2 = 10\%$ and $\beta^2 = 20\%$. We make the following observations:

- When the correlation is 10%, the distribution is fairly broad and slightly skewed with an expected loss of 2.5%.
- When the correlation is 20%, we see two important changes. First, the probability of having very few losses increases so that the peak of the distribution is now close to a portfolio loss of 0.50%. We also see a significant extension of the tail of the loss distribution as larger losses become more likely.

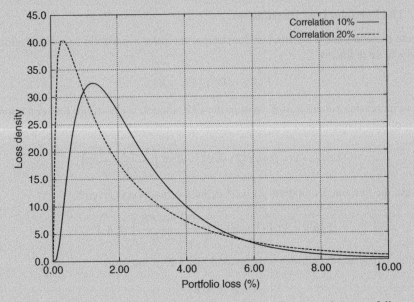

Figure 16.2 The LHP portfolio loss distribution to a five-year horizon for a portfolio spread of 50 bp. We show the cases $\beta^2 = 10\%$ and $\beta^2 = 20\%$. In both cases the expected portfolio loss is 2.50%

16.2.2 The Tranche Survival Curve

We showed in Section 12.7 that a tranche can be priced once we have the time zero tranche survival curve $Q(T, K_1, K_2)$. This is given by

$$Q(T, K_1, K_2) = 1 - \frac{\mathbb{E}\left[\min(L(T), K_2) - \min(L(T), K_1)\right]}{(K_2 - K_1)}.$$

We can write

$$\mathbb{E}\left[\min(L(T), K)\right] = \mathbb{E}\left[L(T)1_{L(T)<K}\right] + K\,\mathbb{E}\left[1_{L(T)\geq K}\right].$$

From above we know that

$$\mathbb{E}\left[1_{L(T)\geq K}\right] = \Pr(L(T) \geq K) = 1 - F(K) = \Phi(A(K)).$$

We can also calculate

$$\mathbb{E}\left[L(T)1_{L(T)<K}\right] = (1-R)\int_{A(K)}^{\infty}\Phi\left(\frac{C(T)-\beta Z}{\sqrt{1-\beta^2}}\right)\phi(Z)dZ$$

$$= (1-R)\Phi_2\left(C(T),-A(K),-\beta\right)$$

where the bi-variate normal cumulative distribution function $\Phi_2(a,b,\rho)$ is defined as

$$\Phi_2(a,b,\rho) = \frac{1}{2\pi\sqrt{1-\rho^2}}\int_{-\infty}^{a}dx\int_{-\infty}^{b}dy\exp\left(-\frac{x^2-2\rho xy+y^2}{2(1-\rho^2)}\right). \tag{16.1}$$

As a result, we have

$$\mathbb{E}\left[\min(L(T),K)\right] = (1-R)\Phi_2(C(T),-A(K),-\beta) + K\Phi(A(K))$$

which can be substituted into the equation for the tranche survival curve.

16.2.3   The Tranche Loss Distribution

The loss distribution for a tranche tells us the probability of incurring a certain loss on the investment in the tranche. It can be broken into three distinct sections:

1. First, there is the probability of zero loss on the tranche. In terms of the portfolio loss distribution, this is given by $\Pr(L(T) \leq K_1)$. This probability increases with the tranche subordination K_1. As a result, tranches with $K_1 > 0$ usually have a non-zero probability mass at zero tranche loss.
2. The body of the tranche loss distribution, which is the probability of tranche losses between 0% and 100%, is simply the probability of the corresponding loss on the portfolio loss distribution.
3. The probability of a 100% loss can be expressed in terms of the portfolio loss distribution as $\Pr(L(T) \geq K_2)$. This probability decreases with increasing K_2 but increases with correlation β^2.

Figure 16.3 compares the loss distribution for a 0–3% tranche and a 3–6% tranche for $\beta^2 = 20\%$. This is not the density but the probability distribution in which we have discretised the losses into buckets of width 0.025%:

- In the case of the 0–3% tranche, there is no probability mass at zero loss since the portfolio loss distribution also has a zero probability at zero loss. The rest of the body of the tranche loss distribution is simply the 'rescaled' 0–3% section of the portfolio loss distribution shown in Figure 16.2. The probability at 100% tranche loss is simply the probability of losses greater than 3% on the portfolio loss distribution and equals approximately 30%.
- For the 3–6% tranche loss distribution, we see that there is a peak of probability mass at zero loss corresponding to the probability of losses below 3% on the portfolio loss distribution. The body of the tranche loss distribution corresponds to the rescaled portfolio loss distribution between 3% and 6%. The probability of a 100% tranche loss is now 10%, lower than the maximum loss of the 0–3% tranche since $\Pr(L > 6\%) < \Pr(L > 3\%)$.

We now consider the factors that drive the value of the tranche spread.

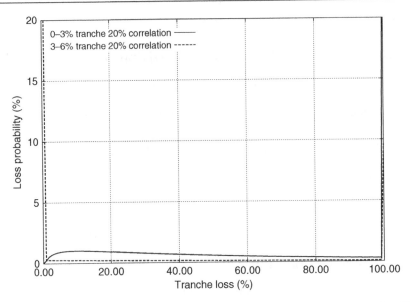

Figure 16.3   The LHP tranche loss distribution for a 0–3% tranche and a 3–6% tranche using $\beta^2 = 20\%$. Losses have been discretised into 0.025%-wide buckets. We assume a horizon of five years and a portfolio spread of 50 bp.

16.3   DRIVERS OF THE TRANCHE SPREAD

Now that we have the pricing formula for a tranche, we can start to analyse how the price depends on the various characteristics of the reference portfolio and the tranche.

16.3.1   Tranche Subordination and Width

Changing the subordination of a tranche is the most direct way to change the risk–return profile of a tranche. This is shown clearly in Figure 16.4 in which we plot the tranche spread as a function of the subordination of the tranche. We do this for tranches of width 3%, 6% and 9%. The spread of the reference portfolio is set at 50 bp.

We see that the tranche spread falls rapidly as we increase K_1. We also note for reasonably wide equity tranches that the 'rule-of-thumb' is that the tranche spread can be approximated by S/K_2. For example, the 6%-wide tranche has a model-implied equity spread of 846 bp, which is close to the 50 bp/6% = 833 bp. This reflects the fact that most of the portfolio loss distribution sits below the 6% strike. Clearly, in the limit $K_2 = 100\%$, the 'equity' spread equals the portfolio spread and this approximation is then exact.

As we increase the tranche width, the breakeven spread falls roughly in inverse proportion to its width. This is because if we fix K_1 and increase K_2, the amount of additional risk being added to the tranche quickly falls as we enter the tail of the loss distribution. However, the tranche spread, which is calculated by dividing by the tranche width, has a $1/(K_2 - K_1)$ dependence.

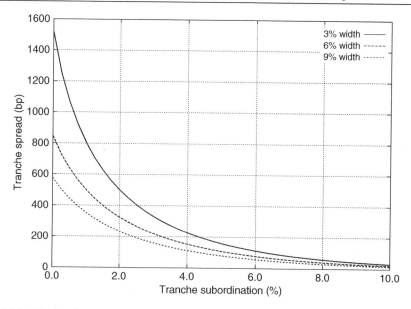

Figure 16.4 The breakeven spread of a 5Y tranche as a function of its subordination and for different tranche widths. We use $\beta^2 = 20\%$ and the portfolio has a spread of 50 bp

16.3.2   Portfolio Spread

Figure 16.5 shows the breakeven tranche spreads for a 0–3%, 3–6%, 6–9%, 9–12% and 12–20% tranche as a function of the spread of the reference portfolio. We see that the breakeven spread of all tranches is an increasing function of the average spread of the reference portfolio. This is no surprise since increasing the spread effectively shifts the mean of the loss distribution to the right. It therefore makes the tranches more likely to incur losses. However, the tranche spread sensitivity, known as the tranche leverage, depends on the subordination and width of the tranche. This figure clearly demonstrates the much greater spread sensitivity of the equity tranche versus the mezzanine tranche and more senior tranches.

16.3.3   Portfolio Correlation

In Figure 16.6 we plot the breakeven spread of a set of tranches as a function of the asset correlation β^2. We observe that:

- The 0–3% equity tranche breakeven spread falls with increasing correlation, reflecting the lower risk of the tranche as the probability of few defaults increases.
- The 3–6%, 6–9% and 9–12% tranche spreads increase with correlation but also start to fall beyond a certain correlation.

One way to explain the fall in the mezzanine and senior tranche spreads beyond a certain correlation is to realise that in the limit of 100% correlation, the spread of tranches which detach below the maximum loss tends towards $S/(1 - R)$. In this case $S = 60\,\text{bp}$ and $R = 40\%$

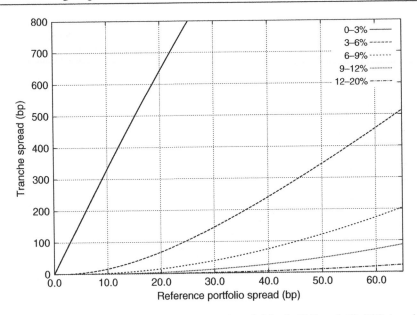

Figure 16.5 The breakeven spread of a 0–3%, 3–6%, 6–9%, 9–12% and 12–20% tranche as a function of the average spread of the reference portfolio. We assume a five-year trade and a correlation of $\beta^2 = 20\%$

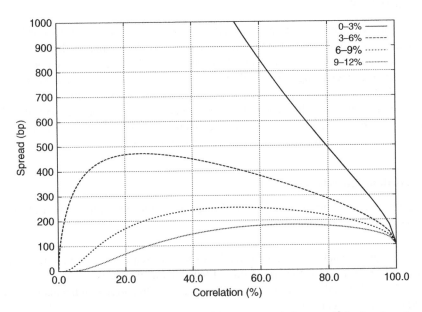

Figure 16.6 Breakeven 5Y spread as a function of the asset correlation $\rho = \beta^2$ for four tranches 0–3%, 3–6%, 6–9% and 9–12%. The portfolio has a spread of 60 bp

so the spreads tend to 100 bp.[2] This means that the mezzanine and senior spreads all have to fall as the correlation tends to this limit.

16.3.4 Time-to-Maturity

Figure 16.7 shows how the breakeven spread of the three tranches depends on the remaining time-to-maturity. This has been plotted on a logarithmic scale in order to capture the wide variation in spreads at different levels of the capital structure. We see that the spread of the equity tranche falls from a value of around 1280 bp at five years to 1200 bp as the time-to-maturity tends to zero. The spreads of the mezzanine and senior tranches also fall as maturity approaches, but tend to zero. This is explained by realising that as the remaining time to maturity falls, there is less time for the defaults necessary to eat up the subordination on these tranches. As a result, they effectively become risk free as the maturity date approaches and all of the portfolio risk is shifted into the equity tranche. Since the reference portfolio spread is 60 bp, in the limit of the time-to-maturity tending to zero, all of the risk moves into the equity tranche and so its spread tends to 60 bp divided by the equity tranche width of 5% which equals 1200 bp.

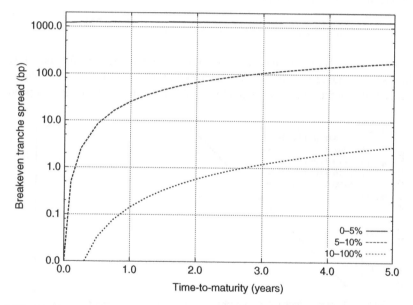

Figure 16.7 The breakeven spread of a 0–5%, 5–10% and 10–100% tranche as a function of the remaining time-to-maturity. The spread is plotted on a logarithmic scale. The average portfolio spread is 60 bp, the correlation $\beta = 45\%$ and $R = 40\%$

---

[2] At 100% correlation the portfolio loss distribution becomes bi-modal with point masses on 0% loss and $(1 - R) = 60\%$ loss. As all of the tranches below the maximum loss lose 100% in this event, they all have the same tranche survival curves and hence the same spread. To any horizon, we can write

$$Q(t, T, K_1, K_2) = 1 - \Pr(L(T) = 1 - R)$$

where the tranche is priced using a *zero recovery assumption*. However, this survival curve equals the credit curve for the homogeneous credits portfolio and these are priced with a recovery assumption of R. Hence, comparing the tranche and CDS pricing formulae, we find that $S(K_1, K_2) = S/(1 - R)$ when $K_2 < 1 - R$.

16.4   ACCURACY OF THE LHP APPROXIMATION

So far, we have assumed that the portfolio we have is large and homogeneous. In practice this is not the case. However, we hope that the portfolios that we typically consider are large enough and homogeneous enough that this LHP approximation is reasonably close to the prices produced by a model which captures the finite number of credits in a portfolio (we will discuss how to do this in Chapter 18). To use the LHP approximation, we need to enter the average default probability, recovery rate and correlation for the real portfolio

$$p = \frac{1}{N_C} \sum_{i=1}^{N_C} p_i \qquad R = \frac{1}{N_C} \sum_{i=1}^{N_C} R_i \qquad \beta = \frac{1}{N_C} \sum_{i=1}^{N_C} \beta_i.$$

We examine the effect of a finite size approximation by comparing the LHP tranche spreads with the 'exact' spreads produced by constructing the exact loss distribution using the recursion method described in Chapter 18. The portfolio is spread homogeneous. We do this for values of N_C ranging from 1000 to 20 000. We then test the $1/N_C$ convergence by plotting the breakeven spread as a function of $1/N_C$ for five different tranches. Specifically, we assume that the first-order spread correction is given by

$$\lim_{N_C \to \infty} S(K_1, K_2) = S(K_1, K_2) (N_C \text{ finite}) + \frac{\alpha(K_1, K_2)}{N_C}.$$

A positive value for α implies that the LHP spread is higher than the finite N_C spread. We have plotted the results in Figure 16.8 and we see that the points lie on straight lines, confirming that the difference between the exact spread and the LHP spread obeys an $O(1/N_C)$ dependence.

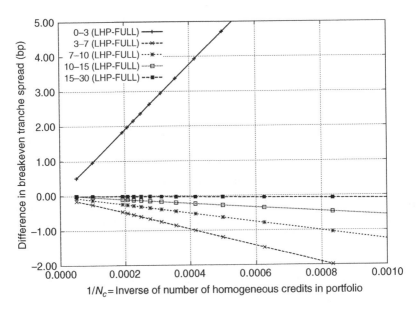

Figure 16.8   Difference between exact model breakeven spread and LHP model breakeven spread as a function of $1/N_C$ where N_C is the number of credits in the portfolio and ranges from 1000 to 20 000. Results are shown for tranches 0–3%, 3–7%, 7–10%, 10–15%, 15–30%. The portfolio is homogeneous with flat issuer spreads at 100 bp and $R = 50\%$

We note from this analysis that the LHP spread is greater than the exact spread of the equity tranche. We explain this by noting that the LHP loss distribution has a lower variance about its mean than the exact loss distribution since it models the conditional loss distribution as a single peak rather than the finite variance binomial distribution. As a result, it assigns a lower probability to low losses than the exact distribution. This makes the equity tranche riskier. We also note that the LHP spread is lower than the exact spread for the more senior tranches. This time the higher variance of the exact loss distribution means that it has fatter tails than the LHP loss distribution. This makes the senior tranches more risky in the exact model.

This analysis only tells us how the error of the LHP approximation scales as a function of N_C for homogeneous portfolios. We have also compared the pricing of realistic tranches using the LHP model to those priced using a full model. This analysis is not presented here but in Section 18.6. We find that the percentage pricing error is typically within 3% of the exact spread level for tranches on fairly homogeneous and high grade credit loss portfolios such as CDX NA IG. The percentage error of tranches on the CDX HY portfolio is much higher since it has fewer credits (100 rather than 125) and its spread distribution is much more disperse.

16.5   THE LHP MODEL WITH TAIL DEPENDENCE

Tail dependence, which was formally defined in Section 14.5, is a measure of the likelihood of extreme joint events. It is an empirically observed feature of equity returns as shown in Mashal and Zeevi (2002). Since it has been argued that equity return correlation is a proxy for the asset correlation in latent variable models, it is of interest to derive an LHP-style model with tail dependence and we do this using the Student-t copula following Schloegl and O'Kane (2005). We recall that the Student-t version of the latent variable model defines

$$A_i = \left(\beta_i Z + \sqrt{1 - \beta_i^2} \varepsilon_i \right) \sqrt{\frac{\nu}{\xi_\nu}}$$

where ξ_ν is an independent chi-square random variable with ν degrees of freedom, and ε_i and Z are independent random draws from a Gaussian distribution with mean zero and unit variance. Note that this is no longer a factor model – since both the idiosyncratic and systemic terms have the same random variable ξ_ν they are no longer independent.

Default occurs before or at time T if A_i falls below some threshold $C_i(T)$. This condition can be written as

$$\varepsilon_i \leq \frac{C_i(T)\sqrt{\xi_\nu/\nu} - \beta_i Z}{\sqrt{1 - \beta_i^2}}.$$

Because A_i is Student-t distributed

$$C_i(T) = t_\nu^{-1}(1 - Q_i(T))$$

where t_ν is the Student-t cumulative distribution function with ν degrees of freedom as defined in Equation 14.5. We assume a homogeneous portfolio so that $C_i(T) = C(T)$ and $\beta_i = \beta$. This allows us to define a mixing variable which is common to all credits

$$\eta = C(T)\sqrt{\frac{\xi}{\nu}} - \beta Z.$$

Conditional on η, the default probability of issuer i is given by

$$\Pr(A_i \leq C_i(T)|\eta) = \Phi\left(\frac{\eta}{\sqrt{1-\beta^2}}\right).$$

Once again we take the limit of a large homogeneous portfolio. By the law of large numbers, the conditional loss $L(\eta)$ on the portfolio is given by

$$\lim_{N \to \infty} L(\eta) = (1-R)\Phi\left(\frac{\eta}{\sqrt{1-\beta^2}}\right).$$

There is a unique mapping from each value of η to each portfolio loss $L(\eta)$. As a result, the cumulative distribution function for the loss distribution, $F(K)$, can be written in terms of the cumulative distribution function for η. We have

$$F(K) = \Pr(L \leq K) = \Pr\left(\eta \leq \sqrt{1-\beta^2}\Phi^{-1}\left(\frac{K}{1-R}\right)\right).$$

We therefore need to compute the cumulative distribution function for η. Schloegl and O'Kane (2005) show that the final cumulative distribution function for the loss distribution is given by

$$F(K) = \Pr(L \leq K) = \Phi(\theta/\beta) + \int_{-\infty}^{-\theta/\beta} \Gamma\left(\frac{v}{2}, \frac{v(\theta+\beta u)^2}{2C(T)^2}\right)\phi(u)du$$

where

$$\theta = \sqrt{1-\beta^2}\;\Phi^{-1}\left(\frac{K}{1-R}\right).$$

This integral over u can be calculated numerically. A simple trapezium rule works fine. What we find is that the effect of the Student-t copula is to shift more probability mass into the high loss and low loss regions of the loss distribution, thereby making senior tranches more risky and equity tranches less risky.

16.6   SUMMARY

The LHP model is a simple yet powerful model for pricing and risk managing of STCDOs. It captures all of the important market variables such as average spread, average correlation, and average recovery rate. It does not capture the effect of spread and correlation dispersion. For this reason it cannot be recommended for industrial pricing. However, its speed and ease of implementation make it a great tool for 'what-if' type analyses and it is a superb tool for building intuition.

16.7   TECHNICAL APPENDIX

16.7.1   Variance of an Independent Loss Distribution

Consider a portfolio of N independent credits, each with a default probability $p_i(T)$ and recovery rate R_i and equal face value exposure. We wish to consider the loss distribution to some fixed horizon time T. We introduce the default indicator function $1_{\tau_i \leq T}$ defined such that

$$1_{\tau_i \le T} = \begin{cases} 1 & \text{if } \tau_i \le T \\ 0 & \text{if } \tau_i > T. \end{cases}$$

As a result

$$p_i(T) = \mathbb{E}\left[1_{\tau_i \le T}\right].$$

The portfolio loss is given by

$$L(T) = \frac{1}{N} \sum_{i=1}^{N} 1_{\tau_i \le T}(1 - R_i).$$

The portfolio expected loss is given by

$$\mathbb{E}\left[L(T)\right] = \frac{1}{N} \sum_{i=1}^{N} \mathbb{E}\left[1_{\tau_i \le T}\right](1 - R_i) = \frac{1}{N} \sum_{i=1}^{N} p_i(T)(1 - R_i).$$

The variance of the loss distribution is given by

$$\mathbb{V}[L(T)] = \mathbb{E}\left[\left(\frac{1}{N} \sum_{i=1}^{N} 1_{\tau_i \le T}(1 - R_i)\right)^2\right] - (\mathbb{E}\left[L(T)\right])^2$$

$$= \frac{1}{N^2} \sum_{i,j=1}^{N} \mathbb{E}\left[1_{\tau_i \le T} 1_{\tau_j \le T}\right](1 - R_i)(1 - R_j) - (\mathbb{E}\left[L(T)\right])^2.$$

Substituting for $\mathbb{E}\left[L(T)\right]$

$$\mathbb{V}[L(T)] = \frac{1}{N^2} \sum_{i,j=1}^{N} \left(\mathbb{E}\left[1_{\tau_i \le T} 1_{\tau_j \le T}\right] - p_i(T)p_j(T)\right)(1 - R_i)(1 - R_j).$$

If $i = j$ then

$$\mathbb{E}\left[1_{\tau_i \le T}^2\right] = p_i(T).$$

If $i \ne j$, the credits are independent and we have

$$\mathbb{E}\left[1_{\tau_i \le T} 1_{\tau_j \le T}\right] = p_i(T)p_j(T).$$

The terms with $i \ne j$ all cancel out leaving just the terms with $i = j$

$$\mathbb{V}[L(T)] = \frac{1}{N^2} \sum_{i=1}^{N} p_i(T)(1 - p_i(T))(1 - R_i)^2.$$

Note that the variance of the portfolio loss distribution is fast to calculate as it is simply a summation over N terms and not N^2 terms. We see that the variance decreases as $O(1/N)$. To see this more clearly, consider the special case of a homogeneous portfolio in which $p_i(T) = p(T)$ and $R_i = R$. The expected portfolio loss is

$$\mathbb{E}[L(T)] = p(T)(1 - R) \tag{16.2}$$

and

$$\mathbb{V}[L(T)] = \frac{p(T)(1 - p(T))(1 - R)^2}{N}. \tag{16.3}$$

The variance of the portfolio loss distribution tends to zero in the limit of $N \to \infty$.

17

Risk Management of Synthetic Tranches

17.1 INTRODUCTION

Hedging all the risks of synthetic CDO tranches is a highly complex task. To better understand these risks, we break them into two types:

1. Systemic risks: The sensitivity of the tranche value to changes which are common to all credits.
2. Idiosyncratic risks: The sensitivity of the tranche value to changes in the characteristics of just one credit.

We begin this chapter by discussing the systemic risks of the tranche. These represent the sensitivity of the tranche value to the changes in the average spread, correlation, the level of interest rates and the passage of time. For simplicity, we do this using the LHP model. While this model does not produce numbers which agree exactly with a full loss distribution model, it is certainly able to give us the correct behaviour for the systemic characteristics.

We then discuss how to calculate the idiosyncratic risks. For this we introduce an extension to the LHP model called the LH+ model. This model enables us to isolate and study the effect of changing the characteristics of one credit in the portfolio while keeping the rest of the portfolio fixed, i.e. we can use it to study idiosyncratic risks. Once we have explained the systemic and idiosyncratic risks, we then explain how to hedge them.

In this chapter, all of the example risk numbers have been generated from the perspective of a protection buyer since it is the dealer, who is typically the buyer of protection, who has to hedge the risk. Investors, who are typically the sellers of protection, do so to assume the risk of the tranche and to receive the spread.

The examples found in this chapter are all based on the tranches whose details are given in Table 17.1. Their contractual spreads are set close to their fair values, so the tranche values are close to zero. The reference portfolio consists of 125 credits with an average spread of 60 bp. We also use an asset correlation of $\rho = \beta^2 = 25\%$.

Table 17.1 The tranches used for examples in this chapter. The reference portfolio consists of 125 names with \$10 million notional all trading at 60 bp

Tranches	0–3	3–7	7–10	10–15	15–30
Contractual spread (bp)	1750	400	150	60	8
Breakeven spread (bp)	1790.2	405.3	148.4	58.1	8.6
Tranche notional (\$m)	37.5	50	37.5	62.5	187.5

17.2 SYSTEMIC RISKS

Using the LHP model, we can examine the sensitivity of the tranche price to systemic changes in the characteristics of the portfolio or to changes in the structure of the deal. We begin with the tranche risky PV01, also known as the tranche RPV01.

17.2.1 Tranche RPV01

As with a CDS contract, we can define a T-maturity tranche risky PV01 as the present value of \$1 paid on the premium leg of the tranche. At time zero we have

$$\text{RPV01}(0) = \frac{1}{2} \sum_{n=1}^{N_T} \Delta(t_{n-1}, t_n) Z(t_n) \left(Q(t_{n-1}, K_1, K_2) + Q(t_n, K_1, K_2) \right)$$

where $Z(t_n)$ is the Libor discount factor to time t_n, n indexes the N_T premium payments,

$$Q(t_n, K_1, K_2) = \mathbb{E}\left[1 - L(t_n, K_1, K_2)\right]$$

is the tranche survival probability and $L(t_n, K_1, K_2)$ is the fractional loss on the K_1 to K_2 tranche notional at time t_n. Since the notional of the tranche falls if the tranche takes losses, the RPV01 reflects the credit risk of the tranche in the same way as the RPV01 of a CDS reflects the credit risk of the reference entity. For senior tranches which are usually low risk, the RPV01 is close to the risk-free Libor PV01.[1] However, for riskier tranches, the RPV01 will be much lower. For a newly issued (on-market) tranche, the RPV01 is the sensitivity of the tranche value to a 1 bp change in the *tranche market spread*.

17.2.2 Systemic Delta, DV01 and Leverage Ratio

The systemic delta is the notional amount of the underlying reference portfolio on which we would need to sell protection so that the combined position is insensitive to small portfolio-wide spread changes. The leverage ratio is a measure of by how many times the tranche has leveraged the credit spread sensitivity of the reference portfolio. We also have a measure called the systemic DV01. This is simply the change in the dollar value of the tranche for a 1 bp widening in the spreads of the reference portfolio.

In the case of the LHP model, the portfolio is assumed to be homogeneous in spreads and so the spread change is automatically the same for each credit in the portfolio. However, when we use a model which distinguishes between the individual credits, the systemic delta measures the sensitivity to a situation in which all portfolio spreads widen by some amount and this can be captured in a number of ways. Here we will assume that this corresponds to a 1 bp widening in the spread curve for each credit. However, if the reference portfolio is a CDS index, we note that a widening by 1 bp in all credits may not correspond exactly to a 1 bp widening in the index spread. This was discussed in Section 10.5 where we demonstrated that the tranche spread is

---

[1] The RPV01 does not necessarily approach the risk-free PV01 as tranches become more senior. This is because super senior tranches experience amortisation of their notional equal in size to the recovery value as soon as there are defaults on the reference portfolio. For example, suppose we have a senior tranche on a low risk and low correlation reference portfolio so that the 20–30% tranche is essentially risk free. Suppose that we also have a super senior 90–100% tranche. In the latter case, the super senior tranche is more likely to amortise due to defaults than the 20–30% tranche and so the super senior 90–100% tranche could have a lower RPV01 than the 20–30% tranche.

approximately equal to the RPV01-weighted index spreads. We compute the systemic delta as follows:

1. Value the tranche using the current market spread curves to give $V_0(K_1, K_2)$.
2. Bump all issuer spread curves by a 1 bp parallel shift and rebuild all of the issuer survival curves.
3. Value the tranche using the bumped issuer curves to calculate $V_1(K_1, K_2)$.
4. Value the reference portfolio using the bumped issuer curves to give P_1. Note that before the bump the reference portfolio has a total value of zero since it is a portfolio of on-market CDS.
5. Calculate the systemic DV01 using

$$\text{Systemic DV01} = V_1(K_1, K_2) - V_0(K_1, K_2).$$

6. Calculate the systemic delta using

$$\Delta_S = \left(\frac{V_1(K_1, K_2) - V_0(K_1, K_2)}{P_1} \right) \times F$$

where F is the face value of the reference portfolio.
7. Calculate the tranche leverage ratio. This is given by

$$L = \Delta_S / F(K_1, K_2)$$

where $F(K_1, K_2)$ is the face value of the tranche.

In Figure 17.1 we plot the systemic delta for a set of tranches as a function of the portfolio spread. We make the following observations:

- The systemic delta for the equity tranche is very large when the portfolio spread is small since in this regime almost the entire portfolio risk is sitting in the 0–3% equity tranche. We might expect the equity delta to approach the notional of the reference portfolio which is $1.25 billion. However, it exceeds this number because the equity protection buyer is also exposed to a spread sensitivity on the premium leg which pays a spread of 1750 bp. When spreads increase, the value of the protection goes up and the value of the premium leg, which we are paying, goes down. Both effects increase the value of the tranche. As a result, the tranche spread delta is higher than it is for the protection leg alone.
- As the portfolio spread increases, the risk of the equity tranche increases but the equity delta starts to fall. At the same time, the deltas of the mezzanine and senior tranches start to increase.
- Beyond a spread of about 60 bp, we see the delta of the 3–7% tranche start to fall. At these spreads, the mezzanine is becoming equity-like as the mean of the loss distribution is moving through it and into the more senior tranches.

The leverage ratio is simply the systemic delta divided by the notional of the tranche. Since the notional of the equity tranche is $37.5 million, we note that its leverage is greater than 30 at low spreads, falling to 18 when the portfolio spread is 60 bp. The mezzanine tranche has a notional of $50 million and so with a delta notional of over $400 million, it has a leverage ratio of just over eight at this portfolio spread. We have to go to the most senior 15–30% tranche to find a leverage ratio below one. If the leverage ratio is greater than one then the tranche has

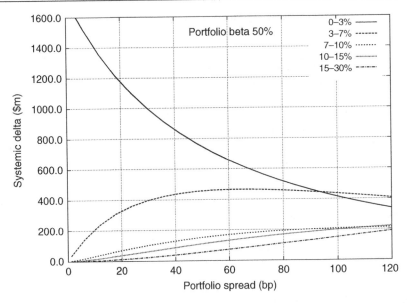

Figure 17.1   The systemic delta for tranches 0–3%, 3–7%, 7–10%, 10–15%, 15–30% as a function of the portfolio spread. We assume a correlation of $\beta^2 = 25\%$. This is from the perspective of a protection buyer

leveraged the reference portfolio, if less than one then the tranche can be considered to have deleveraged the risk of the reference portfolio.

17.2.3   Interest Rate DV01

We do not consider the interest rate risk of a synthetic CDO tranche here because it is handled in exactly the same way as a CDS as described in Chapter 8. Provided we can build a tranche survival curve, we can simply map the tranche onto a standard CDS contract. We can then use the approach described in Section 8.6.

17.2.4   Correlation 01

The correlation 01 is the change in the tranche value due to a 1% absolute increase in the value of all correlations where the initial correlation $\rho = \beta^2$.

Another measure of correlation sensitivity is *rho*. This is the change in the value of $1 face value of the tranche divided by the change in correlation. The correlation 01 and *rho* are therefore calculated as follows:

1. Value the tranche using the current value of β to give $V_0(K_1, K_2)$.
2. Bump all the correlations by 1% by setting $\beta^2 \rightarrow \beta^2 + 1\%$.
3. Recalculate the tranche value to give $V_1(K_1, K_2)$.
4. Calculate the correlation 01. This is given by

$$\text{Correlation } 01 = V_1(K_1, K_2) - V_0(K_1, K_2).$$

5. The value of *rho* is given by

$$rho = \frac{\text{Correlation } 01}{\Delta\rho \cdot F(K_1, K_2)}$$

where $F(K_1, K_2)$ is the notional of the tranche and $\Delta\rho = 0.01$.

Figure 17.2 shows the correlation 01 as a function of the tranche subordination K_1 for a long protection 3%-wide tranche. At very low strikes, we see that the tranche is short correlation reflecting the fact that the value of a long protection equity tranche falls if correlation increases. Then there is the value of K_1^* at which the correlation sensitivity of the tranche equals zero. This is the *correlation neutral point*. For $K_1 > K_1^*$, the correlation 01 becomes positive, indicating that the senior long protection tranches are long correlation. The correlation 01 then tends to zero for higher strikes.

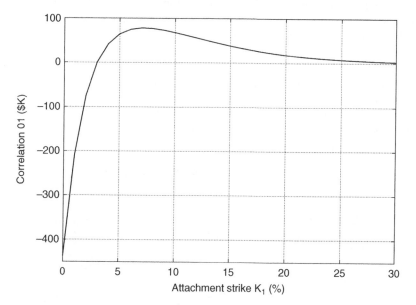

Figure 17.2   The correlation 01 for a 3%-wide long protection position as a function of its attachment strike K_1. We set the contractual spread equal to the breakeven spread for each value of K_1. The tranche notional is $37.5 million

Calculating the equivalent value of rho for this tranche involves dividing the correlation 01 by $37.5m × 0.01 = $375k. It therefore brings the rho to a level ranging from -1.0 at low strikes to about 0.2 at a strike of 8%. This unit of correlation sensitivity makes it easier to compare the correlation risk of tranches of different size.

Note that the correlation 01 summed across the capital structure should be close to zero, reflecting the fact that being long the entire capital structure in tranche format is almost equivalent to being long the reference portfolio which has no correlation sensitivity. It is not exactly zero due to the correlation sensitivities of the tranche premium legs which do not exactly offset each other.

17.2.5   Systemic Gamma

If the portfolio-wide spread movements are larger than those which would make delta hedging sufficient, we need to consider higher order sensitivities. After delta, the second-order sensitivity is the systemic gamma. We define it as

$$\Gamma_S = \frac{\partial^2 V(t, T, K_1, K_2)}{\partial S^2} (1 \, bp)^2$$

where S is the portfolio spread. We choose to multiply the second derivative by $(1 \, bp)^2$ so that we can approximate the change in the value of a systemic delta hedged position simply by writing

$$dV = \frac{\Gamma_S}{2} (dS)^2$$

where dS is an actual spread change (no longer equal to 1 bp) *now expressed in units of basis points*. For example, a movement of 10 bp in the portfolio spread results in a change in value of the delta hedged position of $0.5 \times 10^2 \Gamma_S = 50 \Gamma_S$. The systemic gamma can be calculated numerically by taking second differences as follows:

1. Value the tranche using the current market curves to give $V_0(K_1, K_2)$.
2. Bump all market spread curves by a 1 bp parallel shift upwards and rebuild all of the issuer curves and value the tranche to give $V_+(K_1, K_2)$.
3. Bump all market spread curves by a 1 bp parallel shift downwards and rebuild all of the issuer curves and value the tranche to give $V_-(K_1, K_2)$.
4. Calculate the systemic gamma using

$$\Gamma_S = (V_+(K_1, K_2) - 2V_0(K_1, K_2) + V_-(K_1, K_2)).$$

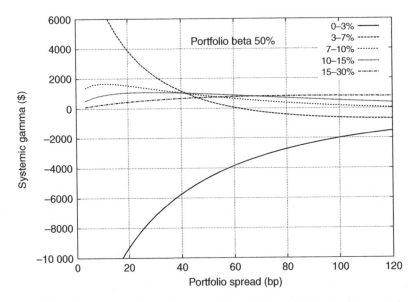

Figure 17.3   The systemic gamma 01 as a function of the portfolio spread for the five example tranches. This is from a long protection perspective. We use a correlation of $\rho = \beta^2 = 25\%$

The systemic gamma is proportional to the rate of change of the systemic delta with respect to the portfolio spread. We are therefore able to get an idea of the gamma dependence by examining the slope of the systemic delta curves plotted in Figure 17.1. These show the systemic delta of a set of tranches from a long protection perspective. However, we have also calculated and plotted the spread sensitivity of the systemic gamma for the different tranches in Figure 17.3.

We see that long protection equity tranches have a large negative systemic gamma for low spreads which tends to zero as the portfolio spread widens. Long protection mezzanine tranches have a large positive systemic gamma which falls rapidly with the portfolio spread and even goes negative for high spreads. Higher tranches have a small gamma which is reasonably insensitive to the portfolio spread.

17.2.6 Carry and Theta

As time passes, provided there is no default and spread and interest rate curves remain fixed, the value of a tranche position changes for the following reasons:

- The approach of scheduled risky coupon payments. As we approach a payment, its present value increases. This has a negative impact for the protection buyer.
- The reduction in the length of the period over which protection remains lowers the value of the protection leg. This is true for all tranches.
- For mezzanine or senior tranches, this fall in protection leg value is accentuated by the fact that time is needed first to wipe out the subordination before any losses can occur.
- If the CDS spread curves are upward sloped, as time passes we roll down the curve with the effect of reducing the average portfolio spread.

We use two measures to quantify the effect of the passing of time on the trade. They are:

- Carry: This is the daily coupon which is accrued. Although coupons are only paid on the quarterly payment dates, we effectively accrue a risk-free coupon each day. This is because the coupon which was accrued since yesterday will be sure to be paid whether or not default occurs since it will be part of the premium accrued at default.
- Theta: This is the daily change in the full price of the tranche. For a long protection position it is the change in the value of the protection leg minus the change in the value of the premium leg.

17.2.7 An Example Systemic Risk Report

We summarise the systemic risk measures of a set of typical standard tranches in Table 17.2. This shows five tranches across the capital structure.

The underlying reference portfolio consists of 125 credits with a $10 million notional and so has a total notional of $1250 million. We show the breakeven tranche spreads computed

Table 17.2 Systemic risk summary for long protection positions on a set of tranches. The reference portfolio has 125 credits, each $10 million notional and with an average spread of 60 bp. We set $\rho = \beta^2 = 25\%$

Tranche	0–3%	3–7%	7–10%	10–15%	15–30%
Breakeven spread (bp)	1790.2	405.3	148.4	58.1	8.6
Tranche RPV01	2.95	4.15	4.39	4.47	4.50
Systemic delta ($m)	691	461	170	133	73
Leverage ratio	18.37	9.20	4.52	2.12	0.39
Systemic DV01 ($)	303 689	202 721	74 768	58 362	32 264
Systemic gamma ($)	−4,013	47	667	901	805
Correlation 01 ($)	−433 553	23 214	78 274	103 158	93 228
Daily carry ($)	−18 229	−5556	−1563	−1042	−417
Daily Θ ($)	−16 632	−7553	−2583	−1971	−1068

using an average portfolio spread of 60 bp and a correlation of 25%. We make the following observations:

- The tranche RPV01 is lowest for the riskiest equity tranche at a value of 2.95. It rises to 4.5 for the least risky senior 15–30% tranche.
- The systemic delta of the 0–3% tranche is $691 million, implying that it contains roughly half the spread risk of the $1250 million notional reference portfolio. It falls to just $73 million for the 15–30% tranche. This is the notional of the reference portfolio which must be traded in order to hedge small portfolio-wide spread movements.
- The equity tranche is highly leveraged with a leverage ratio of 18.37, while the senior tranche is deleveraged with a leverage ratio of 0.39.
- The systemic gamma of the equity tranche is large and negative for a long protection position. The systemic gamma of the more senior tranches are smaller and positive.
- The correlation 01 of the 0–3% tranche is negative, resulting in a loss of over $400 000 for a 1% increase in correlation. The correlation 01 of the 15–30% tranche is positive.
- The magnitude of the daily carry is largest for the 0–3% tranche which is paying the highest spread. It is negative as a protection buyer has to pay the premium.
- The daily Θ is the change in the value of the protection leg minus the change in the value of the premium leg. As we move one day forward, the value of the protection leg falls as we have one day less of protection. Over the same period, the value of the premium leg increases[2] as the future cash flows move one day closer to today and so their time value increases. The Θ is therefore negative.

This completes the discussion of systemic risk measures.

17.3 THE LH+ MODEL

The downside of the LHP model is that we collapse all of the issuer-specific information we may have about the reference portfolio into just its average characteristics. This is unfortunate as it would be extremely useful to have a simple model which would allow us to understand

---

[2] Unless we are on a premium payment date when the value of the premium leg drops by the size of the coupon payment.

the interplay between the characteristics of a single credit and those of the overall portfolio. It could also help us to understand the idiosyncratic risks, namely the delta, gamma and VOD risk to an individual issuer. Fortunately, there is such a model. It is called the LH+ model by Greenberg *et al.* (2004).

17.3.1   The LH+ Loss Distribution

The LH+ model splits the reference portfolio of an STCDO into two segments. They are:

1. A large homogeneous portfolio with average survival probability $Q(T)$, recovery R and market factor weight β.
2. A single credit which has its own characteristics. It has a survival probability $Q_0(T)$, a recovery R_0, and a market factor weight of β_0.

This structure is shown in Figure 17.4. The fraction of the notional of the reference portfolio taken up by the homogeneous part is H while the fractional notional of the idiosyncratic credit is H_0. Therefore, $H + H_0 = 1$. For a portfolio of credits with equal notionals, $H_0 = 1/N_C$. As the model is based on the idea of a large homogeneous portfolio *plus* one credit, we call it LHP plus one credit, or LH+ for short.

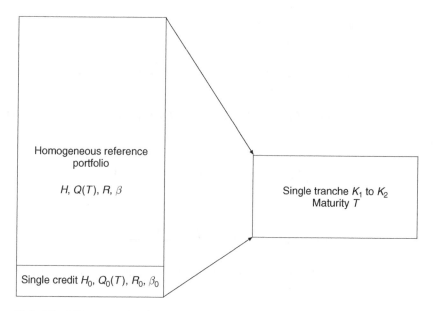

Figure 17.4   The LH+ approximation approximates the true portfolio as a pool of N_C credits, where $N_C - 1$ credits are homogeneous with total notional H, survival probability Q, recovery rate R and beta β. There is an extra credit which has its own notional H_0, survival probability Q_0, and recovery rate R_0 and β_0. We then take the limit $N_C \to \infty$

In the limit of the number of credits in the homogeneous section tending to infinity, we can write the loss on the homogeneous part in terms of the market factor Z as follows

$$L^{\mathrm{Hom}}(T,Z) = (1 - R) \cdot H \cdot \Phi \left(\frac{C(T) - \beta Z}{\sqrt{1 - \beta^2}} \right)$$

where $C(T) = \Phi^{-1}(1 - Q(T))$. In addition, we have the single credit which defaults if A_0 falls below the credit's implied default threshold $C_0(T) = \Phi^{-1}(1 - Q_0(T))$. Given that

$$A_0 = \beta_0 Z + \sqrt{1 - \beta_0^2} \varepsilon_0$$

then the conditional default probability of the single credit is given by

$$p_0(T|Z) = \Phi\left(\frac{C_0(T) - \beta_0 Z}{\sqrt{1 - \beta_0^2}}\right).$$

We can then write the loss of the portfolio given the market factor realisation Z as

$$L(T, Z) = \begin{cases} (1 - R_0)H_0 + L^{\text{Hom}}(T, Z) & \text{with probability} \quad p_0(T|Z), \\ L^{\text{Hom}}(T, Z) & \text{with probability} \quad 1 - p_0(T|Z). \end{cases}$$

To calculate the expected loss of a tranche produced by this model, we must calculate the probability that the loss on the portfolio exceeds a certain K. This can happen in one of two ways:

1. The homogeneous part of the portfolio loses an amount greater than K, irrespective of whether the single credit defaults or not.
2. The single credit defaults resulting in a loss amount $(1 - R_0)H_0$, therefore only requiring the homogeneous part to lose $K - (1 - R_0)H_0$.

For simplicity, we are assuming here that $K > (1 - R_0)H_0$.[3] We can then write the conditional probability of a loss greater than K as

$$\Pr[L(T) \geq K|Z] = 1_{Z \leq A} + p_0(T|Z)1_{A < Z \leq B} \tag{17.1}$$

where

$$A = \frac{1}{\beta}\left[C(T) - \sqrt{1 - \beta^2}\Phi^{-1}\left(\frac{K}{(1 - R)H}\right)\right]$$

and

$$B = \frac{1}{\beta}\left[C(T) - \sqrt{1 - \beta^2}\Phi^{-1}\left(\frac{K - (1 - R_0)H_0}{(1 - R)}\right)\right].$$

We can integrate 17.1 over the Gaussian market factor distribution to give the unconditional probability of the portfolio loss exceeding K as

$$\Pr[L(T) \geq K] = \Phi(A) + \frac{1}{\sqrt{2\pi}}\int_{-\infty}^{\infty}\Phi\left(\frac{C_0(T) - \beta_0 Z}{\sqrt{1 - \beta_0^2}}\right)\phi(Z)1_{A < Z \leq B}\, dZ$$

$$= \Phi(A) + \Phi_{2,\beta_0}(C_0(T), B) - \Phi_{2,\beta_0}(C_0(T), A). \tag{17.2}$$

---

[3] This condition means we can only value equity tranches wider than $(1 - R_0)H_0$. This is not a significant restriction since if $N_C = 125$ and $R_0 = 40\%$ then $(1 - R_0)H_0 = 0.48\%$ which is an extremely narrow equity tranche which would rarely, if ever, be traded due to its very high risk.

Since the density is continuous, we can calculate the density of the portfolio loss distribution simply by taking the numerical derivative as follows

$$f(K) = -\frac{\partial Pr(L(T) \geq K)}{\partial K} = \lim_{dK \to 0} \frac{Pr(L(T) \geq K) - Pr(L(T) \geq K + dK)}{dK}$$

where we choose a suitably small value of dK.

17.3.2   LH+ Tranche Pricing

We can then use this to calculate the tranche survival curve. Noting that

$$Q(t, T, K_1, K_2) = \frac{\mathbb{E}[\min(L(T), K_2) - \min(L(T), K_1)]}{K_2 - K_1} \qquad (17.3)$$

we can write

$$\begin{aligned}
\mathbb{E}[\min(L(T), K)] &= \mathbb{E}[L(T)\mathbf{1}_{L(T)<K}] + K \cdot \mathbb{E}[\mathbf{1}_{L(T)\geq K}] \\
&= \mathbb{E}[L(T)\mathbf{1}_{L(T)<K}] + K \Pr(L(T) \geq K) \\
&= \mathbb{E}[L(T)] - \mathbb{E}[L(T)\mathbf{1}_{L(T)\geq K}] + K \Pr(L(T) \geq K).
\end{aligned}$$

The first term is easy to compute. It is given by

$$\mathbb{E}[L(T)] = (1 - Q(T))(1 - R)H + (1 - Q_0(T))(1 - R_0)H_0.$$

The second term is computed in Section 17.7.1. The probability in the third term has already been computed in Equation 17.2 above. Combining these terms, we get

$$\begin{aligned}
\mathbb{E}[\min(L(T), K)] = &(1 - Q(T))(1 - R)H + (1 - Q_0(T))(1 - R_0)H_0 \\
&- K\left(\Phi_{2,\beta_0}(C_0, A) - \Phi(A)\right) \\
&- ((1 - R_0)H_0 - K)\,\Phi_{2,\beta_0}(C_0, B) \\
&- (1 - R)H\left(\Phi_{2,\beta}(C, A) + \Phi_{3,\Sigma}(C_0, C, B) - \Phi_{3,\Sigma}(C_0, C, A)\right)
\end{aligned}$$

$$(17.4)$$

where

$$\Sigma = \begin{pmatrix} 1 & \beta\beta_0 & \beta_0 \\ \beta\beta_0 & 1 & \beta \\ \beta_0 & \beta & 1 \end{pmatrix}.$$

We therefore require an implementation of the cumulative tri-variate normal function. We could do a nested triple integral of the tri-variate density. However, it is faster to use a simple trapezium rule or quadrature-based integration of the cumulative bi-variate. The formula is given in Section 17.7.2.

Given a reference portfolio consisting of N_C credits with equal notionals, and supposing we wish to calculate idiosyncratic risk of issuer i, the way we use the LH+ model is as follows:

1. Set

$$H = 1 - \frac{1}{N_C}, \quad Q = \frac{1}{N_C - 1} \sum_{j \neq i}^{N_C} Q_j(T), \quad \beta = \frac{1}{N_C - 1} \sum_{j \neq i}^{N_C} \beta_j, \quad R = \frac{1}{N_C - 1} \sum_{j \neq i}^{N_C} R_j.$$

2. Set

$$H_0 = \frac{1}{N_C}, \quad Q_0 = Q_i(T), \quad \beta_0 = \beta_i, \quad R_0 = R_i.$$

3. Calculate the tranche survival curve using Equations 17.3 and 17.4.
4. Perturb the idiosyncratic parameter (this depends on which idiosyncratic risk we are calculating) and calculate the change in tranche value.
5. We can then change the index i and repeat for another issuer.

The advantage of the LH+ model is that it enables us to examine both the systemic risk factors and the idiosyncratic risk factors. Note that:

• We model the idiosyncratic credit exactly in terms of its spread, face value, recovery rate and correlation.
• We approximate the large homogeneous portfolio of $N_C - 1$ credits.

Our hope is that the error in the idiosyncratic risk measure is largely cancelled out when we calculate the *change in the value of the tranche holding the characteristics of the large homogeneous portfolio fixed.* We therefore expect that the idiosyncratic risk measures calculated in the LH+ model should be close to the idiosyncratic risk measures calculated using a full loss distribution model.

17.4   IDIOSYNCRATIC RISKS

17.4.1   The Idiosyncratic Delta

Consider a situation in which we have bought protection on a tranche linked to a reference portfolio with N_C credits. For each credit i, there is an idiosyncratic delta which we denote with Δ_i. This is the amount of CDS protection in credit i that should be sold in order to hedge the spread risk of the tranche to that specific name. We also define an idiosyncratic DV01. This is the change in the value of the tranche for a 1 bp increase in the idiosyncratic spread. If we define $V(T, K_1, K_2)$ as the time zero value of the tranche, then the idiosyncratic delta are given by the following process:

1. Value the tranche using the current market spread curves to give $V_0(K_1, K_2)$.
2. Calculate the RPV01 of the CDS of issuer i to the tranche maturity.
3. Bump the spread curve of issuer i by a 1 bp parallel shift.
4. Value the tranche using the bumped issuer curve to calculate $V_1(K_1, K_2)$.

5. Calculate the idiosyncratic DV01 using

$$\text{Idiosyncratic DV01} = V_1(K_1, K_2) - V_0(K_1, K_2).$$

6. Calculate the idiosyncratic delta using

$$\Delta_i = \frac{V_1(K_1, K_2) - V_0(K_1, K_2)}{\text{RPV01}_i}.$$

Within the LH+ model it is also possible to compute the value of Δ_i by taking an analytical derivative provided we make some simple approximation of the tranche survival probability of the idiosyncratic credit in terms of its spread, e.g. using the credit triangle $Q_i(t, T) \simeq \exp(-S_i(T - t)/(1 - R_i))$. However, we do not do this here since the numerical calculation of the idiosyncratic delta described above is already extremely fast.

17.4.2 Behaviour of the Idiosyncratic Delta

In the example shown in Figure 17.5 we have calculated the idiosyncratic delta for five tranches of a portfolio of 125 credits as a function of the spread of one idiosyncratic credit in the portfolio. The idiosyncratic name has a notional of $10 million, and the remaining 124 credits in the reference portfolio are modelled as a homogeneous group of infinitely many credits which comprise a total notional of $1240 million. We set the correlation of the homogeneous subportfolio at $\beta^2 = 25\%$, close to the typical value used when pricing. We then varied the spread of the single credit from 6 bp to 240 bp, holding the average spread of the homogeneous part of the portfolio fixed at 60 bp. For each value of the spread, we calculated the idiosyncratic delta by bumping its spread curve and repricing each tranche. This was done for two values of the idiosyncratic beta, $\beta_0 = 30\%$ and $\beta_0 = 60\%$. Note also that we used the contractual spreads close to the breakeven spread when the idiosyncratic spread is 60 bp. These were 1750, 400, 150, 60 and 8 bp for the 0–3%, 3–7%, 7–10%, 10–15% and 15–30% tranches, respectively. Figure 17.5 enables us to make the following observations:

- In the case of $\beta_i = 30\%$, the correlation of 9% is low and so when a credit defaults, it is more likely to be due to an idiosyncratic default rather than a systemic default. In this case, if credit i defaults, it will be more likely to default with only a small number of other credits. Credit i will therefore be more likely to impact the equity. For this reason, we see that it has a high delta to the equity. The delta is lower for the mezzanine and drops even further for the senior tranche. The delta is almost insensitive to the idiosyncratic spread since when a credit has a low value of β, no matter how low its spread, it is unlikely to default with enough other credits to make it impact a mezzanine or senior tranche.
- When $\beta_i = 60\%$, the asset correlation with the other credits is $60\% \times 50\% = 36\%$ and a default of credit i is likely to be due to a systemic event. If it is a systemic event, then other credits will also tend to default. The question is then in what order will they default relative to credit i. As there is a one-to-one mapping between the realisation of A_i and the default time, we expect that credits with higher spreads will tend to default before credits with the lower spreads. Hence, if the spread of the idiosyncratic credit is high compared to the average spread of the portfolio, then the idiosyncratic credit will tend to default before the other credits and so impact the equity tranche. It is for this reason that the 0–3% delta

increases with the idiosyncratic spread. If the idiosyncratic spread is low compared to the average spread, then the credit, if it defaults, will tend to default later and so impact the mezzanine or even the senior tranche. This is why we see the mezzanine and senior deltas decrease with increasing idiosyncratic spread.

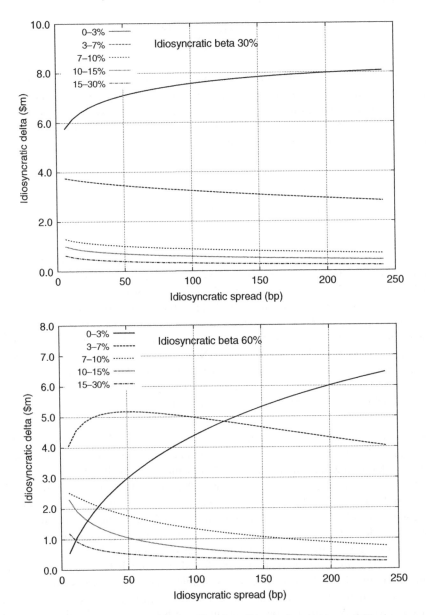

Figure 17.5 The single name tranche delta as a function of the single name spread. We chose a portfolio $\beta = 0.50$ and a portfolio average spread of 60 bp for the homogeneous portfolio. We set a portfolio recovery rate of $R = 0.40$. We calculate the 5Y idiosyncratic delta for the 0–3%, 3–7%, 7–10%, 10–15% and 15–30% tranches as a function of the spread of the single name for $\beta_0 = 0.30$ (top) and $\beta_0 = 0.60$ (bottom). See text for discussion

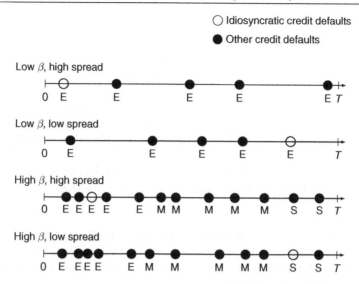

Figure 17.6 To assist our understanding of the idiosyncratic delta, we attempt to depict the typical scenario in which the idiosyncratic credit defaults. Each ball represents the default of a credit in the portfolio before the tranche maturity time T. The distance of the ball along the timeline represents its default time. Assuming a 40% recovery and 100 credits, it takes five defaults to wipe out the 0–3% equity tranche and another five for the 3–6% mezzanine tranche. We label each default with E, M or S for Equity, Mezzanine or Senior, representing which tranche takes which loss and hence which tranche will have a high idiosyncratic delta. See text for a discussion

Our intuition is summarised in Figure 17.6 in which we represent the typical default state in four different scenarios of idiosyncratic correlation and spread. If the idiosyncratic beta is low, the idiosyncratic credit will tend to default independently of the other credits defaulting and so we would not expect many others to default. As a result, it will only managing to impact the very junior tranches, irrespective of its spread. When the idiosyncratic beta is high, default of the idiosyncratic credit will tend to be accompanied by lots of other defaults. To know if a tranche will have a high idiosyncratic delta depends *on the order* in which the credits will default and this will depend on the value of the idiosyncratic spread relative to the portfolio spread. If it is higher then it will default earlier, resulting in a high delta to the junior tranches. If it has a low spread, it will default late, and be more likely to impact the more senior tranches.

It is worth comparing Figures 17.5 and 17.1 since they show the systemic and idiosyncratic deltas as a function of spread. The behaviour is very different. Systemic delta is all about the sensitivity of a tranche value to a portfolio-wide increase in credit risk. All tranches get riskier. Idiosyncratic risk is all about one credit becoming riskier while all the other credits are fixed. It therefore tells us about the risk of the idiosyncratic credit compared with the average of the portfolio.

17.4.3 Idiosyncratic Gamma

The spread movements of various credits in the portfolio may be larger than those which would make simple delta hedging sufficient. We need to understand the sensitivity of a tranche to larger movements in S_i and therefore we need to look at the next order term in the Taylor expansion of the tranche price which is the idiosyncratic gamma. We define the idiosyncratic gamma of credit i as

$$\Gamma_i = \frac{\partial^2 V(t, T, K_1, K_2)}{\partial S_i^2}(1\,\text{bp})^2$$

where S_i is the idiosyncratic spread and we typically set $dS_i = 1\,\text{bp}$. As in the case of the systemic gamma discussed earlier, we have multiplied by $(1\,\text{bp})^2$ so that the P&L impact of a spread movement of an idiosyncratic delta hedged issuer is given by $dV = 0.5\Gamma_i(dS_i)^2$ where dS_i is in units of the *number of basis points*.

The idiosyncratic gamma of the tranche is the second-order dependence of the tranche on spread changes in a specific credit. We calculate the idiosyncratic gamma via second differences as follows:

1. Value the tranche using the current market curves to give $V_0(K_1, K_2)$.
2. Bump issuer curve i up by a 1 bp parallel shift and value the tranche to give $V_+(K_1, K_2)$.
3. Bump issuer curve i down by a 1 bp parallel shift and value the tranche to give $V_-(K_1, K_2)$.
4. Calculate the systemic gamma using

$$\Gamma_i = (V_+(K_1, K_2) - 2V_0(K_1, K_2) + V_-(K_1, K_2)).$$

To quantify the behaviour of gamma, we have calculated the idiosyncratic gammas by doing second differences. We show a typical set of tranche idiosyncratic risk numbers in Table 17.3. When we compare this table with the systemic risk results in Table 17.2, which have been calculated using the same reference portfolio and tranches, we observe that the idiosyncratic risk numbers are much smaller than their systemic equivalents. This is easy to understand since the idiosyncratic delta only hedges one specific credit rather than the entire portfolio of 125 credits.

Table 17.3 Idiosyncratic risk summary. We assume $\beta_0 = \beta = 50\%$

Tranche $K_1 - K_2$	Tranche notional	Contractual spread (bp)	I.DV01 ($m)	I.Delta Δ_i ($m)	I.Gamma Γ_i
0–3%	37.5	1750	2044	4.92	+9.62
3–7%	50.0	400	1993	4.34	−2.97
7–10%	37.5	150	497	1.34	−3.04
10–15%	62.5	60	251	0.87	−2.72
15–30%	187.5	8	152	0.49	−1.54

17.4.4 Value-on-Default (VOD)

Another important idiosyncratic risk measure is the value-on-default or VOD. This measures the impact of an immediate default and the resulting change in value of our tranche position. VOD has already been discussed in the context of CDS. In the context of tranches, we need to be careful how we define it. Let us consider a K_1 to K_2 tranche which at time t has a value of $V(t)$. We then want to quantify the impact of a sudden default in the portfolio. Assume that the face value of the defaulted credit is H_0 and that the recovery rate is R_0. If the default does not result in a loss payment on the tranche, i.e. the tranche still has subordination after the default, the VOD is calculated as follows:

1. Remove the defaulted credit from the reference portfolio. This will change the average portfolio spread and the notional of the reference portfolio.
2. Reduce the attachment and detachment points of the tranche so that $K_1 \to K_1 - H_0(1 - R_0)$ and $K_2 \to K_2 - H_0(1 - R_0)$.
3. Price the tranche using the pricing model giving $V'(t)$.
4. The VOD equals $V'(t) - V(t)$.

If the loss on the reference portfolio before the default is L_1 and the total loss after the default is $L_1 + (1 - R_0)H_0 > K_1$, then the default does result in a loss on the tranche. The loss amount is $G = \max[L_1 + H_0(1 - R_0) - K_1, 0]$ which we assume is less than the tranche width $K_2 - K_1$. Then the VOD is calculated as follows:

1. Remove the defaulted credit from the reference portfolio. This will change the average portfolio spread and the notional of the reference portfolio.
2. Make a payment of G from the protection seller to the protection buyer.
3. Reduce the tranche notional by an amount G.
4. Price the tranche using the pricing model to calculate $V'(t)$.
5. The VOD equals $V'(t) - V(t) \pm G$ where we have a plus for a long protection position and a minus for a short protection position.

VOD is therefore not an especially intensive calculation, requiring only two calls to the pricing routine. However, we do need to do it for all the credits in the portfolio.

Table 17.4 shows the VOD numbers calculated for a set of long protection tranches on a portfolio of 125 credits each with a $10 million notional. We assume that the credit which defaults has the average portfolio spread of 60 bp and a recovery rate of 40%.

Table 17.4   VOD summary for long protection tranche positions. The reference portfolio has 125 credits, each $10 million notional and an average spread of 60 bp. We set $\beta = 50\%$

Tranche	0–3%	3–7%	7–10%	10–15%	15–30%
Loss payment ($m)	+6.0	0	0	0	0
Change in MTM ($m)	+2.596	+1.398	+0.321	+0.195	+0.085
Value on default ($m)	+8.596	+1.398	+0.321	+0.195	+0.085

We show the loss payment on default which only occurs for the 0–3% equity tranche which equals $10m \times (1 - 0.40) = \$6$ million. In addition, there is an increase in the value of the equity tranche. It may seem surprising that the value of the protection has increased even though some of the protection has been used up. To see why, recall that the value of the equity tranche is the value of the protection leg minus the value of the premium leg. While the value of the protection leg has been reduced due to the smaller amount of remaining protection, the value of the premium leg has fallen by even more because of the reduction in the notional on which the very high equity spread has to be paid. The net result is an increase in the value of the equity tranche.

The VOD for the more senior tranches is positive since each default means they lose $6/1250 = 0.48\%$ of subordination and so become more likely to sustain a loss in the future. From a protection buyer's perspective this is a positive since the market cost of the protection has increased while the buyer's cost of protection (the contractual spread) remains the same.

17.5   HEDGING TRANCHES

In the following, we analyse the hedging of synthetic CDO tranches from the perspective of a dealer and hence a protection buyer. We start by considering the risks of a single tranche. We then discuss how to manage the risk of a correlation trading book.

17.5.1   Spread Hedging: Systemic versus Idiosyncratic

The first risk to be hedged is the spread risk of the issuers in the reference portfolio underlying the tranche. Through the long protection position in the tranche, the dealer will be long protection on the credit names in the reference portfolio. The dealer will hedge this by selling protection on the individual names in the reference portfolio via the CDS market as shown in Figure 17.7. Note that the selling of protection by dealers has the effect of pushing down the CDS spreads of the credits in the reference portfolio. This is known as the 'synthetic bid'. As discussed in Section 5.6, this has the effect of narrowing the CDS-cash basis.

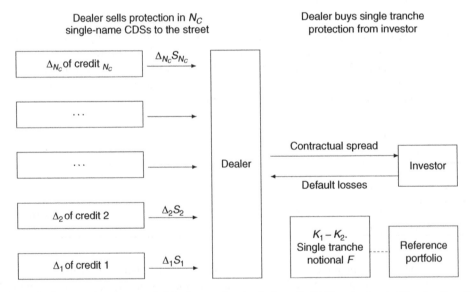

Figure 17.7   To hedge the spread risk of a tranche, the dealer sells CDS protection to 'the street' on the delta amount of each credit

But how much of each credit should we hedge? In this chapter we have set out two different hedging approaches, one called systemic delta (S.Delta) and the other idiosyncratic delta (I.Delta). However, they are not the same. If we consider Table 17.2, we see that the systemic hedges for the tranches are as follows:

Tranche	0–3%	3–7%	7–10%	10–15%	15–30%
Total systemic delta ($m)	691	461	170	133	73

The dealer who chooses to hedge systemic delta will do so by selling protection on equal amounts of each reference credit. Given that there are 125 names in the example reference portfolio, the face value of each CDS hedge will be $1/125 = 0.8\%$ of the total hedge notional. However, if the dealer chooses to hedge idiosyncratic risk, then the total hedge, assuming a homogeneous portfolio, is the idiosyncratic delta times the number of credits. According to Table 17.3, this is given by the following hedges:

Tranche	0–3%	3–7%	7–10%	10–15%	15–30%
Total idiosyncratic delta ($m)	615	542	167.5	108.75	61.25

We also note that if the spreads, recovery rates or β_i of the issuers are not homogeneous, then the idiosyncratic hedge will involve different hedge notionals in each credit.

To explain the difference between these two sets of deltas, we have to recall how we computed them. The idiosyncratic delta is calculated by widening one credit while keeping all of the other credits fixed. A scenario like this has only a small impact on the shape of the portfolio loss distribution. Its main effect is to make this one credit more likely to default before the rest of the credits. The effect of this is to raise the idiosyncratic delta of this name in the junior tranches and to lower it in the senior tranches. Doing this for each credit and summing the idiosyncratic deltas over all of the issuers tells us that these are the hedges which will work best if any one issuer's credit curve widens or narrows in parallel by a small amount.

This is quite different from how the systemic delta is calculated. This involves widening all of the issuer curves simultaneously, which will shift the entire portfolio loss to the right and make all credits more likely to impact more senior tranches. There is no change in their order of default. A systemic hedge like this will work well only if the spread movements are like this.

In practice, spread movements exhibit a mixture of systemic and idiosyncratic moves and the correct hedge will be somewhere between the idiosyncratic hedge and the systemic hedge. To know where in this range would require us to know in advance the likelihood of idiosyncratic versus systemic spread moves. An empirical approach to this problem might be to construct a factor model for spreads which we can calibrate to historical spread data and use to predict the proportion of systemic versus idiosyncratic moves.

Another approach is for the trader to take a view on the relative importance of systemic versus idiosyncratic risk depending on current events in the credit market. For example, suppose the trader expects that a specific credit is about to be downgraded. If this credit is a small issuer in the credit markets and if its downgrade would be for a totally idiosyncratic reason, the trader will tend to adjust his hedges to make sure that credits in the portfolio are hedged according to their idiosyncratic delta. However, if the credit is a large issuer whose downgrade could have a contagious effect on other credits, then the trader would hedge this name idiosyncratically using CDS and then hedge the other credits systemically using the CDS indices. In practice, the delta hedging of these risks is often as much an art as it is a science, i.e. it requires judgement and experience, not just a model.

17.5.2 The Gamma Exposure: Systemic versus Idiosyncratic

When we look at the systemic and idiosyncratic risks, we note that the idiosyncratic gamma (I.Gamma) for a tranche usually has the opposite sign to the systemic gamma (S.Gamma) for that tranche. As discussed in the previous section, this reflects the very different natures of an idiosyncratic versus a systemic spread move. In the idiosyncratic scenario, the delta is an expression of which tranche a specific credit is likely to affect if it defaults. In the systemic scenario, the delta is an expression of how the overall risk of the portfolio is likely to affect a tranche. The table below shows the systemic gammas for the example tranches:

Tranche	0–3%	3–7%	7–10%	10–15%	15–30%
Systemic gamma ($)	−4013	47	667	901	805

and this table shows the idiosyncratic gammas multiplied by $N_C = 125$:

Tranche	0–3%	3–7%	7–10%	10–15%	15–30%
Idiosyncratic gamma ($)	1202	−371.25	−380	−340	−192.5

Since the actual higher order sensitivity of a tranche is a mixture of both systemic and idiosyncratic spread movements, and since the different gammas have opposite signs, we would expect both gammas to tend to partially offset each other. However, there will still be a residual gamma.

17.5.3 Gamma Trading

A number of market players, most notably hedge funds, use the gamma risk profile of tranches as a way to express a view on systemic versus idiosyncratic credit scenarios, while remaining more or less credit spread neutral. How these trades are structured is based on the results in Table 17.5. We only show equity and senior tranches as the gamma profile of a mezzanine tranche can change sign as spreads change.

Table 17.5 Second order tranche spread risk profile

Tranche	Long tranche protection		Short tranche protection	
Equity	I.Gamma > 0	S.Gamma < 0	I.Gamma < 0	S.Gamma > 0
Senior	I.Gamma < 0	S.Gamma > 0	I.Gamma > 0	S.Gamma < 0

Figure 17.8 shows the profile of a long protection tranche position hedged against idiosyncratic spread movements as a function of the idiosyncratic spread of one credit. We see that the equity has a large positive I.Gamma and so makes money when there are idiosyncratic spread movements. The idiosyncratic spread hedged mezzanine tranche has a very low I.Gamma. The idiosyncratic spread hedged senior tranches have a negative I.Gamma meaning that idiosyncratic movements cause us to lose money.

Once we have put on an idiosyncratic delta hedge to every credit in the portfolio, we typically find that there is a net carry which may be positive or negative. In a hedged long protection tranche we are paying out the tranche spread and receiving the spread income from the hedges. We typically find that a positive gamma position is associated with a negative carry.

Now let us consider the second-order risk to a systemic gamma hedged tranche. Figure 17.9 shows the value of long protection positions in a 0–3%, 3–7% and 7–10% tranche each hedged

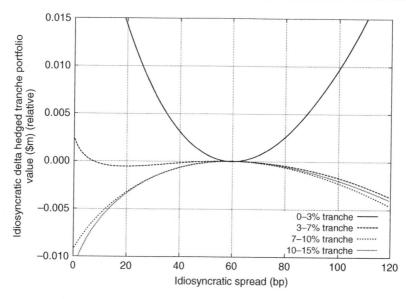

Figure 17.8   We plot the mark-to-market value of a long protection position in a 0–3%, 3–7%, 7–10% and 10–15% tranche each with an idiosyncratic delta hedge calculated at an idiosyncratic spread of 60 bp as a function of the idiosyncratic spread. Each tranche is based on a reference portfolio of $1250 million. The portfolio value is adjusted so that it equals zero when S_0 equals 60 bp

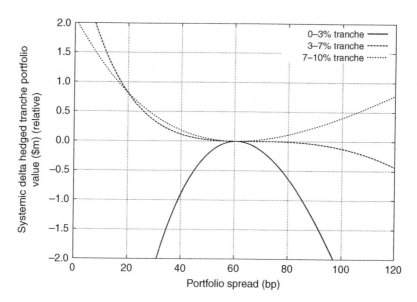

Figure 17.9   We plot the mark-to-market value of a long protection position in a 0–3%, 3–7% and 7–10% tranche each with a systemic delta hedge calculated at a portfolio spread of 60 bp as a function of the portfolio spread. Each tranche is based on a reference portfolio of 125 × $10 million = $1250 million. We have shifted the portfolio value so that it is worth zero when the portfolio spread equals 60 bp

with a delta amount of the underlying portfolio. We see that the long protection 0–3% equity tranche has a negative systemic gamma profile meaning that large spread movements in either direction decrease the value of the net position. The delta hedged long protection 3–7% tranche has a gamma profile which changes as a function of the portfolio spread. The hedged long protection 7–10% tranche has a positive systemic gamma and so makes money for large spread movements.

One final caveat for such trading strategies is that they often assume that the implied tranche correlation will not change. However, this is not guaranteed as will be discussed in later chapters when we encounter the implied correlation skew.

17.5.4   Hedging the Correlation Exposure

After the interest rate risk and spread risk of a tranche have been hedged out, the remaining market risk of a tranche is to changes in the correlation. Whether correlation is estimated empirically, or whether it is implied from the market, it should not be assumed that it is a fixed number. We therefore need to immunise our 'correlation book' against changes in correlation. To hedge correlation, we need to find suitable hedging instruments. However, the only hedging instruments are other correlation products, i.e. other tranches.

If we want an exact offset for the correlation exposure of a long protection tranche, the only solution is to sell protection on the exact same tranche – same subordination, width, reference portfolio and maturity. We would also want to do this at a wider tranche spread, otherwise the overall position will lock-in a negative P&L. However, it is typically very difficult to find a counterparty who will buy protection from the dealer at the required spread and so this approach is not realistic.

Another approach is to *complete the capital structure*. This hedging strategy involves buying protection on tranches on the same reference portfolio but at other parts of the capital structure. For example, if we buy protection on equity from an investor, we are left with a short correlation position. If we then buy protection on mezzanine and senior tranches, as these positions are long correlation and are on the same reference portfolio, the overall correlation exposure is reduced. The ultimate aim is to be long the entire capital structure so that we are effectively long protection on the reference portfolio. It should be noted that being long a 0–5%, 5–10% and 10–100% tranche on the same reference portfolio is not an exactly correlation neutral position due to the correlation exposure of the premium legs which do not offset exactly. A model is required to calculate the precise hedges.

However, even this approach is not practical as it is often difficult to find investors willing to buy tranches on the exact same underlying portfolio at the required level of the capital structure. Instead, what dealers tend to do is to try to structure CDOs which are appealing to investors, but which also are as similar as possible to the portfolios to which they have their largest correlation exposure. In this way, dealers are 'axed'. This means that they will pay a slightly higher spread than they would otherwise pay to investors who buy such portfolios as they enable the dealer to offset some of the overall correlation exposure.

However, in order to do this, the dealer needs to calculate the correlation exposure at an issuer level. For example, suppose V_b is the value of trade $b = 1, \ldots, N_B$ in a book of N_B tranches. The total value of the correlation book is given by

$$\Pi = \sum_{b=1}^{N_B} V_b.$$

The dealer would like to be able to calculate the sensitivity of the entire correlation book to changes in each correlation pair. In the one-factor Gaussian copula model, we can reduce this to calculating the sensitivity $\partial V/\partial \rho_i$ where $\rho_i = \beta_i^2$. This means that we only need to compute $O(N_C N_B)$ tranche values in order to compute all of the correlation sensitivities.

This strategy of building a correlation book by completing the capital structure is one that cannot be executed quickly. It takes time to find the investors willing to buy the tranches that will offset the correlation exposure of the book. It may also mean refusing trades that add to the correlation exposure of the book.

In later chapters we will discuss the arrival of the correlation skew which has created a set of liquid tranches linked to the standard CDX and iTraxx CDS indices. These are another hedging tool which can be used to offset correlation risk. However, a discussion of these requires an introduction to the correlation skew which is the subject of Chapter 19.

17.6 SUMMARY

In this chapter we have set out the risks of single tranche CDOs. We have explained that the sensitivities of a tranche can be broken down into systemic and idiosyncratic risks and used the LHP model to capture the former and the LH+ model to capture the latter. Hedging these risks is as much an art as it is a science since it is not possible to know in advance whether the market is going to behave idiosyncratically or systemically. Hedging the correlation risk of a tranche is also a challenge and we have described how this may be done within a pre-skew framework.

17.7 TECHNICAL APPENDIX

17.7.1 Calculation of the LH+ Tranche Loss

In this section we set out the calculation of

$$\mathbb{E}\left[L(T)\mathbf{1}_{L(T)\geq K}\right]$$

using the LH+ model. To calculate this term we need to consider the loss conditional on the realisation of Z. We denote this with $L(Z)$. If $Z \leq A$, we know that $L(Z) \geq K$ with probability 1, i.e. it is true whether or not the idiosyncratic credit defaults. If $A < Z \leq B$ then we know that the homogeneous part of the reference portfolio has a loss in the range $K > L^{\text{Hom}}(Z) \geq K - H_0(1 - R_0)$. In this case the portfolio loss only exceeds K if the idiosyncratic credit defaults, and the probability of this is $p_0(T|Z)$. We therefore have

$$\mathbb{E}\left[L\mathbf{1}_{L\geq K}\right] = \mathbb{E}\left[\left(p_0(T|Z)(1 - R_0)H_0 + (1 - R)H\Phi\left(\frac{C - \beta Z}{\sqrt{1 - \beta^2}}\right)\right)\cdot \mathbf{1}_{Z\leq A}\right]$$
$$+ \mathbb{E}\left[\left((1 - R_0)H_0 + (1 - R)H\Phi\left(\frac{C - \beta Z}{\sqrt{1 - \beta^2}}\right)\right)p_0(T|Z)\cdot \mathbf{1}_{A<Z\leq B}\right].$$

Since

$$\mathbf{1}_{Z\leq A} + \mathbf{1}_{A<Z\leq B} = \mathbf{1}_{Z\leq B}$$

we can simplify this to give

$$
\mathbb{E}[L1_{L \geq K}] = (1 - R_0) H_0 \cdot \mathbb{E}\left[\Phi\left(\frac{C_0(T) - \beta_0 Z}{\sqrt{1 - \beta_0^2}} \right) 1_{Z \leq B} \right]
$$

$$
+ (1 - R) H \cdot \mathbb{E}\left[\Phi\left(\frac{C - \beta Z}{\sqrt{1 - \beta^2}} \right) 1_{Z \leq A} \right]
$$

$$
+ (1 - R) H \cdot \mathbb{E}\left[\Phi\left(\frac{C - \beta Z}{\sqrt{1 - \beta^2}} \right) \Phi\left(\frac{C_0(T) - \beta_0 Z}{\sqrt{1 - \beta_0^2}} \right) 1_{A < Z \leq B} \right]
$$

where we have also substituted for $p_0(T|Z)$. These terms can then be written in terms of the bi-variate and tri-variate Gaussian cumulative distribution functions.

17.7.2 Tri-variate Gaussian CDF

The density of the n-dimensional Gaussian CDF is given by

$$
f_X(x_1, \ldots, x_N) = \frac{1}{(2\pi)^{N/2} |\det \Sigma|^{1/2}} \exp\left(-\frac{1}{2}(x - \mu)^\top \Sigma^{-1}(x - \mu) \right)
$$

where $|\det \Sigma|$ is the absolute value of the determinant of the covariance matrix Σ. Therefore, the tri-variate CDF for the $N(0, 1)$ Gaussian distribution with 3×3 correlation matrix Σ is defined as

$$
\Phi_3(X_1, X_2, X_3) = \frac{1}{(2\pi)^{3/2}\sqrt{\det \Sigma}} \int_{-\infty}^{X_1} \int_{-\infty}^{X_2} \int_{-\infty}^{X_3} \exp\left(-\frac{1}{2}x^\top \Sigma^{-1} x \right) dx_1 dx_2 dx_3.
$$

The correlation matrix is given by

$$
\Sigma = \begin{pmatrix} 1 & \rho_{12} & \rho_{13} \\ \rho_{12} & 1 & \rho_{23} \\ \rho_{13} & \rho_{23} & 1 \end{pmatrix}
$$

so that the determinant is given by

$$
A = \det \Sigma = 1 - \rho_{12}^2 - \rho_{23}^2 - \rho_{13}^2 + 2\rho_{12}\rho_{23}\rho_{13}
$$

and the inverse becomes

$$
\Sigma^{-1} = \frac{1}{A} \begin{pmatrix} 1 - \rho_{23}^2 & \rho_{13}\rho_{23} - \rho_{12} & \rho_{12}\rho_{23} - \rho_{13} \\ \rho_{13}\rho_{23} - \rho_{12} & 1 - \rho_{13}^2 & \rho_{12}\rho_{13} - \rho_{23} \\ \rho_{12}\rho_{23} - \rho_{13} & \rho_{12}\rho_{13} - \rho_{23} & 1 - \rho_{12}^2 \end{pmatrix}.
$$

Writing it out in full we have

$$
\Phi_3(X_1, X_2, X_3) = \frac{1}{(2\pi)^{3/2}\sqrt{A}} \int_{-\infty}^{X_1} \int_{-\infty}^{X_2} \int_{-\infty}^{X_3} \exp\left(-\frac{C}{2A} \right) dx_1 dx_2 dx_3
$$

where

$$C = x_1^2(1 - \rho_{23}^2) + x_2^2(1 - \rho_{13}^2) + x_3^2(1 - \rho_{12}^2)$$

$$+ 2x_1x_2(\rho_{13}\rho_{23} - \rho_{12}) + 2x_1x_3(\rho_{12}\rho_{23} - \rho_{13}) + 2x_2x_3(\rho_{12}\rho_{13} - \rho_{23}).$$

Compare this to the bi-variate CDF

$$\Phi_2(a, b, \rho) = \frac{1}{2\pi \sqrt{1 - \rho^2}} \int_{-\infty}^{a} \int_{-\infty}^{b} \exp\left(-\frac{x^2 - 2\rho xy + y^2}{2(1 - \rho^2)}\right) dx\, dy.$$

After some changes of variable and some rearrangements, we can write the tri-variate cumulative density function as an integral over the bi-variate density as follows:

$$\Phi_{3,\rho}(X, Y, Z) = \int_{-\infty}^{X} \frac{e^{-x^2/2}}{\sqrt{2\pi}} \Phi_2\left(\frac{Y - \rho_{12}x}{\sqrt{1 - \rho_{12}^2}}, \frac{Z - \rho_{13}x}{\sqrt{1 - \rho_{12}\rho_{13}}}, \frac{\rho_{23} - \rho_{12}\rho_{13}}{\sqrt{1 - \rho_{12}^2}\sqrt{1 - \rho_{12}\rho_{13}}}\right) dx.$$

18
Building the Full Loss Distribution

18.1 INTRODUCTION

This chapter explains how to build a pricing model for synthetic CDOs which takes into account the full heterogeneous nature of a typical reference portfolio. Although the pricing model assumed here is the one-factor Gaussian model, the methods described can be applied to any model which can be expressed in a conditionally independent form. The focus of this chapter is addressing the numerical challenge involved in building an exact portfolio loss distribution for a portfolio consisting of N_C credits where typically $N_C \geq 100$. This must be done with a speed and accuracy which makes it usable for the industrial pricing and risk management of synthetic CDO tranches. Given the number of trades sitting in a typical correlation book plus the hundreds of risk numbers calculated for each, we need to ensure that the pricing algorithm is fast, numerically stable and accurate.

In the first part of this chapter, we discuss the techniques that allow us to calculate the loss distribution exactly. These techniques include recursion and Fourier transform methods. A constant theme will be analysing the speed of routines and, crucially, how this scales with the number of credits in the portfolio. In the second half of the chapter we discuss approximate methods. In this context, we must also analyse the trade-off between speed and accuracy. For this reason, we compare the various algorithms at the end of the chapter. Our overall purpose is to assist the reader to determine which algorithm is most suited to which purpose, and then to show how this algorithm can be most efficiently implemented.

18.2 CALCULATING THE TRANCHE SURVIVAL CURVE

The objective of any tranche pricing model is to calculate the tranche survival curve. We wish to do this in a way which takes into account both the finite granularity of the portfolio, and the fact that the credits in the portfolio can be heterogeneous in terms of spread, loss and correlation. The tranche survival curve at time zero, which we denote by $Q(T, K_1, K_2)$, is defined as

$$Q(T, K_1, K_2) = 1 - \frac{\mathbb{E}\left[\min(L(T), K_2) - \min(L(T), K_1)\right]}{K_2 - K_1}$$

where $L(T)$ is the random portfolio loss at future time T. The expectation in this equation is over the risk-neutral portfolio loss distribution at a horizon date T. To calculate the full survival curve, we have to calculate this expectation at a discrete set of time intervals between valuation date and the maturity of the deal being priced.

Depending on how we choose to model the credits in the portfolio, the distribution may be discrete or continuous. In the continuous case, the density of losses $f(x)$ is given by

$$f(x) = \frac{\partial \Pr (L(T) \leq x)}{\partial x}$$

where the loss is random. Since the loss is between 0 and 1, we have $\int_0^1 f(x)dx = 1$.

The overall portfolio loss process can be written as

$$L(t) = \sum_{i=1}^{N_C} F_i(1 - R_i)1_{\tau_i \leq t}$$

where F_i is the fractional face value exposure to credit i in the portfolio, τ_i is the random default time of credit i, and R_i is its percentage recovery rate. For most synthetic CDOs, the exposure to each credit is the same so that we usually set $F_i = 1/N_C$. However, we retain F_i for those rare cases when heterogeneous face value portfolios may occur. Since $0 \leq R_i \leq 1$ and since we have $\sum_{i=1}^{N_C} F_i = 1$, the portfolio loss $L = L(T)$ is bounded between 0 and 1. Calculation of the tranche survival curve can be decomposed into the calculation of terms of the form

$$\int_0^1 f(L) \min[L, K]dL. \tag{18.1}$$

In the one-factor Gaussian latent variable framework, the default time is determined by A_i which is driven by a common market factor Z and an idiosyncratic factor ε_i. As a result, this expectation can be separated into an expectation on the market factor Z, and then conditional on Z, we have N_C idiosyncratic and independent drivers of risk. By conditioning on the value of the common factor, all of the credits in the portfolio become independent. Using conditional expectations, we can write the unconditional loss distribution as

$$f(L) = \int_{-\infty}^{\infty} \phi(Z)f(L|Z)\,dZ$$

where $f(L|Z)$ is the portfolio loss distribution *conditional on the value of Z*.

18.2.1   Steps in Building the Loss Distribution

The entire process of building the tranche survival curve consists of the following steps:

1. We loop over N_T time steps out to contract maturity time T. The time steps are chosen so that they should include the usually quarterly payments on the premium leg and provide the necessary accuracy on the protection leg as discussed in Section 6.6.
2. Nested inside this loop over time steps we have the loop over the market factor Z. The range of integration of Z should be broad enough and the number of integration steps N_Z should be sufficient to allow the required accuracy.
3. For each credit i, we then calculate the conditional default probability using

$$p_i(T|Z) = \Phi\left(\frac{C_i(T) - \beta_i Z}{\sqrt{1 - \beta_i^2}}\right).$$

This means calling the Gaussian cumulative distribution function $\Phi(x)$. We should first ensure that the thresholds $C_i(T) = \Phi^{-1}(1 - Q_i(t, T))$ are calculated *outside* the loop over Z since the inverse Φ function is an expensive one to call in terms of computational time. It is also important that we have as fast an implementation of the $\Phi(x)$ function as possible.

4. At the core of the process is the calculation of the conditional portfolio loss distribution $f(L(T)|Z)$, which will be the main topic of this chapter.

5. Once we have completed the loop over the N_Z values of the market factor Z, we compute the unconditional loss distribution by integrating over the distribution as follows

$$f(L(T)) = \sum_{i=1}^{N_Z} (\Phi(Z_i) - \Phi(Z_{i-1})) f(L(T)|Z_i).$$

where $Z_0 = Z_{\text{Min}}$ and $Z_{N_Z} = Z_{\text{Max}}$. This is discussed in Section 18.4.

6. We complete the loop over the time steps.

The total time taken to perform the calculation of the tranche survival curve can then be written as

$$N_T \left(N_C \cdot T_C + N_Z \cdot (N_C \cdot T_P + T_D) \right) \tag{18.2}$$

where T_C is the time taken to calculate a default threshold for a single credit, T_P is the time taken to calculate the conditional default probability for each credit, and T_D is the time taken to calculate the conditionally independent loss distribution. However, it is the calculation of the conditional loss distribution which we expect to dominate the overall computation time. Our focus is therefore on finding a method that makes T_D as small as possible. This is the subject of the next section.

18.3   BUILDING THE CONDITIONAL LOSS DISTRIBUTION

The shape of the conditional loss distribution is a generalised version of the binomial distribution in which each probability is different. Although we have claimed that it is easier to build a portfolio loss distribution for a portfolio of independent credits than for a portfolio of correlated credits, there are still some challenges. For a start, we note that with N_C credits in the portfolio there are 2^{N_C} possible default combinations each with its own probability. The challenge is to find an algorithm that can calculate the loss distribution in a number of operations which is low order polynomial rather than exponential in N_C.

There are a number of methods for doing this. In this section, we consider those which are deemed to be *exact*. The first technique we will use is called *recursion*. It builds the conditional loss distribution by exploiting the fact that when the portfolio credits are independent, each addition of a new credit to the portfolio can be expressed as a simple linear updating of the existing portfolio loss distribution. The second method, based on Fourier methods, also exploits the conditional independence of the credits. In both cases, the computational complexity of the problem is driven by the degree of homogeneity in the losses of the credits in the portfolio. We begin with an assumption of homogeneous losses.

18.3.1 The Recursion with Homogeneous Losses

The idea of the recursion approach is to start with an empty portfolio and then to update the loss distribution successively by adding credits. At the addition of each credit, we update the previous loss distribution by taking into account the two possible states of survival and default of the credit being added.

We start by considering the homogeneous loss case, i.e. a portfolio of credits with the same face value and recovery rate. We will discuss the more general case later in this chapter. This means that we can define a loss unit $u = F(1 - R)$ such that all possible losses are integer multiples of u, i.e. we have $0, u, 2u, 3u, \ldots, N_Cu$ as the allowed losses. We define $f^{(j)}(k)$ as the probability of k defaults occurring on the portfolio (resulting in a loss ku) after the addition of the jth credit. The algorithm is as follows:

1. We initialise the probability density f knowing that before we have added any credits, all of the probability mass is on the zero loss. Mathematically, we have

$$f^{(0)}(k) = \begin{cases} 1 & \text{if } k = 0 \\ 0 & \text{if } 1 \le k \le N_C. \end{cases}$$

2. Then we begin a loop over credits $j = 1, \ldots, N_C$. There is no requirement to order the credits in any specific way.
3. For each credit j with a conditional default probability $p_j(T|Z)$, we adjust the loss distribution to handle the two outcomes of default and survival. For the zero loss probability, we simply multiply by the probability of survival of credit j

$$f^{(j)}(0) = f^{(j-1)}(0)(1 - p_j(T|Z)).$$

4. We then loop over losses starting from $k = 1$ up to $k = j$. In this case we have to take into account the fact that k defaults can occur either because k defaults have already occurred and credit j survives, or because $k - 1$ defaults have occurred and credit j defaults. Hence we have

$$f^{(j)}(k) = f^{(j-1)}(k)(1 - p_j(T|Z)) + f^{(j-1)}(k - 1)p_j(T|Z).$$

Note that we could choose to terminate this loop not at $k = j$ but at g, the maximum number of loss units before the detachment point of the tranche being valued is equalled or first exceeded, i.e. $g = \text{ceil}(K_2/u)$ where the $\text{ceil}(x)$ function returns the smallest integer greater than or equal to x. The upper bound on the loop is therefore $\min[g, j]$.
5. We return to step (2) to complete the loop over j, finishing when all N_C credits have been added.

Figure 18.1 shows the typical evolution of the conditional loss distribution as credits are added. For small numbers of credits or if the conditional default probabilities are small, the distribution is typically monotonic and decreasing with its peak at zero. As we add credits or if the average conditional default probability is approximately greater than $1/N_C$, the probability

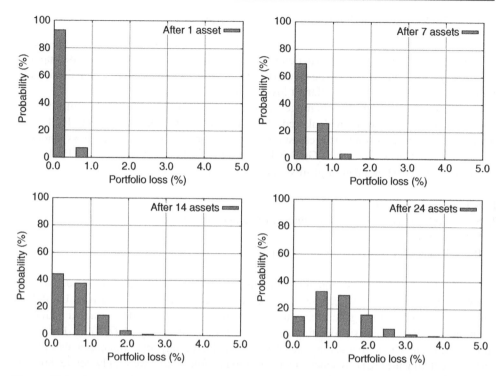

Figure 18.1 An example of how the conditional loss distribution evolves as we add credits to the portfolio. We assume a portfolio of 100 credits, each with a recovery rate of 40%. The average conditional default probability is 7%

mass moves to the right and tends to form a peak at a finite loss,[1] with the overall distribution exhibiting an asymmetric shape with an extended upper loss tail.

Building the conditional loss distribution requires $O(N_C^2)$ operations since we first loop over the $j = 1, \ldots, N_C$ credits and for each of these we then loop over a maximum of $N_C + 1$ loss units. However, as most of the tranches that we have to consider in practice have upper strikes well below 30% of the portfolio notional, there is no need to build the loss distribution out to the maximum portfolio loss. As shown in the algorithm, we can simply terminate the recursion once the upper strike loss has been reached. For a portfolio with a maximum loss of 60%, this means that we can speed up the loss distribution calculation for a 0–3% tranche by a factor of 20, and by a factor of 2 for a 15–30% tranche. If we are only doing individual pricings this is a simple win. However, there are times when we may wish to compute the full portfolio loss distribution, for example if we are trying to calibrate to a set of tranches. Also, if we wish to do fast perturbative risk management we cannot use this speed-up since it prevents us from using the unwinding algorithm discussed in the risk management of tranches in Section 18.7.1.

---

[1] Note that a binomial distribution $\Pr(n) = N!/((N - n)!n!) \cdot p^n(1 - p)^{N-n}$ will have a peak at $n > 0$ if $\Pr(n=0) < \Pr(n=1)$. This means that we have $(1 - p)^N < Np(1 - p)^{N-1}$. Simplifying, the distribution will have a peak at $n > 0$ if $p > 1/(N+1)$. So for $N = 100$, the distribution will have a peak at $n > 0$ if $p > 0.990\%$.

18.3.2   The Recursion with Inhomogeneous Loss Units

In the previous section we assumed that all of the credits in the reference portfolio produced the same loss on default. This led us to define a common loss unit u. However, this assumption is not always valid and we need to be able to handle the case of a portfolio in which the default of different credits can result in different loss amounts.

The standard way to handle inhomogeneous recoveries is to find some loss unit u which is small enough that every individual credit loss that can occur is an integer multiple of u. In other words, we want to find the greatest common divisor (GCD) of all of the loss amounts $L_i = F_i(1 - R_i)$. Calculation of the GCD is based on the method first proposed by Euclid for determining the GCD of a pair of positive integers a and b which is as follows:

1. Set integer `temp` $= b$.
2. Set $b = a$ % b, where x % y is the integer remainder after we divide x by y.
3. Set $a = $ `temp`.
4. If $b = 0$ then GCD $= a$, else return to step (2).

The inputs a and b are loss amounts which have been rounded to integers in such a way that we retain the necessary accuracy. For example, we typically round Euro or US dollar notionals to the nearest integer currency unit since Euro and US dollar denominated notionals are typically $O(10^7)$, and so rounding provides a level of accuracy of $O(10^{-7})$. For other currencies, we may require a scaling factor. For example, we may scale yen notionals by 0.01 before calculating the GCD. To calculate the overall portfolio GCD, we simply iterate through the portfolio credits using the following algorithm:

1. Denote the portfolio GCD as g and initialise it with $g = F_1(1 - R_1)$.
2. Iterate over all the credits $i = 2, \ldots, N_C$. The order of the credits is not important. For each, update g by making the following call

$$g = \texttt{GCDPair}(g, F_i(1 - R_i))$$

    where `GCDPair` (a,b) is the function defined above which returns the GCD of a pair of integers using Euclid's algorithm.
3. The final value of g will be the portfolio GCD in dollars. Each loss can then be expressed as a multiple of this loss unit, i.e. $n_i = F_i(1 - R_i)/g$, where each value of n_i is now an integer.

Once we have the vector of loss units, we are then able to calculate the exact independent loss distribution by extending the previous recursion algorithm:

1. Calculate the total number of portfolio loss units $N_U = \sum_{i=1}^{N_C} n_i$.
2. Initialise the probability density f as before

$$f^{(0)}(k) = \begin{cases} 1 & k = 0 \\ 0 & 1 \leq k \leq N_U. \end{cases}$$

3. Introduce N_J as the number of loss units after j credits have been added. We set $N_J = 0$.
4. Loop over credits $j = 1, \ldots, N_C$.
5. Update $N_J = N_J + n_j$.

6. For credit j, update the loss units which are lower than n_j. They can only change if credit j has survived. We therefore have

$$f^{(j)}(k) = f^{(j-1)}(k)(1 - p_j(T|Z)) \quad \text{for} \quad 0 < k < n_j.$$

7. Consider changes due to either default or survival

$$f^{(j)}(k) = f^{(j-1)}(k)(1 - p_j(T|Z)) + f^{(j-1)}(k - n_j)p_j(T|Z) \quad \text{for} \quad n_j \le k \le N_J.$$

As discussed in the previous section, we could terminate this loop at the number of loss units required to reach the upper strike of the tranche being priced.

8. Repeat the loop over j by returning to step (4) until all N_C credits have been added.

The problem with using loss units is that the number of loss units required can easily 'blow up' to a very high number. This would result in a considerable slowdown in the time taken to price the tranche since the inner loop is over the number of loss units. Also, it may require a significant amount of memory to store the loss distribution, and the time taken to allocate and access this large amount of memory could also have a computational overhead. To demonstrate how non-linear the loss unit calculation is, we have taken a portfolio of 125 credits. We set the recovery rate of 124 of the credits at 40%, and then vary the recovery rate of the 125th credit from 0% to 80% in steps of 1%. For each, we calculate the portfolio GCD and the resulting number of loss units. The results are plotted in Figure 18.2. For example, we see that simply dropping the recovery rate from 40% to 39% would result in an increase of the number of loss

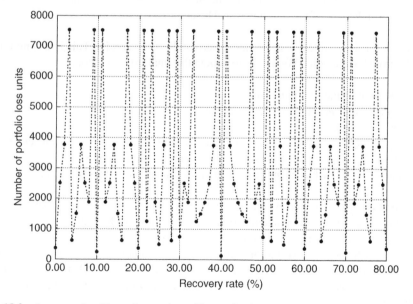

Figure 18.2 An example of how the number of loss units depends on the recovery rate of one credit out of the 125 in the portfolio. All 124 other credits have a common recovery rate of 40%. At 40% the number of loss units equals 125, the number of credits. When the recovery rate of 1 credit changes, the number of loss units quickly increases. We emphasise that the function is highly discontinuous and that with smaller steps than the 1% increments used here, we would see even greater fluctuations in the portfolio loss units. We have joined the points simply to assist the eye

units from 125 to 7501. Even if we drop the recovery to a 'round number' like 35%, the number of loss units is still high at 1500, a factor of 12 increase in the computational time compared with a 40% recovery.

There are ways to avoid this problem. One way is to simply impose a cap on the number of loss units. This necessarily will introduce some error into our calculation as losses have to be rounded to the nearest number of loss units. The question is then one of determining a cap on the number of loss units such that the pricing error is within our required tolerance. It is, however, difficult to determine the pricing error produced by a specific value of the cap *a priori* since the error will depend on the number of credits in the portfolio, their recovery rates, the shape of the loss distribution, and the subordination and width of the tranche being priced. One low tech approach is to simply test for it heuristically by performing a series of pricings, increasing the cap on the number of loss units until the tranche price converges to within the required tolerance. This cap can then be used for all subsequent pricing, and especially for risk management in which multiple calls to the pricing routine will be required.

An algorithm has been proposed by Andersen *et al.* (2003) which does something similar. Unlike the previous suggestion, it is not a direct measure of the error in a tranche price but simply a measure of the error in the loss distribution. The idea behind the algorithm is that we choose a loss unit u such that the associated error for a loss amount $l_j = F_j(1 - R_j)$ associated with some credit j, given by

$$|l_j - \text{int}\left(l_j/u\right) u|,$$

is capped at some tolerance ϵ for all credits. Each error in each credit loss amount will result in an error in the loss distribution and hence in our tranche pricing. By changing the value of ϵ we can control the size of the pricing error. The algorithm is as follows:

1. We search for the smallest loss amount l_i across all of the credits. This is a simple linear search through the credits. We use W to denote the smallest loss amount.
2. Set $n = 1$.
3. Set $g = W/n$ to be the loss unit size.
4. We start the loop over all $i = 1, \ldots, N_C$ credits.
5. For each credit we define $u = \text{int}(l_i/g)$.
6. If for any credit we find that $|l_i - ug| > \epsilon$, the required accuracy has not been achieved, we then exit the loop over credits, we set $n = n + 1$ and return to step (3).
7. The required accuracy has been reached and the corresponding loss unit is g.

The theoretical loss unit will be returned whenever this is greater than ϵ. This routine is simple to implement and is an efficient way to cap the number of loss units.

Another recursive algorithm by Hull and White (2003b) uses a bucketing approach to approximate portfolio loss distribution. However, this is done in a way that preserves the expected loss within each bucket. The size, location and number of buckets all determine the accuracy of the approach. This approach is especially useful when we wish to model stochastic recovery rates.

18.3.3   Fourier Approach

The main alternative to recursion is to use Fourier techniques. The idea of Fourier approaches in general is that we map a problem into another *space* in which it is more analytically tractable.

We then solve the problem in that space and map the solution back. This approach requires that the techniques for mapping to and from this alternative space must be fast and this is provided for by well-known fast Fourier techniques (FFT).

In this case, the problem is the generation of the conditional loss distribution. We start by defining the characteristic function for the total portfolio loss to some horizon time T conditional on the market factor. This is given by

$$\Psi(g|Z) = \mathbb{E}\left[\exp(igL(T))|Z\right]$$

where i is the complex root $\sqrt{-1}$ which is not to be confused with the index i. The portfolio loss at time T is given by

$$L(T) = \sum_{i=1}^{N_C} \mathbf{1}_{A_i \leq C_i(T)} F_i(1 - R_i).$$

Exploiting the one-factor nature of the model, we can factorise the expectation into a product of independent characteristic functions. This is because the $\mathbf{1}_{A_i \leq C_i(T)}$ are independent once we condition on Z. We have

$$\Psi(g|Z) = \mathbb{E}\left[\exp\left(ig \sum_{i=1}^{N_C} \mathbf{1}_{A_i \leq C_i(T)} F_i(1 - R_i)\right) |Z\right]$$

$$= \prod_{i=1}^{N_C} \mathbb{E}_{\varepsilon_i}\left[\exp\left(ig\mathbf{1}_{A_i \leq C_i(T)} F_i(1 - R_i)\right) |Z\right].$$

We can use the GCD algorithm discussed earlier in this chapter to find a loss unit u for the portfolio so that we can write

$$F_i(1 - R_i)\, \mathbf{1}_{A_i \leq C_i(T)} = n_i u\, \mathbf{1}_{A_i \leq C_i(T)}$$

where n_i is the number of loss units of size u associated with the default of credit i. Since credit i defaults with conditional default probability $p_i(T|Z)$ we can calculate the single credit conditional characteristic function for the number of loss units (not the loss amount) as

$$\mathbb{E}\left[\exp(ign_i\mathbf{1}_{A_i \leq C_i(T)}) \mid Z\right] = p_i(T|Z)\exp(ign_i) + (1 - p_i(T|Z)).$$

We now introduce the unconditional characteristic function for the total number of loss units k. We call this $\Psi(g)$. It can be written in terms of the conditional characteristic function as follows

$$\Psi(g) = \int_{-\infty}^{\infty} \phi(Z)\Psi(g|Z)dZ$$

$$= \int_{-\infty}^{\infty} \phi(Z)\left[\prod_{i=1}^{N_C} [p_i(T|Z)\exp(ign_i) + (1 - p_i(T|Z))]\right] dZ. \qquad (18.3)$$

The success of Fourier approaches in general is based on exploiting the efficiencies of fast Fourier transform (FFT) algorithms which are used to invert the transform. In this case we wish to invert the characteristic function to give us the loss distribution. Given that the actual loss distribution is discrete due to the specification of a loss unit u, we can write the discrete form of the characteristic function as

$$\Psi(g) = \sum_{k=0}^{N_U} \Pr(L = ku) e^{igk}$$

where k indexes the number of loss units which ranges from zero up to $N_U = \sum_{i=1}^{N_C} n_i$. The actual loss corresponding to this is ku. To invert the characteristic function to calculate the discrete loss distribution we must write

$$\Pr(L = ku) = \frac{1}{N_U + 1} \sum_{n=0}^{N_U} \Psi\left(\frac{2\pi n}{N_U + 1}\right) \exp\left(-\frac{2\pi ikn}{N_U + 1}\right). \tag{18.4}$$

Computationally, calculating $\Pr(L = ku)$ for all N_U loss units requires us to make N_U calls to Equation 18.4. Each call involves a sum over N_U terms. This implies that the inversion is a quadratic problem which should scale with N_U^2. However, FFT algorithms such as Cooley–Tukey reduce this to $O(N_U \ln N_U)$ as discussed in Press et al. (1992). The algorithm for calculation of the unconditional loss distribution is therefore as follows:

1. Loop over the N_Z values of the market factor Z.
2. For each value of Z loop over all possible numbers of loss units $g = 1, \dots, N_U$. For each value of g calculate the characteristic function given by

$$\Psi(g|Z) = \prod_{i=1}^{N_C} (p_i(T|Z) \exp(ign_i) + (1 - p_i(T|Z))).$$

The complex exponential term can be calculated using complex number algebra by recalling the identity

$$\exp(ign_i) = \cos(gn_i) + i \sin(gn_i)$$

and that multiplication of complex numbers a and b with real and imaginary parts $a = (a_R, a_I)$ and $b = (b_R, b_I)$ is governed by

$$a \times b = (a_R + ia_I)(b_R + ib_I) = a_R b_R - a_I b_I + i(a_R b_I + a_I b_R).$$

3. Return to (1) to increment Z, moving on to (4) only when Z reaches the upper limit of its integration.
4. Calculate the unconditional characteristic functions $\Psi(g)$ at the N_u values of g by integrating $\Psi(g|Z)$ over the Gaussian density $\phi(Z)$.
5. Use an FFT algorithm to invert the transform, producing $f(k)$ at each of the $k = 0, \dots, N_U$ losses.

As a result, the total computation time scales as $O(N_Z N_U N_C) + O(N_U \ln N_U)$. Given that we would expect $N_U \sim O(N_C)$ this becomes $O(N_Z N_C^2) + O(N_C \ln N_C)$. The first term, which corresponds to the calculation of the characteristic function, is the dominant one. This method appears similar to the recursion method in which the number of evaluations also scales as $O(N_Z N_C^2)$ when we include the integration over Z. The question is then one of the speed of each step in the innermost calculation loop. At the core of the calculation of the characteristic function we have the multiplication of complex numbers and calls to the $\cos(x)$ and $\sin(x)$ functions. For each calculation, this seems to be much more expensive than the real-number multiplications in the recursion and suggests that recursion is the faster method. This is confirmed by experience. We also note that Andersen et al. (2003) find a factor of the recursion to be between 5 and 25 times faster than the Fourier approach.

Despite its mathematical complexity, and the requirement of access to a good FFT algorithm, this approach was probably the first widely used loss distribution construction methodology and was discussed in Finger (1999). However, there has been a general trend away from Fourier methods towards recursion methods. There is an overwhelming set of reasons for this: (i) recursion is generally faster than Fourier methods, (ii) recursion is easier to implement than Fourier methods, (iii) using recursion we can stop building the loss distribution at some tranche upper strike and this is not possible with Fourier methods and (iv) recursion does not require access to any specialised numerical libraries.

18.4   INTEGRATING OVER THE MARKET FACTOR

The final step is to generate the unconditional loss distribution by integrating over the market factor Z. This can be done by a naïve trapezium rule in which the interval from Z_{Min} to Z_{Max} is split into N_Z intervals. A suitable choice of range for Z is $Z_{Max} = -Z_{Min} = 6.0$ since the probability mass above and below these limits is $O(10^{-9})$, and so is consistent with the tolerance that we are seeking.

A simple trapezium rule-style integration works well although care must be taken to ensure that the number of integration steps is sufficient to avoid oscillations in the resulting loss distribution caused by the superposition of the independent conditional loss distributions with different values of the market factor Z. Consider Figure 18.3 in which we see how the loss distribution for a homogeneous portfolio of 125 credits depends on N_Z. With $N_Z = 15$ or even $N_Z = 20$, the loss distributions are visibly different from the loss distribution when $N_Z = 25$. We also find that the required value of N_Z increases with the number of credits N_C and can also depend on the heterogeneity of the portfolio. This can be understood by realising that the variance of each conditional loss distribution is proportional to $1/N_C$. So as we increase N_C the distributions we are combining become more tightly distributed about the mean portfolio loss. This makes oscillations in the unconditional distribution become more apparent and more integration steps are required to ensure that this is averaged out correctly. We also find that the oscillations increase with β since a higher value of β means that the range of interest for Z, i.e. the range for which the conditional probability is neither zero nor 100%, becomes narrower. As a result we need a finer sampling of Z as we increase β.

As an alternative to the trapezium rule, one can also use the Gauss–Hermite quadrature approach discussed in Press et al. (1992). This quadrature scheme is based on finding a suitable set of abscissas x_j and weights w_j to solve the following integration problem

$$\int_{-\infty}^{\infty} e^{-x^2} g(x)dx = \sum_{j=1}^{M} w_j g(x_j).$$

It is therefore perfectly suited for a Gaussian density. In theory, quadrature should produce higher precision than the trapezium rule when using the same number of calculations of the

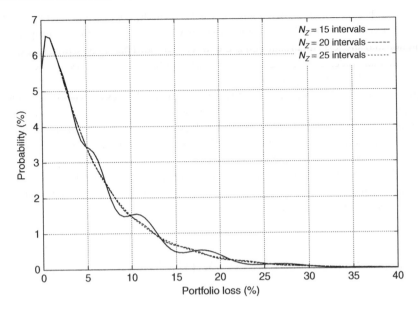

Figure 18.3 The portfolio loss distribution for a homogeneous portfolio of 125 credits for three values of N_Z, the number of intervals in the range $[-6, 6]$ used for the market factor integration. We used $\beta = 0.5$, $p = 0.10$ and $R = 0.40$. We need to increase the number of intervals to 25 in order to remove any visible wiggles in the loss distribution

conditional loss distribution. However, care should also be taken here to ensure that the number of abscissas chosen is sufficient to avoid oscillation effects.

18.5 APPROXIMATING THE CONDITIONAL PORTFOLIO LOSS DISTRIBUTION

The methods discussed so far have focused on attempting to construct the exact loss distribution. As this requires $O(N_C^2)$ evaluations, there is an interest in other methodologies which may be slightly less accurate but faster. Here the important question is what is the trade-off between speed and accuracy, and can we find something which is an acceptable compromise? We discuss two approaches, one known as the Gaussian approximation, which has already been published, and another by the author.

18.5.1 The Gaussian Approximation

The simplest and most analytically tractable approximation of the conditional loss distribution is to use the Gaussian distribution. This approach, first published by Shelton (2004), uses a Gaussian density which fits the first two moments of the conditional loss distribution. It is then possible to obtain a closed-form expression for the expected tranche loss conditional on the market factor.

Specifically, for each horizon date T and each value of the common market factor Z, we approximate the conditional loss distribution by a Gaussian with mean loss $\mu(Z)$ and standard deviation $\sigma(Z)$ determined so that they match the first two moments of the actual conditional loss distribution. We have

$$\mu(Z) = \frac{1}{N} \sum_{i=1}^{N} p_i(T|Z)F_i(1 - R_i)$$

and

$$\sigma^2(Z) = \frac{1}{N^2} \sum_{i=1}^{N} p_i(T|Z)(1 - p_i(T|Z))F_i^2(1 - R_i)^2.$$

These formulae are derived in Section 16.7.1. Because the formula for the conditional loss distribution is analytic in form, it allows us to write an analytical formula for the expected loss of the tranche conditional on the market factor realisation. First, we write

$$\mathbb{E}\left[\min(L(T), K)\right] = \int_{-\infty}^{\infty} \phi(Z) \cdot \mathbb{E}\left[\min(L(T, Z), K)| Z\right] dZ.$$

We then fit the conditional loss distribution with a Gaussian distribution with mean $\mu = \mu(Z)$ and standard deviation $\sigma = \sigma(Z)$ as calculated above. We therefore have

$$\mathbb{E}\left[\min(L(T), K)| Z\right] = \frac{1}{\sqrt{2\pi\sigma^2}} \int_{-\infty}^{\infty} \exp\left(-\frac{(L - \mu)^2}{2\sigma^2}\right) \min(L, K)dL.$$

After some manipulations, this becomes

$$\mathbb{E}\left[\min(L(T), K)| Z\right] = -\sigma\phi\left(\frac{\mu - K}{\sigma}\right) - (\mu - K)\,\Phi\left(\frac{\mu - K}{\sigma}\right).$$

As a result the absolute loss of a K_1 to K_2 tranche conditional on the market factor is given by

$$\mathbb{E}\left[\min(L(T), K_2)\mid Z\right] - \mathbb{E}\left[\min(L(T), K_1)\mid Z\right]$$

$$= \sigma\left(\phi\left(\frac{\mu - K_1}{\sigma}\right) - \phi\left(\frac{\mu - K_2}{\sigma}\right)\right)$$

$$+ (\mu - K_1)\,\Phi\left(\frac{\mu - K_1}{\sigma}\right) - (\mu - K_2)\,\Phi\left(\frac{\mu - K_2}{\sigma}\right). \tag{18.5}$$

We can integrate this over the Gaussian density of the market factor Z to produce the unconditional expected tranche loss, recalculating μ and σ for each value of Z.

To understand the quality of this approximation, we should compare the shape of the Gaussian distribution with the shape of a multinomial distribution. We show in Figure 18.4 attempts of the Gaussian distribution to fit the conditional loss distribution for two different values of the market factor Z equal to -2 and $+1$. While the fit appears good in the first of these cases, it does not appear to be so good in the second case when $Z = +1$. This is the regime in which the conditional default probabilities are small and so the loss distribution is monotonic and decreasing with the highest probability on zero losses. Note that the Gaussian distribution assigns finite probabilities to negative losses. It will also assign a finite probability to losses above 100%. This can lead to problems since it means that the total expected loss of tranche protection legs running from 0% to 100% will not sum to the expected loss of the reference portfolio.

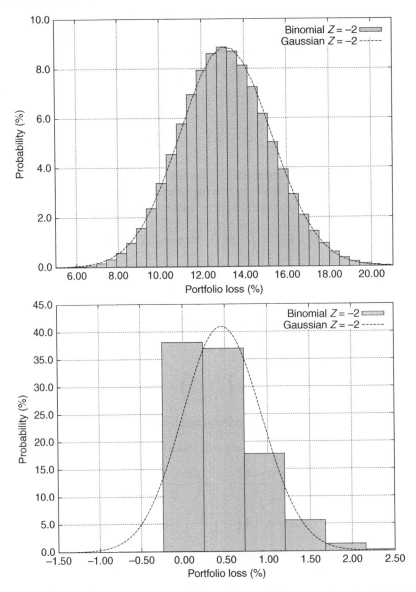

Figure 18.4 We compare the exact conditional loss distribution with the Gaussian fit to its first two moments. In the upper graph we have the conditional loss distribution for $Z = -2$ and in the lower graph the conditional loss distribution for $Z = +1$. The portfolio has an unconditional default probability of 5%, and consists of 125 credits with recovery rate 40%

One advantage of this method is that it discards any discreteness in the portfolio loss distribution since we model it with a continuous function. It therefore avoids all of the complications of GCDs and loss units. The fact that there is a semi-analytical solution for the tranche survival curve makes implementation quite straightforward. However, although it is much faster than a full recursion, it is not necessarily as fast as we might expect. For a start, we still have to calculate the conditional default probabilities $p_i(Z)$ for each value of Z for each credit. From these we then calculate $\mu(Z)$, $\sigma(Z)$ and finally Equation 18.5 for each time step and each value of the market factor. The scaling in the number of evaluations appears to be $O(N_T N_Z N_C)$ which is less than the full recursion by a factor N_C. However, since the inner loop makes two calls to the computationally expensive $\Phi(x)$ and $\exp(x)$ functions, this scaling advantage is partly offset by these function calls. We cannot therefore guarantee that this method will be significantly faster than the full recursion. We must use numerical experiments to determine its actual speed. We do this in Section 18.6.

18.5.2 The Binomial Approximation

Another simple approximation in terms of speed and accuracy is the binomial approximation. The idea is to approximate the exact multinomial distribution with a binomial distribution. The reason for this is that we expect that the shape of the binomial distribution is a better fit to the multinomial distribution than the Gaussian. For sure, we know that when the portfolio spreads and losses are homogeneous, then the binomial approximation will be exact.

To fit the exact conditional loss distribution with a binomial, we need to have a single conditional default probability which is common to all of the credits in the portfolio. The obvious candidate is to choose the average since this guarantees that we fit the mean of the loss distribution. We set

$$p(T|Z) = \frac{1}{N_C} \sum_{i=1}^{N_C} p_i(T|Z). \tag{18.6}$$

We can then build the loss distribution of the binomial by simple recursion. We assume that the portfolio losses are homogeneous, although this restriction can be relaxed. The probability of n defaults out of N_C credits is then given by

$$f(n) = \frac{N_C!}{(N_C - n)!n!} \cdot p(T|Z)^n (1 - p(T|Z))^{N-n}.$$

Rather than use this formula, which requires calls to the computationally expensive factorial function, it is possible to calculate the conditional loss distribution using a recursive approach. The steps in the algorithm are therefore:

1. Calculate $p(T|Z)$ using Equation 18.6.
2. Start the recursion at the zero loss density using

$$f(0) = (1 - p(T|Z))^{N_C}.$$

3. The recursion equation is

$$f(k) = f(k-1) \left(\frac{p(T|Z)}{1 - p(T|Z)} \right) \left(\frac{N_C - k + 1}{k} \right) \quad \text{for } 0 < k \le N_C.$$

4. Alternately, we can terminate the recursion at the number of losses corresponding to the tranche upper strike.

If $p(T|Z)$ is large, it may be more numerically stable to start the recursion from the top of the loss distribution. For example, if $p(T|Z) \to 1$, then the term $p(T|Z)/(1 - p(T|Z))$ will be large and repeated multiplication by this term can cause numerical overflows. We can avoid this by setting $f(N_C) = p(T|Z)^{N_C}$ and then invert the recursion relation by writing $f(k-1)$ in terms of $f(k)$.

The advantage of this approximation is that it should be much faster than a full recursion since the number of evaluations scales as $O(N_C)$. Also, each step is a simple mathematical product operation. We can also precalculate $p(T|Z)/(1 - p(T|Z))$ so that this is not recalculated.

18.5.3   The Adjusted Binomial Approximation

Although this approximation is fast and works well, its accuracy can be further improved. The problem with the binomial approximation is that we have only matched the first moment of the exact conditional loss distribution. Even the Gaussian approach fits the mean and variance. We therefore need to find a way to fit the variance. For simplicity, we consider the distribution of the fraction of defaulted credits, effectively the same as the portfolio loss distribution assuming a recovery rate of zero on each default. As shown in Section 16.7.1, the variance of this distribution is given by

$$v_A = \frac{p(T|Z)\,(1 - p(T|Z))}{N_C}. \tag{18.7}$$

The variance of the exact multinomial distribution that we are attempting to approximate is given by

$$v_E = \frac{1}{N_C^2} \sum_{i=1}^{N_C} p_i(T|Z)\,(1 - p_i(T|Z)). \tag{18.8}$$

One can show via Jensen's inequality that $v_A \geq v_E$. In order to improve the approximation, we need to fit the variance of the approximating distribution to that of the exact distribution. However, we must do this while preserving the expected number of defaults. The method we choose here is to simply transfer probability mass from across the distribution and move it closer to the expected number of defaults in a way which means that the new variance of the approximate distribution equals that of the exact distribution. Our scheme is as follows:

1. Multiply the probability density of the approximating binomial distribution by α.
2. Add back the removed probability mass $(1 - \alpha)$ at the mean number of losses $m = p(T|Z)N_C$ of the loss distribution.

The practicalities are slightly more complicated since the fact that the distribution is discrete means that m will not be an integer number of loss units but will almost surely lie between two of the discrete loss probabilities. If this is the case, we split the $(1 - \alpha)$ of probability between the two integer losses on either side of the mean. These are located at losses of l and $l+1$ such that $l \leq m \leq l+1$. The probability of a loss l gets an additional probability ϵ_l while the probability at $l+1$ gets an additional probability ϵ_{l+1}. This presents us with three linear equations in three unknowns

$$\epsilon_l + \epsilon_{l+1} = (1 - \alpha)$$

$$m = \alpha\, m + \epsilon_l\, l + \epsilon_{l+1}\, (l + 1)$$

$$v_E\, N_C = \alpha\, v_A\, N_C + (l - m)^2 \epsilon_l + (l + 1 - m)^2 \epsilon_{l+1}.$$

These can be solved exactly to give

$$\alpha = \frac{v_E N_C - (l + 1 - m)^2 - ((l - m)^2 - (l + 1 - m)^2)(l + 1 - m)}{v_A N_C - (l + 1 - m)^2 - ((l - m)^2 - (l + 1 - m)^2)(l + 1 - m)}$$

$$\epsilon_l = (1 - \alpha)(l + 1 - m)$$

$$\epsilon_{l+1} = 1 - \alpha - \epsilon_l. \tag{18.9}$$

The additional steps to the binomial approximation algorithm are listed below:

1. Calculate the v_A and v_E using Equations 18.7 and 18.8.
2. Determine l and $l + 1$ which are the losses bracketing the mean $m = p(T|Z)N_C$.
3. Calculate α according to Equation 18.9.
4. Adjust all weights such that $f'(n) = \alpha f(n)$ for $n = 0, \ldots, N_C$.
5. Set $f'(l) = f(l) + \epsilon_l$.
6. Set $f'(l + 1) = f(l + 1) + \epsilon_{l+1}$.

The performance impact of determining the values of α, ϵ_l and ϵ_{l+1} and making all of the adjustments is $O(N_C)$. The resulting increase in accuracy due to this adjustment is significant as we see in Section 18.6.

We now consider how to apply this approximation to the case of an inhomogeneous loss portfolio. One potential limitation of this methodology is that the binomial is a discrete distribution and so at a first glance would appear to present all of the problems with loss units that we have already discussed. As a result, we would not expect it to be able to deal with the challenge of inhomogeneous losses. However, this is not the case. If we define the average loss per credit as

$$L_{Avg} = \frac{1}{N_C} \sum_{i=1}^{N_C} (1 - R_i) F_i$$

then we can write the inhomogeneous version of the binomial default probability

$$p(T|Z) = \frac{1}{N_C} \sum_{i=1}^{N_C} \frac{(1 - R_i) F_i}{L_{Avg}} p_i(T|Z).$$

Using this probability in the binomial approximation ensures that the inhomogeneous portfolio expected loss is conserved. The variance of the distribution of the fraction of defaults is then given as before by $p(T|Z)(1 - p(T|Z)/N_C$. However, the exact variance that we want to match is now given by

$$v_E = \frac{1}{N_C^2} \sum_{i=1}^{N_C} \left(\frac{(1 - R_i) F_i}{L_{Avg}} \right)^2 p_i(T|Z)\, (1 - p_i(T|Z)).$$

Once again we can use the adjustment described above to ensure that the adjusted binomial matches both the mean and variance of the exact inhomogeneous-loss distribution. We show a comparison of this method to others in Section 18.6.

18.6 A COMPARISON OF METHODS

We have discussed a wide variety of approximate methods and in order to recommend any to the reader we should compare their speed and accuracy. The algorithms we shall analyse are the LHP approximation, the Gaussian approximation and the adjusted binomial approximation. These can all be compared to the full and exact recursion. For our analysis of loss methods we consider STCDOs on two different reference portfolios:

1. A CDX NA portfolio of 125 credits with an average 5Y spread of 50 bp.
2. A CDX HY portfolio of 100 credits with an average 5Y spread of 549 bp.

Both portfolios are heterogeneous in terms of spreads. On each, we specify a set of equity tranches. The reason for this is that equity or *base tranches* will be shown to be the building block of the *base correlation* approach which is described later in Chapter 20. Understanding the accuracy of these approximations in pricing base tranches will help us determine how useful these algorithms are in a base correlation framework.

18.6.1 Homogeneous Loss Methods

We begin with the case of a reference portfolio with homogeneous losses. For each algorithm, i.e. full recursion, the Gaussian approximation, the binomial and the adjusted binomial approximation, we calculate the breakeven spread for a set of tranches assuming an asset correlation of $\rho = \beta^2 = 20\%$. Note that we set $N_z = 50$ and $N_T = 20$, i.e. the time steps are quarterly out to five years. We assume a recovery rate of $R = 40\%$.

Table 18.1 compares the breakeven spread of each of the approximations against the exact spread given by the recursion. This table uses the CDX NA Investment Grade index for the reference portfolio. We see that the LHP approximation is the worst of all. We also see that the Gaussian approximation has a similar error to the LHP. This is to be expected since this approximation ignores both the granularity of the portfolio and its spread dispersion. The adjusted binomial performs best and is the clear winner with a spread error within 0.2 bp on all

Table 18.1 Comparison of approximation methods for the standard base tranches on the CDX NA IG index portfolio. The reference portfolio is assumed to be homogeneous loss with a common recovery rate of 40%

Tranche K_1–K_2 (%)	Exact (bp)	Gauss (bp)	Error (%)	LHP (bp)	Error (%)	AdjBinom (bp)	Error (%)
0–3	1596.8	1641.05	2.76	1638.60	2.61	1596.70	−0.01
0–7	741.1	751.84	1.45	754.56	1.81	741.08	−0.00
0–10	515.3	521.53	1.21	526.34	2.14	515.28	−0.00
0–15	336.0	339.63	1.07	344.34	2.46	336.04	−0.00
0–30	161.9	163.42	0.96	166.03	2.57	161.87	0.00

tranches. When we look at the error of the approximations using CDX NA High Yield as the reference portfolio in Table 18.2, we see that the LHP has the largest error and the Gaussian does much better. Once again the adjusted binomial approximation fits to within about 1 bp.

Table 18.2 Comparison of approximation methods for the standard base tranches on the CDX NA HY index portfolio. The reference portfolio is assumed to be homogeneous loss with a common recovery rate of 40%

Tranche K_1–K_2 (%)	Exact (bp)	Gauss (bp)	Error (%)	LHP (bp)	Error (%)	AdjBinom (bp)	Error (%)
0–10	6402.2	6411.8	0.15	7006.4	9.4	6401.0	−0.02
0–15	3965.2	3967.4	0.06	4802.3	21.1	3965.9	0.02
0–25	2043.4	2044.2	0.04	2812.8	37.6	2043.5	0.00
0–35	1298.4	1298.7	0.02	1867.8	43.8	1298.4	−0.00

18.6.2 Inhomogeneous Loss Portfolios

To analyse the inhomogeneous loss case, we take the same two portfolios as before. However, this time we set 10 recovery rates to 10%, 10–20%, 10–30%, and all the remaining credit recovery rates to 40%. For the 125-name CDX IG portfolio, the number of loss units is 810. We set the asset correlation to 20%. In this case we only compare the LHP, Gaussian and adjusted binomial approximations to the exact.

Table 18.3 shows that in the case of an investment grade portfolio, the LHP has the largest pricing error. The Gaussian approximation is the second worst with an error of 56 bp on the equity tranche spread. The adjusted binomial matches the exact pricing to within 1 bp. When the reference portfolio is high yield and inhomogeneous, the adjusted binomial continues to perform well with a pricing error always less than 1 bp. This is shown in Table 18.4.

Table 18.3 Comparison of approximation methods for the standard base tranches on the CDX NA IG index portfolio. The reference portfolio is assumed to be inhomogeneous

Tranche K_1–K_2 (%)	Exact (bp)	Gauss (bp)	Error (%)	LHP (bp)	Error (%)	AdjBinom (bp)	Error (%)
0–3	1749.94	1806.23	3.22	1748.02	−0.11	1749.87	−0.00
0–7	822.11	835.38	1.61	813.62	−1.00	821.96	−0.02
0–10	573.10	580.75	1.33	569.64	−0.60	573.07	−0.01
0–15	373.97	378.30	1.16	373.47	−0.14	373.97	0.00
0–30	179.66	181.50	1.02	179.91	0.13	179.66	0.00

Table 18.4 Comparison of approximation methods for the standard base tranches on the CDX NA HY index portfolio. The reference portfolio is assumed to be inhomogeneous

Tranche K_1–K_2(%)	Exact (bp)	Gauss (bp)	Error (%)	LHP (bp)	Error (%)	AdjBinom (bp)	Error (%)
0–10	7259.6	7270.6	0.15	7508.7	3.43	7260.6	0.01
0–15	4535.8	4540.2	0.10	5170.7	14.00	4536.1	0.00
0–25	2360.7	2361.8	0.05	3067.6	29.95	2360.7	−0.00
0–35	1497.5	1497.9	0.03	2059.8	37.55	1497.5	−0.00

18.6.3   Timings

Rather than show absolute timings which depend very much on the choice of processor, operating system, and programming language, we present the relative timings. We do so for the homogeneous loss case – the computation times of the approximations have almost no dependence on whether the reference portfolios are homogeneous or heterogeneous loss. These timings do not include the overhead of building the underlying single-name credit curves. Our observations are as follows:

- The LHP is the fastest of all, roughly 500 times faster than the full recursion.
- The Gaussian approximation is about six times faster than the full recursion.
- The adjusted binomial approximation is about 10 times faster than the full recursion.

The adjusted binomial approximation appears to be significantly more accurate than the others. It is also about 10 times faster than the full recursion. Since we are assuming a homogeneous loss portfolio, this is a very conservative estimate. If the reference portfolio has inhomogeneous losses, the adjusted binomial algorithm can easily be hundreds of times faster than the full recursion algorithm.

18.7   PERTURBING THE LOSS DISTRIBUTION

The most intensive use of the loss distribution building algorithm is not the pricing of tranches, but the risk management of tranches. The calculation of the idiosyncratic deltas of all of the credits in the portfolio is the most important risk measure. If we have N_C credits in the portfolio and wish to calculate the spread sensitivity to the liquid maturity points at 1Y, 3Y, 5Y, 7Y and 10Y on the CDS term structure of each name, we then have $5N_C$ calls to the loss distribution algorithm. With a book of maybe 500 tranches, each with an average of 100 credits, this requires a loss distribution to be calculated 250 000 times. This raises the question of whether there is a way we can speed up the calculation of these risk measures. Clearly, as we are only perturbing the risk of one credit at a time, it seems as though there is a significant amount of duplication in each loss distribution as $N_C - 1$ out of N_C credits are the same.

18.7.1   Unwinding the Recursion

There is indeed a way to reuse the calculation of the loss distribution and so speed up the calculation of the idiosyncratic risk calculations. We focus on the recursion approach. Let us suppose we have already calculated the density of the conditional loss distribution $f(n)$ and we now wish to perturb the spread of issuer i in the portfolio such that its conditional probability of default is now $p_i^*(T|Z)$. For simplicity we assume that all losses are a multiple of a fundamental loss unit u and that the default of credit i results in a loss equal to $n_i u$. There are a total of $N_U = \sum_{i=1}^{N} n_i$ loss units in the portfolio. The steps are as follows:

1. We first build the full loss distribution using the recursion algorithm and store the distribution $f^{(N_C)}(k)$ for $k = 0, \ldots, N_U$. We do this for each time step, therefore requiring that $N_T(N_U + 1)$

numbers be cached in the memory of the computer. For a five-year deal with quarterly time steps and 500 loss units, this consists of 10 000 numbers, essentially negligible for most modern computers.

2. The next step is to unwind the addition of credit i. We start at the zero loss point of the loss distribution corresponding to $k = 0$. Unwinding the addition of credit i for the zero loss probability is simply a matter of dividing out $(1 - p_i(T|Z))$, the credit's conditional survival probability. We do this for loss units from $k = 0$ to $k = n_i - 1$ we can write this formally as

$$f^{(N_C-1)}(k) = \frac{f^{(N_C)}(k)}{(1 - p_i(T|Z))} \quad \text{for} \ \ 0 \le k < n_i.$$

We can then start to move forward through the loss distribution as follows

$$f^{(N_C-1)}(k) = \frac{f^{(N_C)}(k) - p_i(T|Z)f^{(N_C-1)}(k - n_i)}{(1 - p_i(T|Z))} \quad \text{for} \ \ n_i \le k \le N_U.$$

However, there is a numerical instability in this unwind procedure which can occur due to the repeated subtraction of two potentially very small numbers in the numerator followed by a division by the conditional survival probability. We can show heuristically that this numerical instability appears given a value of $p_i(T|Z) > \kappa$ where κ depends on the average probability of default of the other credits in the portfolio. Its effect is to produce values of $f(k)$ which can be negative, greater than one, or which can be undefined, i.e. a numerical overflow. To avoid these instabilities, we can use the alternative unwind algorithm in step (3).

3. This step needs to be taken only if the conditional probability $p_i(T|Z)$ is greater than some threshold κ and certainly if it is close to 1. The aim is to avoid numerical errors which can occur in step (2). In this step, we unwind the addition of credit i by starting at the *last* point of the loss distribution and working backwards. Unwinding the addition of credit i for the maximum loss is simply a matter of dividing out $p_i(T|Z)$, the previous default probability. Noting that there are only $N_C - 1$ credits once we remove credit i, we set

$$f^{(N_C-1)}(k) = 0 \quad \text{for} \ \ N_U - n_i < k \le N_U.$$

We can then start to move back through the loss distribution as follows

$$f^{(N_C-1)}(k) = \frac{f^{(N_C)}(k + n_i) - (1 - p_i(T|Z))f^{(N_C-1)}(k + n_i)}{p_i(T|Z)} \quad \text{for} \ \ n_i \le k \le N_U - n_i.$$

Finally, we set

$$f^{(N_C-1)}(k) = \frac{f^{(N_C)}(k)}{1 - p_i(T|Z)} \quad \text{for} \ \ 0 \le k < n_i.$$

4. The final step is the re-addition of credit i with its new conditional default probability $p_i^*(T|Z)$. We simply update the probabilities as before. The equations are

$$f^{(N_C)}(k) = f^{(N_C-1)}(k)(1 - p_i^*(T|Z)) \quad \text{for} \ \ 0 \le k < n_i.$$

and

$$f^{(N_C)}(k) = f^{(N_C-1)}(k)(1 - p_i^*(T|Z)) + f^{(N_C-1)}(k - n_i)p_i^*(T|Z) \quad \text{for} \ \ n_i \le k \le N_U.$$

This step is generally numerically stable.

5. This is repeated for all N_T time horizons giving us the perturbed loss 'surface', i.e. the new loss distribution as a function of loss unit and time horizon.

Concerning the value of κ, we find that the value at which numerical instabilities begin depends on portfolio characteristics such as the average portfolio default probability. Numerical experiments suggest a value of κ close to 0.50.

There are therefore only $2N_C$ updating steps to produce the perturbed loss distribution for each credit, a factor of $N_C/2$ reduction in computation effort compared to a full rebuild of the loss distribution. Indeed, if we do it N_C times to calculate the perturbed loss distribution for all credits, the overall computation time is $O(N_C^2)$ which is similar to that of doing a single full recursion pricing. The cost is simply a caching in memory of the unperturbed loss distribution. The only other drawback is that we must build the entire loss distribution up to the maximum loss, i.e. we cannot terminate the loss distribution at some loss which corresponds to the uppermost strike of the tranche we are pricing. In practice, the benefit of caching and unwinding the loss distribution far outweighs the benefit achieved by stopping the construction of the loss distribution at K_2.

Note that we can also use this unwind approach for the calculation of other idiosyncratic risk measures such as the tranche VOD in which one credit needs to be removed from the portfolio, and also measures such as the idiosyncratic gamma. It can also be used to calculate measures which involve the removal of more than one credit.

18.8   SUMMARY

Efficient loss distribution building is an essential requirement when we need to price and risk manage a number of correlation trades. We have described in detail how this can be done using the recursion method in the homogeneous and heterogeneous loss case. We have also analysed a number of approximate methods for building the conditional loss distribution and compared them in terms of speed and accuracy. We concluded by showing how the recursion approach can be adapted to enable the efficient calculation of risk measures.

19

Implied Correlation

19.1 INTRODUCTION

In mid-2003, the participants in the synthetic CDO market witnessed the creation of a market in implied correlation. This was the result of dealers who had begun to send out price levels for a set of five standard tranches based on the highly liquid CDX and iTraxx indices. This event introduced a new level of standardisation and transparency to what had previously been a market in which trades were typically executed on bespoke tranches agreed between private parties. The correlation input to the pricing model, which had previously been an empirical estimate, suddenly became a market observable, and the concept of *implied correlation* was born. Not only was it a revolution in the way the STCDO market operated, it also forced credit derivative modellers to invent new correlation models which were consistent with market prices. These models will be the subject of most of the remaining chapters of this book.

In this chapter, we begin this discussion of implied correlation modelling with a discussion of how to calculate implied correlation. Specifically, we discuss the concept of *compound correlation* in detail. We use compound correlation to explain the so-called 'correlation smile', and explain why compound correlation is not an arbitrage-free model. We then set out in detail the no-arbitrage conditions of a correlation model. This provides the theoretical foundation for the models we will encounter in the following chapters.

19.2 IMPLIED CORRELATION

Table 19.1 shows a set of tranche quotes from October 2004. These consist of quotes for five tranches on each of the two investment grade indices, the North American CDX and the European iTraxx. We can interpret these quotes as follows:

- An investor in a \$10 million notional of the 0–3% equity tranche would receive an upfront payment of \$3.7125 million followed by an annualised running spread of 500 bp a year paid quarterly according to an Actual 360 convention.
- An investor in the more senior tranches does not make or receive any upfront payment. They do, however, receive the annualised spread shown which is also paid quarterly according to an Actual 360 convention.

For all tranches, these spread payments are risky, i.e. they are paid on the outstanding notional of the tranche and so would decline if there were any defaults in the portfolio in exactly the same way as the STCDOs have discussed in earlier chapters.

Table 19.1 Market prices for the CDX NA and iTraxx Europe tranches in October 2004. On this date the CDX IG NA 3 index traded at 53.5 bp and iTraxx Europe 2 traded at 37 bp

Tranche	CDX Investment Grade North America Series 3			iTraxx Europe Series 2		
	Lower–upper strike (%)	Upfront payment (%)	Running spread (bp)	Lower–upper strike (%)	Upfront payment (%)	Running spread (bp)
Equity	0–3	37.125	500.0	0–3	24.25	500.0
Junior mezzanine	3–7	–	259.5	3–6	–	137.5
Senior mezzanine	7–10	–	101.0	6–9	–	47.5
Senior	10–15	–	38.5	9–12	–	34.5
Super senior	15–30	–	11.5	12–22	–	15.5

An obvious first approach to determining implied correlation is to simply take the prices of the standard tranches traded in the market and reverse out the correlation assumption implied using the Gaussian latent variable model. However, any attempt to imply a correlation measure from a tranche price must necessarily require a simplification of the correlation structure assumed for the credits in the underlying portfolio. This is because we can only imply out one number for each tranche given that we have only one market price for that tranche. The only way to proceed is to simplify the correlation structure by representing it with just one parameter. As a result, the market has decided to simply flatten the correlation matrix i.e.

$$C_{ij}^{Impl} = \rho \quad \text{for all} \quad i \neq j$$

and then to solve for the value of ρ which reprices each tranche. This approach has the advantage that it is simple. However, it removes any dispersion in the correlation structure and so is not able to capture any sectoral effects which may be present in the historical correlations.

Agreeing on the definition of implied correlation is not enough to ensure a number which can be agreed between market participants. We also need to specify the precise implementation of the pricing model being used. For example, it is important to answer the following questions:

- Does the pricing model assume homogeneous or actual heterogeneous CDS spreads?
- Are the CDS spreads portfolio swap adjusted to agree with the index swap spreads as discussed in Section 10.6?
- Which loss distribution calculation algorithm is being used – a full exact calculation or some other approximate method?
- What recovery rate assumption is used for the credits in the reference portfolio? Note that the market currently assumes 40% recovery for senior unsecured debt and 20% for subordinate unsecured debt.

The implied correlation also depends on the Libor curve used and the choice of interpolation scheme for both the discount factors and the CDS survival probabilities. However, the effect of these on the implied correlation is typically not significant. The measure of implied correlation just described is known as *compound correlation*. We now discuss this measure in greater detail.

19.3   COMPOUND CORRELATION

Compound correlation is the name given to the flat correlation implied by the price of any tranche using a Gaussian copula model. To calculate the implied correlation for the index tranches, we solve for the value of the flat correlation ρ which, using the market quoted tranche spread, sets the present value of the tranche equal to zero at initiation. It was shown in Section 12.7 that the time zero present value of a short protection position in a standard synthetic tranche is given by

$$PV(K_1, K_2, \rho) = U(K_1, K_2) + \frac{S(K_1, K_2)}{2} \sum_{n=1}^{N_T} \Delta_n Z(t_n) \left(Q(t_n, K_1, K_2) + Q(t_{n-1}, K_1, K_2) \right)$$

$$- \int_0^T Z(t)(-dQ(t, K_1, K_2)) \tag{19.1}$$

where today is time 0 and

$U(K_1, K_2)$ is the upfront payment received by an investor selling protection

$S(K_1, K_2)$ is the fixed annualised spread set at trade initiation.

The tranche survival curve Q measures the expected surviving tranche notional and embeds within it the choice of model used to price the tranche. Here we have assumed a Gaussian copula model, with a flat pairwise correlation ρ. Hence, we write Q as follows

$$Q(t_n, K_1, K_2) = \frac{\mathbb{E}_\rho \left[\min(L(t_n), K_2) - \min(L(t_n), K_1) \right]}{K_2 - K_1}$$

where $\mathbb{E}_\rho[x]$ is the expectation of x using a Gaussian copula model assuming a flat correlation ρ. To determine the compound correlation, we solve the following equation in ρ using a one-dimensional root searching algorithm

$$PV(K_1, K_2, \rho) = 0.$$

Figure 19.1 shows the PV of the five different standard tranches on CDX as a function of the compound correlation from the perspective of an investor (protection seller). We have used the market quotes in Table 19.1. We can make the following observations:

- The short protection equity tranche holder is long correlation since increasing correlation makes it more likely that all of the credits in the portfolio will survive. The tranche PV passes from negative to positive at $\rho = 23.4\%$. Hence, this is the equity tranche compound correlation.
- The 3–7% mezzanine tranche is short correlation for correlations below about 35%. The tranche PV passes through zero at a correlation of about 7.8%. Note that the mezzanine tranche PV recrosses the zero PV line at a correlation of about 75%. We therefore have two solutions to the compound correlation. Note that both solutions typically present very different loss distribution shapes and imply different risk sensitivities. The lower root is the correct one.
- The more senior tranches are all short correlation for all correlations below about 80%. They all cross the zero PV line at one compound correlation value and so have a unique solution.

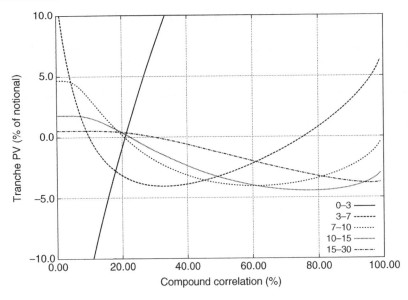

Figure 19.1 The PV of the five standard tranches on CDX as a function of compound correlation from the perspective of a *protection seller*. The tranche compound correlation is the value of compound correlation at which the tranche present value equals zero

We can then produce a compound correlation versus upper strike graph as shown in Figure 19.2. The compound correlation is clearly not the same for all tranches – the market is implying different correlation assumptions for different tranches on the *same portfolio*. The shape of this curve is known as the correlation 'smile' for obvious reasons and although the

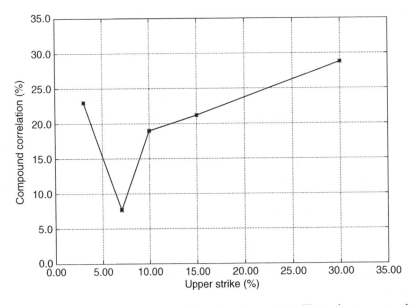

Figure 19.2 The compound correlation for CDX NA IG Series 3. For illustration purposes, the points have been joined by straight lines

levels have changed through time, the general smile shape seems to have become a persistent feature of the market. We now explain the reason for this.

19.3.1 Reasons for a Correlation Smile

It is perhaps not surprising that the compound correlation curve is not a flat line. Indeed, it would be more of a surprise if the compound correlation was a flat line. After all, market prices are not fixed by a model but are a result of market supply and demand. Furthermore, we are using a model which makes a number of key assumptions. These include:

- A Gaussian copula dependency structure.
- A flat correlation structure.
- Deterministic recovery rates.

It is therefore not a surprise that we have different implied correlations for different tranches. In Chapter 21 we will explore how to adapt our model to fit the correlation smile. However, even before we do this, it is already clear from the prices that the market has a view on the pricing of tranches which does not agree with the Gaussian copula. What is even more curious is the smile shape of the correlation when plotted as an increasing function of tranche upper strike. Without going into model specifics, it is possible to explain the smile shape in terms of risk aversion and market segmentation. Consider the different tranches:

- The equity tranche is the riskiest and highest paying tranche. It is typically unrated and so has a limited buyer base consisting of leveraged investors such as credit hedge funds and dealers. The dealers participate in this part of the capital structure in order to hedge both the correlation and VOD risk of their correlation books. The high idiosyncratic risk of equity tranches leads investors to demand a high risk premium. Since an equity tranche investment is long correlation, an increase in the equity tranche spread, holding the reference portfolio spreads fixed, will cause its value to fall and so also its implied correlation. The size of the correlation change may not be large due to the high correlation sensitivity of the equity tranche spread.
- The first mezzanine tranche is leveraged but is typically investment grade quality. This makes it an interesting investment for many investors. However, because of this demand, the actual spread paid is driven down. As a short protection position in a mezzanine tranche is short correlation, a lower spread implies a lower risk and hence a lower correlation. Because this tranche has a low correlation sensitivity, the required correlation drop is significant. The pricing of this tranche is what drives the smile shape.
- The buyer base for senior tranches are typically insurance companies seeking highly rated investments. They are buy-and-hold in their approach and look at investments in terms of the spread paid for a given rating. They generally find that senior tranche spreads look attractive when correlation levels close to historical are used.

Putting all of these effects together creates a correlation smile.

19.4 DISADVANTAGES OF COMPOUND CORRELATION

The key question for compound correlation is whether it can be used as a means for pricing and risk managing tranches within a correlation smile world. The answer is 'no' and there are at least two important reasons why not, which we now detail:

1. *Failure to conserve the expected loss*: One of the most important conditions of any pricing model must be that the sum of the tranche expected loss across the capital structure should equal the sum of the expected loss of the credits in the underlying reference portfolio. This no-arbitrage constraint was already discussed in Section 12.7.1. Recall first that the expected loss of face value $(K_2 - K_1)$ of the K_1–K_2 tranche is given by

$$\text{Expected loss} = \mathbb{E}_{\rho(K_1,K_2)} [\min(L(T), K_2) - \min(L(T), K_1)]$$

where the expectation is taken according to the Gaussian copula model using a correlation $\rho(K_1, K_2)$ which is specific to this tranche. Now consider a set of M contiguous tranches across the capital structure with attachment and detachment points at $K_0, K_1, \ldots, K_M$ where $K_0 = 0$ and $K_M = 100\%$. Summing the expected losses of all of these tranches across the capital structure we get

$$\begin{aligned}
\text{Total expected loss} = {} & \mathbb{E}_{\rho(0,K_1)} [\min(L(T), K_1) - \min(L(T), 0)] \\
& + \mathbb{E}_{\rho(K_1,K_2)} [\min(L(T), K_2) - \min(L(T), K_1)] \\
& + \cdots \\
& + \mathbb{E}_{\rho(K_{M-1},K_M)} [\min(L(T), K_M) - \min(L(T), K_{M-1})] \\
& + \mathbb{E}_{\rho(K_M,1)} [\min(L(T), 1) - \min(L(T), K_M)].
\end{aligned}$$

Since we are using different correlations for different tranches, the equation does not simplify. It is *only if the correlation smile is flat*, i.e. $\rho(K_1, K_2) = \rho$ that the different terms in this equation cancel and the no-arbitrage condition is satisfied, giving

$$\text{Total expected loss} = \mathbb{E}_\rho [L(T)] = \frac{1}{N} \sum_{i=1}^{N} \mathbb{E}[L_i(T)]$$

where $\mathbb{E}[L_i(T)]$ is the expected loss of issuer i to time T which is correlation independent.

Violation of this no-arbitrage requirement is a serious problem for those who wish to use compound correlation as a method for pricing and hedging to the correlation smile. Since many dealers manage their correlation risk by essentially combining various tranches at different levels of the capital structure, a model that fails to aggregate tranches in an arbitrage-free manner must be rejected.

2. *Unable to price non-standard tranches*: A second desirable property for a correlation model is that it can allow us to price other tranches with the same maturity and reference portfolio, but with different strikes using the correlation information implied by the standard tranches. For example, suppose a dealer has been requested by an investor to price a 6–22% tranche on the CDX NA IG reference portfolio. How should the dealer combine the pricing information of the 0–3%, 3–7%, 7–10%, 10–15% and 15–30% tranches to arrive at a price for the 6–22% tranche? Is it possible to determine the correlation to value this tranche via some interpolation method? Unfortunately, this is a very difficult problem to

solve since compound correlation $\rho(K_1, K_2)$ is a two-parameter function and interpolating in a two-parameter space requires more information than is provided by the standard tranche market. Also, because the compound correlation approach is not arbitrage free, any interpolation is likely to result in some arbitrage.

Despite these problems, compound correlation continues to be quoted in the market by some dealers. However, most market participants have switched completely to base correlation, an approach which we discuss in the next chapter, or quote both compound and base correlation. Despite its failings, we would recommend the use of compound correlation for one thing – as a direct measure of the degree of correlation the market has priced into a single tranche quote. It is a more intuitive measure of correlation than base correlation, and is therefore a useful measure for comparing how market expectations about default correlation differ across the capital structure.

19.5   NO-ARBITRAGE CONDITIONS

Before we move on to discuss models for the correlation skew, it is worth establishing the arbitrage-free conditions which should be observed by any STCDO pricing model. This is essential for a number of reasons:

1. It will allow us to determine, based on a minimal number of modelling assumptions, whether or not the prices observed in the market are theoretically arbitrage free. In certain cases, being able to identify such an arbitrage in tranche prices may explain why a highly parametrised arbitrage-free pricing model is unable to fit these market prices.
2. A formal mathematical understanding of the no-arbitrage constraints is a first step towards building a framework for models of portfolio default which do not violate arbitrage.
3. Having a no-arbitrage modelling framework can assist us in determining the degree of *model risk* present in the prices that our models can produce, i.e. we can generate lower and upper bounds on what the arbitrage-free price can be. Whether these bounds are useful or not remains to be seen.

19.5.1   The Expected Tranche Loss

We wish to define the no-arbitrage conditions in terms of the expected tranche loss (ETL). This is defined as the expected loss on an equity tranche of width K at some future time T based on information at time 0. We begin by defining the fractional portfolio loss $L(T)$ as the fraction of the notional of the underlying reference portfolio which has been lost due to defaults at future time T.

Depending on the modelling assumptions we make, especially regarding the choice of recovery rates, we may actually have a maximum loss which is less than the total notional of the portfolio. For example, if we assume that all the assets have a fixed recovery of 40% then we have a maximum portfolio loss of 60%. For this reason, we introduce the maximum loss as L_{Max}. We therefore have

$$0 \leq L(T) \leq L_{\text{Max}}.$$

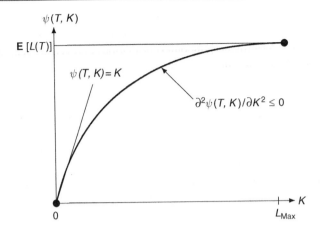

Figure 19.3   The tranche ETL curve $\psi(T, K)$ and its no-arbitrage conditions in the strike dimension

We denote the ETL by $\psi(T, K)$ and define it as follows

$$\psi(T, K) = \mathbb{E}\left[\min\left[L(T), K\right]\right]. \tag{19.2}$$

It is the expected loss at time T of an equity tranche with width K seen from time 0. The boundary conditions on $\psi(T, K)$ are as follows:

1. A zero width tranche has zero loss, i.e. $\psi(T, 0) = 0$.
2. A zero maturity equity tranche has zero loss, i.e. $\psi(0, K) = 0$.
3. An equity tranche cannot lose more than its width, i.e. $\psi(T, K) \leq K$. Since $\psi(T, 0) = 0$, this can also be written as $\partial\psi(T, K)/\partial K \leq 1$ at $K = 0$.
4. The expected tranche loss of an equity tranche with a width greater than or equal to the maximum portfolio loss L_{Max} must be equal to the expected loss of the portfolio, i.e.

$$\psi(T, K) = \mathbb{E}\left[L(T)\right] \text{ for } K \geq L_{\text{Max}}.$$

These are the basic boundary conditions. To ensure no-arbitrage, we have to add two further conditions. We start with the condition that the density of the loss distribution of the underlying portfolio must be zero or positive everywhere. We denote the density of the portfolio loss distribution using $f(x)$. We can therefore write the ETL as

$$\psi(T, K) = \mathbb{E}\left[\min\left[L(T), K\right]\right] = \int_0^{L_{\text{Max}}} f(L) \min\left[L, K\right] dL.$$

Differentiating $\psi(T, K)$ with respect to K we have

$$\frac{\partial\psi(T, K)}{\partial K} = \int_K^{K_{\text{Max}}} f(L) dL.$$

Differentiating again with respect to K gives

$$\frac{\partial^2\psi(T, K)}{\partial K^2} = -f(K).$$

Since we require that $f(K) \geq 0$, the no-arbitrage condition is

$$\frac{\partial^2 \psi(T, K)}{\partial K^2} \leq 0. \tag{19.3}$$

In other words $\psi(T, K)$ must be a concave function of K. Existence of the density also requires that ψ be smooth function of K. However, when the loss distribution is discrete, the density is replaced with a discrete distribution function.

We must also consider what the constraints are in the time dimension. There are a number of conditions. First, since losses cannot be reversed, the ETL of an equity tranche must be a constant or increasing function of T, i.e.

$$\frac{\partial \psi(T, K)}{\partial T} \geq 0. \tag{19.4}$$

However, we also have the condition that the probability of having a loss greater than K must also be an increasing function of time. Since

$$\Pr[L(T) > K] = \frac{\partial \psi(T, K)}{\partial K}$$

the condition becomes

$$\Pr[L(T_2) > K] \geq \Pr[L(T_1) > K]$$

where $T_1 < T_2$. In the limit that $T_1 \rightarrow T_2$ we have

$$\frac{\partial^2 \psi(T, K)}{\partial T \partial K} \geq 0. \tag{19.5}$$

This means that the slope of the ETL surface in the increasing K direction must be flat or increasing when we move in the increasing T direction. This is actually a stronger condition than Equation 19.4. To recap, the two additional conditions are:

5. The density is positive or zero everywhere and so

$$\frac{\partial^2 \psi(T, K)}{\partial K^2} \leq 0.$$

6. We also have a condition on the cross-derivative

$$\frac{\partial^2 \psi(T, K)}{\partial T \partial K} \geq 0.$$

19.5.2 Model Bounds

The ETL approach also gives us a way to impose bounds on the range of no-arbitrage model prices. Suppose that we have implied from market prices of tranches the values of the ETL at just two market points corresponding to strikes K_1 and K_2. We already know that $\psi(T, 0) = 0$ and that $\psi(T, L_{\text{Max}}) = \mathbb{E}[L(T)]$. We have also assumed that we have already plotted the ETL curve segments from $K = 0$ to $K = K_1$, and from $K = K_2$ to $K = L_{\text{Max}}$. These are shown in Figure 19.4. The ETL curve from $K = 0$ to $K = K_1$ must be monotonically increasing and cannot

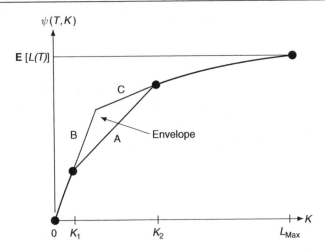

Figure 19.4   Shape constraints on the tranche ETL curve $\psi(T, K)$. Convexity and monotonicity require that the ETL curve be within the marked area. We have drawn two examples of possible ETL curves between K_1 and K_2

have a slope greater than 1. We now examine the no-arbitrage constraints on the shape of the ETL curve between K_1 and K_2 which requires that the curve be within the triangle contained by the lines A, B and C:

1. Line A enforces the convexity constraint. If the curve falls below the straight line joining the K_1 and K_2 points, then the only way for it to get back up to the K_2 point is by becoming locally convex and this is not allowed.
2. Line B is the continuation of the tangent of the ETL curve at K_1. The curve has to be below this line or else the ETL curve would not be globally concave.
3. Line C is the continuation of the tangent of the ETL curve at K_2. The ETL cannot go above this line without causing negative convexity.

The more tranche prices we have, the more points we have on the ETL curve and together with the no-arbitrage constraints the smaller the envelope of allowed curve shapes. These envelopes can be used as a way to assess the amount of model risk in a pricing which involves some interpolation of the ETL curve. For example, for any value of K, the minimum and maximum values of ψ consistent with no-arbitrage can be determined. These minimum and maximum ETLs can be transformed into prices and used to put limits on the range of tranche spreads.

19.6   SUMMARY

In this chapter we have introduced the concept of implied correlation and shown how it leads us to observe a correlation smile in market tranche prices. We also explained what we believe are the factors which cause it. We then described in detail the concept of compound correlation and showed that while it is a useful way to understand the market's pricing of the correlation of STCDOs, it is not an arbitrage-free pricing and risk model when there is a correlation smile. We have then set out in detail the no-arbitrage requirements of a consistent model of portfolio correlation. We have done this in terms of the expected tranche loss.

$$\underline{\ 20\ }$$

Base Correlation

20.1 INTRODUCTION

The aim of this chapter is to explain the concept and implementation of the base correlation framework. Base correlation was first proposed by McGinty *et al.* (2004) as a new parametrisation for implied correlation which overcomes some of the disadvantages of compound correlation. It has since become the standard convention for quoting implied correlation and is also widely used for pricing and risk managing synthetic CDOs.

We begin this chapter by introducing the concept of base correlation. We discuss the calculation of base correlation and the advantages that base correlation has over compound correlation. However, we also describe the many shortcomings of base correlation and how they may be mitigated. We then discuss the risk management of index tranches using base correlation and conclude with a discussion of how base correlation may be used to price and risk manage bespoke tranches.

20.2 BASE CORRELATION

Despite the early success of the compound correlation approach as a method for quoting implied correlation, it has now been overtaken by the base correlation approach. As we will discuss later in this chapter, this is because base correlation presents several important advantages over compound correlation without any significant increase in complexity. Indeed, as with compound correlation, base correlation also relies upon the use of a one-factor Gaussian copula model.

The first insight underlying base correlation is that any tranche can be represented as a linear combination of equity tranches. Consider, for example, a standard synthetic tranche with attachment point K_1 and detachment point K_2. The expected percentage tranche loss to time T can be written as

$$\mathbb{E}[L(T, K_1, K_2)] = \frac{\mathbb{E}[\min(L(T), K_2)] - \mathbb{E}[\min(L(T), K_1)]}{K_2 - K_1}.$$

This can be rewritten as

$$\mathbb{E}[L(T, K_1, K_2)] = \frac{K_2\, \mathbb{E}[L(T, 0, K_2)] - K_1\, \mathbb{E}[(L(T, 0, K_1)]}{K_2 - K_1}.$$

This relationship is depicted in Figure 20.1 which shows that a $K_1 - K_2$ tranche can be decomposed into a linear combination of two equity (or *base*) tranches. The term *base* tranche is another way of referring to an equity tranche. The use of the word *base* stems from the fact that an equity tranche has an attachment point at $K_1 = 0$, i.e. at the *base* of the capital structure.

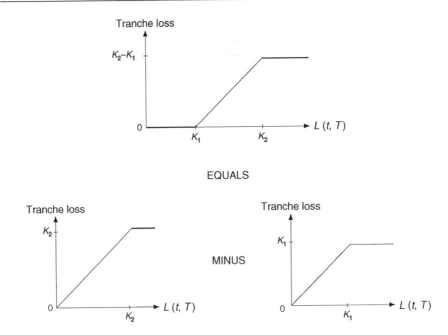

Figure 20.1   In the base correlation approach we decompose face value $(K_2 - K_1)$ of a short protection K_1–K_2 tranche into K_2 face value of a short protection 0–K_2 equity (base) tranche minus face value K_1 of a long protection 0–K_1 equity (base) tranche

The second insight underlying base correlation is that we can *associate a different correlation to each base tranche*. Since we assign a different correlation to the pricing of the 0–K_1 tranche from the one assigned to the pricing of the 0–K_2 tranche, we have

$$\mathbb{E}[L(T,K_1,K_2)] = \frac{\mathbb{E}_{\,\rho(K_2)}[\min(L(T),K_2)] - \mathbb{E}_{\,\rho(K_1)}[\min(L(T),K_1)]}{K_2 - K_1}$$

where $\rho(K_1)$ is the correlation assigned to the 0–K_1 tranche and $\rho(K_2)$ is the correlation assigned to the 0–K_2 tranche. It is immediately clear that this assumption means that there is a contradiction in base correlation in the sense that different base tranches assign different correlations to the same underlying reference portfolios. However, the advantage of base correlation is that by decomposing tranches into base tranches and assigning different correlations to different base tranches, we end up with an approach which, while not arbitrage free, has a number of distinct advantages over compound correlation.

The concept of base correlation does not rely on the use of the Gaussian copula model. It could also be applied to any single-parameter copula model which can be calibrated to a single tranche price. However, for reasons of familiarity, simplicity and speed, the Gaussian copula is the model chosen.

20.2.1   Conservation of Expected Loss

One of the advantages of base correlation over compound correlation is that it *conserves expected loss* across the capital structure. It was shown in Section 12.7.1 that there is an important arbitrage relationship between the expected loss of the protection legs of all of the CDS in a reference portfolio, and the protection legs of single tranche CDOs summed across the entire capital structure.

To demonstrate this, we define a set of contiguous tranches with strikes at K_m where $m = 1, \ldots, M$ with $K_0 = 0$ and $K_M = 1$. The tranche notionals equal $K_m - K_{m-1}$. Let us write the sum of the protection legs, which we call the total expected loss, across the capital structure within a base correlation framework. We get

$$\text{Total expected loss} = \mathbb{E}\left[\sum_{m=1}^{M}(K_m - K_{m-1})L(T, K_{m-1}, K_m)\right].$$

substituting for $L(T, K_{m-1}, K_m)$ from Equation 12.1 and using the base correlation approach this is given by

$$\text{Total expected loss} = \sum_{m=1}^{M}\left(\mathbb{E}_{\rho(K_m)}[\min(L(T), K_m)] - \mathbb{E}_{\rho(K_{m-1})}[\min(L(T), K_{m-1})]\right).$$

Expanding the sum, we have

$$\begin{aligned}\text{Total expected loss} = \ &\mathbb{E}_{\rho(K_1)}[\min(L(T), K_1)] - \mathbb{E}_{\rho(0)}[\min(L(T), 0)]\\ &+ \mathbb{E}_{\rho(K_2)}[\min(L(T), K_2)] - \mathbb{E}_{\rho(K_1)}[\min(L(T), K_1)]\\ &+ \cdots\\ &+ \mathbb{E}_{\rho(K_{M-1})}[\min(L(T), K_{M-1})] - \mathbb{E}_{\rho(K_{M-2})}[\min(L(T), K_{M-2})]\\ &+ \mathbb{E}_{\rho(1)}[\min(L(T), 1)] - \mathbb{E}_{\rho(K_{M-1})}[\min(L(T), K_{M-1})].\end{aligned}$$

We see that all of the intermediate terms cancel leaving just the terms

$$\begin{aligned}\text{Total expected loss} &= \mathbb{E}_{\rho(1)}[\min(L(T), 1)] - \mathbb{E}_{\rho(0)}[\min(L(T), 0)]\\ &= \mathbb{E}[L(T)].\end{aligned}$$

As a result, the expected loss across the capital structure is the expected loss of the reference portfolio which in turn is the sum of the expected losses of the CDS protection legs.

This property of base correlation is very useful since it means that the base correlation will correctly recognise that the correlation sensitivity of the tranche protection legs can be hedged by buying protection across the capital structure. It also means that buying protection with a 3–6% tranche and a 6–9% tranche will be consistent with buying protection on a 3–9% tranche. This is not the case in the compound correlation framework and is an important reason for preferring base correlation to compound correlation.

20.3   BUILDING THE BASE CORRELATION CURVE

The aim of this section is to take a set of market tranche quotes as shown in Table 20.1 and to imply from them the base correlation for each tranche. On this date the respective index curves were as shown in Table 20.2. These quotes will be used as the basis for the numbers generated throughout this chapter.

Table 20.1   Market prices for the CDX NA and iTraxx Europe tranches in March 2007

Tranche	CDX Investment Grade North America Series 7			iTraxx Europe Series 6		
	Lower–upper strike	Upfront payment (%)	Running spread (bp)	Lower–upper strike	Upfront payment (%)	Running spread (bp)
Equity	0–3	24.88	500.0	0–3	12.12	500.0
Junior mezzanine	3–7	–	90.0	3–6	–	55.0
Senior mezzanine	7–10	–	18.25	6–9	–	14.62
Senior	10–15	–	8.0	9–12	–	6.5
Super senior	15–30	–	3.5	12–22	–	2.75

Table 20.2   Index curves in March 2007

Index name	3Y (bp)	5Y (bp)	7Y (bp)	10Y (bp)	Recovery (%)
CDX IG NA Series 7	20	31	50	63	40
iTraxx IG Europe Series 6	12	25	34	46	40

We revisit the pricing equation for a simple synthetic tranche. From the perspective of a protection seller (an investor), this is given by

$$PV(K_1, K_2) = U(K_1, K_2)$$

$$+ \frac{S(K_1, K_2)}{2} \sum_{n=1}^{N} \Delta(t_{n-1}, t_n) Z(t_n) \left(Q(t_{n-1}, K_1, K_2) + Q(t_n, K_1, K_2) \right)$$

$$- \int_0^T Z(t)(-dQ(t, K_1, K_2)). \tag{20.1}$$

Note that this formula assumes that valuation is at time zero. As before, the tranche survival curve Q measures the expected surviving tranche notional and embeds within it the choice of model used to price the tranche. We write the tranche survival curve as a function of the portfolio loss $L(T)$ as follows

$$Q(T, K_1, K_2) = 1 - \frac{\mathbb{E}_{\rho(K_2)} [\min(L(T), K_2)] - \mathbb{E}_{\rho(K_1)} [\min(L(T), K_1)]}{K_2 - K_1}.$$

From this, it is clear that within a base correlation approach, each tranche PV, except the $0-K_1$ and $K_{M-1}-100\%$ tranches, is a function of two base correlations. As a result, it is not possible to solve independently for an implied correlation. Fortunately, the standard tranches are contiguous, meaning that the detachment point of one tranche is the attachment point of the next. This means that solving for the value of $\rho(3\%)$ implied by the equity tranche gives us one of the two unknown correlations needed to price the 3–7% tranche. We therefore have one price and one unknown so we can solve for $\rho(7\%)$. We can then repeat this process for the 7–10% and higher tranches. We call this a bootstrap approach. This means that we solve for the implied base correlations by either moving up the capital structure starting with the equity tranche, or by moving down the capital structure starting with the tranche which detaches at 100%. Since the tranche which detaches at 100% is almost never quoted, we take the first approach which starts with the equity tranche:

1. We start with the equity tranche $m = 1$ which, being a base tranche, has only one base correlation and so can be solved for exactly. The base tranche survival probability is therefore

$$Q(T, 0, K_1) = 1 - \frac{\mathbb{E}_{\rho(K_1)} [\min(L(T), K_1)]}{K_1}$$

and we solve for the value of $\rho(K_1)$ such that

$$PV(0, K_1) = 0.$$

This can be done using a one-dimensional root search for $\rho(K_1)$. Since a base tranche is simply an equity tranche, a short protection position is long correlation for all values of $\rho(K_1)$. As a result, the present value function $PV(t, 0, K_1)$ is monotonic and increasing as a function of $\rho(K_1)$ and so should have a unique root, provided a root exists. Solving for the base correlation for the equity tranche is exactly the same as solving for its compound correlation.

2. We set $m = m + 1$.

3. We have solved for $\rho(K_{m-1})$, we can then solve for $\rho(K_m)$. However, we need to do this while holding the lower base tranche correlation fixed at $\rho(K_{m-1})$. To do this, we rewrite Equation 19.1 in terms of the base tranche survival probabilities

$$Q(t_n, K_{m-1}, K_m) = 1 - \frac{\mathbb{E}_{\rho(K_m)} [\min(L(t_n), K_m)] - \mathbb{E}_{\rho(K_{m-1})} [\min(L(t_n), K_{m-1})]}{K_m - K_{m-1}}.$$

This can be written as

$$Q(t_n, K_{m-1}, K_m) = \kappa Q(t_n, K_m) + (1 - \kappa) Q(t_n, K_{m-1})$$

where $Q(t_n, K) = Q(t_n, 0, K)$ and

$$\kappa = \frac{K_m}{K_m - K_{m-1}}.$$

The tranche PV Equation 20.1 can be rewritten in terms of the base tranche survival probabilities

$$PV(K_{m-1}, K_m) = U(K_{m-1}, K_m)$$

$$+ \kappa \frac{S(K_{m-1}, K_m)}{2} \sum_{n=1}^{N} \Delta(t_{n-1}, t_n) Z(t_n) \left(Q(t_{n-1}, K_m) + Q(t_n, K_m) \right)$$

$$- \kappa \int_0^T Z(t)(-dQ(t, K_m))$$

$$+ (1 - \kappa) \frac{S(K_{m-1}, K_m)}{2} \sum_{n=1}^{N} \Delta(t_{n-1}, t_n) Z(t_n) \left(Q(t_{n-1}, K_{m-1}) + Q(t_n, K_{m-1}) \right)$$

$$- (1 - \kappa) \int_0^T Z(t)(-dQ(t, K_{m-1}))$$

where we have allowed for the existence of an upfront payment on this tranche. This equation gives the tranche value from the perspective of a protection *seller*. Solving for the base correlation then becomes an exercise in finding the value of $\rho(K_m)$ which solves the above equation for $Q(t_n, K_m)$. We note that since $\rho(K_{m-1})$ is fixed, the value of $Q(t_n, K_{m-1})$ is also fixed. As the changing part of this equation is the PV of the $[0, K_m]$ base tranche, the value of $PV(K_{m-1}, K_m)$ is actually long correlation and there is a unique solution, provided a solution exists. Base correlation therefore avoids the problem of multiple solutions which can occur when we try to imply out the compound correlation for mezzanine tranches. *This is another reason to prefer base correlation over compound correlation.*

4. If $m < M$, return to step (2).

Figure 20.2 shows the PV of the five different standard tranches on CDX as a function of their upper strike base correlation $\rho(K_m)$. These are shown from the perspective of a protection seller for whom an equity or base tranche is a long correlation position. As a result, we see the value of the tranche PVs increase since only the value of the K_m base tranche changes. As a result, there is only one solution for the base correlation, provided a solution exists.

The resulting base correlation curves for CDX and iTraxx are shown in Figure 20.3, where we have simply joined the points with a straight line. In Section 19.3.1 we explained why the compound correlation curve is not flat. The same reasons explain why the base correlation curve is also not flat. The shape is quite different from that of the compound correlation curve and is generally termed a 'skew'. The skew shape of the base correlation curve, as implied by market tranche prices, has remained fairly stable through the last few years.

To understand why the base correlation curve is upward sloping, we need to think about how the base correlation is generated using a bootstrap up the capital structure. We should also look at Figure 20.2 which shows the dependence of the tranche PV on its upper-strike base correlation. We start with the equity tranche. Since the equity tranche is a base tranche, by definition, the base correlation for the equity tranche is identical to its compound correlation. In the example shown, it has a base correlation of 16.85%. We then move on to the first mezzanine tranche. As discussed in Section 19.3.1, market demand drives the spread of the mezzanine tranche lower than we would expect. In this case, the 3–7% tranche spread is 90 bp. If we price this tranche using the CDX equity value of the base correlation of 16.85%, we see in Figure 20.2 that the tranche PV is negative. We therefore need to increase the 7% base correlation to make the 0–7% equity tranche less risky and so increase the present value of the 3–7% tranche. The higher correlation required then has a knock-on effect on the more senior

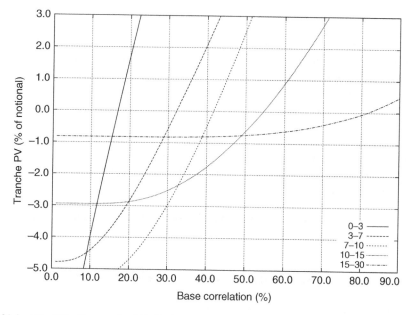

Figure 20.2 The PV of the standard CDX IG tranches as a function of their upper strike base correlation $\rho(K_2)$. We solve for the value of $\rho(K_2)$ which sets the tranche PV equal to zero. The tranche PV is calculated from the perspective of a protection seller

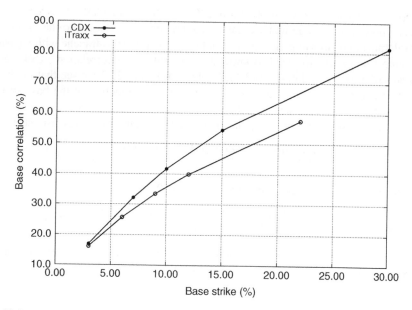

Figure 20.3 Base correlation curve for CDX NA IG Series 7 and iTraxx Europe Series 6. The points have been joined by straight lines

tranches. They require a higher base correlation to compensate for the high base correlations of the lower tranches.

The numbers calculated here were calculated using a model in which we used a set of heterogeneous CDS curves for the credits in the portfolio, we adjusted these to fit the index swaps spreads by performing a portfolio swap adjustment, and we modelled the loss distribution exactly using a full recursion. However, the base correlation quotes which we may encounter in the market may not be calculated in the same way. Differences may arise because:

- The CDS spreads are assumed to be homogeneous and equal to the index swap spreads.
- The CDS spreads may not be swap adjusted as described in Section 10.6.
- The calculation of the loss distribution used may be based on the LHP approximation and so will ignore both spread dispersion and granularity effects.

If we therefore wish to exchange information in the form of base correlation quotes, care must be taken to agree upon an exact methodology.

20.4   BASE CORRELATION INTERPOLATION

Another advantage of base correlation over compound correlation is that it is possible to extend the base correlation approach to price tranches on the same reference portfolio but with non-standard attachment and detachment levels. The approach assumes that we can simply interpolate the base correlation curve and is best described using an example.

Example   Suppose we wish to price a 6–22% tranche on the CDX IG NA Series 7 reference portfolio. Assume that we have a calibration of the base correlation to the standard tranches on this reference portfolio. In order to price this tranche within a base correlation framework, we need to know the 6% strike base correlation $\rho(6\%)$, and the 22% strike base correlation $\rho(22\%)$. Looking at Figure 20.3 we see that the base correlation curve is monotonic and is a reasonably linear function of the base strike. This suggests that as a first guess, we should linearly interpolate the value of $\rho(6\%)$ and $\rho(22\%)$. The 6% strike can be interpolated between the 3 and 7% strikes. We have

$$\rho(6\%) = \frac{\rho(7\%)(6\% - 3\%) + \rho(3\%)(7\% - 6\%)}{7\% - 3\%} = 28.31\%.$$

The 22% strike can be interpolated between 15 and 30%. We have

$$\rho(22\%) = \frac{\rho(15\%)(22\% - 15\%) + \rho(30\%)(30\% - 22\%)}{30\% - 15\%} = 67.04\%.$$

Pricing the tranche using these correlations gives a breakeven spread of 10.6 bp which seems reasonable given the subordination and width of the tranche.

The reason why we are able to interpolate base correlation and not compound correlation is simply because base correlation is a one-parameter function and as such is much easier to interpolate given the low number of data points than the two-parameter compound correlation.

A more comprehensive test of the interpolation scheme is to price tranchelets. A tranchelet is a very thin tranche, typically with a width of 1%. If we price tranchelets across the capital structure, then we are effectively 'zooming in' on the underlying portfolio loss distribution as implied by the base correlation approach, and by doing so exposing any problems in our base correlation interpolation approach.

Figure 20.4 plots the tranchelet spreads for both the iTraxx and CDX IG tranches as a function of their attachment point (subordination). It also shows the interpolated base correlation curve.

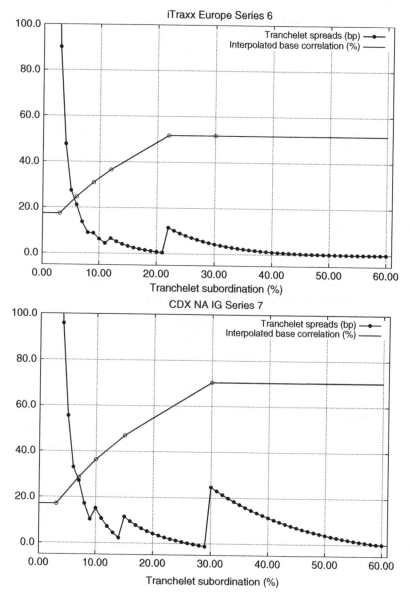

Figure 20.4   The breakeven spread for 1% wide tranchelets on for iTraxx and CDX as a function of their subordination. The linearly interpolated base correlation curve is also shown

Below the minimum quoted strike of 3% and above the maximum quoted strike we have assumed a flat base correlation. Note that at higher subordinations, the base correlation rises to about 70%.[1] We can make a number of important observations from Figure 20.4:

- We see that for both indices, the tranchelet spread is not a monotonically decreasing function of the tranchelet subordination. This implies an arbitrage since a tranche with the same width but with more subordination than another tranche must have a lower expected loss and hence a lower breakeven spread.[2]
- We note that the points at which the violations of arbitrage occur correspond to the standard tranche strikes. This suggests that the cause of the arbitrages is the sudden change in the slope of the base correlation linear interpolation across these node points.
- We further note that in the case of the CDX tranches, there is a range of strikes between 25% and 29% for which the tranchelet spreads actually go negative.

These observations make it very clear that a direct linear interpolation of the base correlation curve is not guaranteed to produce prices for non-standard tranches which are arbitrage free. It also emphasises that the choice of interpolation scheme determines how the interpolated tranche spreads behave and raises the question whether another interpolation scheme might create fewer arbitrages.

Finally, note that the requirement that the sum of the protection legs across the tranchelets equals the expected loss of the reference portfolio is observed and is not affected by the choice of interpolation scheme.

20.4.1 The implied loss density

One way to gain greater insight is to calculate the density of the loss distribution implied by the base correlation curve. From Section 19.5 we know that this is given by

$$f(K) = -\frac{\partial^2 \psi(T, K)}{\partial K^2}$$

where

$$\psi(T, K) = \mathbb{E}_{\rho(K)}[\min(L(T), K)]$$

is the expected tranche loss or ETL of a base tranche.

The density can therefore be calculated numerically. For speed and simplicity, we have used the LHP model to calculate the portfolio loss distributions implied by our linear interpolation of the base correlation for both iTraxx and CDX. These are shown in Figure 20.5. What stands out in these figures are the spikes of the loss density. These are located at the standard tranche strikes of the respective index tranches. These spikes tell us that the density does not exist at these points – the size of the spikes is an artifact of the discretisation used. However, we can note that at the 3% strike, the spike is positive, but is negative at all of the other standard strikes. We suspect that this is due to the fact that the base correlation interpolation in Figure 20.3 is locally convex at the 3% strike but locally concave at the higher strikes.

---

[1] It is important to note that as discussed in Section 18.4, when building the unconditional loss distribution at high correlations, we need to have a sufficiently high number of steps in the market factor integration to ensure numerical accuracy.

[2] Otherwise we would sell protection on the more senior tranche and buy protection on the more subordinated tranche, earning a positive spread with any loss on the senior tranche being covered by the gain on the more subordinated tranche.

These spikes of probability density in Figure 20.5 explain the behaviour of the tranchelet spreads seen in Figure 20.4. For example, in the case of CDX, a 29–30% tranchelet will be completely wiped out if the portfolio loss is greater than 30%. The probability of this is reduced by the negative probability density at 30%. However, when we have a

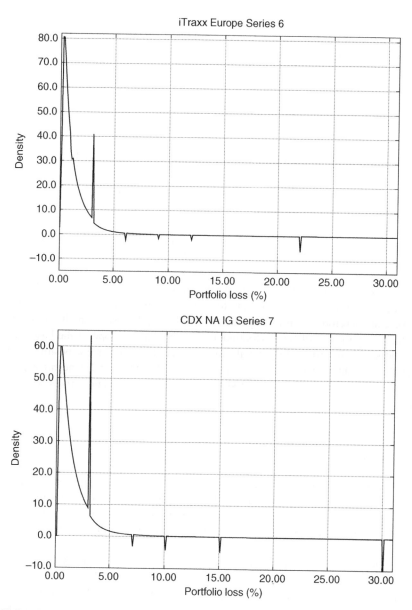

Figure 20.5 The implied portfolio loss density for the calibrated iTRAXX IG and CDX IG index using a linearly interpolated base correlation curve. The spikes in the density are caused by the fact that the ETL is undefined at these points. Their size is an artifact of the discretisation used to calculate the density

30–31% tranchelet, the negative probability is at the point at which this tranchelet would have zero loss. It therefore does not contribute to the tranchelet's expected loss and therefore to its spread. So by moving up 1% in subordination, the probability of the tranchelet being completely wiped out has suddenly increased because this negative probability is no longer above the tranchelet detachment point. As a result, the tranchelet spread jumps upwards.

It is clear that our interpolation is affecting the tranchelet spreads. One way to understand this is to look again at the form of the density. The easiest way to establish a direct connection between the shape of the base correlation curve $\rho(K) = \beta(K)^2$ and the density is to use the LHP model. Recalling that we showed in Section 16.2.1 that

$$\psi(T,K) = \mathbb{E}[\min(L(T),K)] = (1-R)\Phi_2(C, -A(K), -\beta(K)) + K\Phi(A(K))$$

where

$$A(K) = \frac{1}{\beta(K)}\left(C(T) - \sqrt{1 - \beta(K)^2}\Phi^{-1}\left(\frac{K}{1-R}\right)\right)$$

and $C(T)$ is the default threshold. To compute the density we need to calculate the second derivative. Doing so, we end up with a density which can be written as

$$f(x) = c_0(K)\Big|_{K=x} + c_1(K)\frac{\partial\beta(K)}{\partial K}\Big|_{K=x} + c_2(K)\left(\frac{\partial\beta(K)}{\partial K}\right)^2\Big|_{K=x} + c_3(K)\frac{\partial^2\beta(K)}{\partial K^2}\Big|_{K=x}.$$

The key observation here is that the density depends on the first and second derivatives of the $\beta(K)$ curve and, by extension, on the first and second derivatives of the $\rho(K) = \beta^2(K)$ curve. We can therefore confirm that the probability spikes seen in the loss density in Figure 20.5 were a result of the discontinuous changes in the slope of the base correlation curve at the standard strikes. In general, this suggests that we have a positive probability spike for the discontinuous increase in slope at the 3% strike and a negative probability spike for the discontinuous decrease in slope at the higher standard strikes which is what we found.

20.4.2 Cubic Spline Interpolation of the Base Correlation

We can therefore see that the smoothness of the interpolation scheme has a direct impact on the implied portfolio loss distribution. To avoid density spikes, we should try to find an interpolation scheme which is smooth and has a continuous first derivative across the standard strike node points. The simplest scheme which satisfies these constraints is a cubic spline.

However, choosing a cubic spline and passing in the base strikes and base correlations does not uniquely define a cubic spline. The cubic spline also requires us to input the *slope of the base correlation curve* at the lowest and highest strike. We can therefore generate a range of shapes depending on the values chosen and so we have some control over the shape taken by the cubic spline. We may also employ some tricks to ensure a sensible extrapolation by inserting an additional point at the maximum loss strike with some 'reasonable' value of base correlation.

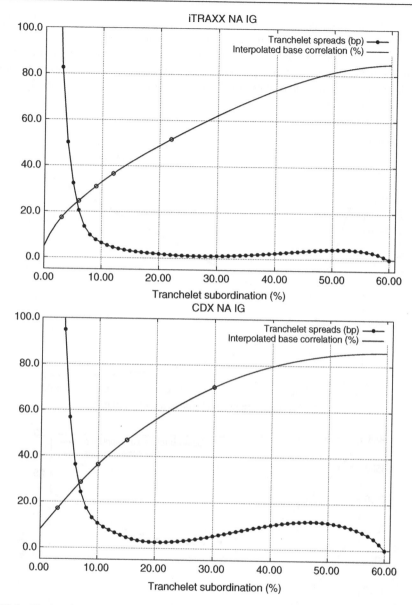

Figure 20.6   The breakeven spread for 1% wide tranchelets as a function of their subordination for CDX and iTraxx. The base correlations and their interpolated curve are shown. Interpolation is performed with a cubic spline

Figure 20.6 shows how the tranchelet spreads depend on the subordination when using a cubic spline to interpolate the base correlation. We make the following observations:

- The tranchelet spreads are now a smooth function of their subordination.
- Unlike the linear interpolation case, there are no negative tranchelet spreads.
- The ETL interpolation is much better than the linear interpolation of base correlation. However, there is an still arbitrage in the case of both iTraxx and CDX since the tranchelet spreads are increasing in the region above 20% subordination.

Ideally, we would like a spline which avoids all arbitrages and guarantees a positive loss density at all points of the capital structure. However, the relationship between the shape of the base correlation curve and the loss density is too complex to enforce on a simple interpolation scheme. In the next section we will explain how we can overcome some of these theoretical problems by performing the interpolation in ETL space. First, however, we briefly consider the issue of extrapolation.

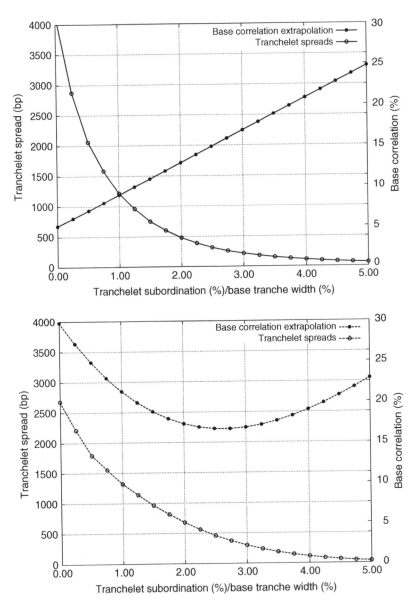

Figure 20.7   A comparison of the effect of different extrapolation schemes below 3% on the thin 0.5%-wide tranchelet spreads as a function of tranchelet subordination. This is for the CDX NA IG index tranches

20.4.3   Extrapolation of the Base Correlation

At very high strikes, we find that avoidance of arbitrage usually requires a concave and flattening base correlation curve. However, it is much less clear how to extrapolate below the lowest strike, which is usually at 3%.

By experimenting with our cubic interpolation of the base correlation curve, we find that many different base correlation shapes are allowed below 3% which are arbitrage free. For example, the extrapolated value of the base correlation to the zero strike $\rho(0\%)$ can be less than, equal to, or greater than the value of $\rho(3\%)$. If $\rho(0\%) > \rho(3\%)$, we tend to find a peak of probability mass at zero loss and a lower spread for thin equity tranches than if $\rho(0\%) < \rho(3\%)$. This is shown in Figure 20.7 where we compare two different extrapolations and their effect on the spreads of 0.5%-wide tranchelets.

Since there is limited pricing available for tranchelets, it is not clear which shape to assume. Certainly, knowing how to extrapolate the base correlation below 3% is not only useful for pricing, it can also help to stabilise the entire base correlation interpolation scheme. As the tranchelet market becomes more liquid, we hope to be able to calibrate the 1% and 2% points to market prices.

20.5   INTERPOLATING BASE CORRELATION USING THE ETL

Another strategy for interpolating the base correlation curve is to map the problem into the expected tranche loss (ETL) space where the no-arbitrage constraints discussed in Section 19.5 are more easily enforced, and where we can also supply additional data points at $K = 0$ and $K = L_{\text{Max}}$. The resulting interpolated ETL can then be mapped back to a base correlation. While the standard base correlation approach values all the cash flows of a base tranche using the same value of base correlation, once we introduce the concept of an ETL, we need to specify a maturity date since the expected tranche loss is a function of which horizon we are looking at. We choose to use the ETL to the maturity date of the tranche T. The interpolation process is as follows:

1. Calibrate the base correlation curve to the market standard strikes for the 5Y maturity tranches. In the case of CDX IG, we would therefore have $\rho(K)$ for $K = 0.03, 0.07, 0.10, 0.15$ and 0.30.
2. For each strike, calculate the value of the $\psi(T, K) = \mathbb{E}_{\rho(K)}[\min(L(T), K)]$ function to the maturity time T of the tranche using the corresponding value of the base correlation for that standard strike.
3. In addition to the standard strikes, we also have two end points to our interpolation at $\psi(T, 0) = 0$ and $\psi(T, L_{\text{Max}}) = \mathbb{E}[L(T)]$. We now have seven points to interpolate between.
4. Using an appropriate interpolation scheme, calculate the value of $\psi(T, K)$ at all strikes from $K = 0$ to the maximum loss at small intervals (typically 1% or less).
5. Imply out the base correlation at each of these strikes and so generate $\rho(K)$.

The main requirements of the interpolation algorithm are that it is smooth, monotonic and concave. This means that as long as the input *skeleton* of points $\psi(K)$ at the standard strikes is monotonic and concave, the interpolation scheme should also be monotonic and concave at all intermediate points. Standard cubic splines do not satisfy these requirements since they are not guaranteed to preserve monotonicity. One promising scheme is the Piecewise Cubic Hermite Interpolant (PCHIP) spline described in Fritsch and Carlson (1980). This scheme does guarantee smoothness and monotonicity. However, it does not guarantee to be concave. Despite this, it is easy to set up and we will use this approach for the rest of this section.

Figure 20.8 shows the interpolated ETL curve for the iTraxx and CDX IG quotes in Table 20.2. We used the LHP model to perform the mapping from base correlation to ETL and back. The first observation we can make about this is that the interpolation works well in

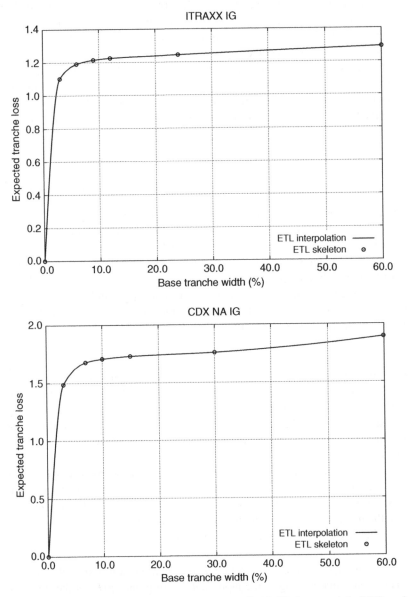

Figure 20.8   The interpolated ETL curve for iTraxx and CDX IG. We have used the LHP model. Since $R = 40\%$, we have $L_{\text{Max}} = 60\%$. The skeleton of market points is shown as circles. Note that the CDX ETL curve is convex at high strikes, implying an arbitrage

preserving the general shape of the input market points. The area of greatest importance for the interpolation is in the region from K equals 3–7% when the ETL curve goes from being almost vertical to almost horizontal. This is where we would expect different interpolation schemes to create the greatest differences. Careful inspection of the CDX ETL curve shows that the ETL curve is not concave beyond 30%. Indeed, we see that the ETL skeleton points are themselves not concave. This has important implications which we will discuss later in this section.

Figure 20.9 shows the base correlation curve implied by interpolating the ETL for both CDX and iTraxx tranches. We see that the curve is smooth and well behaved in both cases.

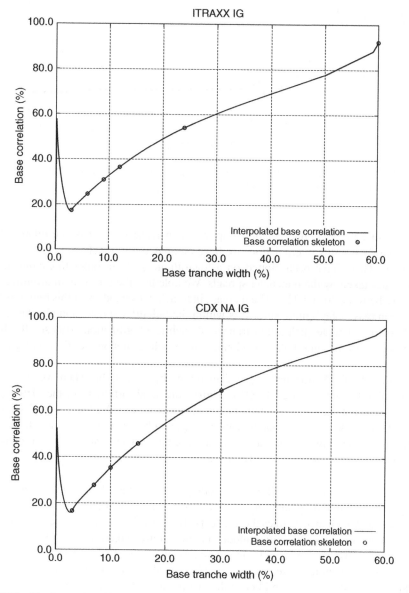

Figure 20.9   The interpolated base correlation curves for iTraxx and CDX IG implied by interpolating in ETL space and then inverting the mapping to return the implied base correlation

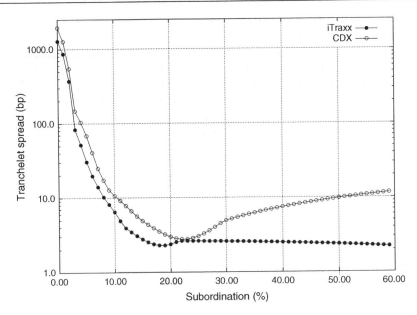

Figure 20.10 The tranchlet spreads for CDX and iTraxx produced by a PCHIP interpolation of the ETL curve. The spreads are plotted on a log scale

We also see that the ETL interpolation implies an increase in the base correlation below the 3% strike. Using this interpolation, we have computed the tranchelet spreads shown in Figure 20.10. These have been plotted on a logarithmic scale in order to capture the full range of values taken by the tranchelet spreads. We note that there is a small arbitrage in the iTraxx curve between 20 and 22%. The increase in tranchelet spreads over this region is 0.4 bp which we can reasonably ignore since it is within the bid–offer spread, and also because we would almost never trade such a thin tranche at such a subordination. This small arbitrage has been caused by the interpolation scheme which, while monotonic, does not guarantee concavity.

We see that the CDX tranchelet spread increases by over 10 bp when we increase the tranchelet subordination from 23 to 60%. Unlike the small arbitrage in the iTraxx curve, this arbitrage has not been caused by the interpolation. If we look back at Figure 20.8, we see that the CDX ETL skeleton was not concave to begin with. It is not easy to identify a single reason for this. Assuming that the tranche quotes are themselves arbitrage free, it could be a result of one or more of the following reasons:

- In this example we used the LHP model. Perhaps the way the LHP model assumes spread homogeneity and infinite granularity is not consistent with the tranche quotes and we need to use a model which incorporates these effects. To check this, we re-ran the calibration and pricing using a full loss distribution model and the arbitrage did not go away.
- There is one unobservable parameter in our pricing, the recovery rate. We have set this equal to 40%. While the choice of recovery rate only typically has a small pricing effect, here it determines the value of L_{Max} and hence the last point on the ETL skeleton. A lower value

of R and hence a higher value of L_{Max} may remedy the situation since it would make the interpolation less convex above $K = 30\%$.

- The base correlation approach effectively assigns the same base correlation to all tranche payments irrespective of their payment date. Perhaps the base correlation model fails to take into account the 'term structure' of correlation embedded in tranche prices which determines how tranche losses are distributed across time.

Despite these problems with this specific interpolation, we note that the ETL interpolation is more arbitrage free than the direct interpolation of the base correlation curve using the linear and cubic splines.

The conclusion of this section is that interpolating base correlation requires a smooth curve and that the exact form of the interpolation can have a significant effect on the prices of tranchelets. We also demonstrated that avoidance of arbitrage is assisted, but not guaranteed, by mapping via the ETL space.

20.6   A BASE CORRELATION SURFACE

Until now, we have simply considered the problem of pricing non-standard tranches as though we only have a five-year tranche market. We have therefore applied the same base correlation to all tranche payments irrespective of their timing. However, there are now additional quotes for the 7Y and a 10Y tranche maturity, and in some cases there is also a 3Y market point.

What then happens if we have to price a standard index tranche trade which had an initial maturity of five years but which has rolled down the curve and now has four years to maturity? Assuming the existence of a three-year tranche market we now need to consider the effect of the term structure of base correlation. However, we need to do this in a way which is consistent. Simply interpolating a base correlation by referring to the tranche maturity is not consistent. For example, a five-year tranche and a two-year tranche on the same reference portfolio, and with the same attachment and detachment points will have identical protection legs out to two years. Our model should reflect this. The obvious solution is to price a cash flow using a base correlation determined not by the trade maturity, but by the timing of the cash flow.

The pricing model would then need to be rewritten to take in a *base correlation surface* of the form $\rho(T, K)$. Each cash flow has then to be calculated using this base correlation and so we need to define a new tranche survival curve

$$Q(t_n, 0, K_1) = 1 - \frac{\mathbb{E}_{\rho(t_n, K_1)}\left[\min(L(t_n), K_1)\right]}{K_1}.$$

Once again, generation of the base correlation surface should pay attention to the avoidance of arbitrage, and we recall from Section 19.5 that there is a no-arbitrage constraint in the time dimension of the form

$$\frac{\partial^2 \psi(T, K)}{\partial T \partial K} \geq 0.$$

This is a difficult constraint to enforce in the construction of a correlation surface. It is much easier to enforce the less restrictive condition

$$\frac{\partial \psi(T,K)}{\partial T} \geq 0.$$

The advantage of this condition is that it allows us to break the construction of the base correlation surface into a two-stage process – correlation interpolation followed by a maturity interpolation. As arbitrages in the maturity dimension are both harder to detect and harder to monetise than those in the strike dimension, it makes sense first to build the interpolations in the strike dimension for each time point on the time grid. Following this the time T interpolations can be performed.

Calibration of the base correlation surface can be performed using a simple bootstrap technique. Assuming that we have 3Y, 5Y, 7Y and 10Y market quotes the process is as follows:

1. Use the 3Y tranche quotes to calculate the base correlation at three years at the standard strikes. The simplest modelling assumption is to assume a piecewise flat structure for the base correlation from $T=0$ to $T=3$. We call this $\rho(3,K)$.
2. Once the 0–3-year base correlation surface has been generated, the bootstrap moves on to the 5Y tranches. Once again, we solve for the flat base correlation between $T=3$ and $T=5$ which reprices the 5Y index tranches. Note that tranche cash flows which occur before $T=3$ must be priced using $\rho(3,K)$.
3. We repeat this process at $T=7$ and then $T=10$. This gives us a skeleton of base correlations at the standard strikes and at the 3Y, 5Y, 7Y and 10Y maturities.
4. To construct the full surface, we use the ETL methodology to imply out the interpolated base correlation curve at the non-standard strikes in the strike dimension. We do not need to interpolate the ETL curve in the time dimension as we have assumed that the base correlations are piecewise flat in the time dimension. However, we can calculate the ETL at all points on the surface using the conditions listed above to detect whether or not arbitrages exist.

Clearly, this is probably the simplest possible way to introduce a base correlation surface. More sophisticated time interpolation approaches can also be explored.

20.7   RISK MANAGEMENT OF INDEX TRANCHES

The risk management characteristics of synthetic tranches was already discussed extensively in Chapter 17. However, this was in the 'pre-skew' world, i.e. when we assumed the same correlation for all tranches. Now that we have a market skew, we need to re-examine these risks to understand how they change.

Table 20.3 shows a broad range of pricing and risk measures for iTraxx Series 6. To see the change from pre-skew to skew, we compare them with the non-skew flat correlation Gaussian copula risk measures where we have chosen a flat correlation of 25%. This is close to historical correlation values used pre-skew. Clearly, the flat correlation results cannot fit the market tranche prices. We see that the calibrated base correlation model assigns a higher spread to the equity tranche than the flat correlation case. However, it also assigns a much lower breakeven spread to the 3–6 mezzanine tranche than the flat correlation case. This redistribution of risk into the equity tranche and out of the first mezzanine tranche is what drives the changes in

Table 20.3   Tranche risk measures for iTraxx Europe Series 6 for a protection seller. We compare these measures for a calibrated base correlation model and for a model using a flat base correlation curve at 25%. A face value of $10m has been assumed for all tranches

Tranche (%)	Correlation Skew Risk Measures						
	Base corr. (%)	RPV01	Spread (bp)	Leverage	S.DV01 ($)	Gamma ($)	Corr01 ($)
0–3	15.76	3.969	805.35	25.45	−112 809	1951	38 661
3–6	25.33	4.499	55.00	4.75	−21 037	−722	−12 808
6–9	33.04	4.515	14.62	1.54	−6844	−230	−5834
9–12	39.45	4.517	6.50	0.79	−3499	−401	−2761
12–22	57.03	4.518	2.75	0.04	−195	51	−513

Tranche (%)	Pre-Skew Risk Measures						
	Flat corr. (%)	RPV01	Spread (bp)	Leverage	S.DV01 ($)	Gamma ($)	Corr01 ($)
0–3	25.00	4.011	714.14	21.48	−95 209	1496	37 477
3–6	25.00	4.457	131.81	8.48	−37 574	−273	−11 500
6–9	25.00	4.503	40.33	3.57	−15 813	−403	−10 593
9–12	25.00	4.514	14.48	1.55	−6850	−220	−6384
12–22	25.00	4.518	2.64	0.34	−1508	−85	−1827

the different risk measures shown in this table. We note that very similar results are found for CDX IG Series 7 but are not shown.

20.8 HEDGING THE BASE CORRELATION SKEW

Hedging the correlation risk for a tranche on a standard index can be done in a variety of ways. Essentially, the aim should be to express the correlation sensitivity of a non-standard tranche – one which is on a standard index but has non-standard attachment points – in terms of equivalent notionals of hedges in the standard tranches. There are a number of ways in which this can be accomplished and we outline one.

We wish to determine the sensitivity of our position to changes in the price of the standard index tranches which are due to changes in *correlation only*. This means that the scenario of interest is one in which the price of a standard index tranche changes while the spread of the underlying index remains fixed. We can therefore examine this risk by holding the spreads of the index portfolio fixed, and bumping the contractual spread of the index tranche by 1 bp. Since the portfolio spreads and recovery rates have not changed, the change in the spread can only be due to a change in correlation. Denoting the strikes of the non-standard tranche as $\hat{K}_1$ and $\hat{K}_2$, and that of the M standard tranches as K_m where $m = 1, \ldots, M$, the process is as follows:

1. Calculate the values of the standard tranches $V(K_{m-1}, K_m)$ for $m = 1, \ldots, M$ and then the value of the non-standard (NS) tranche $V_{NS}(\hat{K}_1, \hat{K}_2)$ using the current market base correlation curve.
2. Set $m = 1$.
3. Bump the contractual spread of the mth standard tranche $S(K_{m-1}, K_m)$ basis point.

4. Build the adjusted base correlation curve at the standard strikes. Because we are using a bootstrap, only the correlation at the standard tranche attachment points above K_m will have changed.
5. Calculate the interpolated base correlation implied by the new base correlation curve.
6. Reprice the standard tranche and the non-standard tranche using the new base correlation curve to give $V'(K_{m-1}, K_m)$ and $V'_{NS}(\hat{K}_1, \hat{K}_2)$ and from these calculate $\Delta V_{K_{m-1}-K_m}$ and ΔV_{NS}. The hedge notional in index tranche $K_{m-1}-K_m$ is then $\Delta V_{NS}/\Delta V_{K_{m-1}-K_m}$.
7. Restore the tranche contractual spread to its initial value.
8. Set $m = m + 1$. If $m \leq M$ return to step (3).

This gives us a vector of equivalent hedge notionals in the standard tranches which will offset small changes in the price of the non-standard tranche dues to changes in the correlation skew. We now consider a specific example.

Example In Table 20.4, we show the vector of price changes for a set of five non-standard tranches on the iTraxx Europe index. These are assumed to have been issued today with a fair-value contractual spread – they have an initial PV of zero. They are all long protection positions.

Table 20.4 Skew hedges for a set of non-standard tranches on the iTraxx Europe index. The top table shows the tranches and their contractual spread. We then hedge these using the iTraxx standard tranches using the market quotes in Table 20.1. The next table shows the change in the value of the non-standard tranche for a 1 bp change in the standard tranche spread. The next table shows the change in the value of the standard tranches for a 1 bp change in the standard tranche spread. The bottom table shows the equivalent notional of hedge where a negative notional represents a short protection position

Non-standard tranches

Tranche $\hat{K}_1-\hat{K}_2$	Long protection notional ($m)	Contractual spread (bp)
0–2	10.0	1055.2
2–5	10.0	166.1
5–10	10.0	16.5
10–15	10.0	4.3
15–20	10.0	2.4

Change in non-standard tranche PV ($) for a 1 bp increase in standard tranche spread

Tranche	$\Delta V_{NS}/\Delta S_{0-3}$	$\Delta V_{NS}/\Delta S_{3-6}$	$\Delta V_{NS}/\Delta S_{6-9}$	$\Delta V_{NS}/\Delta S_{9-12}$	$\Delta V_{NS}/\Delta S_{12-22}$
0–2	−5606	2286	0	0	0
2–5	−505	−5245	833	0	0
5–10	2	−391	−3274	−1025	166
10–15	−15	−18	55	−2002	−3004
15–20	−16	−19	−19	213	−5074

Change in standard tranche PV ($) for a 1 bp change in standard tranche spread					
Tranche	$\Delta V_{0-3}/\Delta S_{0-3}$	$\Delta V_{3-6}/\Delta S_{3-6}$	$\Delta V_{6-9}/\Delta S_{6-9}$	$\Delta V_{9-12}/\Delta S_{9-12}$	$\Delta V_{12-22}/\Delta S_{12-22}$
0–3	3968	0	0	0	0
3–6	0	4500	0	0	0
6–9	0	0	4514	0	0
9–12	0	0	0	4517	0
12–22	0	0	0	0	4518

Equivalent Hedge notional in standard tranche ($m)					
Tranche	$\Delta V_{NS}/\Delta V_{0-3}$	$\Delta V_{NS}/\Delta V_{3-6}$	$\Delta V_{NS}/\Delta V_{6-9}$	$\Delta V_{NS}/\Delta V_{9-12}$	$\Delta V_{NS}/\Delta V_{12-22}$
0–2	−14.13	5.76	0.00	0.00	0.00
2–5	−1.12	−11.66	1.85	0.00	0.00
5–10	0.00	−0.87	−7.25	−2.27	0.37
10–15	−0.03	−0.04	0.12	−4.43	−6.65
15–20	−0.04	−0.04	−0.04	0.47	−11.23

In order to express the hedges in equivalent notionals of the standard iTraxx tranches, we first need to calculate the change in the value of the non-standard tranche due to a 1 bp increase in each of the standard tranche spreads. We then need to calculate the sensitivity of the standard index tranches to a 1 bp increase in their tranche spreads, holding the reference portfolio spread fixed. This will result in a change in the implied tranche base correlation. The size of the change is simply given by the tranche risky PV01. Dividing one by the other gives us the equivalent hedge notional. These values are all shown in Table 20.4.

The hedge notionals are in units of $m, as we have assumed a $10m notional in each non-standard tranche. For example, we see that the 0–2% tranche has a hedge which is a $14.13 million short position in the 0–3% standard tranche, reflecting its higher correlation sensitivity. This is offset by a $5.76m long position in the 3–6% index tranche. We see similar behaviour for the hedges on all of the other non-standard tranches.

This example raises a question. Why should the 0–2% tranche have an exposure to and hence a hedge in the 3–6% standard tranche. After all, if we bump the 3–6% tranche spread, we might only expect the base correlation bootstrap to result in a change in the base correlations at higher strikes. However, this ignores the effect of the base correlation curve interpolation scheme. Here we have used the ETL PCHIP approach. Since this is a spline method, it has non-local effects. As a result, the effect of changing the base correlation at strikes of 3% and higher actually causes the ETL curve to change below 3% and so change the interpolated base correlations. A less local interpolation scheme would reduce these non-local effects, but this means relaxing smoothness and so making more likely the introduction of arbitrage into the implied loss distribution.

20.9   BASE CORRELATION FOR BESPOKE TRANCHES

Until now, we have focused on the calibration of the base correlation curve to the standard index tranches, and then the interpolation of this curve to enable the pricing of non-standard tranches on the standard index portfolio. In this section, we wish to go to the next step of figuring out how best to apply the information embedded in the pricing of standard tranches to price tranches on *non-standard portfolios*, i.e. portfolios which are not identical to the standard indices. We call these *bespoke tranches*. For example, how should we price a 3–6% tranche on a portfolio which is identical to CDX Series 7 except that one credit has been replaced with another credit which is not in the index. What happens if we replace two credits, or three, or 30? Clearly we would expect that the price difference between the bespoke tranche and the index should increase as the bespoke portfolio becomes increasingly different from the index portfolio.

Another source of complexity is regionality. While CDX IG reflects a North American investment grade portfolio and iTraxx a European investment grade portfolio, how should we price a tranche which combines a mixture of European and North American credits? This is another interpolation problem.

20.9.1   The Base Correlation Mapping

We begin by considering the problem of pricing a bespoke tranche with reference to just one standard index tranche. Specifically, what we are looking for is a way to imply out a base correlation curve for tranches on a bespoke portfolio. We call this a mapping since what we wish to do is to map the base correlation curves for the tranches on the standard indices to a base correlation curve for tranches on the bespoke portfolio. To begin with, we denote the base correlation of a $0–K_B$ base tranche on a bespoke portfolio with $\rho_B(K_B)$. We denote the base correlation for a standard $0–K_S$ index base tranche using $\rho_S(K_S)$. The mapping discussed here assumes that the mapping to a bespoke portfolio uses information from just a single standard index base correlation curve. It therefore excludes cases when we have a mixed regional portfolio and may wish to combine information from two or more standard index base correlation curves. This more complex case will be discussed at the end of this section.

The purpose of the mapping is to determine the value of the standard strike K_S^* whose standard base correlation $\rho_S(K_S^*)$ is to be used to price the bespoke base tranche with width K_B, i.e. we have a mapping function $g(x)$ such that

$$K_S^* = g(K_B; \mathcal{I}_B, \mathcal{I}_S)$$

where $\mathcal{I}_B$ and $\mathcal{I}_S$ represent all of the spread and recovery rate information associated with the bespoke and standard index portfolios. We therefore have

$$\rho_B(K_B) = \rho_S(K_S^*).$$

With such a mapping, we can then reuse our entire base correlation framework for pricing and risk managing tranches on this bespoke portfolio. We can define a number of desirable characteristics for this mapping and we list these below:

1. The mapping should interpolate correctly and smoothly between the prices of all known index portfolios, i.e. when applied to the mapping of the base correlation on a tranche on a CDX portfolio, the mapping should return the CDX base correlation curve.

2. The mapping should avoid creating any arbitrages in the interpolation of the bespoke base correlation curve, especially if there is none in the index tranche base correlation curves.
3. The methodology should capture differences between the standard indices and bespoke portfolio. Ideally, these should include differences in the distribution of CDS spreads across different issuers.
4. The methodology should be numerically stable and fast.
5. The mapping approach should be as simple as possible, subject to all of these requirements.

There are currently a number of mapping approaches which we will now summarise. Before doing so, we summarise the general mapping algorithm. This assumes that we have already generated a standard index base correlation curve $\rho_S(K)$ at all values of K by calibrating the market price of the standard tranches.

1. Given a bespoke portfolio base tranche with width K_B, use the mapping to find the corresponding value of K_S. We call this K_S^* where $K_S^* = g(K_B; \mathcal{I}_B, \mathcal{I}_S)$.
2. Set the bespoke tranche base correlation equal to $\rho_B(K_B) = \rho_S(K_S^*)$.
3. Price the bespoke base tranche using $\rho_B(K_B)$.

This process is summarised in Figure 20.11.

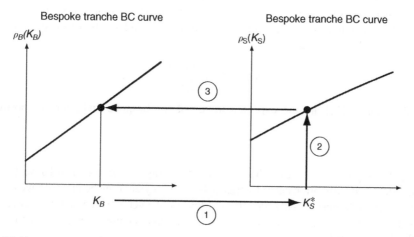

Figure 20.11 Base correlation mapping for bespoke portfolios. We first map the bespoke strike K_B to the equivalent standard strike K_S^* and read off the corresponding value of the base correlation which we use to price the bespoke base tranche

20.9.2 No Mapping

The most trivial mapping is the one in which $g(x) = x$, i.e. we simply set

$$K_S^* = K_B.$$

Consider the following example:

> **Example** Suppose we have a bespoke tranche with an attachment point at 4% and a detachment point at 8%. A no-mapping approach means that we simply price the bespoke by reading off the 4% and 8% strike interpolated base correlations $\rho_S(4\%)$ and $\rho_S(8\%)$ from our standard tranche base correlation curve. These are then used to price the bespoke tranche.

While this approach is certainly simple and easy to implement, it does not seem intuitive. For instance, should a 4–8% tranche on a high yield portfolio be assigned the same correlation as a 4–8% on an investment grade index. After all, a 4–8% tranche on a high yield index is essentially an equity tranche due to the high probability of incurring losses and the fact that the entire tranche is typically sitting below the expected loss of the portfolio. It does not seem reasonable to have a mapping which ignores the difference in credit quality between the bespoke reference portfolio and the standard index reference portfolio.

20.9.3 At-the-Money Correlation Mapping

In order to overcome the intuitive difficulties associated with the no-mapping approach, the at-the-money correlation mapping has been proposed by Ahluwalia *et al.* (2004). The rationale behind this mapping is that the base correlation assigned to a base tranche is such that the ratio of the tranche strike divided by the reference portfolio expected loss is the same for standard and bespoke tranches. The mapping is therefore

$$K_S^* = K_B \times \frac{\mathbb{E}[L_S]}{\mathbb{E}[L_B]}$$

where $\mathbb{E}[L_B]$ and $\mathbb{E}[L_S]$ are the expected losses of the bespoke and standard portfolios, respectively.

> **Example** Suppose once again that we are attempting to use a standard investment grade index base correlation curve to price a 4–8% high yield tranche in which we know that the high yield portfolio has an expected loss to five years which is 20% compared to 5% for the investment grade index. According to this mapping methodology the 4% and 8% bespoke strikes map to
>
> $$K_S^* = 5\% \times \frac{4\%}{20\%} = 1\% \quad \text{and} \quad K_S^* = 5\% \times \frac{8\%}{20\%} = 2\%.$$
>
> As a result, we use the values of $\rho_S(1\%)$ and $\rho_S(2\%)$ to price the 4–8% bespoke tranche. This seems more reasonable since we are using what are equity-like base correlations for what is an equity-like tranche for the high yield portfolio.

There are a number of downsides with this approach. First, we see from this example that the high yield portfolio maps to very low strikes on the investment grade portfolio. This means that the pricing of the bespoke tranche is sensitive to how we extrapolate the base correlation curve below the lowest quoted strike of 3%. This problem can be mitigated somewhat by choosing to use a more appropriate base correlation curve for mapping high yield portfolios, e.g. CDX NA High Yield. Another problem occurs if the bespoke portfolio has a much lower expected loss than the index. In this case we may find values of K_S^* which are higher than the highest quoted standard strike, and which may even be higher than the maximum loss of the portfolio. In this case the pricing is very sensitive to how we have chosen to extrapolate the base correlation curve.

Although it is an improvement on the no-mapping approach, the ATM mapping approach only takes into account the average credit quality of the bespoke and index portfolios. It therefore ignores information about their spread dispersion.

20.9.4   Tranche Loss Proportion Mapping

The tranche loss proportion (TLP) mapping states that the base correlation that should be used for pricing a bespoke tranche is the one for which the ratio of the tranche expected loss divided by the portfolio expected loss should be the same for a standard tranche and a bespoke portfolio tranche. The TLP of a tranche in the base correlation framework is given by

$$\text{TLP}(K) = \frac{\mathbb{E}_{\rho(K)}[\min(L, K)]}{\mathbb{E}[L]}.$$

The mapping between the strikes is based on equating the index and bespoke TLPs as follows

$$\frac{\mathbb{E}_{\rho_S(K_S^*)}[\min(L_S, K_S^*)]}{\mathbb{E}[L_S]} = \frac{\mathbb{E}_{\rho_S(K_S^*)}[\min(L_B, K_B)]}{\mathbb{E}[L_B]}.$$

We no longer have a simple equation which we can solve exactly for K_S^*. Instead we have to solve this equation for K_S^* using some one-dimensional root search. Before we do this, let us take moment to figure out how both sides of this equation depend on K_S.

The left-hand side of this equation is the fraction of the expected loss of the standard index portfolio which is contained within the base tranche of width K_S. It equals zero when $K_S = 0$ and increases monotonically to 1 at $K_S = L_{\text{Max}}$. For each value of K_S the value of $\rho_S(K_S)$ is simply read off the interpolated standard index base correlation curve.

Now consider the right-hand side. As we increase K_S from zero to L_{Max}, the base correlation $\rho_S(K_S)$ used to price the bespoke tranche increases as the base correlation is generally an increasing function of strike.[3] Since the right-hand side of the equation is the expected loss of a $0 - K_B$ equity or base tranche, increasing correlation will cause the right-hand side to be a decreasing function of K_S. For some value of $K_S = K_S^*$, we should find that both sides of the equation are equal.

Figure 20.12 shows the index tranche TLP and that of a number of bespoke tranches with different values of K_B as a function of K_S. The bespoke tranche was constructed by simply taking the iTraxx Europe index portfolio and scaling the spreads by a factor of 5, increasing the average five-year spread from 26 bp to 131 bp. We determine the value of K_S^* for each value of K_B by finding the value of K_S at which the index TLP and the bespoke TLP lines cross. Once

---

[3] This is generally true but it is not guaranteed in all cases. For example, we know that it is possible for the base correlation curve to be a decreasing function of increasing strike at very low strikes.

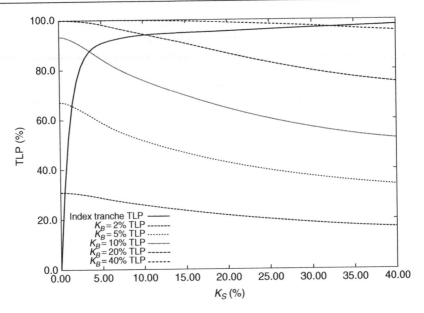

Figure 20.12 The TLP base correlation mapping. We show the index TLP curve and then a succession of TLPs for different base tranches on the bespoke portfolio with widths of 2%, 5%, 10%, 20% and 40%. The intersection of the bespoke TLP curves and the index TLP curve gives the value of K_S^* for that bespoke base tranche

we have the value of K_S^*, we simply set $\rho_B(K_B) = \rho_S(K_S^*)$. If we repeat this for a range of values of K_B, we can calculate the base correlation curve for the bespoke tranche.

Figure 20.13 shows both the bespoke base correlation curves for the three mapping approaches discussed. We used the ETL approach with the PCHIP approach to interpolate the base correlation. Above a bespoke strike of 6%, we see that the base correlation for the bespoke portfolio is always lower than the base correlation for the same strike on the index portfolio. This reflects the higher expected loss of the bespoke portfolio. The no-mapping curve is the same as the original index base correlation curve. The ATM curve is effectively a five-times stretched out version of the index base correlation curve. The TLP bespoke curve lies between the original base correlation curve and the ATM curve.

20.9.5   Interpolating the Bespoke Curve in the TLP mapping

Solving for K_S^* can be numerically time consuming since changing K_S means changing $\rho(K_S)$ which means rebuilding the portfolio loss distribution for both the index tranche and the bespoke tranche. This has to be done for both strikes of the bespoke tranche we are pricing. Depending on the required accuracy and the speed of convergence of the root searching algorithm, this may be very time consuming, especially if we wish to compute the entire bespoke base correlation curve, at say regular 1% intervals. It also means that we are using the initial interpolation of the standard index base correlation curve and the mapping to effectively interpolate the bespoke base correlation curve.

Another approach is to generate the entire bespoke base correlation curve at just the mapped values of K_B which correspond to the standard strikes on the index. This is effectively reversing

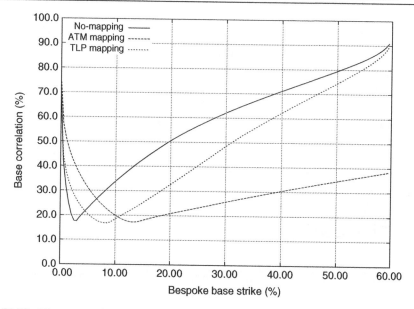

Figure 20.13   We compare the mapped bespoke base correlation curves for a bespoke portfolio in which the spreads of iTraxx have been scaled by a factor of 5. We show the no-mapping curve, the ATM mapping curve and the TLP curve

the order of our earlier mapping. For example, in the case of the iTraxx tranches, the standard strikes are $K_S^* = 0.03, 0.06, 0.09, 0.12, 0.22$ and for each we simply read off the corresponding base correlation from the prices of the standard tranches. No interpolation is required. We can therefore compute the TLP for each value of K_S^* as follows

$$\text{TLP}(K_S^*) = \frac{\mathbb{E}_{\rho_S(K_S^*)}[\min(L_S, K_S^*)]}{\mathbb{E}[L_S]}.$$

Given that the base correlation $\rho(K_S^*)$ is also used to price the bespoke tranche, and since it is fixed, we need only build the bespoke portfolio loss distribution once. We then search for the value of K_B which solves the TLP equation

$$\text{TLP}(K_S^*) = \frac{\mathbb{E}_{\rho_S(K_S^*)}[\min(L_B, K_B)]}{\mathbb{E}[L_B]}.$$

This is very fast to compute. In addition, this mapping is cleaner in the sense that we have not yet done any interpolation since the index base correlations used are those at the standard index strikes.

The result is that we now have a skeleton of base correlation points at five values of K_B. We can then choose an interpolation scheme to interpolate this skeleton of base correlation points. As we can use an interpolation approach like the PCHIP ETL to perform the interpolation, this approach is not only much faster than the previous approach, it is also more likely to result in a bespoke base correlation curve which is arbitrage free. We can summarise this method as 'map first then interpolate' as distinct from the previous method which was 'interpolate first then map'.

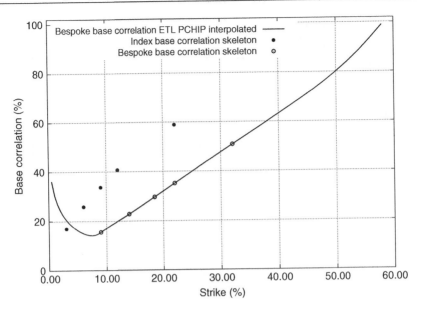

Figure 20.14 The interpolated bespoke base correlation curve produced by mapping the index base correlation skeleton to a bespoke skeleton of points and then interpolating using the ETL PCHIP method

Figure 20.14 shows the result of this mapping for the bespoke portfolio. The skeleton of index base correlations are shown, and their strikes are then mapped to produce a skeleton of bespoke base correlations. Finally, we used the ETL PCHIP interpolation to interpolate the skeleton of points in the bespoke base correlation curve. As discussed earlier, this interpolation methodology implies that the base correlation increases as the strike tends to zero. We can detect whether or not the bespoke base correlation curve is arbitrage free by calculating the density of the implied loss distribution. We find that the density of the loss distribution for the bespoke tranche implied by this base correlation curve is everywhere positive, implying that it is arbitrage free. We also find that when we perform the same exercise with the CDX NA IG Series 7 portfolio, i.e. we use it to price a bespoke in which the index spreads have been scaled by a factor of 5, the resulting loss distribution for the bespoke tranche is arbitrage free even though the loss distribution of the index tranche is not. This is encouraging, though we emphasise that there is no guarantee that the mapping and interpolation will always be so benign.

20.9.6 Choosing a Mapping

We end this section by stating that there is no right answer when it comes to choosing a mapping scheme. However, some schemes are better than others either because they are more reasonable or because they use more information about the reference portfolio or because they are more numerically stable. In general, our experience suggests that the TLP mapping is the most widely used mapping used in the market mainly because it takes into account the dispersion of the spreads of the reference portfolio which the ATM mapping does not. The TLP mapping is also less likely to map to unobservable low or high strikes than the ATM mapping.

In Baheti and Morgan (2007), the authors proposed a test for these mapping methodologies in which the criterion for assessing the mapping was its ability to map one liquid index base correlation curve onto that of another liquid index. The authors found that of all the mappings described here, the TLP mapping performs best at mapping between the investment grade indices of CDX and iTraxx. However, none of the methods tried performed particularly well at mapping between the investment grade and high yield versions of CDX, implying that high yield portfolios are different, and have additional features not adequately captured by the TLP mapping. In most of the tests, the ATM method performed poorly. This confirms our view that the TLP is probably the best of all the mappings described.

20.9.7   Dealing with Multi-region Bespokes

The mappings discussed so far assume that a bespoke portfolio can be mapped directly to one unique standard index base correlation curve. This may be fine for exclusively European or North American investment grade bespoke portfolios, but when there is a regional mix, we want to make sure that information from both CDX and iTraxx is used. There is, however, no obvious solution. Ad hoc approaches such as pricing the bespoke tranche using first CDX and then iTraxx and then taking some *weighted average* of the prices are reasonable but do not have any theoretical justification. Ideally, what we need is a set of liquid quoted tranches on a reference portfolio which is the combination of the CDX IG and the iTraxx indices. Without this information, any interpolation between North American-only and European-only tranches is fairly arbitrary.

20.10   RISK MANAGEMENT OF BESPOKE TRANCHES

The introduction of a mapping methodology for bespoke tranches adds a new dimension to the risk management of tranches within a base correlation framework. We recall that the leverage of a standard tranche is computed by perturbing the index spread by 1 bp and calculating the ratio of the change in the value of the tranche by the change in the value of the index. In the case of bespoke portfolios, we can do something similar. We can perturb all of the issuer curves in the portfolio by 1 bp and then calculate the ratio of the change in the value of the bespoke tranche divided by the change in the value of the bespoke portfolio. What's new is that *by changing the spread of the bespoke portfolio, we change the base correlations* which we use to price the tranche. Within the base correlation framework, a K_1–K_2 tranche value is only sensitive to $\rho(K_1)$ and $\rho(K_2)$. Hence, we can write the change of the tranche value $V = V(S, \rho(K_1), \rho(K_2))$ per small change in the bespoke portfolio spread as

$$\frac{dV}{dS} = \frac{\partial V}{\partial S} + \frac{\partial V}{\partial \rho(K_1)} \frac{\partial \rho(K_1)}{\partial S} + \frac{\partial V}{\partial \rho(K_2)} \frac{\partial \rho(K_2)}{\partial S}. \tag{20.2}$$

If we have a no-mapping approach, the partial derivatives of the bespoke base correlations with respect to the spread change will be zero and we just have the first term which is the pre-skew sensitivity. For the other mappings, we need to calculate how significant the correlation change is when we change the bespoke portfolio spread. If it is material then we will need to take the effect into account. Otherwise we may find that our systemic spread hedges will experience slippage, i.e. the position will not be fully hedged and will experience P&L volatility.

We have examined the size of the adjustment to the leverage of a bespoke tranche due to a change in the spread of the bespoke reference portfolio using the TLP mapping. The methodology used was as follows:

1. Calculate the value of a K_1–K_2 bespoke tranche $V(K_1, K_2)$ using $\rho_B(K_1)$ and $\rho_B(K_2)$.
2. Bump the spreads of the bespoke reference portfolio by 1 bp.
3. Using the TLP mapping, construct a new bespoke base correlation curve.
4. Reprice the bespoke tranche giving $V'(K_1, K_2)$ using the new $\rho'_B(K_1)$ and $\rho'_B(K_2)$.
5. Calculate the change in the value of the tranche $\Delta V = V'(K_1, K_2) - V(K_1, K_2)$.
6. Divide ΔV by the risky PV01 of the underlying bespoke reference portfolio to get the bespoke tranche leverage.

This approach will capture the full change in V due to the combination of the increase in spreads and the corresponding change in the bespoke base correlation curve.

We considered bespoke tranches on a reference portfolio with the iTraxx index spreads scaled by a factor of 5. Table 20.5 shows the results. We see that the mapping has the effect of increasing the tranche leverage for junior tranches and to cause the leverage to decrease for mezzanine tranches. The changes are not large, but should be taken into account.

Table 20.5 This table shows the effect of the mapping on the leverage of a tranche on a bespoke portfolio with an average spread of 131 bp. We show the overall tranche leverage using a TLP mapping. We calculate a risky PV01 of 4.288 for the bespoke reference portfolio.

Tranche ($K_1 - K_2$) (%)	No-map leverage	$\partial\rho(K_2)/\partial S$ (%)	Sensitivities $\partial V/\partial\rho(K_1)$	$\partial V/\partial\rho(K_1)$	TLP leverage
0–3	13.08	−0.005	0.000	1.357	13.23
3–6	11.09	0.027	−1.115	1.806	9.80
6–9	8.15	−0.043	−1.637	1.657	10.91
9–12	3.76	−0.074	−1.576	1.264	4.33
12–22	1.29	−0.108	−0.374	0.207	1.17
22–30	0.39	−0.099	−0.258	0.201	0.21

For hedging purposes, the correlation sensitivity of a bespoke tranche has to be measured as its sensitivity to changes in the base correlation curve of the index tranche, not to changes in its own mapped base correlation curve. The aim is to express the correlation sensitivity of a tranche in terms of hedges in the standard index tranches. The simplest way to calculate these hedges is to calculate the change in the value of the bespoke tranche for a 1 bp bump in each of the standard index tranche spreads. The hedging method should therefore follow the approach described in Section 20.8.

20.11 SUMMARY

Despite the fact that it not an arbitrage-free model for the correlation skew, base correlation continues to be used not just as a method for exchanging information about implied correlation, but also as a tool for pricing and risk managing STCDOs. Because it is not an arbitrage-free model, using it as a full pricing and risk model involves building ad hoc extensions to minimise the dangers of creating arbitrages. We have described a number of such approaches which can be used for pricing non-standard strikes on the standard indices.

We then have to confront the question of how to apply base correlation to the pricing of bespoke tranches. There are currently a number of different methods which have been discussed. Unfortunately, there is no sound theoretical basis for discriminating between them. However, we believe that the TLP method discussed best satisfies the characteristics we would look for in a mapping methodology and we also believe that this is the most widely used method in the market.

Most market practitioners would probably agree that base correlation needs to be displaced as a pricing and risk model. However, this can only occur once a superior approach is found. This would need to have all of the advantages of base correlation – exact market fit, parsimonious, fast, conserves expected loss across capital structure and allows the pricing of non-standard and bespoke tranches. Unlike base correlation, it should be arbitrage free. Unfortunately, the task of finding such a model is not easy and is the subject of most of the remaining chapters.

21

Copula Skew Models

21.1 INTRODUCTION

Since the appearance of the correlation skew, there has been a major effort to find a model which can improve upon base correlation and become the new market standard. In this chapter we introduce and analyse a selection of the proposed models. They all have in common the fact that they fall into the class of copula models. Although comprehensive, our coverage is not complete since new approaches continue to be produced. However, the models discussed here can be considered to be a representative subset of the approaches being used. For each, we discuss the practical difficulties of implementation and calibration. We then compare the approaches in terms of their loss distribution, as captured by the tranchelet spread curves they generate, and their systemic leverage ratios. We conclude with a discussion of how these models can be used to price bespoke portfolios.

21.1.1 Model Requirements

In order to evaluate a correlation skew model, we need to be aware of the main model requirements. These are as follows:

1. The model should be arbitrage free, i.e. given an arbitrage-free set of market quotes, the model should ensure that any non-standard or bespoke tranches are also arbitrage free.
2. The market fit to the prices of index tranches should be within the bid–offer spread.
3. The number of model parameters and their stability is extremely important. The model should be as parsimonious as possible, consistent with the fitting constraint.
4. Parameter stability is vital. Parameters should shadow the market prices in an intuitively clear way.
5. Calculation time should be as low as possible. Typical usability bounds mean that a model should be able to calibrate within a minute and to price a trade in seconds.
6. The model should provide a sensible interpolation scheme for non-standard tranches on the standard indices. It should also extend naturally to price bespoke tranches, i.e. tranches on non-standard portfolios.

With these requirements in mind, we now embark on a tour of the most notable copula skew models. Before we do this, we take a moment to explain the challenge of fitting the skew in terms of the shape of the loss distribution.

21.2 THE CHALLENGE OF FITTING THE SKEW

Before we introduce the copula skew models which are the subject of this chapter, it is important to appreciate the modelling challenge of fitting the skew in terms of the shape of the implied portfolio loss distribution. After all, the beauty of a copula model is that it produces *one* loss distribution for the portfolio from which any tranche can be priced. In this way we overcome the problems of the base correlation framework and we are able to build a model which is guaranteed to be arbitrage free in the strike dimension.

Fitting the skew requires some significant changes in the shape of the loss distribution when compared to the Gaussian copula loss distribution at historical correlation levels. This is made very clear when we study Figure 21.1. This compares the loss distribution implied by the base

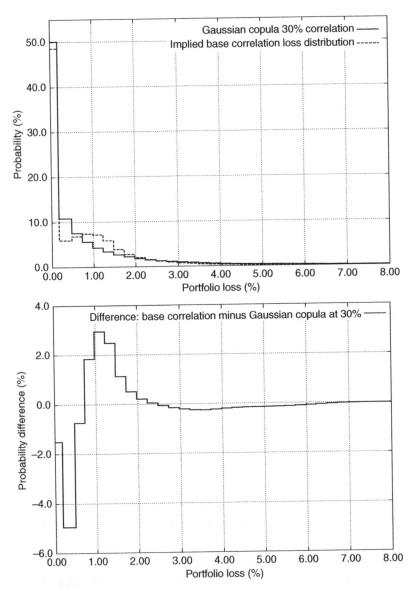

Figure 21.1 Comparison of a Gaussian copula loss distribution for CDX NA IG Series 7 with 30% correlation and the base correlation implied loss distribution which reprices the market exactly. This is calculated using an ETL interpolation. The first figure shows the two loss distributions and the second figure shows the difference in the density

correlation model interpolated with the PCHIP ETL scheme discussed in the previous chapter, which fits the market tranche prices exactly, and the loss distribution implied by the Gaussian copula with a flat 30% correlation, which does not fit the market. We observe that:

- The skew model needs to make 0–3% equity tranches riskier than the Gaussian copula model. In the base correlation approach, this is achieved by reducing the 3% base correlation. In terms of the loss distribution, this can only be done by shifting the probability mass to higher losses within the 0–3% loss range, e.g. by reducing the probability of zero defaults and increasing the probability of a small number of defaults.
- The skew model needs to reduce the risk of junior mezzanine tranches. This does not seem compatible with the requirement for equity tranches. However, if the probability density in the range 3–7% is reduced by shifting mass into the 0–3% range – and so not increasing the probability mass above 7% – then this can be achieved.
- Senior tranches are already priced close to the level implied by a 30% Gaussian copula correlation. No significant alteration in the loss distribution above 7% is required.

What this exercise demonstrates is the subtle shifting of probability mass required by a model of the correlation skew in order that it can refit the market. It is clear that the base correlation loss distribution has a lot of structure and the challenge is to see if a copula model has the same degree of flexibility.

21.3 CALIBRATION

In this chapter, when calibrating a copula model to the market price of tranches on the CDX or iTraxx indices, we use the following objective function to perform the calibration

$$\hat{O}(\mathbf{x}) = \frac{1}{5} \sum_{i=1}^{5} |PV\,(K_{i-1}, K_i, \mathbf{x})|$$

where $K_0, K_1, \ldots, K_5$ is the vector of strikes for the index tranches being fitted with $K_0 = 0$, and $\mathbf{x}$ represents the set of model parameters. The objective function is the sum of the absolute PV values per tranche expressed as a percentage of the tranche face value. Recall that all on-market tranches should have a present value of zero and so any deviation of the tranche value away from zero is a pricing error.

For simplicity, all tranches irrespective of their width are weighted equally. However, in alternative approaches a weighting scheme is often used which links the importance of a tranche to its liquidity, quantified as some decreasing function of the width of the bid–offer spread on the tranche.

Calibration is therefore performed using a multi-dimensional non-linear optimiser which permits linear equality and inequality constraints. In each model case, we will attempt to fit the CDX tranche prices given in Table 20.1.

In order to map the calibration pricing error into correlation terms, we use compound correlation rather than base correlation for the simple reason that the error in the base correlation for a senior tranche is the result of the accumulation of errors for the more junior tranches and so does not tell us how well a specific tranche fits the market. By treating each tranche individually, we can more easily see if the model studied presents the compound correlation smile shape required to fit the market, and we can see the correlation error on each tranche.

The calibration study conducted here is very limited as it consists of fitting a single set of tranche prices on a single day. As a result, it gives us only a rough guide to the fitting ability of each model. Clearly, any wish to put any of these models into production requires extensive calibration tests over many market environments.

It may also appear confusing to the reader when we call a model which produces a correlation smile a *correlation skew model*. Unfortunately, this apparent contradiction is a result of the widespread use of two measures of implied correlation and we recall that a set of market prices which produce a compound correlation smile also produce a base correlation skew.

21.4   RANDOM RECOVERY

One of the most significant assumptions of all of the correlation models discussed so far has been the use of a fixed recovery rate. However, we discussed in Section 3.2.2 empirical evidence suggests that there is a negative correlation between macro default rates and recovery rates. This means that when the portfolio default rate is higher than historical average, the average portfolio recovery rate is lower than historical average and vice-versa. We would expect this phenomenon to change the shape of the portfolio loss distribution. The question we ask here is whether this explains the existence of the compound correlation smile and base correlation skew.

To examine this question, we first note that the expected loss of a reference portfolio is fixed by the average spread of all of the credits in the portfolio. The question then is how does a default rate and recovery rate relationship of the type described above change the shape of the loss distribution given that the expected loss is fixed? We answer this by observing that there will be two changes in the shape of the loss distribution:

1. Scenarios with higher than average numbers of defaults will have lower than average recovery rates and this will extend the upper tail of the loss distribution.
2. Scenarios with lower than average numbers of defaults are linked to higher than average recovery rates and this will increase the probability of low losses.

Now let us consider the CDX tranches given in Table 20.1. We see that the underlying index has a 5Y spread of 37 bp. This implies that the expected loss to five years is approximately equal to $5 \times 37\,\text{bp} = 1.85\%$, i.e. the tranche expected loss is well inside the 0–3% region.

As a result, if we have a Gaussian copula with a 30% correlation, the effect of turning on the random recovery will be to make mezzanine and senior tranches more risky and to make the equity tranche less risky, whereas what we actually want is to make the mezzanine tranche less risky while keeping the equity and senior tranche spreads relatively constant. We cannot fit the skew. Even if we do not have a negative correlation between default rates and recovery rates, a random recovery will still have the effect of increasing the variance of the loss distribution about its mean loss. This will have a similar, albeit smaller, effect on the negative correlation case. We conclude that *by itself* random recovery is not the answer to explaining and fitting the correlation skew. To solve the problem of modelling the skew, we need to look to alternative models of the dependency structure of defaults.

21.5   THE STUDENT-T COPULA

Mashal and Zeevi (2002) showed that the joint distributions of equity returns exhibit fatter tails than those implied by a Gaussian copula. They suggested that the Student-t copula may be a more appropriate model for pricing synthetic CDO tranches as examined in Andersen *et al.* (2003). However, whether a copula that appears more consistent with empirical data is also capable of fitting the correlation skew is the main question of this section.

The properties of the Student-t distribution and its copula have already been set out in Section 14.6.2. Figure 21.2 plots the difference between the probability density for the Student-t distribution with ν degrees of freedom and the Gaussian probability density. It shows that the tails of the Student-t distribution decay much more slowly than the Gaussian and the tails become more pronounced as we decrease ν.

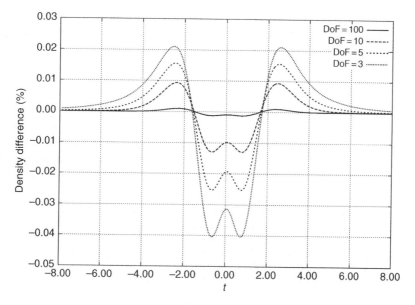

Figure 21.2   A plot of the Student-t distribution density minus the Gaussian distribution density for four values of the degree of freedom parameter ν

In the Student-t copula model the equation for the asset value is given by

$$A_i = \left(\beta_i Z + \sqrt{1 - \beta_i^2}\, \varepsilon_i \right) \sqrt{\frac{\nu}{\xi_\nu}} \tag{21.1}$$

where Z and ε_i are independent Gaussian random variables with mean zero and unit standard deviation, and ξ_ν is an independent chi-square distributed random variable with ν degrees of freedom. Since A_i is now distributed according to a Student-t distribution with ν degrees of freedom, we calibrate the default probabilities by solving for the default threshold for credit i as follows

$$C_i(T) = t_\nu^{-1}(1 - Q_i(T))$$

where $t_v(x)$ is the Student-t cumulative distribution function with v degrees of freedom, given in Equation 14.5. For a fixed value of v, determining the threshold $C_i(T)$ requires a one-dimensional root search which makes many calls to the function $t_v(x)$. There are a number of fast numerical routines which can be used to calculate $t_v(x)$, usually in terms of the incomplete gamma function using continued fractions as described in Press *et al.* (1992).

Once again, we can cast this model into a conditionally independent framework. However, we have to condition on the two common sources of randomness, Z and ξ_v. The conditional probability of default is therefore given by

$$\Pr\left(A_i \leq C_i(T)|Z, \xi_v\right) = \Phi\left(\frac{C_i(T)\sqrt{\xi_v/v} - \beta_i Z}{\sqrt{1 - \beta_i^2}}\right).$$

Given the conditional default probability for each credit, it is possible to build the conditional loss distribution using the standard techniques described in Chapter 18. Calculation of the unconditional loss distribution then involves a nested integral over both Z and the chi-square distributed ξ_v. The chi-square distribution is only defined for $\xi \geq 0$ with first and second moments $\mathbb{E}[\xi_v] = v$ and $\mathbb{E}[\xi_v^2] = 2v$, and can be long tailed.

21.5.1 Calibration

We have attempted to calibrate the Student-t copula model to the market prices of index tranches. To do so, we assume that the correlation structure is flat, i.e. $\beta_i = \beta = \sqrt{\rho}$. This gives us two parameters for our fitting, ρ and v. We find that the Student-t copula model is unable to fit the correlation smile. This is clear in Figure 21.3 which shows the compound correlation curve for a range of values of correlation ρ and degrees of freedom parameter v. We have also

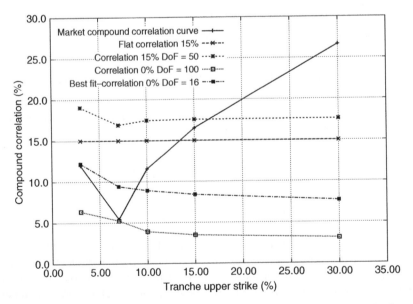

Figure 21.3 This shows the different compound correlation curves produced by the Student-t model for different values of the correlation ρ and the degrees of freedom parameter v. The market compound correlation curve is also shown

plotted the market implied compound correlation curve which we are attempting to fit. We make the following observations:

- When $\nu \to \infty$ and $\rho = 15\%$, we have the Gaussian copula and hence a compound correlation curve which is flat at 15%.
- When $\nu = 50$ and $\rho = 15\%$, the average level of the compound correlation increases above 15% due to the tail dependence of the Student-t copula. We see a very small 'smile' effect but at the wrong correlation level.
- If we drop the correlation ρ to zero, and set $\nu = 16$, we are able to fit the equity compound correlation. However, the model fails to fit any of the other tranches. In terms of our PV-based objective function this is the best fit we can achieve.
- Setting the $\rho = 0\%$ and $\nu = 100$ allows us to fit the mezzanine tranche but the other points cannot be fitted.

The main reason for the failure of the Student-t copula to produce a smile is that ρ and ν are performing the same function – both control the portfolio-wide degree of default dependency. Increasing ρ and decreasing ν tends to extend the tail of the loss distribution and make the probability of small losses increase. It is not able to perform the subtle adjustments to the probability distribution required to fit the skew. We therefore reject the Student-t copula model as a correlation skew model.

21.6   THE DOUBLE-T COPULA

Hull and White (2003b) have proposed a model in which the individual factors in the one-factor Gaussian latent variable model are replaced by independent, Student-t distributed factors. We have

$$A_i = \beta_i \sqrt{\frac{\nu_Z - 2}{\nu_Z}} Z + \sqrt{1 - \beta_i^2} \sqrt{\frac{\nu_\epsilon - 2}{\nu_\epsilon}} \varepsilon_i \qquad (21.2)$$

where Z and ε_i are independent Student-t distributed random variables with ν_Z and ν_ε degrees of freedom, respectively. The factor weights in Equation 21.2 ensure that A_i has mean zero and unit variance. This *is not* a Student-t copula model since the sum of two Student-t random variables is not Student-t distributed.[1] It is therefore known as the *Double-t* copula model.

Default occurs before time T if $A_i \leq C_i(T)$. Calibration of the threshold for each asset requires that we solve

$$\Pr\left(A_i \leq C_i(T)\right) = 1 - Q_i(T)$$

for $C_i(T)$ where $Q_i(T)$ is the issuer survival probability to time T. There is no simple analytical formula for the distribution of A_i. Instead, we denote the cumulative distribution function of A_i with $H(C_i(T); \beta_i, \nu_Z, \nu_\varepsilon)$. The default threshold is therefore given by

$$C_i(T) = H^{-1}\left(1 - Q_i(T); \beta_i, \nu_Z, \nu_\varepsilon\right).$$

---

[1] The sum of two independent Gaussian variables is Gaussian distributed. This useful property does not extend to Student-t distributed variables.

Inverting the function $H(C_i(T); \beta_i, v_Z, v_\varepsilon)$ to calculate the default probability threshold involves performing a convolution of the two Student-t distributions for Z and ε_i as follows

$$H(C_i(T); \beta_i, v_Z, v_\varepsilon) = \int_{-\infty}^{\infty} f_{v_\varepsilon}(\varepsilon_i) d\varepsilon_i \int_{-\infty}^{\alpha(\varepsilon_i)} f_{v_Z}(Z) dZ$$

where $f_v(x)$ is the density of the Student-t distribution with v degrees of freedom given in Equation 14.4, and

$$\alpha(\varepsilon_i) = \frac{C_i(T) - \sqrt{1 - \beta_i^2}\sqrt{\frac{v_\varepsilon - 2}{v_\varepsilon}}\varepsilon_i}{\beta_i\sqrt{\frac{v_Z - 2}{v_Z}}}.$$

Unfortunately, the calculation of the default threshold $C_i(T)$ is a very computationally expensive procedure since it involves a root search on the function $H(C_i(T); \beta_i, v_M, v_Z)$, and each evaluation of H requires calculation of a nested integration. The function $H(C_i(T); \beta_i, v_M, v_Z)$ is also dependent on the value of β_i, v_M and v_Z. This is very expensive when calibrating the model since it means that the thresholds have to be recalculated as the correlation parameters change.

Once we have the default thresholds $C_i(T)$, the conditional default probability of credit i is given by

$$p_i(T|Z) = t_{v_\varepsilon}\left(\frac{C_i(T) - \beta_i\sqrt{\frac{v_Z - 2}{v_Z}}Z}{\sqrt{1 - \beta_i^2}\sqrt{\frac{v_\varepsilon - 2}{v_\varepsilon}}}\right).$$

We then calculate the conditional loss distribution as described in Chapter 18. The unconditional loss distribution is calculated by integrating the conditional loss distribution over the Student-t distributed variable Z.

21.6.1 Calibration

We start our calibration by assuming a flat correlation matrix, i.e. $\beta_i = \beta = \sqrt{\rho}$. We then have three parameters for the calibration. They are v_Z, v_ε and ρ. We then attempt to fit the model to the market prices of the CDX NA IG tranches given in Table 20.1. We have done this and found the best fit shown in Table 21.1. We see that the fit is reasonably good across all of the tranches. We also computed the market compound correlation curve and compared it to the compound correlation implied by the calibrated Double-t model. This is shown in Figure 21.4. It is clear that this model produces a compound correlation smile.

Table 21.1 Calibration of the Double-t model to the market prices of CDX NA IG index tranche prices. The following parameters are used $v_Z = 7.0$, $v_\varepsilon = 2.5$ and $\rho = 15.0\%$

Tranche	Market		Double-t model	
	Upfront	Spread	Upfront	Spread
0–3	24.88	500.00	24.99	500.00
3–7		90.00		97.71
7–10		18.25		23.45
10–15		8.00		11.25
15–30		3.50		4.21

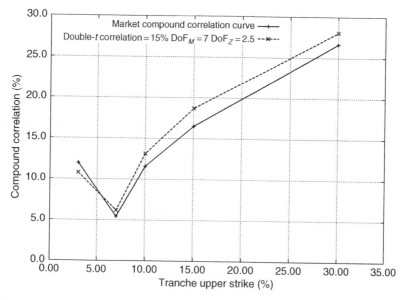

Figure 21.4 Compound correlation fit for the Double-t model. The parameters are $\rho = 15\%$, $\nu_Z = 7.0$ and $\nu_\varepsilon = 2.5$

To explain how this model is able to produce a smile it is necessary to explain the role of the different model parameters:

- Parameter ν_ε controls the width of the distribution of the idiosyncratic factor in A_i. The lower the value of ν_ε, the more likely it is that A_i is driven below $C_i(T)$ by an idiosyncratic default. Idiosyncratic default events hit the equity tranche and have little effect on mezzanine and more senior tranches. As a result, lowering ν_ε tends to make equity tranches riskier and so increases their spread.
- Parameter ν_Z controls the width of the distribution of the systemic factor in A_i. The lower the value of ν_Z, the more likely it is that when $A_i > C_i(T)$ or when $A_i \le C_i(T)$, it is a systemic event. Systemic events tend to increase the overall level of correlation and so affect the risk of the equity and the senior tranches. We find that lowering ν_Z makes senior tranches riskier and so increases their spread. It also makes the equity tranches safer. However, this can be offset by increasing the idiosyncratic risk by reducing ν_ε.
- The parameter ρ controls the 'background' or 'average' level of correlation.

This explains the parameters at the best fit which are $\nu_Z = 7.0$, $\nu_\varepsilon = 2.5$ and $\rho = 15.0\%$. Given a background correlation of 15%, we need to reduce the compound correlation of the equity tranche. We do this by increasing idiosyncratic risk which we do by reducing the value of ν_Z to 2.5. The correlation of $\rho = 15\%$ is also lower than the senior tranche base correlation. However, by reducing the value of ν_M to 7.0, we make large negative realisations of Z and therefore systemic defaults more likely, making senior tranches more risky. If we increase the equity spread and the senior spread, then the conservation of expected loss across the capital structure means that the mezzanine spread has to decrease.

The Double-t model can therefore produce a correlation skew. Furthermore, it gives us some insight into the sort of model needed to fit the correlation skew. It suggests that a model which fits the market skew must allow us to control the relative importance of idiosyncratic versus systemic risk. However, there are two problems with the Double-t model. First, we have only three parameters to play with and this is not enough to provide the required quality of fit. Second, the slow computational speed of the calibration of the default thresholds and the time taken to perform the integration over the Student-t density to calculate the unconditional loss distribution are both much more computationally expensive than in the Gaussian density. For both these reasons, this model is not widely used in practice, especially when we can find other models which can produce a better fit without these computational issues.

21.7   THE COMPOSITE BASKET MODEL

The composite basket model (CBM) by Tavares $et\ al.$ (2004) specifies that the default of each issuer in the reference portfolio of a tranche can occur in one of three different ways:

1. The issuer experiences an idiosyncratic shock which is modelled as the first jump of a Poisson process with a constant hazard rate or intensity λ_I. This shock causes the issuer to default. The probability of this shock arriving before time t is given by $1 - Q_I(t)$ where $Q_I(t) = \exp(-\lambda_I t)$.
2. The portfolio experiences a systemic shock in which all of the credits in the portfolio default. This is also modelled as the first jump of a Poisson process with a constant hazard rate or intensity λ_S. The probability of this shock arriving before time t is given by $1 - Q_S(t)$ where $Q_S(t) = \exp(-\lambda_S t)$.
3. Default of the issuer occurs before time t if the asset value A_i falls below the default threshold $C_i(t)$. The probability of the issuer surviving this risk to time t is given by $Q_C(t)$. $C_i(t)$ will be used to fit the marginal issuer default probabilities to the market CDS curves. The asset value is given by

$$A_i = \beta_i Z + \sqrt{1 - \beta_i^2}\, \varepsilon_i$$

and default occurs if $A_i \leq C_i(t)$. To calibrate this threshold, we solve for $C_i(t)$ such that

$$C_i(t) = \Phi^{-1}\left(1 - Q_C(t)\right).$$

Since all of these events are independent of one another, the unconditional survival probability is the product of all three individual survival probabilities. Given a time t survival probability for issuer i, which we denote with $Q_i(t)$, fitting the market implied CDS survival probability requires that

$$Q_i(t) = Q_I(t)Q_S(t)Q_C(t).$$

With this model, the spread can be expressed approximately as a linear sum of a systemic, idiosyncratic and copula spread, i.e.

$$S \simeq S_S + S_I + S_C.$$

To calibrate the default threshold in the Gaussian copula default channel we write

$$Q_C(t) = \frac{Q_i(t)}{Q_S(t)Q_I(t)} = 1 - \Phi(C_i(t)).$$

The copula default threshold is therefore given by

$$C_i(t) = \Phi^{-1}\left(1 - \frac{Q_i(t)}{Q_I(t)Q_S(t)}\right).$$

We can then invoke conditional independence. Conditioning on the value of the market factor Z and the systemic default event which we label with S, we have a conditional default probability for each credit given by

$$p_i(t|Z, S) = 1 - Q_I(t)\,\Pr(A_i > C_i(t)|Z, S)$$

which becomes

$$p_i(t|Z, S) = 1 - Q_I(t)\left(1 - \Phi\left(\frac{C_i(t) - \beta_i Z}{\sqrt{1 - \beta_i^2}}\right)\right).$$

We can then use this conditional default probability to construct the conditional loss distribution. Once we have the conditional loss distribution, we have to integrate over the market factor Z and the systemic event S. The first is simply the Gaussian density. In the case of the systemic factor, the distribution is bi-modal – either all of the portfolio defaults resulting in a probability weight of $1 - Q_S(t)$ at the maximum portfolio loss, or the systemic event does not occur with probability $Q_S(t)$.

21.7.1 Calibration

To calibrate this model, we first assumed that $\beta_i = \beta = \sqrt{\rho}$. We then calibrated this model to the market price of tranches given in Table 20.1 and found that the best fit for this pricing occurs when we set $\lambda_S = 0.049\%$, $\lambda_I = 0.20\%$ and $\rho = 13.09\%$. The best-fit spreads are shown in Table 21.2.

Table 21.2 Calibration of the composite basket model to the market prices of the CDX NA IG index tranches. The following parameters are used: $\lambda_S = 0.05\%$, $\lambda_I = 0.20\%$ and $\rho = 13.09\%$

Tranche	Market		CBM model	
	Upfront	Spread	Upfront	Spread
0–3	24.88	500.00	24.88	500.00
3–7		90.00		91.92
7–10		18.25		12.36
10–15		8.00		5.48
15–30		3.50		4.58

The quality of the fit is very good, especially for the equity and first mezzanine tranches. It also does reasonably well for the more senior tranches. The resulting compound correlation curve is shown in Figure 21.5. We make the following observations:

- The calibration implies that the annual probability of a systemic event is approximately 0.05%. This systemic shock plays a role in enabling the fitting of the senior tranches. Assuming a 40% recovery rate, it is equivalent to a systemic spread S_S of just 3 bp.
- To fit the equity tranche, we need to increase the idiosyncratic risk. This is achieved through an annualised idiosyncratic default probability of approximately 0.20%. Assuming a 40% recovery, this is equivalent to an idiosyncratic spread S_I of 12 bp.
- The Gaussian copula of 13.09% is greater than the mezzanine tranche compound correlation and below that of the more senior tranches. This risk accounts for the rest of the spread.

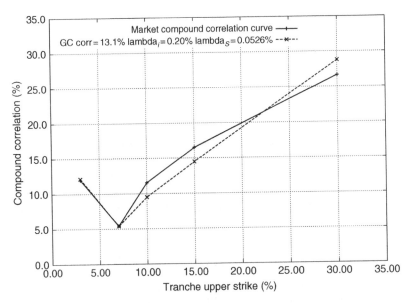

Figure 21.5   Compound correlation fit for the composite basket model to the market curve. We find a good fit for $\lambda_S = 0.05\%$, $\lambda_I = 0.20\%$ and $\rho = 13.09\%$

This model has a number of advantages over the Double-t model discussed previously. It is extremely simple to implement, especially as it is a simple extension of the Gaussian copula model. Computationally, it is almost as fast as the one-factor Gaussian latent variable copula model. The CBM model also manages a better fit that the Double-t model. One problem with the model is that it is not possible to calibrate to portfolios with inhomogeneous spreads in which the smallest credit spread is less than $S_S + S_I$. However, the main problem with the model in this form is that the market fit is still not good enough to use for production pricing.

21.8   THE MARSHALL–OLKIN COPULA

In the Marshall–Olkin copula, introduced in Section 14.6.3, we model M shocks as independent Poisson processes with intensities λ_m, $m = 1, \ldots, M$. Each shock can affect only a subset of the credits in the reference portfolio and this is controlled via a matrix of 0- or 1-valued indicator variables I_{im}. As a result, firm i will default as a result of a jump in the mth Poisson process if $I_{im} = 1$.

The advantage of the Marshall–Olkin copula is the potentially rich correlation structure and the large number of parameters which can be introduced.

Example   Consider, for example, a portfolio of $N = 6$ credits. We can apply different systemic shocks to different subsets of the credits in the portfolio using the following matrix

$$I_{im} = \begin{pmatrix} 1 & 1 & 0 & 1 & 0 & 0 & 0 & 0 & 0 \\ 1 & 1 & 0 & 0 & 1 & 0 & 0 & 0 & 0 \\ 1 & 1 & 0 & 0 & 0 & 1 & 0 & 0 & 0 \\ 1 & 0 & 1 & 0 & 0 & 0 & 1 & 0 & 0 \\ 1 & 0 & 1 & 0 & 0 & 0 & 0 & 1 & 0 \\ 1 & 0 & 1 & 0 & 0 & 0 & 0 & 0 & 1 \end{pmatrix}.$$

The first column represents shock $m = 1$ and since all of the elements of the column equal 1, this shock is seen by all $N = 6$ credits. It is a systemic shock. The second shock in the second column, $m = 2$, is seen by credits 1, 2 and 3. The third shock $m = 3$ is seen by credits 4, 5 and 6. Clearly, we can use shocks 2 and 3 to create two sectors, one consisting of credits 1, 2 and 3, and the other consisting of 4, 5 and 6. The last six shocks are pure idiosyncratic shocks which affect only one credit each.

The Marshall–Olkin copula is very similar to the CBM model with the difference being that the only shocks in the CBM model are systemic or idiosyncratic. However, in the CBM model, a Gaussian copula default mechanism has been added which can be tuned between purely idiosyncratic and purely systemic by varying the correlation parameter. Also, since the correlation skew pricing tells us only the portfolio-wide correlation and nothing about the correlations between the groups of credits in the portfolio, we do not have the information needed to calibrate the Marshall–Olkin copula and to exploit its full power. For this reason, and the reason that the CBM model embeds a Marshall–Olkin model, we do not discuss this model in detail.

21.9   THE MIXING COPULA

The mixing copula model captures the correlation skew by introducing uncertainty into the correlation. Specifically, in this model, the current market price of tranches is viewed as a probability weighted average over a finite number $n = 1, \ldots, N_S$ of correlation states. Each state is denoted by a state variable ξ which takes integer values $1, 2, \ldots, N_S$, and modelled using a Gaussian copula model. Within this model, the expected loss of a tranche can be computed by averaging over the N_S states

$$\mathbb{E}\left[\min\left(L(T), K\right)\right] = \sum_{n=1}^{N_S} \Pr\left(\xi = n\right) \mathbb{E}\left[\min\left(L(T), K\right) \mid \xi = n\right]$$

where $\Pr(\xi = n)$ is the probability of state n. The sum of the state probabilities obeys the following constraint

$$\sum_{n=1}^{N_S} \Pr(\xi = n) = 1.$$

We therefore have $2N_S - 1$ free parameters consisting of N_S correlation values and $N_S - 1$ probabilities (this includes the constraint on the probabilities).

Since it is only the correlation which changes in each state, the marginals, i.e. the issuer survival curves do not change for different states. This means that the expected loss in each state is the portfolio expected loss. It also means that default thresholds are the same in each state, providing a useful computational efficiency.

21.9.1 Calibration

Let us consider the case of $N_S = 3$, i.e. we have three correlation states. This is shown in Figure 21.6. To minimise the number of calibration variables, we set the correlation of state $\xi = 1$ to 0% and that of state $\xi = 3$–100%. Note that in these two correlation limits the calculation of the loss distribution is independent of Z, avoiding the need to integrate over Z. This means that we have only one free correlation parameter $\rho(\xi = 2)$ and two state probabilities, $\Pr(\xi = 1)$ and $\Pr(\xi = 2)$. We therefore have a total of three parameters to play with.

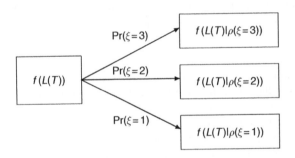

Figure 21.6 Mixing model with three states

We performed a three-dimensional minimisation to find a fit to the market prices of CDX NA IG Series 7 and the results are shown in Table 21.3 with the resulting correlation smile in Figure 21.7. We see that the quality of the fit is extremely good, with the largest error occurring

Table 21.3 Calibration of the mixing model to tranche prices. The following parameters are used: $\Pr(\xi = 1) = 48.52\%$, $\Pr(\xi = 2) = 43.85\%$ with $\rho(\xi = 2) = 14.63\%$

Tranche	Market prices		Mixing model fit	
	Upfront	Spread	Upfront	Spread
0–3	24.88	500.00	24.88	500.00
3–7		90.00		90.25
7–10		18.25		18.25
10–15		8.00		5.97
15–30		3.50		2.38

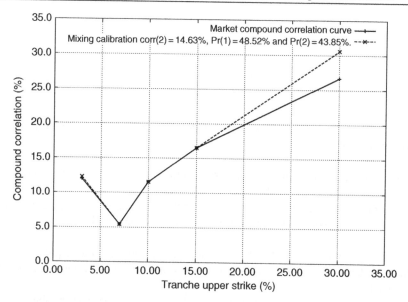

Figure 21.7 Compound correlation fit for the mixing model to the market curve. We find a good fit for $\rho(2) = 14.63\%$, $\Pr(1) = 48.52\%$ and $\Pr(2) = 43.85\%$

for the most senior tranches. We also find similar results for iTraxx Europe. Both suggest that the parameters of the model are individually well tuned to the different parts of the capital structure. We make the following observations:

- The 0% correlation state has a probability of 48.52%. This is the most idiosyncratic state and is used to fit the equity tranche.
- The 100% correlation state has a probability of 7.63%. It is used to fit the senior spread and in this model performs a similar function to the systemic event in the CBM model.
- The intermediate state has a correlation of 14.63%. This is also similar to the Gaussian copula correlation found in the CBM.

The mixing model has a number of advantages. It is fast, easy to calibrate and fits the market prices better than both the Double-t model and the CBM. Despite these strengths, the model is not able to fit the senior tranches with enough accuracy to recommend it. Finally, we note that this model is closely related to the stochastic correlation model by Burtschell *et al.* (2005).

21.10   THE RANDOM FACTOR LOADING MODEL

The random factor loading (RFL) model by Andersen and Sidenius (2004) is a one-factor latent variable model in which there is a weighting on the systemic factor which is a deterministic function of the random market factor Z. Specifically, we have

$$A_i = a_i(Z)Z + b_i\varepsilon_i + m_i$$

where Z and ε_i are independent Gaussian random variables with mean zero and unit variance. The function $a_i(Z)$ is the factor loading function. The coefficients b_i and coefficient m_i are used to enforce a mean of zero and a unit variance on A_i, i.e.

$$\mathbb{E}\left[A_i\right] = 0 \Rightarrow m_i = -\mathbb{E}\left[a_i(Z)Z\right]$$

and

$$b_i = \sqrt{1 - \mathbb{V}[a_i(Z)Z]}$$
$$= \sqrt{1 - \mathbb{E}\left[a_i(Z)^2 Z^2\right] + m_i^2}.$$

By weighting Z by a factor weight $a(Z)$, the random factor loading model has a correlation which is a function of Z. There are two effects:

- If the function $a_i(Z) > 0$ and increasing in Z, then the correlation between credits increases in *good* states of the world, and decreases in *bad* states of the world.
- If the function $a_i(Z) > 0$ and decreasing in Z, then the correlation between credits decreases in *good* states of the world, and increases in *bad* states of the world.

Generating a skew involves a combination of lowering the correlation for equity tranches and raising the correlation for senior tranches. The question is therefore whether random factor weights can achieve this.

To cast this model into a conditionally independent framework, we need to be able to calculate the conditional default probability for each credit. This is given by

$$\Pr\left(A_i \le C_i(T)|Z\right) = \Phi\left(\frac{C_i(T) - a_i(Z)Z - m_i}{b_i}\right)$$

where $C_i(T)$ is the default threshold, determined by solving the following equation for the unconditional default probability

$$\Pr\left(A_i \le C_i(T)\right) = \int_{-\infty}^{\infty} \Pr\left(A_i \le C_i(T)|Z\right)\phi(Z)dZ$$
$$= \int_{-\infty}^{\infty} \Phi\left(\frac{C_i(T) - a_i(Z)Z - m_i}{b_i}\right)\phi(Z)dZ.$$

To proceed further with this model, we need to specify a form for the factor loading function $a_i(x)$; the main constraint on the form of the function $a_i(x)$ is that the variance of A_i must be defined. Mathematically this requires that

$$\mathbb{E}\left[a_i(Z)^2 Z^2\right] \le 1 - m_i^2.$$

There are many possible parametrisations for the function $a_i(Z)$. Perhaps the simplest is to allow it to be a single-step function with a step at $Z = \Theta_i$, i.e. we have

$$a_i(Z) = \begin{cases} \alpha_i & \text{for } Z \le \Theta_i \\ \beta_i & \text{for } Z > \Theta_i. \end{cases}$$

This is shown in Figure 21.8. After some mathematics, we can show that this implies

$$m_i = -\mathbb{E}[a_i(Z)Z] = (\alpha_i - \beta_i)\,\phi(\Theta_i)$$

and

$$b_i^2 = 1 - \alpha_i^2\left(\Phi(\Theta_i) - \Theta_i\phi(\Theta_i)\right) - \beta_i^2\left(1 - \Phi(\Theta_i) + \Theta_i\phi(\Theta_i)\right) + m_i^2$$

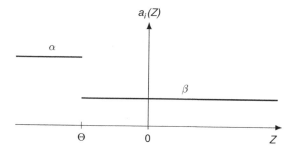

Figure 21.8   Single-step factor loading function $a_i(Z)$

where

$$\phi(x) = \frac{e^{-x^2/2}}{\sqrt{2\pi}}.$$

In this case, the default threshold is determined by solving

$$\Pr(A_i \le C_i(T)) = \int_{-\infty}^{\Theta_i} \Phi\left(\frac{C_i(T) - \alpha_i Z - m_i}{b_i}\right)\phi(Z)dZ$$
$$+ \int_{\Theta_i}^{\infty} \Phi\left(\frac{C_i(T) - \beta_i Z - m_i}{b_i}\right)\phi(Z)dZ$$

which can be re-expressed in terms of bi-variate normal distributions to give

$$\Pr(A_i \le C_i(T)) = \Phi_2\left(\frac{C_i(T) - m_i}{\sqrt{\alpha_i^2 + b_i^2}}, \Theta_i; \frac{\alpha_i}{\sqrt{\alpha_i^2 + b_i^2}}\right) + \Phi\left(\frac{C_i(T) - m_i}{\sqrt{b_i^2 + \beta_i^2}}\right)$$
$$- \Phi_2\left(\frac{C_i(T) - m_i}{\sqrt{\beta_i^2 + b_i^2}}, \Theta_i; \frac{\beta_i}{\sqrt{\beta_i^2 + b_i^2}}\right).$$

21.10.1   Calibration

For the purpose of simplifying the calibration, we assume that the factor loading parameters are homogeneous across the portfolio, i.e. $\alpha_i = \alpha$, $\beta_i = \beta$, and $\Theta_i = \Theta$.

This means that we have three parameters to play with. There is a constraint on α, β and Θ which is that $b_i^2 > 0$. As a reference point, we note that the Gaussian copula with correlation ρ is returned when we set $\alpha = \beta = \sqrt{\rho}$. Once again we attempt to fit the market prices of the CDX NA IG Series 7 tranches. The calibration results are shown in Table 21.4 and Figure 21.9. While the fit is good for the equity and senior tranches, it is not very good for the junior mezzanine tranche. We make the following observations:

- We see that $\alpha > \beta$, implying a higher correlation in *bad* states of the world, i.e. when $Z < -2.58$.
- When $Z \ll 0$, losses are likely to be affecting the senior tranche. We see that the effective correlation is then $\alpha^2 \simeq 30\%$, consistent with the compound correlation of the senior tranche.

- In the regime of $Z \gg 0$, any losses will tend to affect the equity tranche. In this regime the effective correlation between the credits is $\beta^2 \simeq 10\%$. This low correlation provides the idiosyncratic risk needed to fit the equity tranche. It is close to the compound correlation of the equity tranche.

Table 21.4 Calibration of the random factor loading model to tranche prices. The following parameters are used: $\alpha = 54.25\%$, $\beta = 31.16\%$ and $\Theta = -2.58$

Tranche	Market prices		RFL model fit	
	Upfront	Spread	Upfront	Spread
0–3	24.88	500.00	24.88	500.00
3–7		90.00		123.04
7–10		18.25		15.99
10–15		8.00		9.17
15–30		3.50		4.26

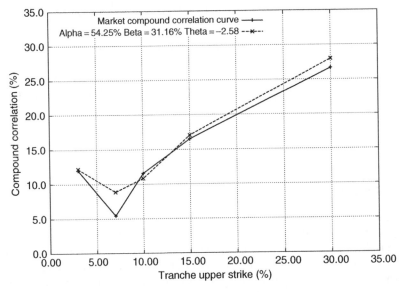

Figure 21.9 Compound correlation fit for the RFL model to the market curve. The best-fit parameters are $\alpha = 54.25\%$, $\beta = 31.16\%$ and $\Theta = -2.58$

According to Andersen and Sidenius (2004), the quality of the market fit improves significantly when an additional step is added to the factor loading function $a_i(Z)$, thereby allowing three different values for the factor loading. Numerically, this means adding another partition to the integral over Z and the effect of this on computation time should be small.

21.11   THE IMPLIED COPULA

The implied copula approach by Hull and White (2006) performs an exact fit to the market price of index tranches using a non-parametric fit to the distribution of the conditional hazard rates. Conditional hazard rates were discussed in Section 13.3.2 where it was shown that the distribution of conditional hazard rates is linked to the dependency structure of the credits in the portfolio.

We begin by defining a non-specific, single-factor, latent variable model of the form

$$A_i = \beta Z + \sqrt{1 - \beta^2}\varepsilon_i$$

where Z and ε_i are independent random variables with mean zero and a standard deviation of one. We denote the cumulative distribution function of ε_i with $H_i(x)$. The cumulative distribution function of A_i is given by $F_i(x)$. Conditional on Z, the survival probability of credit i from time zero to time T is given by

$$Q_i(T|Z) = 1 - H_i\left(\frac{F_i^{-1}(1 - Q_i(T)) - \beta_i Z}{\sqrt{1 - \beta_i^2}}\right). \tag{21.3}$$

We can also write the conditional survival probability in terms of the conditional hazard rates as follows

$$Q_i(T|Z) = \exp\left(-\int_0^T \lambda_i(s|Z)ds\right).$$

From this, we can write $\lambda(T|Z)$ as an explicit function of the conditional survival probability, i.e.

$$\lambda_i(T|Z) = -\frac{1}{dT}\frac{dQ_i(T|Z)}{Q_i(T|Z)}. \tag{21.4}$$

Together, these equations show that each conditional survival probability given by a copula model via Equation 21.3 maps to a conditional hazard rate via Equation 21.4. From Sklar's theorem there must be a copula for every distribution of $\lambda_i(T|Z)$. This implies that we can characterise a default-time copula in terms of the probability density function it implies for the conditional hazard rates. Indeed, we can circumvent the whole need to motivate the model as a latent variable model, and simply *model the copula by specifying the distribution of conditional hazard rates*.

21.11.1   Calibration

The calibration strategy of the implied copula model is that we create a non-parametric distribution for the conditional hazard rates which allows us to refit the market prices of the index tranches. We start by assuming that the conditional hazard rates have a flat term structure, and are the same for all credits in the reference portfolio. We then define a non-parametric distribution for the conditional hazard rate by defining K scenarios in which we denote the corresponding conditional hazard rate with λ_k where $k = 1, \ldots, K$. Each value of λ_k occurs with a probability π_k. Fitting the market is then a process of specifying the values $\lambda_1, \ldots, \lambda_K$, and then the corresponding probability weights $\pi_1, \ldots, \pi_K$ to assign to each.

Calibration involves fitting the market prices of the $m = 1, \ldots, M - 1$ tranches plus the CDS index reference portfolio which we represent as the Mth tranche. The price of tranche m is a weighted sum over the hazard rate scenarios, i.e.

$$V_m = \sum_{k=1}^{K} \pi_k V_m(\lambda_k).$$

Mathematically, the challenge is to solve the M equations

$$\sum_{k=1}^{K} \pi_k V_m(\lambda_k) = 0 \quad \text{for all } m = 1, \ldots, M \tag{21.5}$$

where $V_m(\lambda_k)$ is the value of tranche m in scenario k. Given each index tranche is a new on-market tranche, its mark-to-market value should be zero. There is also the normalisation constraint on the probabilities

$$\sum_{k=1}^{K} \pi_k = 1 \quad \text{with } \pi_k \geq 0. \tag{21.6}$$

Since the values of π_k are probabilities and must lie in the range $[0, 1]$, this system of equations is non-linear and a solution is not guaranteed for $K = M + 1$, the case in which the number of linear equations equals the number of probabilities. To ensure a solution in which $0 \leq \pi_k \leq 1$ we typically need to choose K scenarios where $K > M + 1$.

There are a number of ways to generate the conditional default scenarios. For example, the scenarios could simply be values of λ_k which are equally spaced in the range $[0, \lambda_K]$ where λ_K is some maximum value. Hull and White (2006) chose values of λ_k for which the sum of tranche values are equally spaced between their minimum and maximum values.

The non-parametric nature of this model means that it should be able to fit the market exactly. In fact, one of the problems we have to face with this model is that there are often multiple distributions for $\lambda(T|Z)$ which fit the market. One criteria for selecting just one solution is to choose the one which generates the smoothest density distribution for the vector of hazard rate probabilities π_k. The smoothness of the distribution can be characterised by the second derivative. If we minimise the absolute value of the second derivative across the distribution then we effectively penalise discontinuities and slope changes in the density function. In practice, this can be done by calculating the numerical second derivative of π_k as a function of λ_k, taking the square to ensure positivity and then summing across the density. We therefore wish to find the vector π which minimises the objective function

$$\hat{O}(\pi) = \sum_{m=1}^{M} V_m^2 + c \sum_{k=2}^{K-1} \frac{(\pi_{k+1} - 2\pi_k + \pi_{k-1})^2}{\lambda_{k+1} - \lambda_{k-1}}$$

while satisfying all the probability constraints in Equation 21.6. The coefficient c is used to tune the relative importance of fitting the prices of the tranches versus smoothness of the conditional hazard rate probability distribution.[2]

We have performed a fitting exercise to the CDX NA IG Series 7 tranches for various values of c. To do so, we used $K = 101$ hazard rate values from 0 to 9.5% with a 0.10% spacing, and with extra points at 20%, 30%, 40% and 100%. Figure 21.10 shows the resulting hazard rate distributions. All fitted the market prices exactly. In all cases, we found that the

---

[2] In Hull and White (2006), the authors also suggest some other optimisation strategies.

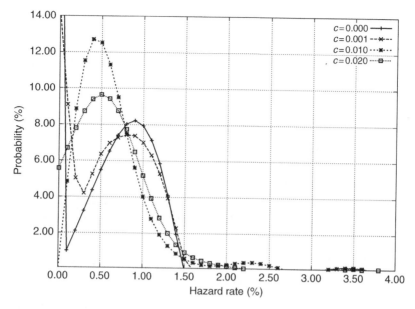

Figure 21.10 Conditional hazard rate distributions which fit CDX NA IG Series 7 tranches for four values of the smoothness parameter c ranging from $c = 0$ to $c = 0.02$

optimiser seeks to put a small probability weight of about 0.16% on the largest hazard rate of 100%. Although they all fit the market prices exactly, we would expect them to differ in terms of their risk sensitivities.

21.12   COPULA COMPARISON

It is important to understand the impact of the choice of copula on both pricing and risk. To understand the pricing effect of the copula, we have calculated the breakeven spreads for 1% wide tranchelets with lower strikes from 0% to 59% for the mixing, the Double-t, the CBM, the RFL and the implied copula models. These are shown in Figure 21.11.

The first point to note is that all the curves are monotonically decreasing or flat. There are no arbitrages in any of them. This is the strength of a proper no-arbitrage model. As these models do not fit the market equally well, the precise differences in the shapes of the tranchelet curves are not solely due to model differences but also reflect fitting differences. However, we expect that the overall shape is model determined.

First, the mixing model, the CBM model and the implied copula tranchelet spreads are similarly behaved, with both falling smoothly and then flattening above the 20% strike at a non-zero spread. This can be explained by the 100% correlation state of the mixing model, the systemic shock in the CBM model, and the very high default rate scenario in the implied copula model. All have the effect of assigning a small but important probability mass on the maximum portfolio loss of 60%.

The tranchelet spreads in the Double-t copula model do not flatten out but instead fall slowly to zero at the maximum loss. This reflects the very long tailed shape of the Double-t copula loss distribution and the lack of a probability mass on the maximum loss. The RFL model

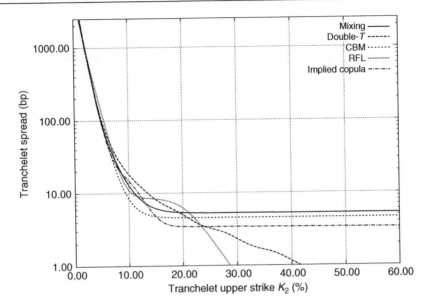

Figure 21.11 Tranchelet spread curves (plotted on a logarithmic scale) for the mixing, Double-t, CBM, RFL and implied copula models. We use the best-fit calibration parameters for the fit to CDX NA IG Series 7 discussed earlier

is similar to the Double-t copula in that tranchelet spreads fall to zero. However, the rate at which the spreads fall to zero is even greater than the Double-t copula. It remains to be seen whether a two-step RFL model which should better fit the market would have a shape closer to the Double-t.

The second comparison for the models is the leverage factor they produce for each tranche. To calculate the leverage factor, we bump all of the issuer spreads by 1 bp and then calculate the resulting change in tranche value. This is then divided by the change in the value of the underlying index portfolio. This procedure is not possible in the implied copula model because the calibration to the underlying reference portfolio is performed jointly with that of the tranches. An alternative approach to the calculation of systemic risk is to simply increase the unconditional hazard rate. We write

$$\lambda = \sum_{k=1}^{K} \pi_k \lambda_k.$$

To bump the index spread by approximately 1 bp, we let

$$\lambda_k \to \lambda_k + \frac{0.01\%}{(1-R)}$$

for all $k = 1, \ldots, K$ holding the values of π_k fixed. We then calculate the change in the tranche values and divide that by the change in the value of the index. We will find that the index spread has increased by about 1 bp and that the values of the tranches have changed.

Table 21.5 shows that the implied copula, mixing and CBM models have the highest equity leverage but the lowest senior leverage. For comparison, we show the equivalent base correlation leverage ratios.

Table 21.5 Comparison of tranche leverage ratios for the different copula models calibrated to the CDX NA IG market prices in Table 20.1. We also show the base correlation leverage ratios for comparison

Tranche	Mixing	CBM	RFL	Double-t	Implied	Base corr.
0–3	26.965	25.164	24.402	22.828	30.367	23.034
3–7	5.865	7.726	7.731	6.665	4.261	5.447
7–10	1.165	1.099	0.944	1.755	0.287	1.377
10–15	0.336	0.160	0.080	0.818	0.145	0.636
15–30	0.026	0.004	0.163	0.270	0.001	0.247

21.13   PRICING BESPOKES

The focus until this point has been finding a copula model which has the flexibility to fit the market prices of the standard index tranches. Because of the arbitrage-free copula nature of these models, they all produce a coherent loss distribution which can be used to price any tranche on the same reference portfolio. The next step is to seek to apply these models to the pricing of tranches on reference portfolios which are not one of the standard indices.

For single-region bespoke portfolios we may reasonably decide to apply the model parameters from the nearest corresponding index, e.g. for a European investment grade index we use the calibration parameters from the iTraxx Europe index. For all of the models described except the implied copula, the different spread of the bespoke portfolio relative to the index will be handled automatically by the model parameters which are held fixed – only the default thresholds change. In the case of the implied copula, Hull and White (2006) suggest that bespoke portfolios with a different average spread can be handled by scaling the conditional hazard rates by some common factor γ so that we have $\lambda_k^* = \gamma \lambda_k$.

We now turn to the more tricky problem of mixed-region bespokes. We suppose that we wish to price tranches on a combined portfolio of CDX NA IG and iTraxx Europe. Without a standard and liquid mixed-region portfolio there is no market guidance on where mixed region tranches should price. As a result, pricing mixed-region bespokes is necessarily *ad hoc*. One simple approach is to interpolate between the different regional calibrations. For example, we could choose to value the mixed region bespoke using first the CDX parameters, then the iTraxx parameters, and then take some average of the two values based on the relative percentage of European versus North American credits. Other approaches involve modelling the mixed-region reference by applying the different regional calibration parameters to the corresponding credits. Some models make this easier than others. For example, the RFL model naturally extends to bespoke portfolios as it allows us to apply model parameters at a single-asset level.

21.14   SUMMARY

We have set out in detail the main copula models which have been used. We have explained their theory, implementation, pricing and risk. We conclude by noting that we have only covered a subset of the known copula skew models. However, we consider these copulae to be the most representative.

However, one important issue which has not been addressed is the ability of copula models to fit a term structure of tranche prices. With the development of liquid tranches at seven and 10-year maturities, it is important for our correlation model to fit the entire term structure. This poses a problem for copula models. Either we need a copula with many more parameters, or we need to make the copula parameters time dependent. The former approach is possible, but technically and computationally difficult. The latter approach has the problem that making the copula parameters time dependent can break the arbitrage-free property of copula models in the time dimension. For this reason and also because of the nature of many of the next generation correlation products, correlation modelling is beginning to focus on more dynamic models of default correlation of the type discussed in Chapters 23 and 24.

22
Advanced Multi-name Credit Derivatives

22.1 INTRODUCTION

This chapter discusses some of the other multi-name products that exist. Some are extensions to the STCDO discussed earlier: These include the CDO-squared, tranchelets and leveraged supersenior. We also discuss two more recent product innovations which involve the dynamic trading of the CDS indices, namely the credit CPPI and the CPDO. All of the products discussed in this chapter have in common the use of a leveraged exposure, typically to one or more of the standard indices such as CDX or iTraxx. We discuss how these products work, what their risks are, and, where appropriate, we describe how to value them using a pricing model.

22.2 CREDIT CPPI

Investors who assume leverage often like to limit their losses by requiring that their principal be protected. For example, an investor with a bullish view on the long-term performance of the stock market may decide to buy a product which combines a high credit quality zero coupon bond with a call option. If the trade has a five-year horizon, and assuming the five-year zero rate for the bond is around 5%, this bond will cost about $78 for every $100 face value. The remaining $22 can then be used to buy a call option on the stock market. Depending on the strike level of the option and the implied market volatility, the investor may be able to have a participation in the stock market which is equivalent to investing two to three times their initial investment of $100. The investor therefore gets a leveraged participation in the stock market, comfortable in the knowledge that in the worst-case scenario they will get back their initial investment of $100 after five years. In this worst-case scenario, what is lost is the interest that would have accrued on a $100 investment in a 5Y risk-free bond.

Such option-based strategies only work when there is a liquid market for long-dated options. This is because the seller of the option needs to hedge the volatility sensitivity of the position by dynamically trading other long-dated options. However, when there is no long-dated volatility market, this approach is not possible. However, there is an alternative approach to producing a very similar payoff profile. It is called CPPI.

CPPI stands for constant proportion portfolio insurance and is a generic dynamic portfolio management methodology developed by Black and Jones (1987). CPPI is designed to allow an investor to participate in the performance of a stock or index while imposing a limit on the downside losses. Its advantage is that while it requires a liquid underlying index, it does not require the existence of a long-dated volatility market. As a result, with the advent of the liquid CDS indices, credit-based CPPI strategies have become possible.

22.2.1 Mechanics

We assume that the underlying asset in the CPPI is a short protection position in one or more of the liquid CDS indices. However, we also note that the beauty of the CPPI approach is that the choice of underlying is very flexible. It could, for example, be a trade which starts with an exposure to a 5Y index and it could also be a more complicated strategy involving a curve steepener, e.g. sell the 10Y index and buy the 5Y index. In some cases, CPPI structures have been issued with STCDOs as the underlying asset. This flexibility is one of the reason why so many different CPPI structures exist. All that is required is that the underlying asset be liquid.

As well as defining the underlying asset, the maturity date of the trade must be specified. This can typically range from five to 10 years. We also need to define the *constant proportion*, L, also known as the *multiplier* or *gearing factor* of the CPPI. Assuming a CPPI trade with a notional of $100, at trade initiation, the steps are as follows:

1. At trade initiation time $t = 0$, the investor pays $100 to the issuer of the CPPI note.
2. This $100 is paid into a deposit account where it earns interest at some short-term deposit rate, e.g. one month Libor. We denote the value of this account at time 0 as $D(0)$.
3. The issuer calculates the initial value $Z(0, T)$ of a zero coupon bond with a final maturity time T equal to that of the CPPI trade. If $y(0, T)$ is the time zero T-maturity risk-free zero coupon discount rate then $Z(0, T) = \exp(-y(0, T) T)$. This value is known as the *bond floor* and represents the cash required to buy a risk-free zero coupon bond which pays $100 at time T.
4. The issuer calculates the initial value of the *reserve*. This is the total value of the CPPI note minus the value of the bond floor. It is given by $R(0) = D(0) - \$100 \times Z(0, T)$. If the 5-year Libor zero rate equals 5% then $Z(0, 5) = 0.7788$ and $R(0) = \$22.12$.
5. The issuer now calculates the size of the initial investment in the index. This is a function of the constant proportion L. For example, $L = 20$ means that the CPPI assumes an exposure to the underlying index equivalent to 20 times the reserve, i.e. $\$22.12 \times 20 = \$442.4$. This corresponds to a leverage of 4.42 on the initial investment of $100. The cash in the deposit account is used as collateral on the unfunded investments in the index.

Following trade initiation, the value of the underlying asset in the CPPI, which we assume is a short protection position in a CDS index, moves due to a combination of:

- Spread movements on the index.
- Coupon income received on index premium payment dates which has been rolled up.
- Losses due to any defaults in the index portfolio.
- Interest rate movements, although the interest rate sensitivity of the index is typically small.

These changes in value cause the rebalancing mechanism of the CPPI structure to come into action. This typically occurs frequently, often daily. Since the idea behind CPPI is that the constant proportion is constant, the issuer needs to rebalance the credit index to ensure that this is the case. Assuming that the previous rebalancing occurred at time t_1, and we are now at time t_2, we have the following rebalancing procedure:

1. The index value per dollar of face value equals $V(t_2)$ and the credit portfolio is now worth $L \cdot R(t_1) \cdot V(t_2)$. Coupons received, index upfront payments and any default losses on the

index are transferred into and out of the deposit account which has value $D(t_2)$. Recall that the deposit account is also growing at Libor.

2. In order to maintain the constant proportion, the issuer needs to recalculate the reserve and adjust the size of the credit index exposure. The new value of the reserve is given by $R(t_2) = D(t_2) - Z(t_2, T) + L \cdot R(t_1) \cdot V(t_2)$.

3. If $R(t_2) \leq K$, where K is a predefined trigger level, the entire trade is deleveraged by unwinding the credit portfolio and the proceeds are used to buy a risk-free zero coupon bond which matures at par at time T.

4. If $R(t_2) > K$, the issuer simply needs to rebalance the notional of the credit index to $L \cdot R(t_2)$. This means buying a notional amount $L \cdot (R(t_2) - R(t_1))$ of the index. Depending on the change in the index value this can be a leverage or deleverage. The portfolio leverage of the CPPI is given by

$$\text{Portfolio leverage}(t_2) = \frac{L \cdot R(t_2)}{\text{NAV}(t_2)}$$

where the net asset value (NAV) of the note is given by $\text{NAV}(t_2) = D(t_2) + V(t_2)$. In practice, an upper bound may be imposed on the value of L in order to cap the *gap risk* of the trade. This is discussed below.

5. The issuer then sets $t_1 = t_2$ and waits until time $t_2 = t_2 + \Delta T$ where ΔT is the time between portfolio rebalancings. If $t_2 < T$ we return to step (2). Otherwise, the CPPI, consisting of the deposit account and credit portfolio, is unwound and the proceeds are paid to the investor.

In its simplest form described here, no cash flows are paid to the investor in the credit CPPI during the life of the trade. All coupon payments from the credit portfolio plus mark-to-market changes are held within the structure and are rolled up until the maturity date. However, in practice many of the variations on this strategy do pay a running coupon.

One of the criticisms of the CPPI strategy is that it buys in a rising market and sells in a falling market. For this reason, the CPPI approach does not perform well in volatile markets. It generally performs better when the market is directional.

22.2.2   Pricing and Gap Risk

A CPPI is a dynamic trading strategy in which all of the payments to the investor are replicated exactly by the issuer who simply follows the CPPI rebalancing strategy. As a result, the issuer simply passes through the cash payments from the CPPI strategy. In a sense we may think that the issuer has a perfect hedge and it may not seem necessary to build a pricing model. However, this hedge is not truly perfect and the issuer does retain a *gap risk* and a model is needed to quantify this.

Gap risk is the risk that the asset, in this case a credit portfolio, loses value so quickly that the issuer of the structure is unable to sell the underlying asset as soon as the reserve account value $R(t)$ falls below its trigger K, and ultimately is only able to close it out at a negative value, i.e. $R(t) < 0$. The consequence is that there will not be enough cash left in the structure to purchase the zero coupon bond required to guarantee the payment of par at the specified maturity. Since the CPPI mechanism guarantees the repayment of the principal to the investor, this risk is 'owned' by the issuer.

This inability to unwind the position at the threshold level could be a result of a sudden spread widening. It could be further compounded by a liquidity crisis. For this reason, most

CPPI issuers build a risk model to assess this risk at a single deal level and to aggregate this risk across the entire book of CPPI trades. The gap risk of a CPPI depends on:

- The volatility of the underlying index and its tendency to exhibit sudden shocks.
- The value of the constant proportion L: The larger the value of L, the greater the impact of any sudden widening in the index on the value of the credit portfolio. This explains why an upper bound is imposed on the portfolio leverage.
- The distance of the NAV from the bond floor: Clearly as a deal approaches maturity, the bond floor will pull to par and the distance of the NAV from the bond floor will decrease.
- The distance of any deleveraging trigger from the bond floor: Deleveraging the trade when the reserve falls below 5% is safer than waiting until the reserve falls to zero. However, setting the threshold too high may cause the deal to deleverage unnecessarily.
- The frequency of rebalancing: The longer the period between rebalancing, the longer it will take before the manager can react to a decline in the market by reducing leverage. However, the more frequent the rebalancing, the greater the transaction costs.
- The liquidity of the market: A loss of liquidity in the market may impair the ability of the note issuer to sell the underlying asset. This can be modelled by imposing some time delay on the unwind of the structure.

Models for analysing gap risk are usually based on a Monte Carlo simulation of the index spread. The process for the index spread typically involves a Cox process for each of the underlying credits. This normally incorporates jumps and also captures the risk of default. As the gap risk is not usually hedgeable using other market instruments, calibration of the model is typically done within the *real-world measure* by looking at historical data. In return for assuming this gap risk, the dealer will usually embed some cost within the CPPI structure.

A simulation is also used to estimate the transaction costs associated with managing the CPPI. These costs are a function of the bid–offer spread of the underlying index, the frequency of rebalancing the portfolio, and the volatility of the underlying. For example, many deals attempt to reduce transaction costs by only requiring rebalancing if the value of the reserve has changed by more than a certain amount. These costs are then factored into the pricing of the CPPI note.

22.3   CONSTANT PROPORTION DEBT OBLIGATIONS

Constant proportion debt obligations (CPDOs) have been one of the most recent innovations in the credit markets. In common with CPPI structures, they provide a dynamically managed leveraged exposure to one or more credit indices. However, while the purpose of the CPPI strategy is to protect the investor's principal, the aim of the CPDO structure is to pay the investor a high coupon until maturity and then redeem at par. Just as with a credit risky bond, neither the coupons nor the principal payment are guaranteed and so the investor can lose some or all of their initial investment.

The first CPDO products were issued in late 2006 and were made famous by their ability to pay a coupon of Libor plus 200 bp and achieve a AAA rating on both coupons and principal. However these high ratings have been revised down since then as some of the assumptions underlying the rating models have been tightened. Furthermore, the volatile credit market environment of 2007–8 has significantly reduced the issuance of CPDOs especially as it has highlighted the weaknesses of some of the early CPDO structures. Despite this, we discuss the CPDO because it employs a novel dynamic rebalancing mechanism which takes advantage of the particular dynamics of credit spreads.

The investment strategy used in a CPDO is one in which the *leverage increases when the CDS index value falls*, and *falls when the CDS index value rises*. This strategy, which may appear counter-intuitive, is based on the assumption that index spreads are mean reverting and that the coupon income or 'carry' received from the leveraged position in the index over the life of the trade will more than cover any losses due to defaults and spread widenings. Later in this section we will analyse the performance of this trading strategy.

22.3.1 Mechanics

The aim of the CPDO structure is to grow its net asset value (NAV) to a 'target value' (TV). The target value is the amount of money needed to guarantee all of the remaining scheduled cash flows. It is the present value of all remaining coupons, principal and fees discounted on the risk-free Libor curve. At initiation of a $100 investment in a CPDO, the steps are as follows:

1. The investor pays $100 to the issuer of the CPDO.
2. This issuer invests the $100 in a deposit account at some short-term rate, e.g. three month Libor. This cash is to be used as collateral for the leveraged investments undertaken within the CPDO structure. The value of the deposit account at time t is $D(t)$.
3. The CPDO takes a leveraged index exposure to a credit index. We denote the notional of the index portfolio position at time t with $N(t)$ and the coupon of the *on-the-run* index with $C(t)$. The value of $N(t)$ is given by

$$N(t) = \min\left[U, \frac{TV(t) - NAV(t) + B}{PV01(t, T) \cdot C(t)}\right] \tag{22.1}$$

where

- $TV(t)$ is the target value.
- U is an upper limit on the amount of leverage.
- $PV01(t, T)$ is the time t value of a 1 dollar Libor annuity to maturity time T.
- $NAV(t) = D(t) + V(t)$.
- $V(t)$ is the value of the index portfolio.
- B is a 'boost' to the leverage.

We assume that coupons, default losses, and index unwinds all impact the deposit account. Note also that the value of the deposit account $D(t)$ grows at Libor.
4. The issuer checks to see if the trade should terminate. There are three possibilities:

- Cash-in: This occurs if $NAV(t) \geq TV(t)$. The assets in the CPDO are liquidated and used to fund the guaranteed payment of the specified coupons and principal. There is no further credit risk.
- Cash-out: This occurs if $NAV(t) < K$ where K is a threshold, say $10. The value of K is chosen so as to minimise the gap risk to the issuer who does not want the NAV to fall below zero. The CPDO is liquidated and the proceeds are paid to the investor. This is the CPDO's version of a default event.

- Maturity: The CPDO structure can reach maturity without either a cash-in or cash-out event having occurred. This usually means that the target value has not been reached, so although all of the coupons have been paid, there is not enough cash to make the final payment of coupon plus principal in full. This is also a default.

5. If the trade does not terminate, the issuer waits until the next rebalancing time and returns to step (3).

Equation 22.1 is the all-important equation since it determines the size of the investment in the underlying index. Its aim is to leverage the index investment so that it can earn enough carry from the index position over the remaining life of the trade to grow the NAV to the target value. It is only a heuristic approximation since the index coupon $C(t)$ used to calculate the carry will only last until the next roll of the index – it is not fixed for the life of the trade.

Example   Consider the case of a T-maturity CPDO with a notional of $100 which pays a floating rate coupon of Libor plus 200 bp. Suppose that the CDS index has a coupon of 50 bp and we are at CPDO initiation. The target value is the price of the floating leg of an interest rate swap which pays a coupon of Libor plus 200 bp and redeems at par. This equals

$$TV(t) = \$100 + 200\,bp \cdot PV01(t, T).$$

where $PV01(t, T)$ is the risk-free value of a 1 bp annuity from time t to time T. If we set $B = 0$, $NAV(t) = \$100$ and $U = 10$, Equation 22.1 gives

$$N(t) = 4.0.$$

This implies that we need to leverage the index 4.0 times. This make sense since four times 50 bp will pay the 200 bp spread on the CPDO while the Libor part of the coupon can simply be paid out of the Libor interest earned on the deposit account. If there are no defaults and no spread volatility, this strategy guarantees the CPDO cash flows.

To account for default and spread volatility, dealers will usually run Monte Carlo simulations of spreads and default to determine values of B and U which provide a suitable compromise between the need to have sufficient leverage to minimise the risk of the coupons and principal, and having so much leverage that the risk of a cash-out is too high for the desired credit rating.

There is also a gap risk. By gap risk, we refer to the loss which would occur if the value of the credit portfolio was to fall suddenly, driving the value of the NAV below zero. The trade would cash-out with no further payments. However, the negative value of the NAV would be borne by the issuer of the CPDO.

It is clear from Equation 22.1 that the leverage will increase if the value of the NAV falls or if the coupon on the index falls. As a result, the CPDO structure buys into a falling market and sells into a rising market. This is opposite to the CPPI strategy and means that volatility can actually benefit the CPDO. The frequency at which the credit portfolio is rebalanced varies and as with a CPPI, depends on a variety of factors including transaction costs and index volatility.

22.3.2   Understanding the CPDO

To explore the behaviour of the CPDO strategy and to better understand the rationale for its high credit rating, we have performed Monte Carlo simulations. The index spread S was modelled as a mean-reverting normal process with jump diffusion as follows

$$dS = \kappa(S_\infty - S)dt + \sigma_S dW_t + J(dN_t - \lambda dt)$$

where κ is the speed of mean reversion, S_∞ is the level of the long-term spread, σ_S is the basis point spread volatility of the Brownian motion W_t, N_t is a Poisson process with intensity λ and the jump size is J. We also assumed a risk-free interest rate r. Although the dynamics are normal, the positive jumps and the mean reversion make it unlikely for the spread to drift below zero.

We performed a simulation with the following parameters: $\kappa = 1.0$, $S_0 = 40$ bp, $S_\infty = 40$ bp, $r = 5\%$, $\sigma_S = 20$ bp, $\lambda = 1.0$ and $J = 10$ bp. The spread levels, speed of mean reversion and volatilities have not been formally calibrated to market data but are fairly typical long-run averages. We have not modelled default directly although we have incorporated a spread jump which has a similar loss – a default of one credit with recovery rate 40% on $100 face value of the five-year CDX index causes a loss of $1/125 \times \$100 \times (1-0.4) = \$0.48$ while a widening of 10 bp results in a loss of 4.5×10 bp $\times \$100 = \$0.45$ where 4.5 is the risky PV01 of the index. We note that a value of $\lambda = 1.0$, implying on average one default per year, is very conservative.

We rebalanced the strategy every three months and rolled the index every six months. We ignored fees and hedging costs. In order to have a metric for assessing the risk of the CPDO, we calculated the probability of a loss on the scheduled coupon or principal.

We ran the Monte Carlo simulation with 10 000 spread paths. Our analysis showed that provided the parameters of the CPDO are chosen carefully, the CPDO trading strategy can, according to this model, provide a very attractive risk–return profile. We observe that the following factors contribute to the success of this strategy:

1. Mean reversion: Figure 22.1 shows that the risk of the strategy requires that index spreads are mean reverting. For example, the probability of a loss on a 10 year CPDO is approximately 1% in the $\kappa = 0$ case when the CPDO pays just Libor. However, for $\kappa = 1$, this drops to zero for CPDO coupons up to Libor plus 250 bp.
2. Leverage boost: We find that the risk of the CPDO depends on the value of the boost B. Specifically, a value of $B > 15\%$ is needed to reduce the probability of a loss to zero on a CPDO paying Libor plus 100 bp, rising to $B > 25\%$ for the CPDO which pays Libor plus 300 bp.
3. Maturity: We find that we need the CPDO maturity to be long enough to allow the CPDO strategy to have time to work. This effect is shown in Figure 22.2 in which we see that the probability of a loss falls to zero for CPDOs paying Libor plus 200 bp provided the time-to-maturity exceeds seven years. Unlike traditional static[1] credit trades, shorter maturity trades are *more* risky than long maturity trades.

This analysis is simplistic since it does not model default risk correctly. It also ignores the adjustments to the index at the index roll. In practice, dealers need to build models which

---

[1] By static credit, we mean trades in which an investor buys a credit risky bond or sells protection on a CDS and then holds the position until maturity.

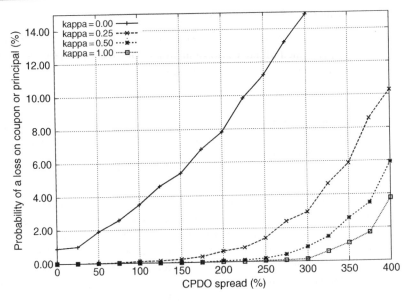

Figure 22.1 Probability of a loss on coupon or principal as a function of the CPDO spread over Libor for four values of the mean-reversion parameter $\kappa = 0.0, 0.25, 0.50$ and 1.0. This assumes a 10 year maturity CPDO

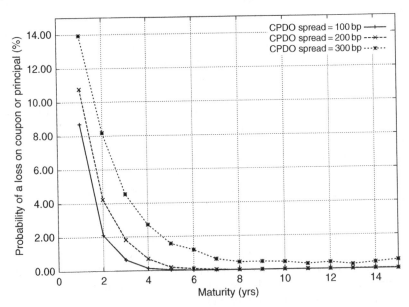

Figure 22.2 Probability of a loss on coupon or principal as a function of the initial maturity of the trade in years. We show this for a CPDO paying a coupon of Libor plus 100, 200 and 300 bp

overcome these shortcomings. They also need to perform empirical calibrations of the model parameters in order to produce better estimates for B, U and the risk of the strategy.

Although the CPDO strategy can present a low loss risk, CPDO trades can present a lot of mark-to-market volatility. Indeed, this is an essential side-effect of the trading strategy and is one important way in which CPDOs differ from traditional highly rated credit investments.

Given the widening in spreads and higher credit volatility which began in August 2007, the popularity of CPDO style investments has fallen significantly. It remains to be seen whether the CPDO will become a long term feature of the credit derivatives market.

22.4 THE CDO-SQUARED

The CDO squared is an extension of the standard CDO tranche concept in which the reference portfolio is itself a portfolio of single tranche CDOs. The effect of this double layer of tranching is to further leverage the spread premium embedded in the reference portfolios creating a CDO of CDOs, or *CDO squared* as it is more commonly known.

The CDO squared is a bespoke transaction. This means that the investor has the freedom to choose the many characteristics of the structure. This includes the number of *sub-tranches* in the reference portfolio, their attachment and detachment points, the choice of the credits in the reference sub-portfolios, and the attachment point and detachment point of the *super-tranche*.

The overall structure is shown in Figure 22.3. Market terminology calls the outermost CDO the *super-tranche*. This has its own specified attachment and detachment points which we denote with $\hat{K}_1$ and $\hat{K}_2$. The reference portfolio for the super-tranche is known as the *super-portfolio*. It consists of N_S *sub-tranches*. Each sub-tranche, which we index with $i = 1, \ldots, N_S$ has an attachment and detachment which we denote with $K_1^{(i)}$ and $K_2^{(i)}$.

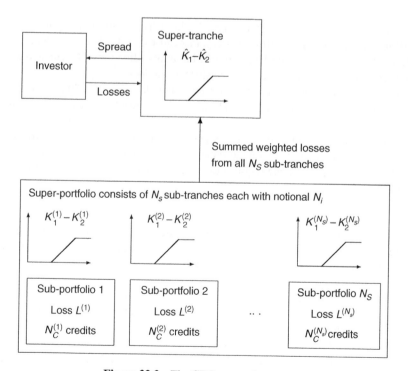

Figure 22.3   The CDO-squared structure

Losses are transferred from the sub-tranches to the super-portfolio by summing the losses on each of the sub-tranches weighted by its fractional notional. This super-portfolio loss is then applied to the super-tranche to determine if the investor has a loss. A typical CDO-squared structure consists of 5–15 sub-tranches, each with 50–100 underlying credits in their respective sub-portfolios.

There are several factors which determine the risk of a CDO-squared transaction. These include the credit quality of the portfolio, the assumed recovery rates, the correlation of the credits, the subordination and width of the super-tranche, and the subordination and width of the sub-tranches. These risks are much the same as in a standard single CDO tranche.

The available universe of highly liquid CDS names which are of interest to the CDO-squared investor typically numbers between 200 and 300. However, the number of underlying credits required for a CDO-squared with say eight sub-tranches each with reference portfolios of say 50 credits would be 400. It then becomes inevitable that there will be some overlap between the sub-portfolios. This causes an additional source of co-dependency between different sub-tranches which must be taken into account in any model.

The performance of a CDO squared is very dependent on the way any losses in the reference portfolio are distributed across the sub-portfolios. To see this consider the following example:

Example   Assume that we have a CDO-squared with five sub-tranches. Assume that each sub-portfolio consists of 100 credits and each sub-tranche has a subordination of 4% and a width of 5%, and that the super-tranche has a subordination of 8% and a width of 10%. Consider two scenarios in which 20 of the underlying credits default:

1. In the first scenario we assume that four credits in each of the five underlying reference portfolio default. Assuming 40% recovery, this causes a 2.4% loss in each of the five reference portfolios. Since each sub-tranche has a subordination of 4%, no loss occurs and the super-tranche and hence the investor take no loss.
2. In the second scenario we assume that 10 credits default in just two of the sub-tranches. Once again we assume 40% recovery. The loss is therefore 6.0% on each sub-portfolio, translating to a percentage tranche loss of $(6\% - 4\%)/5\% = 40\%$ on the two sub-tranches on the sub-portfolios which experience losses. Since there are five equal notional sub-tranches, the loss on the super-portfolio equals $(40\% + 40\%)/5 = 16\%$. The loss on the super-tranche requires the investor to lose $(16\% - 8\%)/10\% = 80\%$ of the tranche notional.

This example emphasises that the risk of a CDO-squared is very sensitive to the way the defaults are distributed across the different sub-portfolios. Clearly, the investor should ensure that highly correlated credits should be as broadly distributed across the sub-portfolios as possible.

The double-tranching mechanism has the effect of delaying the losses on the reference portfolio for as long as possible. However, once the sub-tranches start to take losses, the sensitivity of the super-tranche to further losses is much greater than for a typical STCDO. To see this, consider a CDO squared with five sub-tranches each with a reference portfolio of 100 credits. We also assume that there is a rough 10% overlap between the sub-portfolios, i.e. each pair of sub-portfolios has five credits in common. For simplicity we set all of the super-tranche and sub-tranche attachment and detachment points to be 5% and 10%, respectively. Assuming that defaults occur at a uniform rate across the different sub-portfolios, we plot in Figure 22.4 the loss on the super-tranche as a function of the *number of defaults*.

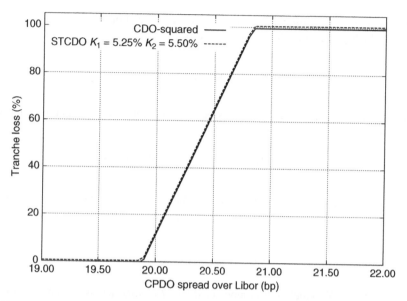

Figure 22.4 Comparison of a CDO-squared payoff with that of an STCDO on the combined sub-portfolios. We consider a scenario in which assets default uniformly across the sub-portfolios. Both lines fall exactly on top of each other. We have moved them apart slightly to make them both visible. See text for details

Given the assumption of uniform losses, the loss on the CDO-squared is very similar to that of a very thin STCDO. Indeed we have also plotted the loss for a K_1–K_2 STCDO on a reference portfolio equivalent to the sum of all of the sub-portfolios. By setting the attachment level at $K_1 = 5.25\%$ and the detachment level at $K_2 = 5.5\%$, we find that we can exactly reproduce the CDO-squared payoff. This equivalence only exists if we assume that defaults occur at a constant rate across the sub-portfolios. This insight becomes useful when we wish to use a base correlation approach to price CDO-squared. This is discussed later in Section 22.4.6.

22.4.1   The Valuation of a CDO-squared

As described above, two levels of subordination need to be breached before default losses are experienced by an investor. Specifically, a loss occurs if:

1. There are time T losses on one or more of the $i = 1, \ldots, N_S$ reference portfolios, which we denote by $L^{(i)}(T)$ which are large enough to exceed their respective subordination $K_1^{(i)}$.
2. The sum of the sub-tranche losses weighted by the tranche percentage notionals is greater than the subordination of the super-tranche $\hat{K}_1$.

This can be expressed mathematically. The loss at time T of the super-tranche, $L^{ST}(T)$ can be written as a function of the loss on the super-portfolio $L^{SP}(T)$. We have

$$L^{ST}(T) = \frac{\min(L^{SP}(T), \hat{K}_2) - \min(L^{SP}(T), \hat{K}_1)}{\hat{K}_2 - \hat{K}_1}.$$

The super-portfolio loss at time T, given by $L^{SP}(T)$, is the sum over the losses on the N_S sub-tranches which we denote with $L_i^{Tr}(T)$. Therefore

$$L^{SP}(T) = \frac{\sum_{i=1}^{N_S} N_i L_i^{Tr}(T)}{\sum_{i=1}^{N_S} N_i}.$$

The losses on the sub-tranches can be expressed as a function of the losses on the individual sub-portfolios, i.e.

$$L_i^{Tr}(T) = \frac{\min(L^{(i)}(T), K_2^{(i)}) - \min(L^{(i)}(T), K_1^{(i)})}{K_2^{(i)} - K_1^{(i)}}$$

which can be expressed in terms of the losses on the individual credits which constitute the sub-portfolios,

$$L^{(i)}(T) = \sum_{k=1}^{N_C} (1 - R_k) F_{ik} \mathbf{1}_{\tau_k \leq T}.$$

The index $k = 1, \ldots, N_C$ labels the number of *distinct credits* across the entirety of all N_S reference portfolios, i.e. the same credit in two different sub-portfolios is only counted once. As a result, we can write

$$N_C \leq \sum_{i=1}^{N_S} N_C^{(i)}.$$

Quantity F_{ik} is the fractional exposure of the reference portfolio underlying sub-tranche i to credit k. In the case of equally weighted exposures

$$F_{ik} = \begin{cases} 1/N_C^{(i)} & \text{if credit } k \text{ is in sub-portfolio } i, \\ 0 & \text{otherwise.} \end{cases}$$

In many cases the matrix F_{ik} will be fairly sparse, i.e. it will have mostly zero elements since most credits will only occur in only one of the sub-portfolios.

22.4.2   Calculating the CDO-squared Tranche Survival Curve

As with single-tranche CDOs, we can price a CDO-squared via its tranche survival curve. We therefore need to calculate

$$\mathbb{E}[L^{ST}(T)] = \frac{\mathbb{E}[\min(L^{SP}(T), \hat{K}_2)] - \mathbb{E}[\min(L^{SP}(T), \hat{K}_1)]}{\hat{K}_2 - \hat{K}_1}.$$

Calculating the loss distribution for the super-portfolio requires that we take into account the co-dependency between the losses on the different sub-portfolios. These are two distinct sources of dependency between the losses on two different sub-tranches:

1. There is a correlation between different issuers in the different sub-portfolios due to their being exposed to some common factor. In the standard one-factor Gaussian copula model this correlation is measured as the product of the market factor weights $\beta_i \beta_j$.
2. There is a correlation between sub-tranches because the same credit can be in two or more of the sub-portfolios. In a typical CDO squared, the sub-portfolio overlaps are typically more than 10% of the names, e.g. two different sub-portfolios of 100 credits each having 10 or more credits in common.

It is certainly possible to use Monte Carlo time-to-default models to price CDO-squareds. For each Monte Carlo trial we generate the default times of all N_C distinct credits. We simply need to make sure that credits which are common to different sub-tranches default at the same time and this can easily be handled in a Monte Carlo implementation. As a result, these two sources of correlation are handled correctly. Pricing CDO-squareds with Monte Carlo within a correlation skew model is also possible. Any one of the copula skew models described in Chapter 21 can be implemented as a times-to-default model.

Although Monte Carlo methods can capture the exact structure of the deal and the co-dependency between the losses on the different sub-tranches, it is a slow method, especially given the large universe of underlying credits (typically there are 400 or more credits), and the two-layer payoff function which must be calculated. There is therefore a desire for alternative analytical approaches which, while not exact, are close enough to provide a good approximation.

22.4.3 A Simplified Approach

The challenge is to find a faster way to capture the distribution of losses on the super-portfolio by modelling the co-dependence between the losses on the sub-tranches. One approach is to model the joint distribution for the losses on the sub-tranche reference portfolios. We define

$$f \left(L^{(1)}(T), L^{(2)}(T), \ldots, L^{(N_S)}(T) \right)$$

as the multi-variate density function which joins together the losses on the individual sub-tranches. Our next modelling assumption is to assume a one-factor model for the underlying credits. Assuming for simplicity a Gaussian copula model, we have

$$A_k = \beta_k Z + \sqrt{1 - \beta_k^2} \, \varepsilon_k.$$

where $k = 1, \ldots, N_C$. As a result we can write the expected loss of the super-tranche in terms of the conditional expected loss of the super-tranche, i.e.

$$\mathbb{E}\left[L^{ST}(T) \right] = \int_{-\infty}^{\infty} \phi(Z) \, \mathbb{E}\left[L^{ST}(T) | Z \right] dZ. \tag{22.2}$$

Conditional on Z, all of the N_C distinct credits in the CDO-squared are independent. Therefore conditional on Z, the only dependency between the losses on the sub-tranche reference portfolios arises from them holding the same credits. Given that the loss for each sub-portfolio is

$$L^{(i)}(T) = \sum_{k=1}^{N_C}(1 - R_k)F_{ik}\mathbf{1}_{\tau_k \leq T}$$

we can then calculate the mean and variance of the conditional loss distribution for each sub-portfolio. These are given by

$$m_i(Z) = \mathbb{E}\left[L^{(i)}(T)|Z\right] = \sum_{k=1}^{N_C}(1 - R_j)F_{ik}p_k(T|Z)$$

where $p_k(T|Z)$ is the conditional default probability of issuer k given by

$$p_k(T|Z) = \Phi\left(\frac{\Phi^{-1}(1 - Q_k(T)) - \beta_k Z}{\sqrt{1 - \beta_k^2}}\right).$$

The variance of the conditional loss distribution for sub-portfolio i is given by

$$V_i(Z) = \mathbb{E}\left[(L^{(i)}(T))^2|Z\right] - m_i(Z)^2 = \sum_{k=1}^{N_C}(1 - R_k)^2 F_{ik}^2 p_k(T|Z)(1 - p_k(T|Z)).$$

We can also extend this to calculate the correlation matrix between the conditional losses distribution for two different sub-portfolios indexed with i and j. This is given by

$$C_{ij}(Z) = \frac{\sum_{k=1}^{N_C}(1 - R_k)^2 F_{ik}F_{jk}p_k(T|Z)(1 - p_k(T|Z))}{\sqrt{V_i(Z)V_j(Z)}}.$$

The correlation $C_{ij}(Z)$ will only be zero if there are no common credits between sub-portfolios i and j.

This information suggests an analytical approach to modelling the conditional joint distribution of sub-tranche losses. Following Shelton (2004), we decide to model the individual sub-tranche conditional loss distributions using a Gaussian distribution and the conditional joint distribution of sub-tranche losses using a multi-variate Gaussian distribution with the correlation matrix computed above.

We choose a multi-variate Gaussian distribution for the simple reason that it has already been shown in Section 18.5.1 that the Gaussian distribution is a reasonably good approximation to the exact loss distribution. The choice of a multi-variate Gaussian is made mainly because it is the natural extension of the Gaussian distribution to multiple dimensions, and because it takes a relatively simple and analytically tractable form.

The individual sub-portfolio losses conditional on the market factor are Gaussian distributed so that

$$\Pr\left(L^{(i)}(T,Z) < X|Z\right) = \Phi\left(X; m_i(Z), \sqrt{V_i(Z)}\right) \tag{22.3}$$

where $\Phi(X, a, b)$ is the cumulative distribution function for a Gaussian random variable with mean a and standard deviation b. Hence, we have

$$\mathbb{E}\left[L^{ST}(T,Z)|Z\right] = \int_{-\infty}^{\infty} \cdots \int_{-\infty}^{\infty} \phi_{N_C}\left(g_1, g_2, \ldots, g_{N_S}; C(Z)\right)$$
$$\times \Theta\left(L^{(1)}(g_1, T, Z), \ldots, L^{(N_S)}(g_{N_S}, T, Z)\right) dg_1 \ldots dg_{N_S} \tag{22.4}$$

where Θ is the loss function for the super-tranche as a function of the losses on the sub-portfolios, $\phi_N(g_1, \ldots, g_N; \mathbf{C})$ is the N-dimensional Gaussian density function with correlation matrix $\mathbf{C}$, and

$$L^{(i)}(g_i, T, Z) = m_i(Z) + g_i\sqrt{V_i(Z)}. \tag{22.5}$$

We have to calculate the conditional expected CDO-squared tranche loss at a range of values of Z and then integrate over the Gaussian density of Z to arrive at the unconditional expected CDO-squared tranche loss.

Though analytical, this approach is computationally slow. This is because we have to compute the N_S-dimensional integral in Equation 22.4 and the computational time scales exponentially in N_S. The total computation time is typically too long to make it practical. We can overcome this using a Monte Carlo integration.

22.4.4 A Monte Carlo-based Integration

This is one situation in which Monte Carlo comes to the rescue. For dimensions greater than three or so, it is generally faster to use Monte Carlo methods to perform a multi-dimensional integration. This involves drawing $p = 1, \ldots, N_P$ realisations of $i = 1, \ldots, N_S$ multi-variate Gaussian random numbers g_i^p from the joint distribution with correlation matrix $\mathbf{C}(Z)$. We do this using the Cholesky decomposition algorithm presented in Section 14.10.1. We then calculate the sub-portfolio losses using Equation 22.5. From these we calculate the super-tranche loss. We then repeat this over all of the Monte Carlo realisations and average as follows

$$\mathbb{E}\left[L^{ST}(T)|Z\right] \simeq \frac{1}{N_P}\sum_{p=1}^{N_P}\Theta\left(L_p^{(1)}(g_i^p, T, Z), \ldots, L_p^{(N_S)}(g_{N_S}^p, T, Z)\right).$$

This procedure has to be repeated for each value of Z and the result is integrated over the density of Z using Equation 22.2 to arrive at the unconditional tranche survival probability to time T.

The main reason why this Monte Carlo approach is faster than a full Monte Carlo times-to-default simulation is because we have reduced the dimensionality of the problem from N_C credits to N_S sub-tranches. Since N_C is typically around 400 and N_S is typically around 10, this is an immediate factor of 40 reduction in problem dimensionality. Also, as the dimensionality of the problem, which equals the number of sub-tranches N_S, is typically of the order of 10, it is especially suitable for the use of low discrepancy quasi random number generators as discussed in Jaeckel (2002).

22.4.5 Improving the Accuracy

The approach described here is based on our use of the Gaussian multi-variate distribution to model the conditional joint distribution of sub-portfolio losses. However, we can break this modelling assumption into two assumptions:

1. We assumed the conditionally independent distribution of sub-portfolio losses is Gaussian.
2. We assumed the joint dependency structure of sub-portfolio losses is a multi-variate Gaussian.

In general we find that the first assumption is the more significant of the two, i.e. the error from approximating the sub-tranche loss distributions is greater than the error due to our approximation of the joint dependency structure. In fact the quality of the first approximation has already been discussed in Section 18.5.1 in which we found that the use of a Gaussian distribution to model the conditional loss distribution can break down in certain regimes.

To improve on these two assumptions, we can use a copula approach to separate the specification of the marginal from the choice of dependence structure. We therefore define a marginal distribution function which can map the exact sub-portfolio conditional loss distribution to the Gaussian distribution, i.e. if g_i is the Gaussian random draw for sub-portfolio i, then we want to ensure that

$$F_i(L^{(i)}(g_i, T, Z)) = \Phi(g_i)$$

where $F_i(x)$ is the cumulative distribution function for the conditional loss distribution of sub-portfolio i. For each value of g_i, the corresponding loss is given by inverting this equation to give

$$L^{(i)}(g_i, T, Z) = F_i^{-1}(\Phi(g_i)).$$

We can also choose to approximate $F_i(x)$ using a distribution which is faster to compute than the exact sub-portfolio conditional loss distribution but which fits the sub-portfolio loss distribution better than the Gaussian used above. For example, we could use the adjusted binomial approximation discussed in Section 18.5.1.

22.4.6 Skew Calibration

The slower but direct approach to pricing a CDO-squared is to use a full times-to-default model. With this approach, we can apply most of the copula pricing models discussed in Chapter 21. Given a suitable calibration, the resulting CDO-squared price will incorporate the correlation skew.

When using the approach described in the previous section, the natural first step in incorporating the skew is to use the base correlation approach. However, it is far from clear how to map the strikes of the super-tranche and sub-tranches to the base correlation curves. The only approach which seems reasonable is to determine a way to map a CDO-squared tranche onto an equivalent single tranche CDO. This approach seems promising since it can be shown that a CDO-squared tranche can be well approximated by a very thin STCDO as discussed in Section 22.4.

22.5 TRANCHELETS

Tranchelets is the name given to very thin tranches on the standard indices. From early 2006, the market has begun to quote and trade tranchelets on both CDX and iTraxx indices. However, their liquidity can be described as 'patchy' and they are mostly used for inter-dealer hedging of correlation books. In terms of mechanics and risk, tranchelets are identical to the standard tranche CDOs discussed earlier. Their width, which is typically 1%, means that they are generally highly leveraged.

What makes them interesting is that the 0–1%, 1–2% and 2–3% tranchelets give us the ability to see for the first time how the market prices the very low strike part of the base correlation curve. Initial pricing given in Muench *et al.* (2006) implies that the base correlation curve is fairly flat below the first standard quoted strike of 3%.

22.6   FORWARD STARTING TRANCHES

A forward starting tranche allows the investor to sell protection on an STCDO starting at a forward date t_F at a spread agreed today. The underlying tranche matures at time T. The attachment and detachment levels of the tranche, K_1 and K_2, are fixed at option initiation.

There are two variations on the forward starting tranche which differ in the way the attachment and detachment levels are affected by defaults between option initiation and option expiry. In the first variation, defaults in this period reduce K_1 and K_2 in the usual way. However, if K_2 falls below zero before t_F, the contract cancels. In the second variation, a forward starting tranche contract specifies that the tranche strikes are fixed until the forward date, i.e. the tranche subordination does not decrease if there have been defaults on the reference portfolio. Only defaults after t_F will cause K_1 and K_2 to decrease and cause the investor to incur a loss payment once K_1 is reduced to zero and further defaults occur. We consider this variation to be the more standard of the two.

The second type of forward starting tranches cannot be priced by replication, i.e. as a combination of a long and short position in two spot-starting tranches since we are required to distinguish between defaults on the reference portfolio which occur before the forward date and so do not change the tranche attachment and detachment levels, and those which fall after the forward date which do. One approach to pricing this sort of product is to extend an existing model to a so-called 'two-period' approach as suggested in Andersen (2006b). An alternative approach is to use one of the dynamic models of correlated default discussed in the next two chapters.

22.7   OPTIONS ON TRANCHES

An option on a tranche gives the option holder the right, but not the obligation, to enter into an STCDO at a future expiry date t_E. The underlying tranche matures at time T and pays a tranche spread agreed today. The attachment and detachment levels of the tranche, K_1 and K_2, are also defined and fixed at option initiation. Since the tranche strikes are fixed, any defaults which occur on the reference portfolio between trade initiation and option expiry do not affect the strike levels. Only defaults after t_E will cause the tranche subordination level to decrease.

On option expiry, the option buyer has the choice of entering into an on-market tranche paying the current market spread, or to exercise the option and enter into the tranche paying the strike spread S_0. Since the value of the on-market tranche is zero, the value of the tranche option at expiry is

$$\max \left[V_{(Tranche)}(t_E, T, K_1, K_2, S_0), 0 \right]$$

where $V_{(Tranche)}(t_E, T, K_1, K_2, S_0)$ is the value of the tranche at the strike spread on the option expiry date. The expected present value of the option at time zero is given by

$$V_{(Option)} = \mathbb{E} \left[\frac{1}{\beta(t_E)} \max \left[V_{(Tranche)}(t_E, T, K_1, K_2, S_0), 0 \right] \right].$$

The value of the option depends on the width of the distribution of the tranche value at option expiry. To model this distribution, we need to capture the uncertainty in the evolution of the tranche spread in a manner which is consistent with the incidence of default on the reference portfolio and the spread volatility of the reference portfolio.

However, recalling the discussion in Section 13.6, we note that copula-based portfolio default models would only assign some value to the option, *through conditioning on the number of defaults in the reference portfolio prior to the option expiry date*. This is not sufficient since it ignores changes in the tranche value due to changes in the market's view of the expectation of default, which is expressed through changes in the underlying spread of the reference portfolio. The only way to overcome this is to add an additional source of uncertainty to the model to represent spread volatility. However, combining spread and default dynamics in a coherent and usable manner is a major challenge which will be discussed in Chapters 23 and 24.

22.8   LEVERAGED SUPER SENIOR

As its name suggests, the leveraged super-senior (LSS) tranche is a product in which the investor assumes a leveraged exposure to the super-senior part of the capital structure. This is a trade which is usually popular when the senior tranches of an index appear 'cheap', i.e. given where the index swap is trading, the combined risk implied by the spreads of the equity, mezzanine and senior tranches appear low and so imply a higher spread to the senior tranche than usual. Given that the actuarial risk of senior tranches is low, this situation becomes very interesting to investors who exploit the leverage to be paid a relatively large coupon for taking exposure to a very low risk and highly rated part of the capital structure. Typical leverage ratios are between 10 and 20. For dealers, buying protection at the super-senior level of the capital, structure is of interest as it helps them to hedge out the senior risk in their correlation books.

Although the default risk of the leveraged super-senior tranche is low, it can exhibit mark-to-market volatility. For this reason, the structure requires the investor to post an upfront amount of collateral. Given the leverage of the trade, it is possible for the mark-to-market value of the trade to fall by more than the value of the collateral. This can leave the dealer exposed to a loss. To guard against this risk, the dealer usually inserts a trigger in the deal which causes the trade to deleverage. This trigger may be linked to one of the following:

1. The market super-senior tranche spread.
2. The number of defaults or total loss in the reference portfolio.

To value this trigger, we need to know the mark-to-market of the super senior tranche at the moment the deleveraging event is triggered. In the first case, both the trigger and resulting mark-to-market are both spread driven. However, given that we know the tranche spread at the moment the trigger is reached, we can easily approximate its mark-to-market. The reason we do not know the mark-to-market exactly is because we would need the full super-senior tranche spread curve on the trigger date in order to calculate the exact tranche mark-to-market. Knowing just the tranche spread to its maturity date only gives us the exact mark-to-market if the forward tranche spread curve is flat.

In the second case, we do not have direct knowledge of the value of the super senior at the moment the deleveraging event is triggered. However, we would expect that the super-senior spread will have widened if so many defaults have occurred in the reference portfolio. As a result, we need a model which captures the joint behaviour between the loss on the reference portfolio and the value of the tranche spread. This means that pricing a leveraged super-senior with a loss-based trigger requires not just a model of correlated default, but also one of spread. Such models are the subject of the remaining two chapters.

22.9 SUMMARY

In this chapter we have covered some of the main advanced multi-name credit derivative products. The first two products – the credit CPPI and the CPDO – fall into the family of dynamic credit products and apart from their gap risk exposure, they require little derivative pricing and hedging technology.

We have then covered the main extensions to the standard STCDO structure. We have shown how to price a CDO squared structure. We have also considered structures such as the forward starting tranche, the option on a tranche and the leveraged super senior which require a model which combines default and credit spread dynamics within a coherent framework. Such models must also be consistent with the correlation skew at the different tranche maturities. A number of models which attempt to address these requirements are the subject of the next two chapters.

23

Dynamic Bottom-up Correlation Models

23.1 INTRODUCTION

The development of advanced correlation products has created a need for dynamic correlation models which can overcome the lack of a coherent modelling of default dynamics in the base correlation and copula frameworks. We recall that the base correlation approach does not guarantee arbitrage-free prices in the time dimension. We also note that the copula framework does not guarantee arbitrage-free prices when we make the copula parameters time dependent. This need for dynamic correlation models has recently become more important due to a number of product innovations which have required a better treatment of the dynamics of joint default. In particular:

- The growth in liquidity of the term structure of standard tranches, which now includes points at five, seven and 10 years has created a requirement for a model which can simultaneously fit the entire correlation skew term structure.
- There is an interest in trading forward starting tranches, not least because these are the underlying for options on tranches. There is therefore an exposure to the forward starting loss surface[1] which is correlated with the incidence of defaults before the forward start date.
- Extensions of the STCDO have been designed which include features similar to those found in traditional cash flow CDOs. These features are usually defensive as they are designed to deleverage the transaction if a loss level if crossed and protect the investor from further losses. Such features make the product path dependent in the sense that the recovery rate and timing of defaults may affect the subsequent payments.
- A correlation model should incorporate empirically observed default phenomena such as default clustering. It should also be able to incorporate any term structure effects in default correlation which could be linked to market expectations about the future state of the economy.

---

[1] The loss surface is the set of loss distributions to all maturities. It is a surface since each point on the surface represents the probability of a certain loss at a specific horizon time.

The dynamic model which can satisfy these requirements can be a *default-only* model, i.e. it only needs to model the risk of joint default. There is no need to model *unconditional* spread dynamics as none of these products listed above has an explicit dependence on spread volatility. We do recall that a default-only model will imply spread dynamics once we *condition on the default and survival of other credits* as discussed in Section 13.6. However, there are a number of products which also have an exposure to the dynamics of joint default *and to unconditional spread dynamics*. Examples of these products include:

- Tranche products with an unwind trigger linked to a specific level of losses on the reference portfolio: Although the trigger is linked to a specific default loss and so may initially appear to be a product which can be handled within a default-only model, the unwind value is determined by the breakeven spread of the tranche at the moment the trigger is breached and so depends on the evolution of the tranche spread taking any defaults into account. The first widely traded example of such a correlation product is the leveraged super-senior product discussed in Section 22.8.
- Options on tranches: This would definitely require a model which can capture both spread volatility and default correlation within a unified framework. Specifically the model needs to handle the evolution of the spreads in the reference portfolio and the cumulative losses in the reference portfolio up until the option expiry date. This must be done in a coherent manner meaning that we would expect that on average there will be more defaults when spreads are wide and fewer defaults when spreads are narrow.
- Extensions of the STCDO which embed defensive features similar to traditional cash flow CDOs such as deleveraging triggers linked to the breakeven spread of the tranche rather than to a level of losses.

The task of finding a model which can satisfy all of these needs is much harder than the default-only case. Not only must the model fit the correlation skew, it must also fit any tranche implied volatility term structure which may appear. To find a model which can do all this and remain analytically tractable is a significant challenge.

The models which will be discussed in this chapter are all 'bottom-up'. What this means is that they specify a dynamics for each credit in the portfolio. The joint default behaviour at a portfolio level then emerges from the way the default dynamics of the individual credits are correlated. This contrasts with the 'top-down' approach described in the next chapter in which the state variable modelled is some aggregate property of the portfolio loss distribution. It is not issuer specific. There are pros and cons for each approach which will be discussed in this and the next chapter.

The search for a dynamic correlation model which can price and risk manage all of the products discussed in this section is very much a work in progress. As a result, new models continue to appear and it would be impossible to provide a comprehensive list that would not quickly become out of date. Instead, our aim here is to present an overview of the different types of approach, and then to focus on two very different models which address the challenge. As a result, this chapter is broken into three sections. We begin with a survey of the different approaches to the bottom-up modelling of default correlation. Following this we detail a default-only model. This is the intensity gamma model of Joshi and Stacey (2005). We then discuss the implementation, calibration and pricing of tranches using the affine jump diffusion model, an approach which incorporates both default dynamics and spread dynamics.

23.2   A SURVEY OF DYNAMIC MODELS

It is worth taking the time to survey the various dynamic models which have been proposed for modelling correlated default[2] since it is interesting to see the range of mechanisms which have been proposed. It is also useful, for the purpose of establishing some framework for understanding the similarities and differences between these mechanisms, to categorise them into the following four groups:

1. The first is the *intensity-based* mechanism which extends the doubly stochastic Poisson model into a multi-name setting. Default correlation is typically induced through the introduction of common jumps in the issuer intensities.
2. The second type is based on the idea of *contagion* in which the default of a firm causes a change in the default intensities of other firms causing them to become more or less likely to default.
3. The third type are *time-changed approaches* in which a stochastic time process is introduced which acts as a measure of the information arrival rate into the market. Shocks in this process, which are seen by all the credits, can lead to joint default.
4. The fourth and final type are *hybrid* structural approaches in which we model the dynamics of the 'asset values' for all of the firms using correlated dynamic processes. Correlated credits will have asset values which will tend to jointly fall below or rise above their default thresholds.

These joint-default mechanisms are not mutually exclusive – we may find models which combine more than one of these joint default mechanisms. We now survey a range of models categorised by their default mechanisms. We emphasise that this list is not complete since this is currently a very active area of research within investment banks and academia.

23.2.1   Intensity Models

One of the earliest approaches to the modelling of correlated default was the use of the *doubly stochastic framework* by Duffie and Singleton (1998). This model used the correlated dynamics of the intensity process to induce default correlation. However, realistic default correlations are not possible with typical normal or lognormal dynamics. To see this, consider two intensity processes for credits A and B which we denote with $\lambda_A(t)$ and $\lambda_B(t)$. The processes evolve according to $d\lambda_A(t) = \mu dt + \sigma dW_A$ and $d\lambda_B(t) = \mu dt + \sigma dW_B$ with correlation $\mathbb{E}[dW_A dW_B] = c.dt$. The default indicator correlation to horizon T, is given by

$$\rho(T) = \frac{p_{12} - p_1 p_2}{\sqrt{p_1(1 - p_1)p_2(1 - p_2)}}$$

where we have $p_1 = \Pr(\tau_1 \leq T)$ and $p_2 = \Pr(\tau_2 \leq T)$ and

$$p_{12} = \Pr(\tau_1 \leq T, \tau_2 \leq T)$$

$$= p_1 + p_2 - 1 + \mathbb{E}\left[\exp\left(-\int_0^T (\lambda_A(t) + \lambda_B(t)) \, dt\right)\right].$$

---

[2] For a comprehensive review, we also refer the reader to Elizade (2006).

Following the same analytical techniques used in Section 3.8, we have

$$p_{12} = p_1 + p_2 - 1 + (1 - p_1)(1 - p_2) \exp\left(c\sigma^2 T^3/3\right).$$

Setting $p_1 = p_2 = p$ and substituting for p_{12} gives

$$\rho(T) = \frac{(1 - p)}{p} \left(\exp\left(c\sigma^2 T^3/3\right) - 1\right).$$

Note that as discussed in Section 12.2.3, when $p_1 = p_2$, maximum default dependence corresponds to a default indicator correlation of 100%.

Example   To estimate a typical value for $\rho(T)$, we set $T = 5$ and $p = 5\%$ and assume a hazard rate volatility of $\sigma = 50$ bp. We then assume perfect correlation of the intensity processes, i.e. $c = 100\%$. Substituting these values gives a five-year default correlation of $\rho(T) = 1.98\%$.

This example shows that even with a fairly high level of volatility and using perfect correlation for the intensity processes, the maximum five-year default correlation is still less than 2%. We conclude that it is not possible to generate the levels of default correlation needed to fit the correlation skew using a diffusion-based intensity process without going to unrealistically high volatility levels. The problem with the intensity-based approach is that we are correlating changes in the intensities and not the default event itself. When the intensities are pure diffusive processes, this is a very weak mechanism for correlating default.

One way to overcome this problem is to incorporate large synchronous jumps in the different credit intensity processes. Even if the common jumps are synchronous and large, the actual defaults are not necessarily going to be synchronous. The jumps simply make each credit more likely to default, but they do not force them to default immediately and synchronously except in the limit that the jump size tends to infinity.

Stochastic processes which combine a normal, lognormal or square-root diffusive intensity process with jumps are generally known as affine jump diffusion (AJD) models. The application of AJD models to the pricing of CDOs was pioneered in Duffie and Garleanu (1999). However, this approach was not adopted widely by the market since it was perceived to rely upon a relatively slow Monte Carlo implementation, especially when compared to the semi-analytic one-factor latent variable approach which we initially adopted. However, recent work by Mortensen (2006) and Chapovsky et al. (2006) has shown that semi-analytical approaches to solving this model are possible. This has sparked renewed interest in the use of AJD processes as discussed in Section 23.4.

23.2.2   Contagion Models

Another approach is to use contagion as a mechanism for correlating default. Perhaps the earliest example of this approach is the 'infectious default' model due to Davis and Lo (2001a). In this model, an issuer can default either idiosyncratically or by being 'infected' by the default of another issuer according to some infection probability. This model is able to generate strong correlations which can be controlled via the infection probability. In its initial form the model was *static* as it only modelled a single period and so only one contagion step was possible. In a later version by Davis and Lo (2001b), a full dynamical version was proposed. In this model, the portfolio can be in either a normal risk state or an enhanced risk state. Migration from normal to enhanced occurs if there is a default in the portfolio. When this happens the intensities of all the other credits become scaled by a factor $\kappa > 1$. After an exponentially distributed random time the portfolio reverts to a normal risk state.

Within the same general framework of contagion models, Jarrow and Yu (2001) model the intensity of each of two correlated issuers as a process which jumps following the default of the other issuer. Feedback effects prevent the authors from generating an explicit solution for the distribution of default times. To overcome this *looping defaults* effect, the authors divide issuers into primary and secondary firms. While the default of primary firms is driven by macro variables, the default of secondary firms depends on the same macro variables plus the default processes of the primary firms. Unfortunately, such an approach is hard to use in practical pricing since it is not obvious that one can distinguish primary and secondary firms. Later work by Yu (2005) overcomes this problem.

Another approach is to use so-called *frailty* models to model default correlation. In these models firms have some unobservable common source of 'frailty' which makes default more likely and which evolves randomly through time. Examples include Schönbucher (2003b) and Duffie *et al.* (2006).

23.2.3   Time-changed Intensity Models

The first application of a time-changed intensity default mechanism to pricing credit derivatives is to be found in Joshi and Stacey (2005). The idea underlying this approach is that we model an alternative time process known as the *business time*. The business time is modelled as an increasing process which comprised of jumps of varying sizes. Default correlation comes about because all of the credits 'see' the same business time. Jumps in the business time can be interpreted as the sudden arrival of new information which causes a systemic jump in the default compensator defined as

$$\Lambda_t = \int_0^t \lambda(s)\, dI(s)$$

where $dI(s)$ is the business time increment at calendar time s and $\lambda(s)$ is the issuer hazard rate. These common jumps in the compensator make joint defaults more likely. This model is discussed more fully in Section 23.3 where we show that it is able to generate enough default correlation to allow us to find a good fit to the correlation skew.

Another example from this family of models is Cariboni and Schoutens (2006) who model the default intensities of the different credits as Ornstein–Uhlenbeck processes within a time-changed gamma process.

23.2.4   Hybrid Models

Hybrid models choose to model a state variable which is supposed to represent some transformation of the 'firm asset value'. They are hybrid in the sense that while they take their inspiration from structural models of default, they are actually used as reduced form models, i.e. they are calibrated directly to market prices and no attempt is made to say anything about the capital structure of the firm being modelled. By correlating the dynamics of the firm value, the model is able to correlate default. Given a rich enough dynamic process, it is hoped that such a model will be able to generate the level of dependency required to fit the correlation skew.

Hull *et al.* (2005) introduced a hybrid model of default in which the asset process of a firm evolves according to a lognormal process. This model, which has already been described in Section 13.7, produces similar results to the Gaussian copula model. More recently, Luciano and Schoutens (2005) and Moosbrucker (2006) have used variance gamma processes to model the evolution of the asset value with the latter group finding a good fit to the correlation skew. Baxter (2006) has extended these approaches by allowing the asset process to be modelled as a combination of a Brownian motion plus two gamma processes. One of these gamma processes is common to all credits. Therefore if jumps in this process are sufficiently large that they all cross the default threshold, they will induce systemic default events. As a result simultaneous defaults are possible. This model can be calibrated to fit the correlation skew.

23.3   THE INTENSITY GAMMA MODEL

One model that exhibits default clustering and is relatively tractable is the intensity gamma (IG) model of Joshi and Stacey (2005). As previously discussed, the idea behind the model is that we introduce a time-changed process which exhibits finite jumps. These jumps represent the arrival of new information and cause common jumps in the default compensator which can lead to joint default. We begin by defining the gamma process which is the driver of the business time.

23.3.1   The Gamma Process

Before we can introduce the gamma process, we need to introduce the gamma distribution. The gamma distribution is the choice of distribution from which we will draw the time shocks. A variable x has a gamma distribution with shape parameter γ and inverse scale parameter λ if the probability density function for x is given by

$$f(x; \gamma, \lambda) = \frac{\lambda^{\gamma}}{\Gamma(\gamma)} x^{\gamma-1} e^{-\lambda x} \quad \text{where } \lambda > 0 \text{ and } \gamma > 0. \tag{23.1}$$

We write the gamma distribution as $\Gamma(\gamma, \lambda)$. For integer γ, the gamma distribution represents the sum of γ exponential random numbers with scale parameter $1/\lambda$, i.e. $g = (1/\lambda) \sum_{i=1}^{\gamma} e_i$, where g is a gamma distributed random variable and each e_i is an independent exponential distributed random variable. Note that exponential distributed random variables e can be simulated by drawing independent uniform random numbers u and then simply using the equation $e = -\ln u$. The mean and variance of the gamma distribution are as follows

$$\mathbb{E}[x] = \gamma/\lambda \quad \text{and} \quad \mathbb{E}[x^2] - \mathbb{E}[x]^2 = \gamma/\lambda^2.$$

We also note that the sum of two independent gamma distributed random variables X_1 and X_2 is also gamma distributed. Specifically, if

$$X_1 \sim \Gamma(\gamma_1, \lambda) \quad \text{and} \quad X_2 \sim \Gamma(\gamma_2, \lambda)$$

then

$$X_1 + X_2 \sim \Gamma(\gamma_1 + \gamma_2, \lambda).$$

A *gamma process* is a Lévy process with independent increments drawn from a gamma distribution. We define a stochastic gamma process $X(t)$ with the following properties:

- $X(0) = 0$.
- $X(t)$ has independent increments $X(t_n) - X(t_{n-1})$ where $t_n > t_{n-1}$.
- $X(t + s) - X(t) \sim \Gamma(\gamma s, \lambda)$ for any $s, t \geq 0$.

The mean and variance of a gamma process are as follows

$$\mathbb{E}[X(t)] = \gamma t/\lambda \quad \text{and} \quad \mathbb{E}[X(t)^2] - \mathbb{E}[X(t)]^2 = \gamma t/\lambda^2.$$

A gamma process is a jump process. Parameter γ controls the rate of jump arrivals and $1/\lambda$ controls the size of the jumps. This is made very clear in Figure 23.1 in which we have simulated the evolution of three gamma processes. In each case we have set $\gamma = \lambda$ so that the expected value of $X(t)$ is t. We see that there is a relationship between the frequency and size of jumps. When $\gamma = \lambda = 0.2$, there are a small number of large jumps and when $\gamma = \lambda = 5.0$ there are many very small jumps.

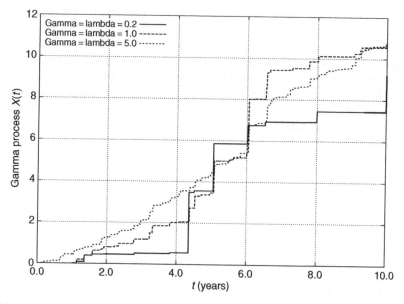

Figure 23.1 Simulated evolution of three gamma processes $\Gamma(\gamma t, \lambda)$. In each case we have set $\lambda = \gamma$ and go out to $T = 10$ years. We show gamma process for $\gamma = \lambda = 0.2, 1.0$ and 5.0

It is also possible to combine different gamma processes to create a new stochastic jump process. Note that the sum of gamma processes with different scale parameters is not a gamma process and as such provides a richer set of dynamics. We define the sum of gamma processes as

$$\hat{X}(t) = \sum_{i=1}^{n} X(t, \gamma_i, \lambda_i) + at$$

where a is a constant drift term which has been added on. This drift term can be thought of as just another gamma process which has parameters $\lambda \to \infty$ and $\gamma/\lambda \to a$.

23.3.2   The Information Arrival Process

To apply the idea of a business time to the modelling of credit, we introduce a new hazard rate $c_i(t)$. This models the instantaneous hazard rate of issuer i per unit of business time or *information arrival* $I(t)$, where $I(t)$ is modelled as the sum of n gamma processes plus a drift, i.e. it follows the same dynamics as the process $\hat{X}(t)$ defined above. The probability that a credit survives to time T conditional on the path of the information arrival process from time 0 to T which we denote with $\{I(s)\}_{s\in[0,T]}$ is therefore given by

$$Q_i(0, T | \{I(s)\}_{s\in[0,T]}) = \exp\left(-\int_0^T c_i(s) dI(s)\right).$$

Note that $c_i(t)$ is a function of calendar time t and not the business time $I(t)$.

Since $I(t)$ follows a sum of gamma processes, it will experience jumps whose size and frequency will be determined by the value of the parameters $\gamma_1, \ldots, \gamma_n$ and $\lambda_1, \ldots, \lambda_n$. Conditional on the path of $I(t)$, the credits are independent. In a limited sense, the information arrival process is analogous to the market factor in the one-factor copula approach. Note that it is also possible to recreate the independence case in this model by setting $\lambda_i \to \infty$ for all $i = 1, \ldots, n$. In this limit the jump sizes in the gamma process tend to zero, the variance of the gamma process tends to zero, and the gamma process becomes a constant drift so that business time and calendar time are equal.

If we assume that $c_i(t)$ is piecewise flat with a value c between times t_1 and t_2, then the probability that the credit has survived to time t_2 given that it has survived to time t_1, conditional on the information arrival path $\{I(t)\}$ is given by

$$\exp\left(-c\left(I(t_2) - I(t_1)\right) | \{I(s)\}_{s\in[t_1, t_2]}\right).$$

Therefore the survival probability from t_1 to t_2 is given by

$$Q(t_1, t_2) = \mathbb{E}_{t_1}\left[\exp\left(-c(I(t_2) - I(t_1))\right)\right]$$

where the expectation is over the randomness in $I(t_2) - I(t_1)$.

23.3.3   Simulating the Information Arrival Process

The direct approach to the implementation of this model is to simulate the information arrival process by discretising calendar time into many small steps dt and then making a draw from a gamma distribution to determine the corresponding $dI(t)$ for each time t. An efficient algorithm for drawing gamma distributed random variables is described in Marsaglia and Tang (2000). The process for simulating the information arrival process to time T is then as follows:

1. Set $t = 0$ and $I(t) = 0$.
2. Draw $j = 1, \ldots, n$ gamma random variables $g_j \sim \Gamma(\gamma_j \, dt, \lambda_j)$.
3. Set $dI(t) = \sum_{j=1}^{n} g_j + a \, dt$ so that $I(t + dt) = I(t) + dI(t)$.
4. Set $t = t + dt$. If $t < T$ then return to step (2). Otherwise terminate.

23.3.4 Calibrating to the Issuer Curves

If calibration of the issuer survival curves require use of this Monte Carlo algorithm, it would be computationally very expensive. However, assuming a piecewise constant value of $c = c(t_1, t_2)$ between times t_1 and t_2, we can write the survival probability to time t_2 given that the credit has survived to time t_1 as

$$Q(t_1, t_2) = \int_0^\infty \exp(-cx) f_I(x) dx$$

where $f_I(x)$ is the density function of the business time increment between t_1 and t_2, i.e. $x = I(t_2) - I(t_1)$. Since x is the sum of gamma distributed functions, and since the Laplace transform of the gamma distribution is known, it is possible to show that

$$Q(t_1, t_2) = \exp(-a \, c(t_1, t_2)(t_2 - t_1)) \prod_{j=1}^{n} \frac{1}{(1 + c(t_1, t_2)/\lambda_j)^{\gamma_j(t_2 - t_1)}}. \qquad (23.2)$$

The n gamma processes driving the business time have parameters (γ, λ).

Calibration to the survival probabilities involves determining the shape of function $c_i(t_1, t_2)$ for each credit $i = 1, \ldots, N_C$. We therefore loop over all of the credits in the reference portfolio. For each credit, we then bootstrap the term structure of $c(t)$. Setting $c(t)$ to be piecewise flat means that we can solve successively for each value of $c(t)$ using a simple one-dimensional root search. The advantage of the Laplace transform is that we can avoid the use of Monte Carlo simulation when calibrating all of the credits, resulting in a significant reduction in computation time. This is especially useful when we want to calculate perturbatory spread risk.

23.3.5 Pricing Tranches

To price tranches, we need to have access to the joint distribution of default times. To determine the default time τ_i^p of credit i in path $p = 1, \ldots, P$ of a Monte Carlo simulation given $c_i(t)$ and the simulated gamma process $I_p(t)$, we have to solve for

$$\tau_i^p = \inf\left(t : \int_0^t c_i(s) dI_p(s) \geq e_i^p \right)$$

where e_i^p is an independent exponential random draw and $\inf(x : S)$ means the smallest value of x which satisfies condition S. Using this method it is then straightforward to generate the default time for each credit in each Monte Carlo trial. These default times can then be fed into a tranche pricer of the type discussed in Section 14.7.1.

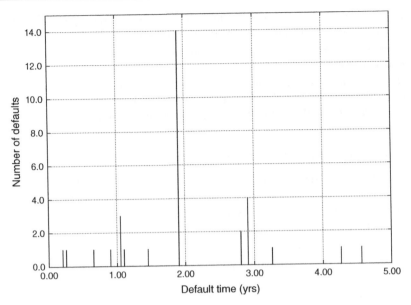

Figure 23.2   Default clustering as exhibited by the intensity gamma model. We show the incidence of defaults versus default time for defaults which occur before $T = 5$

Using the IG model we have simulated one path of the gamma process and calculated the implied default times of credits in a 125-name portfolio. Figure 23.2 shows the number of defaults versus the default time for defaults which occur before year 5 in one simulated path. The credits in the portfolio have heterogeneous spreads. We see that there are several occasions on which only one credit defaults. There are also occasions when two, three and even four credits default together. What is striking is that there is also a time at which 14 credits (out of 125) default together. This is a clear example of the ability of this model to capture the empirically observed phenomenon of default clustering.

Although worth implementing as a first step in building intuition about this model, the method described in Section 23.3.3 for generating a gamma process is not very efficient. A more efficient procedure involves using a series representation of the gamma process as described in algorithm 6.14 of Cont and Tankov (2004).

23.3.6   A Fast Approximation

To speed up the pricing algorithm we can make a number of simplifying assumptions which allow us to approximate the price. The advantage in having a fast approximate pricer is that it gives us a quick estimate which we can also use as a control variate for improving the price produced by the slower more exact pricer. Assuming that T is the time to the maturity date of the trade being priced, the simplifying assumptions are:

1. We assume that CDS spread curves are homogeneous and flat so that $c_i(t) = c_i$.
2. We assume that if a credit defaults before time T it defaults at time $T/2$.
3. We assume that the recovery rates are homogeneous.

The pricing algorithm is then:

1. Set $p = 1$.
2. Draw $j = 1, \ldots, n$ gamma distributed random variables $g_j^p \sim \Gamma(\gamma_j T, \lambda_j)$.
3. Set $I_p(T) = \sum_{j=1}^{n} g_j^p + aT$.
4. Set $k^p = 0$. This counts the number of defaults before time T in path p.
5. Set $i = 1$.
6. Draw a random exponential e_i^p.
7. If $I_p(T) < e_i^p / c_i$ then credit i defaults before time T and we set $k^p = k^p + 1$.
8. Set $i = i + 1$. If $i \leq N_C$ return to step (6).
9. Calculate the surviving tranche notional $Q_p(T/2)$ assuming k^p credits default at $T/2$.
10. Set $p = p + 1$. If $p \leq P$ then return to step (2).
11. Set $Q(t) = 1.0$ for $0 < t < T/2$. Set $Q(t) = 1/P \sum_{p=1}^{P} Q_p(T/2)$ for $T/2 \leq t < T$.
12. Given the tranche survival curve Q, pricing can be done as discussed in Section 12.7.

The main assumption made here is that all defaults before time T occur at time $T/2$. The quality of the approximation can easily be improved by spreading out the defaults so that they occur more uniformly through time. This would not significantly impact the speed, but would increase the accuracy of the approximation.

23.3.7 Calibration to the Skew

Calibration to the skew involves searching for the set of values of parameters (γ, λ) and a which best fit the market prices. The number of free parameters is actually not $2n + 1$ but $2n$. This is because if $X(t) \sim \Gamma(\gamma t, \lambda) + at$ then the scaling properties of a gamma distribution mean that sending $a \to ma$ and $\lambda \to \lambda/m$ gives

$$X(t) \sim mat + \Gamma(\gamma t, \lambda/m) = mat + m\Gamma(\gamma t, \lambda)$$

which is equivalent to $X(t) \to mX(t)$. This simply washes out in a rescaling of c.

Gradient-based optimisers do not work well for Monte Carlo-based models since there is often too much statistical noise in the objective function. One alternative optimiser is the down-hill simplex algorithm described in Press *et al.* (1992). This minimisation approach extends to multiple dimensions. One problem with this optimiser is that it needs to be started with a good guess and this can be done either by *trial and error* or by some more systematic search of parameter space. Once an optimal solution is found, it would be hoped that subsequent market moves would only require small local changes in the parameters which could be found by starting with the previous solution values.

We have used this optimiser to calibrate the IG model with $n = 2$ when the information arrival process is driven by two gamma processes plus a constant drift, and find that there is a good fit to the market. This is shown in Table 23.1 in terms of the calibrated prices. While the fit to the equity and first mezzanine tranches are within 1 bp, the fitting error for the more senior tranches is larger. This suggests adoption of a calibration weighting scheme which puts more emphasis on the more senior tranches. Nevertheless, the quality of the fit is already good enough to suggest that the intensity gamma model can capture the skew despite the fact that it is fairly parsimonious.

The parameter values used in this calibration are as follows: $\gamma_1 = 0.0008$, $\gamma_2 = 0.217$, $\lambda_1 = 0.00109$ and $\lambda_2 = 0.186$. We see that there are two gamma process with very different

Table 23.1 Calibration of intensity gamma process to CDX NA IG. We use $n = 2$ gamma processes. Model parameters are $\gamma_1 = 0.0008$, $\gamma_2 = 0.217$, $\lambda_1 = 0.0011$ and $\lambda_2 = 0.186$. We also set $a = 1$

Tranche	Market		Calibration	
K_1–K_2 (%)	Upfront (%)	Spread (bp)	Upfront (%)	Spread (bp)
0–3	24.88	500	24.88	500
3–7	0	90	0	90
7–10	0	18.25	0	20.23
10–15	0	8.00	0	12.47
15–30	0	3.50	0	6.46

dynamics. Since γ is a measure of the jump frequency and $1/\lambda$ is a measure of the jump size, we can conclude that the first process is one involving rare large jumps which are likely to generate multiple defaults. This can be thought of as the systemic 'factor'. The second process has many more smaller jumps, and results in a small number of defaults. This can be thought of as the idiosyncratic 'factor' since the credits are more independent. Once again we see the interplay between systemic and idiosyncratic risk being the mechanism for modelling the correlation skew.

Further improvements to the calibration can be achieved by adding a third gamma process to the dynamics of the business time process. We can also make the model richer by incorporating stochastic recovery rates.

Further insight into this model may be gained by calculating the tranchelet spreads across the capital structure. These are shown in Figure 23.3. We see that the spreads are monotonically

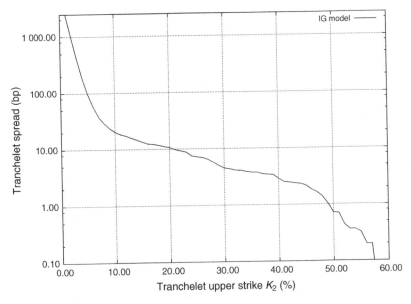

Figure 23.3 Tranchelet spread curves (plotted on a logarithmic scale) for the intensity gamma model. We use the best-fit calibration parameters for the fit to CDX NA IG Series 7. The breakeven spreads were computed using 100 000 Monte Carlo paths

decreasing, consistent with no-arbitrage constraints. The curve becomes less smooth as we move to the higher parts of the capital structure since losses in this region are becoming increasingly rare and so the standard error of the Monte Carlo increases. For $K_1 \geq 58\%$ we are approaching the maximum loss and the breakeven tranchelet spread falls to zero, indicating that not one out the 100 000 simulated paths resulted in a portfolio loss greater than 58%. Since the spread falls to zero, we conclude that there is no probability mass at the maximum loss as we found in some of the copula skew models.

23.3.8   Risk Management

Calculating risk within the IG model is very straightforward. For example, to calculate idiosyncratic or systemic delta, we simply perturb the spread curves and then recalibrate the values of the information arrival processes. The $2n$ model parameters (γ, λ) remain unchanged. One advantage of this model is that the perturbation and recalibration of the hazard rate function $c(t)$ to a single name is analytic and so can be performed quickly.

Table 23.2   Systemic tranche leverage ratios implied by the intensity gamma model for comparison with those implied by the base correlation model. This is for the CDX NA IG Series 7 tranches

Tranche (%)	IG model delta	Base corr. delta
0–3	24.85	23.03
3–7	5.13	5.48
7–10	0.56	1.38
10–15	0.49	0.64
15–30	0.38	0.25

Table 23.2 shows the tranche leverage ratios for CDX NA IG implied by the IG model. They are similar to the numbers produced by base correlation and the copula skew models described in the previous chapter. The slightly higher delta for the senior tranches is probably due to the fitting error in the market calibration which overstates the senior spread levels.

23.3.9   Fitting the Correlation Term Sturcture

The IG model is a full dynamic multi-issuer default model. It is arbitrage free in both the strike dimension and the time dimension. As a result we can certainly use it to price tranches on the same reference portfolio with non-standard strikes. When pricing tranches with non-standard maturities, we should take into account the existence of market prices for other maturities. These can be accommodated by allowing the model parameters to be time dependent. Unlike the copula approach, making the model parameters time dependent does not 'break' the no-arbitrage properties of the model in the time dimension. For example, we can use different values of (γ, λ) for $0 < T < 5$ than we do for $5 \leq T \leq 10$. Calibration can be performed using a bootstrap in which we determine first the parameters for $0 < T < 5$ and then determine the parameters for $5 \leq T \leq 10$.

23.3.10   Bespoke Tranches

Extending the IG model to handle tranches on non-standard reference portfolios requires us to make additional modelling assumptions. We should not decide to assign completely different business time processes to different reference portfolios since this would imply default independence between these portfolios. We would expect that US and European portfolios should have some positive correlation through their common exposure to a global economy. One way to induce a correlation would be to drive their respective business times using two or more gamma processes, and to make one of these gamma processes common to both portfolios. This would mean that both portfolios would experience the same shocks in the business time, and we could further generalise this by assigning some weighting scheme to make one portfolio more or less sensitive to these shocks than the other.

23.3.11   Spread Dynamics

The IG model can price and risk manage products which depend on the identity and timing of defaults in a portfolio. The question here is whether it can also be used to price products with a dependence on the distribution of forward tranche spreads such as tranche options. Although this model would imply a forward distribution of tranche spreads, using it to price tranche options is not recommended. For a start, all of the parameters of the model, even in the two-gamma process version, are required to fit the correlation skew. There is no slack left to ensure that any implied volatilities for tranche spreads could also be fitted. Furthermore, the shocks experienced due to the business time process are systemic shocks. If the $c_i(t)$ are deterministic, there are no idiosyncratic dynamics in the implied hazard rates of issuers. As a result, as a bottom-up model for spread dynamics, this model does not seem realistic unless we add an additional source of randomness to the dynamics, e.g. we make $c_i(t)$ stochastic.

23.3.12   Conclusions

The IG model is a full dynamic model of correlated default which exhibits a number of important characteristics including default clustering and stationarity. It is flexible enough to fit the base correlation skew with reasonable accuracy at a single maturity. To attempt to fit multiple maturities we can make the model parameters time-dependent. To assist fitting, additional parameters can be introduced by increasing the number of gamma processes which drive the business time.

   One weakness of the model is that it requires a Monte Carlo-based implementation and so is not as fast at pricing as some of the analytical copula models. However, there are several ways to improve upon this including the use of control variates and low discrepancy random numbers.

23.4   THE AFFINE JUMP DIFFUSION MODEL

The second dynamic correlation model we wish to describe in detail is the affine jump diffusion model by Duffie and Singleton (1998), first applied in the context of CDOs by Duffie and Garleanu (1999). This approach is based on modelling the evolution of the default intensity processes for all credits in terms of an affine jump diffusion process $X(t)$. This is given by

$$dX(t) = \kappa \left(\theta - X(t) \right) dt + \sigma \sqrt{X(t)}\, dW(t) + J\, dN(t). \tag{23.3}$$

Let us consider each of these terms:

- The first term makes $X(t)$ a mean-reverting process. In the absence of a jump process $X(t)$, i.e. $J = 0, X(t)$ mean reverts to a value θ at a rate determined by the value of κ.
- The second term is a continuous stochastic square root process of the type used to model interest rate dynamics in Cox *et al.* (1985). The $\sqrt{X(t)}$ term supposes that $X(t) > 0$ which is the case for the pure diffusive process if $2\kappa\theta > \sigma^2$.
- The final term is the pure jump process where jump sizes J are independent and exponentially distributed with mean jump size μ. Jump times are driven by a Poisson process $N(t)$ with intensity ℓ.

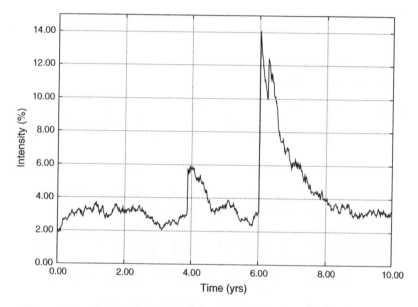

Figure 23.4   Simulation of the mean-reverting jump diffusion intensity process

This process is known as a *basic affine jump diffusion* (AJD) process. An example of the dynamics is shown in Figure 23.4. The first two moments of the process can be calculated analytically. In the long time limit, the expected value of $X(t)$ is given by

$$m = \lim_{t\to\infty} \mathbb{E}\,[X(t)] = \theta + \frac{\ell\mu}{\kappa}$$

while the variance is given by

$$v = \lim_{t\to\infty} \mathbb{E}\,[X(t)^2] - \mathbb{E}\,[X(t)]^2 = \frac{\sigma^2 m}{2\kappa} + \frac{\ell\mu^2}{\kappa}.$$

We wish to extend this model to multiple issuers. In doing so we wish to overcome the low default dependency problem of a purely diffusive model. This can be done by requiring that the intensity processes of different issuers have a *common* jump. Following Duffie and Garleanu (1999) and Mortensen (2006), we suppose that

$$\lambda_i(t) = \alpha_i X_c(t) + X_i(t)$$

where $X_c(t)$ is the common AJD process with parameters $(\kappa_c, \theta_c, \sigma_c, \mu_c, \ell_c)$ and $X_i(t)$ are also AJD processes with parameters $(\kappa_i, \theta_i, \sigma_i, \mu_i, \ell_i)$. The jump and diffusive components of the $X_i(t)$ and $X_c(t)$ are all independent. A parameter α_i is used to weight the relative importance of the common AJD process.

This is a model which is capable of spanning the range of default correlations from independence to maximum dependence. On average, in the long time limit, the number of systemic jumps experienced by credit i divided by the total number of jumps experienced by credit i is given by

$$w = \frac{\ell_c}{\ell_i + \ell_c}.$$

If $\ell_c = 0$ then $w = 0$ and none of the jumps are common. In this limit the credits are all independent. If $\ell_i = 0$ for all $i = 1, \ldots, N_C$ then $w = 1$ and we have perfectly correlated jumps in the issuer intensities.

23.4.1   Analytical Formulation

Although the model can be implemented using Monte Carlo techniques by simulating according to Equation 23.3, it is possible to calibrate the survival probabilities analytically. Consider a basic affine jump process $X(t)$ with parameters $(\kappa, \theta, \sigma, \mu, l)$. It is possible to show that

$$\mathbb{E}\left[e^{-\int_0^T X(s)ds}\right] = \exp\left(A + BX(0)\right) \tag{23.4}$$

where A and B are functions given in Section 23.6. In the case of our multi-name model of default, we can use this result to write the issuer survival probability

$$Q_i(T) = \mathbb{E}\left[\exp\left(-\int_0^T \lambda_i(s)ds\right)\right] = \exp\left(-\int_0^T (\alpha X_c(s) + X_i(s))ds\right)$$

$$= \exp\left(A\left(T; \kappa, \alpha_i\theta, \sqrt{\alpha_i}\sigma, \ell, \alpha_i\mu\right) + B\left(T; \kappa, \sqrt{\alpha_i}\sigma\right)\alpha_i X_c(0)\right)$$

$$\times \exp\left(A\left(T; \kappa_i, \theta_i, \sigma_i, \ell_i, \mu_i\right) + B\left(T; \kappa_i, \sigma_i\right)X_i(0)\right).$$

This result makes it numerically fast to calibrate the model to the issuer survival probabilities. One approach is to simply calibrate the model to the maturity of the contract being priced, e.g. five years. In this case, we need only one parameter. The natural choice of free parameter is to use the level of mean reversion, θ_i, as this does not play a significant role in the dynamics. For example, the long-term variance of the AJD process is independent of θ.

23.4.2   Conditional Independence

Although appealing, the initial reaction to this model which was published in the very early days of the correlation market was that its implementation for multi-name pricing is Monte Carlo based and so too slow to be practical. This is one reason why practitioners switched to copula models. However, Mortensen (2006) has shown that it is possible to cast this model into a conditionally independent framework. By conditioning on the integrated path[3]

---

[3] The conditional loss distribution depends only on the conditional survival probabilities of the credits and so depends only on the integral $\int_0^t X_c(s)ds$ and not on the entire path $\{X_c(s)\}_{s\in[0,t]}$.

$$Z(T) = \int_t^T X_c(s)ds \tag{23.5}$$

all of the credits are independent with conditional default probabilities given by

$$p_i\left(T \mid Z(T)\right) = 1 - \exp\left(-\alpha_i Z(T) + A\left(T; \kappa_i, \theta_i, \sigma_i, \mu_i, \ell_i\right) + B\left(T; \kappa_i, \sigma_i\right) X_i(0)\right).$$

We can then use the methods discussed in Chapter 18 to build the conditional loss distribution for the portfolio. The final step is to integrate these conditional loss distributions over the distribution of $Z(T)$. We can do this making use of the fact that the density of a probability distribution can be found by Fourier inverting its characteristic function φ_Z, i.e.

$$f_Z(z) = \frac{1}{2\pi} \int_{-\infty}^{\infty} e^{-iuz} \varphi_Z(u) du$$

where the characteristic function can be solved for analytically as described in Mortensen (2006).

23.4.3 Calibration Results

Mortensen (2006) shows that it is possible to calibrate this model to CDX NA IG quotes from August 2004. The results are shown in Table 23.3. The fit, based on an adjustment of five model parameters, is reasonable, but is certainly not within the bid-offer spread, especially the equity tranche. It is possible that the incorporation of stochastic recovery rates could improve the fit. It also remains to be seen if the AJD model calibrates well to the entire term structure tranche prices which would require us to make the model parameters time dependent. Note that doing this would not violate the no-arbitrage properties of this model as it would for a copula model.

Table 23.3   Calibration of affine jump diffusion process to CDX NA IG on 23rd August 2004 taken from Mortensen (2006). Model parameters are $\kappa = 0.20$, $\sigma = 0.054$, $l = 0.037$ and $\mu = 0.067$, $w = 0.93$. This calibration assumes heterogeneous spreads in the reference portfolio

Tranche	Market		Calibration	
	Upfront (%)	Spread (bp)	Upfront (%)	Spread (bp)
0–3	40.00	500	49.60	500
3–7	0	312.5	0	343.8
7–10	0	122.5	0	122.9
10–15	0	42.5	0	65.7
15–30	0	12.5	0	15.3

23.4.4 Bespoke Tranches

The pricing of tranches on pure US or European bespoke portfolios should be straightforward in this model since the parameters which have been calibrated to the corresponding index can be kept fixed with only the issuer survival curves being calibrated using the θ_i parameter. For mixed region bespokes, one approach could be to calibrate jointly to iTraxx tranches and CDX tranches each with a 'regional' jump process and one common 'global' jump process.

23.4.5   Conclusion

The affine jump diffusion model is an appealing model for correlated default. The individual spread dynamics, which are closely related to the intensity process dynamics, appear realistic as they imply infrequent positive jumps in spreads followed by a more gradual mean reversion to a lower spread level. Although default is more likely to occur when spreads are wide, it can occur at any time – it can be a surprise. Correlating default through the use of a common jump does also seem realistic. The model is also rich enough to be used for the pricing of products which have an exposure to the volatility of tranche spreads as discussed in Chapovsky et al. (2006).

23.5   SUMMARY

This chapter has discussed the broad range of approaches to bottom-up dynamic models of default correlation. We have highlighted two specific models and shown how they can be calibrated to the price of index tranches. It is still too early to say which, if any of these models, will become widely adopted for the purpose of pricing these products.

23.6   TECHNICAL APPENDIX

The deterministic functions A and B defined in the survival probability in equation 23.4 are given by

$$
A(T;\kappa,\theta,\sigma,\mu,l) = \frac{\kappa\theta(-c_1 - d_1)}{bc_1d_1}\log\left(\frac{c_1 + d_1e^{bT}}{c_1 + d_1}\right) + \frac{\kappa\theta}{c_1}T
$$
$$
+ \frac{l(ac_2 - d_2)}{bc_2d_2}\log\left(\frac{c_2 + d_2e^{bT}}{c_2 + d_2}\right) + \left(\frac{l}{c_2} - l\right)T
$$

and

$$
B(T;\kappa,\sigma) = \frac{1 - e^{bT}}{c_1 + d_1e^{bT}}
$$

where

$$
c_1 = \frac{-\kappa - \sqrt{\kappa^2 + 2\sigma^2}}{2}
$$

$$
d_1 = \frac{\kappa - \sqrt{\kappa^2 + 2\sigma^2}}{2}
$$

$$
b = \frac{d_1(\kappa + 2c_1) - (\kappa c_1 - \sigma^2)}{c_1 + d_1}
$$

$$
a = \frac{d_1}{c_1}
$$

$$
c_2 = 1 - \frac{\mu}{c_1}
$$

$$
d_2 = \frac{d_1 + \mu}{c_1}.
$$

24

Dynamic Top-down Correlation Models

24.1 INTRODUCTION

Dynamic default correlation models can be grouped into two main approaches which have become known as *bottom-up* and *top-down*. In the bottom-up approach, discussed in the previous chapter, each credit in the portfolio is modelled specifically and the portfolio loss distribution is the result of the aggregate behaviour of these individual correlated credits. The principal advantage of this approach is that it allows us to measure directly both idiosyncratic and systemic risks.

The disadvantage of bottom-up models is that calculation of the portfolio loss distribution is a computationally expensive task, especially when it is required to fit the correlation skew. If we then wish to layer a spread dynamics on top of the individual default dynamics in order to price spread and default contingent products, the computational effort required becomes significant.

For this reason, the market has begun to investigate the use of dynamic top-down skew models. In this approach, we forgo the issuer level specifics of the reference portfolio, focusing instead on the aggregate loss distribution and its dynamics. The hope is that what we lose in terms of the issuer-specific information, we compensate for by having tranche spread dynamics which are rich enough to allow us to calibrate to both the correlation skew and any tranche option volatility market that may develop.

Because we model the evolution of the spread and losses of the reference portfolio at an aggregate level, the hedges produced by the model will be at a systemic risk level. As a result, top-down models are best suited for products in which the underlying portfolio is one of the standard indices. Hedging idiosyncratic risks within these models is not so easy since it requires us to use conditioning techniques to extract the necessary information about a specific credit. As a result, it is best to use these top-down models in cases when the idiosyncratic risk is considered to be small.

In order to begin to price products with a dependence on tranche spread volatility, the first requirement is that a top-down model should be able to fit exactly the distribution of portfolio losses as implied by today's market for tranche prices. It should then be straightforward to price:

- Standard index tranches with non-standard strikes and non-standard maturities.
- Forward starting index tranches.
- Standard index tranches with loss-based triggers for which the contingent payments are not dependent on future spread levels, e.g. tranches in which the coupon increases by a fixed amount if a pre-specified loss threshold is crossed.

The first requirement of any correlation model is that it is arbitrage free in terms of how it models the current loss distribution surface. This is the probability of a specific loss on the reference portfolio at all future times. What is even more demanding is to require the model to evolve the loss surface through time in a way that retains its no-arbitrage properties.

This is a major technical challenge which can be compared to the challenge of evolving interest rate forward curves through time in an arbitrage-free manner. This problem was solved by Heath et al. (1992) who established a relationship between the drift and volatility of the forward interest rate process which ensured no-arbitrage. However, the challenge is even greater in the world of tranches as we need to worry about the no-arbitrage evolution of not just a curve but an entire loss surface, i.e. we cannot just ensure no-arbitrage in the time and maturity dimension, we also have to do it in the strike dimension. If we can achieve this, the aim is then to use this model to price spread and default contingent products. These include:

- Options on tranches on the standard indices.
- Leveraged super-senior tranches with loss triggers for which the value on the future trigger date is a function of the super-senior spread.
- Tranches which embed deleveraging triggers linked to the spread of the reference portfolio or the tranche spread.

A number of 'top-down' dynamic credit models have been proposed beginning with the models by Frey and Backhaus (2004), Schönbucher (2005), Andersen et al. (2005) and Bennani (2005). These have been followed by a second wave of top-down models including Brigo et al. (2006), Errais et al. (2006) and Di Graziano and Rogers (2006). The aim of this chapter is not to present a full survey of all of these pricing models but to impart a sense of what a top-down model does and how it does it. We therefore focus on just one of these models, namely the Markov chain model in Schönbucher (2005).

24.2   THE MARKOV CHAIN APPROACH

The Markov chain approach introduced by Schönbucher (2005) is a top-down model of the portfolio default loss process $L(t)$. Schönbucher assumes a homogeneous loss portfolio of N_C credits and defines a loss process

$$L(t) = \sum_{i=1}^{N_C} \mathbf{1}_{\tau_i \leq t}$$

where $L(t)$ has $N_C + 1$ integer states $\{0, 1, 2, \ldots, N_C\}$. Strictly speaking, $L(t)$ is not a loss process as it is not a measure of the loss but of the number of defaults. However we retain this terminology to be consistent with the original paper.

This loss process is piecewise constant, has one-step increments (we assume no joint defaults) and is non-decreasing as shown in Figure 24.1. The actual loss on the portfolio at time t is given by

$$\text{Loss}(t) = \frac{(1 - R)}{N_C} L(t)$$

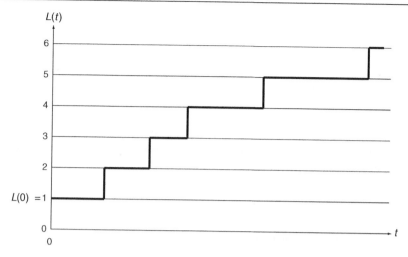

Figure 24.1   An example path for the evolution of the loss process $L(t)$ in which $L(0) = 1$

where R is the homogeneous recovery rate and we assume equal face value exposures for each credit. We can therefore define a loss unit $u = (1 - R)/N_C$. Note also that $L(0) > 0$ if we are pricing an existing trade in which defaults have occurred on the reference portfolio.

Our exposition of this model is separated into two parts:

1. In the first part we model the evolution of the loss process to horizon times T based on information available today time 0. A Markov chain is used to evolve the portfolio loss distribution and the initial generator matrix $A(T) = A(0, T)$ which governs the evolution of the portfolio loss process is fully known. The loss process distributions are unconditional and the generator matrix $A(T)$ can be implied by the prices of market tranches.

2. We then model the evolution of the entire loss surface by allowing the generator matrix $A(t, T)$ to evolve stochastically through time $t > 0$. Note the extra time argument t in the generator. The loss process distributions are then conditional on the future information set $\mathcal{F}_t$. By calculating product payoffs conditional on these future distributions and then taking a discounted expectation over $\mathcal{F}_t$, we can price instruments such as options on tranches.

We begin by setting out the no-arbitrage conditions of the initial and future portfolio loss distribution.

24.2.1   No-arbitrage Conditions

We define the discrete distribution of the loss process at future horizon time T as

$$p_n(0, T) = \Pr\left(L(T) = n\right) \quad \text{for all } n = 0, 1, \ldots, N_C.$$

Later, we will wish to evolve the loss distribution forward to time t in order to price forward starting tranches and options on tranches. We therefore introduce the conditional loss distribution $p_n(t, T)$. This is defined as

$$p_n(t, T) = \Pr\left(L(T) = n \mid \mathcal{F}_t\right) \quad \text{for all } n = 0, 1, \ldots, N_C$$

where we condition on information up to time t. The no-arbitrage properties of $p_n(t, T)$ for $t \geq 0$ and $T \geq t$ are as follows:

- $p_n(t, T) \geq 0$, i.e. all probabilities are non-negative and the sum of the distribution probabilities at a fixed horizon time equals one, i.e. $\sum_{i=1}^{N_C} p_n(t, T) = 1$.
- We also have $p_n(t, t) = \mathbf{1}_{L(t)=n}$, i.e. at time t we know that the entire loss distribution for losses to time t is all on the loss amount $L(t) = n$ which corresponds to n defaults.
- $p_n(t, T) = 0$ if $n < L(t)$, which says that the probability of a loss lower than the current value of the loss process at some later time T is zero since $L(t)$ can only increase with time.
- Finally, the function

$$\Pr\left(L(T) \leq n | \mathcal{F}_t\right) = \sum_{m=0}^{n} p_m(t, T)$$

is a constant or decreasing function of T.

These are necessary conditions for the current and future loss distributions to be arbitrage free and are an alternative representation of the no-arbitrage conditions set out in Section 19.5 which were expressed in terms of the ETL.

24.3 MARKOV CHAIN: INITIAL GENERATOR

We now show how the initial loss distribution is determined by the initial value of the generator matrix.

24.3.1 Dynamics of the Loss Process

We model the dynamics of the loss process via time inhomogeneous Markov chains. The dynamics of the loss process is governed by the deterministic loss transition rates which we denote with $a_{ij}(T)$. This represents the rate at which probability mass is transferred from loss level i to loss level j at future horizon time T. The no-arbitrage condition on the generator matrix $A(T)$ with elements $a_{ij}(T)$ is given by

$$a_{ij}(T) = 0 \quad \text{for all } i > j$$
$$a_{ij}(T) \geq 0 \quad \text{for all } i < j$$
$$a_{ij}(T) = 0 \quad \text{for all } j, i = N_C. \tag{24.1}$$

The first condition ensures that loss probability only flows to higher loss states, i.e. the portfolio loss cannot decrease. The second condition ensures that the rate at which probability flows from low to high losses must be positive. The last condition ensures that the maximum loss is an *absorbing state*. There is a further condition due to the conservation of probability which is that $\sum_{j=0}^{N_C} a_{ij}(T) = 0$. The probability distribution of the portfolio losses at a future horizon time T as seen from time 0 is given by

$$P(0, T) = \begin{pmatrix} p_0(0, T) \\ p_1(0, T) \\ \vdots \\ p_{N_C}(0, T) \end{pmatrix}.$$

This is implied by the market prices of index tranches observed in the market today. We can therefore write the dynamics for the evolution of the loss process distribution to more distant horizon times T in the form

$$\frac{dP(0,T)}{dT} = A(T)P(0,T).$$

Both $A(T)$ and $P(0,T)$ are matrices and so this equation involves matrix multiplication. In the time homogeneous case when $A(t) = A$, the solution to this equation is given by

$$P(0,T) = P(0,0) \exp(A \cdot T).$$

This can be calculated using the series expansion of the exponential function of a matrix.[1]

24.3.2   Single-step Transition Model

We now investigate a restricted version of the Markov chain model in which the loss process can only increase by one default per infinitesimal time step. This is consistent with our earlier assumption of no joint defaults. We also return to the time inhomogeneous case in which the generator matrix is time dependent and is given by $A(T)$. The generator matrix is now given by

$$A(T) = \begin{pmatrix} -a_0(T) & a_0(T) & 0 & \cdots & 0 \\ 0 & -a_1(T) & a_1(T) & \cdots & 0 \\ \vdots & 0 & 0 & \ddots & \vdots \\ 0 & 0 & \cdots & -a_{NC-1}(T) & a_{NC-1}(T) \\ 0 & 0 & 0 & \cdots & 0 \end{pmatrix}. \qquad (24.2)$$

The dynamics for the portfolio loss process $L(t)$ can then be represented as a simple binomial tree as shown in Figure 24.2.

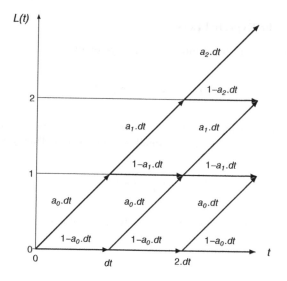

Figure 24.2   Evaluation of the portfolio loss process $L(t)$ for a single-step transition model

---

[1] See Moler and van Loan (2003) for a discussion of numerical approaches which can be used to calculate the exponential of a matrix.

Although these single-step dynamics do not prevent all loss states being reached in finite time, they make it harder to have catastrophic events in which the loss process jumps by a large amount in a short period of time. The advantage of this version of the model is that only one parameter, $a_n(T)$, controls the evolution of the loss process at time T beyond a level n. It means that the model is parsimonius and the evolution of $P(0, T)$ is also easier to calculate.

The evolution of the loss process probabilities can be solved analytically. For example, the probability of no defaults between time zero and time T is given by

$$p_{L(0)}(0, T) = \exp\left(-\int_0^T a_0(s)ds\right).$$

The probability of n defaults at time T is given by

$$p_n(0, T) = \int_0^T e^{-\int_s^T a_n(u)du} p_{n-1}(0, s)a_{n-1}(s)ds \quad \text{where} \quad n > L(0).$$

The evolution of the unconditional loss process is therefore governed by the vector of N_C transition rates $a_0(T), \ldots, a_{N_C-1}(T)$. It is not hard to see how the values of these parameters will affect the loss distribution. For example, high values of $a_n(T)$ will tend to move the loss process above $L(T) = n$ while very low values of $a_n(T)$ will tend to keep the loss process at or below n. If $a_n(T) = 0$ then the portfolio loss process will not be able to increase beyond n.

Note that we can also solve the inverse problem which is to determine the values of $a_n(T)$ based on the loss distribution. This is given by

$$a_n(T) = -\frac{1}{p_n(0, T)} \sum_{k=L(0)}^n \frac{\partial p_k(0, T)}{\partial T}. \tag{24.3}$$

24.3.3   Calculating the Expected Loss

The expected loss of the portfolio at future time T is given by

$$\mathbb{E}[L(T)] = u \sum_{l=1}^{N_C} p_l(0, T)l.$$

To see how the evolution of the expected loss is linked to the transition rates, consider the expected value of the change in loss over a small time interval dt. This is given by

$$\mathbb{E}[dL(t)] = u \sum_{l=0}^{N_C} p_l(0, t)a_l(t)dt.$$

We see that the evolution of the expected loss is a weighted sum of the transition rates.[2]

---

[2] If we set the transition rates to be level independent and time independent, i.e. $a_l(t) = a$, then we have

$$\mathbb{E}[dL(t)] = ua\,dt \rightarrow L(T) = L(0) + uaT.$$

24.3.4   Pricing the Index Swap

Given an initial Libor discount curve $Z(t)$, we can value the underlying index swap with fixed coupon $C(T)$ in terms of the forward transition rates $a_n(t)$. We first write the value of the T-maturity premium payment leg (ignoring coupon accrued at default for simplicity) at time zero as

$$\text{Premium leg PV}(0, T) = C(T) \sum_{n=1}^{N_T} Z(t_n)\,(1 - \mathbb{E}\,[L(t_n)]\,/N_C)\,.$$

This can then be written as

$$\text{Premium leg PV}(0, T) = C(T) \sum_{n=1}^{N_T} Z(t_n) \sum_{l=0}^{N_C}(1 - l/N_C)p_l(0, t_n).$$

The protection leg present value can be written as

$$\text{Protection leg PV}(0, T) = \int_0^T Z(s)\mathbb{E}\,[dL(s)]$$

which becomes

$$\text{Protection leg PV}(0, T) = u \int_0^T Z(s) \sum_{l=0}^{N_C} p_l(0, s)a_l(s)ds.$$

From these equations we can calculate the index upfront as defined in Chapter 10. These equations can also be easily extended to handle tranches.

24.3.5   Calibration

Calibration of this model to the market prices of tranches should be exact assuming that the market prices are themselves arbitrage free. Schönbucher (2005) shows that for any arbitrage-free loss distribution, a representation with transition rates always exists. What calibration means in the context of this model is determining the generator matrix $A(T)$ which enables the model to reprice the market tranches and the underlying index swap. We can consider two main approaches to calibration:

1. Perform some sort of minimisation of the index and tranche pricing error by varying the elements of generator matrix $A(T)$ using an optimiser. We call this the *direct approach.*
2. Calibrate $A(T)$ to the loss distribution implied by another model which has also been fitted to the market prices. This is the *indirect* approach. This approach makes use of equation 24.3. The problem with this approach is that it fails as soon as one $p_n(0, T)$ equals zero. Whether this is likely or not very much depends on the market prices and the choice of model. It also assumes the existence of a model which can provide an arbitrage-free loss distribution to all future times and which fits the market exactly.

Because of the problems with the second approach, we have performed a *direct* calibration of the model to the CDX NA IG tranche spreads in Table 20.1. Since we are only calibrating to the five-year tranches, we assumed time homogeneity so that $A(t) = A$. We are also using the

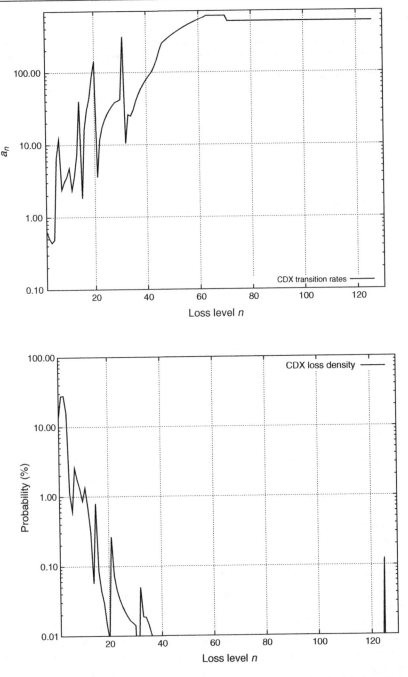

Figure 24.3 Transition rates and portfolio loss distribution at maturity for the Markov chain model calibrated to the CDX NA IG tranche spreads in Table 20.1

single-transition version of the model in which the matrix A is bi-diagonal as in equation 24.2. Calibration therefore involves determining the vector of N_C transition rates $(a_0, a_1, a_2, \ldots, a_{124})$. With 125 parameters, an exact fit to five tranches and one index swap should certainly be possible.

In this model, different transition rates can be associated directly to the price of different tranches. For example, suppose that $N_C = 125$ and $R = 40\%$. Changing a_7 does not affect the price of a 0–3% equity tranche since the equity tranche is completely wiped out with seven defaults as this equates to a loss of $7 \times (100\% - 40\%)/125 = 3.36\%$. For this reason we investigate a fitting approach which uses a bootstrap. Care is needed since it is also important that the transition rates reprice the index swap. For example, it would not be helpful if the model was calibrated to fit the equity tranche and produced an exact fit with a value of $a_6 = 0$. The effect of this would be to cap the portfolio loss process at $6 \times (100\% - 40\%)/125 = 2.88\%$. It would then be impossible to fit the index swap and the higher tranches would all be risk free. This problem can be overcome by fitting to the equity tranche and the index swap simultaneously. A sketch of the calibration strategy for the CDX tranches would be as follows:

1. Fit the 0–3% tranche and index swap simultaneously by allowing a_0 to a_6 to vary.
2. Fit the 3–7% tranche and index swap simultaneously by allowing a_7 to a_{14} to vary.
3. Repeat this process for more senior tranches as we ascend the capital structure.

Figure 24.3 shows the results of a calibration of the transition rates to the tranche spreads and index spread shown in Table 20.1. We also show the terminal loss distribution of the portfolio. Both curves have been plotted using a logarithmic scale in order to capture the wide variation in the values of a_n and $p_n(0, T)$. As expected, we see that both a_n and $p_n(0, T)$ are everywhere positive, confirming that the input prices are arbitrage free. The curves are not smooth, reflecting the non-parametric and reasonably unconstrained nature of the calibration. In most cases the discontinuities occur when crossing the loss boundary between different tranches.

We see that there is a close relationship between the value of the transition rate and the loss density function. When the value of a_n peaks, it coincides with a very low value of p_n. This is because when a_n is high, the probability mass is moving beyond this loss size at a high rate. For the opposite reason, sudden drops in a_n result in peaks of probability mass in the loss distribution. Note also that the model assigns a non-zero probability to the maximum loss.

This discussion has only considered calibrating to the market tranches at one maturity. In practice we can calibrate this model to the term structure of tranche prices by allowing the single-step transition rates to be time-dependent.

24.4 MARKOV CHAIN: STOCHASTIC GENERATOR

Having calibrated this model to the initial term structure of the loss distribution, we now wish to evolve this 'loss surface' forward in time to price products whose value is linked to future loss distributions. For options and other products whose value depends on the future probability distribution of tranche spreads, we also need to have spread dynamics which are *not conditional* on the default or survival of other credits. We can do this by making the Markov chain generator matrix stochastic. We therefore write the generator matrix as $A(t, T)$. It now has two time arguments. The first, t, is the future time at which the generator matrix is known. The second argument, T, is the time to which this generator matrix applies, i.e. at future time t, $a_{ij}(t, T)$ tells us the rate at which probability mass flows from loss level i to loss level j at a later time T.

24.4.1 Stochastic Single-step Transition Rates

We return to the single-step transition version of the Markov model and we define a process for each transition rate

$$da_n(t, T) = \mu_n(t, T)dt + \sigma_n(t, T)dW$$

where $\sigma_n(t, T) \geq 0$ and W is a d-dimensional Brownian motion. If $d = 1$ we have a one-factor dynamics so that the random changes in the transition rates at all loss levels n are always in the same direction with the size of the change dependent on $\sigma_n(t, T)$. In this case the average loss of the index portfolio either increases or decreases depending on whether dW is positive or negative.

The model has two sets of dynamics:

1. A stochastic process for the transition rates $a_n(t, T)$ which evolve through time t.
2. The evolution of the loss process according to the transition rates $a_n(t, T)$ at time t.

We introduce the conditional loss distribution $p_n(t, T)$. This is defined as

$$p_n(t, T) = \Pr\left(L(T) = n \mid \mathcal{F}_t\right).$$

The stochastic process for the transition rates $a_n(t, T)$ implies a stochastic process for the *transition probabilities* $P_{nm}(t, T)$. Given a current generator matrix $A(t, T)$, these transition probabilities are defined as

$$P_{nm}(t, T) = \Pr\left(L(T) = m \mid L(t) = n\right).$$

The dynamics of $A(t, T)$ and $L(t)$ are consistent with each other if and only if

$$p_m(t, T) = P_{L(t),m}(t, T).$$

The transition probabilities can be solved analytically in terms of the transition rates to give

$$P_{nm}(t, T) = \begin{cases} 0 & m < n \\ \exp\left(-\int_t^T a_n(t, s)ds\right) & m = n \\ \int_t^T P_{n,m-1}(t, s)a_{m-1}(t, s)\exp\left(-\int_s^T a_m(t, u)du\right)ds & m > n. \end{cases} \qquad (24.4)$$

Given a term structure of matrices $A(t, T)$, for a given value of $n \geq 0$, we can use these equations to first evaluate the transition probability for $m = n$ and then for $m = n + 1$, $m = n + 2$ and so on.

24.4.2 No-arbitrage Condition

The dynamic process for the future transition rates $a_n(t, T)$ implies a dynamic process for the future transition probabilities which we write in the form

$$dP_{nm}(t, T) = u_{nm}(t, T)dt + v_{nm}(t, T)dW.$$

The challenge now is to take the no-arbitrage conditions for $P_{nm}(t, T)$ and to use them to specify restrictions on the dynamics of $a_n(t, T)$ which ensure that future loss distributions are arbitrage free.

Given these dynamics, the values of $u_{nm}(t,T)$ and $v_{nm}(t,T)$ can be expressed in terms of the dynamics of the transition rates. Using equation 24.4 and after some Ito calculus, Schönbucher (2005) shows that

$$u_{nm}(t,T) = \begin{cases} 0 & m < n \\ a_n(t,t) - \int_t^T \mu_n(t,s)ds + \frac{1}{2}\left(\int_t^T \sigma_n(t,s)ds\right)^2 & m = n \\ -a_{m-1}(t,t)P_{mm}(t,T)\mathbf{1}_{m=n+1} + \int_t^T e^{-\int_s^T a_m(t,u)du} \\ \times \left[-P_{nm}(t,s)\mu_m(t,s) + \hat{\mu}_{n,m-1}(t,s) - \sigma_m(t,s)v_{nm}(t,s)\right]ds & m > n \end{cases}$$

(24.5)

and

$$v_{nm}(t,T) = \begin{cases} 0 & m < n \\ P_{nm}(t,T)\left(-\int_t^T \sigma_n(t,s)ds\right) & m = n \\ \int_t^T e^{-\int_s^T a_m(t,u)du}\left(\hat{\sigma}_{n,m-1}(t,s) - P_{nm}(t,s)\sigma_m(t,s)\right)ds & m > n \end{cases}$$

(24.6)

where for $m > n$, we have

$$\hat{\mu}_{n,m-1}(t,T) = a_{m-1}(t,T)u_{n,m-1}(t,T) + P_{n,m-1}(t,T)\mu_{m-1}(t,T)$$
$$+ \sigma_{m-1}(t,T)v_{n,m-1}(t,T)$$

and

$$\hat{\sigma}_{n,m-1}(t,T) = P_{n,m-1}(t,T)\sigma_{m-1}(t,T) + a_{m-1}(t,T)v_{n,m-1}(t,T).$$

The no-arbitrage restriction on the drift of the transition rate gives

$$\mu_m(t,T) = -\frac{\sigma_m(t,T)v_{L(t),m}(t,T)}{P_{L(t),m}(t,T)}.$$

(24.7)

This condition arises out of the requirement that $a_m(t,T){\cdot}P_{L(t),m}(t,T)$ is a martingale and is a consequence of the fact that $P_{L(t),m}(t,T)$ must be a martingale. In other words, under the risk-neutral measure, the probability today of m defaults at time T must be the same as the expectation of the probability of m defaults at time T conditional on $L(t)$ defaults at time t. Mathematically, we have

$$\mathbb{E}\left[P_{L(t),m}(t,T)|\mathcal{F}_t\right] = p_m(0,T).$$

Note that we have assumed that the loss process is independent of interest rates.

24.4.3   Valuation

The best way to understand this model is to use it to price a product which requires a dynamic loss model. We choose the European option on a tranche. Consider an option to enter into a short protection position in a tranche which pays a contractual spread $S(K_1,K_2)$ which is fixed today and which has attachment and detachment points K_1 and K_2 which are also fixed today. The option expires at time T_E and the underlying tranche matures at time T_M. We assume that a volatility structure for the transition rates $a_n(t,T)$ given by $\sigma_n(t,T)$ has been specified.

The process involves a Monte Carlo simulation over $p = 1,\ldots,N_P$ paths. The steps in the valuation are as follows:

1. Calibrate the initial time zero generator matrix $A(T) = A(0,T)$ which reprices the liquid tranches and the index swap. In the single-step transition version, this involves determining

the vector of transition rates which we denote with $a_n(0, T)$ for all $T \in [0, T_M]$. A direct method for calibrating to one time horizon has already been discussed. However, if we have a term structure of tranche prices then we would allow $a_n(0, T)$ to have a term structure.

2. Initialise Monte-Carlo path $p = 1$.
3. Initialise $L(0)$ to the number of defaults incurred by the reference portfolio before time 0 and set $t = 0$.
4. Set $t \rightarrow t + dt$.
5. If $t = T_E$ then continue to step (10). Otherwise continue to step (6).
6. At this next time t, calculate transition probabilities $P_{nm}(t, T)$ from equation 24.4 and transition volatilities $v_{nm}(t, T)$ from equation 24.6. Then, using equation 24.7, calculate the no-arbitrage drift $\mu_n(t_k, T)$.
7. Evolve the transition rates to the next time step according to the discretised stochastic process

$$a_n(t + dt, T) = a_n(t, T) + \mu_n(t, T)dt + \sigma_n(t, T)dW.$$

8. Simulate the loss process at the next time step. This is given by

$$L(t + dt) = \begin{cases} L(t) & \text{with probability } \exp(-a_n(t, t)dt) \\ L(t) + 1 & \text{with probability } 1 - \exp(-a_n(t, t)dt). \end{cases}$$

This can be done by drawing an independent uniform random number u. If $u < 1 - \exp(-a_n(t, t)dt)$ then default occurs and the loss process is increased by 1.

9. Return to step (4).
10. Calculate the loss distribution at option expiry, i.e. $P_{L(T_E),m}(T_E, T)$, according to equation 24.4. For this we need $L(T_E)$ and $a_n(T_E, T)$ for $T \in [T_E, T_M]$. Using this loss distribution calculate the value of the tranche at expiry $V(T_E, T_M, K_1, K_2)$.
11. Calculate the option payoff. This is given by $X_p = \max[V(T_E, T_M, K_1, K_2), 0]$.
12. Set $p = p + 1$. If $p \leq N_P$ return to step (3).
13. Calculate the average payoff $X = \frac{1}{N_P} \sum_{p=1}^{N_P} X_p$ and discount the result by multiplying by $Z(0, T_E)$.

The most important thing to note about this simulation is that the no-arbitrage drift ensures that the dynamics of the $a_n(t, T)$ do not destroy the initial calibration. In this sense, this model is exactly analogous to the HJM model used for the modelling of interest rate dynamics.

The model specification here assumes the input of a single-factor loss-level-dependent volatility structure $\sigma_n(t, T)$. Setting $\sigma_n(t, T) = 0$ turns off the spread volatility, making the model a pure default-only model. Applying different values of $\sigma_n(t, T)$ to different loss levels n would have the effect of redistributing losses across the capital structure, effectively changing the level and shape of the correlation skew. Schönbucher (2005) also points out that the loss-level dependence of $\sigma_n(t, T)$ can be used to control idiosyncratic risk effects.

24.4.4 Conclusion

Overall, this approach is very promising. First and foremost, the choice of the transition rate $a_n(t, T)$ as the fundamental quantity which is evolved means that guaranteeing an arbitrage-free evolution of the entire loss distribution consists of ensuring that $a_n(t, T) \geq 0$ at all times T and for all loss levels n. In the deterministic case, this is easy to control. When $a_n(t, T)$ is diffusive, it requires an appropriate choice of dynamics and a careful fitting. An exact calibration to tranche prices should be possible as long as they are arbitrage free. Furthermore, by allowing $A(t, T)$ to evolve stochastically, we have the ability to price products which have a default and spread dependence. Depending on the exact dynamics, there should also be enough parameters to enable the model to fit a tranche option volatility market if one does appear. Also, the model appears reasonably tractable and hopefully will be fast enough to use in a production setting.

24.5   SUMMARY

We have motivated the need for top-down models which are a new departure for credit modelling. The hope is that by modelling just the aggregate loss distribution as the fundamental state variable, we will be better able to build models which combine default and spread dynamics in a coherent manner. This will make it possible to price and risk manage a whole set of new derivative products on the standard tranches including options on tranches, leveraged super-senior, and other products which embed some combination of portfolio default and index spread dependency.

We have gone into the details of the Markov chain model. We have seen how it captures the interplay between spread and default risk in a coherent and consistent manner, how it can exactly fit the current prices of market tranches, and how it can be implemented in a manner which renders it no-arbitrage.

It is also worth emphasising that there are other top-down approaches to consider. Some of these other approaches appear promising, and require further investigation in order to establish their respective strengths and weaknesses. It is therefore too early to state or even attempt to predict which approach will be adopted by the market.

Appendix A
Useful Formulae

Gaussian probability density function

$$\phi(x) = \frac{1}{\sqrt{2\pi}} e^{-x^2/2}.$$

Gaussian cumulative distribution function

$$\Phi(x) = \frac{1}{\sqrt{2\pi}} \int_{-\infty}^{x} e^{-z^2/2} dz.$$

Gaussian integration

$$e^{+m^2/2v} = \frac{1}{\sqrt{2\pi v}} \int_{-\infty}^{\infty} e^{-z^2/2v + mz/v} dz.$$

Expansion of the exponential function

$$e^x = 1 + \sum_{k=1}^{\infty} \frac{x^k}{k!}.$$

Gaussian bi-variate probability density function

$$\phi_2(x, y, \rho) = \frac{1}{2\pi \sqrt{1 - \rho^2}} \exp\left(-\frac{x^2 - 2\rho xy + y^2}{2(1 - \rho^2)} \right).$$

Gaussian bi-variate cumulative distribution function

$$\Phi_2(a, b, \rho) = \frac{1}{2\pi \sqrt{1 - \rho^2}} \int_{-\infty}^{a} dx \int_{-\infty}^{b} dy \exp\left(-\frac{x^2 - 2\rho xy + y^2}{2(1 - \rho^2)} \right).$$

Gaussian tri-variate cumulative distribution function

$$\Phi_3(a, b, c, \rho) = \int_{-\infty}^{a} \frac{e^{-x^2/2}}{\sqrt{2\pi}} \Phi_2\left(\frac{b - \rho_{12}x}{\sqrt{1 - \rho_{12}^2}}, \frac{c - \rho_{13}x}{\sqrt{1 - \rho_{12}\rho_{13}}}, \frac{\rho_{23} - \rho_{12}\rho_{13}}{\sqrt{1 - \rho_{12}^2}\sqrt{1 - \rho_{12}\rho_{13}}} \right) dx.$$

Gaussian n-variate cumulative distribution function

$$\Phi_n(\mathbf{a}, \Sigma) = \left(\prod_{i=1}^{N} \int_{-\infty}^{a_i} dx_i \right) \left(\frac{1}{2\pi} \right)^{N/2} \frac{1}{\sqrt{\det \Sigma}} \exp\left(-\frac{1}{2} x^\top \Sigma_{ij}^{-1} x \right).$$

Student-t probability density function

$$f_v(t) = \frac{\Gamma((v+1)/2)}{\sqrt{v\pi}\,\Gamma(v/2)} \left(1 + \frac{t^2}{v}\right)^{-(v+1)/2}.$$

Gamma function

$$\Gamma(x) = \int_0^\infty t^{x-1} e^{-t} dt \quad x > 0.$$

Gamma distribution probability density function

$$f(x; \gamma, \lambda) = \frac{\lambda^\gamma}{\Gamma(\gamma)} x^{\gamma-1} e^{-\lambda x} \quad \text{for } x, \gamma, \lambda > 0.$$

Bibliography

Ahluwalia, R., McGinty, L. and Beinstein, E. (2004) A relative value framework for credit correlation, Research Paper, JP Morgan.

Altman, E., Brady, B., Resti, A. and Sironi, A. (2003a) The link between default and recovery rates: theory, empirical evidence and implications, Working paper.

Altman, E., Resti, A. and Sironi, A. (2003b) Default recovery rates in credit risk modelling: a review of the literature and empirical evidence, Working paper.

Andersen, L. (2005) Discount curve construction with tension splines, Working paper.

Andersen, L. (2006a) CDS options, CMDS, general PDEs and index options, Lecture notes.

Andersen, L. (2006b) Portfolio losses in factor models: term structures and intertemporal loss dependence, Working paper, Bank of America.

Andersen, L. and Sidenius, J. (2004) Extensions to the gaussian copula: random recovery and random factor loadings, *Journal of Credit Risk*, 1:29–70.

Andersen, L., Sidenius, J. and Basu, S. (2003) All your hedges in one basket, *Risk*.

Andersen, L., Piterbarg, V. and Sidenius, J. (2005) A new framework for dynamic credit portfolio loss modelling, Working paper.

Baheti, P. and Morgan, S. (2007) Base correlation mapping, *Lehman Brothers Quantitative Credit Research Quarterly*, Q1.

Baxter, M. (2006) Dynamic modelling of single-name credits and CDO tranches, Working paper.

Baxter, M. and Rennie, A. (1996) *Financial Calculus, an Introduction to Derivative Pricing*, Cambridge University Press.

Bennani, N. (2005) The forward loss model: a dynamic term structure approach for the pricing of portfolio credit derivatives, Working paper, Royal Bank of Scotland.

Black, F. (1976) The pricing of commodity contracts, *Journal of Financial Economics*, 3(2):167–179.

Black, F. and Jones, R. (1987) Simplifying portfolio insurance, *Journal of Portfolio Management*, 13:48–51.

Brigo, D. and Mercurio, F. (2001) *Interest Rate Models: Theory and Practice*, Springer Finance, 2001.

Brigo, D., Pallavicini, A. and Torresetti, R. (2006) Calibration of CDO tranches with the dynamical generalized-Poisson loss model, Working paper.

Burtschell, X., Gregory, J. and Laurent, J.-P. (2005) Beyond the gaussian copula: stochastic and local correlation, Working paper.

Cariboni, J. and Schoutens, W. (2006) Jumps in intensity models, Working paper.

Chapovsky, A., Rennie, A. and Tavares, P.A.C. (2006) Stochastic intensity modeling for structured credit exotics, Working paper.

Cherubini, U., Luciano, E. and Vecchiato, W. (2004) *Copula Methods in Finance*, John Wiley & Sons.

Cont, R. and Tankov, P. (2004) *Financial Modelling with Jump Processes*, Chapman and Hall.

Cox, J.C., Ingersoll, J.E. and Ross, S.A. (1985) A theory of the term structure of interest rates, *Econometrica*, 53(2):385–407.

Davis, M.H.A. and Lo, V. (2001a) Infectious defaults, *Quantitative Finance*, 1(4):382–387.

Davis, M.H.A. and Lo, V. (2001b) Modelling default correlation in bond portfolios, *Mastering Risk Volume 2: Applications*, Financial Times/Prentice-Hall, pages 141–151.

Di Graziano, G. and Rogers, C. (2006) A dynamic approach to the modelling of correlation credit derivatives using Markov chains, Working Paper, University of Cambridge.

Duffie, D. (1996) *Dynamic Asset Pricing Theory*, Princeton University Press.

Duffie, D. (1998) Credit swap valuation, Working paper.

Duffie, D. and Garleanu, N. (1999) Risk and valuation of collateralized debt obligations, Working paper, Graduate School of Business, Stanford University.

Duffie, D. and Singleton, K. (1998) Simulating correlated defaults, Working paper, Graduate School of Business, Stanford University.

Duffie, D., Eckner, A., Horel, G. and Saita, L. (2006) Frailty correlated default, Working paper, Stanford University.

Elizade, A. (2006) Credit risk models I: default correlation in intensity models. CEMFI working paper No. 0605.

Errais, E., Giesecke, K. and Goldberg, L. (2006) Pricing credit from the top down with affine point processes, Working paper, Stanford University and MSCI Barra.

Finger, C. (1999) Conditional approaches for CreditMetrics portfolio distributions, *CreditMetrics Monitor*, pages 14–33.

Frank, J. and Torous, W. (1989) An empirical investigation of US firms in reorganization, *Journal of Finance*, 44:747–769.

Frey, R. and Backhaus, J.(2004) Portfolio credit risk models with interacting default intensities: a Markovian approach, Working paper, University of Leipzig.

Fritsch, F. and Carlson, R. (1980) Monotone piecewise cubic interpolation, *SIAM Journal on Numerical Analysis*, 17(2):238–246.

Ganguin, B. and Bilardello, J. (2005) *Fundamentals of Corporate Credit Analysis*, McGraw-Hill.

Geske, R. (1977) The valuation of corporate liabilities as compound options, *Journal of Financial and Quantitative Analysis*, 12:541–552.

Glasserman, P. (2004) *Monte-Carlo Methods in Financial Engineering*, Springer.

Gordy, M. (2003) A risk-factor model foundation for ratings-based bank capital rules, *Journal of Financial Intermediation*, July.

Greenberg, A., O'Kane, D. and Schloegl, L. (2004) LH+: a fast analytical model for CDO hedging and risk management, *Lehman Brothers, Quantitative Credit Research Quarterly*, Q2.

Gupton, G., Finger, C. and Bhatia, M. (1997) *CreditMetrics, Technical Document*. Morgan Guarantee Trust, New York.

Hagan, P. and West, G. (2004) Interpolation methods for yield curve construction, Working paper.

Hamilton, D.T., Varma, P., Ou, S. and Cantor, R. (2005) Default and recovery rates of corporate bond issuers, *Moody's Investor's Services*.

Harrison, J.M. and Kreps, D. (1979) Martingales and arbitrage in multi-period securities markets, *Journal of Economic Theory*, 20:381–408.

Harrison, J.M. and Pliska, S. (1981) Martingales and stochastic integrals in the theory of continuous trading, *Stochastic Processes and their Applications*, 11:215–260.

Heath, D., Jarrow, R. and Morton, A. (1992) Bond pricing and the term structure of interest rates: a new methodology for contingent claims valuation. *Econometrica*, 60(1):77–105.

Ho, T.S.Y. and Lee, S.B. (1986) Term structure movements and pricing interest rate contingent claims, *Journal of Finance*, 41:1011–1029.

Hull, J. and White, A. (2000a) Valuing credit default swaps I: No counterparty risk, Working paper.

Hull, J. and White, A. (2000b) Valuing credit default swaps II: Modeling default correlations, Working paper.

Hull, J. and White, A. (2003a) The valuation of credit default swap options, *Journal of Derivatives*, 10(3): 40–50.

Hull, J. and White, A. (2003b) Valuation of a CDO and an nth-to-default CDS without Monte Carlo simulation, Working paper, University of Toronto.

Hull, J. and White, A. (2006) Valuing credit derivatives using an implied copula approach, Working paper.

Hull, J., Predescu, M. and White, A. (2005) The valuation of correlation-dependent credit derivatives using a structural model, Working paper.

Jaeckel, P. (2002) *Monte-Carlo Methods in Finance*, John Wiley & Sons.

Jamshidian, F. (2002) Valuation of credit default swaps and swaptions, Working paper, NIB Capital Bank.

Jarrow, R. and Turnbull, S. (1995) Pricing options on derivative securities subject to credit risk, *Journal of Finance*, 1:53–85.

Jarrow, R. and Yu, F. (2001) Counterparty risk and the pricing of defaultable securities, *Journal of Finance*, 61:1765–1799 .

Joshi, M. (2003) *The Concepts and Practice of Mathematical Finance*, Cambridge University Press.

Joshi, M. (2005) Applying importance sampling to pricing single tranches of CDOs in a one-factor Li model, Working paper, QUARC Group, RBS.

Joshi, M. and Kainth, D. (2003) Rapid and accurate development of prices and Greeks for nth to default credit swaps in the Li model, Working paper, QUARC Group, RBS.

Joshi, M. and Stacey, A. (2005) Intensity gamma, a new approach to pricing portfolio credit derivatives, Working paper, RBS QUARC Group.

Lando, D. (1998) On Cox processes and credit risky securities, *Review of Derivatives Research*, 2: 99–120.

Laurent, J-P. and Gregory. J. Basket default swaps, CDO's and factor copulas. *Working paper*, 2002.

Li, D. (2000) On default correlation: a copula function approach, *Journal of Fixed Income*, 9(4):43–54 2000.

Lindskog, F., McNeil, A. and Schmock, U. (2001) A note on Kendall's tau for elliptical distributions, *ETH preprint*.

Luciano, E. and Schoutens, W. (2005) A multivariate jump-driven financial asset model, Working paper.

Marsaglia, G. and Tang, W.W. (2000) A simple method for generating gamma variables, *ACM Transactions* on Mathematical Software, 26(3):363–372.

Mashal, R. and Naldi, M. (2002) Extreme events and default baskets, *Risk*, June.

Mashal, R. and Zeevi, A. (2002) Beyond correlation: extreme comovements between financial assets. Working paper, Columbia University.

McGinty, L., Beinstein, E., Ahluwalia, R. and Watts, M. (2004) Introducing base correlations, Research paper, JP Morgan.

Merton, R. (1974) On the pricing of corporate debt: the risk structure of interest rates, *Journal of Finance*, 29:449–470.

Moler, C. and van Loan, C. (2003) Nineteen dubious ways to compute the exponential of a matrix, twenty five years later, *SIAM Review*, 45(1):3–49.

Moosbrucker, T. (2006) Pricing CDOs with correlated variance gamma distributions, Working paper.

Mortensen, A. (2006) Semi-analytical valuation of basket credit derivatives in intensity-based models, *Journal of Derivatives*, 13(4):8–26.

Muench, D., Allen, P.S., Sbityakov, A. and Beinstein, E. (2006) An introduction to tranchelets, *JP Morgan Credit Derivatives Research*.

Nelsen, R.B. (1999) An introduction to copulas, *Lecture notes in Statistic 139*, Springer, New York.

O'Kane, D. and McAdie, R. (2001) Explaining the basis: cash versus default swaps, *Lehman Brothers, Structured Credit Research*.

O'Kane, D. and Schloegl, L. (2002a) A counterparty risk framework for protection buyers, *Lehman Brothers Quantitative Credit Research Quarterly*, Q2.

O'Kane, D. and Schloegl, L. (2002b) Spread premia for portfolio tranches, *Lehman Brothers Quantitative Credit Research Quarterly*, Q1.

O'Kane, D. and Turnbull, S. (2003) Valuation of credit default swaps, *Lehman Brothers Quantitative Credit Research Quarterly*, Q2.

O'Kane, D., Pedersen, C. and Turnbull, S. (2003) Valuing the restructuring clause in CDS, *Lehman Brothers Quantitative Credit Research Quarterly*.

Pedersen, C.M. (2003) Valuation of portfolio credit default swaptions, *Lehman Brothers Quantitative Credit Research Quarterly*, Q4.

Pedersen, C.M. and Sen, S. (2004) Valuation of constant maturity default swaptions, *Lehman Brothers Quantitative Credit Research Quarterly*, Q2.

Press, W.H., Teukolsky, S.A., Vetterling, W.T. and Flannery, B.P. (1992) *Numerical Recipes in C: The Art of Scientific Computing*. 2nd edn, Cambridge University Press.

Schloegl, L. and O'Kane, D. (2005) A note on the large homogeneous portfolio approximation with the student-*t* copula, *Finance and Stochastics*, 9(4):577–584.

Schönbucher, P. (1999) A Libor market model with default risk, Working paper, University of Bonn.

Schönbucher, P. (2003a) A note on survival measures and the pricing of options on credit default swaps, Working paper, ETH, Zurich, Department of Mathematics.

Schönbucher, P. (2003b) Information-driven default contagion, Working paper, ETH, Zurich.

Schönbucher, P. (2005) Portfolio losses and the term structure of loss transition rates: a new methodology for the pricing of portfolio credit derivatives, Working paper, ETH, Zurich.

Shelton, D. (2004) Back to normal, proxy integration: a fast accurate method for CDO and CDO-squared pricing, *Citigroup Structured Credit Research*.

Sklar, A. (1959) Functions de répartition à *n* dimensions et leurs marges, *Publ. Inst. Statist. Univ. Paris 8*, pages 229–231.

Tavares, P., Nguyen, T., Chapovsky, A. and Vaysburd, I. (2004) Composite basket model, *Merrill Lynch Credit Derivatives*.

Tuckman, B. (2002) *Fixed Income Securities: Tools for Today's Markets*. 2nd edn, Wiley Finance.

Vasicek, O. (1987) Probability of loss on loan portfolio, Working paper, KMV Corporation.

Williams, D. (1991) *Probability with Martingales*, Cambridge University Press.

Yu, F. (2005) Correlated defaults in intensity based models, Working paper, University of California, Irvine.

Index

Printed and bound by CPI Group (UK) Ltd, Croydon, CR0 4YY

23/10/2024

14578716-0001